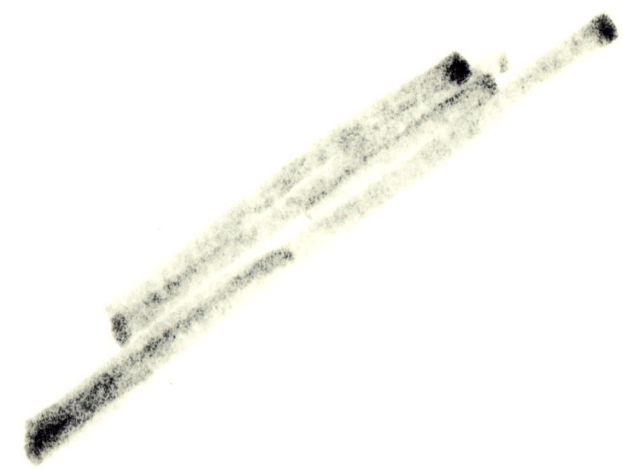

Paul Miliukov and the Quest for
a Liberal Russia, 1880–1918

Miliukov at the time of the First Duma (1906).
Reproduced from the collections of the Library of Congress.

PAUL MILIUKOV

and the Quest for a Liberal Russia, 1880–1918

Melissa Kirschke Stockdale

Cornell University Press

ITHACA AND LONDON

Copyright © 1996 by Cornell University

All rights reserved. Except for brief quotations in a review, this book, or parts thereof, must not be reproduced in any form without permission in writing from the publisher. For information, address Cornell University Press, Sage House, 512 East State Street, Ithaca, New York 14850.

First published 1996 by Cornell University Press.

Printed in the United States of America

⊗ The paper in this book meets the minimum requirements of the American National Standard for Information Sciences—Permanence of Paper for Printed Library Materials, ANSI Z39.48-1984.

Library of Congress Cataloging-in-Publication Data

Stockdale, Melissa Kirschke.
  Paul Miliukov and the quest for a liberal Russia, 1880–1918 / Melissa Kirschke Stockdale.
    p. cm.
  Includes bibliographical references and index.
  ISBN 0-8014-3248-0 (cloth : alk. paper)
    1. Miliukov, P. N. (Pavel Nikolaevich), 1859–1943. 2. Statesmen—Russia—Biography. 3. Historians—Russia—Biography. 4. Russia—Politics and government—1894–1917. I. Title.
DK254.M52S76 1996
947.08′3′092—DC20   96-27319

cloth 10 9 8 7 6 5 4 3 2 1

"The strengths and weaknesses of liberalism in Russia were more or less those of Miliukov himself."
—Donald Treadgold

"It was Miliukov's tragedy that he believed himself to be a liberal when he was, in fact, a radical."
—Leonard Schapiro

"[Miliukov's] views never seemed to me to diverge much from what one could hear at any time at the National Liberal Club in London."
—Bernard Pares

Contents

Illustrations		ix
Preface		xi
Note on Transliteration, Titles, and Dates		xxi
CHAPTER ONE	Youth and Student Years	1
CHAPTER TWO	Political Awakening	28
CHAPTER THREE	Miliukov's Historical Thought	53
CHAPTER FOUR	Scholarship and Opposition	81
CHAPTER FIVE	Russian Liberalism	103
CHAPTER SIX	The Revolution of 1905	128
CHAPTER SEVEN	The Search for Unity, 1907–1914	170
CHAPTER EIGHT	The War Years	208
CHAPTER NINE	Miliukov Displaced	238
Conclusion		273
Epilogue		280
Notes		289
Selected Bibliography		361
Index		371

Illustrations

Miliukov at the time of the First Duma	ii
V. O. Kliuchevskii in the 1880s	11
Gentry leaders	93
Fedor Kokoshkin	130
Miliukov, circa 1907	132
Cartoon: Miliukov's attitude toward Russia's socialists	174
Andrei I. Shingarev	195
Vladimir N. Nabokov	250
Miliukov, minister of Foreign Affairs, 1917	256
Miliukov aboard the SS *America*, 1921	285

Preface

In February 1895 in Moscow, friends and admirers of Paul Miliukov gathered for a farewell banquet in his honor. The thirty-six-year-old historian, author of two acclaimed monographs and one of the most popular instructors at Moscow University, had just been barred from teaching and ordered into administrative exile in consequence of his "harmful" political views. Viktor Gol'tsev, editor of the journal *Russkaia mysl'* (Russian thought), proposed a toast to his young colleague expressing the hope that Miliukov would one day become the historian of the fall of the Russian monarchy.[1]

Twenty-three years later, in February 1918, Miliukov was in a way realizing this wish as he commenced writing his three-volume history of the Russian revolution. The nature of that work and the circumstances of its composition, however, were not such as anyone could have predicted in 1895. The historian's own actions—including his desperate effort to *save* the monarchy in 1917—necessarily figured prominently in the narrative. The head of Russia's liberal Constitutional Democratic Party, a two-term deputy to the Duma and organizer of its wartime Progressive bloc, Miliukov was a seasoned politician and leader when revolution catapulted him to political center stage. And though he managed to establish a government of progressive public figures, his chronicle of the collapse of tsarism would not be written in the celebratory spirit Gol'tsev's toast assumed. Miliukov was ousted from office two months after becoming minister of foreign affairs; the remnant of the government he organized was forcibly overthrown in October; his party had been outlawed by the end of the year. His history of the Russian revolution, begun in hiding in Bolshevik-held Rostov and completed in 1920 in emigration, was an account not of liberal triumph but of national tragedy.[2]

History and politics—the individual effort to write the history of one's country and also to shape its future—were joined in the person of Paul Miliukov to a remarkable degree. Even had he been a pedestrian historian, or one specialized in a topic far removed from the concerns of his day, scholars who have become political leaders in this century are sufficiently rare to make his career of interest. But Miliukov was a historian of uncommon power and breadth, innovative in his methodology and bold in conception, "the best of the gifted new generation of historians," as one critical reviewer felt compelled to observe.[3]

His first, pioneering works probed the financial and institutional history of the seventeenth century and the Petrine period. He turned next to the history of ideas and then, as his interests broadened and confidence grew, undertook a three-volume interpretative history of Russian culture from its beginnings to his own day. By the time Miliukov finally chose political activity over a scholarly career, at the age of forty-six, he had written six books and numerous articles and reviews in which he developed views on the historical process and the nature of Russia itself that informed his political thought.

Steeped as he was in Russian history, Miliukov studied that history within a larger context. Encyclopedic in his interests and enjoying a gift for languages, he read widely in foreign belles lettres, philosophy, and scholarly literature, traveled extensively in Europe and to America, and kept up correspondence with friends made in the course of his travels. His knowledge of things Western was thus based on personal observation as well as study, and in his case—as compared with the experience of many Russian radicals who traveled abroad—familiarity did not breed contempt. He admired Western culture and democratic institutions deeply, though not uncritically, and believed it both desirable and possible to establish parliamentary government in a Russia that had outgrown autocracy.

But the who, what, and how of Russia's political transformation were questions to which he only gradually worked out answers: Russia's most famous liberal was not a liberal always. Like many of his fellow citizens, Miliukov became politicized in the early 1890s. He found much that was attractive in Marxism and populism without being won over to either; liberalism, rather inchoate and quiescent at that time, interested him not at all. Returning to Russia in 1899 after two years' exile spent in the Balkans, he frequented socialist circles and became active in the burgeoning opposition movement, for which he won two stays in prison. Liberals of a militant stripe were by then beginning to organize; this activity, and what he saw of radical liberalism in Bulgaria, suggested to him that liberalism was more dynamic than he had assumed. Studying liberal theory from a sociological perspective, and plunging into the history of Russian political thought, Miliukov worked out his views on a new sort of liberalism. This work, with that by Petr Struve, provided a theoretical basis for the effort to make liberalism a mass movement in Russia.

Miliukov respected classical liberalism's espousal of individual rights and political liberty, but found these liberal touchstones insufficient to the needs of twentieth-century society. The modern, interventionist, democratic state had necessary social and economic tasks to perform that laissez-faire doctrines and natural law theory could ill accommodate. Liberalism needed to recognize that individual rights are not absolute but generated by society, and that a balance must be struck between those rights and the needs of the community. At the same time, liberalism had to retain its distinctive respect for the individual and commitment to rule by law, so that the democratic state did not become a new sort of despotism. Miliukov believed that Russians were exceptionally well suited to effect this reorientation in liberal perspectives, since Russian liberalism was more "humanitarian" in its ethos and less "bourgeois" in composition than was the case in Europe.

The liberals' task, as Miliukov and others saw it, was to unite the entire opposition in order to defeat autocracy. Once political rights were won, social reform could be accomplished. With his strong ties among both socialists and liberals, Miliukov was uniquely placed to help effect this unification, quickly emerging as one of the most prominent leaders of the liberation movement in 1905. In October of that year he helped found the Constitutional Democratic (Kadet) Party, just as autocracy was forced to issue the October Manifesto promising civil liberties and creation of an elected legislative body. By spring 1906 the Kadets had become Russia's largest political party and won a stunning victory in elections to the First Duma.

Hopes of implementing the liberal program soon plummeted. The October Manifesto did not put an end to widespread violence, the first two Dumas survived only months and accomplished nothing, and by summer 1907 the government had reasserted its authority. The Kadet party was persecuted and harassed in the provinces, while a restriction of the franchise reduced it to a small minority in subsequent Dumas. In these conditions, many drifted out of the liberal party and politics altogether. Among the remaining, a tension existed between those who thought the best course was to make common cause with the left and those who favored a move to the right. Miliukov devoted considerable energies in these years to mediating differences and moderating expectations, in the hopes of retaining some liberal influence in the Duma and the country and averting a formal split in the party.

The Kadets experienced far more defeats than successes in the decade following the 1905 revolution, but this period was also one of continued intellectual development for Miliukov. The excesses and failures of the revolution taught him both to fear mass upheaval and to distrust the revolutionary socialists he had previously regarded as allies, lessons that would profoundly influence his behavior in 1917. On a more creative level, the social and ethnic tensions revealed by the revolution caused him to think in new ways about the lack of social cohesion in Russia. Most of all, he was challenged by the appearance of a phenomenon often difficult to reconcile with liberal values, an aroused and assertive nationalism. In the Third and Fourth Dumas, concern for the integrity of the empire and its international prestige expressed itself in discrimination against the empire's non-Russian nationalities and advocacy of an aggressive foreign policy in the Balkans. Miliukov opposed both these orientations, not only as a liberal, but also because of the danger to the state inherent in the excesses of each.

His views on the nationality question were informed by his historical research into the Russian "national idea," but also by his observations in the Balkans. From his first travels in the region in 1897, Miliukov had been intrigued by the various and competing Slav national movements and the ways religion, language, history, and myth contributed to articulation of national identity. Drawing on these observations, he argued for the socially constructed and variable nature of national identity, but also for the durability of national consciousness once it penetrated to the mass of the population. In fighting Great Russian chauvinism he therefore propounded an approach to the nationality question predicated not on rejection of nationalism, or on assimilationist hopes, but on accommodation of and respect for the national consciousness of all the peoples of the Russian empire.

In these same years Miliukov developed his strong interest in foreign policy. His belief that Russia's foreign policy should be worthy of a great power was one of the few orientations he shared with the conservative Duma majority, even as his more cautious views on that policy divided him from it. Although he agreed that German and Austrian encroachment on Russia's interests in the Balkans should be countered, he did not consider Russia strong enough to fight for them. His knowledge of the Balkans made it impossible for him to subscribe to popular neo-Slav assumptions about the common interests uniting Russia and her brother Slavs, nor could he share the general Russian partiality for the Serbs. The Balkan wars of 1912, whose causes and conduct Miliukov investigated as a member of an international commission of inquiry, confirmed his mistrust of Serbian aggrandizement, while the terrible evidence of atrocities committed by all the belligerents intensified his revulsion of war. From 1912, no politician outside the socialist camp so passionately opposed Russia's entering any armed conflict, a position that provoked the most scathing attacks upon his patriotism.[4]

Through all the tumult and tedium of these years, and despite their sobering lessons, Miliukov retained his zest for politics and his faith that they must eventually produce a free and equitable order in Russia. Countering those who maintained that Russians were too backward, ignorant, and unused to freedom to be able to govern themselves, he insisted that experience of genuine parliamentary democracy would itself furnish the necessary political education. Miliukov supplemented his thoroughly liberal confidence in the beneficent influence of liberty and good institutions with a one-man campaign of mass political education. He wrote hundreds of editorials and articles, went on lecture tours, delivered speeches in the Duma to promulgate his vision of what a democratic Russia should be and do.

As the leader of a party, Miliukov was concerned not just with larger questions of theory and program but also with tactics. Fortunately, the extensive records of the Kadet party help us weigh the often contradictory memoir accounts of his strengths and weaknesses as a leader. Outsiders imagined Miliukov to hold nearly dictatorial sway among the Kadets; some of his colleagues later made the same charge, while others contended he was not forceful enough.[5] Over time Miliukov did become more dominant, even domineering, but this was not the case at the start. If he usually carried his way, it was primarily owing to the practicality of his tactical proposals and his efforts to identify a middle position. On those occasions when he did not manage to persuade his colleagues, he fell in with the decision of the majority. But as charting a tenable course became more difficult and rifts in the party widened, from 1912, criticism of his tactical fine-tunings mounted. Miliukov, in turn, became more stubborn and irritable, took defeat less gracefully, and increasingly resorted to ultimatums when he had not managed to persuade.

A complex personality, Miliukov united features that could be both assets and drawbacks in a leader. His native optimism, enormous self-confidence, and great personal courage were clearly advantages in a frequently hostile political environment. His colleagues also esteemed his integrity, indifference to money and rank, and tremendous capacity for work. Non-Russian members justly valued his freedom from racial or religious prejudice. Yet Miliukov could also be caustic, critical of others, unwilling to admit mistakes, and vulnerable to flattery. Priding himself on his pragmatism, he was at times doctrinaire; though adept at reconciling even the most divided gathering, his tactlessness was proverbial. The independent cast of mind that gave his theoretical writings much of their power could also be a political liability, since swimming against the current rarely wins votes. Finally, he had a natural reserve that frequently made him appear lacking in warmth and emotion. Miliukov's coldness "inhibited any feeling of personal sympathy or love for him," one colleague wrote, adding, "But then, he had no need of either."[6]

Getting to know Miliukov, to know more of his private life and how it influenced behavior and decision making, has been one of the hardest tasks of this biography. Although his personal archive is vast, it contains little of a truly personal nature, the same being the case with the diaries he kept intermittently.[7] Very few of his private letters written before 1918 survived the upheavals of revolution, civil war, and emigration. Such evidence as does exist, however, suggests that the cold and somewhat austere figure of memoir accounts was a later development. As was the case with his contemporary Woodrow Wilson—another scholar who entered politics—the burdens of leadership and personal frustrations exerted a chilling effect on his public persona.[8]

When Miliukov at last began writing his memoirs, at age eighty-one in Montpelier, France, he chose to omit the more intimate details of his life even though "my silence . . . will perhaps lead my future biographer, if there is one, to substitute anecdotes for facts."[9] In a number of places in the memoirs Miliukov similarly addresses the future historian or possible biographer, noting the possibility of error concerning a particular date, regretting his inability to render a quotation exactly, acknowledging that his recollection of an episode might be more "subjective" than he realized. This pronounced historical sensibility was as characteristic of his political career as of his memoirs. As a historian attempting to transform his country, Miliukov was constantly aware of past origins of present problems, but was also anticipating future judgment of the way those problems were addressed: "history will remember" what we say and do or fail to do, he often warned contemporaries.[10]

For many decades Miliukov and his party were in fact "remembered" only partially and incompletely. It was long impossible for any scholar in his homeland to undertake a biography of Miliukov, and the only Western biography, published in 1969, had to be written without benefit of access to Soviet archives.[11] Various aspects of Miliukov's political activity have been thoughtfully treated in works on the events and movements in which he played a part, but there exists no full-scale study of the nature of his liberalism or of the party he led.[12] His scholarship, though frequently alluded to, has been little studied, and his writings on nationalism and the Russian nationalities question are virtually unknown.[13]

History, however, has its "whims," as even the positivist Miliukov conceded, and individuals and movements consigned to its dustbin do not always stay put.[14] When I began this study of Miliukov's life in Russia, more years ago than is comfortable to admit, Iurii Andropov headed the Communist Party of the Soviet Union and Soviet reformers looking for a "usable past" turned to alternative currents within early Bolshevism, not to the defeated and discredited rivals of Bolshevism itself.[15] The nationality question in Russia scarcely appeared to exist. Bosnia was a place name one spelled out for students when giving a lecture on the origins of the Great War. Since then, the period of perestroika and the demise of one-party states have resurrected most of the issues Miliukov confronted, as well as lending fresh interest to the ways he tried to resolve them. Democrats in Russia again confront the staggering tasks of building a liberal order in a state lacking traditions of respect for law and the individual, of strengthening social cohesion in an ethnically, culturally, and economically divided population, of fostering national pride without resort to misrepresentation of the past or to adventuristic foreign policy, and of mediating collisions between opposing notions of what is "right."

While specific policies proposed by Miliukov rarely have relevance today, the general perspectives informing them remain attractive: that social justice cannot be achieved without first securing political liberties, that both are indispensable to genuine liberalism, and that tolerance and practicality are no less important criteria of politics than are lofty ideals.

The number of individuals and institutions to whom I owe thanks for assistance and support is vast; in the course of the many years that I have been engaged in this study I have met with kindness, encouragement, stimulation, constructive criticism "in measure overflowing." No formal acknowledgment can adequately convey my gratitude.

The International Research and Exchange Board generously funded three research trips to Russia between 1984 and 1995; without this support, and that of the Fulbright-Hayes Fellowship Program, this book could not have been written. The Department of History of Harvard University made it possible to do much-needed research in New York; the support of the Harvard Russian Research Center, thanks chiefly to the efforts of my adviser, Richard Pipes, helped finance the final stages of writing my dissertation. Adam Ulam and the fellows and staff of the Russian Research Center provided an intellectual home that was as rewarding personally as it was academically. The generous support of the Russian Research Center and the John M. Olin Foundation also made possible a wonderfully productive year of work in 1992, one all the more memorable thanks to residency at Lowell House and the opportunity to enjoy the stimulating community of the Lowell senior common room headed by William and MaryLee Bossert. The Research Council of the University of Oklahoma and the Oklahoma Foundation for the Humanities generously provided funding for travel to collections and summer support for writing.

xviii   Preface

I am grateful to the library staffs of Harvard University, Columbia University, and the state libraries of Moscow and St. Petersburg, the library of the Academy of Sciences in St. Petersburg, and also to the archivists and staff of the Houghton Archive at Harvard University, the Bakhmeteff Archive of Columbia University, the Russian State Historical Archive of St. Petersburg, and the State Archive of the Russian Federation in Moscow. I particularly wish to thank the archivists and staff of the Hoover Institution, Stanford, and the Archive of the Academy of Sciences in Moscow not only for their invaluable professional assistance but also for making the conduct of research in these two institutions so pleasurable. I am also grateful for the help of the inter-library loan staff of Bizzell Memorial Library at the University of Oklahoma, who efficiently procured for me dozens of necessary items over the course of several years.

Among the individuals I wish to thank are the teachers who guided and challenged me, not only in the study of history. Marilyn Brannon, Connie Cronley, and John Huffman taught me to write. David Epstein and Marvin Lomax nourished my love of history; James Wilkinson taught me to think critically; and Ben Henneke inspired me in ways too numerous to mention.

Scholars and fellow students shared their expertise and their work, offered suggestions, and pointed me in the direction of sources. I thank James Flynn, Edward Kasinec, Raymond Pearson, Terence Emmons, Robert Nye, Arch Getty, James Cracraft, Thomas Bohn, Gary Cohen, and Olga Andriewsky for their assistance and good will. Paul Nascimento, Dirk Voss, and Ina Germanovich provided assistance with research and translation. Margaret Smith expertly produced many of the illustrations. Most especially, I thank Tom Gleason, Shmuel Galai, and V. V. Shelokhaev for their mentorship as well as for many, many happy hours of conversation on the subject of Russian history, liberalism, and Paul Miliukov; their knowledge, critical acumen, and guidance enriched this study—and its author—in a variety of ways.

One of my greatest debts is to the teachers, colleagues, and friends who gave so generously of their time and expertise in reading this manuscript or portions of it, through its many tortuous drafts. To them belongs much of the credit for whatever is creditable in this study; I am responsible for the shortcomings. Richard Pipes, Cathy Frierson, Tom Gleason, Steve Marks, Edward Keenan, Shmuel Galai, Robert Shalhope, David Levy, Tom Schwartz, Tom Stockdale, and Adrian Jones critiqued my work gently but rigorously, improving my style, correcting inaccuracies, tightening my logic, and suggesting lines of argument I had not even considered. They also provided encouragement and help when it was sorely needed, as did, in different ways, Julie Jones, Laurie Burnham, Christine Porto, Jacki Rand, Dan Snell,

Katie Barwick, Martha Skeeters, Linda Reese, Paul and Chris Regan, Oleg Zimarin, Sergei and Valia Zapolskii, and Dmitrii Rundkvist.

I have been extraordinarily lucky in my editors at Cornell University Press. I thank Andrew Lewis for his fine copy-editing; Carol Betsch for her expertise, patience, and warmth in shepherding the manuscript through the production process; and most especially John Ackerman, for his humor and encouragement, his rigorous editing, and for caring so much about Paul Miliukov.

Finally, I wish to mention my family. Bob Bruce first made me think of graduate work. Members of my extended family, most especially Bud and Georgette Stockdale and Anne Wurr, constantly heartened and touched me with their interest and expressions of support. My son, Nicholas, has been a source of joy and also of sanity, since he helped keep the importance of producing a monograph in some sort of reasonable perspective. I thank Jane Bruce, Harry Kirschke, Amy Kirschke, Tom Schwartz, and Tom Stockdale with all my heart for their love, encouragement, and help. Finally, I lovingly dedicate this book to the memory of my grandparents, Harry and Helene Stamos and Edward and Nadine Kirschke.

MELISSA KIRSCHKE STOCKDALE

Norman, Oklahoma

Note on Transliteration, Titles, and Dates

I have used the Library of Congress transliteration system in this book, without diacritical marks. Proper names are also rendered according to this system, though not consistently. Because Miliukov is known in the secondary literature as Paul Miliukov I have referred to him that way, excepting quotation of primary sources referring to "Pavel Nikolaevich"; similarly, familiar names such as Nicholas II and Kerensky appear in their familiar English form. Non-Russian names of citizens of the Russian empire are given in Russianized form—thus Dragomanov, not Drahomanov—except in the case of citations in the notes of a published work, where the author's name is rendered as it was published. For the convenience of the nonspecialist reader, Russian books are referred to in the text by a translated title, although all titles are given in the original in the notes.

Until February 1, 1918, Russia used the old Julian calendar, which was behind the Western calendar by twelve days in the nineteenth century and thirteen days in the twentieth; all dates in the text prior to 1918 are "old style" unless otherwise noted.

Paul Miliukov and the Quest for
a Liberal Russia, 1880–1918

C·H·A·P·T·E·R   O·N·E

Youth and Student Years

Pavel Nikolaevich Miliukov was born in Moscow on January 15, 1859.[1] His father's family claimed descent from the service nobility of Tver', a claim rejected by the Tver' Assembly of Nobility because it was insufficiently documented.[2] Nobility or not, the Miliukovs were neither distinguished nor prosperous. Miliukov's grandfather, Pavel Alekseevich Miliukov, left Tver' for Siberia in an unsuccessful effort to make his fortune in gold. Miliukov's father, Nikolai Pavlovich (b. 1820), trained as an architect in Moscow. There, he first occupied a humble position as teacher of architecture; his situation improved somewhat when he was appointed as a municipal architect, around 1868, and he finally enjoyed a brief success when he struck out on his own. Although only modestly and intermittently prosperous, he remained deeply committed to his chosen profession, which claimed the chief part of his energy and attention.[3]

Miliukov's mother, Mariia Arkad'evna, came from a family of undisputed nobility, the Sultanovs of Iaroslavl', and she made no secret of considering this, her second marriage, a misalliance. Her first husband had been a Baranov, a harsh landlord whose own serfs murdered him in the fields. The son by this marriage, Aleksandr, served in the hussars and had little connection with Madame Miliukov's second family.[4]

Miliukov had one brother, Aleksei, one year younger than he. They spent their first years in a house connected to the technical school on Lefortovo Street where their father taught. Over the next few years they relocated first to the village of Davydkovo, near Moscow; when their home in Davydkovo was destroyed in a fire, the Miliukovs took refuge with friends, then moved again, to the home of the wealthy Spechinskii family on Starokoniushennyi Pereulok. Miliukov described the Spechinskiis as kind, but patronizing. The Miliukovs' dependent status made a strong impression on the young Pavel Nikolaevich, who felt his family's inferiority before the Spechinskiis and was vaguely offended by their charity. Miliukov was eight or nine years old when his father was appointed a Moscow municipal architect and they moved to an apartment of their own.

Even then the family was not happy. Miliukov's mother, strong-willed and temperamental, dominated the home. His father, though less passionate and outspoken, did not suffer her outbursts in silence. In Miliukov's early years his parents quarreled often; he recalled one fight when his father heaved crockery at the walls while he and his brother cowered on a bench. Later, open fights became less frequent, but an undercurrent of tension remained. Never an attentive parent, his father increasingly conceded domestic sovereignty to his wife and retreated further into his work.[5]

Miliukov does recall some happy times, however, sometimes with his parents but more frequently with Aleksei. Miliukov seems to have gained his interest in art and architecture from his father, and rare trips to concerts and the theater gave him a lifelong love of music. After one such visit, Miliukov persuaded his parents to buy him a violin, and playing this instrument would always be one of his chief sources of pleasure. There were, as well, special trips through Moscow during the holidays, when his father, in his capacity as city architect, inspected all the temporary festival structures and the Miliukov boys enjoyed free passes to the various spectacles. Above all, there were joyful ramblings in the countryside; during the brief period of family solvency, from about 1869 to 1874, Miliukov's father was even able to take a lease on land at Pushkino, near Moscow, where he designed and built two dachas in the "Old Moscow" style.[6]

Miliukov's early education was remarkably haphazard. Its chief feature was, in his opinion, the lack of guidance from his parents. The boys learned to read and write at home, but were exposed to nothing in the way of literature beyond Krylov's fables (*Basni*), and then went to an impoverished Jewish tutor who taught them in his shabby lodgings. The want of guidance at home extended to things moral. The boys were taught proper behavior and observance of holy days, but nothing beyond these superficialities. Miliukov doubted whether the family library included a Bible, and only in the upper courses of gymnasium did he learn the significance of the liturgy and rites of the Church. The vague need he felt to "express some sort of more personal, intimate attitude to faith" was left to him to work out for himself. Without understanding the ritual of the Church, Miliukov was attracted to it, and for several years, from about the age of ten, he practiced devotions on his own, even slipping out to a nearby church to light candles before icons.[7]

Miliukov insisted that he and his brother had no "spiritual connection" with their parents. He felt that the fragility of this bond was caused by his parents' conjugal unhappiness and by their relative indifference to their sons' spiritual and emotional development. He also attributed great significance to one incident of early childhood. On the occasion of some childish misdemeanor, Miliukov's father, at the instigation of his wife, thrashed his sons soundly. The experience left a lasting impression, one which resonated in his later reading of Rousseau's *Confession*. Corporal punishment "severs the moral bond and destroys confidence in one's parents," Miliukov maintained, creating a system of "hypocrisy and deceit." However simplistic the explanation, the bitterness was real: Miliukov and his brother had little love for their father and only slightly warmer feelings toward their mother.[8]

One consequence of the state of affairs at home was an unusual degree of independence for the children at an early age. The brothers seemed to have been left largely to their own devices. "So long as we satisfied external requirements," Miliukov wrote, "we had 'internal freedom,' and made the most of it." Aleksei was a spirited and engaging boy, always surrounded by a host of friends. Though the younger of the two, he took the lead in everything, his more sober and awkward brother following him into adventure and misadventure as well. Miliukov's own tastes inclined more toward the violin, art books, and the composition of poetry he never showed to anyone. If the two brothers were not spiritually close, they became good comrades, further united by the circumstance of parental neglect. Miliukov felt that his development progressed under the influence of people and events external to the family. "I can say, without great exaggeration, that I was obliged to myself for everything."[9]

Miliukov was not a serious student in his first years at Moscow First Gymnasium, slowly sliding from fourth to twentieth place in his class. The change came in 1874, at the age of fifteen, when he was due to take the demanding examinations required for entering the fourth class of gymnasium. He threw himself into his studies with unaccustomed zeal and passed. Looking back, he felt that these exertions administered some sort of "moral push" that began his "fully conscious life." Such a life meant, first of all, recognizing the deficiencies in his intellectual background, which he set out to rectify.[10]

Miliukov's interests in these years were largely determined by the school curriculum. Greek and Latin held pride of place in gymnasium instruction during the tenure of Minister of Education Dmitrii Tolstoi. Science, considered suspect, was scarcely taught; mathematics instruction tended to be solid but unappealing. History was reduced to dull genealogies and the memorization of dates. The history of literature was equally suspect, but this subject's appeal was harder to petrify: "illicit" works, such as those by V. G. Belinskii, were somehow smuggled into the syllabus, which stimulated students to read independently.[11]

Miliukov became a voracious reader. He dipped into French and English literature, but German literature, especially German philosophy, attracted him more. He read Lessing, Goethe, and Wieland, read and reread Schiller and his favorite, Heine, whose work by the end of gymnasium was his constant reference. Above all, guided by his teacher of Greek, Petr Kalenov, he immersed himself in the classics. Kalenov imparted to his students his own love of the classical world and its culture. Leading students in discussion of Antigone and the dialogues of Plato, he introduced them to the study of critical thought and ethical behavior. Kalenov helped Miliukov draw up an extensive reading list of works in both Greek and Latin, which Miliukov then sought in the secondhand bookshops that had become his familiar haunts.[12]

In these years Miliukov took as his slogan Schiller's exhortation "Strebe zum Ganzen, lebe im Ganzen, / Eigne das Ganze dir an" [Strive for wholeness, live in wholeness / Embrace the whole.]. Probably in response to his initial dismay on discovering his own ignorance, Miliukov equated the "whole" with an encyclopedic approach to knowledge. As he matured, he sought to integrate his knowledge, to theorize and distinguish patterns or "laws" shaping the empirical world, but he never abandoned his encyclopedic approach. The breadth of his learning, the sheer scope of his interests, never ceased to impress his contemporaries. Many years later I. V. Gessen, who edited the daily *Rech'* (Speech) with Miliukov, observed that Miliukov "could easily have written an entire issue of the paper himself, from the editorial to the music and theater reviews."[13]

With the exception of Kalenov, Miliukov's chief intellectual stimulus came from schoolfellows rather than teachers. In his last years at gymnasium he joined an informal circle that coalesced around Prince Nikolai Dolgorukov.[14] Members gathered frequently at one another's homes to discuss topics of mutual interest; often, someone would present a "report." Dolgorukov imparted to the circle a vaguely Slavophile coloration, and all the members were avid followers of Dostoevsky's *Diary of a Writer*. Not particularly politically conscious, they were only dimly aware of other, more radical orientations.[15]

Miliukov finished the last year of gymnasium in a rather unsettled state. His studies and efforts at self-improvement had paid off scholastically—although no gold medal was awarded in his class, he captured the silver. But these had also sown the seeds of religious doubt. Miliukov's religious beliefs, receiving neither encouragement nor direction from any quarter, could not stand up to secular wisdom. Adherence to Orthodoxy was the first to go; exposure to the anticlericalism permeating Voltaire's *Philosophical Dictionary* helped focus the dissatisfaction he already felt with the formal side of religion.[16] In an article written a number of years later, Miliukov pointed out what were, for him, the principal shortcomings of the Russian Orthodox Church: its formalism, rigidity, and "unconscious" brand of spirituality. As he put it, "Less, perhaps, than any other has our church ever lived a conscious spiritual life; and its external forms, which make it primarily a state institution, are little adapted to any free internal development, however small. The majority of our believers cease to be Orthodox from the very moment that they consciously endeavor to formulate the tenets of their religion."[17]

The most formidable threat to his personal faith, however, came from the sociology of Herbert Spencer. Miliukov read the first volume of his *Psychology*, in translation, during his last year at gymnasium. He considered Spencer a thoroughgoing atheist, but found he could not discount his views: "However unwillingly I parted with the remnants of a religious tradition taken on faith, they visibly yielded before the broadening sphere of scientific knowledge." Miliukov confessed to resenting Spencer for disturbing his peace; only later would he learn to esteem him, with Comte, as a "forefather" of modern sociology and one of the formative influences on his own thought.[18]

One aspect of Miliukov's youthful orientation that survived gymnasium unscathed was his vague Pan-Slavism, and the summer before entering university he had a chance to contribute to the "cause." On April 24, 1877, Russia declared war on Turkey. Miliukov and the other members of his circle had followed the events leading to the formal opening of hostilities with great interest, sharing completely Dostoevsky's initial view that the liberation of the South Slavs was a special Russian task, a moral duty to their "brothers." Miliukov was therefore proud to be invited by Dolgorukov to accompany, for the summer, an expedition of the Russian paramedical unit organized by the Moscow gentry.[19]

Miliukov's humble contribution to Russia's efforts on behalf of its brother Slavs was a learning experience, but in ways he scarcely anticipated. He had dreamed of being near the front; instead, the boys went to the Caucasus to the village of Suram, not far from Tiflis (Tbilisi). Miliukov, innocent of any knowledge of bookkeeping, became the outfit's treasurer. He also found himself organizing the laundry service and supervising the provisioning. This was his first chance to display the superb organizational skills that would later be one of his political hallmarks.[20]

Although they were far from the actual fighting, Miliukov and Dolgorukov saw the horrible aftereffects of battle when they helped unload wagons of wounded after the defeat at Ziviin. After that, Miliukov never lost the chance to visit the wards, where he listened to patients relate stories of the fighting, read them their letters, and wrote their replies. His contact with the wounded in the summer of 1877 was the closest he came to personal experience of war for some twenty-five years.[21]

In his memoirs Miliukov relates one incident of the journey home from the Caucasus that sheds light on the other, less bookish side of his nature. One morning, at a way station where his group had stopped to eat, Miliukov forgot to remove his cap upon being seated. An officer took umbrage at this insolence and advanced on him, shouting; Miliukov sprang to his feet, brandishing his stool, and shouted back. Others intervened to avert a fight and after the officer had been led away by his friends, Miliukov removed his cap and apologized to his comrades. This courage was a quality that even his detractors would acknowledge in the years ahead.[22]

Moscow University: Formative Influences

In September 1877, Miliukov entered Moscow University. He would be affiliated with the university for the next seventeen years, during which time he would find his calling and his sense of self and place, make friends of a lifetime and marry, and produce some of his most signal contributions to the study and writing of Russian history. He cherished hopes of spending his whole professional life there, and even in emigration his affection for his alma mater was undiminished. In many ways Moscow University was the making of Paul Miliukov.

The two decades between promulgation of the university statute of 1863, which granted greater academic freedom, and the statute of 1884, which revoked it, were very likely the best possible time to be connected with a Russian university. In this period Russia's universities matured as full-fledged centers of learning and culture—Russia might have had one of the lowest literacy rates in Europe, but its best universities were the equals of those of its more developed neighbors.[23]

Moscow University, the oldest, largest, and most prestigious in the empire, epitomized the dynamism of the period. Physically, its growth was impressive, and it was particularly blessed in its faculty.[24] The young generation of scholars filling old and new chairs in the 1870s included many unusually gifted men, some of whom would attain international stature. Miliukov believed, as did many other alumni, that the significance of Moscow University lay not so much in the courses of instruction or formal institutional traditions as in the personal connections forged there between students and select professors and among students themselves. In his mind, it was individuals and the influence they wielded—an influence as much moral as scholarly—that gave Moscow University its special place as the "seedbed of the Russian intelligentsia."[25]

This was the Moscow University he entered in autumn of 1877, matriculating in the history-philology *fakul'tet* (department). The Russian equivalent of a humanities school, it was the smallest department at all Imperial Universities, at Moscow enrolling less than 10 percent of the student body.[26] Miliukov was initially attracted not by any particular interest in history, but out of love of classical languages. He in fact found his courses in history in his first two years scarcely more stimulating than they had been in gymnasium. The great S. M. Solov'ev, aged and ill, was in his final year of teaching; Miliukov managed to sit in on his course and was frankly disappointed: the "living element" Solov'ev identified as the motive force in Russian history was conspicuously missing in Solov'ev's Russian history lectures. World history was taught by V. I. Ger'e, an "old style" teacher not only in his dismissive attitude toward his students but also, or so Miliukov felt, in his incomplete command of his subject, though he confessed to learning a great deal from Ger'e's reading list for the seminar, which included Rousseau's *Social Contract*, and Tocqueville's and Taine's work on the French revolution among others.[27]

The decisive impetus in Miliukov's determination to become a historian no doubt came at the beginning of his third year with the arrival at the university of two outstanding historians, V. O. Kliuchevskii and P. G. Vinogradov. Nonetheless, Miliukov seems to have chosen history prior to their arrival, and his reception of Kliuchevskii raises an interesting point about the source of his orientation at this time. Kliuchevskii struck such a chord in the students of this generation, Miliukov wrote, because his approach to his subject satisfied students' thirst for a truly "scientific history."[28]

Generally speaking, the demand that any discipline be "scientific" was scarcely unusual for the day—the congeries of assumptions, values, and aspirations generally labeled "Populism" constituted the prevailing orientation among the *semidesiatniki* (people of the seventies), and even those who did not subscribe wholeheartedly to populist ideology shared the populist enthusiasm for "science." The "people of the seventies" were firmly convinced that scientific knowledge held the key to social progress.[29] Like most of the university students of his day, Miliukov probably read the essays of N. K. Mikhailovskii and other populists in the pages of the influential *Otechestvennye zapiski* (Notes of the fatherland). In his own characterization of his class at university he said that despite the continued enthusiasm for the natural sciences, its members had crossed over from the thoroughgoing materialism of the 1860s to empiricism. The lectures of M. M. Troitskii in philosophy, which substituted the teaching of logic for more traditional philosophical inquiry and were unblinkingly hostile to any "metaphysic," appealed to them enormously.[30]

The most important stimulus to Miliukov's scientific orientation and interest in history was a remarkable circle of professors that coalesced in the 1870s in the history-philology and law *fakul′tety*, what I call the "Moscow young professors." The heart of the circle was Maksim Kovalevskii, dean of Russian sociology; Vsevolod Miller, a brilliant linguist specializing in Sanskrit; and I. V. Ianzhul, a jurist. Over time the circle grew to include Paul Vinogradov, lecturer (*shtatnyi dotsent*) in world history; N. I. Storozhenko and Aleksei Veselovskii, from the literature department; and S. A. Muromtsev and A. I. Chuprov, from the law school. They were young, being forty or under in 1878. All assumed their positions at Moscow University between 1872 and 1881. They quickly became friends, read one another's books and papers, and socialized together at the university and at home. There was nothing comparable to this circle at Petersburg University, Kovalevskii felt; they were like a close family, and "the university was the center of all interests for each one of us."[31]

No one single orientation or philosophy characterized the entire group, but all were empiricists, imbued with the "scientific" spirit, and more or less hostile to "metaphysics." All were interested in a comparative approach and the interconnectedness of their various disciplines, and, by extension, most believed in the idea of regularity (*zakonomernost′*) in history and social life. One fruit of this circle and its orientation was the journal *Kriticheskoe obozrenie* (The critical review), founded in 1877 and jointly edited by Miller and Kovalevskii for its first eighteen months. *Kriticheskoe obozrenie* reflected their conviction that the approach of scholars, no matter the discipline, should be broadly conceived, and their belief in the close connection that existed between the problems investigated by historians of culture and those studied by historians of beliefs, morals, and law. The journal was dedicated as much to the study of society (*obshchestvovedenie*) as to history or philology per se, and attracted contributions from scholars from other universities as well as from Moscow. In the orientation of this group of professors it is possible to discern most of the elements of Miliukov's mature sociological views.[32]

Miliukov's exposure to this circle initially came through Miller, one of the four men who most profoundly influenced him at Moscow University. Miller's course on Sanskrit, along with a course by F. F. Fortunatov on historical linguistics, taken in Miliukov's first year at university, were among the bright spots of his entire university experience. The immediate attraction of topics seemingly so unattractive to young men was the "scientific" nature of linguistics. Miller's course on Sanskrit languages turned out to be a sweeping introduction to the culture of primitive man, an experience that "broadened and deepened historical horizons with the aid of folklore, legends, and the myths of popular literature." Miller's courses made his students enthusiasts of this "new stage in the history of science," but his influence on Miliukov went beyond this. They became friends, Miller introducing the budding scholar into his family circle and the extended "family circle" of the Moscow young professors.[33]

It was Miller and Vinogradov who introduced Miliukov to Maksim Kovalevskii, and Kovalevskii who introduced him to the third volume of Comte's *Positive Philosophy*, with its exposition of the three stages of world history, the theological, metaphysical, and positive. Comte's work exercised a tremendous formative influence on Miliukov's historical thought and helped convince him to become a historian. In a letter to Kovalevskii written some years later, Miliukov recalled their first meeting, when "the student Miliukov" came to him to borrow books and was told that what he needed was "something quite different. . . . Comte was read, reread, outlined and summarized, and had the most decisive influence on the whole scholarly worldview of that student."[34]

The work of Paul Vinogradov embodied the conviction that history must be both broadly conceived and studied "scientifically." Just five years older than Miliukov, Vinogradov became a lecturer in the history department in 1880. He specialized in medieval English history and had just concluded several years of research and study at Oxford. He brought with him the latest word in European, scientific historical methodology, a circumstance that immediately predisposed Miliukov and his fellows in his favor; he was, moreover, a born teacher. Both Miliukov and Vasilii Maklakov, his future political colleague, left extensive descriptions of their studies with Vinogradov, which tally in almost every particular. Vinogradov's seminars were a genuine workshop for training in the practice of historical scholarship. There he inculcated in students the belief in the necessity of using archival sources and of exercising a rigorous and critical approach to their materials. Both men felt that it was in these seminars that they learned what "real scholarship" was.[35]

Miliukov, in his memoirs, credits Vinogradov more with the teaching of method than of theory, but Vinogradov's orientation clearly influenced him in no small degree. His approach, in keeping with that of the circle of Moscow young professors, was sociological. In lectures, as in seminars, the leitmotif was the disclosure of "regularities" in the historical process. As Maklakov recalled, "Vinogradov always had a mass of analogies, comparisons, illustrations from different epochs and peoples to show with crystal clarity that in history everything occurs according to immutable laws of social life, that in it there is nothing that is inexplicable." This sociological approach virtually excluded study of individual historical figures; Vinogradov once said that his ideal for his course was to lecture on the history of the Middle Ages "without having a single proper name."[36]

Joint work in Vinogradov's seminars laid the basis of lasting friendships with other developing scholars. Vinogradov also invited his students to gatherings at his home, where they met other members of the Moscow faculty and scholars from different institutions. Miliukov became increasingly close to Vinogradov, who was his primary mentor at the university and eventually became his champion on the history-philology *fakul' tet*.[37]

Miliukov was already determined to study history by the time Kliuchevskii arrived at Moscow University in December 1879, but it was Kliuchevskii's example that caused him to specialize in Russian history for his graduate work.[38] For a variety of reasons, Kliuchevskii's influence was less direct and immediate than Vinogradov's had been; Miliukov's final assessment was that Kliuchevskii had been an inspiration, rather than a teacher.[39] The sheer artistry of Kliuchevskii's lectures reanimated in his listeners a sense of the interest and drama of the history of their own country that the program of teaching in gymnasium had effectively ossified. But for Miliukov and others inclining toward an academic calling, most of whom could never hope to emulate the master's style, it was Kliuchevskii's sociological approach that was of most lasting importance.

The theoretical basis of Kliuchevskii's work was not something explicitly articulated at this time; he laid it out only some twenty years later when he finally approved publication of his lectures on Russian history, and then only in abbreviated fashion.[40] In what students understood of Kliuchevskii's approach, he fully satisfied their demand that Russian history, like any history, be studied from the point of view of a general scientific problem, "as an internal, organic evolution of human society." Kliuchevskii's approach to institutional history combined consideration of both the dynamic and structural elements, as well as the "social material" that filled political institutions.[41] Students felt that his periodization of Russian history was not a schema superimposed on material, a mere abstract construct, but a conclusion directly stemming from observation and investigation. It thus satisfied their empiricist bent. Finally, Kliuchevskii's enormous range of topics and genres showed his students the breadth of questions that could be asked about Russia's history and the variety of sources that could be consulted for their answers.[42] In many ways, his work represented the application of the methods and orientation of the "Moscow young professors" to the study of Russian history, though he was not himself a part of that circle.[43]

Kliuchevskii, however, did little to teach fledgling historians how to accomplish their task. He showed them the goal, but not how to reach it. Basically, students could learn his methods only by observing him, since his pedagogical maxim seems to have been "Get there yourself."[44] Even when students were able to benefit from being forced to use their own initiative,

V. O. Kliuchevskii in the 1880s. Frontispiece to *Sbornik statei, posviashchennykh Vasiliiu Osipovichu Kliuchevskomu* (Moscow, 1909).

at least one crucial feature of his approach defied imitation, the intuition that Miliukov felt was a strong element of Kliuchevskii's method: "His penetration was amazing, but its source wasn't accessible to all. Kliuchevskii read the sense of Russian history with, so to say, an inner eye, himself living through the psychology of the past."[45] Kliuchevskii's limitations as a teacher are worth noting, for it later fell to Miliukov, along with Vinogradov, to teach aspiring historians of Russia the new methodology. This pedagogic role was one of Miliukov's most important contributions to the formation of the "Moscow school" of historiography.[46]

By his third year at Moscow University, Kliuchevskii's brilliant example had decided Miliukov on the study of Russian history; practical and "civic" considerations also figured in this decision. Miliukov thought it unwise for a Russian to specialize in European history; obstacles to such a career included access to sources and the barrier of language, which could prevent one's work from becoming known to a broader European audience. Russian history was a field that needed work, and Russians were the logical people to do it. Still, as an undergraduate, Miliukov felt that his best course was to concentrate on his studies with Vinogradov. In this way he could learn the most of modern methodology, as well as acquire the broad European background against which to draw the Russian outline. It was a practical decision, but choosing Vinogradov over Kliuchevskii may have contributed to Kliuchevskii's subsequent reservations about taking Miliukov on as a graduate student.[47]

As Miliukov was taking his first independent steps into scholarly research, responsibility of a less welcome sort was thrust on him at home. The brief period of family prosperity had ended while Miliukov was still in gymnasium; his father's architectural business collapsed, and the Miliukovs were forced to move to more modest quarters on Chistyi Prud. In Miliukov's second year at university his father's health failed; he died in the winter of 1878–79 at the age of fifty-nine. He was by then so alienated from his family that his death seems to have made no great impression on his wife or sons, beyond the financial difficulties it occasioned.[48]

Miliukov had to assume a share of the family's support, and his remaining years at the university were a time of financial hardship. His mother took in two medical students as lodgers, and his own earnings from the private lessons he had been giving since gymnasium days, which had financed his purchases in secondhand bookstores, were now funneled into the family treasury. The following year he continued to help support his family, through tutoring and by selling the summaries he made of lecture courses; after Aleksei finished school and moved in with friends, Miliukov shared an apartment with his mother on Malaia Bronnaia.[49]

Somehow, despite his studies and the work that helped support himself and the family, Miliukov found time to participate in student affairs. These were, at first, of a strictly practical nature. A student mutual aid society, though formally prohibited, had long existed, and Miliukov's classmates elected him chairman of it.[50] Miliukov's political views at this time were still largely inchoate. His response to an ugly street incident in Moscow in the spring of 1878 reflects this, as well as marking an initial turning point in their evolution.

On April 3 butchers and shopkeepers of the Okhotnyi Riad, an area neighboring Moscow university, set upon some 150 students accompanying a group of students from Kiev University passing through Moscow en route to internal exile.⁵¹ This bloody clash between the "people" and the students, who considered themselves the people's friends and intercessors, provoked furious debate in the press. Miliukov and his university friends, most of them comrades from his gymnasium circle, were deeply troubled by both the incident and the polemics that followed. Unable to resolve for themselves the questions thus raised, they turned to their "oracle," Dostoevsky, for an answer.

The friends commissioned Miliukov to compose a letter to the author of *Diary of a Writer*, which they all signed.⁵² They were no more satisfied by the interpretation of the street clash offered by the progressive press than by that of the reactionaries, the letter explained, for if the latter excused the violence as the protest of the "people" against the intelligentsia, the former condescendingly exonerated the students on the basis that little was to be expected of them, and nothing at all expected of the "savage people." Equally bad, Miliukov wrote, many of their fellow students seemed only too ready to assume their own superiority to the butchers of the Okhotnyi Riad, instead of being roused to inquire into their own share of responsibility. Miliukov thus appealed to Dostoevsky: "We are accustomed to making use of your decisions for the establishment of our own views, and to respecting them. . . . We are turning to you for an answer to this question which torments us, about what our intellectual and moral decline is, and whether it isn't just an intermediate stage of development."⁵³

The response from Dostoevsky, anxiously awaited, came as a surprise. Miliukov, describing the episode many years later, wryly remarked that this was exactly the answer they should have expected if they had understood him at all.⁵⁴ For Dostoevsky, while honoring the "pure and self-sacrificing nature of Russian youth," nonetheless accused them of worshiping the false idol of Europeanism when Russia's only salvation reposed in the people itself. "It's a stange business . . . our Russian intelligentsia democratism unites with the aristocrats against the people: they go to the people 'in order to make them good' and despise all their customs and foundations." Educated young Russians needed not only to lose their contempt for the people, Dostoevsky advised, but to learn again to believe in God.⁵⁵

This reply filled them with consternation: they had not anticipated and did not accept the antithesis Dostoevsky posed. "Not only did we not see any sort of contradiction between the people and Europe," Miliukov wrote, "but, on the contrary, we expected from Europe the raising of the people to a higher cultural level." He would not look again to Dostoevsky for guidance.⁵⁶

Miliukov could not long confine himself to such innocuous student activities as the collection and dispersal of mutual aid funds; the nature of the student movement changed rapidly with the changing political atmosphere in Russia. Initially, students concerned themselves chiefly with broadening their rights. With the tsar's bestowal of broad discretionary powers on General M. T. Loris Melikov in 1880, in the hopes of effecting a reconciliation between government and society, student demands for greater autonomy seemed likely to be realized: A. A. Saburov, the new minister of education, proposed legalizing student organizations.[57] A student group formed to work out the guidelines of an all-student organization, and Miliukov served on the newly instituted student court.[58]

Demands speedily escalated to include a call for legal representation of the entire student body on all issues concerning students, and student meetings became more overtly political. Miliukov's attitude was somewhat ambivalent. He later claimed that the students of his year had already largely disassociated themselves from "populism," but also felt they could not help but share in the political ideals of the struggle being waged by the young revolutionaries of Narodnaia Volia (People's Will). A "doer" by nature, Miliukov found that his sympathies lay with the active fighters.[59]

At the same time, his tactical views put him with the more moderate minority generally associated with the history-philology *fakul'tet*, which wished to confine the student movement to student-related concerns and stick to legal means. According to Miliukov this group was known as the "constitutionalists," in contrast to the "radicals" of the medical and natural science *fakul'tety*. Prince Dmitrii Shakhovskoi, then a first-year law student and later a Kadet colleague of Miliukov's, characterized the dominant medical student group as the "old university"; the liberal, "new university," he said, was headed by Miliukov.[60]

The assassination of the tsar on March 1, 1881, produced a schism in the student movement. The police now forbade student assemblies, but the left students nonetheless planned one last, big meeting. Miliukov and his friends attended, but with the intention of diverting student energies away from general political questions to a firm defense of the rights they had already acquired.[61] Shakhovskoi was among those who felt that the student struggle for its own concerns was less than timely at this moment in the nation's fortunes, but he was much struck by Miliukov's attitude. "Among the intransigents I well recall the calm, resolute figure of P. N. Miliukov, who was risking his whole brilliant future under the influence of one consideration: that rights left undefended when threatened will never be consolidated."[62]

The police arrested all the participants in the unauthorized meeting. Miliukov's first brush with the tsarist police was not a particularly chastening experience. En route to Butyrka prison the arresting officers good-naturedly permitted several students to stop off for purchases of bread and sausage for the group, and they spent the night in jail in debate, versification, and general hilarity. Several days later each student appeared in turn before the University rector, Nikolai S. Tikhonravov. Tikhonravov, for whom Miliukov had written a long paper on Muscovite literature in the fifteenth and sixteenth centuries, offered him an out by suggesting that Miliukov had merely happened to find himself on the spot of the forbidden meeting. Miliukov liked and respected Tikhonravov, but was not prepared to disavow his actions. He insisted that he had knowingly attended the meeting and in consequence was suspended for the remainder of the semester, thus precluding his graduating with his class.[63]

Delayal of graduation by one year was not a particularly heavy penalty to pay for his first foray into "illegal activity," but Miliukov's developing political views cost him dearer in personal terms. He had met a girl at Pushkino eight years previously and their friendship had matured into love, at least on his part. The young woman's mother was an ardent admirer of Dostoevsky and took exception to Miliukov's increasingly negative attitude toward his views. The day after the tsar's assassination she attacked Miliukov for his "political" opinions and he felt himself no longer welcome in her home. With the rupture in his relations with the family the romance evaporated, and for a number of months Miliukov was troubled and depressed by the unhappy conclusion to his first love.[64]

A change of scene is one time-honored remedy for recovering from adversity in love, and Miliukov soon had recourse to that cure: a friend of his brother's proposed that they go abroad. Miliukov was twenty-two and had only been outside Moscow province twice. Characteristically, his intention was not to taste of European society or drink in the beauties of nature, but to study. He decided to concentrate on Greco-Roman sculpture and the painting of the early Renaissance; with these goals in mind he mapped out an arduous itinerary. The young men went first to Warsaw and then to Vienna, where they parted company, and for three happy months Miliukov was a solitary wanderer over the Italian peninsula. Venice overwhelmed him, the Giottos of Padua and Raphaels of Bologna caused him to "swoon," but it was Rome, above all, that impressed him. He spent a month there tramping the streets and ruins in the July heat. He even spent one evening locked in a museum, having become so absorbed in its exhibits that he failed to notice the building's closing time.[65]

Miliukov reentered the university in September refreshed and with a new seriousness of purpose, only to find the university atmosphere much changed and himself a stranger. His friends had graduated and gone. The student movement was quelled, but Miliukov sensed a change in the general atmosphere that went beyond a temporary cessation to student unrest: "There was something foreign, different in their dispositions, conversations, cast of thought."[66]

The assassination of Alexander II and the repression that followed in its wake proved to be a line of demarcation not only between two regimes but between two self-styled "generations": the "people of the seventies"—uncompromising, more enthralled by populism and revolutionary romanticism—and the "people of the eighties," who opposed revolution and believed in civic responsibility and gradual reform through "small deeds." The more cautious, modest stance of the latter, though occasioned by shock at revolutionary excesses and the limited opportunities for action permitted by Alexander III's regime, had a philosophical underpinning as well. Miliukov and his fellows had drunk in the hostility to "metaphysics" of the empiricist M. M. Troitskii, whose lectures now had serious competition in the philosophy department in the more idealist orientation of N. Ia. Grot and L. M. Lopatin. Many disillusioned youths of this generation were also attracted by the quietism of Tolstoy and his call for self-perfection.

Miliukov, entering university in the late 1870s, was a member of a transitional group, slightly younger and politically more moderate than the "classic" men of the seventies; he was of them, yet slightly apart. He now found himself most definitely set apart from the burgeoning ethos of the new generation. Later, he would reveal a certain confusion about his "generational" identity, in some instances "taking up the cudgels in the name of 'seventyness,'" at other times characterizing himself as younger than the men of the seventies but older than those of the eighties and nineties.[67]

Standing outside student circles, and with no student movement to divert him from his studies, Miliukov threw himself single-mindedly into academic work.[68] He concentrated on independent reading in political economy, history, and sociology, and also continued to take part in Vinogradov's seminar, where he made several new friends, including Aleksandr Guchkov.[69] He worked most closely with Vinogradov, but began writing his first thesis under Kliuchevskii, a work on landholding in the Muscovite state in the sixteenth century, based on the cadastral books (*pistsovye knigi*).[70] In its official evaluation of the work, most probably written by Kliuchevskii, the history department gave him high marks for analytical ability, mastery of method, and the enormous amount of statistical data gathered, although it found some of his conclusions "curious."[71]

Miliukov passed his qualifying exams in the spring and applied to be kept on at the university for graduate work in Russian history. He was therefore surprised when Vinogradov and Ger'e pressed him to opt for a specialty in world history. He later learned that Kliuchevskii had had qualms about taking him on as a graduate student. Miliukov could only speculate on the reasons for his professor's reservations, believing that his political views and previous lack of concentration on Russian history must have offended Kliuchevskii. He nonetheless persisted in his desire to study Russian history, and the department accordingly recommended to the Ministry of Education that

Miliukov, "in view of his capability and conscientiousness," be kept on for two years as kandidat, with an annual stipend of 600 rubles.[72]

The Aspiring Years

Miliukov, at twenty-four, had distinguished himself in his studies, put behind him his romantic disappointment, and gained support for beginning his chosen field of work. He was to be a scholar: he had, at last, an identity and clear purpose. "Real life" was starting for him now, he felt, and in searching for guides to that life he was drawn to the autobiography of John Stuart Mill, and found his mood best expressed in Longfellow's "A Psalm of Life," which he translated at this time:

> Lives of great men all remind us
> We can make our lives sublime.
> And, departing, leave behind us
> Footprints on the sands of time.[73]

Miliukov spent the next nine years in graduate work at Moscow University. This was, arguably, the happiest period of his life.[74]

He divided his first three years between preparation for graduate examinations and teaching, discovering that the latter employment was not only a material aid to the former, but a source of pleasure in its own right. Miliukov immediately procured a position at Moscow Fourth Women's Gymnasium, which he would hold for the next eleven years. He also gave lessons in history at the Agricultural Institute on Smolensk Boulevard and became a temporary instructor in the history of literature at a private girls' school. Miliukov expended considerable care on preparation for classes. He took a fairly maverick pedagogic approach for Russian secondary schools of the day, supplementing textbook accounts with his own interpretative treatment and minimizing attention to individual historical figures and dates. His students apparently liked this approach, for he was a popular teacher.[75]

Teaching, however personally satisfying, was ultimately a secondary concern. Preparation for the formidable master's examinations was the consuming task of these first three years of graduate school.[76] The candidate geared his studies to twelve to fifteen large questions set for his major field and six questions in each of two minor fields. Miliukov studied the obligatory minor in world history under Vinogradov, and his second minor, political economy, under Chuprov, another member of the circle of young professors around Miller and Kovalevskii.[77]

Even as he prepared for the exams, Miliukov looked beyond them to his future in the department. Successful examinees were considered for appointment as lecturers (*privat-dotsenty*), and it was up to the faculty to determine whether a lecturer's courses would be classified as requirements or electives. This was a decision of considerable financial significance, since instructors received virtually no remuneration for the typically small elective courses.[78] The inadequacy of support for graduate students was a source of bitterness among younger Russian academics; Miliukov was himself quite eloquent on the subject:

> [Young scholars] for years preserve a holy fire in themselves, meanwhile getting into cheap lessons, settling down to married life and, in the end, some sooner, some later, coming to realize the impossibility of combining loyalty to one's calling with care about a bit of bread. In good time the more expert ones try to find themselves a different, more lucrative occupation; the more conscientious and naive ones end with bitter disappointment and apathy.[79]

An important factor in the department's decision was the public lecture given by the candidate lecturer. Miliukov chose a theme reflecting one of his growing interests, the history of Russian historiography.

Highly conscious that the approach to history represented by Vinogradov and Kliuchevskii was a radical departure from the work of the previous generation of Russian historians, Miliukov looked for common characteristics in the work of this older generation and believed he found it in its preoccupation with the state. He argued that S. M. Solov'ev, K. D. Kavelin, B. N. Chicherin, and V. I. Sergeevich represented a distinct orientation united by a common ruling idea, which he called the "juridical school" of Russian historiography.[80] Assessing this school, he suggested its contribution was to introduce into Russian history writing the German idea of history as development, an "organic process."[81] The flaw in the juridical school's application of this approach was that it was ruled by its schema, placing elaborate forms before content. That school, Miliukov maintained, was now dead, its place taken by a more empirically grounded, less philosophical approach to history.[82]

Miliukov's lecture on the juridical school was well received, and he was appointed a lecturer, without, however, being given any of the more desirable required courses.[83] He considerably enhanced his social standing on joining the faculty of Moscow University, something of no small consequence to a man who had felt keenly the effects of social patronization in his youth. His new position gave him access to Moscow's most brilliant intellectual circles, and he entered this broader domain with enthusiasm. But the significance of Miliukov's teaching at Moscow University, which was to continue until his dismissal in January 1895, went beyond the social satisfaction it undoubtedly afforded him. Miliukov was the first student of Kliuchevskii and Vinogradov to assume a faculty position. Future historians took his classes and were profoundly influenced by his methodological and theoretical training. Iu. V. Got'e, who earned his master's degree under Kliuchevskii, warmly recalled Miliukov's guidance and encouragement, writing that he considered Miliukov, no less than Kliuchevskii, to be his teacher.[84]

Miliukov taught courses in the history of Russian colonization and the history of Russian historiography. He clearly took Vinogradov as a model when he insisted that the first task of the teacher at university level was to force students to think independently and to have confidence in their own powers.[85] It took him several years to feel entirely at ease before a class; at first, even a small audience could unsettle him, and more than once he would stumble and blush in the course of a lecture. Many students found this an endearing trait. According to one of his earliest students, Alexander Kizevetter: "Miliukov's lectures produced on those students who were already prepared to dedicate themselves to the study of Russian history a strong impression, by virtue of the fact that before us was a lecturer who ushered us into the ongoing work of his laboratory; the ebullience of this investigative work infected and inspired the attentive listeners."[86] Students began to gather regularly at Miliukov's tiny apartment—which looked rather like a secondhand bookstore—and there "in the friendly intercourse of our circle . . . worked out common views on history as a science."[87]

The transformation from student to faculty member coincided with another important change in Miliukov's life: in spring of 1886 he became engaged. Anna Sergeevna Smirnova was one of eight children of S. K. Smirnov, rector of the theological seminary at the Trinity Monastery of St. Sergius, near Moscow. Although shy and even self-effacing in public, Anna was at the same time extraordinarily energetic and strong-willed, "a woman who always knew her own mind." Her ten years at a Moscow boarding school awakened interests and ambitions her conservative family could not endorse—she became a fine pianist and wished to continue practice of her music and her studies in history. When her parents refused to consider further education, she struck out on her own, just managing to support herself by giving piano lessons while attending the Ger'e higher courses for women.[88] Kliuchevskii, an old family friend, was extremely fond of her and took her under his wing; when she finished the Ger'e courses, Kliuchevskii began directing her in advanced work in history.[89]

Miliukov met Anna at his adviser's home sometime in 1885; he was at that time a regular visitor there. The relationship was, at first, simply the acquaintance of two young people who studied in the same field and shared a passion for music. Anna, valuing her hard-won independence and immersed in her studies, was not inclined to think of matrimony. As comrades, their relationship was free of the banter and flirtatiousness of which the awkward Miliukov felt himself incapable. Imperceptibly, though, an attraction grew, and they began to meet outside the Kliuchevskii home. Secretly engaged, the couple married that winter in the presence of her family only.[90]

The newlyweds first lived with Miliukov's mother, but her coolness soon deteriorated into open hostility, and in autumn 1887 Miliukov and Anna rented a tiny flat of their own on a street off Zubovskii Boulevard. This proved to be an unexpected means for broadening their social circle and forwarding Miliukov's journalistic activities. They were drawn into the liberal circle of their upstairs neighbor, I. V. Storozhenko, professor of foreign literature and yet another of the Moscow University young professors gathered around Miller and Kovalevskii. At Storozhenkos', the Miliukovs met K. D. Bal'mont, a successful translator not yet transformed into the decadent hero of youth, and the famous mathematician Nikolai Bugaev, whose precocious young son, Boris (better known by his future nom de plume, Andrei Belyi), left a malicious picture of these "Apostles of humanism."[91] Through the Storozhenkos the Miliukovs were drawn into another group as well: the professorial "jurists" circle of the Ianzhuls, which included V. A. Gol'tsev, Chuprov, and I. I. Ivanov, as well as Kovalevskii, S. A. Muromtsev, and Vladimir Solov'ev as frequent visitors.[92]

The "liberalism" of the younger Moscow professorate in these years is difficult to define, since it was more a progressive orientation than an articulated philosophy or political program. Generally speaking, it stood for the rule of law, for more rational administration and more freedom for the average citizen, and for gradual change within the existing framework. George Fischer's characterization of the main current of gentry liberalism between the Great Reforms and the 1890s applies to the Mosocw circles Miliukov was entering: "It shared with most Western liberals of this period the apprehensions about unqualified democracy and large-scale social reforms. And it admired Western parliaments and constitutions without being certain when and how they might be transplanted to Russia."[93]

By virtue of being admitted into these enclaves, Miliukov was at first regarded as a liberal, and to the extent that he rejected both radical and conservative orientations, the label was not inaccurate. He was in fact far too involved with his studies, his various jobs, and his personal affairs to be more than casually interested in political and social issues in these years. In the mid-1880s, eagerly finding his way in the world, he appreciated his welcome into Moscow's progressive professorial circles. In his memoirs, he admitted some of the justice of Belyi's characterization of the narrowness and complacency of this little "liberal" world, but insisted, too, that he would be sorry to see it remembered only as Belyi had sketched it.[94]

Storozhenko's circle also had a very important function in that it introduced Miliukov into the journalistic activity that would, along with politics, eventually occupy him for the remainder of his long life. Some of the mainstays of the recently founded journal *Russkaia mysl'* (Russian thought) were part of the Storozhenko set, and both Miliukovs became contributors. Miliukov was invited to review works on history and archaeology; he recalled his trembling delight at seeing his first printed piece, and his horror on discovering two typographical errors in the text![95]

As he increasingly partook of the delights and ardors of intellectual Moscow, there were family changes. Miliukov and his mother were still estranged when she died of pneumonia a year or so after his marriage. He was troubled for many months by this circumstance, as well as by legal difficulties in settling with her creditors. The Miliukovs' first child, Nikolai, arrived in 1889, which helped bring Miliukov back into contact with his brother, already the father of two children. Aleksei, a rising young architect and avid hunter, moved in altogether different, less intellectual circles, but Miliukov was pleased by the strengthening of their family ties.[96]

Against this busy and happy backdrop of participation in circles, teaching, parenthood, journalistic employment, and the pleasurable relaxation of the quartet and quintet in which Anna and Miliukov played, it is rather startling to realize that Miliukov's chief occupation of this six-year period was in fact his master's dissertation. The scope of his interests and activities, and the indefatigable energy with which he pursued them, continually amazed his friends.[97]

Gosudarstvennoe khoziaistvo Rossii v pervoi chetverti XVIII veka i reforma Petra Velikogo (The state economy of Russia in the first quarter of the eighteenth century and the reforms of Peter the Great) was a project of colossal proportions. A master's dissertation normally occupied its author for three years; Miliukov required twice this time to complete what would be a 700-page monograph based almost entirely on unpublished archival sources. It was an undertaking that had given him both pleasure and pain. The pleasure was in the archival work itself, conducted in Moscow and during two summers in St. Petersburg. Miliukov learned to love this work and could not keep his enthusiasm to himself, spilling over with discussion of his discoveries in his classes and at the historians' gatherings at Vinogradov's.[98] The conclusions to which his investigations drew him were far-reaching and important; the work would be a pathbreaker, and its author knew it full well. The pain came from the deterioration of his relations with Kliuchevskii, occasioned in part by his choice of dissertation topic.

At his dissertation defense, Miliukov insisted that the concerns originally prompting this project had nothing to do with Peter himself. He knew that he wanted a topic in the field of material history that was amenable to statistical methodology, and that he wanted to work with archival sources. With these criteria in mind he decided to try and combine study of population history with an investigation of the state budget during the years 1680–

1710. As he established, to his mind, an enormous and coincident decline in both population and revenues by 1710, he began to ponder both how the two phenomena were connected and how the state addressed this crisis. This led him to grapple directly with the administrative and financial reforms of the entire Petrine era, and in this way he worked out fully the contours of the topic that actually encompassed even more than the dissertation's title suggests.[99]

Research for the dissertation required that Miliukov spend time in a world hitherto unknown to him: St. Petersburg. He spent two summers in the capital, between 1887 and 1891; his rather critical first impressions of the city that would become his home for many years never substantially altered. Much later, drawing an analogy between the characteristics of the Moscow and Petersburg schools of historiography and their respective cities of origin, he wrote:

> Petersburg is the city of the hierarchical bureaucracy; in Moscow, the liberal professions are first in society. Petersburg is official and fastened into uniform; in Moscow, the soul is unbuttoned. Petersburg is disciplined, while Moscow is peopled by free men. Petersburg is precise; Moscow is forever inclined to seek the causes of causes and to "consider the root." Moscow has originality, invents, is not afraid to offend by an excess of personality; Petersburg looks upon imagination with distrust, but once it has hit upon an idea, it is skilled in adapting itself to its application.[100]

Miliukov became acquainted with the elder statesman of St. Petersburg historians, K. N. Bestuzhev-Riumin, but felt more at home with the younger historians gathered around Sergei F. Platonov. Though Platonov and Miliukov were to differ significantly in their historical interpretations, particularly concerning the role of Peter in reforming Russia, they respected and liked each other, and Platonov was of great help to Miliukov in getting his early work published.[101] Platonov also introduced Miliukov into a talented group of graduate students and young scholars, including A. S. Lappo-Danilevskii, N. P. Pavlov-Sil'vanskii, and V. M. Druzhinin, all of whom met frequently at the latter's home to discuss their craft.[102]

This group welcomed Miliukov with a certain anticipation as Kliuchevskii's first student and therefore a most informed source on the new, more sociological approach that was emerging as the Moscow school of historiography. He was happy to preach the advantages of the sociological approach; later contrasting the Petersburg school's tradition with that of Moscow, he felt that their differences were chiefly explicable by their perspective on the object of the historian: "[The Petersburg school] attributes to the *establishment* of facts that primary significance which in the Moscow school belongs to their *explanation*." Miliukov enjoyed his reputation as a proponent of the new school, even presenting reports to the Platonov circle on its approach and methodology.[103]

In addition to time spent with this stimulating and congenial group, Miliukov came into the orbit of a decidedly more leftist group that included V. I. Semevskiii, a specialist on the peasantry, and his student Venedict A. Miakotin. Both had strong Populist leanings, and Miakotin had close contacts with several adherents of the revolutionary People's Will. Miakotin and Miliukov became particularly close; Miakotin even lived with the Miliukovs for a time in Moscow.[104]

Miliukov returned to Moscow after his first summer in St. Petersburg full of his findings, only to meet with a disheartening reception from Kliuchevskii. In truth, though Miliukov already enjoyed a certain reputation as Kliuchevskii's first student, the relationship was not a smooth one. Kliuchevskii was by no means an easy man to work with. More formal and reserved in his relations with students than was the case with the other young professors, he was also not in the habit of offering praise, holding that a teacher should not "encourage conceit." In his memoirs, Miliukov refers to an "irritability and nerviness" in his adviser that grew more pronounced over time. According to Kizevetter, the student closest to Kliuchevskii, his mentor's sharp tongue spared no one, and gaining his trust was not easy: "He was suspicious to the point of paranoia."[105] It is suggestive that in the twenty some years during which Kliuchevskii occupied the chair of Russian history at Moscow University, only six students successfully defended master's dissertations in his field.[106]

Miliukov's behavior, however, was not best calculated to smooth the way with this sensitive and difficult scholar. He first incurred his teacher's displeasure through his teaching: in his course on the history of Russian colonization, Miliukov contradicted Kliuchevskii's interpretation.[107] Displaying his customary independence, as well as the insensitivity that on occasion colored his actions, it did not occur to him to discuss his ideas with Kliuchevskii before offering a course that refuted several theories advanced by his adviser and senior faculty colleague. Kliuchevskii visibly cooled toward Miliukov.[108]

The most important source of friction was Miliukov's dissertation. Kliuchevskii, with some foundation, considered the topic unsuitable for a master's dissertation. When Miliukov came to see him after his first summer of archival work in Petersburg, flushed with success and eager to share his findings, Kliuchevskii advised him to confine himself to a more modest inquiry. Miliukov felt that he had fallen from the empyrean. "I'd been prepared to contribute to science, to open new paths—and suddenly, instead of this, I was having suggested to me a heap of monastery charters and a poor little booklet in result!" Thoroughly disappointed, he refused to yield, electing to continue work on the Petrine reforms. Kliuchevskii's coldness toward

Miliukov became unmistakable, and it appears that it was at this time that the Miliukovs' visits to their teacher's dacha and home ended.[109]

The breach seems to have come in late spring of 1892. In 1891, at any rate, Miliukov did not rule out the possibility of Kliuchevskii's support for making his career at Moscow University. He had other options—an offer to teach Russian history at the Aleksandrovskii Lyceum in Petersburg and a chance to go to "one of our provincial departments." He wrote Kliuchevskii on March 10, 1891, explaining that before he made a decision on these offers he wished to have a firmer idea of his prospects at Moscow.[110] Kliuchevskii's answer was apparently encouraging, for Miliukov declined both positions.

A letter from Kliuchevskii on April 22, 1892, suggests a confrontation occurred one month before Miliukov's public dissertation defense. Miliukov wished to submit his dissertation for the newly created Solov'ev prize in history. Kliuchevskii wrote to say that they needed to talk about getting the work ready for submission, continuing: "I hesitate to ask that you come by next Sunday evening, although I will be home and even hope to see several of my acquaintances there. For my part, it would be awkward to request this of you after last Saturday. However, I really would be very glad to see you on that evening."[111] Miliukov apparently did not go by the Kliuchevskiis' that evening, for a brief note of Kliuchevskii's of May 4, coldly headed "Dear Sir" (*milostivyi gosudar'*) pointed out that the deadline for the prize submissions was the following day and that if Miliukov still intended to submit his dissertation he should so inform him.[112]

The substance of the disagreement may be guessed at. Miliukov had hoped that Kliuchevskii would recommend that he receive both master and doctoral degrees for his ambitious dissertation. There was a precedent for such a step: Professor Ger'e had recommended simultaneous degrees for a huge dissertation on Renaissance Italy by his student Karelin, at about the same time that Miliukov submitted his dissertation.[113] Vinogradov, ever Miliukov's champion, had tried, along with Ger'e, to persuade Kliuchevskii to do the same for Miliukov, but Kliuchevskii refused. When the two men pointed out that Miliukov's monograph was already being published, Kliuchevskii answered that he could write another; science would only gain from this. Vinogradov indignantly related to Miliukov the whole of the departmental interplay on this issue, and it may be that Miliukov approached Kliuchevskii directly on the subject.[114]

Miliukov's public defense of the dissertation was scheduled for May 17, 1892. The large audience knew of Kliuchevskii's decision regarding the granting of a doctoral degree and, in Vasilii Maklakov's account, "students hastened to the conclusion that Kliuchevskii was biased and unjust. They brought to the dispute a mood against Kliuchevskii, and he knew it." But if they came in hopes of witnessing unseemly pyrotechnics, they were disappointed: according to the chronicler of the defense, Miliukov conducted himself with great tact and restraint. He opened with a discussion of how he had chosen his topic and the nature of the data he used. He then concisely and clearly—more clearly, it might be said, than in the dissertation itself—outlined his findings and conclusions, one of them being the famous assertion that "the price of raising Russia to the rank of a European power was the ruination of the country."[115]

Kliuchevskii's examination was conducted with his customary subtlety and technique, in what Maklakov referred to as his "dialectical method," but which Kizevetter less euphemistically termed a game of "cat and mouse." He began with a general evaluation of the whole work that rather damned with faint praise. Noting the contribution to scholarship Miliukov's archival discoveries constituted, he reproached him for not making the fullest use of the facts he had ascertained: Miliukov, he argued, had saddled the reader with the responsibility of discerning conclusions only implicitly drawn. He then went on to a series of separate, seemingly unconnected observations and questions on minutiae, whose overall effect was to suggest that Miliukov had failed to consider alternate explanations for his data. He concluded with the devastating words that Miliukov's dissertation constituted an "adequate basis" for the master's degree.[116]

The entire experience long haunted Miliukov; writing nearly fifty years later, he still characterized Kliuchevskii's examination as a "profanation." He claimed, too, that at the end of the defense he vowed to himself that he would never write another dissertation. Following the formal defense, the professors of the faculty crowded around him to give the traditional kisses of welcome to their new colleague, but Kliuchevskii brusquely offered his hand. For his part, Miliukov also broke with a university tradition by pointedly not inviting Kliuchevskii to the banquet celebrating his defense. The breach between them was not to heal any time soon.[117]

Three distinct impressions emerge from an examination of Miliukov's life up to the award of his graduate degree: the extent to which his years at Moscow University shaped his interests and perspectives; his near indifference to social and political issues for much of this period; and a sort of overall "lack of roots."

At Moscow University, exposure to the orientation of Kliuchevskii and the circle of young professors around Kovalevskii and Miller stimulated and nourished a love of history and scholarship and provided Miliukov with a vocation. He found not only a new and intellectually satisfying approach to the history of human society, but, in Comtean positivism, a successor to the religious faith he had lost. Miliukov's views would develop and alter in the decades to come, but he never relinquished positivism's confident perspective on "regular" and "lawful" historical processes, and related views on the historicity and relativity of all human values.

For most of this period, Miliukov's pursuits were intellectual and practical. His humble contribution to the cause of liberating the Slavs and letter to Dostoevsky were the sole instances of concern with political or social issues extending beyond the university milieu. His "liberalism" was nothing more definite than the progressive orientation of a member of educated society and did not even find application in "small deeds." Miliukov was decidedly not, in these years, political.

A third impression to be derived from the early years of Miliukov's life concerns his lack of roots. The indeterminate social status of his parents, the peripatetic years of his early youth, the absence of strong family feeling and sense of religious heritage, and lack of a "generational" identity all contributed to Miliukov's entering Moscow University without any strong sense of self, place, or tradition. While Miliukov clearly found an identity and vocation in scholarship, there is an obvious parallel between the rather rootless quality of his background and his later contention, as an historian, that the distinguishing feature of the Russian "national type" was its "full indeterminacy" and plasticity. Miliukov's rootlessness, too, helps explain his subsequent capacity for crossing political lines and forging coalitions. Encyclopedic and far-ranging in his interests, lacking strong ties to any social estate, and born to a transitional "generation," Miliukov was suited to the role of mediator by temperament, talents, and background.

Finally, Miliukov's teaching and his relations with his own adviser, Kliuchevskii, are themes in their own right. In the tradition of Vinogradov, and in contrast to Kliuchevskii, Miliukov worked closely with students and believed in the virtues of hands-on training and discussion of both theoretical and methodological approach. Once he began offering courses at Moscow University he performed a much needed function in defining and disseminating the new, sociological orientation that contemporaries called the Moscow school of historiography and which is today often called—rather misleadingly—the "Kliuchevskii" school.

The subject of his relations with Kliuchevskii was one to which Miliukov returned repeatedly; in his own mind, his falling-out with his adviser was a turning point in his life. One need not be a psychologist to note certain suggestive parallels between Miliukov's relationship with his difficult adviser, the major "authority figure" of his young manhood, and his frustrating relationship with his father.[118] Miliukov bitterly recalled his father's aloofness, his failure to offer encouragement and guidance, and the way he severed the "moral bond" uniting parent and child by thrashing his sons; these motifs emerge, in varying guises, in Miliukov's writings on Kliuchevskii.

Miliukov's attitude toward his father and ambivalent feelings toward his adviser, when considered in the light of his frequent assertions that he always strove to preserve his independence, raise a point very important to understanding his subsequent behavior as a leader. Valuing his freedom, Miliukov did not submit easily to authority.

C·H·A·P·T·E·R T·W·O

Political Awakening

Defense of the dissertation marked a turning point in Miliukov's life. Having been a student his entire life he was at last, at thirty-three, a full-fledged scholar and *magistr*. What should have been a most satisfying transformation, however, proved otherwise. His relations with Kliuchevskii did not improve, and he came to find his position at the university intolerable. The fault was Kliuchevskii's, he felt, although his own wounded pride featured in the continued estrangement, since his former teacher made at least one friendly overture.[1]

Whatever Kliuchevskii's personal feelings, circumstantial evidence tends to support Miliukov's later contention that Kliuchevskii effectively blocked his career at the university well before the government terminated it formally. It is significant that he was not advanced beyond the position of lecturer; with his outstanding teaching and publication record, he would surely have been promoted if Kliuchevskii supported his candidacy.[2] Miliukov felt keenly the consequences of being overlooked. In the short term, remaining a lecturer condemned him to continued financial hardship. For the long term, the department's failure to promote him was an unmistakable signal that he was not being groomed to be a permanent member of the faculty. Apparently, Miliukov's disaffection was common knowledge. In December 1894, when a speech by Kliuchevskii in honor of the recently deceased Alexander III provoked a furor among students, Miliukov was popularly—and incorrectly—assumed to be responsible for the unpleasant rejoinder anonymously circulated in response. Such incidents helped to make the university atmosphere "festering."³

Financial pressures and his frustrating position at the university contributed to Miliukov's stepping up his journalistic activity and extracurricular teaching. After the university, the editorial offices of *Russkaia mysl'* became his second home. He had been publishing reviews and the occasional article with the journal for three years and gradually became "one of its own." Now, he also assumed direction of its entire bibliographic department, a position of some influence, since it gave him a large voice in determining what books were reviewed, and by whom.⁴

Although Miliukov later claimed that his political orientation at this time was closer to that of the Petersburg journal *Vestnik Evropy* (The herald of Europe), the standard bearer of Western-style liberalism in Russia, *Russkaia mysl'* was in fact the ideal place for him.⁵ Its editor, V. A. Gol'tsev, considered by radical Moscow students to be more "left" than liberal, made it an organ of moderate populist opinion but welcomed contributions from social democrats and virtually all "progressives." The journal was therefore eclectic, which suited Miliukov quite well, and under the hospitable Gol'tsev its editorial offices were a gathering place for Muscovites and visiting contributors from Petersburg and the provinces. Miliukov met many of the luminaries of Russian literature and criticism at the offices of *Russkaia mysl'*, or at the public banquets Gol'tsev regularly arranged to honor some public principle or individual whose work embodied that ideal.⁶ It was also through Gol'tsev, at his Thursday "at homes," that he first made the acquaintance, in 1890, of Ivan Petrunkevich, Dmitrii Shakhovskoi, and other prominent provincials who subsequently became his close colleagues in the Union of Liberation and the Constitutional Democratic Party.⁷

Miliukov's new position at the Moscow Pedagogical Institute was more than just another means of supplementing the family income. The three-year course he began teaching there in 1892 was his first opportunity to expound the "new view on history" he had been working out.⁸ The course was an interpretative history of Russian culture, conceived on a vast scale. Its three parts traced the formation and evolution of the state, its institutions, and the social estates; examined the history of Russian religiosity and high culture; and concluded with a history of the development of public opinion. Miliukov hoped to penetrate beyond the deceptively random picture produced by study of political history, in order to discern the fundamental patterns of Russian historical development. He therefore largely excluded *l'histoire evenementielle* (event-oriented history), instead concentrating on the history of institutions and the history of ideas.⁹

He also took an explicitly instrumental approach to history, his stated objective being to "explain the present by means of study of the past."[10] Whether discussing the peasant commune or the printing press, he traced the history of a phenomenon virtually up to his own day. This present-mindedness constituted a departure from Miliukov's earlier work as well as from current pedagogical practice: courses on recent history were thought to be necessarily unscientific.[11]

A major theme of the course was the historicity of all aspects of Russian culture. Not only governmental bodies but social values and even the "national ethos" were historically grounded and subject to change. Nationality, Miliukov maintained, was not the explanation for the distinctive features of the historical process in Russia, for the Russian nationality was itself the product of those distinctive features.[12] The import of this perspective was to undercut rather than to support loyalty to institutions and ideas that were indigenous and therefore inherently "Russian." If all phenomena are historical, generated by specific material conditions and a given level of social, political, and cultural development, then as circumstances change institutions and ideas must likewise change or cease to be relevant to the needs of a new age.

The state's monopoly on power was a case in point. According to Miliukov, the peculiar and adverse conditions in which the Russian state originated required that it be able to command every resource, human as well as natural, merely in order to survive. Even after the continued existence of the Russian state ceased to be problematic, the state's control over political and cultural life remained largely constructive. It was the state that forced education and innovation on a body politic that was still underdeveloped and more or less inert. When Russia's citizenry at last matured and began to think and act independently, however, the state persisted in treating it as a captious minor. The state had begun by fostering growth, but continued by stunting it. Miliukov insisted that Russia "has grown up from certain forms and outgrown certain traditions—to deny this is to close our eyes to reality and deny the laws of historical development."[13] For politically conscious students—and of these there was an ever-growing supply in the 1890s—it was easy to infer that autocracy was one of the traditions that Russia had outgrown.

In the classroom Miliukov could not openly read encomiums on democracy, but his comparisons of Russian and European development left little doubt that he saw democracy as the highest stage of political life and the system best calculated to promote the general good. Examining the history of political struggle in the West, he explained that "socially purposeful action has as its goal the best possible good of the masses; as its means, the legal struggle of political parties; as its result, the improvement of the state organization," adding, "We will not find any of these phenomena of socially purposeful action in the history of Russia."[14]

Was Russia destined to follow the Western experience, or was the Russian pattern of development to remain unique? Miliukov was already disposed toward the former view, but his answer to this question, at this time, was cast in terms more guarded than would later be the case. As a positivist, he sought to discern universal "laws of internal development." Russia was European, he affirmed, and would therefore roughly follow the "European" pattern. But his strict empiricism pulled him in the opposite direction, forcing him to insist, as well, that the cluster of conditions shaping any given state's development varied endlessly, so that each state was truly unique: similarity could never be identity.[15]

The great bulk of Miliukov's writing throughout this period was scholarly. Yet in addition to the four books, seventeen articles, and fifty-eight reviews he published on historical themes between 1892 and 1897 (an astonishing average output of more than 300 pages per year), he wrote a number of articles on more contemporary issues. In 1889 Nikolai Storozhenko, a professor of foreign literature at the university and Miliukov's upstairs neighbor, passed on to him the job of writing an annual survey of Russian literature for the "Continental Literature" section of the English journal *The Athenaeum*.[16] The term "literature" was understood to encompass virtually everything relating to higher culture, including belles lettres, literary criticism, philosophy, history, political economy, and even debate on social issues. Comprehensive in their coverage and free from the usual censorship constraints, the eight surveys Miliukov wrote for the *Athenaeum* constitute a fascinating overview of Russian intellectual currents in this period, as well as a valuable source for his response to them.

Both the tone and preoccupations of Miliukov's *Athenaeum* pieces help date his political awakening. His article of July 1889, though written in a minor key, did not explicitly express dissatisfaction with the state of affairs in Russia. A year later his discontent surfaced openly with the assertion that Russia is a "society whose stagnation is ever growing more complete." His observations for summer 1891 were still more somber: "The barrenness of our literature is merely a reflection of the emptiness of our daily life."[17]

One stimulant to Miliukov's consciousness of Russia's ills probably came from his first contacts with professionals from the zemstvos, Russia's institutions of county and provincial self-government. About a year before making the acquaintance of Petrunkevich and others at the Gol'tsev's, Miliukov took part in a series of informal colloquia (*besedy*) of zemtsy and professional men held in Moscow at the end of the decade.[18] In all, some forty people gathered in private homes on eight occasions to discuss such zemstvo concerns as the electoral system, taxation, education, and public health. Miliukov, along with his friend Venedikt Miakotin, was a regular participant.[19] No record of these discussions has been preserved, but Miliukov would have carried away from them a sharp impression of the frustration provoked by the 1889 institution of land captains and other governmental measures undermining zemstvo autonomy and effectiveness.

The ills Miliukov chronicled in 1890 and 1891 in the *Athenaeum* were not social or economic, however, but spiritual. With the exception of one short diatribe on post-emancipation exploitation of the peasantry and the corruption of the bureaucracy, Miliukov directed all his attention to the spiritual malaise of educated Russian society. The manifestations of this malaise were the prevailing currents of "individualism" and "indifferentism." The old, clearly defined schools and parties had vanished, he lamented, and with them had gone not only the exchange of ideas but any impetus for action broadly conceived. "Individualism is in the ascendant. Each man sits in his own corner and develops out of his inner consciousness theories of his own, or perhaps remains without any equipment at all of general ideas."[20]

For Miliukov, the practical result of "individualism," be it the egotistical brand he attributed to Nietzsche and Maurice Barrès or the more morally inspired "self-perfecting" of Tolstoy, was harmful social inaction.[21] His hostility to Tolstoy, whose influence on youth alarmed him, amounted almost to rancor. In Tolstoy's moral doctrines, he wrote, "fragments of modern science are brought to the aid of old questions about the necessity of religious opinions," all of which was strangely mixed up with "elements of modern political economy, the moral teachings of Buddhism," and the social utopias of Cromwell's parliament.[22]

The generation of the 1880s was "remarkable for its premature senility and indifferentism," he charged. He could sympathize with the reluctance of these men to sacrifice themselves to a cause after the decimation of their heroic "elder brothers" of 1878–81. Nonetheless, this generation drew his scorn for being more than resigned to its fate, instead choosing to make a virtue of necessity. "The first task set themselves by this group was to raise their mental attitude (a temporary and accidental historical phenomenon) into a political theory and to found upon it something in the shape of a positive program."[23] In the work to better Russia, which Miliukov clearly viewed as a duty incumbent on every educated Russian, the temporary tactic of "small deeds" was defensible but a philosophy of small deeds emphatically was not.

Miliukov's fundamental concern in depicting a gray and mediocre literature reflecting a stagnant society was the absence of any generally agreed upon ethical and philosophical foundation to life. As he characterized it, the effort "to give a moral reason and principle to our conception of the universe," an effort as yet unsuccessful, was the motive informing not only

Russian fiction of this period, but philosophy and philosophy of history as well.[24] The works of Vladimir Solov'ev and Sergei Trubetskoi, the Moscow Philosophical Society's commemoration of the anniversary of Schopenhauer's birth, the "interminable debates" on free will conducted on the pages of that society's journal—all these testified, he felt, to a new preoccupation in Russian philosophy. In essence, this could be described as a turn away from positivism and empiricism toward a "metaphysical ethics with a mystical religious colouring."[25]

Miliukov's examination of philosophical currents demonstrated a lively interest in the issues under discussion and a more than creditable grasp of the approaches and the literature, but the tone of his appraisal was, above all, disappointed. The philosophers were original, sometimes even compelling, but had thus far been no more successful than other writers in supplying a moral foundation or system that could attract large numbers of the thinking public. The sticking point seemed to be, for Miliukov, the assumption of the existence of absolutes: the philosophers were renewing "the quest of our old Slavophiles after some universal moral truth in opposition to the scientific truth found by the 'West.'"[26] But even as he dismissed most of the theories advanced as artificial, idiosyncratic, or impractical, he acknowledged that "the demand for some philosophical and ethical basis can scarcely be regarded as artificial."[27]

He opened his *Athenaeum* review in 1892 on a more hopeful note; there were definite signs, he told his readers, of a "rise of the social temperature."[28] The stirrings in society revealed by the public critique of the program of the "men of the 'eighties" had now burst into the open in both debate and action. The catalyst was the trans-Volga famine of 1891–92 and the resultant cholera epidemics.[29] The scope of this calamity definitively punctured the shell of "social indifferentism" as society was galvanized into relief work. Praising the energies and efforts of relief workers, Miliukov correctly predicted that the impression made by the famine would have a long-term significance: it signaled an "entire reorientation in views" and aroused a new interest in the people that would, he felt, outlive the crisis itself.

The famine that acted as a catalyst on educated Russians similarly affected Paul Miliukov. From early 1893, when he became an active member of the influential Moscow Literacy Committee, he increasingly devoted his energies to public work.[30] He in a sense signaled his new engagement in the concerns of society with his first public lecture, "The Decline of Slavophilism," delivered January 22, 1893, in the Moscow Historical Museum.[31] Miliukov was already acknowledged as something of an expert on Slavophilism, which he regarded as the first instance of truly creative Russian reworking of European philosophy.[32] But his lecture on the heirs to Slavophilism was as much a normative characterization of contemporary values and a call to action as a scholarly evaluation of a doctrine; it therefore had political overtones his audience could not have failed to detect. This lecture was, as well, the closest Miliukov ever came to an elaboration of his ethical views.

Miliukov argued, on both theoretical and pragmatic grounds, that latter-day Slavophilism, as represented in the thought of Nikolai Danilevskii, Konstantin Leont'ev, and Vladimir Solov'ev, was untenable. He saw Slavophilism as the child of German romantic philosophy and the patriarchal family structure in which its epigones matured. Since neither this philosophical system nor its engendering family order survived the 1860s, all later attempts to revivify Slavophilism were necessarily abstract and lifeless, even when they adduced new kinds of evidence in support of the old theory.

Miliukov also contended that Slavophilism itself, as originally formulated, was internally inconsistent and rested on a fallacious assumption. It attempted to combine two concepts that could coexist only temporarily, the idea of unique nationality and that of world-historical significance.[33] In seeking national characteristics that were distinctly "Russian" and which would furthermore promise Russians a world-historical significance, the Slavophiles hit upon the integrated spiritualism of peasant orthodoxy and the practical communalism of peasant institutions. They believed that by virtue of these qualities the Russian people would help humanity transcend the atomizing rationalism of Western civilization.[34] The problem was, Miliukov argued, that the Slavophiles, though infinitely more tradition-minded than the Westernizers, were nonetheless ahistorical in their thought. They erroneously construed inalterable "absolutes" from temporary, historical phenomena.

The heirs of Slavophilism found it impossible to preserve this unstable combination of particularism and universalism, instead developing one or the other to its logical conclusion. Danilevskii and Leont'ev, he argued, embraced the idea of national uniqueness, which shorn of its universalizing elements became simple national egoism.[35] Their theories could not avoid becoming conservative to the point of reaction: valuing nationality as a thing in itself, they either rejected the possibility of the evolution of nationality or, in the case of Leont'ev, attempted to forestall it.[36] Solov'ev, on the other hand, developing the religious thought of Slavophilism, represented its universal and progressive side. But a strictly religious development of Slavophile teaching, lacking its national element, logically resulted in the chimera of a world theocracy as the only resolution of the world-historical mission.[37]

Finally, both currents of latter day Slavophilism retained what Miliukov saw as the fatal flaw of the original theory, its absolutist assumptions. Educated Russians, Miliukov argued, would neither accept the immutable "nationality" of the one camp nor assume, with the other, the moral primacy of a purely religious end: "Just as national absolutism is foreign to contemporary sociology, so too is religious absolutism foreign to contemporary ethics."[38] Populism and democratic liberalism "of the newest type" were the real successors to the Hegelian-based theories of the 1840s and 1850s. It was time to recognize, Miliukov concluded, that Slavophilism "is dead and will not rise again."[39]

Although Miliukov's theoretical objections to the rival currents within the new Slavophilism made up the bulk of the lecture, it was the practical consequences of this orientation that most patently concerned him. For Miliukov, Slavophilism followed to its logical conclusion resulted in social inaction. This was clearly the import of the inherent conservatism of Danilevskii and Leont'ev, which he found easy to dismiss out of hand.[40] Solov'ev's dream of bringing the city of God to earth, however, was not so easily cast aside. Solov'ev's theory was essentially ethical and humanitarian, as the nationalistic strain of the new Slavophilism was not; it attempted to combine a modern and secular idea, that of "liberal-egalitarian progress" with the ascetic ideal of historical Christianity. But Solov'ev's form of Slavophilism led to a preoccupation with the future at the expense of the present, a subordination of resolution of problems in the here and now to achievement of a distant, future goal. It led, Miliukov insisted, to a preference for the "moral" over the "just," a reversal of "the whole hierarchy of human aspirations and obligations."[41]

Considered in conjunction with Miliukov's pieces for the *Athenaeum* and his history course for the Pedagogic Institute, the lecture on Slavophilism may be read as his response—albeit a provisional one—to the Russian search for a "philosophical and moral basis." Rejecting any metaphysical or religious absolute as the foundation for a system of ethics, insisting on the historicity of all theories and values, Miliukov implicitly argued for an understanding of ethics as socially generated and dynamic.[42] The "good" is not absolute and unambiguous; rather, there is a multitude of competing, and variable, conceptions of the good. Moral action entails making choices not just between right and wrong but between different versions of what is right, and as Miliukov's references to the "hierarchy of aspirations and obligations" and "egalitarian progress" make clear, he believed social welfare to be the referent by which these choices should be made. Equally implicit in this understanding of ethics as socially founded was the idea of praxis: if the good could only be defined empirically, through social experience, then it must be realized in practice. It must be put into action.

The pragmatic, "contextual" ethic that Miliukov hinted at in "The Decline of Slavophilism" was remarkably similar to the ethical theory of "instrumentalism" John Dewey was working out at precisely this time.[43] Noting the similarities in the ethical approach of these two men is not meant to suggest that Miliukov's thinking on moral values ever approximated

Dewey's systematization or scope, or that he was directly influenced by Dewey, though it is possible that he was already familiar with his work. The similarities are, nevertheless, instructive, especially given both men's almost transcendent faith—empiricists though they were—in the beneficence of democracy.[44]

Dewey saw social reform as "the transformation of ethics from abstraction to reality," arguing that "communication, sharing, joint participation are the only actual ways of universalizing the moral law and end."[45] Miliukov's approach to ethics, like that of Dewey, emphasized the sense of obligation as the motive force of ethical action. Both men were aware of the social dimension of such activity; Miliukov always maintained that in a backward country like Russia, efforts at self-perfection had to take a back seat to the reform of institutions.[46] Historical relativists, both men rejected attempts to prescribe an unchanging system of ethics. Finally, Miliukov shared Dewey's belief that in ethical theory "volition, activity, and results must all be viewed as pieces of a single puzzle." In other words, a theory that did not entail action corresponding to and productive of its avowed ends was not "ethical," no matter how humanitarian its intentions might be.[47]

An ethical perspective grounded in action was admirably suited to Miliukov and Dewey's common desire to bring about actual and immediate social reform, but their exclusion of absolute moral values was also an exclusion of ethical certitude; without recourse to a transcendent, the "right" course of action was not always clear cut, particularly when it came to determining the relationship of means and ends. As will be seen, this lack of certitude helps explain Miliukov's periodic flirtations with more radical political orientations and his repeated failure to come to grips with the question of the legitimacy of terror as a tool of political struggle.[48]

Politicization

Having pronounced his obituary on neo-Slavophilism, Miliukov switched his attention to other modes of discourse. From 1893, his annual midsummer surveys for the *Athenaeum* were increasingly preoccupied with the public debate sparked by the famine. Polemics exchanged between Populists and liberals, followed by even fiercer disputes between Populists and Marxists, focused on the course of Russia's economic development. For some, such as V. P. Vorontsov, the famine was a striking demonstration of their conviction that Russia could not or should not attempt to compete with the capitalist West on its own ground. For others, such as Petr Struve and the young Lenin, the famine furnished further proof that Russia was becoming, and must become, an industrial, capitalist country.[49] The principle of government intervention in the economy was not at issue; in Russia,

Miliukov told his British readers, even liberals recognized that the state had an active role to play in economic life.[50]

For Populists and Marxists, the dispute was primarily over means: both looked forward to socialism, but had very different notions about how to achieve that aim. Populists saw primitive economic collectivism, embodied in the peasant commune and *artel'*, as the promise of the future, Miliukov wrote; they therefore desired the safeguarding of these institutions. The Marxists anticipated the collectivism that would follow mature individualist capitalism and so argued against policies intended to impede the dissolution of the commune.[51] At bottom, he felt, the dispute over Russia's economic future came down to "opposite sociological views in the interpretation of history": it was not the economic evidence itself that dictated the various positions, but preconceived orientations applied to the evidence:

> [The Populist group] values primitive collectivism because it regards it as an inalienable trait in the character of the Russian people; and at present, of course, it sees in it not the immemorial peculiarity of the popular spirit, but a means of saving Russia from proletarianism. The other group derives its deductions from the teachings of Marx and Engels and from a corresponding understanding of history.[52]

Whatever the shortcomings of either perspective, Miliukov welcomed this debate as a healthy sign of the reanimation of society and its deepening engagement in the concerns of Russian life.

In the mid-1890s, Miliukov's wrangles with various Marxists notwithstanding, many Russians thought him inclined toward Marxism.[53] Up until 1893 his published work had been concerned almost exclusively with material history, and his treatment of that history, implicitly and at times explicitly, drew on the framework and terminology of economic materialism.[54] He clearly had a number of affinities with Marxism. The three most important were its historical sensibilities, its materialist orientation, and the importance it attached to institutions in shaping the trajectory of a society's development. Marxists rejected any notion of an immutable popular spirit, contending that a people's values, ethos, and institutions were all subject to evolution and that this evolution proceeded according to historical laws; Miliukov could endorse all of this. Marxists opposed "metaphysics" and dualism, as did Miliukov—he was very impressed by Plekhanov's *On the Monist View of History*, which appeared in 1895.[55] Finally, he liked Marxism's appreciation of the importance of political as well as social reform, and the implicit Westernism of its entire approach.[56]

Nonetheless, Miliukov had serious reservations about Marxism, especially as it was understood in Russia in the first half of the 1890s. For one thing, he recoiled from its determinism. To the young Marxists who launched the critique of agrarian socialism, or "Populism," it seemed that the famine had proved Marx right about the inevitable march of history.[57] For them, Marxism was not a revolutionary doctrine; adherence to Marxism did not as yet entail *doing* anything. The vogue among young people of Struve's *Critical Remarks* (*Kriticheskie zametki*), which pictured the advent of capitalism in Russia as not merely inevitable but welcome, troubled Miliukov not a little: "In order to promote the realization of the ideal collectivistic state, the most logical and impulsive of the Marxists are ready of their own free will to become the servants and supporters of capital."[58] The young Marxists' determinism was not far removed from the social indifferentism of the 1880s: he complained that the Marxists offered no program.

In general, he found them overly prone to abstractions. Miliukov was convinced, for instance, that the dispute on the peasant commune could not be decided without a closer study of the economics of contemporary Russia. This had to be achieved independently of the "doctrinaire tendencies" of the contending parties. The Marxist view seemed to ignore "the idiosyncratic peculiarities of Russia, and appears to be no less fallacious than the Populist view, which is inclined, on the contrary, to exaggerate the importance of these peculiarities."[59]

The Marxists' scathing critiques of "Populism" sharpened Miliukov's dissatisfaction with that orientation in all its various permutations. He had been briefly attracted to the commonsense reworking of Populism in the hands of N. K. Mikhailovskii and the circle at the journal *Russkoe bogatstvo* (Russian wealth), which he characterized in 1894 as an effort to "steer a middle course between the Scylla of Marxism and the Charybdis of 'peasantism.'"[60] Plekhanov's dissection of the dualism underlying Mikhailovskii's subjective sociology convinced him the effort was fruitless.

Populism's attraction for Miliukov had always been more emotional than theoretical. He could accept neither its dichotomy of Russia and the West as contrasting and irreconcilable entities nor its related suspicion of the Westernized intelligentsia: the anti-intellectual streak in Russian populism was utterly foreign to him. Miliukov recognized that there was, in fact, no single and coherent "Populism"—that "love of the people" was a general orientation, not a "logical deduction from some clearly defined theoretical system." Furthermore, he noted that Populism had evolved and factionalized as a consequence of the debates between Populists and Marxists.[61]

He felt that all "peasantist" or Populist approaches ultimately derived their theoretical foundation, however, from Slavophilism. They accepted Slavophilism's belief in the "spiritual robustness of the masses," but in place of the saving grace of the national spirit saw only the socialist principle extant in peasant communal institutions. This, Miliukov said, was a confusion of socialism with nationalism that had to produce incongruities. The greatest of these was the assumption that it was not the educated classes but the victimized and ignorant peasantry that would usher in a progressive, socialist future. The Populists retained, as well, the metaphysical absolutism of the Slavophiles—their belief that Russia could advance directly to socialism without passing through a capitalist phase assumed that primitive collectivism was an inalienable trait of the Russian people.[62]

Populism's emotional appeal for Miliukov nevertheless managed to withstand both Marxist onslaughts and his own critiques, and he maintained close ties with the people at *Russkoe bogatstvo*. Populists burned with moral indignation. They could not reconcile outrage over the suffering of the masses with logical theorems about the laws of history and the march toward a progressive society. Above all, they longed to do something, and Miliukov honored them for this. Paying tribute to the classic "peasantism" embodied in the work of Iuzov [T. Kablitz], he wrote in 1894, "His book will be the most precious memorial of a school of thought whose logic was more faulty than its aspirations."[63]

Miliukov's growing political consciousness and his conclusion that what was most needed was action resulted in new activities on his part. From late 1892 he became involved with a number of organizations doing public work and strove to take a more active part in political debate. His contributions to the political debate revealed how far he was from being a "liberal," despite his later claim to have been a liberal since his university days.[64]

In his memoirs Viktor Chernov provides interesting testimony on Miliukov's contact with radical student organizations in the 1890s, contacts that Miliukov did not mention in his own memoirs. In spring of 1893 Chernov, who would later head the Socialist Revolutionary Party, was a first-year law student at Moscow University and already one of the leaders of the largest and most militant of illegal student organizations, the United Council. The leaders of the United Council were mostly *narodovol'tsy* (adherents of the People's Will party,) or at any rate inclined toward the agrarian socialists, and in 1893 were chiefly occupied with trying to stem the rising popularity of young Marxists.[65] They organized a whole series of "Evenings of Debate" with the Marxists; Miliukov was one of a select number of popular professors invited to attend.[66]

Members of the United Council despised liberals. It is noteworthy that they did not think of Miliukov as a liberal: Chernov later recalled that "we did not consider him "foreign" to us."[67] Yet Miliukov's views on the peasant commune were scarcely Populist. In his lecture course, Miliukov accounted for the origins of the commune with an argument that roughly followed that of Boris Chicherin, who had sought to prove that the commune was created by the government for tax purposes and therefore in no way embodied a putative "collectivist" popular spirit.[68] Nonetheless, at the first "Evening of Debate" Miliukov declared that while the place of the commune in Russia's development was an open question, protecting its integrity in order to allow it to develop freely was the "elementary obligation of any sincere democrat."[69]

Encouraged by this statement, the United Council group invited Miliukov to chair the third Evening of Debate, when the group intended to present its political and social program. Miliukov, whom Chernov described as "conducting himself very boldly at that time," accepted the invitation. While he did not directly declare his sympathies for the program of the group from the United Council, his summation appeared to them an endorsement. Praising all those present for their activism and political awareness, Miliukov then spoke of the need to create real organizations to take action. Chernov claimed that he also gave the nod, obliquely, to the use of terror: "[Miliukov] gave us to understand that attacks on the government by the old means worked out by the *narodovol' tsy* would meet with a most sympathetic attitude on his part."[70]

With Miliukov sending such encouraging signals, the United Council leadership resolved to "try to involve him in our revolutionary plans." Chernov approached him with a concrete proposal: would he be willing to revise a now dated pamphlet on the struggle of social forces in Russia? Miliukov said he would first like to look the pamphlet over, but promised a speedy decision. Chernov took this initial response very favorably: "I already considered that Miliukov would be 'ours' and inwardly exulted in such a first, big acquisition."[71]

Even Miliukov's disagreement with the group's timetable for social revolution did not deter its pursuit of him as an ally. Miliukov thought the United Council was seriously mistaken in its efforts to fight simultaneously for political emancipation and social revolution. According to Chernov, Miliukov said, "You are eclectics. For you, the struggle with autocracy is an immediate task but along with it—and this will be directly at its expense—you want to set broad, separate tasks which can't help but introduce disintegration and quarrels into the camp of supporters of political freedom." Miliukov's priority was clear: the first task was political emancipation of the whole country, "without distinction of groups or classes."[72] Chernov was nonetheless confident that this dispute involved only tactics, deriving chiefly from Miliukov's historical perspective, and that their final goal was identical.[73]

Participation in the United Council's "Evenings of Debate" amounted to an advertisement of Miliukov's political disaffection. Such an advertisement was bound to be noticed. Already liked by history students as a challenging and accessible teacher, by virtue of being "political" Miliukov now became one of the most popular instructors at Moscow University.⁷⁴ He was invited to attend student parties, where socializing was only the ostensible aim of the gathering. V. I. El'iashevich, then a student in history, recalled one such party in autumn 1894, where Miliukov, Chuprov, and Vinogradov were special guests. To lend the party an air of verisimilitude, students unwise enough to admit that they knew how to dance were made to do so in one room, while in another the real "party," a political discussion, took place.⁷⁵ Vinogradov left early, after a false alarm about the arrival of the police, but at 4 A.M. Miliukov was still talking to Vasilii Maklakov, complimenting his generation of students for marching in "close ranks." While El'iashevich was not entirely sure where those close ranks were, Miliukov made such an impression on him that he immediately began attending his lecture course.⁷⁶

Miliukov's open airing of his political discontent—behavior bordering on the reckless—eventually had serious repercussions. His frankness prompted the United Council's efforts to involve him in their propaganda, and their overtures came to the attention of officialdom. When the police broke up *narodovol'tsy* groups all over the country with mass arrests on April 21, 1894, they seized papers of the United Council. These included a directive to "enter into relations with P. N. Miliukov," which figured in the subsequent government decision to exile Miliukov for his "harmful influence on youth."⁷⁷ Looking back on his association with Chernov, Miliukov would wryly remark that he didn't know who had exercised a harmful influence on whom.⁷⁸

The extent of Miliukov's political discontent in this period is attested to by behavior still more risky than political discussions with students, for in late 1893 or early 1894 he apparently joined an underground political organization, the Social-Revolutionary Party of People's Rights (hereafter referred to by its usual name of Narodnoe Pravo).⁷⁹ The party was organized by several veterans of the Chaikovskii circle and the revolutionary Narodnaia Volia, chief among them P. F. Nikolaev, A. I. Bogdanovich, N. S. Tiutchev, and Mark Natanson.⁸⁰ Simultaneously heartened by the quickening of the social temper in the wake of the famine and disillusioned by peasant passivity during this crisis, they concluded that the most immediate tasks for the transformation of Russia were political ones. They further concluded that these tasks could best be accomplished by the mobilization of public opinion on a broad front.

The program drawn up at the founding congress in Saratov in September 1893 declared that the new party would unify all oppositional elements in the country to "secure the destruction of the autocracy and guarantee everyone the rights of a citizen and of a human being."⁸¹ Since specific social questions were more likely to divide than unite public opinion, the program concentrated on political demands: representative rule on the basis of universal suffrage, political and civil liberties for all, and the independence of the courts.[82] Equally pragmatically, the program was also vague on tactics. Its reference to using all "moral and material aids" to destroy autocracy could be variously construed as accepting or rejecting terrorism.

Having worked out a program appropriate to a broadly conceived liberation movement, the founders then set about recruiting members. In all, there were some 112 people in the party or "close to it"—the latter included V. G. Korolenko and N. K. Mikhailovskii, who were willing to aid, but not to join, the illegal party—which made it a very large group for its day.[83] According to S. I. Mitskevich only two prominent Moscow "liberals" were recruited: Gol'tsev, editor of *Russkaia mysl'*, and Miliukov.[84] The party had opportunity to do little more than publish its program and one pamphlet before the police roundup of *narodovol'tsy* in April 1894 routed its leaders. Police seized the party printing press in Smolensk and arrested some fifty-two members. Members still at liberty tried to continue party activities, but the organization was effectively defunct.[85]

The significance of Miliukov's involvement in Narodnoe Pravo, an involvement he failed even to mention in his memoirs, lay not in what he did for this short-lived party but rather in what it said of his disposition and political views at this time. The party's attraction for him was no puzzle: its insistence that winning political freedom was the first step toward any reform and its effort to unify society for action corresponded to his own views. The founders' conviction that divisive programmatic issues should be set aside in order to create a broad front for the struggle for political freedom was nearly identical to the approach advocated by Miliukov and other liberationists less than a decade later; many scholars have seen in Narodnoe Pravo the Union of Liberation in embryo.[86]

Nonetheless, the differences between Narodnoe Pravo and the Union of Liberation were significant. The Union of Liberation did constitute a broad front; Narodnoe Pravo, which was not nearly so heterogeneous in its makeup, was a socialist party. This was tacitly acknowledged in its full title, The Social-Revolutionary Party of People's Rights, and implicit in its programmatic declaration that "rights" included "the people's right to the satisfaction of its material needs." O. V. Aptekman, who wrote the only known account of the party by a member, insisted that its members were socialists; virtually all the individuals associated with Narodnoe Pravo eventually joined socialist parties.[87] That Miliukov was ready to take the risky step of becoming involved with a party of this nature suggests both the extent of his dissatisfaction with Russia's political order and the suspect nature of his later claim to have been, at this time, a "liberal."[88]

The University Extension Movement

As much as Miliukov enjoyed his continued teaching and writing, participation in Moscow's intellectual circles, and chairing an occasional meeting, these occupations were not sufficient to satisfy his restless, active nature. He wanted to be doing something more concrete toward bettering life in Russia; as he wrote in his memoirs, it was fine to talk about politics, "but it was necessary to seek other, broader forms for the opening of public activity. Our coalescing Moscow group found them in educational work."[89] Miliukov's pedagogic interests made it natural that he should be attracted to one of the chief social issues of the day, education.

During the late 1880s and early 1890s, when the authorities prohibited any activity that could even remotely be construed as political, privately funded organizations dedicated to promoting "self-improvement" multiplied rapidly.[90] In the zemstvo milieu, where the need for primary education was painfully clear, basic literacy was the main goal of those promoting self-improvement. Cultural advancement of the people was also the end of the activities of the literacy committees of the St. Petersburg Free Economic Society and of the Moscow Agricultural Society—which Miliukov joined in 1892—and the publishing house Posrednik, founded by A. Sytin in 1894.[91] But educational efforts were not confined to this most rudimentary level; other organizations and publications undertook dissemination of culture to those already in possession of some level of education. Miliukov became the moving spirit behind the largest and most ambitious of the undertakings promoting higher education, the Moscow Commission for the Organization of Home Reading.[92]

The idea of establishing some modest version of university extension in Russia came from Elizaveta N. Orlova, a friend of Anna Miliukova who had some contacts with the English and American extension movements. Orlova approached Anna in early 1893 with a suggestion for composing a serious guide for home reading. She had come to the right place: both Miliukovs were immediately excited by the possibilities. They began to frequent the circle around the Ianzhuls, a couple active in Moscow pedagogic concerns, and Miliukov gathered information on the Chautauqua lectures in New York State and university extension programs.[93] When the family summered in France that year, Miliukov took the opportunity to cross the channel and attend the summer session of the university extension program in Cambridge in order to gain firsthand experience of one of the best-established extension programs.[94]

The program he envisioned went far beyond Orlova's proposals; it would unite the popular appeal of American correspondence courses and public lectures with the more serious content of the English courses, and would be aimed at an all-Russian audience. Armed with information and ideas, he then set about drumming up the support of Moscow university circles. The formal side of the business had to be considered as well: since there was no likelihood of gaining official permission to establish an independent organization for the promotion of education, it was necessary to find an appropriate parent institution, one which had the power to form commissions with tasks of an educational nature. The Moscow "Society for the Dissemination of Technical Knowledge," which was under the patronage of one of the grand dukes, fit the bill in every particular and was willing to extend its legitimacy to a university extension movement humbly named "The Commission for the Organization of Home Reading."[95]

The first organizational meeting, chaired by Miliukov and Orlova, met in September 1893 in the grand hall of the Polytechnic Museum. The turnout was impressive, including many of the most popular professors of Moscow University and nearly all the university lecturers. Nikolai Umov in physics, Mikhail Menzbir in zoology, Lev Lopatin in philosophy, Storozhenko in literature, and Chuprov in political science all contributed to the establishment of the Commission's programs. Miliukov was elected chairman, and it was unanimously decided to embark on a large scale, to create a genuine "university outside university walls."[96]

The Commission founders decided to offer two types of programs of study. One was to be a systematic course of reading, approximating university curricula, which would offer four-year programs of study in all subjects save medicine. The other was to consist of specialized courses of reading, either in one area of knowledge or on specific topics of interest to readers. Detailed syllabi were soon compiled for each program; an amazing twenty thousand reading lists were distributed in the first two years of the Commission's existence.[97] Serious readers desiring more active guidance in their studies could, for the payment of a small yearly fee (three rubles), correspond with scholars connected with the Commission, submit written work for evaluation, and sit for examinations.[98]

By these arrangements the organizers of the Commission hoped to meet the needs of the different types of readers they assumed would be interested in "home reading." These included individuals who had had no opportunity to attend university, and formally educated persons who wanted guidance in a subject unfamiliar to them. As Miliukov put it, the accountant intrigued by chemistry, the young woman in the provinces whose herb garden had awakened an interest in botany, the young man hoping to improve himself but living far from any university town—these were the Commission's intended audience.[99]

Responsibility for generating the actual courses of study was shared out among the organizers according to their specialties. Miliukov and Vinogradov designed the programs for Russian and "world" history; their course of study was highly characteristic both of their approach to history and of the Commission's basic assumption about the seriousness of its subscribers.[100] The course's goals were to acquaint readers with the general course of historical events and the most salient features of the "chief historical epochs." Reliance on textbooks was to be kept to a minimum, with the bulk of the readings coming from primary sources and literary works. The full four years' course was arranged chronologically, with the first year divided among anthropology, primitive culture, and classical antiquity, and the entire fourth year devoted to the nineteenth century—a significant departure from standard university curricula.[101]

Within a year of its founding, the Commission initiated publication of its own "Library for Self-Education" in order to ensure that its readers had access to all required readings at affordable prices. A. Sytin, who already published the Commission's programs of reading, fell in readily with the plan; the books in the "Library for Self-Education" were offered to libraries and the general public as well as to the commission's subscribers, and sold extremely well. The first book produced by the Library was Miliukov's translation of Charles Minto's *Logic*, which "sold out almost the day it reached the book stalls."[102]

By the end of 1895, the Commission had 382 subscribers in regular correspondence; an even larger number of its programs had been purchased by individuals for independent use. By 1899, 1473 people had taken correspondence courses and more than 4000 books had been mailed to subscribers.[103] Despite this heartening success, the Commission was not without its critics, particularly those who questioned its concentration on higher education when the majority of the population still lacked basic literacy. Organizers of the Commission countered criticisms by pointing out that there were many people who had no opportunity to attend a university and by defending the benefits conferred on the nation at large by higher education. Aleksandr Kizevetter, who was deeply involved in the movement, saw promotion of higher education as a crucial step in forging a genuine national culture:

> We did not agree with that point of view that saw higher education as some sort of luxury, a sort of intellectual delicacy which the country could do without until it had fulfilled more pressing tasks; the same urgent necessity attaches to introducing large numbers of people to higher education, for only under such conditions can one achieve a commonly shared higher culture.[104]

Miliukov shared this conviction; his course for the Pedagogical Institute was imbued with the belief that education was both the prerequisite to, and guarantor of, a vibrant national life. But in his defense of the goals of the

Commission he nonetheless struck a different note, one revealing an appreciation of culture as something to be desired by all people irrespective of any utilitarian considerations. Referring to the Commission's provincial audience, Miliukov spoke of the "spiritual thirst" of provincials barred from higher education, of the moral satisfaction they would derive from their studies, which would further help isolated, intelligent people in the provinces to "shed sensations of emptiness and solitude."[105] He also believed that the fulfillment to be gained from learning must be possible for all social classes; university extension would truly democratize education. "For the first time in history, the new movement makes higher education the *attainment of the entire nation*."[106]

In the second year of its existence the Commission was ready for a test run of an undertaking particularly dear to Miliukov, public lecture series for the provinces. These were to be fairly substantive courses of four or five lectures each, such as he had attended at Cambridge. Serious lecture courses would, he believed, raise interest in self-education and impart to the Russian university extension movement a genuine "university" charcter.[107] Nizhnii Novgorod was settled on as a first site for gauging public appetite for a lecture series thus conceived. Over the Christmas holidays in 1894–95 Miliukov and a popular lecturer in literature, N. I. Ivanov, would give a series of public lectures in Nizhnii.[108] Gaining permission to lecture publicly outside the capital was at that time extraordinarily difficult, but both the official in charge of the Moscow Educational District and the governor of Nizhnii Novgorod approved the prospectuses submitted to them. Ivanov was to lecture on the history of political ideas in France; Miliukov would give five lectures on social movements in eighteenth- and nineteenth-century Russia and one lecture on the university extension movement.[109]

The timing of this series in part accounts for its stunning reception; Nicholas II had ascended the throne just two months before and a mood of expectancy, of anticipation of reform, excited the citizens of Nizhnii Novgorod as it did all Russians. More than 500 people turned out for each lecture, including such local luminaries as the province's vice-governor, M. I. Chaikovskii (a brother of the composer), and an archbishop. The success of the series exceeded all expectations. "In the city it was like a continuous holiday while the lectures went on, the public thronged to the talks and had parties and banquets for the speakers."[110] The content of the lectures was, for the day, heady stuff indeed; their general thrust was to demonstrate that education was the prerequisite to democracy, since it nourished the demand for freedom while making people capable of using freedom wisely. Ivanov concluded that the French Revolution had failed not because of its ideas and goals, but due to the insufficiency of education among the people. Miliukov's lectures were essentially a condensation of the third year of his course on Russian history for the Pedagogic Institute, but with a more radical coloration. He celebrated the efforts of Radishchev, the Decembrists, Herzen, and the "people of the sixties," while demonstrating that the government rewarded public initiative with prison sentences and exile. He nonetheless insisted that thanks to the dissemination of culture in Russia, the social movement was today stronger and broader than ever before.[111]

Such frank speaking produced a sensation. As one man who attended the lectures wrote to a friend, in a letter intercepted by the police, "Ivanov and Miliukov have said so many bold and true things. . . . [W]e've heard and spoken of all this many times before, but talked of it behind closed doors, surreptitiously. That Moscow professors give such speeches from a public podium in the provinces, in the presence of young people and teachers, this has never happened!"[112] Nearly two months after the lectures, Minister of Internal Affairs P. N. Durnovo grimly remarked that "the excitement caused by these speeches in Nizhnii has still not died down."[113]

Partially as a consequence of these lectures, Miliukov was soon forced to resign as chairman of the Commission and withdraw from active participation in its affairs, but he had the satisfaction of seeing his undertaking prosper. Its library, lecture bureau, and correspondence courses continued to flourish as least until 1905.[114] The extension movement had, as well, a significance beyond its educational contributions. It brought together Moscow University circles, for the first time, in active public work of some duration. In Kizevetter's opinion, "Every one of the young scholars of the 1890s who participated in this had very vivid recollections of their work in it and its important role in uniting this generation of university figures."[115]

For a generation of young academics, many of them future Kadets, this first experience of public work had occurred under the confident and enthusiastic direction of Paul Miliukov. They had been accustomed to respecting him as a scholar; they came to think of him as their first "leader" in public work and the first university "martyr" in the reign of Nicholas II. One might suspect that these early, strong impressions greatly contributed to their readiness to look to him for political leadership in the years ahead.

Expulsion and Exile

The audacious nature of the lectures in Nizhnii Novgorod convinced officials that Miliukov's actions could no longer be tolerated. Ivanov was not subjected to any serious reprisals, but early in February 1895 two ministries took measures against Miliukov. The Ministry of Education had him dismissed from his position at Moscow University. In a communication of February 6, 1895, Minister of Education I. D. Delianov instructed P. A. Kapnist, supervisor of the Moscow Educational District, that "former lecturer Miliukov is to be prohibited from any pedagogic activity and from reading public lectures of any kind whatsoever."[116] The Ministry of Internal Affairs initiated investigation into Miliukov's "criminal activity" in Nizhnii Novgorod, ordering that he be sent from Moscow into administrative exile until his case had been resolved.[117]

Miliukov had already been sent away from Moscow before he managed to obtain from Durnovo a statement of exactly what charges were being made against him; the list spoke volumes about the repressive atmosphere of the day. In addition to the charge connected with the talks in Nizhnii Novgorod, of reading "lectures of criminal content before an audience not capable of relating to them critically," he was accused of agitational activity, of giving lectures that could "evoke in listeners thoughts of antigovernmental activity," and of encouraging students to petition for corporate rights and abolition of the university statute of 1884.[118]

Miliukov's teaching at the University came to an abrupt halt on February 14. In his parting lecture to his students, he told them "There was nothing for me to teach you about loving Russia, but I wanted to help you know her and prepare for activity on her behalf. For you this activity now lies ahead; for me, the help to you was already [a form of] action, one which corresponded to my personal inclinations."[119]

The initiative for Miliukov's expulsion came from the Ministry of Internal Affairs. On January 25, Durnovo sent the Minister of Education abstracts of the Nizhnii lectures drawn up by several individuals who had attended them; they were, in his opinion, "tendentious."[120] Delianov wrote Durnovo defending Kapnist's approval of the lectures, but added that he had suggested to Kapnist that "individuals like Miliukov absolutely not be allowed to lecture," because even when reading from a printed text they "are always able to slip in a pernicious word."[121] Privately, he took Kapnist to task for laxness in approving public lectures in general, as well as for allowing Miliukov to give what must have been a provocative final lecture at the Pedagogic Institute, having been informed that the lecture called forth "frenzied applause."[122]

A further consequence of the official reaction to the Nizhnii Novgorod lectures was to make it still more difficult for any individual to lecture publicly in Russia. Durnovo sent a memo to provincial governors instructing them to act more cautiously in approving public lectures, and a memo to Delianov asking that he direct Kapnist to scrutinize any future lecture proposals emanating from the Commission on Home Reading, and be careful in approving public lectures or literary readings in general.[123] Director of Police Petrov went further, telling Delianov that "I propose, after the lectures of Ivanov and Miliukov, that Lieutenant General Bartanov not allow lectures whose contents could evoke any sort of excitement in society."[124]

Miliukov's ouster, which occasioned a flurry of paper-shuffling and saber-rattling in bureaucratic circles, produced a genuine sensation in Moscow. Fellow scholars saw a promising career ruined; students were indignant at the persecution of a popular teacher. The public and private expressions of sympathy and support that deluged Miliukov were heartening, and he was fully alive to the fact that by his "martyrdom" he had gained immensely, at least temporarily, in public stature. As he shortly after wrote to Kovalevskii, the authorities had in a way done him a service by advertising him to all the people "whose opinion and sympathy I respect. . . . Having lost a small audience, I gain by this the possibility of more frequently appearing before a large one."[125] Before leaving Moscow Miliukov was feted at a banquet organized by Gol'tsev, who expressed the hope that Miliukov would one day become the historian of the fall of the Russian monarchy. Many well-wishers from society swelled the ranks of the hundreds of students who came to see him off at the train station on February 23, 1895.[126]

While Miliukov's friends persisted in regarding his expulsion as an unmitigated disaster, Miliukov maintained in his memoirs that he left his native city with a sense of liberation. Allowances must be made here for hindsight, but he offered cogent reasons in support of this claim. His situation at the university had become so uncomfortable, he contended, that any change of venue had to be an improvement. In addition to the frustrations caused by his differences with Kliuchevskii, he was clearly weary of the "scramble for a bit of bread" that was the lot of the lecturer. The second factor occasioning his feeling of liberation was one he became fully conscious of only later. Making a university career entailed writing a second doctoral dissertation, but Miliukov had, by 1895, lost his taste for monographic work on this scale. He wanted to write on different sorts of questions and in different formats, for a nonspecialist audience and with a new, more immediate and pragmatic goal in mind.

Finally, his native optimism was not as yet seriously shaken. He appreciated that the very arbitrariness of Russian government, which could so suddenly disrupt his life and career, itself afforded the hope that what had been done might equally arbitrarily be undone. As he wrote Kovalevskii in May 1895, he did not know how long he would have to stay in Riazan'; when and if it became necessary to refute the formal changes, he was confident that he could do so. Concerning the current state of affairs in Russia, he added, "It seems to me that our situation is not all that bad. At any rate, it has been a long while since I have seen, at least from the end of the 70s, such hopeful signs as Russian life has given the past few years."[127]

In this frame of mind Miliukov was clearly disposed to make the best of his enforced residency in Riazan'. His two and a half years there were pleasant and productive ones, in part for financial reasons.[128] The sympathies of educated Moscow had not been confined to demonstrations of moral support: material aid was also forthcoming. The liberal Moscow daily *Russkie vedomosti* (Russian gazette) created a largely fictive editorial position for Miliukov, which provided him with a regular salary. One of the thick journals, *Mir Bozhii*, paid generously for serializing volume 1 of *Ocherki po istorii russkoi kul'tury* based on the first year of his Pedagogic Institute course. For the first time since he was nineteen, Miliukov was financially comfortable. He and Anna rented a handsome house with large gardens, ideal for their growing family—their second child, Sergei, was born there that year.[129]

Release from financial durance coincided with—and in part contributed to—another circumstance novel for Miliukov: he had plenty of time at his disposal. He wrote prolifically. He acquired a bicycle, and cycling became a veritable passion. Both he and Anna played in quartets and quintets, and he also joined the local orchestra, even petitioning for—and receiving—permission from the governor to travel with the orchestra outside his place of exile for a series of concerts in Kolomna![130] I. V. Cherepnin, the distinguished archaeologist, became one of Miliukov's closest friends in Riazan', and under Cherepnin's guidance he learned how to excavate a site and evaluate his findings. He participated in a number of digs and wrote up his results for the local society on the archaeology and history of Riazan'. Miliukov made other contributions to local scholarship as well, one being a total reorganization of the province's historical archives for the Riazan' Archival Commission.[131]

In short, Miliukov became a highly valued member of Riazan' society, and the light this throws on his personality is perhaps the most interesting thing to be gleaned from his stay there. It might be expected that a well-known—not to say notorious—intellectual from Moscow would receive a most flattering reception from the culture-hungry educated of the hinterlands, as Miliukov did. But it is clear that Miliukov won the affection as well as the admiration of his provincial colleagues. Entering with gusto into provincial concerns and activities, and speedily making friends, he was in no way above or outside the social microcosm of Riazan'. More than one Riazan' friend would look back on this time as exceptional, as did the correspondent who wrote Anna in 1900 that "I will never forget those few, blessed years when I was in the circle that united so quickly and so well around the unforgettable Pavel Nikolaevich."[132]

The flattering picture of Miliukov that emerges from his Riazan' exile corresponds to his students' depictions of him as a teacher. These describe him as an unaffected and accessible individual who shared his scholarly enthusiasms with his students and exerted himself to help them in their work.[133]

It would thus seem that the coldness, reserve, and arrogance opponents and colleagues so often noted in him in their memoirs reflected changes that came later.[134] At any rate, in the 1890s Miliukov was a well-liked man, and this is important for understanding how he so quickly assumed leadership of the Russian liberal movement.

Despite the pleasurable tenor of life in Riazan', the years of internal exile were not unmarked by frustration. A stream of visitors to the Miliukovs from the capitals helped keep him apprised of the political atmosphere, which he found disheartening.[135] In July of 1895 his review for the *Athenaeum* was bleak: "Misrule and ignorance—these are the principal plagues of contemporary Russia."[136] The following summer, Miliukov noted the continued predisposition of *obshchestvo* (society) to voice only its minimum demands, radicals' growing awareness of the need to construct practical programs, and government suppression of all public initiatives; it was a state of affairs whose outcome defied prognostication.

> I can only liken the condition of Russian society this year to a river whose current has been suddenly stopped by some insuperable obstacle. The stream has not been sufficiently strong to break down the dam, nor so weak as to be stopped entirely. . . . In the absence of a direct channel, it would appear to have been seeking a circuitous route and trickling in little streamlets through the interstices of the dam.[137]

By spring of 1897 Miliukov was restive, having existed in a sort of limbo for over two years while St. Petersburg officialdom determined his fate. An unexpected opportunity to resume teaching had in the meantime presented itself. The chair in Russian history at Sofia University became vacant when its previous holder, the dissident Ukrainian exile Mikhail Dragomanov, died in 1896. The Bulgarian government offered his chair to Miliukov.[138] The Russian government in effect acceded to this proposal by giving Miliukov a choice: one year in prison in Ufa or two years exile "abroad." He of course chose the latter and headed that summer for Vienna to begin preparing his lecture courses for the fall semester; Anna and the children were to join him later.[139] Miliukov was in high spirits—he could not then know that during the next eight years he would live in Russia only intermittently, and that part of that time would be spent in prison.

Miliukov left Russia in April of 1897 uncertain of what his future might hold and uncertain, too, of the probable course of the social movement in Russia in the near future. The decade of the 1890s had so far witnessed the reanimation of public debate in Russia, followed by a broadening current of dissatisfaction with the old order perpetuated by the new regime. It was a period of transition; there was no knowing when and if these "trickling streamlets" would again flow together, nor what "direct channel" they might take.

For Miliukov personally, this decade was also a time of important transitions. Shortly after he established himself as one of the leading historians of Russia he was barred from academia, having already begun to redefine the subject and goals of his scholarship, seeking not so much to elucidate his country's past as its present. The transition from graduate student to professional historian was almost exactly coincident with the transformation from private person to public figure, as Miliukov entered the larger world of Moscow's intellectual circles and public organizations.

As he became more conscious of the ills bedeviling Russian life he became politicized and to a certain extent radicalized (though his move to the left was, at least in part, the product of professional disappointments). Given his political affiliations in this period, contemporaries' estimations of his views, what he said and, significantly, what he failed to say, it is difficult to conclude that he was at this time a "liberal" in any but the most general sense of the term. The question of when Miliukov embraced liberalism has a significance that goes beyond biographical chronology. To assume that his views were, in 1892 or 1895, essentially the same as those he began to avow explicitly in 1902 is to ignore a complex and by no means linear evolution toward a worldview and a corresponding program.

Although Miliukov had not, by the time of his exile from Russia, arrived at the worldview he so actively sought, by a process of elimination he had narrowed the choice of viable options. But concomitant with this negative process was development of a more constructive sort. As Miliukov's research into Russian history and the Russian historical process matured, broadening both in chronological scope and in subject matter, he worked out what was an eclectic but empirically and logically consistent sociological perspective, a perspective that would ultimately serve as the basis for what was to be a sociological rather than philosophic liberalism.

C·H·A·P·T·E·R T·H·R·E·E

Miliukov's Historical Thought

In the introductory lecture of his course on Russian history, first delivered in 1892, Miliukov told his students he would not be offering them a narrative history such as they were accustomed to from their school-days. The sort of history that set itself no further goal than the "possibly true reproduction of that which was" might be interesting and instructive but had very little in common with history as a science. The subject of scientific history was not changes in dynasties and the conduct of wars but the study of the "internal, fundamental processes of a people's development in all its fullness and animation." Its goal was not only to ascertain the process of development, but to understand it: "As a science, history, like other sciences, tries to find the laws underlying the phenomena it studies and to discern in these phenomena a certain regularity."[1]

Theoretical Views

Any discussion of Miliukov's historical views must begin with a consideration of the influence of Auguste Comte; Miliukov remained, throughout his life, a self-proclaimed positivist.[2] From Comte he took his belief in humanity's development from a theological to a metaphysical and thence to a rational and scientific mode of thinking, and his belief in the growing complexity and interrelatedness of all social phenomena. Again following Comte, Miliukov believed that all social phenomena were subject to laws of causality and that scientific history could properly seek and hope to identify these laws. For Miliukov, differences between the methods of the natural and social sciences were differences of degree rather than kind. As early as 1887 he rejected overly strict distinctions between abstract or nomological sciences, which study laws, and concrete or phenomenological sciences, such as history.[3]

Miliukov felt that empirical observation made the idea of the "regularity" or "lawfulness" (*zakonomernost'*) of the historical process virtually inescapable. The numerous similarities observable among different human societies at comparable stages of development required explanation; once reference to a providential plan, or anything external to the world, was excluded as a tenable mode of explanation of human history, the historian had to suppose the existence of sociological laws.[4] Just as chemical and physiological phenomena were "lawful," so too were more complex phenomena, including even conscious action. "The purposeful behavior of the individual, from the point of view of science, is only one of the modifications of the causal connection of phenomena: it is the same *zakonomernyi* process, carried over from the area of the external world to the area of psychic life."[5]

Where those laws were to be sought, and how they were to be discovered, were questions for which Miliukov did not immediately have answers. In fact, despite having asserted the historian's duty both to seek laws and to presuppose them, Miliukov was unsatisfactory and curiously incomplete in his treatment of the laws of history. He never defined what he meant by "law" and used the term inconsistently; sometimes it appeared to be a heuristic device, an aid to the historian in ordering events, and at other times it seems to have assumed independent existence. Methodologically, he first assumed, with Thomas Henry Buckle, the influential British proponent of comparative history, that the historian's approach must be inductive. But by 1895, with the serial publication of volume 1 of his *Studies of Russian Culture*, Miliukov was advocating a deductive approach. Historians could draw on the known laws of other disciplines, above all psychology, and apply them to the explanation of the historical process.[6]

Whatever the weaknesses of his treatment of the concept of historical "laws," Miliukov's insistence on the lawfulness of the historical process was not a strictly deterministic one. First, he argued not only that each constituent element of any phenomenon had its own lawful process, but that no process could be derived from another.[7] The problem with Marxism, he held, was that in its admirable fight against metaphysical dualism it had fastened on philosophical materialism, a form of monism that ultimately reduced explanation of even the phenomena of religious belief and high culture to material causes. Miliukov was not suggesting that sophisticated economic materialists tried to derive spiritual phenomena from the material, but they did argue that material factors were the key or primary cause in historical development, relegating other factors to a secondary role.[8]

Miliukov, with his pluralist perspective on causal relationships, rejected the idea of key causal factors as too narrow and dogmatic: "From the point of view of science there are not primary and necessary, secondary and accidental causes," but only causes turning out to have a larger or smaller sphere of influence in any given case.[9] Insisting that the many aspects of human culture were interdependent, but at the same time too differentiated and complex to be reduced to any "primordial unity," Miliukov was skeptical of overly schematic approaches to cultural history.[10] He in fact never attempted an overall schema of the history of Russian culture, instead offering separate periodizations, for example, of the evolution of the state, spirituality, and social consciousness.

In the second place—and it is here that Miliukov was most original—he accommodated operation of the unique and individual within an overall regular framework by seeing the "lawful" as only one of three factors constituting the historical process. It was the most abstract, but in practice it was wedded to the concrete, the particular. Alongside the operation of the sociological "law" there was the fact of its realization in a given milieu in a given time and place. Milieu included what might be called structural or "necessary" conditions, such as climate and geography, and slightly more variable or accidental conditions, such as the presence of hostile neighbors. Finally, there was a third element, the most truly ephemeral and accidental, and that was the role played by individual human personalities, what Miliukov lightly referred to as the factor of "Cleopatra's nose" and "Napoleon's cold."[11] "Constituting one indivisible whole, all these sides develop in closest connection and interdependence."[12]

This tripartite theory of the functioning of the historical process largely determined the structure of Miliukov's three-volume *Studies of Russian Culture*, being most apparent in the volume detailing the formulation of the Russian "national ideology," in which Miliukov addresses the question of the origins of Russia's definition of itself as a distinct nation and people. The sociological process of self-definition was one undergone by every people. In Russia, however, the process of self-definition was set in motion when the society was at a relatively low level of cultural and economic development, with the result that Russians borrowed a great deal of their "national idea" from other, older and more advanced cultures. This was the effect of milieu on the operation of the universal law. Finally, the choice of what cultures were to be borrowed from, what elements of a given culture were borrowed, and how, constituted the most "accidental" factor in the development of the national idea, and the one most susceptible to influence by human will, such as the character and inclinations of a given ruler and of his advisers.[13]

In this way, Miliukov accommodated the structural and the dynamic, the universal and the particular, the strictly causal and the adventitious in his explanation of the functioning of the historical process. The joint action of universal law and particular milieu preserved his explanation from being overly abstract or ahistorical; we may recall that in the early stages of the Marxist-Populist debate of the 1890s Miliukov had remarked that "the Marxite view seems to ignore the idiosyncratic peculiarities of Russia, and appears no less fallacious than the Populist view, which is inclined, on the contrary, to exaggerate the importance of these peculiarities."[14]

It also allowed him to steer a middle course between the conception of a totally unconscious, elemental social development offered by Spencerian evolution, on the one hand, and the pronounced voluntarism of the Russian "subjective school" of sociology, on the other. Spencer's model of social evolution ignored the factor of human consciousness and left no historical role to individual human actors, Miliukov felt, while he detected in subjective sociology's idea of the "critically thinking individual" Carlyle's great man in more up-to-date costume.[15] Miliukov's characterization of the historical process afforded a place to individual will and action. That sphere was, admittedly, limited, since he did not conceive human will as lying somehow beyond or outside the realm of sociological "laws." But Miliukov's belief in progress—a subject I shall return to—promised greater scope for human society's conscious direction of its destiny in the future.

That Miliukov was basically satisfied with his tripartite characterization of the historical process may be assumed, since he never altered it in any essentials. The few scholars, however, who have examined Miliukov's sociological theory have been highly critical. Particularly interesting is P. B. Struve's evaluation, written when he still considered himself a Marxist.

The most familiar objection to the view of history as science is that history studies phenomena that are unique and nonrepeatable, but the positivist search for the laws of history raises the specter of determinism. Struve had both these questions in mind when he charged Miliukov with an overly broad conception of the idea of "regularity," one which became contradictory by including the idea of the individual. Struve insisted that the principle of strict *zakonomernost'* acted on individual representations and images like water acted on fire. Causality presupposed an identity between cause and consequence that extinguished individuality.[16]

Examining Miliukov's scattered remarks on human will and the individual, it is clear that he was not trying to suggest that human behavior is determined—such a proposition would make holding individuals responsible for their actions logically absurd. Rather, he was arguing against an overly abstract and ahistorical conception of the human personality that inflated the role of human will in history and attributed more purposefulness to historical change than as yet existed. The individual is motivated by instincts and unconscious desires—riddles that Miliukov thought psychology might one day resolve—and by conscious ideals, which are socially generated, historical in nature, and whose origins and evolution history could discover. What Miliukov sought to stress was that these ideals are not the sole or even main engine of the historical process:

> Unfortunately, many philosophers of history continue to look on the will as an independent thing, as though outside the historical process. Asserting the purposefulness of human deeds they forget that there is still a whole abyss dividing each separate purposeful act, with its personal motives, from its social consequences, from a purposeful social result; a whole series of conditions existing fully only at the highest rungs of societal life is necessary for the bridging of this abyss.[17]

The importance Miliukov attached to making this point about the role of the individual becomes clearer when it is considered as part of a larger debate about the meaning and uses of history. Miliukov was an impassioned opponent of any normative or ethical interpretation of history. He wanted to demarcate scientific history not only from "metaphysics"—a distinction common to the Russian sociological orientation of the time—but also from the practical application of the findings of history.[18]

In his view, the chief difference between an approach that was truly scientific and one that is philosophical is that the former undertakes to explain history whereas the latter seeks to evaluate it. A philosophical or "metaphysical" approach looks for the meaning of history; Miliukov considered this question entirely improper to a scientific viewpoint.[19] The historian is an investigator, not a judge, and any investigation consciously or unconsciously premised upon subjective normative considerations or ideals, upon any idea superimposed from outside, goes beyond the boundaries of "scientific" study.

Miliukov did not by this exclude the role of ideals in human activity, nor did he deny the heuristic value of some ruling idea. It was primarily a stricture against the mixing-up of science with ethics and ethics with science. At his dissertation defense in 1892, Miliukov outlined these views in an emphatic call for a strictly conceived "scientific" approach to the study of the human past. Reiterating his conviction that history is a sociological science, he said:

> When objective or genetic sociology denies the existence of conscious creativity or stands the laws of evolution in the place of the conscious ideals of mankind, it undoubtedly exceeds its authority and leaves its own natural sphere. When, on the other hand, subjective or dynamic sociology tries to put

forward its own ideas as concurring with the natural tendency of the historical process, or when it wants to erect a theory of progress on a subjective moral evaluation of the fragmentary phenomena of the historical past, it perhaps does something very useful in the educational sense, but this business, so it seems to me, has nothing in common with science.[20]

There are several unresolved contradictions in Miliukov's thoughts on the practical application of history. The first of these concerns the scholar's motivations in selecting subject matter. Miliukov claimed that even among the Moscow University history students of his generation it was already axiomatic that "the study of history could not and should not set itself applied goals."[21] But elsewhere, Miliukov predicted that by switching attention from the study of events to the history of society (*byt'*), "history will cease to be the subject of the simple love of knowledge, a variegated collection of 'anecdotes of days past,' and will become a subject capable of arousing scientific interest and being put to practical use."[22]

This second statement rests, in part, on Miliukov's belief that events, being by nature more accidental, are thus less amenable to scientific methods of investigation and less likely to yield "scientific" knowledge. With other proponents of the new, sociological orientation in history, Miliukov believed that the focus of inquiry should shift from politics and the actions of individuals, which he called "a sort of dust on the surface of the historic ocean," to the more "immobile" and substantive, namely, to the institutions and life of the whole people.[23] But this view also reflected a normative approach to choice of subject matter: demanding that historians not "extravagantly" expend their energies on studying what need not be studied, Miliukov implicitly used the criterion of usefulness to society in determining what subjects merited scholarly investigation.[24]

What, then, was the use of history? For Miliukov, this was the question that lay at the heart of the dispute about the nature of cultural history, and its answer depended on whether one approached its study from the perspective of science or of art. The scholar set his goal as study, the politician set his as "creation"; one discovered the laws of historical science, the other established the rules of political art. But the line of demarcation between the two is easier to draw in theory than to honor in practice, as Miliukov ruefully acknowledged. Political art needs knowledge of the laws of social science in order to establish its own rules. And as a member of society "the sociologist necessarily feels a need or obligation to apply his knowledge to evaluation of the social reality that surrounds him. In the majority of cases he is, willy-nilly, called upon to play the role of a public figure, and naturally this role influences the direction of scholarly work. The point of view of purposefulness is brought into the realm of causal explanation, where it does not belong."[25]

Scientific history sought to know human beings, to establish what they were and what they have become, and explain why they have done what they have. The use of this, for Miliukov, was in part a positivistic anticipation of a time when history would be so genuinely scientific that it would permit "scientific prevision," in the sense intended by Comte and John Stuart Mill. More important, it was connected to his assumption that "knowledge of the truth will set man free."[26] The burden of the past would be lightened immensely when the past became truly known, for much of that burden was, in Miliukov's eyes, the accumulated detritus of times dead and gone: "It is clear that our own conscious activity should be directed not at preservation of the archaeological remnant of a remote antiquity, but toward creation of a new Russian cultural tradition corresponding to contemporary social ideals."[27]

For Miliukov did, increasingly, believe in progress. He understood progress to be the gaining of knowledge of and mastery over the material world, the shedding of superstition and advancement toward genuine, scientific knowledge of the workings of human society. He believed that human beings were becoming more enlightened and thereby "conscious," and that it was in the full consciousness of an entire people and not just its elite that the possibility of truly "making" history reposed. When a common goal has been worked out, transmitted over generations, and disseminated by education and upbringing so that it truly constitutes a cultural "tradition," society can at last hope to bridge the gap between articulation of social ideals and achievement of those ideals. The penetration of higher culture to the masses, the creation of an enlightened "general will," "constitutes the most precious hope of mankind."[28]

While Miliukov's conception of what constituted progress changed very little over the course of time, his hope for the possibility of such progress deepened into conviction. In the mid-1880s, in his critique of N. I. Kareev's philosophy of history, Miliukov wrote that even if one agreed to the application of a ruling idea to the interpretation of history, he didn't understand the suitability of applying the ideal of progress.[29] In his "Lectures on Russian history," some seven years later, Miliukov told his students that for the time being, the idea that humanity could make its history was "a golden dream of the future transferred onto the past."[30] In 1905, striking a much different note, Miliukov told his American readers that "if the law of Russian history is progress, as we have tried to demonstrate, political reform may not be avoided."[31]

Miliukov's growing belief in progress was in part predicated on his belief that the picture of social evolution yielded by a scientific history was not simply another example of "a golden dream of the future" transferred onto the past. In advocating the scientific-realistic tendency, Miliukov recognized that when historians are subjective in approach, or ignorant of theory, the validity of their interpretations suffers. But this cautionary view was not accompanied by any doubts of the possibility, in principle, of arriving at genuine knowledge of the past; epistemological considerations in Miliukov's work are conspicuous by their absence.

The confidence that one can gain objective knowledge of the human past has been called a characteristically "nineteenth-century" view: Stuart Hughes contrasts it with a view he sees as more typically "twentieth century" in its heightened intellectual self-consciousness and recognition of the disparity between external reality and internal appreciation of that reality.[32] The Annales school, on the other hand, one of the most influential historical orientations of the twentieth century, approaches the study of the past with a set of positivist assumptions remarkably similar to those of Miliukov and the Moscow school of historiography. The nomological approach of the Annales school, its belief in the possibility of obtaining direct, objective knowledge of the past, its interest in both structure and dynamic in history, and its commitment to "histoire totale" and relative lack of interest in political history are all highly reminiscent of the Moscow school.[33] The major difference, at least in the case of Miliukov, lies in the Annalists' resistance to any attempt to impose a theory of progress, or even of discernible direction, on history.[34] Arguably, it was Miliukov's mature conviction in the near inevitability of progress, based on a Eurocentric model, that most clearly marks him as a product of the nineteenth century.

Less characteristic of the Moscow school of historiography was Miliukov's abiding interest in the history of ideas. Kliuchevskii was typical of Russian historiography as a whole in separating intellectual history from political, social, and economic history, and in neglecting the former.[35] Theoretically, Miliukov held that ideas, representing "spiritual forces," are as important in the historical process as material conditions; in practice, they became his chief interest. Yet in studying ideas one cannot divorce them from the social, political, and economic realities of the time in which they were formulated and gained currency. Neither should they be looked at abstractly, as constructs: one must study how people attempted to realize ideas in practice and, especially, how ideas changed when confronted with "real life."[36]

Miliukov's first major works were monographs decidedly centered on material life, which created the mistaken impression that this was his first interest, consideration of the "spiritual realm" and historical synthesis only coming later. That Miliukov was, from the start, interested in ideas, theory, and a broad, synthesizing approach to the study of history is demonstrated by his effort, at age eighteen, to create his own schematization of the historical process. He extended Théodule Ribot's representation of the human psyche as a triple spectrum of will, feeling, and thought, to Comte's idea of successive, collective psychological stages but differed from Comte by concluding that each people realizes the process in its own time and way. This youthful and derivative effort was almost immediately shelved and forgotten, but the questions it raised would be preoccupations of a lifetime. Significantly, Miliukov here sought his ideas in sociology and his proof in high culture, ignoring political organization and economic criteria.[37]

Major Works and Themes

The period 1892–1903 saw Miliukov's greatest activity as a scholar; Michael Karpovich has called it Miliukov's "remarkable decade."[38] In addition to many reviews, original articles, and encyclopedia pieces, a historical atlas of the Balkans, and numerous public lectures, Miliukov published eight books in just fifteen years: *The State Economy of Russia in the First Quarter of the Eighteenth Century and the Reforms of Peter the Great* (which I shall refer to as *State Economy of Russia*), *Controversial Questions in the History of Muscovite State Finances, Main Currents in Russian Historical Thought, From the History of the Russian Intelligentsia*, the three volumes of the *Studies of Russian Culture*, and *Russia and Its Crisis*. As amazing as the sheer volume of output was his erudition and the range of his interests: his review articles displayed familiarity with sources and literature on topics as diverse as the origins of the Slavs, Byzantine influence on Russian ideas of sovereignty, early nineteenth-century Russian diplomacy, and the history of Russian art.[39]

State Economy of Russia, published in book form in 1892, immediately established Miliukov's reputation. The thesis that Peter's reforms were neither an abrupt break with the past nor a consciously thought-out whole, was not new. S. M. Solov'ev had first argued that the Petrine reforms were the outgrowth of the gradual Westernizing of the seventeenth century, and Kliuchevskii had demonstrated the ad hoc nature and underlying military motivations of most of Peter's administrative and financial reforms.[40] What was new was how Miliukov tried to shift the debate from intentions to results, by moving the focus of the investigation to reforms whose results were more readily quantifiable, that is, from the cultural realm to the material. In Miliukov's opinion, the Slavophile-Westernizer debate over whether Peter had created modern Russia or betrayed the country's traditions had played out its usefulness for scholarly knowledge. It was time to plant the study of Peter on firmer, more scientific ground by recasting the questions asked about his reign and returning to the primary sources.[41] Miliukov therefore confined himself to studying the institutions of state finance, undertaking a huge investigation of unpublished archival documents, many of them never before consulted by scholars.[42]

Miliukov drew two very controversial conclusions. Whereas Solov'ev and K. D. Kavelin had asserted that the reforms were "necessary" and "organic," in this work the question of the necessity of the reforms was answered in somewhat ambivalent fashion. Miliukov concluded that while the international situation had indeed demanded creation of a military capability such as that wrought by Peter, the country was not financially capable of supporting it. "The price of raising Russia to the rank of a European power was the ruination of the country."[43]

Miliukov's conclusion reflected the dilemma Peter's activities posed for him. As a thoroughgoing proponent of European culture and "European" state administration, Miliukov could not but sympathize with Peter's efforts to make Russia a great European power. But as an opponent of autocratic government he criticized the sacrifice of the welfare of the people to the interests of the state. In effect, he defended the goals but deplored the means and many of their indirect results. Yet his own research seemed to suggest that, given the low level of development of productivity in Petrine Russia, there was no way Russia could have achieved great power status which would not have entailed wholesale privation for the masses. At least one contemporary reviewer of this work took issue with the ambivalence of Miliukov's evaluation of the reforms, tartly remarking that if preservation of the polity had indeed necessitated the reforms, there could not be, simultaneously, a yes and no answer to the question of their timeliness.[44]

The second controversial area had to do with Miliukov's negative assessment of Peter's personal role in the reforms. The absence of visible evidence of Peter's participation in various administrative and institutional reforms led Miliukov to take Kliuchevskii's thesis one step further. Not only had Peter had no overall plan of reform to begin with, he was not even the architect of most of the reforms themselves, which were actually the creation of trusted subordinates.[45] The "Great Legislator" was not really a legislator at all.

This was in part, as Nicholas Riasanovsky notes, a reflection of the "temper of the times," that is, of the hostility of the radical intelligentsia toward the tsarist system.[46] It was also entirely in keeping with Miliukov's early view of the functioning of the historical process, which accorded to the individual's actions a much more limited sphere of influence than he was later inclined to admit. Nevertheless, Miliukov's evaluation of Peter's role rested as much on sources consulted as on theoretical disposition; the discovery of new archival evidence modified his views. In subsequent works touching on Peter, he increasingly expanded his picture of Peter's personal role in reform, emphasizing the correspondence of Peter's means to the conditions of the day, the more "conscious" long-term goals of the last reforming years, and Peter's right to be considered the creator of an intellectual class in Russia.[47]

State Economy of Russia was an outstanding "first book" that did not deserve Kliuchevskii's austere evaluation of it.[48] Kliuchevskii felt that the work's chief merit was in its wealth of new materials rather than in its analysis. He remarked, with some justice, that while Miliukov proved everything he asserted, he did not assert everything that he proved. At his dissertation defense, Miliukov stressed that he embarked on the project with no preconceived ideas and judgments, allowing the materials to determine the contours of his study. As his review articles for *Russkaia mysl'* indicate, Miliukov still favored the inductive method in history writing; the critiques of his dissertation likely helped nudge him toward his subsequent advocacy of a deductive approach.[49]

Nonetheless, Miliukov's study remained for some seventy years the most comprehensive and authoritative overall account of the Petrine financial reforms.[50] Miliukov also succeeded in this work in his twofold purpose of removing scholarly debate over the Petrine reforms from the philosophical plane, and in giving an impetus to the "new history" based on extensive archival work. M. M. Bogoslovskii's dissertation on the regional reform of Peter the Great and Kizevetter's book on the provincial reform of Catherine are among the best of the works inspired by the achievement of Miliukov's pioneering monograph.[51]

Miliukov's second book, *Controversial Questions*, retained the financial-institutional focus of his work on Peter's reforms but revealed more pronounced theoretical views on the study of history. The book was a response to A. Lappo-Danilevskii's monograph on seventeenth-century financial institutions, *The Organization of Direct Taxation in the Muscovite State*. Miliukov warmly praised Lappo-Danilevskii's achievement without entirely supporting his conclusions; what is of interest to this discussion, however, is Miliukov's remarks on the author's historical approach.[52]

Miliukov took issue with Lappo-Danilevskii's assertion that "the specialist in the history of a given people should study in its history primarily *specific* phenomena peculiar to the national type, and not features it has in common with other peoples." Miliukov found this statement in itself highly disputable, but directed his main critique to a second assertion, based on this initial assumption of a national type, that "the most specific phenomenon of Russian national history is the Muscovite state of the seventeenth century."[53]

In rejecting the idea of a "type" as an abstraction from reality, Miliukov showed his preference for the study of "social dynamics" over "social statics" in sociological history. "This primary concentration of attention on an idea of a type, worked out in advance, does not presage anything good," he averred. "Exaggerating the 'stability' of phenomena, the investigator risks losing the necessary flexibility of thought and acuteness of view; following the unity of a type, the historian risks missing the main thing underlying historical study, the diversity, complexity, and mobility of the historical process."[54] A typological perspective, Miliukov concluded, cannot accommodate the dynamic of historical development. As he put it elsewhere, studying a "mechanism in its functioning" is not history.[55]

Main Currents in Russian Historical Thought did not generate the sort of attention produced by his work on the Petrine reforms, but it was one of Miliukov's finest works. It is certainly the least dated: no book on Russian historiography, written before or after, rivals its treatment of the period 1700–1836. The work actually has two subjects, for Miliukov here consciously used the history of historiography as a vehicle for tracing the evolution of the worldviews of Russian society at large. It also represented a complete departure from his first two monographs in terms of subject and approach. Basically, Miliukov's focus shifted from the history of institutions to the history of ideas and culture. In this area, his work tended to be more interpretative and synthetic, its merit lying in the originality of the conceptualization and the use of materials rather than in utilization of new sources.

Main Currents begins with a brief overview of the *synopsis* of 1688 and ends with an examination of Peter Chaadaev, P. V. Kireevskii, and the influence of German Idealism on Russian thought. A projected second volume, which would have taken the exposition to Miliukov's own day, was never completed.[56] Two premises underlie the book. Miliukov advanced the proposition that all scientific work, consciously or unconsciously, is directed by theories, and that these theories are the product of the prevailing worldview of the given period in which they are advanced. The scholar who ignores theory becomes the involuntary tool of outdated theory, and his work suffers in consequence. Miliukov asserted that this knowledge frees contemporary scholarship from the burdens imposed by the thought of the past:

> The historian must look at products of historical literature as remnants [*otsloeniia*] of the thought of the past and for each of these find that point of view by which this product was created—by resurrecting these phenomena of old historical literature in their temporary and local significance he deprives them of their absolute significance and, consequently, frees contemporary thought from the aggregate of historical axioms taken on faith from old historical works.[57]

By asserting the existence of an "uninterrupted connection between science and learning" Miliukov's history of historiography became a larger history of Russian thought. The general current of Russian historiography, he held, "is always in more or less close connection with the development of the general worldview."[58]

Miliukov divided the development of Russian historical writing over the last two centuries into two periods. The first, from V. N. Tatishchev through N. M. Karamzin, was the period of the practical or ethical understanding of the tasks of the historian. The second period, extending from the mid-1820s to his own day, was that of history looked on as a science. Miliukov identified four subperiods in the eighteenth-century development of historical study and, by extension, in the evolution of Russian thought, by examining four outstanding representatives of the Russian Enlightenment: Tatishchev, M. V. Lomonosov, M. M. Shcherbatov, and I. N. Boltin.

His evaluation of these representatives was as revealing of his own worldview as it was of the views of eighteenth-century Russia. In Miliukov's characterization, Tatishchev's utilitarian estimation of knowledge for its practical results was symptomatic of the outlook of the Petrine era, which was "foreign to the idea that enlightenment softens the heart, that art ennobles the soul."[59] Lomonosov's historical approach, with its rhetorical emphasis, was typical of the Elizabethan era, which "took on the pretty decorations of Western culture."[60] Under Catherine there were two different social types, embodied by Shcherbatov and Boltin.

For Miliukov, the pragmatism of Shcherbatov's rationalistic worldview was lacking in historical perspective, since "the peculiarity of pragmatism in the eighteenth century is that for psychological motivation it primarily takes the self-interested motives of human nature and sees them as the same for all times and peoples."[61] Boltin's "scientific" view held that morals are created by the natural conditions of historical life and that human will can only somewhat alter the action of natural conditions.[62] Miliukov believed that Boltin's view was closer to a true, organic understanding of the historical process. At any rate, it was closer to his own, for he shared Boltin's historicist belief in moral relativism.

Also revealing was Miliukov's remark that he felt a greater sense of kinship with the historians of the late eighteenth century than with scholars of more recent generations. The former brought to their historical studies "a broad understanding of the phenomena of social and political life, a feeling for reality" absent from their successors.[63]

Between the two periods of Russian historiography stood Nikolai Karamzin, and Miliukov was at great pains to rout forever the myth of Karamzin as "the Peter the Great of Russian historians." This was the most controversial section of his study.[64] Karamzin profited by his predecessors' work without managing to correct their faults or found a school of historiography.[65] Even his views on the course of Russian history were largely borrowed from a schema worked out by eighteenth century historians, and they had discovered it laid out for them in the sources. In Karamzin, Moscow appeared as the natural continuation of Kiev, and the rise of Moscow was presented as something necessary in the general course of Russian history. The actions of the rulers were the prime mover of history: princely will plunged Russia into the depths and raised it to greatness.[66] Miliukov paused here to explore how this understanding of Russian history was formulated and incorporated into the original sources themselves in the fifteenth and sixteenth centuries. This reading of the sources would become the provocative central thesis on the foreign origins of national ideology in his own *Studies of Russian Culture*.

The second, "scientific" period of Russian historical science had its genesis in the change in worldview wrought by German romanticism. Miliukov's ability to appreciate views for which he had little intellectual affinity is illustrated by his treatment of Schelling's nature philosophy. For the generation of the 1820s, he wrote, the artificial analogies drawn by Schellingism from nature "quenched a spiritual thirst." Schellingism's unitary idea was not a "dead, mechanical unity of atomistic theory, but a living, dynamic unity of life permeating the universe."[67] The consequences of these views were not confined to literature and art; the generation of the 1820s had perspectives on history very different from those of their predecessors.[68] The concentration on external history—that is, political history—gave way to the study of "internal" history, "the history of the mind and heart of mankind."[69]

Chief among the disputes engendered by the new orientation was the question of what gave the Russian nationality its ordained place in world history, a dispute Miliukov illustrated by looking at how N. A. Polevoi, M. P. Pogodin, Kireevskii, and Chaadaev addressed this issue. Pogodin and Polevoi tried, unsuccessfully, to find in the Russian past a warrant for a "world-historical" future. Kireevskii and Chaadaev began from the premise that no such warrant existed, with Kireevskii demanding the borrowing of universalizing elements from the European present, and Chaadaev seeking them in the European past. The problem for all of these attempts, Miliukov argued, was the absence of a connection between Russia's past and future, between national history and a universal, historical mission of the Russian people.[70]

Main Currents was a study of gradual but not uninterrupted progress, for advances in historiography in one area often occasioned neglect of previous advances in others. The standards of historical criticism established by Boltin, for example, were allowed to lapse with the infusion of romantic philosophy into historical thinking. By the time of Kireevskii and Chaadaev, Russian scholarship had experienced but not succeeded in uniting the three elements that, taken altogether, constituted truly scientific history in Miliukov's eyes: rigorous, critical methodology; subject matter drawn from "real life"; and a dynamic, "lawful," theoretical view of the historical process.

Main Currents was also the story of the joint contribution of Western and

Russian influences to the development of native historiography. If French and German scholarship were mainly responsible for scientific theory and methodology, it was Russian scholars who uncovered sources and provided the historical schema. And theories foreign in origin were revised, added to, transformed—and sometimes distorted—in the hands of Russian scholars, in order to suit them to the realities of the Russian experience. What might be called the "subplot" of the work, the larger intellectual history of the period 1700–1836, unfolded in parallel fashion. The "main currents" examined were all European imports, but the story of their acceptance and reworking was one of increasingly widespread cultural attainments and of increasingly sophisticated and original thinking.

Although Miliukov never wrote the projected second volume of this work, his views on the further development of Russian thought and historiography found expression in lectures, scattered articles and in volume 3 of the *Studies of Russian Culture*.[71] Particularly remarkable was an essay that appeared in his collection *From the History of the Russian Intelligentsia*, "Liubov u idealistov tridtsatykh godov" (Love among the idealists of the 1830s). It bore the Miliukov hallmarks of bold thesis, interest in ideas, and easy familiarity with the sources and secondary literature, but was almost unique among his works in its conception, which was less "nineteenth century" than anything else he did.

In this essay Miliukov attempted to throw light on the question of the extreme abstractness of the idealists of the 1830s by looking into their conduct of "affairs of the heart." Diaries and love letters were the primary sources. Using N. K. Stankevich, Belinskii, and Alexander Herzen as case studies, Miliukov looked at what they believed should be their attitude and behavior in the matter of love, then compared this belief with their actual behavior. Discrepancies between their ideas and conduct were instructive on the evolution of idealism in Russia; Miliukov argued that actual experience forced them to revise or abandon their idealist position on love and that this had implications for all their thought.

Miliukov suggested that the hitherto untold love story of Vissarion Belinskii held the key to the correct explanation of his theoretical views. Belinskii, like Stankevich, began from an ultraromantic theory by which love was the means of merging with the spirit that permeated the world. Belinskii's first experience of unrequited love forced him to realize that differences in education, social position, and material circumstances, those despised "externalities," exercised far greater influence than his circle's theories allowed for. His passionate embrace of the theory of "reasonable reality" of Hegel, therefore, was not the highest manifestation of the abstractness of the circle theories, but the reaction of his nature against their abstractness.[72] Belinskii drew the most extreme conclusions from his "reasonable reality," again feeling, by 1841, lost and dissatisfied with himself. Another romantic crisis at this time convinced him that he could neither restore his old feelings on love nor live without "feeling": abandoning idealism, Belinskii sought and ultimately found a love that was "human."[73]

The love story of Alexander Herzen was really that of two people, Alexander and his wife, Natasha.[74] As with Belinskii, Miliukov traced the connection between the stormy development of a passion and the development of Herzen's thought, arguing that these were not merely parallel but connected. Herzen was, inherently, a man who celebrated the mind over the heart; metaphysics were foreign to him. Natasha, in contrast, directed all her energies to things of the heart, dwelling in the world of feeling and religious mysticism. The strength of her love for Herzen, coupled with the vagaries of his personal fortunes, awakened in him new sensibilities. "Herzen the mystic" enjoyed a temporary ascendancy over "Herzen the realist," and he modified his behavior in consequence.[75] His subordination to idealism was short-lived however, and the clash of the realistic view on feeling with the idealistic one produced a family crisis, since only the old worldview had given their union meaning for Natasha.[76]

Herzen's sufferings of the heart were colored by the idealism of the 1830s, and in turn colored his move away from idealism. But the fact of that real suffering and the lessons he drew from it was part of what gave Herzen, in Miliukov's eyes, a special place among the idealists. "That cup of delights, before which they stood in irresolution, he boldly drank to the bottom; and if at bottom he found bitter sediment, then that bitter stuff had nothing in common with later regret about a life spent in vain."[77]

By grounding this study of idealism in the character, romantic vicissitudes, and social experiences of individual thinkers, Miliukov offered a novel and valuable perspective on the evolution of an abstract philosophy. In its emphasis on behavior whose model was derived from philosophical literature, "Love among the Idealists" was almost an anticipation of the semiotic approach.[78] For the "scientific" Miliukov, it represented a departure, not only from the historical scholarship of the time, but from his own customary approach as well. Not surprisingly, it baffled his contemporaries. Today, it is virtually forgotten, and this is a pity, for in its penetrating characterizations, lucid prose, and sympathetic, thoughtful treatment, this essay shows Miliukov at the height of his scholarly powers. It is also more revealing than Miliukov perhaps realized. Clearly, he admired Herzen not only for his thought, but for the way he combined an ultimate commitment to things of the mind with a daring, active, feeling nature. The irony in this choice of topic was that very shortly Miliukov would himself begin to experience the effects of family storm and adversity in love.[79]

Miliukov's *Studies of Russian Culture* was the most widely read interpretation of Russian history since Karamzin's. Over the course of seven editions, from 1896 to 1918, it underwent significant revision and supplementation, reflecting the suggestions and criticisms of Miliukov's colleagues, new discoveries in historical scholarship, and under the influence of developments in the political realm, his changing conception of the connection between the Russian past and present. It was therefore Miliukov's most fully developed expression of the Russian national identity—spiritually, materially, and psychologically.

The phenomenal success of the *Studies* was due in part to its ability to provide an interpretation of the history of Russian culture, broadly defined, for the growing educated public. Miliukov's explicit goal was to "explain the present in terms of the past." This was not, in his view, strictly scholarly history; in the *Studies* he undertook to present "what was most essential and elementary in the process of Russian history" in readable and accessible form.[80] In the opinion of one reviewer, the public wanted a history that would aid in working out "a conscious attitude toward the actuality which surrounds it. The author of the *Studies of Russian Culture* divined this basic and vital need and the *Studies* is right on target—this is why it has found so many readers."[81]

The *Studies* grew out of the course of lectures Miliukov first gave at the Pedagogical Academy in 1892–94.[82] The treatment is thematic and methodological rather than chronological. Its three volumes deal with material culture, spiritual culture, and the origins and development of the "national idea" and public opinion.[83] Three major premises connect all three volumes: the changeability of Russia throughout its existence, caused by its own internal dynamic; the external nature of the formative influences on the state order, culture, and national ideas; and the fact of the imposition of borrowed culture from above. Also of great importance was the novel decision to exclude Kievan history from the history of the state order and of national ideas, since "in the north-east there were entirely different conditions of historical development than in the south."[84]

Miliukov's treatment of material culture included demographic history, economic history, and development of the whole institutional and social structure of the Russian state. Russia's harsh climate, short growing season, and vast expanses meant, first, that only low levels of population could be supported by primitive economy and, second, that the population was peripatetic, naturally inclining to the easier course of extensive rather than intensive agriculture. The huge difference in population density between European Russia and Western Europe had enormous significance for the history of the Russian state.[85] Because the population was not only numerically small but "wandering," productivity was low and the potential pool of recruits for the army small. Given these factors, in the face of the threat posed by hostile and aggressive neighbors, the state had to become hyperactive, summoning into existence and harnessing social estates, urban settlement, and industry, in the interests of self-defense. The Russian state developed in a fashion opposite to the course of development of the state in Europe, being created from the top down rather than from the bottom up.[86] This, in Miliukov's interpretation, was the single most important fact of Russian history.

Its consequences were enormous. In the West, Miliukov said, the existence of entrenched aristocratic landed interests forced the developing modern state to recognize, from the start, legitimate interests separate from and independent of its own. The existence of cities, with corporate interests and traditions of independence, gave birth to the idea of political freedom. In Muscovite Russia, in contrast, cities had their origins in the princely *dvor* or military settlements and there was no entrenched landed interest. As a result, there was no conception of political freedom or of participation of citizens in government. Instead, the state became a "military camp" and conscripted every social order to its service.[87]

Miliukov described this process without making any explicit value judgment, but judgment was implicit: the offspring of this parentage was a sorry creature, uncouth, undeveloped, a "rude and barbarous kingdom." Where latter-day historians are sometimes prompted to express admiration for the very feat of physical survival as a state in circumstances so unpropitious, Miliukov saw little to admire in the Muscovy he described.[88] And in identifying what was distinctively Russian in the development of its state and society, he did not find the mere fact of uniqueness a recommendation.

Miliukov's analysis of spiritual culture addressed religiosity and high culture.[89] His fundamental concern was to chronicle the history of the break between the elite and the people, which he saw, above all, as a product of the evolution of the official church. Informing the whole work was a refutation of both the Slavophile and "official" view of religiosity as a distinctively Russian characteristic, in his assertion that "despite the generally accepted opinion, we can say that Russian life in the past was not too much but too *little* penetrated by the foundations of faith."[90]

According to Miliukov, there has been a break between the "intelligentsia" and the people in every European country, and this break is always evoked by changes in the state of belief (*verovanie*).[91] In the West, the medieval Church was a living, dynamic force, a part of daily life and therefore able to influence it and the development of higher culture and creativity. With the waning of the Middle Ages national churches emerged and took different paths, the English church retaining the loyalty of its elite, the French church, because it refused to relinquish its cultural hegemony, driving educated believers away.[92]

And then Miliukov turned to Russia, distinguished, he alleged, neither by love for nor hatred of the church, but by indifference.[93] The twin factors of material circumstances and the nature of the Eastern Orthodox Church were responsible for this unfortunate situation, which had huge repercussions for the development of Russian culture. "The difference in the character of the break of Russian and European society with their past is above all explained by the difference in the cultural role of their faith."[94]

Miliukov argued that, for a variety of reasons, Christianity did not penetrate to the masses of the population for centuries after the formal conversion of the Eastern Slavs.[95] The conversion of the population was at first effected on a formal rather than spiritual level; in the sixteenth century, when the people began to demonstrate greater spiritual awareness and needs, the church hierarchy saw only rebellion, and turning to the government for help, stamped it out.[96] The official church thus lost any chance to foster and direct creativity; Russians were to turn to other sources of inspiration, secular and borrowed.

One could say that, with Chaadaev, Miliukov found Russia's choice of Eastern Christianity a fateful one. It was not Peter who divided the intelligentsia from the people, but the evolution of the official church—the century from the 1551 Stoglav council to the Schism marked the great watershed in the creative and spiritual life of Russia.[97] The consequences of this rupture, for cultural development, were disastrous. Russian art and literature became secularized too abruptly and, lacking a native secular tradition of high culture, merely imitated foreign ways. Not until the nineteenth century, as men of the people began to penetrate the upper social echelons, and those in "society" began to seek out the sources of their native cultural heritage did a truly indigenous and creative Russian culture begin to flourish again.[98] In this way, the course of development of high culture paralleled that of the state and social order, being shaped primarily by external factors, but only in response to changes generated internally, by the people.

The heart of the *Studies of Russian Culture* is volume 3, which many consider Miliukov's masterpiece.[99] Its two parts treated the genesis and evolution of "popular consciousness," which Miliukov defined as consisting of two successive processes or moments, national consciousness and social consciousness.[100] Miliukov argued that in all countries nationality was a product rather than cause of the historical process, and that it carried the unmistakable stamp of the period in which its characteristics came to be recognized. Such an understanding of nationality and national consciousness had far-reaching implications.

When nationality is identified as a phenomenon of natural science—speaking of blood or race—or as an anthropological-geographical one, it assumes the character of an absolute, something unchanging. From this followed the romantic concept of a national genius or national tradition that is equally unalterable, which allows scholars to search the past for the "genuine" national tradition, one perhaps deviated from over the course of time, that should serve as the touchstone for nationally minded policies. For example, followers of N. I. Kostomarov could identify the *veche* period in Russia as the expression of a truly Russian democratic tradition, placing the whole blame for subversion of this tradition on the Mongol yoke and its pernicious influence on the Muscovite grand princes.[101] Whether one's outlook was conservative or progressive, however, the usual view of popular consciousness made it possible to look to an absolute national tradition to sanction social and political programs in the present.

The sanction of tradition was undone when nationality was understood as the first moment in the evolution of popular consciousness. In Miliukov's dryly sociological definition: "Nationality constitutes a social group that has at its disposal language, as the singular and necessary means for uninterrupted psychological interaction, and which elaborates for itself a permanent fund of unique psychological experiences that regulate the correctness and the recurrence of the phenomena of this interaction."[102]

In dividing the evolution of popular consciousness into two successive processes or periods, Miliukov distinguished them as being expressed by different social groups with different desiderata, so that national consciousness assumed a basically traditional character, whereas social consciousness was primarily reformist. National consciousness, since it is evoked by recognition of an "other," arises from the clash of nations and is most often worked out during the process of a people's struggle for unification and independence. The customs, religion, and language of that period, which developed during earlier, unconscious eras, are taken to be what is distinctively indigenous and truly national, though in fact the group has already absorbed much that was foreign.[103] The transition from the first to the second period is accompanied by a struggle that, in the most favorable circumstances, ends with a reworking of the traditional system of social relations and its replacement with a system founded on the conscious choice of the majority (namely, democracy): "National 'tradition' retires to the background before victorious 'public opinion.'"[104]

The history of popular consciousness yielded the same double conclusion arrived at in the analysis of material and spiritual history: the Russian experience was both universal and unique. That the formative period of national consciousness coincided with and was influenced by an external threat was in no way peculiar to Russia. What Miliukov saw as unique or accidental, in the case of Russia, was that the activity of the external threat to the state coincided with a given—and low—degree of development of internal "social" forces.[105]

Class struggle, religious thought, and the territorial aspirations of the grand princes of Moscow were among the important factors shaping the "national idea" from the time of Ivan III to Peter, but in Miliukov's exposition foreign influence played the primary role. It was European ideas that were responsible for "the rapid ideological metamorphosis that clothed the grand prince of the appanage period in the costume of the tsar." Bulgarian and South Slav theories, for example, were the source of the Muscovite rulers' claim to be the "sole orthodox tsar in the entire universe" and of the representation of Moscow as the "new Tsargrad and the third Rome."[106] These theories and legends were revised in Russian hands, reconciling the South Slavic formula for Muscovy's political role as heir of the Byzantine emperors with native Muscovite pretensions to the lands of their Kievan "ancestors."[107]

The emergence of a new class, the service gentry, was another important factor in determining the shape of the "national idea." Beholden to the autocratic order for its status and well-being, the gentry proved very conservative. The dynastic and social crises of the Time of Troubles (1598–1613) had taught it to fear an insufficiency of power rather than an excess; it did not seek an independent political role in government but rather a secure social order and the guarantee of its economic interests.[108] It therefore did nothing to impede the monopolization of political power by the ruler and his burgeoning bureaucracy. In this way, the early seventeenth century saw the triumph of a national ideology that justified the absolutist idea of an all-Russian "tsar," one imposed by the state and greatly influenced by foreign ideas.[109]

Miliukov's interest was always piqued more by the business of explaining how things came to be than by establishing what they had been. He found plenty of scope for this interest in the problem of determining why, during Peter's reign, the triumphant "national program" was so swiftly succeeded by the "critical" program, under the auspices of the state itself and, above all, why a reform that was "necessary" was accomplished violently and arbitrarily.

By the beginning of Peter's reign, Miliukov argued, increased contact with the West had already made it clear that reform was unavoidable. The violence and extremism of the Petrine reforms stemmed from Russia's low level of cultural and social development, which made virtually impossible a conscious combination of borrowed elements and viable national traditions such as Iurii Krizhanich had advocated. For proponents of change, the choice seemed clear-cut: reform along Western lines *or* preservation of the "national" tradition. With corporative society still underdeveloped, it was once again the dynamic state that determined the course of action and ruthlessly imposed it on the population.[110] It was only from roughly the

1780s that an independent, vital, genuinely "social" consciousness arose, one created not by the state, but by the intelligentsia that the state had created and enlightened.[111]

Publication of the *Studies of Russian Culture* engendered a lively debate in the press. The most telling critiques turned on Miliukov's treatment of the evolution of the state and social structure in Russia. These critiques varied widely both in approach and interpretation, but all posited one factor absent in Miliukov's account: the existence of internal obstacles to the untrammeled development of the autocratic Muscovite state. V. Miakotin and N. Pomialovskii objected to Miliukov's disavowal of the influence of indigenous traditions, such as the institution of the *veche* of the appanage period and the whole tradition of Novgorodian spiritual culture.[112] A number of scholars held that Miliukov ignored the existence of social forces with which the developing state had had to contend. N. V. Pavlov-Sil'vanskii, for example, argued that Muscovite Russia had experienced a feudal period and was therefore far more "European" in its development than Miliukov maintained.[113] A critic writing under the initials "P.B." insisted, in contrast, that the course of Russian history was less European than Miliukov represented it as being. He also complained that Miliukov's explanation of autocracy bordered on the teleological; namely, that since material conditions required that the state become omnipotent in order to survive, it accordingly became omnipotent—since it was necessary, it happened.[114]

The unanimity on this one point underscores the rather abstract quality of Miliukov's characterization of state development, as initially formulated—excessive abstraction was the very flaw for which he had taken the juridical school to task. In subsequent editions of the *Studies* Miliukov responded to his critics and modified his exposition, although its theoretical foundations and line of argument remained essentially unchanged. He came to agree with Pavlov-Sil'vanskii that north-eastern Rus' had evolved a sort of feudalism, although he saw it as weakly developed.[115] Taking P.B.'s objections more to heart, he explained that he was not arguing that the Muscovite state had necessarily to survive, but that in order to survive it *was* necessary that it become all-powerful.[116] He also took greater care to emphasize that the rulers' consciousness of the tasks of state building was a developing one: the Moscow princes at first acted "thriftily," and solely in their own interests, only gradually articulating, with the aggrandizement of their position, a genuine political program and a more abstract ideological foundation for that program.[117]

Miliukov was less accommodating on the issue of the influence of native traditions. In his opinion, the state order of Muscovite Russia was not the product of struggle between competing, dissimilar traditions, but simply the product of the development of the old forms of governance of northeastern

Rus'. Only the uninterrupted existence of institutions, such as the boyar duma and *zemskii sobor* (council of the land), could allow them to be considered "tenacious traditions" handed down from earlier eras, and Miliukov saw no such continuity. In this sense, Russia did not have a "usable past."[118]

Studies of Russian Culture clearly carried the stamp of its time. This is discernible in its overall "positivistic" conception, in Miliukov's preservation of an "us/them" dichotomy in his treatment of the later conflict between "social forces" and the state, in his use of anachronistic terminology, and in his extreme Europhilism.[119] The *intelligent*'s classic disdain of "philistines" also made itself felt in Miliukov's reading of the genesis of culture: there existed indigenous popular culture, the creation of the traditional, peasant masses, and high culture, which was generated by the intelligentsia and drew upon popular culture. No genuine source of "culture" lay between these two poles.[120]

His recognition of the extent to which the context of the time had colored his interpretation was belated and only partial. In emigration, Miliukov changed the title of the revised volume 3 from *Nationalism and Social Consciousness* to *Nationalism and Europeanism*. He acknowledged that the dichotomy between nationalism and progressive social views implied in the original subtitle was not really correct, being the result of political orientations of the first decade of the twentieth century. He preserved, however, the contrast between "society" and "state."[121]

Whatever its shortcomings, the *Studies* was a brilliant and pioneering work. It far surpassed its Russian predecessors and compared favorably with similar works being written in this period in England and Europe.[122] Miliukov understood cultural history very broadly, but notwithstanding the huge importance of the material environment and social factors in the analysis, this was equally a history of things "spiritual" and intellectual.[123] In this synthesis of intellectual, religious, and material history, Miliukov not only broadened his own scholarly horizons, but also departed significantly from the orientation of the Russian historical establishment of his day.

Much was original here. Using a strongly comparative approach, Miliukov made the first sustained effort to reconcile the old debate on the particularity or universality of the Russian experience on sociological grounds. Despite its initially over-abstract formulation, his explanation of the genesis of autocracy in Russia was original and persuasive. Where earlier accounts of this genesis had relied chiefly on the innate character of the Russians or the geographical imperatives of a huge multinational state, Miliukov founded his explanation on the scarcity of resources, human as well as material, and the presence of an external threat to the state's very existence.[124] Also original was his thesis on the foreign origins of national ideology. This was the fruit of his extensive work on Russian historiography, which furnished the discovery of the first formulation of this ideology in the Muscovite sources, and of his sociological studies and training in European history, which provided him with a theoretical framework for assertions and evidence to support them.

Perhaps the most novel contention of the work was its emphasis on the protean and dynamic nature of the Russian state, not only institutionally and in terms of geographic extent, but even regarding its own self-definition. "Official nationalism" of the nineteenth century proclaimed Russia to be, and to have been, more or less immutable. In reality, Miliukov argued, Russia had been in a state of constant change, disequilibrium, transformation, since at least the middle of the sixteenth century, and more nearly since the gathering of the lands. This perspective very subtly shifted understanding of Russia's relationship to the West, from being a strictly reactive one to a more complex mixture of indigenous change, impact, and response.[125]

Personal and Political Orientations

Miliukov's enormous historical ouevre has much to offer in the way of clues for understanding his values, his interests, and the evolution of his thought. It offers a valuable corrective and supplement to his memoirs, in part because Miliukov was not a man greatly given to self-reflection or to the commitment of the fruits of such reflection to paper.

Above all, Miliukov's historical works were a celebration of rationality. He did not assume that all human action is rationally motivated—indeed, he recognized that spiritual needs are as "real" as physical ones, and that what satisfied those spiritual needs was quite frequently not rational. Still, he rejoiced when the rational triumphed; he explicitly valued the "scientific" worldview over the metaphysical or religious one and anticipated the time when education and culture would have fully penetrated to the masses. It is significant that he characterized Herzen, whom he admired deeply, as a man for whom the "claims of the mind" always outweighed the "claims of the heart."[126]

His belief in human rationality, which permits self-mastery and mastery of the material world, made him optimistic for the future. He was spared paralyzing doubts concerning the possibility of genuine knowledge and the futility of conscious activity founded upon this knowledge. Miliukov's pragmatism and preference for the "realistic" were in keeping with a rationalistic perspective. He championed the "scientific-realistic" approach to the writing of history and held that the subject of history must be "real life." He embraced also the understanding of "realism" as the practical. For example, although he admired the seventeenth-century reform projects of V. V. Golitsyn, he saw their failure as inevitable because they were not "realistic," given the conditions of the day.[127] As Miliukov gradually moved toward adoption of a professedly "liberal" political worldview, between 1892 and 1903, he increasingly identified realism and practicality as specifically characteristic of Russian liberalism, in contrast to the "utopianism" of conservative nationalists and revolutionary socialists.[128]

The historicism of Miliukov's approach illustrated more than scholarly belief in the impropriety of imposing externally derived criteria of judgment on past ideas and behavior. It reflected an intellectual tolerance generally characteristic of Miliukov, one in keeping with his rather eclectic work. Certainly, Miliukov polemicized heatedly with proponents of the application of subjective sociology to history writing, but he had the ability to recognize what was valid and useful in virtually any approach. His perceptive exploration of German idealism and its influence on Russian thought was but one example of his capacity for appreciating views alien to his own.

Miliukov's historical and political thought were intimately connected. Neither was unchanging, and changes in Russian political realities, as well as a finer understanding of those realities, derived from participation in politics, affected all his thought. But it is possible to identify ideas about Russian history that served as the foundation or justification of his political policies, as well as to point out at least one crucial instance when Miliukov ignored one of the lessons of the past.

It is clear that most of Miliukov's views on the history of Russia were completely congenial to his hopes for Russia's future, and that in many cases ideas he had imbibed as a student in the gymnasium and university strongly affected conclusions he drew from actual historical study, which only refined these ideas. One example is his thinking on the state. Miliukov held that in Russia the process of state building had inverted the European pattern, preceding from the top down. Although the state had had its progressive role, it eventually forfeited that role to "society." Miliukov was therefore able to see a historical pedigree for contemporary society's struggle with the state, although he denied that there was any "national tradition" that sanctioned society's progressive programs.

Of more significance, Miliukov saw this struggle as a struggle for democracy and believed society was more or less foreordained to win. In Miliukov's reading of the historical process, European states in the modern period increasingly admitted lower social estates and classes in the governing process, as they became more enlightened and cultured. The result was greater democratization, the increased concern of the state with domestic welfare, and more abstractly, greater rationality and less scope for the element of the accidental in the movement of history as "consciousness" characterized more and more of the citizenry.[129] Russia was no exception to this process, and though other elements of the historical process gave to the

Russian past much that was unique, there was implicit the conviction that Russia, too, was moving toward democracy.

There was, in addition, a specifically Russian feature that would help promote a "European" outcome, and that is what Miliukov saw as the absence of a genuine national tradition. Russian national ideology was a creation of the state during the process of its unification. Because of the tardiness of that process, and because of other factors singular to the Russian historical experience, almost as soon as it gained formal victory this national ideology was taken apart and discarded. Wholesale borrowing from abroad, coupled with an accelerated pace of remaking cultural institutions again and again, meant that one could not speak of an enduring, organic national tradition connecting past and present.[130] In consequence, Russia was, in effect, free of the burden of the past: she could remake herself wholly on the basis of the needs of the present and, by implication, relatively rapidly. Given this understanding of the Russian past, Miliukov's call for a radical democratization of the political process in 1905 was not, theoretically, a violation of what he took to be historical realities. Yet we can identify at least two problems with this orientation, one entirely consistent with his historical perspective, and one that transgressed against it.

Miliukov's perspective on "social consciousness" resembled his depiction of the role of the state in Russian history in being a view from the top down. He was not a populist. The ideas he valued most highly were those generated by the educated and, for the most part, were foreign in origin; in anticipating the convergence of "democratic" and "popular" thought, he actually had in mind the replacement of the latter by the former. Miliukov did not make the mistake of assuming the peasantry to be a tabula rasa. He fully appreciated the autonomous creative forces of the people which in the seventeenth century withstood the state's efforts to bend them to the official mold. But in his belief that the Russians—like all people—would be educated into a rational, socially enlightened, democratic state of consciousness, he did assume a certain receptivity that would allow the rationalization of popular thought to be effected in very short order.

The second problem is related to the first, but is less consistent with Miliukov's views on the working of the historical process. In his political program, Miliukov initially did not reckon with what might be called the structural obstacles to reform that are the dilemma of all developing countries. Charging Miliukov with this error is not anachronistic, for one of the distinctions of his historical work was its very appreciation of this dilemma. In the *Studies*, Miliukov repeatedly demonstrated that even when enlightened autocracy tried to enact progressive cultural reforms, these reforms were sabotaged by the combination of bureaucratic and popular incomprehension or self-interest, on the one hand, and the scarcity of human and fiscal resources, on the other. Miliukov's best example was Catherine the Great's unsuccessful effort to create a "new man" in Russia by totally recasting the educational system.[131]

But Miliukov the politician, at least in the heady period of the 1905 revolution, acted as though the Duma could legislate the country into a progressive, democratic, equitable condition. His speeches and articles made no allusion to the problems of financing and staffing, to the sort of bureaucratic or popular resistance that figured in his historical studies. Under the impress of actual participation in politics, Miliukov soon abandoned this view; the example is cited here to demonstrate that while his historical knowledge influenced his political thought and program, Miliukov by no means always harkened to the lessons of the past.

Throughout his life, Miliukov refused to call his approach a "philosophy of history" as such; for him this had overtones of the despised "metaphysical" approach, with its assumption of absolute ethical values and search for "meaning" in history. His view of history was pluralistic and avowedly sociological, with Comtean positivism the most formative element. His range of subject matter was extraordinary, embracing everything from state finances to the love life of the idealists. His methods were no less diverse, drawing on linguistics, archaeology, anthropology, psychology, and economics for both theory and evidence. And in all his works he preserved a view of history that sought to reconcile the unique and the universal, the "lawful" and the accidental, the structural and the dynamic—to account for everything in the historical process.

But if Miliukov's approach was eclectic, it was also, for the most part, internally consistent. His view of the historical process as both "regular"—in the sense of conforming to patterns or developmental laws—and complex, imposed certain constraints on the historian that Miliukov acknowledged and to which he adhered. First, Miliukov advocated that scholars choose subject matter that lent itself to "scientific" treatment, and though his topics were diverse, he honored the rule. Prior to the 1917 revolution he almost never wrote history of an event; his approach was conceptual, and "structure" and "process" were the prime foci.

Second, it can be argued that at least *consciously* he avoided normative interpretations. In the larger sense, he failed here completely, since his reading of Russian history was based on the assumption that a socially conscious society in the ideal "European" mode—democratic, secular, enlightened—was not only the superior form of social organization, but the state toward which all Western peoples evolve. But in the narrower sense of not passing judgment on historical eras or individual actors on the basis of externally imposed criteria, Miliukov practiced historicism. He did not, for example, deprecate the seventeenth-century gentry servitors for failing to institutionalize their role in the governing process because such was not their interest or concern at the time.[132]

In considering the use of history, Miliukov was less consistent. Theoretically, he espoused the view of historical study as a science, strictly conceived; it was an end in itself, and its object was knowledge of the truth. The study of the past should not be undertaken in a utilitarian spirit, and the application of its findings was not the business of the scholar. In practice, Miliukov found this view difficult to reconcile with the educated individual's responsibility to be of service to his society and his own passionate desire to better Russia.

In the context of the history writing of the day, both Miliukov's sociological approach and his eclecticism were consistent with what was called "new history" in Western Europe. This approach stressed a dynamic, generative view of history, a change in subject toward more institutional and social history, and greater flexibility in methods of investigation. Viewed more specifically in the context of the "Kliuchevskii legacy," or the Moscow school of historiography, Miliukov fit the tradition not only in his interest in sociology and economics, but also in his relative lack of attention to political and diplomatic history and to biography. Also in keeping with the tradition of Kliuchevskii was Miliukov's neglect of the influence of nonwestern cultures on the course of Russian development.[133] Where Miliukov diverged from this tradition was in his comparative approach, his employment of theory, and his interest in ideas and "spiritual" culture. Kliuchevskii consciously excluded the history of ideas from study of the past; Miliukov made ideas, and the efforts to realize them in practice, his chief concern.[134] Those works devoted to the history of ideas were his most original and compelling.

A reading of Miliukov's historical works reveals the image of a man who was confident, optimistic, largely unreflective; a thoroughgoing agnostic and Westernizer who celebrated human rationality, was tolerant of past beliefs uncongenial to his own, and a proselytizer of his scholarly orientation in the present. It was this combination of attributes that quickly dated some of his scholarly works and infused others with a quality which has withstood the test of time. These were also the attributes of Paul Miliukov himself when he turned away from scholarly pursuits to devote himself to active participation in the political development of his country. As he shifted his energies from the study of history to its making, he carried with him the convictions and predilections that had shaped his career as a historian.

CHAPTER FOUR

Scholarship and Opposition

In his memoirs, Miliukov referred to the decade of 1895–1905 as "the years of wandering."[1] His existence was a peripatetic one, as he went from Moscow to Riazan' and then to Bulgaria, then to St. Petersburg, and then, after a stint in prison, to Finland. Then, between June 1902 and April 1905, he divided most of his time between the United States, England, and the Balkans, spending just six months in the Russian empire, with three of these spent serving another term in prison. For the eight years following his departure from Riazan' in 1897, Miliukov was more frequently separated from his family than with it, and more often out of Russia than in it.

The years between 1897 and 1905 were unsettled in more than just physical terms. Miliukov had found his identity at Moscow University, in the realm of historical scholarship. The rupture with Kliuchevskii loosed those moorings; the expulsion from academe in 1895 set him further adrift. For the next ten years Miliukov was to divide his time and energies between his continuing interest in scholarship, his new interest in Balkan nationalism and national liberation movements, and his commitment to the growing opposition movement in Russia. These interests made conflicting claims on him and at times pulled him in different directions. Even as he grew in stature as one of the most influential spokesmen of the opposition movement, he partially disengaged himself from that movement to pursue his scholarly career.

Balkan Interlude

Miliukov gave two courses at Sofia University, one on the Middle Ages that he had prepared in Vienna and Paris, and one on Slavic antiquity and archaeology. He had feared enrollments would be small, since he had to give his lectures in Russian, but this did not prove to be a major impediment. Miliukov enjoyed his teaching and quickly made friends among his faculty colleagues.[2]

It was perhaps not surprising that Miliukov, as "heir" to Dragomanov, made his closest friends among liberally inclined political activists such as Ivan Shishmanov, professor of foreign literature and Dragomanov's son-in-law. Through the Shishmanovs he became friendly with Alexander Malinov and the radical liberal circle of Petko Karavelov, who had at one time headed the government and was still the "grand old man" of Bulgarian democratic liberals. Miliukov was not an uncritical admirer of his new friends, but nonetheless described himself and Anna as being "united with the Karavelovs in very sincere friendship."[3] It might also be added that this was Miliukov's first contact with veterans of real parliamentary politics, people who had actually held office and been responsible for the translation of their ideals into practice under all the constraints of actual political conditions.[4]

The pleasant resumption to Miliukov's professorial career proved short-lived. Even abroad, he managed to run afoul of the Russian government. He had held aloof from the Russian consulate in Sofia and the circle of "official Russophiles" gathered round it, and the Russian consul, Iu. P. Bakhmetev, looked equally askance at him. Miliukov later wrote a friend that the consul had been agitating the Bulgarian government for his dismissal from the university almost all autumn; Miliukov soon furnished him with a pretext for insisting upon it.[5] December 6 was Tsar Nicholas's name day, and while Miliukov dutifully attended the cathedral service in its honor, he did not accompany the other professors to the Russian consulate for the customary toast to the tsar's health. This was interpreted as a "demonstration against Russia," Miliukov wrote; Bakhmetev demanded that he be dismissed. Bakhmetev's demand was a blow to Bulgarian pride, but since the government's concerted efforts to improve its strained relations with Russia were finally bearing fruit, Miliukov would have to be sacrificed.[6] His teaching was terminated, a compensation being grant of a half-year sabbatical at full pay. He decided to spend part of this "sabbatical" in travel and study in Macedonia.[7]

The "Macedonian Question" had again become one of the major issues of Bulgarian politics at the time of Miliukov's arrival in Sofia; Austria, Bulgaria, Serbia, Greece, and Turkey were all jockeying for dominance in the area.[8] Miliukov spent the winter of 1897–98 preparing for his trip, in part by studying Turkish and modern Greek, and most of 1898 in Constantinople and traveling through Macedonia, while his family remained in Sofia. The purpose of his travels, as he wrote in the first of a series of "Letters from Macedonia" published in *Russkie vedomosti*, was to observe the struggle for sovereignty in Macedonia. Although Miliukov insisted that he undertook his travels with "no prior intention of proving any sort of national theory or serving any business save the business of truth," he was in fact very much predisposed toward Bulgaria.[9]

Miliukov carried away three strong impressions from his first trip through Macedonia: the continuing importance of churches in defining national identities, even as those identities and their attendant aspirations became more consciously political than religious; the formidable nature of the task of bringing the many primitive and isolated regions of the area into the "modern age"; and the extent to which Bulgarian Macedonians reposed hope in Russia's "obligation" to liberate the Slavs from the Turks.[10]

Within a year, Miliukov had again left Sofia for Constantinople in preparation for another trip, which would include Asia Minor as well as Macedonia. He traveled as part of an archaeological expedition headed by F. I. Uspenskii, director of the Russian Archaeological Institute in Constantinople. They went to the southern shore of the sea of Marmara in search of modern Greek inscriptions and continued deep into Asia Minor. They then went to Macedonia to investigate Christian antiquity of the Slavic period. The difficulties of the trip were numerous, including travel on horseback over rough terrain and dealings with the corrupt Turkish bureaucracy, but Miliukov was eager to exercise the archaeological skills he had acquired in Riazan' and obviously relished his adventures.[11] Once the main dig was completed, an ancient necropolis near Lake Ostrovo, and the excavators' share of the findings shipped off to Constantinople, Miliukov spent months in the Turkish capital organizing and inventorying the materials. He resolved to present a report of the dig to the archaeological congress scheduled to convene in Kiev in late summer 1899.[12]

Miliukov's "Balkan interlude" was brief—less than two years, of which only one year was spent in Bulgaria—but it was important in a variety of ways. In his memoirs, Miliukov maintained that his stay in Bulgaria had given him his first interest in foreign policy considerations, and this was to be a major interest throughout his political career. Sofia was alive to every nuance and rumor of foreign policy, he wrote, making Bulgaria a sort of optimal "prep school" for the student of foreign affairs.[13] More specifically, the partiality for Bulgaria and dislike of Russia's pro-Serbian policies which he acquired in 1897–98 stayed with him always.[14]

Miliukov's experiences in the Balkans influenced him in other ways he did not explicitly identify. They contributed significantly to his interest in nationalism and the sources of national identity. A year after his first trip to Macedonia to observe the struggle of competing nations and nationalities in the Macedonian ethnic stewpot, Miliukov began volume 3 of *Studies of Russian Culture*, dealing with the origins and development of Russian "nationality." This was the only part of the book which was a completely new addition to his lecture course on Russian history.[15] While his travels in Macedonia did not create his interest in nationality, they did strengthen it.

Miliukov's firsthand experience of domestic political life in Bulgaria also influenced him profoundly. Bulgaria convinced him that Russia was not too backward for a constitutional regime. He was already theoretically inclined to assume this, having been a democrat since at least the early 1890s, but the Bulgarian experience gave him the empirical evidence he required. Despite the many imperfections of Bulgarian constitutionalism, he felt, the younger generation had already internalized the customs and responsibilities of free political life. Even the less tutored older generation had demonstrated its legislative common sense. "You see that these people are perfect ignoramuses when it comes to state law, or any sort of law you like," he wrote. "You can't help but laugh, seeing how they joust with windmills without remarking actual dangers . . . But soon you begin to notice that by some sort of secret path, imperceptible to us, from this chaos of cries, rhetorical exclamations, ignorant criticisms, and offensive personal tricks comes together a decision which you cannot help but acknowledge as the most intelligent and most suitable for the given case."[16]

As he wrote in 1904, the viable existence of a constitutional regime for twenty-five years in a country no less backward than Russia proved that the actual experience of constitutional life itself was a political education.[17]

Miliukov's Bulgarian interlude seems to provide a piece of the puzzle in the story of the evolution of his political liberalism. It is not unlikely that the impression made on him by the left-liberal circle in which he moved in Bulgaria convinced him of the practicability of liberalism in Russia, something toward which his Russian observations and readings in sociology had been drawing him. Just as Bulgaria had shown him how constitutionalism could work in a backward, agrarian country, Karavelov and his political confreres showed Miliukov a workable liberalism, one that was neither "small deed" in approach nor timid in method. His receptivity to the radical liberalism of the Karavelov circle did not blind him to its shortcomings—nor save him from repeating its mistakes. In 1904 he wrote of Bulgarian liberalism of the 1870s that it had made a tragic error in wanting too much at once, in failing to appreciate that in settling for partial reforms it contributed to the stability and practice of constitutionalism:

> At a time when strengthening the general consciousness of the rights already granted to the people was still to be worked on, by this means filling the

broad limits and formulas of the constitution with living content, the leaders of the [liberal] party decided that these rights were insufficient and limits too narrow, and that the constitution had to be changed in the sense of still greater democratism.[18]

In 1905, "dizzy with success" as were so many others active in the Russian liberation movement, Miliukov would echo the maximalism of the Bulgarian liberals in insisting on nothing less than the establishment of a constituent assembly based on universal suffrage. Although Miliukov did not always recollect the lessons he learned by observation of Bulgarian political life, one could argue that Bulgaria was at least as important a way station as England in his development as a liberal.

The Petersburg Opposition

Miliukov returned to Russia in spring of 1899. He reported the findings of his excavations in Macedonia to the archaeological congress in Kiev and received official confirmation of his request to be allowed to settle in St. Petersburg. With the warm reception given him by friends and acquaintances in St. Petersburg, the high spirits he had enjoyed since arriving in Kiev burgeoned into a feeling of near joy.[19]

Why Miliukov chose Petersburg over his native Moscow is unclear, but his choice proved to be an important one. The atmosphere in the capital in 1899 was a far cry from what he had observed when he spent two summers researching his dissertation there a decade earlier. Since February, student unrest in the city had become endemic and in St. Petersburg, as elsewhere, the politicization and radicalization of the student population heightened the general level of disaffection.[20] Miliukov was almost immediately drawn into contact with St. Petersburg's restive student population. In general, 1899 saw a visible escalation of tension between government and "society." According to Miliukov, by the time of his arrival in the capital, government reaction had already given society a "revolutionary shade."[21]

Miliukov could not help but be affected by the oppositional climate of his new home, but another set of circumstances also contributed to his "heel to the left."[22] The circles in which he moved in Moscow in the first half of the 1890s had been far from homogeneous in outlook and disposition, and he had therefore been subject to varied and competing political influences. The circles he frequented in Petersburg were more unambiguously leftist. In addition to his contacts with the student movement, Miliukov strengthened his ties with the "Legal Populist" group around *Russkoe bogatstvo* (Russian wealth), assumed an editorial position at the journal *Mir Bozhii* (God's world), a stronghold of young Marxists, and became active in the two most outspoken organizations of the city, the Union of Writers and the Free Economic Society. To supplement his income from *Mir Bozhii*, he also became coeditor of the encyclopedia being produced by S. N. Iuzhakov. The Miliukovs had been living entirely on his earnings from articles and book royalties, and with three children to support—a daughter, Natalia, had been born while they were abroad—a regular salary was welcome.[23]

The arrangement with Iuzhakov deteriorated very quickly. Miliukov had reservations about the quality of the encyclopedia and claimed that the enthusiasm he brought to his work was not altogether welcome to Iuzhakov, who was more interested in exploiting his name than his expertise. Letters Iuzhakov wrote to his new editor suggest that Miliukov had strong opinions and was not particularly diplomatic about expressing them; within a few years Petersburg circles coined for Miliukov the sobriquet "the soul of tactlessness."[24] In January 1901 he gave Iuzhakov his resignation, refusing to continue even as director of the historical division of the encyclopedia.[25]

Miliukov's editorial involvement with *Mir Bozhii*, a monthly devoted to "self-improvement," initially promised well. Founded as a journal for youth, *Mir Bozhii* had gradually assumed the standard format of a thick journal without abandoning its lively and popularizing tone. Its publisher, Aleksandra Davydova, styled herself a patroness of young Marxists and from 1897, with the addition of prominent young marxist historian M. I. Tugan-Baranovskii to the editorial board, the journal had taken on what the censors described as an economic-materialist coloration.[26]

Miliukov's position at the widely circulated journal offered the possibility of exercising an appreciable influence on public opinion. He energetically set about finding reviewers, subeditors, and contributors, and was deluged with manuscripts, requests for translation jobs, and recommendations of protégés. Some of his correspondents applauded his taking on the position, indicating that he might indeed shape the political orientation of the journal. One man using the pen name N. Severnyi wrote Miliukov in early 1900, "Who is grouped around you now at *Mir Bozhii*? We expect here that *you* will succeed in establishing a group and something equivalent in influence and significance to *Otechestvennye zapiski* in its own time, but fully European."[27]

If Miliukov entertained similar hopes of his role at *Mir Bozhii*, he was soon forced to recognize them as misplaced. He never felt himself at home there, and did not get on well with the editor of the literary half of the journal, A. Iu. Bogdanovich, a former member of Narodnoe Pravo whom he characterized as doctrinaire, "severe in comportment, and reticent in manifestation of his feelings and thoughts." Bogdanovich at first kept his disapproval of Miliukov to himself, but an open rupture came sometime in

1901. One of them would have to go, and Miliukov says he told Aleksandra Davydova that there could be no doubt that it was he, the newcomer, who should leave. Miliukov left the journal on good terms with the publisher, and *Mir Bozhii* continued to serialize his *Studies of Russian Culture*.[28]

Miliukov's closest friends in Petersburg were gathered around a rival publication, the Populist-oriented *Russkoe bogatstvo*.[29] His long-time friend Venedikt Miakotin was on the editorial staff, as was A. V. Peshekhonov, with whom Miliukov also became close. N. K. Mikhailovskii, old and ill but still a figure of immense intellectual authority, was editor-in-chief. Other staff members included the popular writer V. G. Korolenko and the hugely influential N. F. Annenskii.[30] All of these men were extremely active in the Union of Writers.

The friendship between Miakotin and Miliukov is an interesting one. Miakotin was the more ideologically zealous of the two. Miliukov, honoring Miakotin's moral integrity, saw him as a "warrior in social conflicts"; I. V. Gessen, less charitably, called him "one of the most striking representatives of the intelligentsia 'circle mentality' [*kruzhkovshchina*]." It was Miakotin who introduced Miliukov into the passionately political, notoriously humorless *Russkoe bogatstvo* circle; he also later tried to induce Miliukov to join the Socialist Revolutionary Party. Following publication of the manifesto of October 17, 1905, Miakotin would become one of his most bitter political critics, but even in these years of close collaboration, friendship did not preclude heated arguments over controversial questions.[31]

Miliukov's capacity for entering into close friendships with individuals whose political orientation differed from his own had been evident since his student days. It was not altogether typical of the intelligentsia of the period; friendships, particularly in the more radical circles, did not tend to cross ideological lines. The catholicity of Miliukov's personal relationships was a tremendous asset in a political setting lacking formalized structures and established channels of communication, one where circles and personal ties long played the chief role in organization and recruitment.[32]

It was due to the influence of Miakotin and the members of the *Russkoe bogatstvo* circle that almost immediately upon settling in St. Petersburg Miliukov was invited to join the prestigious Writers' Union, one of the two main organizational bases of the Petersburg radical intelligentsia. The other base was the Free Economic Society, to which Miliukov had belonged since the mid-1890s.[33] Both organizations were prime examples of how technical and professional societies were increasingly used for political purposes from the latter half of the 1890s, a phenomenon of which the government was well aware. Miliukov's involvement in both organizations introduced him to the capital's political activists, enhanced his political reputation, and restored to him something he had savored in Moscow and for nearly five years been denied: that immediate, unfiltered experience of debating Russia's "burning questions."

The Writers' Union had been in existence less than five years when Miliukov was invited to join, but in that time had emerged as an influential voice of protest against the regime.[34] By 1900 its 449 members included influential writers from all over the country, and it had largely shed its professional preoccupations. At this time its leadership was increasingly assumed by a group made up of the *Russkoe bogatstvo* circle, former "Economists" Ekaterina Kuskova and S. N. Prokopovich, and a group of revisionist Marxists—among them Petr Struve—known as the "Freedom Group." From summer 1900 the banquets and weekly dinners organized by the Writers' Union became "the central events in the political life of the St. Petersburg intelligentsia."[35]

Miliukov rapidly assumed a prominent place in the activities of the Writers' Union. He was a member of the executive committee, chaired meetings, and presented reports. His home became a gathering place for political discussions among members of the Union and invited outsiders.[36] Miliukov's growing influence in oppositional circles was ironically attested to by Maksim Gorkii in 1899, after his first visit to the capital. Gorkii told his Petersburg guide, radical journalist Vladimir Posse, "I have liked three things about your St. Petersburg. First, its smoked whitefish. Second, Merezhkovsky, for his being in earnest about believing in the immortality of the soul. Third, Miliukov's teeth, with which he will some time eat us all up."[37]

Miliukov appears to have been particularly interested in extending the organization of the intelligentsia beyond the confines of the capital. In February 1900, under the cover of a statisticians' congress held in St. Petersburg, Miliukov, Miakotin, and Peshekhonov were among a group of urban professionals elected at a private gathering as the St. Petersburg bureau of an organization intended to unite the intelligentsia. The gathering discussed establishing a foreign-based newspaper as an important means of furthering their organizational efforts, but neither the newspaper nor the organization went beyond the discussion stage.[38] When the Writer's Union held a three-day "caucus" of writers from the capitals and provinces, in November 1900, Miliukov presented a report urging that the Union do more to promote the affiliation of provincial journalists and writers with the Petersburg-based organization.[39]

The oppositional mood, including Miliukov's own, was expressed more sharply in private meetings held behind the scenes of the November writers' caucus. At one such meeting, also attended by Peshekhonov, G. A. Fal'bork, V. I. Charnoluskii, and A. A. Nikonov—all future members of the Union of Liberation—Miliukov advanced the thesis that it was time to begin to fight "on the borders of legality"; clearly, by late 1901 he had already come to the conclusion that a more activist and confrontational stance would be required to pressure the regime into granting serious political reforms. The group gathered at this meeting entrusted Miliukov and Peshekhonov with drafting a "constitution," the text of which has not survived.[40]

Having just returned from exile, Miliukov could scarcely have imagined that his activities would escape the authorities' notice. In January 1900 the St. Petersburg director of police summoned Miliukov to explain his role in a Writers' Union meeting in honor of émigré socialist Peter Lavrov, who had died that month; he was also told of the minister of internal affairs' dissatisfaction with "the general orientation of the Union." According to a police informer, when Miliukov related this conversation to the next meeting of the Writers' Union the whole gathering was convulsed with laughter.[41] On February 21, 1900, he was again asked to call upon the director of police; the substance of this meeting is unknown.[42] It was Miliukov's contact with radical students, however, rather than his ongoing work among the oppositional intelligentsia, that eventually led to his arrest.

The police reported that in 1900 Miliukov frequented meetings where "radical youth debated and defended revolutionary programs."[43] For Miliukov, personally, the most important of these meetings turned out to be a special, illicit meeting to honor the memory of Petr Lavrov held in December 1900 at the Mining Institute, one of the most volatile institutions of higher education in St. Petersburg. Perhaps because he had actually met Lavrov on one occasion, and written a brief obituary for him in *Mir Bozhii*, Miliukov was invited to give the opening speech.[44]

The authorities had good reason to find the speech objectionable, for it was, of course, more about the current situation in Russia than about the deceased. In a small room filled to bursting point, Miliukov invoked Lavrov in order to posit a general "law" of the revolutionary dynamic. He contrasted Lavrov's evolutionary approach to socialism with Bakunin's more impatient agitation, then discussed the way the "idyllic" Going-to-the-People movement of the 1870s, inspired by the ideas of both men, was transformed by police repression into a conspiratorial movement that set terror as its task. Miliukov concluded that terror is the result of any frustrated revolutionary movement. His listeners immediately asked what stage of the process they were presently in; Miliukov says he answered them with an historical exposition from which they drew a "practical conclusion." One of his auditors, then student Boris Savinkov, later helped plan the assassinations of Minister of Internal Affairs Viacheslav Plehve and the Grand Duke Sergei Aleksandrovich. Referring to this talk many years later he told Miliukov, half jokingly, "That night, I became your student."[45]

Once again, Miliukov found he had exceeded the bounds of the permissible. Some time between January 23 and February 7, 1901, police arrested him at his home and placed him in solitary confinement at Shpalernaia prison. In a note in French he left for Anna, he explained that he had been taken into custody and asked that she go see the authorities on his behalf and bring him money when she visited, since he had with him exactly one ruble.[46]

Miliukov did not immediately learn precisely what charges were being pressed, but he had been extraordinarily lucky in two respects. For one thing, it became clear during the course of his interrogations that the police informer present at the meeting at the Mining Institute was a semiliterate who had failed to understand most of what he had heard; his evidence was far less damning than it might have been. The second piece of luck involved his interrogator's appraisal of the draft constitution written by Miliukov and Peshekhonov, which had been among the personal papers seized by police at his arrest. Miliukov had assumed this would constitute the chief evidence against him, but his interrogator, a General Shmakov, took it to be a copy of some historical document. Miliukov was only too happy to confirm this surmise.[47]

Looking back on his interrogation, Miliukov rather wryly surveyed his disinclination to acknowledge openly his oppositional activities. The old revolutionaries, he said, had been eagles, proudly admitting their deeds. The new generation of oppositionists were "some sort of sparrows," anxious to escape the net if they could, and Miliukov realized that he preferred to be numbered among the sparrows. He had already mastered the prisoners' system of communicating with each other by knocks on the walls and had been employed in finding out from the occupants of neighboring cells what to expect during interrogation and how best to avoid incriminating oneself. Miliukov profited from their counsels and was sure he revealed nothing. He was finally told that he was free until such time as his sentence had been determined, with the stipulation that he could not reside in Petersburg. He had been in prison about three months.[48]

On his release, Miliukov's sensation of freedom was unexpectedly intense, but his prison stay had not really been onerous. The first night was the worst: exploring the confines of his solitary cell, not even knowing of what he had been accused, Miliukov felt "as though I had been cut off forever from the entire living world." The next day brought flowers and sweets from friends and well-wishers, and once Miliukov became part of the prisoners' "telegraph" his sense of solitude vanished. Anna was able to visit three times a week, even slipping him important news under the guard's nose by speaking in Bulgarian. The books he ordered from the public library were regularly delivered, enabling him to carry on with his work on volume 3 of the *Studies of Russian Culture*. He was also mapping out a new project; as Anna wrote to a friend, "[Pavel] is all excited by a collection of belle lettrists–populists which he took from the library there; he's already put together a plan for a work on the Populism question."⁴⁹

Miliukov emerged from prison in spring 1901 to find many of his friends and colleagues gone from Petersburg and the radical intelligentsia in complete disarray, as a result of the Kazan' Square incident.⁵⁰ The assassination February 14 of M. P. Bogolepov, the minister of education, by an expelled university student precipitated a wave of student strikes and protests all over the empire that culminated in a mass demonstration in St. Petersburg's Kazan' Square on March 4. Cossacks and mounted police brutally dispersed the demonstrators and arrested some 750 people.⁵¹ Among those arrested were many of Miliukov's colleagues from the Writers' Union, including Miakotin, Tugan-Baranovskii, Annenskii, Peshekhonov, and Peter Struve, all of whom had joined the demonstration and were thereafter banished from St. Petersburg.

The brutality on Kazan' Square, which outraged Russian society, marked the definitive politicization of many of the demonstration's participants and thus contributed to the organization of the liberation movement.⁵² One of its immediate consequences was the abolition of the Writers' Union, which deprived the St. Petersburg intelligentsia of its remaining legal organizational center. Informal groups gathered almost immediately elsewhere. Struve elected to go to Tver', one of the centers of zemstvo radicalism. Miakotin and Annenskii selected the Finnish town of Sestroretsk, very close to Petersburg, and it was to Finland that Miliukov headed upon his release from prison. By fall of 1901 the Miliukovs were settled in Udel'naia, a town where several other members of the *Russkoe bogatstvo* circle resided and whose train station was a mere eighteen minutes' ride from Petersburg.⁵³ Within months, the first of the oppositional circles to be known as "Friends of Liberation" would be organized in the area around Udel'naia, in connection with an oppositional, constitutionalist journal to be published outside Russia.

The Founding of *Osvobozhdenie*

Foundation of an oppositional journal abroad was a milestone in the history of Russian liberalism. Various circles had for some time considered the possibility of establishing such an organ.⁵⁴ It would not only be able to articulate oppositional views far more freely than could any legal publication within Russia, but would ideally serve as the foundation for a future political party or action group. By early summer 1901, in part thanks to the catalyst of the Kazan' Square debacle, Russian society was sufficiently aroused and politicized to encourage a group of zemstvo radicals and urban intellectuals to begin organizing such a publication in earnest. Although the journal *Os-*

vobozhdenie (Liberation) was not explicitly envisioned as "liberal," with its foundation liberalism as a political movement, as opposed to an orientation or "state of mind," came into being in Russia.[55]

The initiative for the founding of *Osvobozhdenie* came from the circle of zemstvo activists and urban professionals gathered around Ivan Petrunkevich in Moscow.[56] Petrunkevich divided his time between Moscow and his estate in Tver', and with Struve's arrival in Tver' in April 1901 they resumed the discussions they had been having in Moscow the previous autumn with V. I. Vernadskii, Dmitrii Shakhovskoi, and others of the Petrunkevich circle.[57] According to Petrunkevich, he met with Struve every day during the provincial zemstvo session in order to talk about the political situation and "the necessity of creating a free press abroad for the struggle against a government whose policy was becoming ever more arbitrary and was worsening the already unbearable situation."[58]

Having once decided to proceed with organization of the journal, Petrunkevich, Shakhovskoi, and their confederates discussed the crucial question of the editor: the two names that came up were those of Miliukov and Struve. Miliukov must have seemed nearly ideal for the postion. His name was well known and respected, his recent stay in prison having only augmented his reputation. He was already personally known to most of the Petrunkevich group through his participation in the Storozhenko circle in the early 1890s. He was a constitutionalist, without, however, being firmly identified with any group or party—the very indeterminacy of his political affiliations was no doubt an attraction. Finally, he was already an experienced editor. Petrunkevich's only reservations about Miliukov concerned removing "such a huge talent" from the home front, perhaps forever, by asking him to emigrate.[59] Still, he commissioned D. E. Zhukovskii to approach Miliukov about the editorship sometime in early summer 1901.

The proposal conveyed by Zhukovskii was apparently both unexpected and unwelcome. Miliukov was likely flattered by the implicit honor of the proposal, but rejected it immediately. In his memoirs, he claims that "having just returned to Russia, I did not want to be separated from it again with the risk of forever remaining an emigrant." He might also have added that he was by no means ready to make a definitive choice between scholarship and the cause of Russia's political emancipation. Ignorant of Petrunkevich's ongoing talks with Struve, Miliukov recommended that the editorship be offered to him, since, he claimed, he knew that Struve was already contemplating emigrating.[60]

Struve's reputation was, if anything, even more brilliant than Miliukov's. That he had made his reputation as a fiery young Marxist economist was apparently not a problem for the group proposing to found the paper, since his gradual process of disengagement from both Marxism and the Marxist

Gentry leaders, including founding members of the Union of Liberation Ivan Petrunkevich (front row, center) and, in the back row, Fedor Rodichev (2d from left), Pavel Dolgorukov (4th from right), and Dmitrii Shakhovskoi (far right). From I. P. Belokonskii, *Zemskoe dvizhenie* (Moscow, 1914).

camp was nearly complete by midsummer 1901.[61] It is not clear whether a firm agreement was reached by August 1901 or only later, after Struve had already left Russia, but in May 1902 Shakhovskoi, S. A. Kotliarevskii, and N. N. L'vov visited Struve in his new home in Stuttgart with 100,000 rubles for the start-up of the journal and a programmatic article, which was, in its main features, the work of Miliukov.[62]

Between summer 1901 and the appearance of the first issue of the journal in June 1902 much had to be done in the way of establishing a support and distribution network, but the extent of Miliukov's involvement in these activities is unclear. V. Ia. Bogucharskii visited oppositionists in the capitals, provinces, and Finland, apparently with the aim of organizing circles sympathetic to the projected journal.[63] The Finnish circle of "Friends of Liberation" was the first such group constituted. Its members included many of the leaders of the defunct Writers' Union—Kuskova, Annenskii, Miakotin, Prokopovich, and Bogucharskii—and their role in the liberation movement would be considerable.[64] One might assume that Miliukov participated in a local circle composed of many of his friends and colleagues, and devoted to the ideal of introduction of a constitutional order, but he is not named as an actual member of the Finnish group of the "Friends of Liberation" in any of the sources.[65]

Nonetheless, when organizational work had proceeded sufficiently to allow Petrunkevich to gather a small group at his Tver' estate, Mashuk, to work out a programmatic article for the forthcoming journal, he turned to Miliukov. There were just two others involved, in addition to Miliukov and Petrunkevich: Shakhovskoi and Aleksandr Kornilov, a historian who had been in government service as a specialist on the peasantry. Miliukov apparently composed a draft article and brought it with him. "In Mashuk my draft of the program was discussed, then—already in my absence—it was taken to Moscow and again discussed and approved in circles of zemtsy and individuals of the free urban professions and sent abroad for inclusion in the first (June) issue of *Osvobozhdenie*."[66] Miliukov's claim that subsequent discussions of the article did not produce any significant alterations is borne out by its highly characteristic style and approach. Less clear is the extent to which the views he outlined expressed his own orientation at this time, since his task, as he saw it, was to create a program corresponding to the orientation of the zemtsy, not of those further to the left.

The final version of the article, "From the Russian Constitutionalists," was printed in the first issue of *Osvobozhdenie* as a submission "wholeheartedly endorsed" by the editor, rather than as the official programmatic declaration of the journal. Aimed specifically at the zemstvo milieu, it followed a long article by Struve, "From the Editor," conceived for a broader audience and in many ways complementing Miliukov's piece.[67] Both articles proclaimed the necessity of replacing autocracy with a constitutional order. Both saw the introduction and guarantee of individual and political liberties as the first, necessary condition for any other reforms; social issues were referred to tangentially, if at all. Finally, both articles insisted that the reform of Russia could not be the task of any one group or class acting alone or in its own interests.

There were, however, significant differences as well, in emphasis, lines of argument, and even basic assumptions. Even allowing for the considerations of audience and purpose which shaped the two presentations, a comparison of these articles suggests that here were two different approaches to "liberalism," which would be important for the future development of liberalism as a political movement in Russia.

Struve made clear his overriding concern with freedom in the opening sections of his article. He introduced *Osvobozhdenie* as a journal "dedicated exclusively to the great cause of the struggle for the universal liberation of our homeland from police subjugation, for the freedom of the Russian individual and of Russian society." Freedom was not simply "one of many questions of domestic policy, one point of a program;" it was the most important of all goals. An end in itself, it was also the means to an end: the improvement of daily life and the development of culture were equally inconceivable without freedom.[68]

From this idealist perspective, Struve understood the cause of liberation as not only politically but ethically imperative, the responsibility of all Russians. "Our task is not to separate, but to unite. The cultural and political liberation of Russia can be neither exclusively nor principally the affair of one class, one party, one doctrine. It must become a national affair, a common task for the entire people."[69]

Struve was intentionally vague in describing the nature of this united front against autocracy and the means it would employ. It would be, he said, a liberal and democratic movement, "Liberal because it is directed at the winning of freedom, democratic because it defends the most vital needs, material and spiritual, of the popular masses." Struve was also noncommittal on the nature of the concrete goals which would realize the overarching goal of freedom. *Osvobozhdenie* did not intend to give a program, he said, but instead expected to receive one from its readers.[70]

Miliukov's article also assumed that the elimination of autocracy is the basic precondition for reform and progress in Russia. The article's purpose was to legitimize the struggle for political freedom and to identify the "most immediate tasks" in achieving this goal. Its intended audience was moderate, educated Russian society, those groups "who can find expression for their outraged feelings neither in class nor revolutionary struggle." The article was therefore conceived as the first attempt at a political platform that would unite moderate public opinion and serve as the center around which a constitutional party could eventually coalesce.[71]

Miliukov founded his call for action on the incompatibility of a modernizing, increasingly complex society with the existing social and political order. "Russian social life no longer fits into the old molds. We need new forms in order to adapt to new ways of life." Student unrest, peasant disorders, political terrorism—these expressions of discontent were symptomatic of the anachronism of the existing order and could only be quelled through systemic change.[72]

He then proposed three criteria for a "zemstvo political program." It must be principled, practical, and reflective of the opinion of more than just the zemstvo milieu. Only in this way could it hope to distinguish itself from competing programs of other groups, preserve the unity of its heterogeneous parts, and attract the support of the intelligentsia, who could marshal the "broad social forces" crucial to the eventual adoption of the program. Miliukov therefore purposely avoided potentially divisive issues. To decide such matters as the agenda of the envisioned legislative body before the objective of representative government had been won would be "to divide the skin of the bear before the bear has been slain."[73]

The two fundamental principles of Miliukov's minimum program were individual and political rights and an elected legislature. The list of rights, characterized as "the basic principles of any developed political life," included personal inviolability, guaranteed by independent courts; equality of all before the law, without discrimination on the basis of nationality, class, and religion; freedom of the press; the right of assembly and association; and the right of petition. In the absence of these rights, Miliukov insisted, a representative institution could neither express the opinion and will of the country nor function politically. The institution itself he characterized as a "non-class, popular representation, in a permanent, supreme institution, to be convened annually, with rights of supreme control, legislation, and budget approval."[74]

Miliukov then outlined, with scrupulous care, the gradual inception of a constitutional order. The initial reform would have to come from the tsar, in the form of a "unilateral act." The second step, drafting of a charter (that is, a constitution) and electoral law, could not be entrusted to the discredited bureaucracy. Nor was it wise to "leap into the unknown" by depending on the choices of a mass electorate subject to governmental pressure and unused to thinking and acting politically. He therefore suggested that the most feasible course would be to entrust these tasks to representatives elected by the zemstvos and city dumas; they would then yield their places to the representatives of the people elected on the basis of the new law, who would begin the broader work of reform.[75]

Miliukov concluded with a rejection of any notion of a political "separate path," such as a *zemskii sobor*, for the resolution of Russia's problems. He countered this "sentimental and harmful illusion" with a confident legitimation of constitutionalism on sociological grounds.

> Representative institutions in our country, as everywhere else, inevitably will assume a special coloration, corresponding to the peculiarities of Russian cultural and political life. But the free forms of political life as such are no more national than use of the alphabet or the printing press, steam or electricity. They are simply forms of higher culture. They are broad and flexible enough to absorb very varied national content. They become inevitable when social life has become so complex that it can no longer be accommodated within the framework of a more primitive order. When such a time approaches, when the new year of history knocks at the door, it is no use putting obstacles in its way. It will come just the same.[76]

By linking the constitutionalist program with the dynamism of the modernization process, Miliukov presented its application in Russia as not simply relevant, but virtually inevitable.

The explanation for most of the differences in these articles by Miliukov and Struve must be sought in the authors' different perspectives and assumptions. The two most significant were their approaches to liberty and to the specifically national quality of political liberation. Struve's view of liberty, founded on an idealist conception of the absolute value of freedom of the individual was, ultimately, philosophical. Moreover, it was a *moral* value; Struve's article was saturated with the conviction that national liberation is an ethical imperative.

Miliukov, too, saw liberty as a good in its own right, but this was not his article's center of gravity; he was arguing for empirical freedom and did so from a more instrumental perspective. He justified the call for personal freedom and equality before the law as the "elementary and necessary preliminary conditions" for the free social life of a civilized state. While Miliukov repeatedly referred to liberty as a principle that cannot be compromised, his article lacked the strong moral overtones of Struve's. The reader had to infer his absolute commitment to freedom of the individual, for Miliukov defended personal liberty as the condition for political liberty, which was in turn the condition for, and guarantee of, the constitutional order required by a complex, modern society. It was perhaps significant that the word "liberal" appeared in Struve's article, but not in Miliukov's.

The second fundamental difference concerned the national quality of the movement for political liberation. For Struve, the premise that Russia had outgrown an autocratic system of government had tremendous cultural significance. Autocracy stifled cultural development as well as individual self-realization and social reform. It was not only politically obsolete but "anti-cultural, anti-social, and immoral." Elsewhere he would define culture, with Semen Frank, as "the totality of absolute values, created and being created by mankind, and constituting its spiritual-social life."[77] His vision, therefore, was of a national liberation in the fullest sense of that phrase: the liberation of a great people, the unfettering of a great national culture, to be accomplished by and for that people.

The national idea was almost entirely absent from Miliukov's piece. As he began, so he concluded with the sociological postulate that as any society grows more complex it requires political freedom. There were no references, in Miliukov, to a "great people." He spoke not of national liberation but of "serious political reform," not of Russian culture but of "any civilized society." In this way, Miliukov's perspective on liberation was in a sense more structural than Struve's; his concern here was with the state, understood as a diverse and complex social organization, rather than the nation, understood as the embodiment of a culture.

In the short run, these differences would figure primarily in disputes over the tactical orientation of the liberation movement, most particularly in the question of the opposition's attitude toward the Russo-Japanese War. In the long run, they would be more telling. After 1905, when Russian liberalism had more clearly differentiated into three currents or strands, these perspectives on state versus nation and political versus moral-cultural imperatives assumed greater significance.[78]

Miliukov's introduction of practicality as a programmatic criterion no less important than principle is particularly instructive. In his first overtly political public declaration he advanced what would prove to be one of the fundamental tenets of his political behavior: the understanding that politics is the art of the possible. Increasingly, Miliukov came to identify this pragmatic orientation as a specifically liberal characteristic, arguing that it was practicality, even more than goals, that distinguished Russian liberalism from Russian socialism, for the latter displayed the same abstract, utopian bent characteristic of the conservative supporters of autocracy.[79] In the course of the next fifteen years he would repeat tirelessly that Russians needed to learn to distinguish between long-term goals and immediate tasks, between "a party program and a party platform."[80] They also needed to learn to compromise, to determine which of their desiderata could be conceded without jeopardizing their essential program.

These commonplaces of political wisdom were anything but commonplace in the ideologically laden atmosphere of late Imperial Russia. They would involve Miliukov in endless disputes, both with those who were more doctrinally zealous, and those who differed in their estimation of what constituted the possible and practical. While Miliukov's advocacy of political pragmatism by no means ensured that his tactical lines were indeed tenable, especially in late 1905–6 and 1912–14, his role in the Constitutional-Democratic Party would most frequently be to identify and win support for practical positions.

The points of view expressed in *Osvobozhdenie*, while sharing certain important beliefs and goals, were too varied to please everyone. Nonetheless, the paper's influence on the organization and direction of the Russian liberation movement was indisputable. Smuggled into the country and passed from hand to hand, its steadily growing audience included such disparate types as highly placed bureaucrats, revolutionaries in exile, and zemtsy and urban professionals throughout the empire.[81] In the estimation of the police "this illegal journal does not frighten society with bloody calls for social revolution and has found a huge circle of readers in all classes."[82]

Miliukov's articles thus reached a large audience; in all, he published some twelve pieces in *Osvobozhdenie* in the course of its three-year existence.[83] Many of them were of cardinal importance in shaping the liberation movement and all were featured prominently by Struve, even when their conclusions differed markedly from his own. In large part because of his sensitivity to the shifts in the general mood of the public, Miliukov gradually assumed the role of chief spokesman in the journal for the slightly left-of-center majority within the Union of Liberation. After Struve, Miliukov's was the most authoritative and influential voice in *Osvobozhdenie*.

In Miliukov's own evaluation of his contribution to *Osvobozhdenie*, written many years later, he contended that his efforts were directed toward two ends: ensuring that the constitutionalist program was not abandoned upon receipt of partial concessions from the government, and preventing a leftward shift in the program. Concerning the latter point, Miliukov depicted himself as a moderating influence in *Osvobozhdenie*, in contrast to Struve's more leftist orientation.[84] While the first of these claims was correct, the second was less than accurate. Miliukov was the first contributor to *Osvobozhdenie* to demand exclusion of the zemstvo conservatives from any future liberal party, the first to outline a "defeatist" stance on the Russo-Japanese War, the first to reject the concessions promised by V. K. Plehve's successor in autumn 1904. Miliukov assumed a moderating stance only in July 1905, when the political revolutionary movement had unmistakably assumed the rhetoric and delineations of class struggle.

Although Miliukov's later accounts of his activities in these years unduly minimized the radicalism of his views, it is true that his involvement in the liberation movement was not nearly as wholehearted as that of men like Petrunkevich, Struve, Bogucharskii, and Shakhovskoi. It may be that time spent in prison had shaken him more than he later cared to admit. It may be simply that scholarship still exercised the stronger pull. So far as the sources make it possible to establish Miliukov's activities in the seventeen-month interval dividing his first and second prison terms—the period which saw the organization and launching of *Osvobozhdenie*—his involvement in the liberation movement was limited, and strictly literary in nature. His overall publishing record for this period supports the conjecture that scholarship claimed his chief loyalties, since the great bulk of his work was devoted to historical themes.[85]

Miliukov continued work on *Studies of Russian Culture*; he also had a new project, which claimed a good portion of his time and was to take him far from Russia and the unfolding liberation movement. In May 1900 he had been invited by the St. Petersburg publisher F. D. Batiushkov to meet with several Americans visiting Russia for the purpose of arranging lecture courses on Slavic history and culture at the University of Chicago. The Americans were William Harper, president of the University of Chicago, and the philanthropist Charles Crane, founder of Westinghouse, who was funding the venture. They had already arranged for Thomas Masaryk to give a course on Czech history and Maksim Kovalevskii to teach one on Russian state law.[86] As a result of this meeting, it was agreed that Miliukov would offer a course in Chicago in summer 1903 on the history of Russia. Miliukov began thinking about not only the content of his lectures—he envisioned an entirely new course that would not duplicate the *Studies of Russian Culture*—but about improving his command of English as well. Rather than having his lectures translated, he determined to compose them in English himself.[87]

Mastery of foreign languages was a lifelong source of pride to Miliukov—Riha has estimated that he had a command of fourteen modern languages, in addition to Latin and classical Greek—and his efforts to become fluent in English were certainly considerable.[88] He employed a young Englishwoman in Petersburg, a Miss E. M. Hughes, to give him conversation lessons and help prepare the text of the lectures, then amplified on this with a planned bicycle tour of England in summer 1902 with Miss Hughes and a companion. Before his departure for England, Miliukov learned that he had been sentenced to six months in solitary confinement for his speech on Lavrov at the Mining Institute; he feared this would prevent his trip. The authorities, however, obligingly took his word that he would present himself for incarceration on an appointed date in the fall, and granted him an exit visa.[89]

That Miliukov, facing six months' separation from his wife and children, nonetheless went ahead with his tour suggests a certain degree of estrangement from his family. There is also an incongruous cast to the whole episode, when viewed from the perspective of events unfolding in Russia. Miliukov gave Petrunkevich and his colleagues his draft article for the oppositional journal, then set off for England even before its final form had been determined. When the first issue of *Osvobozhdenie* appeared in June 1902, with Miliukov's article, its author was enjoying the beauties of the English countryside in the company of two young ladies.[90]

True to his word, Miliukov returned home in time to serve his sentence at the Kresty prison, beginning October 1, 1902.[91] This time, familiar with prison routine and heartened as before by constant gifts of sweets and flowers from friends and well-wishers, Miliukov settled down comfortably to continue work on volume 3 of the *Studies of Russian Culture*. As he genially recollected his second prison stay, "this was, in its own way, a temporary change of apartments." The hardships were rather Anna's lot, since in addition to caring for the family she had also to care for her husband's affairs. With a briefcase loaded full of books, she set off in the mornings, her days spent petitioning at government offices, waiting in prison for meetings with her husband, or working in the public library to collect materials and check citations. As one friend put it, "while the husband wrote the *Studies of Russian Culture* in prison, the wife, in life, trod the mournful path of this culture."[92]

As it turned out, Miliukov served only half of his six-month sentence; the circumstances of his premature release form a curious episode illustrative of his occasional lapses into recklessness. One day Miliukov was abruptly transported from his cell to the opulent mansion of the minister of internal affairs and ushered into the presence of the hated Plehve. He was astonished to find himself being treated more like an esteemed guest than a prisoner. Plehve offered him a comfortable chair, ordered tea and complimented him on the *Studies*. What followed was still more surprising. According to Miliukov, Plehve explained that Miliukov's former professor, Kliuchevskii, had spoken to the tsar on his behalf, telling him that Miliukov was "necessary to scholarship" and ought not to be held in prison. The tsar asked that Plehve get acquainted with Miliukov; if his impression was favorable, he would be released. Plehve, in turn, had occasion to be nonplussed by his guest, for when he startled Miliukov with the question, "What would you say if I offered you the position of minister of education?" Miliukov replied that he would probably turn it down, "since one could really do nothing in this post. But if Your Excellency were to suggest that I take your place, then I would give it some thought." The interview terminated here, but a week later Miliukov was again taken to the minister's mansion. Plehve, now brusque and distant, said he had given the sovereign a favorable report. Miliukov was free, but he was warned to watch his step: "You will never be reconciled with us. At least, do not engage in an open fight with us—otherwise, we will sweep you away!"[93]

Miliukov was greatly moved by his teacher's intercession and wrote immediately to express his feelings. Kliuchevskii in fact had been motivated mainly by concern for Anna's difficult circumstances rather than for Miliukov himself, and the letter he wrote Plehve on Miliukov's behalf was scarcely flattering: "He is not among the worst of his kind. This is a naive, ponderous, academic liberal, even stupid in his actions. . . . In their mistakes, men such as Miliukov all the same preserve something cultured and right-thinking, and on this I have incontrovertible evidence."[94] Still, his reply to Miliukov's letter of thanks showed that he, too, had been troubled by the rupture between them.

> I was very glad for you and for Anna Sergeevna, on reading how well you are settled at Udel'naia, and have begun better to respect the Russian reading public, since your books are bringing you a steady, if modest, income. I thank you very much for touching on our relations in your letter. This gives me the

right and the grounds to tell you openly that they have long lain heavy on my heart.⁹⁵

These letters paved the way for a resumption of personal contact in summer 1905, when Kliuchevskii turned to Miliukov for help in preparing for a conference with the tsar on determining representation to the "Bulygin" Duma. In future, when visiting Moscow, Miliukov would make a point of calling on the Kliuchevskiis, where their pleasant conversations revolved primarily around politics.⁹⁶

Miliukov's second incarceration thus had serendipitous results, by beginning the process of healing an old wound. Both his stays in jail, in fact, brought him certain positive benefits, since they enhanced rather than tarnished his reputation in progressive public opinion. As he wryly remarked to an American audience in 1904, given present conditions in Russia "to be branded as a political criminal by the police is a mark of distinction, gradually becoming a quite necessary qualification for everybody who claims to advocate liberal public opinion." The number of individuals "yearly receiving this preliminary qualification," he added, "is growing at a very rapid rate."⁹⁷

C·H·A·P·T·E·R F·I·V·E

Russian Liberalism

Miliukov was released from prison in January 1903. Some six months had elapsed since publication of the first issue of *Osvobozhdenie*, and during that time the opposition's confidence in the resolution of more conservative zemstvo reformers had substantially eroded. In July 1902, after discussions with Plehve and Sergei Witte suggesting their desire to come to a reasonable compromise with the zemstvo opposition, Moscow provincial zemstvo board chairmen Dmitrii Shipov convened a small conference and persuaded it to rescind one of the more political resolutions passed by a zemstvo congress that May. Oppositional fears and indignation at this seeming "sell-out" were reflected in some of the contributions to *Osvobozhdenie*. Dmitrii Shakhovskoi, in a private letter to Struve, gave it as his opinion that Struve's confidence in the zemstvo milieu was misplaced. He urged organization of a liberal-democratic party as soon as possible, suggesting that *Osvobozhdenie* try to attract revolutionaries to this party.[1]

Struve agreed with these opinions only in part. In December he wrote that the time had come for "the organization of the liberal forces of Russian society into a cohesive entity which will be able to act systematically." He made it clear that he still numbered supporters of the Slavophile ideal of autocracy among the liberal forces: so as not to drive moderates from the liberationist camp, he proposed that the liberal organization make its demand the "convocation of a *zemskii sobor*."[2]

Miliukov entered the debate in decisive fashion February 16, 1903, with his third contribution to *Osvobozhdenie*, a letter to the editor published under the title "On Forthcoming Questions." This letter, along with Struve's rejoinder in the same issue, inaugurated a new stage in the liberation movement.[3] Miliukov endorsed Struve's suggested liberal organization in principle, but pointed out that it presupposed agreement about the goals and composition of the organization: "Before one can organize, it is essential to know who is going with whom, and where."[4] The requisite consensus did not, however, exist. Abandoning his earlier advocacy of unity within the zemstvo milieu, Miliukov now argued that *Osvobozhdenie* was casting its net too widely.

The goal of the future liberal party had to be constitutional reform. Referring to moderate zemtsy such as Shipov and M. A. Stakhovich, Miliukov insisted that "idealists of autocracy" and "unreconstructed Slavophiles" did not make constitutional reform their goal and hence had no place in a liberal party. Nor was there any place for passive adherents of constitutionalism. Political freedom had to be fought for, Miliukov warned, and "only confidence in one another can generate that cohesion which is necessary for concerted action."[5]

Rather than face up to these differences, *Osvobozhdenie* was trying to preserve what was now an "unnatural union" by advancing as its slogan the ambiguous term *zemskii sobor*. Such a proposal was merely a means of postponing resolution of the programmatic and tactical line that a political party had to have. Miliukov revealed his waning confidence in the possibility of persuading the tsar to grant reforms when he asked what the liberals meant to do if the government did not cave in "at the first serious pressure of social forces." A party that did not anticipate such questions and hammer out answers to them would have no part in the determination of Russia's future political order.

In Miliukov's eyes, the supporters of *Osvobozhdenie* should therefore not be precipitate in creating a liberal organization. "It would be more than enough at this stage if it were possible to organize stalwart cadres of a party to consist of convinced constitutionalists." It was not doctrinairism that moved Miliukov to advise that *Osvobozhdenie* frankly employ the word "constitution": the choice of slogan would itself help solve the question of composition. "To recruit an entire army around an unclear slogan and with inclusion of unreliable, and in part even suspect elements, would be, in our opinion, a huge tactical mistake, weakening the energy of the movement, and destroying its moral significance."[6] The suspect elements were those frightened by the word "constitution," and those not willing to act for it openly.

Struve now abandoned his former position; his rejoinder largely seconded and extended Miliukov's views. Repeating that it was indeed time to think about creating a liberal party, he stipulated that it be openly and decisively constitutional. This demand necessitated exclusion of the "semiconstitutionalists." There was, moreover, a second, equally important characteristic of the proposed party: it had to be "openly and decisively democratic." Democratic demands were the necessary consequence of the liberal principle, Struve maintained. They were also a crucial tactical consideration, for without a democratic program—and a program was, he pointed out, a means as well as an end—the party of political liberation would lack the broad basis it needed. The party therefore had to make a clear declaration in favor of universal suffrage and present a broad program of social reforms. Finally, Struve said bluntly what Miliukov had put more obliquely: given the conditions under which a political party of liberation would have to operate, its tactics would include illegal as well as legal means.[7]

The effect of these two articles was to redefine Russian liberalism and shift it to the left. Since at least the time of the Great Reforms, to be "liberal" meant rejecting violent means of struggle while supporting some measure of political reform and the recognition of individual liberties. To be a liberal now meant adhering to the principle of constitutionalism, including some form of representative government. Miliukov and Struve agreed on this point, and on the consequent exclusion from the future liberal organization of reform-minded Russians ready to be satisfied by a less arbitrary, more enlightened autocracy and greater scope for local self-government. It was only from this time, when liberalism's identity with constitutionalism was made explicit, that Miliukov first called himself a "liberal."[8]

Russian liberalism's assumption of the second of the principles advanced by Struve, that of democracy, was less clear-cut at this time, but equally significant. Not every liberal, for example, was ready to follow Struve in declaring for universal suffrage, but opponents of an unlimited franchise—of which Miliukov was still one—were henceforth to be a distinct minority in the leadership of organized liberalism. The democratization of liberalism, entailing a commitment to far-reaching social reform as well as political egalitarianism, was in part due to the changing social composition of the liberal movement. As a concomitant to liberals' distancing themselves from more conservative reformers, Miliukov and Struve advocated a turn toward the "non-class intelligentsia"; urban professionals and the salaried employees of the zemstvos already displayed the constitutionalist convictions and activism Miliukov saw as essential for a liberal organization.

In this way, the leftward theoretical shift was prior to, and a precondition for, attraction of more "democratic" elements to the liberal standard. The inclusion of these elements in the liberation movement would make that shift more pronounced in both theory and tactics, but it was not the expansion in social composition, from zemtsy to intelligentsia, that pushed Russian liberalism to the left.[9]

That Miliukov was of this intelligentsia, yet somehow marginally apart, was the impression Iosif Gessen gained when he met Miliukov at approximately this time. A jurist making a name for himself in Petersburg circles as editor of the progressive law weekly *Pravo*, Gessen noticed Miliukov at a party at Miakotin's in early 1903. He wore a pale gray suit, in contrast to the darker, more wintry hues of the other guests' attire, and rimless pince-nez. He had thinning, light brown hair, handsome features, and very white, rather elegant hands. Sitting off to one side and drinking but sparingly—another singularity, in the *Russkoe bogatstvo* set—he listened and watched attentively. Gessen introduced himself and they spent the evening in conversation. He was impressed not only by the clarity of thought of his companion, but also by the pleasant, unpretentious manners of this celebrated author. Equally striking, in Gessen's eyes, was the total absence of ethnic prejudice in Miliukov: "In the course of an extended conversation I never once experienced the unpleasant chill that prejudice always evokes." A converted Jew, Gessen felt this could not be said for much of the Russian intelligentsia. He worked to develop the acquaintance, which eventually turned into a long and fruitful journalistic collaboration.[10]

The authorities, meanwhile, were doing little to diffuse the general discontent. In late February an imperial manifesto at least acknowledged the need for reforms, but vague references to respect for religious freedom and employing the public's expertise in amelioration of the agrarian crisis satisfied virtually no one.[11] Miliukov's reaction was angry; this was a "third-hand, pseudo-liberal stunt." It neither proposed substantial reform measures nor institutionalized the rights it seemed to concede. But part of the blame, he felt, lay with the educated public: it was only the unthinking inertia of a substantial portion of society which allowed the government to imagine it could get away with palliatives. Miliukov urged that Russians actively unite and raise their voices, for Plehve was leading the country to a point where "neither you, nor Plehve, nor any tsarist paper manifesto will be of any further use. Truly, gentlemen, you must make haste: that juncture is not far off."[12]

In a sense, with this article Miliukov himself ceased to act. Having twice insisted, within the span of a month, that the time for organization and action was fast approaching, he packed his bags and departed for the United States. Barring one brief visit to Petersburg in October 1904, he was to remain outside Russia for the next two years. Furthermore, he contributed nothing to *Osvobozhdenie* for the next nine months. As he traveled in the United States, England, and the Balkans, delivering lectures and pursuing his historical investigations, formation of "stalwart constitutionalist cadres" and creation of a liberal organization proceeded without his participation or his input.

Miliukov's and Struve's articles on the composition and program of a liberal organization touched off prolonged debate on these issues in the pages of *Osvobozhdenie*. They appeared at a time when the oppositional mood was steadily deepening, fueled by the generally repressive nature of Plehve's rule and economic tensions owing to the worldwide recession. The mood became still sharper in the wake of the shocking Kishinev pogrom of April 6–7. Several hundred people perished in Kishinev thanks to the refusal of local authorities to halt an aroused mob's Easter rampage through the Jewish quarter of that city. All of these circumstances prepared the ground for formal organization of the opposition.[13] On July 20–22 of that year, while Miliukov was giving lectures on Russian history in Chicago, Struve and some twenty *Osvobozhdenie* contributors and sponsors gathered clandestinely in Schaffhausen, Switzerland, to discuss the nature and organization of the liberation movement.[14]

The conference participants voted to create a union, a coalition of independent groups with similar programs, rather than a party. The proposed semiconspiratorial organization was to be called the "Union of Liberation," with branches all over Russia; it would create the cadres of "convinced constitutionalists" acting to consolidate the opposition, whose formation Miliukov had urged in February. So far as program was concerned, the participants shared Struve's conviction that it must be "democratic in spirit" and include broad social reforms. They therefore adopted the principle of "four-tailed" suffrage—universal, secret, equal, and direct—and approved compulsory alienation of land to the peasantry, if necessary, and satisfaction of such labor demands as the eight-hour workday.[15]

The Schaffhausen conference was the most important step toward the organization of the Union of Liberation, which at last held its founding congress in St. Petersburg on January 3–5, 1904.[16] Some fifty delegates representing liberation groups in twenty-three cities and towns ratified the organizational decisions of the Schaffhausen Conference; after heated debate they approved a program, which was finally made public, in revised form, in December of that year. Declaring the Union of Liberation's primary aim to be the political liberation of Russia, the program stated that "the Union will seek before all else the abolition of autocracy and the establishment in Russia of a constitutional regime" to be founded on the basis of the four-tailed suffrage. Given the more divisive nature of social reforms, the program proclaimed a commitment to "the defense of the interests of the toiling masses" without, however, going into specifics.[17]

The congress also elected a council of ten members to direct the Union's activities, giving it the right to select new members and enter into agreements with other parties and groups. The council was the nerve center of the loosely knit Union of Liberation; Miliukov did not join it until March 1905, on the eve of his final return to Russia.[18]

American Lectures

Armed with Mothersill's Seasick Pills, Miliukov safely crossed the Atlantic to arrive in New York in April 1903, two months prior to the Schaffhausen conference. It was the first of five journeys to the United States he would make in the course of his life.[19] Curiously, his memoirs are completely silent on the subject of U.S. government and politics, in strong contrast to his recollections of his stay in England. He did, however, discern in Americans a strength he believed to be a living legacy from the colonists of the seventeenth century; American culture, for all its restlessness and change, was solidly engrafted in "the root of former generations."[20] It was precisely this connectedness with one's past that he elsewhere diagnosed as one of two components missing from Russian culture, in the broad sense of the word, the other being what he termed "social cement."[21] In 1903, Miliukov attributed greater importance to connectedness with the past; following the revolution of 1905, the tragic import of Russia's lack of social cohesion would loom much larger in his thought.

After a pleasant stay in New York with the Crane family, he made his way to Chicago for the University of Chicago's summer session.[22] As in Riazan' and Sofia, he exerted himself to become a part of his new community and made friends quickly; a later letter to Miliukov from a member of the university's history department refers to him as "the Russian colleague of whom we were so fond."[23] Miliukov's closest colleague at the university was William Muss-Arnolt, a young Assyriologist, who earned his heartfelt gratitude by helping him revise the over-long and still wooden text of his lectures.

Miliukov was initially in near despair over his course. Unsure of his English, he was afraid to depart from his written text and felt the lectures themselves were "overloaded in content and gloomy in tone." By the end of his course he was able to speak far more extemporaneously, thanks to Muss-Arnolt's help and the many speaking engagements he accepted in the city. As he admitted, he willingly lectured at clubs and luncheons with an eye not only to disseminating information about the state of affairs in Russia, but to practicing his English as well.[24] Having been one of the most popular instructors at Moscow University, Miliukov was clearly determined to be more than merely passable in Chicago. At the same time, his diligence in learning English and preparing his course, and his willingness, a year later, to return to the United States to lecture at a time when his political colleagues urged him to stay in Russia, suggests that he may have contemplated an academic career in the United States.

The course Miliukov gave in Chicago made up part of the text of his book *Russia and Its Crisis*, published in Chicago two years later. The Chicago lectures had been conceived as an interpretative introduction to Russian history; the parts on "crisis" came from his second U.S. lecture series, in autumn 1904. Although the chapters on the history of Russian liberalism and socialism cannot be read as Miliukov's political profession of faith as of 1903, since he expanded and revised them later, the text can be used to help ascertain his views for the period prior to the formal establishment of the Union of Liberation.[25]

The chapters on Russia's "nationalistic idea," religious tradition, and political tradition present the arguments of the *Studies of Russian Culture* more succinctly and forthrightly. Tracing the process of modernization—"civilization" is the word he used—Miliukov concentrated on the internal dynamic of Russian social and political culture, with an emphasis on the development of public opinion. His exposition stressed the constant flux in Russia's history, dismissing conceptions of Russia as "traditional" or relatively unchanging. Moreover, Russia's centuries-old recourse to the ideas and products of its western neighbors was only secondarily a response to foreign influence, its fundamental cause being the pressures of its internal growth and maturation.

The result of ceaseless change and frequent cultural and political borrowing, Miliukov concluded, was the absence in Russia of ongoing, genuinely "national" traditions. His rejection of the existence of a viable national tradition had the effect of legitimizing present-day opposition to autocracy, not only "morally" but practically, as well as that opposition's invocation of European experience.[26] Moreover, quoting Cardinal Newman, Miliukov made it clear that Russia's protean nature was not, in itself, any cause for shame: "To live is to change, and to be perfect is to have changed often."[27]

In his treatment of the Russian opposition, Miliukov undertook to explain why liberalism and socialism developed in a rather singular way in Russia, and to show the significance of that singularity. Both liberal and socialist doctrines made their way to Russia when it was in a different stage of social and political development than had been the case when these doctrines were elaborated in Western Europe. Above all, both developed in a country lacking a strong sense of the individual and a tradition of political rights. The result was that despite their initially nearly antithetical perspectives, "Russian liberalism and Russian socialism were not at all mutually exclusive."[28]

From its inception, Russian liberalism was different from European liberalism. Russia had no urban middle classes comparable to those of Western Europe; liberalism was introduced by members of the very class against whose interests it was in part directed, the serf-owning gentry, which had been inspired by European political ideas. As a result, "Russian liberalism was not *bourgeois* but *intellectual*." While it closely resembled Western European liberalism in its focus on individual and civic rights, it was nonetheless less self-interested and more abstract.[29]

Socialism, too, emerged in Russia as a classless, intellectual doctrine, as a vision of social justice on the part of "repentant noblemen."[30] Heavily influenced by the teaching of Proudhon, this socialism was anarchistic and hostile to the state. Where it differed greatly from early European socialism, however, was in its equal hostility to working for the achievement of political rights. This very critical difference Miliukov explained by the fact that in more advanced countries

> political liberty was settled when the social questions arose. Social radicalism simply accepted the results of a struggle won by political radicalism, its predecessor. . . . In Russia alone it so happened that social teachings prepossessed the more active spirits at a time when the work of political liberalism had yet to be done; and the Russian socialists, not satisfied to consider this liberal work superfluous, went even so far as to deem it dangerous for the people.[31]

Abstract utopianism and hostility to political reform were the legacy of socialism's premature inception in Russia.

The incomplete nature of the Great Reforms of the 1860s and 1870s created the conditions for the rapprochement of Russian liberalism and socialism. Having failed to win political rights, Russian liberalism decisively diverged from European, "classical" liberalism, becoming less individualistic, more concerned with broad social reform, and more "democratic" in its social composition. By the mid-1890s, Miliukov added, government repression of any public initiative or discussion had made liberalism radical. During these decades, as socialists came face to face with the realities of the peasant worldview and the long arm of the tsarist police, the influence of Proudhon began to yield to that of Marx. Marxism helped bring the various socialist camps to the realization that winning political freedom was the necessary precondition to effecting social revolution. In practical terms, this meant working with the liberals.[32]

In following the evolution of Russian socialism and liberalism, Miliukov did not suggest that their differences eventually concerned the means of struggle alone. He emphasized that populists and social democrats remained mutually antagonistic, and that the revolutionary parties had long-term goals opposed to those of the liberals. At the same time, he clearly believed that the willingness of liberals and socialists to work together for an immediate political goal reflected more than tactical expediency. The Russian liberalism described by Miliukov, while preserving its gradualist and practical approach, had internalized much of the socialist perspective.

In 1894, lecturing at Moscow University on the history of Russian public opinion, Miliukov had treated liberalism in rather cursory fashion, asserting that Russian liberal theory had remained unchanged since the 1840s.[33] Comparing this statement with the exposition of liberalism's development he offered in Chicago in 1903 demonstrates how significantly Miliukov's own views had altered in the course of a decade.

His American students quite probably did not appreciate that they had been offered the first historical treatment of the relationship between liberalism and socialism in Russia. The lectures were simply judged a success, and Miliukov was invited to offer another course at Chicago, this time on the Balkan Slavs. It was agreed that after completing travels in the western part of the Balkans, to familiarize himself with this area, he would offer his new course in winter 1904–5. President Harper also arranged that Miliukov be invited to deliver eight lectures on Russia for the prestigious Lowell Institute in Boston in late fall of 1904, before coming on to Chicago.[34]

In July 1903 Miliukov headed for Massachusetts in order to do research at Harvard. It so happened that the materials he found were far richer than he could have anticipated; Harvard Library contained a large collection of revolutionary Russian newspapers and pamphlets, dating from the 1880s and 1890s and published abroad, the gift of a Russian émigré. Articles by S. M. Stepniak-Kravchinskii, Plekhanov's early Marxist writings, the short-lived journal *Sotsialist*—all these readings deepened Miliukov's belief in the gradual convergence of socialism and liberalism, at least in their immediate aims.[35]

Even as he explored this rich cache of materials, part of Miliukov's attention was straying toward the Balkans. Tensions in Macedonia had been building all year, erupting in August in armed insurrections against the Turkish authorities. If Miliukov had had any thought of returning to Russia to stay in the interim between his American lecture trips, he now abandoned it. Instead, he hurried to Macedonia in September, and from there directed his steps to London in late fall 1903.[36]

England and the "New Liberalism"

Miliukov had come to London to work in the British Museum, both on revisions to his lectures on the history of Russian liberalism and socialism and on the final volume of *Studies of Russian Culture*. He planned to spend the winter and spring there in research, joining his family in Europe for the summer. Anna spent this time in Udel'naia, looking after the children and working on projects of her own, including her memoirs. She sent him a draft of these and was delighted by his favorable opinion, since, as she wrote a friend, "he is in general so severe."[37]

His London impressions included those gained from his contact with the Russian émigré community. He consciously limited that contact, since he feared being drawn into oppositional activity, but was curious to meet such celebrated figures of the revolutionary movement as Nikolai Chaikovskii, Peter Kropotkin, and Ekaterina Breshko-Breshkovskaia.[38] It was also in London that Miliukov had his first and only personal encounter with Vladimir Lenin, in the latter's small, shabby apartment. He found Lenin a dogged debater, more interested in forcing his interlocutor to concede points than in any exchange of views. They parted politically unreconciled, but amiably enough; Lenin seemed to him nothing more than a strictly "armchair theoretician."[39]

In Miliukov's own eyes, the most important consequence of his six-month stay in London was the opportunity to observe English political life. Watching sessions of the House of Commons, avidly reading the liberal *Westminster Gazette*, and discussing politics with his new acquaintances among prominent liberal and radical journalists and scholars influenced him profoundly. He became fully conscious of the effect of his English observations only later, he felt, but "these observations helped me to a very considerable extent in working out my own political worldview."[40] In light of the importance Miliukov attached to his stay in England, and observations of contemporaries such as Bernard Pares to the effect that Miliukov's political views were "a product of the English liberalism of his time," it is worth inquiring into the nature of this English liberalism.[41]

The Liberal Party's new espousal of social reform, reflected in a spate of social legislation between 1906 and 1914, is well known. Historians long interpreted the programmatic shift to the "new liberalism" primarily as a defensive response to socialist ideas and the attractiveness of these ideas to a mass electorate. Without denying the influence of socialist theories on such liberal thinkers as J. A. Hobson, L. T. Hobhouse, and J. M. Robertson, more recent scholarship emphasizes that the new liberal theory should be understood as being (like the varieties of socialism) a direct response to the host of political and social issues confronting serious thinkers at the turn of the century, and equally a reflection of then-dominant scientific and ethical trends.[42]

The collectivist perspective of the commitment to state-sponsored social reform, however, posed special dilemmas for liberalism. Social legislation entailed not only an abandonment of laissez-faire principles and a move from a negative to a positive concept of liberty; it also involved developing, in Michael Freeden's expression, "new conceptions of human nature, concurrently with new theories of society."[43] The utilitarian and natural law philosophies underlying classical liberalism, with their emphasis on the rationally acting, self-interested individual, were a somewhat problematic foundation for a new liberal theory. Many liberal theorists turned instead to sociology for a "science of society" that would provide a new understanding of community and guidelines for social progress while accommodating the liberal belief in the freedom of the individual. In so doing, they in effect attempted to strike a balance between rival claims made for the primacy of the community or the individual as the "unit of analysis and locus of value."[44] The overall tendency of sociologically based liberalism was to argue that liberties are not inherent in the individual but socially generated, and therefore not absolute but relative to the character of a given society, and liable, with society, to change. At the same time they sought to show that a large measure of individual freedom is a functional good for society as a whole, one of the constituent elements of social progress.[45]

There is little to suggest that Miliukov consciously perceived that sociology was replacing liberalism's old philosophical foundations, but he was aware that liberal theory and practice were changing in both England and France. This perception helped provide him with an evaluative framework for his treatment of the evolution of Russian liberalism. It also served as a validation of Russian liberalism, not by showing that it was following in the footsteps of its European predecessors, but by showing that progressive European liberals were moving toward the form of social reformism that Miliukov saw as the essence of Russian liberalism.

According to Miliukov, liberalism as initially conceived was completely antithetical to the collectivist perspective underlying both social reformism and socialism. Liberalism, as its very name implied, was a "consistent doctrine of individual liberty." Developing out of the struggle of the urban middle classes against landed privilege and arbitrary patriarchal government, it presented a contractual and limiting notion of the state as existing to defend individuals and their enjoyment of their liberties.[46] Philosophically, the liberal conception of the individual and of the relation of the individual to the state rested on the pragmatic view of human nature characteristic of eighteenth-century French rationalism and the doctrines of natural law. Not surprisingly, Miliukov had both theoretical and practical objections to a liberalism thus understood.

For one thing, Miliukov's historicism and Comtean positivism did not allow him to accept any vision of the human personality as unchanging or lying outside the realm of social laws. The pragmatism of eighteenth-century rationalism was flawed in that "for psychological motivation it primarily takes the self-interested motives of human nature and sees these as the same for all times and peoples."[47] In his polemics against the subjective school of sociology, Miliukov had charged that its overly volitional interpretation of the historical process harbored the old metaphysical dualism, and it was on the basis of its dualism that he rejected notions of natural law as being somehow transcendent or external to human beings. "Natural rights" derived from natural law were in fact the creation of society, not something immanent in the individual or existing prior to society. He further argued that this "sociological" foundation did not make these rights any less substantive or well defended than when they reposed on the seemingly "absolute" basis advanced by idealist or subjective-juridical theories.[48]

Miliukov also rejected the contractual idea of the state. There is not "a" state, but many ideas of the state; moreover, states can and do change their nature over time.[49] The contractual idea also failed to appreciate the "organic" quality of society, that is, the interdependence of not only social relations but all social phenomena, from prevailing aesthetics to economic organization.

Whatever its theoretical shortcomings, Miliukov was ready to acknowledge that thoroughly individualistic liberalism, with its defense of rights and idea of the "social compact" of free individuals, had been progressive in its own day, acting as a counterweight to the arbitrary encroachments of the old absolutist state. In the present day it did not correspond to the reality of the new phenomenon of the interventionist, modern democratic state. The achievement of the political program of liberalism was now understood to be one stage in, not the end of, political development. In a very telling phrase Miliukov asserted that "political freedom and individual liberty no longer seem to be the absolute good that they were considered when the era of liberty dawned in France."[50]

In Russia, a country lacking a "pure" liberal tradition, where the individualistic spirit was weakly developed and where political and social conditions rendered all political ideologies largely "abstract and humanitarian," liberalism could accommodate the collectivist orientation fairly easily. Effecting this change was more difficult in countries with established liberal parties and traditions, where distrust of the state still lingered and the "socialistic spirit to a large extent remains unconscious of itself." But in England, at any rate, liberalism had gradually come to signify "the idea of state intervention by way of social legislation."[51]

Miliukov did not, in these years, offer an explicit definition of Russian liberalism at the dawn of the new century, but sifting through his various writings it is possible to arrive at a formula that captures the essence of that creed: "constitutional democracy and social reformism." For Miliukov, democratic constitutionalism meant essentially the old liberal political program: guaranteed individual and political rights, representative government, and the rule of law. Constitutionalism was necessary not only for providing a flexible and pluralist framework for the functioning of the socially diversified and dynamic modern state, but as a check on the latter-day "enlightened absolutism" to which the centralized, democratic state could be prone.

Democracy was necessary not simply because the democratic consciousness was, in Russia, already present and increasingly aware of itself, and therefore a political fact of life.⁵² Democracy was a constitutive feature of progress, for in Miliukov's reading of the historical process, the agency of human will in directing the course of the future was limited and random until such time as that will became the conscious expression of all society: "The only path by which we can arrive at a replacement of the elemental historical process by a conscious one is by the gradual replacement of the socially purposeful acts of separate individuals with the socially purposeful behavior of the masses."⁵³

Social reformism constituted, for Miliukov, the moral content of liberalism and evolutionary socialism; it represented that transformation of ethics from abstraction to reality which he regarded as the truly moral. Social reformism meant working "not for the better future, but for the better present" and was therefore more genuinely humanitarian than revolutionary socialism, whose moral vision of the future led to neglect of constructive social work in the here and now.⁵⁴

In this way, Miliukov's version of liberalism differed from the moderate socialism of a Kuskova or Bogucharskii in little more than its conception of "the feasible"; after 1917, Vasilii Maklakov would declare that Miliukovian liberalism had not been liberalism at all.⁵⁵ What I have sought to demonstrate here is that Miliukov's liberalism, in both its sociological foundations and in many of its conclusions, was remarkably similar to the reorientation of liberalism then under way in England and France. He worked out his views, however, independently; they were reinforced by, rather than a product of, his exposure to contemporary English debate. The resemblance of his liberalism to that of Western European "new liberalism" does not of course constitute an argument for its viability in the Russia of his day. But it does challenge characterizations of his views as an illiberal reworking or variant of a more "genuine" liberal creed.

The War and the Russian Opposition

A week before the Japanese attack on Port Arthur, which launched the Russo-Japanese War on January 26/27, 1904, Miliukov warned *Osvobozhdenie* readers that war was nearly inevitable, and its consequences potentially catastrophic. The interests, monies, and rivalries of so many powers would be so intimately concerned with any Russian war in the Far East, he felt, that a clash between Russia and Japan could conceivably touch off a European conflagration.⁵⁶

The outbreak of the war put a halt to the agitational efforts of the newly formed Union of Liberation almost immediately, and for a time seemed to threaten it with disintegration. Waged in a remote area and on behalf of less than pressing state interests, the war was unpopular. Widespread disapproval of the war did not, however, lead to any consensus within the liberation movement on the attitude to be taken to the war effort. Some believed all oppositional activity must cease for the duration, purely on patriotic grounds or, in part, out of fear that such activity would harm the liberation movement by outraging patriotic sensibilities. These various responses constituted the "defensist" position. In contrast, the "defeatist" position believed that military setbacks would hasten a liberationist victory and counseled against suspension of oppositional activity. Miliukov was, for a number of reasons, a defeatist.

He was also the first liberationist to attack publicly the ambiguous attitude toward the war adopted by the editor of *Osvobozhdenie*. The sharp exchange between Struve and Miliukov on the pages of the journal provides an excellent comparison of the views of the chief theoreticians of Russian liberalism not only in terms of the war itself but also in their approach to politics and conception of the very nature of Russian nationalism.

For Struve, it was of critical importance that Russians draw a clear distinction between the government and the state, between the hateful regime conducting the war and the army sent off to fight it. The war was senseless, but that did not mean one should welcome the defeat of one's country and countrymen, or trample on their patriotic feelings.[57] He therefore advocated both continued opposition to the government and support of the fatherland and the army, for "the army is the people in arms." It was not only possible but necessary to fuse this aroused nationalism with the struggle for the liberation of the country. This perspective informed his controversial "Letter to Students," where he exhorted students to participate in patriotic demonstrations, adding to the cries "Long live Russia!" "Long live the army!" their own slogans, "Long live freedom!" "Long live free Russia!"[58]

Miliukov promptly rejected Struve's advice to the opposition. It was impossible, he rightly argued, to maintain Struve's distinction between the government and the army. From the fact that the people are in the army it does not follow that the army is the people; so long as the army was the weapon of the government, "the symbolic fist of Russian insolence," to support it was impossible. Struve's advice to students was worse than impractical: such a stand, on the part of any portion of the Russian opposition, would be behavior no less "false, evasive, and contradictory" than the government's own, and therefore not only absurd but harmful.[59]

The distinction to be drawn was not between the regime conducting the war and the army itself, but between "official Russia" and "Russia of the future." The opposition's task must be to work for that future by unequivocally disavowing the war and through efforts to disperse, not link up with, misplaced patriotism, which Miliukov characterized—in a jibe at Struve—as "that loathsome fog which . . . is settling over the Russian swamp and addling, apparently, even quite strong heads." The very most that could be asked of the opposition was that it remain silent, but if a rallying cry was needed it should be the old slogan "Down with autocracy!" "Truly," he concluded, "this is no less patriotic."[60]

Struve drew a sharper line between their positions by insisting that their differences were not merely tactical but the product of dissimilar worldviews. Struve insisted that patriotic demonstrations revealed, albeit in confused and unconscious form, genuine civic sentiment. This sentiment was of overwhelming significance for Russia's future; thinking Russians should bend all their energies to "melding healthy patriotic feeling with civic liberationist aspirations." Whatever the practical merits of Miliukov's position, its cold logic was shortsighted: "We *need* a common ground with those who still do not understand us. The search for such a common ground is, for me, a most vital spiritual need."[61]

In his reply to Struve, Miliukov sought to show that he and Struve differed not so much in their appreciation of the significance of national solidarity as in their estimation of what constituted "healthy national feeling" and what could be done to engender it.[62] Without denying the spiritual dimensions of the problem, Miliukov suggested that as a symptom of the ills of Russian political culture, it required a political solution.

Miliukov detected in Struve's national perspective an element of romantic chauvinism that was foreign to many Russians, one which led him to idealize manifestations of simple Russian chauvinism in his desire for national solidarity. Look where he would, Struve was not going to find a genuinely "normal" expression of healthy national feeling. This was not because Russians were deficient in love of country, but because Russia's abnormal political conditions cast patriotism in misshapen forms. "Only a free political life can little by little demolish the sad legacy of centuries of ignorance and decades of struggle, which prevent the normal manifestation of healthy national feeling."[63]

Consciousness of the limits of national solidarity constituted the patriotic Russian's "tragedy of the soul." Nonetheless, to think practically and politically those limits had to be recognized, and Struve had yet to make this recognition. In the meantime, Miliukov cautioned, any search for a common ground for resolution of the national question would only "fatally obscure our own understanding, muddle our political conduct, and overshadow more urgent questions of domestic politics."[64]

With this exchange, Miliukov demonstrated a still greater intransigence toward the autocratic regime. The war against Japan was not the only one being waged: government and public opinion, official Russia and "popular Russia," were equally at war with each other. At the same time, in distinguishing between public opinion "in the broad sense," which supported the war effort, and public opinion "in the restricted sense" (that is, the opposition), which did not, Miliukov admitted to a cleavage that contradicted the putative unity of his "popular Russia."

Miliukov's position on the liberationists' attitude to the war was in fact founded on this latter recognition: that the liberation movement's success would be the condition for, not the result of, rapprochement on the "national question." He therefore chided Struve for an unfounded optimism, as well as political impracticality, in seeking a common ground with chauvinistic patriotism as a sort of shortcut to national solidarity. In effect, he suggested that unity in opposing the war could serve as a provisional surrogate for genuine national solidarity; the course of events of the next twelve months would demonstrate the practical validity of this approach. In one respect, however, Miliukov's perspective was no less optimistic than Struve's, since it assumed that continued opposition, including opposition to the war, would gain Russia the needed political reforms *in time* to lay the ground for real national solidarity.[65]

Even as Miliukov and Struve concluded their debate on the opposition's position on the war, news of reversals in the Far East was fueling widespread discontent. Between mid-April and early June the Russian army suffered three defeats, and the summer saw no improvement. Plehve, meanwhile, had not responded to the zemstvos' readiness to cooperate with the government in wartime with the slightest concession or manifestation of trust, with the result that even some moderates began to renew their critiques of the government.[66] On the far left, attacks were more menacing: a wave of political terrorism swept the Russian empire in spring and summer 1904.

Growing violence prompted one Moscow zemstist to urge in June, in *Osvobozhdenie*, that constitutionalists curtail their demands until the war had been won, also making clear their condemnation of any resort to force. "Distant from both terror and class struggle . . . their task consists in the organization of state-minded public opinion."[67] Miliukov strongly disagreed. He instead urged that the time had come for the liberation movement to issue a specific, positive declaration about the political part of its program, its minimum demand being a popularly elected legislative body. He also argued that while liberationists advocated neither terror nor class struggle, they realized that "only *active struggle*, whatever its forms," would clear the way for the victory of "state-minded" public opinion.[68]

Miliukov's defense of "active struggle" appeared in print just four days after Plehve fell victim to a terrorist attack on July 15. The bomb that killed the hated minister of internal affairs reverberated deeply. Far from causing educated society to recoil in horror, his assassination struck people as the logical outcome of the conditions created by his repressive regime, and therefore lent a new urgency to the desire for reform. According to Shakhovskoi, Plehve's end was the beginning of the "reanimation of the public mood." Debate in the Union of Liberation mirrored the call to prepare for action implicit in Miliukov's article: "Everyone already felt the impossibility of remaining mere witnesses to the drama."[69]

Plehve's death persuaded Nicholas of the need to appease some sections of public opinion. An *ukaz* and manifesto published August 11 abolished corporal punishment and canceled arrears in peasant redemption payments. More important was the tsar's choice, after long deliberations, of a new minister of internal affairs, Prince P. D. Sviatopolk-Mirskii. This was not another Plehve: Sviatopolk-Mirskii believed in the necessity of bridging the gulf between government and society. He immediately proclaimed a "New Course," and to back this up announced a partial political amnesty and easing of censorship laws.

Mirskii's appointment, coming in the wake of military debacles and a spreading wave of terror, was not interpreted by everyone as a gesture of good faith. If some public figures were inclined to see in it the harbinger of a genuine political "spring," others condemned it as a minimal concession wrung from the regime by the conjuncture of foreign and domestic troubles. Miliukov's reaction to these developments was contained in an article of early October, "The New Course." Assessing Sviatopolk-Mirskii's "New Course" as little more than a "return to the status quo ante Plehve," he presented the constitutionalists' political demands. "What we want is an open and official recognition of complete freedom of religion and conscience, as well as freedom of the press, of meetings, unions, travel, personal immunity as well as immunity of property and dwellings. . . . We want a formal abolition of autocracy. . . . We want the tsar to give Russians what he gave the Bulgarians."[70]

Miliukov was in fact speaking to the fainthearted among the opposition as well as to the government when he declared that "there are no intermediate positions between autocracy and consistent constitutionalism." The government might imagine that it could offer half-measures, and some individuals might settle for these, but the constitutionalists could not. They knew that there were other "parties and forces," with still more radical demands, whose patience was spent. They had no choice but to insist that the government speedily honor the claims against it, for there were other "creditors" ready to foreclose.

> We will not offer you any of our people, we will not render you any credit, we will not grant you any respite till you accept our full program. And even then, we are not sure if we will be able to save Russia from your political dilettantism and, without shocks, lead her along the road of peaceful political development.[71]

"No Enemies on the Left"

The opposition's wartime "ceasefire" with the government now definitely over, the Council of the Union of Liberation reviewed its neglect of agitational work and intensified discussion of ways and means for mobilizing public opinion. In August it began plans for a national zemstvo congress, with an eye to inducing it to issue some sort of proclamation in favor of sweeping reform. Zemstvo support of the liberation movement was still considered of paramount importance, but there was a growing feeling that depending too exclusively on the zemtsy was not wise. The Council therefore looked to the left for allies and decided to accept an invitation to participate in a conference of oppositional and revolutionary groups being organized for September.[72]

The moving force behind what has come to be known as the Paris Conference was the Finnish Party of Active Resistance, and particularly its leader, Koni Zilliacus. Zilliacus invited eighteen oppositional and revolutionary organizations within the Russian empire to meet in Paris in order to coordinate their activities; most of the participants did not know that he had Japanese financial support for his activities.[73] The social democratic parties, initially interested in the proposal, eventually decided to boycott. In the end, only eight organizations, many of them representing national minorities, sent delegates.

The Union of Liberation's four delegates were Petr Dolgorukov, V. Ia. Bogucharskii, Struve, and Miliukov. Along with the other delegates they took great care not to attract the attention of the Paris branch of the tsarist political police, their precautions even extending to the use of pseudonyms in the conference protocols. They might well have spared themselves these efforts, since one of the Socialist Revolutionary delegates, Evno Azef, was a police agent.[74]

The Paris Conference was the first formal meeting of representatives of the Union of Liberation with revolutionary and national groups.[75] For Miliukov, participation in its discussions marked a departure from his hitherto strictly "literary" involvement in the liberation movement; for the first time, he appeared as a representative of the Union of Liberation. As it turned out, he had significant differences with the other members of the Union of Liberation delegation, which as a whole was far from united in its views. The most divisive issues were the Polish question, universal suffrage, and organization of antiwar demonstrations.

In his memoirs, Miliukov frankly acknowledged his differences with his colleagues and other delegates at the Paris Conference on the question of Polish autonomy, saying that he was astounded by the extent of the concessions they were willing to make to satisfy the Poles. His unyielding position dragged out debates on the Polish question for several sessions, and the final resolution did not specifically mention the issue of Polish autonomy, but settled instead for the general formula that all the organizations signing the resolution recognized the right of national "self-determination."[76]

The question of whether to espouse the principle of universal suffrage also initially divided Miliukov from his colleagues. On the first day of the Paris Conference, Miliukov said that while the constitutionalists did not have any objection to universal suffrage, it was not an opportune time to proclaim the principle of universal suffrage in a formal resolution. Viktor Chernov, the other of the two Socialist Revolutionary delegates, said he would insist on inclusion of this demand.[77] Miliukov's colleagues apparently persuaded him to reconsider his position, for the next day's session opened with Miliukov declaring that constitutionalists were not against the principle of universal suffrage and that their delegates therefore agreed to include this in the Conference resolution.[78]

Finally, there was the question of the attitude to the war. Miliukov apparently did not desire that the Conference adopt an antiwar slogan, but envisioned participating groups orchestrating "demonstrations against recruitment or the war."[79] The Finns, the Polish National League, and the other delegates from the Union of Liberation flatly refused to countenance any form of "street manifestations," and both Struve and Dolgorukov said the constitutionalists would not agree to exhortations against the recruitment of soldiers.[80]

For all the differences dividing the Union of Liberation delegation internally as well as from the other parties represented at the Conference, there was sufficient agreement on certain basic ends to allow for a joint "Declaration of Principles," which Miliukov helped draft. The declaration's preamble made it clear that the signatories preserved their independence as organizations, and that they "did not for one minute renounce their own tactics or programs." The three principles on which they were agreed were the destruction of autocracy, its replacement by a democratic regime based on universal suffrage, and laws guaranteeing free national development for all nationalities. In the name of these basic principles and demands, "the parties represented at the conference will unite their efforts to hasten the inevitable fall of absolutism."[81]

Determining how they were to "unite their efforts" was a still more difficult task. Miliukov presented the most comprehensive list of suggestions on tactics. Reiterating the tactical independence preserved by all the signatories, he suggested that each group undertake not to hinder the tactical line pursued by other groups. His positive proposals for the conference participants were that they establish a central bureau and create provincial groups that would act jointly, disseminate literature jointly, and issue common declarations.[82] After prolonged debate on the nature and competence of the proposed central committee or bureau, conference participants decided on a three-person bureau to be located in St. Petersburg, its function being to coordinate the relations of the parties and handle the exchange of information between them. It was also agreed that the various parties would individually publish the "Declaration of Principles" and protocol of the conference in their own organs.[83]

Despite the limited nature of the agreements reached at the Paris Conference, most of the delegates were pleased with the fruits of their labors. For the first time, liberals, socialists, and nationality groups had managed to work out and even agree upon joint declarations, and most supposed that this was only the first of such conferences. For Miliukov, "The results exceeded our expectations and dispelled our misgivings. . . . Personal acquaintance and negotiations did more than years of literary polemics."[84] Two months later he would tell his American audience that "this declaration of oppositional and revolutionary parties certainly marks the climax of the political struggle in Russia. Its practical result is to isolate the government in its struggle with the Russian opposition."[85]

Miliukov played an important part in the conference. He was elected one of its two vice-chairmen, helped draft its protocols and declaration, and succeeded in blocking any direct mention of Poland or Polish autonomy.[86] He must also have had forced upon him a clearer sense of the differences between his views and those of his colleagues in the Union of Liberation. One effect of the conference on Miliukov seems to have been the realization that the liberationist program had to include what he had once referred to as a "leap into the unknown": from this point on he always publicly supported the demand for universal suffrage.

The Paris Conference had two further consequences for Miliukov. One was the misleading impression it gave him of the willingness of the leftist parties to make concessions to the constitutionalists. It reinforced his belief in the growing moderation of Russian socialism, a belief he had gained from reading publications of the Russian radical press of the 1880s and 1890s at Harvard Library. The absence from the conference of the most intransigent of the socialist parties, the Social Democrats, certainly contributed to this impression. After Miliukov returned to Russia to stay, in April 1905, it would take him some time to appreciate the extent to which he had misunderstood the attitude of many revolutionaries.

A second, much-delayed consequence was the damage done to his political reputation when the public finally learned who had participated in the Paris Conference. A much more conservative mood prevailed in Russia in spring 1909 when Premier P. A. Stolypin, using Azef's reports to the police, dramatically revealed to the Third Duma Miliukov's collaboration with revolutionaries in Paris. Miliukov's enemies on the extreme right took immediate advantage of the scandal caused by this announcement, introducing an interpellation demanding to know why the government did not arrest member of the Duma Miliukov.[87]

The Public Opinion Campaign

After the conclusion of the Paris Conference, Dolgorukov returned directly to Russia to prepare for the important forthcoming zemstvo congress and, presumably, to acquaint the Council of the Union of Liberation with the results of the Paris Conference.[88] The Council was preparing for the second congress of the Union of Liberation, to be held two weeks before the zemstvo congress on October 20–22 in St. Petersburg.[89]

The second congress of the Union of Liberation differed little from the January founding congress in composition, but greatly in mood.[90] Buoyed by the rising tide of discontent in the empire, the delegates to the second congress contemplated a course of action intended to wring from the government a constitutional order in the near future. The tactical means envisioned were still "legal" and nonviolent, but the policy of working with revolutionary organizations—"no enemies on the left"—was definitely endorsed.

The two issues dominating the second congress were the public opinion campaign proposed by the Council of the Union and the future course of the Union of Liberation itself. The congress approved the Council's tactical proposals and the two documents of the Paris Conference.[91] After significant debate concerning the Union's future as an organization, revolving around whether it should try to organize a genuine political party or retain its semiconspiratorial nature, the congress voted to make the Union of Liberation known to the public and to preserve its loose coalitional basis. The announcement of the existence of the Union would include a revised version of the January congress's enumeration of its principles and goals and would be published simultaneously with the two documents from the Paris Conference.[92]

Miliukov's behavior in these weeks is somewhat enigmatic. He returned to Russia for only a few days in late October prior to leaving for his lectures in Boston and Chicago. Curiously, after playing so prominent a role in Paris, Miliukov was scarcely visible at the Union of Liberation congress. Perhaps he was not elected with Petrunkevich, Bogucharskii, and Dolgorukov to the Union's all-important Council because of his intended departure.[93] He apparently was present only at the last day's sessions, and if he gave a speech at the congress or participated in the debate, it was not alluded to in any contemporary account.

Miliukov was, however, a prominent participant at a meeting held several days later, one of the first of several organized by the Union of Liberation to influence delegates to the upcoming zemstvo congress. At a gathering in the home of I. A. Korsakov, Miliukov was instrumental in convincing a number of moderates that Russia was indeed ready for a constitution. According to Ekaterina Kuskova, Miliukov "completely smashed" fainthearted objections about Russia's fitness for representative government and the inopportune timing of constitutional demands.[94] His most telling argument was one he would employ frequently in the coming eighteen months, the example of Bulgaria. Bulgaria had received its democratic constitution from a Russian tsar, and twenty-five years' practice showed that a constitutional system could work even in a country of "very elementary social and cultural conditions." The argument was doubly effective in its combination of a persuasive analogy with an implicit play to national pride. "The zemtsy," Shakhovskoi wrote, "did not want to lag behind Bulgaria."[95]

Miliukov fully shared the liberationists' conviction that the attitude of the zemstvo congress was of tremendous importance to the public opinion campaign. He was not willing, however, to delay his departure for the United States in order to continue propagandizing: his last effort in this direction was a strong article printed in the influential journal *Pravo* (Law) after he had already left the country. In "The Tasks of the Zemstvo Congress" Miliukov represented it as crucial that the government hear the opinion of the country: since conditions prevented the country from speaking for itself, it became the congress's duty to speak for it. He exhorted the zemstvo delegates to demand a constitution, to pronounce "the word that has long been on everyone's tongue."[96]

The resolutions passed by the November 1904 zemstvo congress corresponded almost exactly to the "zemstvo political program" Miliukov had proposed in the first issue of *Osvobozhdenie* some two years earlier. Virtually without debate the congress approved resolutions calling for political freedom, the independence of courts, and an end to discrimination on the basis of religion and social estate. On the all-important question of Russia's future political order, a two-thirds majority voted for a resolution on a democratically elected legislative body whose functions would include budgetary approval and supervision of the legality of the administration's activity, as opposed to a more modest resolution on an elected consultative body. Rather than demand a constituent assembly, the congress resolved to appeal to the "supreme authority" to grant its requests, and elected a delegation to present its resolutions to Sviatopolk-Mirskii.[97]

Although the zemstvo congress did not pronounce "the word on everyone's tongue," it had gone much further than Miliukov and the liberationists had dared hope; in September, in a discussion with the Struves of the upcoming zemstvo congress, Miliukov had doubted that more than forty-five delegates to the congress would vote for a constitutionalist resolution.[98] In his enthusiastic characterization of the congress resolutions for his Boston audience, couched in language he most likely would not have permitted himself in Russia, Miliukov described them as "the first political program of the Russian Liberal Party": "The Petition of Rights" of November 19–21, 1904 will remain a beautiful page in our annals; and whatever be its immediate practical consequences, its political importance cannot be overestimated."[99] If Miliukov's conflation of the zemstvo congress with the Union of Liberation as Russia's "Liberal Party" was misleading, the connection he posited between the congress resolutions and the spread of constitutional demands was not. The decisions reached by a majority of the country's only elected officials conferred a sanction on the constitutional movement, and the Union of Liberation's "Banquet Campaign" became a runaway success.

The organization of banquets for expression of forbidden political sentiments was not a new device in Russia, but the Union of Liberation's Banquet Campaign, modeled after the French campaign of 1848, was the first attempt to orchestrate a series of banquets all over the country. The resolutions adopted at these banquets went beyond those of the zemstvo congress, many of them calling for a constituent assembly based on four-tailed suffrage, political amnesty, and an immediate end to the war.[100] "Society"—educated Russia—had never before publicly voiced such demands, and the impact of the campaign was heightened not only by extensive press coverage, but by the militancy of the press itself. As Miliukov told his Boston audiences, the spirit manifested in liberal gatherings also pervaded the press.[101]

Years later, as part of his effort to depict himself as representative of the more moderate current of the liberation movement, Miliukov tried to distance himself from the radical mood of the Banquet Campaign. Criticizing the Campaign's tendency to unite people by emotion rather than reason, he claimed to have been dismayed by its oratorical excesses. His claims do not square with the evidence. Virtually none of the resolutions issuing from the banquets went beyond his own positions at the time, and his American lectures of late 1904 did not display the least reservation concerning what he termed the most "united and coordinated political action" ever witnessed in the history of the country. It was true, he said, that "socialistic publications" tried to insert demands in the liberals' resolutions, but in many cases it was agreed to include these demands, "as practically they did not contradict—and often even were implied in—the demands of the liberals themselves."[102] In January 1905 Miliukov unequivocally asserted, "Public opinion has done its duty. The fault is not this time with public opinion."[103]

Until April 1905, however, Miliukov was party to the most successful public movement in Russian history only from afar. During his whirlwind visit to Petersburg in October 1904, friends unsuccessfully tried to dissuade him from returning to the United States for his lecture engagements.[104] Miliukov later defended his decision to leave by saying that while everyone knew the situation had to change, he could not have known that it would change so rapidly.[105] Given his own perceptions, on the eve of the zemstvo congress, of the rapidity of change in Russia, this defense was somewhat disingenuous; though he could not have foretold Bloody Sunday, it was not the moment for a leader to leave the scene of the action.

"Leader" is the operative word here: at several key points in the liberation movement Miliukov's *Osvobozhdenie* articles provided leadership, but Miliukov did not want, or wanted only ambivalently, the responsibility and commitment that leadership entailed. In essence, he still preserved the personal outlook revealed by his behavior at the Paris Conference, where he voiced his own convictions more frequently than those of the perceived "liberal group." He evinced a fighting spirit, but his militancy was still that of an armchair strategist, not a general who conceived and oversaw tactics. Miliukov proposed a course of action, then left; negotiated agreements and drafted resolutions, then disappeared; read reports of the struggle and evaluated them, rather than witnessing the campaign. It would appear that he looked upon his participation in the liberation movement as a personal expression of principles rather than a formal responsibility incurred by the member of an organization. And when it came to weighing his different interests and responsibilities—his commitment to lecture about Russia as against his commitment to the struggle in Russia—the former still seemed more immediate.

Miliukov arrived in Boston shortly before the start of his very successful Lowell Institute Lectures on November 30, 1904. His visit began auspiciously, with an invitation to be the house guest of Harvard president Abbott Lawrence Lowell, an honor he found deeply gratifying.[106] Miliukov was thoroughly impressed by the exceptional caliber of his Lowell Institute audiences. He, in turn, provided them with a scholarly but topical eight lecture exposition of the "Russian Crisis"—characterized as both economic and political—which combined a barrage of statistics about peasant indebtedness, bureaucratic misrule, and industrial strikes with what amounted to bulletins on the unfolding oppositional movement. The *Boston Evening Transcript* praised the lectures and urged its readers to attend them. Other American newspapers reported the contents of Miliukov's lectures, and by the time he finished the series in Boston he had established a truly national reputation as a reliable and perceptive interpreter of current affairs in Russia.[107]

Shortly after Christmas Miliukov headed for Chicago to begin his course on the Balkan Slavs. Once again, he would find himself abruptly terminating lectures before the scheduled conclusion of a course, but in this case the decision was his own. On January 22, 1905 (January 9 of the Russian calendar), tsarist troops fired on an unarmed procession of workers bringing a petition of grievances to the tsar at the Winter Palace. News of this tragedy, which immediately came to be known as "Bloody Sunday," was cabled to Miliukov in Chicago. He consulted with Crane, and they agreed he would depart as soon as he had finished the text of the book based on his Boston lectures and his previous Chicago course.[108]

Appreciating the need to return to Russia, Miliukov nonetheless tarried; nearly three months elapsed between Bloody Sunday and his arrival in St. Petersburg. The manuscript of the book was completed in February and handed over to the press; after he had proofed the galleys he headed for Paris, where he delivered a lecture on the "Russian Crisis" and met with Struve to discuss, among other issues, the future of *Osvobozhdenie*. Miliukov's business in Paris was not purely political. While there he looked up a young woman he had met several months previously in Chicago. Marie Petite had been sent to lecture in the United States by the Alliance Française; the two met at a dinner party and immediately became friendly. Mlle Petite expressed interest in translating *Russia and Its Crisis*, and by the time he saw her in Paris she had already made provisional arrangements for its publication in France.[109]

Miliukov at last arrived in St. Petersburg in early April 1905, to plunge immediately into the struggle for a constitutional order. This time, his commitment was unambiguous: he would not again vacillate between pursuit of his studies and his political activity. Within a month of his return he occupied one of the most prominent places in the liberation movement, presiding over the unruly, dynamic, and increasingly militant "Union of Unions." Six months later he gave the opening speech at the congress that realized one of his long-cherished goals, the foundation of a constitutional-democratic party.

CHAPTER SIX

The Revolution of 1905

When Miliukov returned to Russia in April 1905, he had had little firsthand experience of events in his native country for some two and a half years. He had to take his bearings in a much altered political landscape and then determine what his role should be in what was now a revolution. This latter task was complicated by the erroneous expectations people had formed about his political temperament during his long absence, as well as by his own political inexperience.

Miliukov had to define himself anew, both for himself and for the various "publics" before whom he appeared. He was a scholar whose participation in politics had been largely theoretical; now, he meant to be not only a political activist, but a leader. But Miliukov would have little in the way of apprenticeship, no time, as a junior senator or backbencher, to learn politics and assess his own strengths and shortcomings before assuming a leader's responsibilities. He often found himself feeling his way gingerly, even groping. He also found that he returned to Russia with the reputation, in certain circles, of an "inveterate revolutionary," which colored expectations of the line he would take; misunderstandings on this point would cause trouble.[1]

By his own reckoning, his views were not crystallized in every particular. He could survey the scene and determine where he belonged. His long absence had preserved for him a certain freedom of choice upon returning to Russia. The process of political differentiation within the liberation movement was gaining momentum, but eventual lines of demarcation were not yet clear. Furthermore, Miliukov still believed it possible to preserve and even widen the "united front" of the opposition, a goal he intended to further by whatever means recommended themselves.

The United Front

Miliukov immediately recognized the degree to which the oppositional mood in society had deepened and moved to the left since November of the previous year. Reaction to "Bloody Sunday" had wrung further concessions from the government, but these only fueled the opposition. A rescript of February 18 promised to establish a consultative representative body to participate in the making of laws; this extension to "worthy" citizens of a purely consultative voice, widely hoped for in December, no longer satisfied even most moderates. A decree to the Senate of the same date, allowing subjects to offer advice on necessary reforms, was freely interpreted as a de facto lifting of censorship and restrictions on assembly. Inhabitants of the capitals availed themselves of the greater opportunities to speak, publish, and assemble.

The third congress of the Union of Liberation, which openly met in Moscow on March 25–28, just days before Miliukov's return to Russia, reflected both the heightened tension and the growing rifts in the Union itself. In a written appeal to the congress the absent Struve insisted on the urgency of creating an organized, disciplined constitutional party frankly standing on a "revolutionary path," with program and tactics spelled out accordingly.[2] The congress shared Struve's concern about the need for programmatic and tactical coherence, but found it impossible to agree on many specific points, including extension of the franchise to women, the nature of peasant land ownership, and the right of national minorities to self-determination. Nor were the majority of delegates prepared to go as far in tactics as Struve and many members from St. Petersburg desired. In the end, the congress shelved the question of organizing a party and issued its program, based on the positions worked out at the Paris Conference, as provisional and nonbinding. Clearly, the Union of Liberation could continue to exist only so long as individual members and groups retained the freedom to act according to the dictates of "their conscience and their social convictions."[3]

Work on organization and program continued after the congress, the center of gravity for the former being St. Petersburg and for the latter, Moscow. Miliukov participated in both kinds of activity. His base was Petersburg, since the Miliukov family was still settled in Udel'naia, Finland, a short commute from the capital. He also journeyed regularly to Moscow.

Almost immediately upon his return to Moscow, Miliukov was puzzled by an eighteenth-century document handed him by a smiling Dmitrii Shakhovskoi. It took a moment to realize that this translated constitutional proj-

Fedor Kokoshkin. From P. N. Miliukov et al., *M. M. Vinaver i russkaia obshchestvennost' nachala xx veka* (Paris, 1937).

ect for the Austrian empire, with its provisions for popular representation, reformed local self-government, and "Gallician" autonomy, was actually a disguised draft of a Russian constitution. Its author was Fedor Kokoshkin, a young Moscow jurist, who together with other lawyers and jurists, among them Maksim Kovalevskii, Sergei Muromtsev, and P. I. Novgorodtsev, were at work on more precise formulation of the project. The ultimate object was to provide a constitutional project around which a future party could unite. A second committee was working out a more detailed agrarian program for the future party. All this work went on under the aegis of the zemstvo constitutional group, of whom Petrunkevich and Shakhovskoi were among the moving figures.

Miliukov read and discussed their proposals with great interest, debated some of their points, and contributed whatever he could on the basis of his familiarity with the U.S. and Bulgarian systems.[4] Observation of the workings of these systems had made him a staunch proponent of a unicameral legislature for Russia. An upper chamber was too likely to be elite in composition and act as a brake on the reforms a more democratic lower chamber would pass, he felt, thus introducing an element of class friction into the parliamentary arrangement.[5] Miliukov and Kokoshkin differed on this question, although Miliukov would eventually come to share his views about the desirability of two chambers. In other respects, the two men thought very similarly, as was the case for most of the Moscow circle assembled around Petrunkevich. Miliukov felt comfortable among them, "at last truly myself." Above all it was Kokoshkin, twelve years his junior, who became his intimate friend.[6]

In late April Miliukov's Moscow friends decided it was time that he be formally presented to the public. They arranged a public speech for him at the Novosiltsev mansion, to which they invited "all Moscow." Miliukov's subject was the necessity of a rapprochement between constitutionalists and revolutionaries if Russia's liberation was to be won. Some of the 300 people in attendance were perhaps more skeptical than he about the prospects of such an alliance, but the audience responded enthusiastically. His first political speech was deemed a thorough success, and he was invited to speak before other gatherings in Moscow.[7]

While Miliukov personally felt most at home in the circle gathered round Petrunkevich in Moscow, his mood at this time corresponded more to that of the Petersburg nucleus of the Union of Liberation. Dominated by intelligentsia rather than zemtsy, the Petersburg branch of the Union was better organized, more active, and more militant than its Moscow counterpart. Immediately upon his return to Russia Miliukov resumed his old contacts at the Free Economic Society, one of the organizational centers of the Union of Liberation in Petersburg, and at *Russkoe bogatstvo*, around which Miakotin, Peshekhonov, and other close friends were still gathered.[8] He also became active in the newly formed Writers' Union, a successor to the suppressed Writers' Union to which he had previously belonged and part of the burgeoning all-Russian professional union movement.

In autumn 1904, the Union of Liberation had raised the idea of organizing Russia's professionals for the advancement of political goals, in the absence of other, legal means of political organization. It was directly under

Miliukov, circa 1907. From Paul Miliukov, *La crise russe* (Paris, 1907).

the Union's auspices that the first three professional unions on a nationwide scale were organized in December 1904, the All-Russian Union of Engineers and Technicians (in which Miliukov's brother Aleksei was to play a role), the Academic Union, and the All-Russian Union of Medical Personnel. By May 1905, fourteen professional unions already existed.[9]

The Writers' Union was established at the All-Russian Congress of Journalists, a gathering of some 140 writers in St. Petersburg on April 5–8.

Miliukov, though he had returned to Russia just days before convocation of the congress, played a prominent role in determining the new union's profile and was elected to its central bureau. Characterizing the Union as a body organized for political rather than professional aims, Miliukov told the congress that its goal should be "replacement of the existing autocratic-bureaucratic state system with a representative form of government." He stipulated that the people's representatives had to be elected on the basis of the "four-tailed" suffrage and were to enjoy full legislative powers. But by deliberately avoiding use of the term "constituent assembly" he set a relatively moderate tone. His election to the editorial committee entrusted with drafting the new union's platform helped him preserve this focus on political freedom. The committee chose to ignore the controversial agrarian and labor provisions approved on the second day of the congress, arguing that many delegates would not join the union were they to be included in the platform. The tactical line suggested in the platform was equally moderate, calling for agitation in the press for a constituent assembly and urging organization of more unions along professional lines, to be united in a Union of Unions.[10]

As one perceptive foreign correspondent noted, the import of the Writers' Union platform lay in its orientation rather than its demands: "The platform seems comparatively harmless, but the point of it is that it aims not at influencing the government to give, but at influencing the people to take." The same observer noted that "in the Congress there were able men and good speakers. M. Miakotin is a man of ideas, M. Vinaver is incisive and practical, Professor Miliukov is prudent and clear . . . but there was no one in the Congress who showed himself to be possessed of the sacred fire of a great leader."[11]

Miliukov immediately began propagandizing the concept of politically oriented professional unions, defending it against critics—most of them Social Democrats—who felt unions should have strictly professional goals, and others who argued for the creation not of unions but of distinct and cohesive political parties.[12] In Miliukov's view, the paramount task in spring 1905 was the politicization of the great majority of Russians. He welcomed the current process of political differentiation already occurring as a healthy one, but felt that Russia was still too inexperienced politically for genuine political parties. The numerous "middle elements," lying between the right and the left, had not yet formed distinct views and were not ready or able to enter political parties.[13]

For the time being, politically oriented unions organized along professional lines were the best means for the ultimate formation of parties. The unions had already performed a huge service among the politically articulate by acquainting them with one another and clarifying the relationships of various political views and social groups. By activizing the still apolitical, they could cover the whole country with a network of organized groups and "furnish material for the formation of cadres." With this function in mind, Miliukov took issue with those who complained that the unions were too indeterminate politically: this was rather their virtue, since they were seeking to mobilize as many people as possible. When even minimum goals had yet to be achieved, the loose program and structure of the unions allowed people of differing beliefs to work together within them.[14]

Miliukov also took aim at the elitism underlying the Social Democratic perspective on unions. Social Democrats argued for strictly professional unions because they assumed an apolitical membership could be shaped as they chose. They viewed this membership as an "amorphous mass," an arena for the influence of parties or even as a tool (*orudie*) of those parties. Miliukov saw it rather differently: "I do not condemn the 'amorphous elements' of the unions to the passive role of adhering to one of the existing parties, but place a certain hope on their independence and activity."[15] From "middle Russia" altogether new parties might arise. Clearly, Miliukov believed that this huge, untapped population, located between the right and the left, could turn out to be constitutionally minded.

Organization of a national Union of Unions finally began in late April. The initiators were Petersburg liberationists, particularly L. I. Lutugin and other leaders of the Union of Engineers, a body that had been particularly energetic in helping organize unions. The congress of sixty representatives from fourteen unions convened on May 8 in Moscow and elected Miliukov chairman.[16] Discussion showed that most of the delegates shared Miliukov's conception of a Union of Unions that would stand above class or special interests to help coordinate the struggle against autocracy, but developing any more specific consensus about its program and tactics proved more difficult. Delegates agreed that decisions of the congress would be subject to ratification and amendment by each union, whose representatives would then gather in a second, more conclusive congress. The body's self-definition was deliberately imprecise, holding that "the Union of Unions is an organ uniting autonomous all-Russian unions on a federative foundation to lead the struggle for the political liberation of Russia on the basis of democratism." Even then, Miliukov managed to forestall massive walkouts only by repeatedly stressing the provisional nature of the Union's proposed statement of purpose and by accepting a number of special opinions to be included in materials distributed to individual unions for consideration.[17]

Until convocation of the Union's second congress, executive power for the new body would be vested in a temporary central bureau, composed of two representatives from each member union and based in Petersburg. Miliukov was elected to the central bureau from the Union of Writers.

Several weeks after the founding congress of the Union of Unions, Miliukov became involved for the first time in political activity of a more physical sort. On May 19 Russians learned that the Japanese had decimated most of the Russian Baltic fleet in the Tsushima straits in a single afternoon. Shock and grief at the loss of life were compounded by a sense of national humiliation; this latest blow dispelled any lingering hopes for eventual victory in the war. Two leading liberationists in Petersburg, V. I. Charnolusskii and G. A. Fal'bork, persuaded Miliukov to help organize a public demonstration over Tsushima. Some three hundred people converged on the site of the weekly Sunday concert at Pavlovsk Park; during the intermission the demonstrators began to shout antiwar slogans and call for a constituent assembly. A. I. Novikov's denunciation of government incompetence was cut short by the arrival of the police. A melee developed as concertgoers and demonstrators either fled the hall or fought back against the police. Only with great difficulty did Miliukov and several others manage to bundle the orator out safely, and then scatter to safety themselves.[18]

The Pavlovsk demonstration marked Miliukov's first and last foray into the realm of organized "street" protest. This was decidedly not his milieu; in the memoirs, his distaste for the incident is palpable. Many of the participants considered the protest a success, drawing as it did such large numbers willing to demonstrate publicly for peace and a constituent assembly. Miliukov, however, termed it a "frivolous gesture."[19] In his opinion, the second congress of the Union of Unions, hastily assembled in Moscow on May 24–26, was a more genuine and effective expression of national outrage.

The second congress, numbering eighty delegates and chaired again by Miliukov, was radically inclined. Government actions taken on the eve of the congress heightened the atmosphere. First, details were intentionally leaked to the press about the proposed form of the representative body promised in the February 18 rescript. Referred to as the "Bulygin duma," after Minister of Internal Affairs A. G. Bulygin, who chaired the commission drafting the plan, it was to be only a consultative body and elected by an indirect and restricted franchise. Then, as if deliberately to undermine confidence in the government's good faith, on May 21 the appointment of the hated D. F. Trepov as assistant minister of internal affairs, with special police powers, was officially announced.[20]

Miliukov's anger and frustration at this juncture is reflected in his proposed response to the Tsushima debacle. He suggested that the Union of Unions direct an appeal to the people. The appeal was the most radical document he ever composed. The destruction of the Baltic fleet, he argued, impelled the nation to speak out and to act, for the question now before it was not only that of freedom, but of the future existence of the state itself.

> We talked while there was even a shadow of hope that [the authorities] would listen. Now this hope has vanished and we must seek another route. We must act, each as he can and according to his own political convictions. Do as you like, but act! All means are now legitimate against the terrible threat latent in the very fact of the continued existence of the present government.... We say use all forces, all means to eliminate immediately the plundering gang which has seized power. In its place put a Constituent assembly elected by the people ... so that it might, as soon as possible, put an end to the war and to the political regime which has held sway until now.[21]

By calling for popular installation of a constituent assembly by "all forces, all means," Miliukov had endorsed violence. Later, he would have preferred to forget composing such an appeal, though he never denied sharing the militant mood of the moment; the text was, he said, a "frank expression of the general feeling."[22] Several delegates in fact voiced moral reservations about the phrase "all means are now legitimate," but the appeal passed with only three dissenting votes.[23]

The next order of business concerned the sort of connection the Union of Unions congress wished to have with the much larger zemstvo congress meeting concurrently with it.[24] On the second day of deliberations the union delegates learned that the zemstvo congress proposed sending a petition to the tsar. The petition asked that he speedily summon representatives of the people to decide, in agreement with him, questions of war and peace and the future legal order of the state. Miliukov, on the grounds that any and all means had to be tried, supported this proposal, but a great many union delegates were outraged by anything as modest as a petition.[25] It became his difficult task to avert any resolution or gesture so hostile as to preclude future cooperation between zemtsy and the Union of Unions. He carefully presided over a series of votes whereby the delegates decided not to express solidarity with the zemtsy of the coalition congress, but also decided against issuing a statement condemning its actions. Summarizing the decisions of the Union congress a short time later, Miliukov somewhat disingenuously characterized its position toward the actions of the zemtsy as one of "benevolent neutrality." The unions appreciated that they were all working for the same goals, he declared, even if their methods differed.[26]

The attitude of the Union of Unions toward the zemstvo coalition congress was more hostile than neutral, but Miliukov nonetheless was pleased with the results of the second congress. Not only had the Union of Unions not split with the zemtsy, it had also, as he hoped, emerged from the congress with greater independence for its constituent parts: delegates had approved statutes curtailing the radical-dominated central bureau's scope of activity.[27] It therefore still seemed to Miliukov, in late May, that moderates and leftists could continue to work together, and that the united front would be preserved. As he wrote Struve after the second congress:

> A left center stands out in the Union of Unions, and my endeavors—not entirely fruitless—have been directed at ensuring that it all the same be a *center*, and not a new variant of the Petersburg group. The business is very difficult: I even thought, at first, hopeless. But now I'm beginning to think differently. The "SDs" have helped with their stupidities and secessions, and the "SRs" are behaving very intelligently and not hindering business. The Petersburg and Moscow loudmouths [*krikuny*] are losing a little of their influence and discrediting themselves among their own supporters.[28]

At the height of his radicalism, Miliukov saw his position as a left centrist one, and his role as anchoring the Union of Unions there, to preserve links between moderates and radicals.

At the second congress, he had demonstrated his skills in managing a volatile political assembly. Nonetheless, his influence in the Union of Unions began to decline even as it became the largest political organization in the country and assumed greater prominence in the public eye. The radicalization of the union movement continued even as he himself began to check his position. The Petersburg group of liberationists, he told Struve, did not really want him as a part of their group: the republicans considered his line too moderate. For his part, Miliukov had gradually come to the conclusion that "our republicans do more shouting and noise-making than seeing to business."[29]

Publicly, he continued to defend the leftists and left positions against attack, as in his spirited justification of the left's inclination to boycott elections to the Bulygin Duma. In his article "To vote or not to vote?" he declared (mistakenly) that not a single "left" party believed in an *immediate* social revolution.[30] Miliukov was clearly reluctant to criticize the Social Democrats publicly, but he also continued to cherish illusions about their "reasonableness" for a long time. He remained convinced that they would come to appreciate the folly of their rhetoric and their demands and modify them accordingly. He also distinguished between the extremism of their leaders and the pragmatism of the party rank and file. In autumn 1904 he had advised Struve not to worry about the Social Democrats. "The stupidity and naïveté of the people from *Iskra* are not worth paying attention to; the party itself is greater and higher than its spokesmen, who have given themselves over to intrigue [*politikantstvo*]."[31] In June 1905 he began rethinking his attitude toward the revolutionary Marxists for several reasons.

First, the positions taken at the third congress of the Russian Social Democratic Workers' Party in London in April 1905 gradually became known to liberationists, and could scarcely be taken as a sign of growing moderation.[32] The order of the day, the congress held, was organization of an armed uprising. By early summer a number of prominent liberals were losing faith in the possibility of working with the Social Democrats even for short-term goals. Aleksandr Kornilov, for example, told Struve that the Social Democrats were bewitched by the idea of an immediate social revolution. "I am convinced that if the zemtsy managed to obtain the most liberal and democratic constitution, guaranteeing the possibility of a legal fight for achieving social-democratic ideals, the revolutionaries would be most displeased. Thinking this way, I am increasingly convinced that there can be no alliance between them and liberals at the present time."[33]

What brought home to Miliukov the irreconcilability of liberals and revolutionaries was his speaking tour of provincial Russia. In May and June he traveled to a number of cities to promote constitutional ideas and the necessity of cooperation between moderates and those further to the left.[34] No texts of these speeches exist, but he apparently took the historical line so effective in his American lectures, one that legitimized constitutionalism by showing the "borrowed" nature of autocracy, and at the same time legitimized Russian liberalism by arguing for its classless nature and commitment to social reform. He also warned against pinning hope on the tsar's being won over to constitutional principles.[35]

Public lecturing was not like talking to college classes or American clubs, Miliukov discovered, but he soon learned how to speak before large audiences of varying educational levels and political sympathies. He was not a speaker able to play upon the emotions; clear reason, aimed at persuading rather than captivating an audience, was his style.[36] Nonetheless, his lectures drew large crowds and were regarded by the organizers as an enormous success.[37]

Debate attending his lectures, especially as he moved further south, gave him his first direct experience of socialist perspectives outside the capitals. In Kharkov, he and his opponents argued furiously through the night, "parting exhausted but not reconciled at the first rays of the rising sun." Miliukov discovered in his Social Democratic opponents a clearly defined and coherent perspective on the revolution utterly at odds with his own conciliatory intentions. They were confident that the proletariat was not, as he still believed, primarily interested in economic and professional betterment, and that only the proletariat could make and lead the revolution. By their logic, no matter how far to the left the liberals moved, they could never be anything but "bourgeois," acting on their class interests and betraying the interests of the working class; no sort of compromise or agreement was possible. The extent of the gulf dividing Social Democrats from moderate socialists and liberals was not wholly apparent in summer 1905. All the same, Miliukov later wrote, "the more clear and comprehensible all this became, the more my hopes for an agreement between constitutionalists and revolutionaries faded away."[38]

It was not simply fighting words but violent events that caused Miliukov to rethink some of his positions in June 1905. After Tsushima a new wave of strikes commenced in Russia proper, culminating in a near-general strike and armed clashes in Odessa in mid-June. The mutiny on the battleship *Potemkin* aggravated disorders in Odessa, with some two thousand killed in street-fighting.[39] This was violence on a frightening scale, yet the *Potemkin* mutiny only encouraged Social Democrats in their hopes for a possible armed uprising. At the same time, Socialist Revolutionaries were inflaming peasant passions in the countryside with their propaganda efforts. In early July Miliukov wrote in *Osvobozhdenie* that "the country is not on the brink of anarchy, as was often said in the past, but in anarchy itself."[40]

By the time of the third congress of the Union of Unions, held July 1–3, Miliukov had changed his mind about participation in the Bulygin Duma, belatedly adopting the position held by most of his zemstvo friends. Whatever its deficiencies, he now felt it was too good an opportunity to let slip. Moreover, if all progressives boycotted the Duma, it would be wholly dominated by conservative landed gentry. The congress majority did not, however, share his views. Nine unions voted to boycott elections to the Duma, with three unions voting in favor of participation and four abstaining. The vote was sufficiently divided to allow Miliukov some hope for mitigating or reversing the decision subsequently, but it nonetheless represented a defeat of his position; in his memoirs, he inaccurately claimed not even to have been present at the third congress.[41]

Logically, the decision to participate in elections to the Bulygin Duma entailed differentiation of the opposition movement into distinct political parties, a step Miliukov now felt was warranted. He took an active role at the fifth congress of zemstvo-constitutionalists, held in Moscow in early July, which decided that the time had come to establish a constitutional-democratic party embracing a broad group of like-minded people. The difficult question was, whom did participants consider "like-minded"? Most constitutionalists agreed with Miliukov's declaration that the Union of Liberation would be an important constituent of the future party and in order to procure its members' support decided that the party program would include social and economic questions.[42] The congress selected a committee of twenty, including Miliukov, to work out agreements with representatives from other groups of similar orientation, and with them establish a temporary committee to organize the new party.[43]

The question of the zemstvo-constitutionalists' relationship to the radical Union of Unions was more problematic for a number of delegates, primarily because of the legitimation of violence implicit in its "Appeal to the People." Miliukov, in the name of the congress bureau, presented a report endorsing formal membership in the Union of Unions. He argued that the Union of Unions appeal to the people did not *oblige* anyone to use violence, and that the participation of zemstvo-constitutionalists in the Union of Unions was likely to moderate its position. The debate was stormy and his aplomb deserted him. Unwilling to let pass several denunciations of resort to physical violence, Miliukov noted with exasperation the pointlessness of organizing a political party during a revolution if its members were going to be so "delicate" about the use of force. The position was not only impractical, it was hypocritical: he asked if many zemtsy were not "counting on some one else's force, hoping in your hearts for a certain outcome but refusing to take part personally in acts of physical coercion?" He finally stung the gathering into a favorable vote by remarking that "after all I have heard here, I have doubts, not about whether or not we should join with the Union of Unions, but about whether or not the Union of Unions itself will refuse the honor of maintaining comradely relations with us."[44]

Uncertainties concerning the competence and composition of the Bulygin Duma, which complicated decisions about the desirability of participating in it, were settled within the month. Miliukov had an unexpected opportunity to follow their resolution. The tsar convened a special conference for this purpose at Peterhof on July 24; although the participants consisted largely of senior government officials and a number of grand dukes, the historian Vasilii Kliuchevskii was invited to attend. Kliuchevskii contacted Miliukov upon his arrival in Petersburg, asking his former student to help him orient himself politically. They met—for the first time in ten years—for detailed discussions every evening at Kliuchevskii's hotel. In this way Miliukov became privy to not only the machinations and compromises by which the Duma and the franchise were finally established, but to confidential papers as well.[45] When the final statutes were promulgated August 6, he had already prepared for publication a detailed analysis of the laws and two articles urging participation in the Duma.

Miliukov was quick to acknowledge all the shortcomings of the Duma statutes and electoral law, among them not simply the restrictive franchise and purely consultative voice, but also the absence of explicit guarantees of basic political freedoms.[46] He nonetheless felt that with the creation of a representative institution "the Rubicon has been crossed." Putting the Bulygin Duma in historical perspective, he demonstrated its superiority to abortive government projects for consultative assemblies worked out in 1863 and 1881: it was a permanent standing body, not an assembly occasionally convened to consider a specific project.[47] Second, he argued that the very existence of a representative institution would necessitate changes in the existing order. For example, the new law permitted some freedom of discussion during elections; this logically entailed the freedom to form parties, he reasoned, and the one and the other "presupposed" other civil liberties.[48] It would be up to the Duma to make the fullest use possible of the powers granted it. Failure to utilize what had been won, on the grounds that it didn't meet expectations, would be an unforgivable mistake.[49]

The left very likely would not have been dissuaded from boycott by Miliukov even if the government had not immediately demonstrated how ill-founded those assumptions were. In an "Open Letter to Professor P. N. Miliukov," for example, Leon Trotsky recalled the sorry fate of liberalism in Germany in 1848 when it sided with autocracy against the revolution, adding bitingly, "But history teaches the professors of history nothing."[50] Indeed, the laws of August 6 were accompanied by an order rescinding the freedom to discuss state reform which had been granted in February, and government officials took advantage of this order to try and silence leaders of the Union of Unions. On August 7, as Miliukov met in his apartment with members of the Union of Unions sympathetic to his views on the Bulygin Duma, police surrounded the building and took all those present at the meeting to the Kresty prison.[51]

The order of August 6 and the arrests of August 7 were remarkably stupid actions. Taking back the right to discuss reform even as a major concession was granted, and then arresting prominent citizens engaged in a private meeting gravely weakened confidence in the government's good faith. Constitutionalists, genuinely outraged by Miliukov's arrest, seized upon it as an opportunity to pressure the government by mobilizing both international and domestic public opinion in favor of his release.[52] Moreover, the government had unwittingly stifled the most moderating voice in the Union movement: with Miliukov and many of his principal supporters in prison, Union leaders who favored more militant tactics were free to concentrate their energies on organizing a general strike. The authorities soon realized that the arrests had been a mistake. Miliukov was treated with exceptional courtesy in prison and released after only a month. By that time, however, he had concluded that whatever influence he once exercised in the Union of Unions was gone; he ceased to participate on its central bureau, although he did not formally resign.[53]

While Miliukov was still in prison the task of organizing a party continued. The fourth and final congress of the Union of Liberation met August 23–24 and agreed on the "transition of the Union of Liberation from a clandestine society to an open political party in the European sense of the word," one which would still strive to unite as many people as possible. A committee was selected to cooperate with the committee selected by the zemstvo-constitutionalists in working out a program for the future "Constitutional Democratic Party" and organizing a founding congress. Finally, the congress crossed its own Rubicon by recommending that its members participate in the Bulygin Duma, but only in order to use the Duma to fight for "constitutional freedoms and institutions on a democratic foundation."[54]

Miliukov was released from prison two weeks after the Union of Liberation congress to find that the general mood had again changed dramatically. Promulgation of the laws of August 6 had produced a temporary lull in the country, during which time peace was formally concluded with Japan. It was at this moment that the government granted a concession that backfired spectacularly: restoration of autonomy to Russia's institutions of higher learning. With universities now outside police control, students on many campuses took advantage of the situation by throwing open halls and classrooms for political meetings. A stinging tide of popular frustration was released as thousands of people flocked to campuses to hear and give speeches, hold meetings, and issue resolutions. Daily accounts of meetings all over the country competed for space on the pages of the press with other reports confirming the breakdown of order throughout empire. The police seemed incapable of dealing with a rising tide of crime or of preventing terrorist attacks against themselves and government officials. The strike movement resumed and gained momentum. In the countryside, where the harvest was poor, peasant disorders began to assume alarming proportions. It was in this feverish atmosphere that the representatives selected by the zemstvo-constitutionalists and Union of Liberation worked to organize the Constitutional Democratic Party.[55]

The Formation of Parties

The elliptical record of the organizing committee's ten meetings between September 9 and October 6 reveals that the participants disagreed on the nature and goals of the party they were to establish.[56] The most substantive differences concerned agrarian issues, with some participants urging provisions on a right to land and a "labor norm," while others insisted that the party not lose sight of landowners' interests. Miliukov expended considerable effort trying to reconcile these views, reminding the group of the sort of party whose program they were drafting. "We are forgetting our goal. . . . This is not the peasant union or a landowners' party. We must take a middle line. Expropriation is possible, but it must not be spelled out too precisely."[57]

In the end, the agrarian section did not mention a right to land or set ownership norms, but did condone compulsory expropriation of private land, when necessary and with compensation. This compromise provision would long remain the most controversial element in the Constitutional Democratic program.

Organizational matters, including creation of a party press, which would clearly be crucial in the elections, also occupied a great deal of the committee's time. Miliukov was commissioned with establishing a party paper in St. Petersburg, while Dmitrii Shakhovskoi and several others would see to provincial organs and organize a press bureau.[58] The committee also set about establishing local party branches, many of them to be formed from existing groups of liberationists. They were to convene meetings to discuss the proposed party platform and elect delegates to the party founding congress, making an effort to attract to these meetings and elect as delegates representatives of the laboring population, especially peasants. From the outset, the founders intended that the Constitutional Democratic Party be "democratic" in composition as well as in its program.[59]

The founding congress was scheduled to open October 12 in Moscow, but by that date the railroad strike launched by the Central Bureau of the Railway Union had halted all service to the city. By October 16 every line in the empire was affected and workers, white-collar employees and professionals in numerous state and private enterprises were striking as well: factories, shops, city utilities, and even theaters closed. The party organizers realized that most delegates outside Moscow would be unable to attend the congress, making its authority somewhat suspect, but considered it crucial to be able to respond to these unprecedented developments. They decided to proceed as planned, and on October 12 eighty delegates, about 40 percent of those originally anticipated, gathered in the candle-lit mansion of Pavel Dolgorukov to found Russia's first open political party.[60]

Miliukov delivered the keynote address. That the organizers selected Miliukov, rather than more senior founders such as Petrunkevich or Shakhovskoi, or the popular and fiery orator Fedor Rodichev, is testimony in part to his still-valued role as mediator between liberals and socialists. Not a zemstvo man, and until recently titular head of the Union movement, Miliukov symbolized the organizers' desire to retain the "democratic" intelligentsia members of the Union of Liberation in the new party. Clearly, however, Miliukov was chosen, as well, not only because his colleagues had confidence in his ability to present a clearly reasoned and persuasive speech but because he had become one of the dominant members of the constitutionalist group. Since the text of his speech was soon disseminated all over Russia in brochures, it became the official party gloss on its founding.

His speech had two aims: to characterize the new party, in terms of goals, composition, and tactics, and, in the face of leftist criticism about splitting the opposition, to justify its creation.[61] He therefore represented the Constitutional Democratic Party as the natural product of the liberation movement and its principal components outside the organized socialist parties, the "liberationists" and the zemstvo-constitutionalists. Alien to class interests, they resembled the "social reformist" groups of Western Europe and also stood squarely within the tradition of the Russian intelligentsia.[62] Now that they had received, through creation of the Bulygin Duma, the possibility of using parliamentary means, it was time to create an open party.

It was to be a mass political party, capable of uniting diverse views. At the same time, certain boundaries had to be acknowledged. The new party was not against preservation of the integrity of the Russian state and private property, as critics to the right insisted, but it opposed completely "bureaucratic centralism and Manchesterism" (that is, laissez-faire liberalism).[63] The boundary to the right of the Constitutional Democrats began where groups spoke in the name of "the narrow class interests of Russian agrarians and industrialists" at the expense of the interests of the laboring classes. The boundary to the left was different: here were not opponents but "allies." Minimizing their differences without denying their existence, Miliukov explained that the Constitutional Democrats did not support the lefts' demands for a democratic republic and socialization of the means of production—some because they did not consider them desirable and others because they did not consider them practical. But so long as supporters of these two demands did not attempt to include them in the new party's program, a split could be avoided and they could all work together for common short-term goals.[64]

The task of the new party was to transform the ideals of the intelligentsia into realizable demands. Such a task, Miliukov acknowledged, was not easy to appreciate for Russians, as yet unfamiliar with practical politics; many would criticize the party for not going far enough. "And yet," as he insisted, "our program is, indisputably, the most left of all those proclaimed by Western European groups analogous to us."[65]

The general strike had actually made the organizers' task at the congress easier, since it meant the majority of more radical liberationists from St. Petersburg could not be present. The detailed party program was accepted with little dispute, the exception being the point on women's suffrage. Miliukov was among those who felt it inexpedient to insist on immediate extension of the vote to women, arguing that it would cost the party peasant votes. To his chagrin, and the amusement of those present, his fiercest opponent turned out to be his wife. Anna Sergeevna was a founder of the League for Women's Equality, established in May 1905, and did not share her husband's view that a commitment to genuinely universal suffrage could be postponed out of tactical considerations. Miliukov was defeated by a narrow margin; afterwards he angrily reproached Iosif Gessen and Vladimir Nabokov, who had stepped out to investigate the mood on the street, for not being present during the voting. He did, however, manage to secure a clause that left support of women's suffrage up to individual party members.[66]

The congress approved party organizational statutes and elected a temporary central committee of thirty members. It was understood that all these decisions were subject to ratification by a second, more representative party congress, to be convened as soon as possible. The congress also issued two resolutions on subjects requiring immediate comment: the general strike and the October Manifesto. On October 14 the Constitutional Democratic Party declared its solidarity with what it identified as the goals of the general strike: liberty, a constituent assembly elected by universal suffrage, and a political amnesty. Whatever the strike's outcome, the resolution read, the party offered its sympathy and "all possible support" for the people's demands and the people's liberation.[67] At the least, verbal support for the strike was a political necessity for a party with mass aspirations, but the resolution also reflected the real sentiment of the congress participants, most of whom were deeply impressed by the organization and self-discipline of the strikers. They were, Miliukov later wrote, "the heroes of the day."[68]

The second resolution gave the party's response to the October Manifesto, news of which reached the stunned congress on October 17, when a reporter from the liberal paper *Russkie vedomosti* burst in on its evening session waving the still-damp proof sheet of the text. The October Manifesto went far beyond the concessions of the Bulygin arrangement in its promises to introduce basic civil liberties, make the Duma a legislative rather than consultative body, and broaden the electoral franchise. Most of those present hailed the October Manifesto with a joy singularly lacking in Miliukov's response. Vasilii Maklakov later recalled Miliukov's initial reaction to the Manifesto, during a celebratory banquet for the new party at the Literary Circle. "Miliukov decided to introduce a serious note into the gaiety. He began with the joking question, 'Has it been resolved whether to criticize the Manifesto?' and embarked on his criticism of it, with his polemical talent and manner. He dwelt not only on what was written in it, but on what it failed to mention; he explained the silences, denounced, established guilt, and concluded his demolition of the Manifesto with the words, 'Nothing has changed; the war continues.'"[69]

By his own account, Miliukov did not know if the new concessions represented "another cunning ruse or delay, or genuinely serious intentions"; certainly, the manifesto's far-reaching promises were couched in ambiguous, even "evasive" terms familiar from previous imperial acts and susceptible to a variety of interpretations.[70] At any rate, he was not inclined to assume the government's good faith. Here, Miliukov's own experience with the Bulygin acts probably played their part. He had obviously been mistaken in August when he was willing to accept the consultative duma then proffered. He would not, a second time, settle for too little too soon.

The majority of the delegates to the congress came to share his skepticism. The party's October 18 resolution on the Manifesto spelled out its insufficiencies and called upon the government to prove its sincerity by acting to fulfill its promises immediately: introduce civil liberties, hold fully democratic elections to a constituent assembly, and grant a complete amnesty to political and religious prisoners.[71]

A paramount concern of the new liberal party was clarification of its relations with other parts of the liberation movement and its attitude toward the government. The process of differentiation and self-definition took place in the midst of disorder and violence, for the October Manifesto did not immediately pacify the country in the way anticipated. In the two-and-one-half months following the Manifesto's promulgation Russia experienced abortive armed uprisings, mutinies in the armed forces, terrorist bombings, bloody pogroms, and the most serious agrarian unrest since the peasant rebellions of the late eighteenth century. After initial vacillation, the government answered violence in kind, in December shelling the Moscow uprising into submission and sending into troubled areas military punitive expeditions to restore order which claimed thousands of lives. It is difficult to exaggerate the degree to which the resort to violence, on the right as well as on the left, from above as well as below, exacerbated differences and harmed prospects for compromise and cooperation.

The confusion and tragedy of these months, so crucial to the ultimate fate of the new order promised in the Manifesto, both fueled and were compounded by the ingrained mistrust various groups inside and outside government harbored toward one another. Although Miliukov and most of the Constitutional Democrats were wont to stick to the old dichotomy of "government" versus "society" (*obshchestvo*), neither of these were monolithic. Thus the liberals mistakenly anticipated that cooperation with those to their left would continue during transition to the new order. They also expected more in the way of concessions from Sergei Witte, the new premier, than he could deliver, failing to take into account obstacles at the court and in the bureaucracy with which he had to contend. In like fashion, Witte and other senior officials failed to appreciate fully the popular pressures dictating certain Kadet positions, as well as the differences between the liberals and revolutionaries. They blamed the Kadets for not stemming the revolutionary impetus, as if, Miliukov wrathfully wrote, "the Russian revolutionary movement could be stopped by Russian 'liberals.'"[72]

In weeks and months following promulgation of the October Manifesto the united opposition splintered into a host of new parties and groups. The formal divide to the Constitutional Democrats' right was, as Miliukov's congress speech had suggested, the most clear-cut and least regretted. Its outlines had been apparent since the September zemstvo and municipal council congress held in Moscow, which revealed that attitudes toward the nationalities question, as much as differences over agrarian issues and the nature of the franchise, distinguished more conservative delegates from the majority. Aleksandr Guchkov had argued heatedly with Miliukov over the proposal that Poland and other regions should be granted autonomy, a step Guchkov saw as prejudicial to the future of the empire and which Miliukov now strongly defended.[73]

It came as no surprise that Guchkov, with Count Petr Geiden, Dmitrii Shipov, and others, quickly established a loosely knit constitutional party of liberal-conservative coloration. As implied in its name, the Union of 17 October (called the Octobrists, for short) welcomed the October Manifesto as the sufficient foundation of a new, rule-of-law state that would implement needed reforms, pledging to support and aid the government in its reform efforts.[74] Miliukov welcomed creation of the Octobrists. He had long urged that Shipov and "Slavophiles" leave the liberation movement; defection of the right flank of zemstvo-constitutionalists would promote greater cohesion and self-definition among the Constitutional Democrats.[75]

Relations with the left were something Miliukov and most of the party leadership regarded as more important, and found far more vexing. Hopes were soon dispelled that the positions adopted at the first congress would attract the left liberationists to the party. At the end of October, the entire group of Moscow liberationists publicly declined to become Constitutional Democrats. The "Big Group" in Petersburg acted no less decisively; E. D. Kuskova, V. Ia. Bogucharskii, S. N. Prokopovich, and V. V. Khizhniakov—all elected in absentia to the central committee—refused to enter the party.[76] Miliukov took part, with Iosif Gessen, in a meeting between party leaders and delegates from the "liberationist secessionists." The mood of the meeting was passionate and acrimonious, Gessen recalled, in part because of Miliukov, whose "tutelage was resented." Miliukov later acknowledged that the Petersburgers "blamed me personally for what could be considered the rightward shift of the party."[77]

The defections to the left were fairly small numerically, though of significance, since the polemics of their former allies, along with vituperative attacks of the Social Democratic press, helped discredit the Kadets (the nickname given the new party by Annenskii) in popular eyes. Critics on the left—including Miliukov's old comrades from *Russkoe bogatstvo*—blamed the Kadets for splitting the opposition, consistently characterized them as "bourgeois" and the defenders of class interests, and reminded readers that

Russian liberalism had always, historically, failed to stand fast.[78] Nonetheless, the Kadets did not give up their efforts to woo unaffiliated socialists, those whom Terence Emmons refers to as "the non-sectarian left."[79]

The sticky problem of the attitude to be taken toward the government was perhaps the least satisfactorily resolved. In the days immediately following issue of the October Manifesto, Witte hoped to restore order by winning public confidence in his government rather than by resort to force. To this end, several concessions were made to popular demands, among them grant on October 21 of a partial amnesty. He also approached a number of prominent liberals and moderates to explore ways by which he could secure their support. Fedor Kokoshkin, G. E. L'vov, and F. A. Golovin, representing the bureau of zemstvo and municipal council congresses, took an intransigent stance. They told the premier that convocation of a constituent assembly elected by four-tailed suffrage, introduction of civil liberties, and a complete political amnesty was the minimum acceptable for zemstvo bureau support of the new government. Witte obviously could not be expected to see this as a sign of willingness to work with him, but did not get much further with more moderate figures. His offers of ministerial portfolios to Dmitrii Shipov, Aleksandr Guchkov, and M. A. Stakhovich were politely refused, largely due to their concern about being mere figureheads holding minor positions in a cabinet dominated by bureaucrats.[80]

Miliukov's own attitude toward Witte and the possibility of working with the government was by no means straightforward. On the one hand, he made no effort to moderate the stance of the congress bureau delegation. On the other, when Miliukov had an opportunity to speak with Witte several days later, he displayed a rather different take on what the government should do to attract public support. His behavior at that meeting demonstrated the curious mixture of doctrinairism and practicality so typical of him at this time.[81]

Miliukov told Witte that confidence in the government's intentions could only be earned by action. Rather than waiting for society's cooperation, he recommended forming a working cabinet of decent bureaucrats who were not discredited in the public's eyes and issuing reforms. Miliukov continued that he would offer his advice as a private person, which allowed him to admit that the constitutional procedure insisted upon by his party was cumbersome, time-consuming, and risky. The best course would be for the government to issue immediately a constitution liberal enough to satisfy society at large; he recommended taking Belgium or Bulgaria as models. No less revealing was Miliukov's response to Witte's objection that the public would no longer be satisfied by a constitution handed down from above. Miliukov reassured him, "The public would not be satisfied primarily because it does not believe in the possibility of receiving such a liberal constitution from the bureaucracy. If it received one, it would make noise for a while and then calm down."[82] What was important, in his opinion, was the grant of a constitution that was openly acknowledged *as* a constitution, not where it came from. Once Witte made it clear that the tsar would not permit him to use the word "constitution," Miliukov told him any further discussion was fruitless: "I cannot give you any sort of practical [*del' nyi*] advice."[83]

Witte negotiated a mere nine days before giving up in disgust. By that time, however, many Kadets had had opportunity to wonder whether they had been precipitate in rejecting the premier's overtures. Such a sensibility, still by no means articulate or sure, permeated the sessions of the last ever congress of zemstvo and municipal council representatives, held in Moscow on November 6–13. Miliukov, on the bureau of the Kadet-dominated congress, helped elaborate a set of resolutions widely interpreted as resolutions of the party itself. The main resolution demanded that the government immediately convoke an assembly elected by universal suffrage "for drawing up, with the confirmation of the sovereign, a constitution of the Russian empire," a formula meant to dispel the impression that the Kadets were trying to establish a republic.[84] By also dropping the demand for a constituent assembly, Miliukov later wrote, the Kadets provided the first formulation of "our parting of the ways with the left parties." These gestures were intended to facilitate an agreement with the government, should negotiations be resumed.[85] In a less conciliatory spirit, however, the congress also called for revocation of emergency legislation, abolition of the death penalty, political amnesty, and a purge of the administration. It also rejected overwhelmingly Guchkov's proposal that the demand for abolition of the death penalty include a condemnation of violence as a means of political struggle.[86]

In his memoirs Miliukov took credit for the resolutions as "a personal success in my efforts to make the party's tactics more realistic," admitting that this success was only partial: his own opinions were not yet "sufficiently realistic." He revealed his doubts at the time about Witte's likely response to the congress by strongly opposing the decision to send a delegation to the premier with a copy of its resolutions. The support being offered Witte was too conditional, he thought, and coming rather too late; he correctly predicted a humiliating rebuff.[87]

Hopes that government and society could begin to work together rapidly receded in November. Unrest in the armed forces continued, and rural disorders became more widespread and violent. In late October the Petersburg Soviet voted to introduce the eight-hour workday in all factories "by revolutionary means." This conflict merged into the general strike called by the Soviet on November 1, which was soon followed by a strike of postal and telegraph workers in mid-November. Kadet leaders were alarmed by these developments, but unsure how to respond. The sketchy record of central committee meetings shows that they hoped to use their program to wean people away from the radicals, but still felt that it was not the time to engage in a struggle against the left.[88]

The question became more urgent after December 2 when the Petersburg Soviet issued its "Financial Manifesto," calling upon the population not to make payments to the government, and to withdraw all deposits from banks in gold. The next day the government arrested the Executive Committee of the Petersburg Soviet and two hundred of its deputies, causing that body to issue a call for another general strike to begin December 8. The Moscow Soviet went further, on December 6 appealing to workers to begin a general strike the following day which would overthrow the government.

Miliukov provided a running, if interrupted, commentary on these events on the pages of his first paper, coedited with Iosif Gessen. It was a difficult moment to be learning the newspaper trade. Constant labor strikes and fast-breaking news impelled the editors to labor all night over issues, even setting type themselves. Moreover, Miliukov found it hard—"almost impossible"—to strike the right note, given the complex, passionate currents swirling through the capital. He wanted to call the paper *Mir* (Peace), he wrote a friend in Moscow, but "Not a hope! 'Struggle' might just be possible, but 'Peace'—that is treachery, betrayal!"[89] Then, there was the matter of the censorship. *Narodnaia svoboda* (Popular freedom), as the paper was finally called, appeared December 1 and was suppressed after its second issue for printing the financial manifesto of the Petersburg Soviet. It reappeared several days later under the name *Svobodnyi narod*; six issues came out under this title before the censors closed it on December 20 for an article by Petr Struve.[90]

Difficulties notwithstanding, in the first issues of his liberal daily Miliukov tried to identify the nature of the current crisis and what must be done in order to save the revolution from itself. "Russia is living through one of the most decisive moments of its history," he wrote. "The old order is rapidly crumbling, while no new order has as yet been created. The government and the revolution are at loggerheads, and seemingly neither can control a revolutionary movement becoming ever more elemental and destructive."

In his reading, the government was obviously "organically incapable" of meeting popular demands half-way. It simply had not learned that it is not concessions per se that harm monarchy, but tardy, grudging, insincere concessions. Nor did it appreciate that a return to the old "home remedy" of repression could no longer work. He advised this government to "retire!"[91]

Embarking on a critique of the revolutionary parties required more care and tact, since it could be misconstrued as an attack on the revolution itself. There could be no talk, Miliukov said, of equating the extremes of the government with those of the revolutionaries. But it wasn't necessary to deify revolution, or forget that it is only a means of struggle, not an end in itself. Revolutionaries were overestimating their strength when they set such goals as the immediate realization of a democratic republic. By too easily resorting to extreme methods of struggle, they risked alienating the nonrevolutionary progressives and provoking reaction.[92]

The only hope Miliukov saw was in the "conscious elements" who respected but did not make a fetish of revolution. He appealed to them to organize to preserve what the revolution had already won, to remember that all creative revolutionary forces should be directed to creation of new rights protected by new law, "not to the perpetuation of the revolution."[93] On December 8, with the general strike well under way in Moscow, his plea became more urgent. The proletariat was already exhausted by its previous struggles. An uprising could turn into a "slaughterhouse." Before making a decision that could be fatal for the whole course of the liberation movement, he wrote, "I entreat all those on whom the decision depends to reconsider and to stop before it is too late."[94]

The first major clashes occurred on December 9. Barricades went up in the streets, and the government began to use artillery. On December 14 Miliukov wrote, "In the ancient capital of Russia unbelievable events are taking place. Moscow is being bombarded by cannon. They are bombarding with a fury, with a persistence, with an accuracy, with which the Japanese positions were never favored."[95] By the time the insurrectionists conceded defeat and called an end to the strike, 1,059 Muscovites had been killed and many hundreds arrested.[96] Later, Miliukov identified the Moscow uprising as the turning point in the struggle for political liberty, primarily because it marked a final tactical split between the liberals and revolutionaries: "The curve of success in the struggle against the government declined from this point."[97]

Preparing for a Parliament

Three weeks after the crushing of the uprising, the second Kadet party congress convened in St. Petersburg in a sober mood. Miliukov and members of the central committee approached the congress with some trepidation; incomplete representation at the first congress had masked many internal differences that would now be aired. Miliukov also worried that there might be considerable sentiment in favor of joining the left's boycott of the upcoming elections.[98] In his opening report to the congress, he urged participation in the elections as a necessity for a parliamentary party, stressing how crucial it was for organizational purposes and dissemination of its message to the population. And even if the Constitutional Democrats won only a few seats in the Duma, they could exercise moral influence as a political opposition.

Much to his relief, virtually all the delegates endorsed participating in both the elections and the Duma itself. Far more difficult was agreement on precisely what they should do in the Duma, an issue that concerned not only programmatic goals but also differing conceptions of the party's role and mandate. Some felt they ought to enter the Duma only to broaden its franchise so that it could be dissolved and replaced by a genuinely representative institution. Fedor Kokoshkin presented the views of the central committee in a report which held that doing real work was imperative: prompt and substantive social and political reforms were necessary "in order to prevent collapse of the country into a state of complete anarchy."[99]

The contradictory votes on these questions revealed not only substantive differences among delegates, but uncertainties within individuals themselves.[100] The congress voted unanimously that it was not necessary to introduce "organic work" into the Duma, as in a normal institution, but also voted that it was necessary to pass urgent reforms for the pacification of the country. The decisions on tactics revealed the same contradictory impulses. Maksim Vinaver pointed out that the party had no clear-cut line of tactics, which invited confusion from both the right and the left. He recommended that it state openly that revolutionary means were not its own, even as he proclaimed that the party did not condemn revolutionary tactics used by others and urged that the party try to establish blocs with "friends on the left." Miliukov heartily endorsed this equivocal position, and it passed with a majority.[101]

Proceeding to a discussion of the party program approved in October, the congress actually introduced very few modifications. One was the decision to add the words the "Party of Popular Freedom" to the party's name, since this was more comprehensible to the people than the loanwords "Constitutional Democratic." The clause making women's suffrage a matter of individual choice, backed by Petr Struve and Miliukov, was defeated by a narrow margin (202–198).[102] The agrarian points of the program provoked two days of furious debate, primarily over the question of compulsory expropriation. Miliukov appealed to the "good sense of the congress," asking that it not adopt any categorical formulas that would force a schism in the party; delegates decided to make only one relatively minor change.[103]

The electoral campaign for the Duma, for which the Kadets organized like no other party, dominated January, February, and most of March. Although Miliukov was disqualified from running in the election—he was under litigation for publishing the Petersburg Soviet's financial manifesto in the short-lived *Narodnaia svoboda*—he nonetheless took active part in the campaign. He assisted V. A. Maklakov in his course for training party orators, spoke at numerous election meetings in Petersburg, and campaigned actively on behalf of the party in the provinces, as part of its speakers' bureau. The Kadets often found themselves forced to defend their program from withering attacks by Social Democrats, who in spite of their boycott of the elections, were happy to make use of the liberals' meetings to expound their own position and disrupt the Kadet campaign.[104]

By the time the campaign was in full swing Miliukov had acquired a vehicle for the effort in political persuasion and instruction that he saw as a critical part of the party's mission. *Rech'* (Speech) began appearing February 23, 1906. While it was not the official party organ, that role belonging to the weekly *Vestnik partii narodnoi svobody*, it was looked upon as the Petersburg voice of the Kadets.[105] Miliukov's coeditor was again Iosif Gessen, and their assistant, M. I Ganfman; Petrunkevich became treasurer and Nabokov was on its board. *Rech'* flourished, thanks to talented writers, a reputation for reliable reporting, and a competent business side. Miliukov wrote almost daily editorials—as well as composing all manner of articles, news stories, even chess problems, as the need arose—so that in the pages of *Rech'* it is possible to follow his thoughts on the campaign and the First Duma, as well as to reconstruct his developing sense of what Russian constitutionalism should, and might, be.

Despite government harassment of the party and interference with electoral campaigns in general, by mid-March it became clear that the Kadets were going to win big. Not surprisingly, their greatest victory came in the cities—26 of the 28 deputies to the Duma elected in special municipal elections were Kadets—but they also fared well in many of the provinces. Overall, the party had about 130 of 448 deputies from European Russia, which made them the largest single group in the Duma.[106] The Kadets' success was due in part to the left parties' boycott of the elections, but their strong showing in Russia's first-ever national elections also testified to the appeal of their program: some 100,000 people joined the party in spring 1906.[107]

The stunning victory administered a huge boost to party spirits and self-esteem, even as it complicated the question of how the Kadets were to behave in the Duma—theirs was the anomalous position of being both the "oppositional" party *and* the "majority" party. Although they repeatedly reminded themselves and the Russian public that they could not claim to "speak for the people," given the restricted franchise and the circumstance of the left boycott, many activists and elected deputies indeed interpreted their victory as a mandate to express the popular will.[108] The victory also increased party members' sense of power relative to that of the government. As one speaker after another declared at the third party congress, in April of 1906, the Kadets could and must take on the government.[109]

Although Miliukov, too, saw their victory as proof of the country's support, he did not conclude that the party should press confrontation in the Duma itself.[110] For one thing, unlike many of his fellow party members, he was not convinced that the government would not be able to fight the Duma. Conversely, he was more optimistic about the possibility of achieving significant reform through the Duma.[111] In his tactical report to the third congress he therefore stressed that the party had to pick its battles with care. By selecting issues that were within their competence and of deep interest to the people, Kadet deputies could maximize chances for success while ensuring that the whole onus fell on the government in the event of serious conflict. Accordingly, Miliukov ruled out efforts to overturn or ignore the Duma and State Council Charter issued on February 20, which circumscribed the representatives' sphere of action. At the same time, he argued that the Charter was not an insuperable obstacle to reform, since it left introduction of laws on civil liberties, broadening of the franchise, and agrarian matters within the competence of the Duma.[112]

Did electors want the party to adopt a parliamentary or revolutionary form of action? "Is the revolution over," Miliukov asked the congress, "or does it continue?" Since the party was in two minds about the answer, it should not try to base its tactics on the putative "mood" of the country but rather on a short-term, pragmatic strategy that could be altered or discarded as circumstances changed.[113]

Passionate debate over the course of two sessions showed how little this report pleased many of the delegates. There was talk of a failure to heed principles, and condemnation of calculating tactics as the product of a "cold mind" (*kholodnogo uma*). Opposition to his recommendations concerning the laws of February 20 was especially fierce, with many deputies showing themselves skeptical about the possibility of achieving anything within their confines. Deputies objected to behaving like "diplomats" when what was needed was boldness, principle, and plain-speaking: "We must be ready to die for liberty." Finally, many suggested that Miliukov and the central committee were simply out of touch with the popular mood. As one delegate put it, in answer to Miliukov's question about the mood of the country, "The country which *I* live in is revolutionary!"[114] Nonetheless, the diversity of opinions concerning what could and should be done prevented formation of a majority against the resolutions proposed by Miliukov and the central committee. The congress passed them all on its second day of sessions.[115]

As if more were needed to add to the militant mood, on the final day delegates learned that the draft of the Fundamental Laws, already familiar to the public, had been signed into law without any significant changes. This step by the government was a particular blow to Miliukov. He had predicated much of his tactical report on the possibility of achieving reform while still working within the legal confines established by the laws of February

20: the new Fundamental Laws, essentially a conservative constitution, now precluded the possibility of altering the franchise, limited the legislature's budgetary powers, and were not subject to amendment.[116] Miliukov denounced them as a fraud and "debasement of the worst part of the worst European constitutions," adding "now we have the right to be harsh!" The resolution he introduced on behalf of the central committee censuring the Fundamental Laws promised that "no obstacles created by the government" would prevent the legislature from fulfilling the people's wishes—a clear signal for conflict, but one many delegates still thought too weak.[117]

The brief and unhappy history of the First Duma, the "Duma of popular hopes," is well known. It lasted a mere seventy-two days, its activities being distinguished almost from the start by the provocative and unyielding stance of its deputies and the often equally provocative behavior of the government headed by new premier Ivan Goremykin (Witte was unceremoniously relieved of his position several weeks before the Duma convened). Contemporaries and historians have disagreed about the degree of culpability of various participants in the tragedy, with some inclined to blame the tsar and his ministers, others the intransigence of socialist deputies, and still others the Kadets' unwillingness to meet the government even half-way.[118]

Miliukov's own role in the First Duma, though frequently exaggerated, was substantial. There was no shortage of people—foreign observers, party members, government officials—who believed that though he was not a deputy, his was the dominant voice. Bernard Pares, an English specialist on Russia, maintained that Miliukov was the real leader of the House; present every day at the Taurida Palace to observe sessions and confer with his party's deputies, Miliukov directed the Duma "from the tea room."[119] Miliukov later noted this assertion wryly, pointing out "Not only could I not control the whole Duma but I could not even begin to control our own Duma faction in the Duma itself." His statement comes closer to the truth; Miliukov's dominant role in the Kadet central committee, along with the fact that many of the party's Duma deputies were his friends, did indeed give him great influence in the faction, but responsibility for Kadet tactics was not his alone, nor was his counsel always heeded. It was primarily Petrunkevich, Kokoshkin, Miliukov, and Maksim Vinaver, a talented courtroom lawyer and member of the party central committee, who worked out tactical lines on the spot. In particular, Miliukov claimed, he and Vinaver strove to reconcile conflicts between the Kadets and the left. In the first flush of victory the Kadets had believed they had a majority, but now realized that formation of a majority would require cooperation with the volatile Trudovik ("labor") group and the large "nonaligned" group of mostly peasant deputies, who together accounted for some two hundred votes.[120] If he really had been able to "direct" the Duma, Miliukov wrote, that direction would have consisted in "moderating the Duma's political temperament and increasing the government's political wisdom. But neither the one nor the other turned out to be possible, and especially not a combination of the two, either for myself or for anyone else."[121]

The difficulties entailed in fashioning tactics that would satisfy the militant mood of most Duma deputies (Kadets included), without needlessly offending the government or overstepping parliamentary constraints, are illustrated in the response to the "Speech from the Throne."[122] The text drafted by Miliukov, Kokoshkin, Vinaver, and three Trudovik deputies contained most of the Kadet program, which meant it included illegal demands—not precisely a statement designed to avoid conflict. The problem of competence was surmounted, Miliukov claimed, by the way the text divided its desiderata between "Duma intentions"—issues which the Duma had the authority to effect itself—and "requests" made of the sovereign power concerning issues lying outside the Duma's competence, such as abolition of the State Council. An examination of the text, however, shows that proper and illegal demands were jumbled up together, so that it not unnaturally struck the Council of Ministers as an effort by the Duma to arrogate executive authority.[123] The consequences were significant. On May 13 Goremykin gave a provocative speech to the Duma which rejected most of the demands in the address to the throne as "absolutely inadmissible." The Duma promptly responded with a vote of no confidence in the cabinet. Thus scarcely three weeks into the new legislature's first term, open hostility was declared and constructive work paralyzed.

At the same time, the Duma's address to the throne did not go nearly far enough in the eyes of most of the socialist intelligentsia, especially because it failed to include the demand for four-tailed suffrage. They blamed this omission on the majority party and launched a campaign against it, in mass meetings and articles denouncing the Kadets for breaking electoral promises and ignoring popular demands, and warning against further perfidies to be expected from the liberals.[124]

If Miliukov's efforts to ameliorate the atmosphere were not always as moderate as he imagined, they were at times effective. Frequently he was able to paper over differences between the Kadets and the Trudoviks, or forestall obstructive or unconstitutional steps contemplated by the latter; several times, thanks to the prestige he initially enjoyed among many Trudovik deputies, he was called upon to chair important joint sessions of the two parties' factions.[125] But his most powerful tool was his pen: Miliukov strove to explain and justify Duma actions to a confused population, to modify the extreme left and call the government to its senses, to combat calumnies against the Kadet party and, above all, to legitimize parliamentary life as the only sure, long-term solution for Russia's problems.

His hopes for the Duma were manifold. It would accomplish reform, necessary for the welfare of the people and for the salvation of the state, as the only means by which struggle could be directed into peaceful and constructive channels. Participation in elections and following the activities of the Duma would be a form of political education. It would teach the citizenry to appreciate the rule of law, while the liberties it procured for the people would gradually cause them to value these rights more than they now did. It would be able to effect changes in the unyielding peasant worldview against which every government blandishment or intellectual argument had proved powerless. It would moderate expectations and teach practicality to all segments of the population, and above all to the intelligentsia, as they learned the difference between utopian abstractions and real possibilities.[126]

Miliukov did not enumerate all these fruits of the Duma in any single piece; had he done so, he might have realized how very great his expectations were for a much circumscribed institution functioning in an unfamiliar and hostile environment. At the time, and later, Miliukov remained convinced that the external enemies of the Duma constituted the greatest obstacle to its effective functioning and the greatest danger to its continued existence. Continued left pressure on the Trudoviks made them more radical and increasingly less willing to cooperate with the Kadets, while it was apparent that right pressure for a dissolution of the Duma was mounting.

At his most polemical, Miliukov treated the government simply as the "common enemy" of all oppositional groups and of the people. It had to be defeated, power had to be wrested from it; the Duma's "blows" were gradually wearing it down.[127] In a more sober vein, however, Miliukov was concerned to point out to the government that its apparent doubts about the new order, its flirtation with reactionary enemies of the Duma, destroyed confidence in its good intentions and therefore also undermined the conviction that it was possible to achieve reform by legal and nonviolent means. When the government printed in its official organs telegrams from reactionary "Black Hundreds" groups demanding abolition of the Duma, when its generals and governors gave interviews to the foreign press hinting at imminent dissolution, the monarchy put itself at risk. It was precisely this wavering between cooperation and reaction which had destroyed Charles I and Louis XVI.[128]

The government also had to assume responsibility for the ways in which its inclination to stick by familiar and arbitrary means of dealing with dissent only perpetuated the old modes of thinking it was trying to combat. Miliukov held that much of the extremism and impracticality characteristic of Russian socialist ideas derived from their long confinement to closed, sectarian circles. Instead of understanding that freedom of the press exposed those ideas to critiques from many points of view, forcing socialists to defend themselves, take actual conditions into account, and become more moderate, the government's capricious censorship was once again driving the socialist press underground and in upon itself. In the same way, tutelary censorship on behalf of a society unaccustomed to freedom of speech would not teach the public to use that freedom wisely or inoculate it against the "poison of the printed page": "One is schooled to freedom only by practicing freedom."[129]

Miliukov spent just as much time trying to moderate the behavior of the far-left parties, most especially the Bolsheviks, toward the Duma and the Kadet faction. He took them to task for their inability to adapt to the new situation, to shed their devotion to conspiratorial tactics and utopian illusions. It was imperative that they realize discrediting the Duma and non-revolutionary progressives ultimately served the same end as the attacks of the Black Hundreds. He tried repeatedly to convince the Bolsheviks of the contradictions in their positions: at one and the same time they dismissed the Duma as lacking real power, reviled it for refusing to effect sweeping reforms, and deprived it of the popular support necessary to make it strong. "In the name of the rights of the people they forbid it to do for the people what it can, and demand that it do what it is beyond its power to do."[130]

The patent self-destructiveness of such behavior was beyond his ken, but suggested to him that Bolsheviks were not only unrealistic but irrational. The words sectarianism, true-believers, orthodoxy, and heresy figured prominently in Miliukov's polemics with the left during the First Duma.[131] He did not then draw explicit parallels between religious fanaticism and Bolshevik zealotry, perhaps because he could not bring himself to so decisive a break with putative allies on the left, but the resemblance of leftist "political fanaticism" to a religious rather than secular worldview is all the same apparent in his writing.

It is impossible to judge how these articles affected his readers: they seem to have had little effect on the far left or the reactionaries at court, the two groups whom he most desperately wished to influence. Looking to the French revolution for examples, Miliukov feared that the Kadet party might share the fate of the Girondists, becoming "the victim of its historical position between two extremes."[132] Still, it is likely that his many short pieces in the widely circulated *Rech'*, constantly clarifying, justifying, giving grounds for hope and confidence, deflecting the calumnies from right and left, did contribute in some measure to the belief that even if this Duma could not be made to work, a Duma was itself important.

A New Ministry or Dissolution?

After the May 13 vote of no confidence in the Goremykin cabinet, Miliukov hammered away on the absolute necessity of a change of ministry. He had always desired in principle a ministry composed of and responsible to the majority party in the legislature, which he took to be one of the essential characteristics of a genuinely parliamentary system. The majority would support its own ministers, and Russia would then have, instead of an oppositional Duma, "a mighty governmental party in the Duma, relying upon the support of the whole country."[133] The legislature could not work with an executive branch it had no confidence in or control over, and if the people's representatives were denied the opportunity for constructive work, popular faith in the legislature would be irreparably damaged. The longer the impasse continued, the more the deputies lost their moral authority and ability to influence the people.[134]

Such an appraisal was widespread by late May. And while Goremykin and the more conservative ministers opposed any change in the cabinet's composition, a handful of senior officials were willing to consider formation of a ministry of confidence as the only alternative to dissolution of the Duma, an act whose consequences might be fatal to the regime. In June, the deadlock between the executive and legislature showing no signs of breaking, two different sets of discussions with public figures on forming a new ministry were undertaken. For a while, it appeared these discussions might actually bear fruit. Miliukov was drawn into both attempts, where he showed himself in his worst light.

The first inquiries were launched from an unexpected quarter. On June 16 the conservative palace commandant, General D. F. Trepov, met privately with Miliukov. Apparently, Trepov was acting entirely on his own initiative. Miliukov made it clear that the ministry would have to be formed strictly from the majority party—that is, from the Kadets; what was under discussion was commitment to a whole program, not selection of various individuals deemed acceptable to the government.[135] Trepov seemed to accept such a perspective, once Miliukov had assured him that the Kadets appreciated that selection of the ministers of the army, navy, and court must be left to the tsar. Trepov was also far more yielding than Miliukov had anticipated on other questions, such as the introduction of universal suffrage laws: he even agreed to the expropriation of private property on behalf of the peasants, on the stipulation that land reform would come from the tsar, not the Duma. The only sticking point, Miliukov thought, was a political amnesty, since the Kadets insisted on total amnesty while Trepov said the tsar would never agree to pardon "bombists." Greatly encouraged by this meeting, Miliukov published an article June 18 talking about the real foundation for a Kadet ministry.[136]

Trepov was less committed to a purely Kadet ministry than Miliukov presumed; the list of potential candidates he drew up and presented to Nicholas sometime between 16 and 20 June included three public figures from other parties, Dmitrii Shipov, Nikolai L'vov, and V. D. Kuz'min-Karavaev. Suggested Kadets were Duma president Sergei Muromtsev as chairman of the Council of Ministers, Miliukov or Petrunkevich as minister of internal affairs, Mikhail Gertsenshtein for finance, and Vladimir Nabokov as minister of justice; Miliukov was also considered for foreign affairs. Nicholas showed the list to Finance Minister V. N. Kokovtsov, who earnestly counseled him against any such step; the tsar said he had made no decision as yet.[137]

Meanwhile, a wholly unrelated proposal to form a ministry composed of government officials and various public men was presented to the tsar on June 25 by Foreign Minister Aleksandr Izvolskii, the most "liberal" member of the Goremykin cabinet. Izvolskii apparently knew nothing of Trepov's efforts, but his memo proposed several of the same individuals for the same posts, mentioning Muromtsev as chairman and the necessity of including Shipov. On Miliukov, the memo read:

> The participation in the Ministry of M. Miliukov would be especially well regarded, for, although he has no seat in the Duma, his influence is very great with the public as well as with the Duma itself. In spite of all his defects—an immense ambition and a certain tendency toward intrigue—he is a man endowed with a very keen perception and an extremely clear political sense. His entrance into the Ministry might even be unavoidable, for he would become the most vigorous defender of the Government against the attacks of the extreme left. He is the only one who would be capable of organizing a Governmental party under conditions that are as novel as they are difficult.[138]

Several days later Nicholas authorized Izvolskii, along with Minister of Internal Affairs Petr Stolypin, to begin discussions with public men; however, the meeting between Miliukov and Stolypin did not go well. Stolypin did not contemplate a purely Kadet ministry. Miliukov, under the impression that Trepov's approach had been authorized by the tsar, and that Stolypin had already made up his mind against the Kadets, treated the latter coolly. He made it clear that there could be no thought of Stolypin's own inclusion in any new ministry.[139]

Shipov was to meet with the tsar on June 28; before that meeting, he sounded out Kadet willingness to participate in a coalition cabinet. Count Geiden, of the Octobrists, met with Miliukov, reporting back to Shipov that

Miliukov categorically rejected a coalition cabinet but was willing to form a Kadet ministry. Meanwhile, Muromtsev told Shipov he could not accept responsibility for forming a coalition cabinet, in part because he felt no ministry could expect to last more than a few weeks at the present time, and in part because the Kadets would not consider a coalition, since "P. N. Miliukov already thinks of himself as premier."[140]

Shipov thus concluded that a coalition ministry was untenable, and in his meeting with the tsar tried to persuade him that a Kadet ministry would not really be so objectionable, since once in power the party would speedily become more responsible and moderate. He felt Muromtsev was much better suited to head the government than Miliukov, who had little religious feeling and therefore "would not always base his actions on the demands of moral duty." He also noted that "Miliukov loves power and is autocratic"; he might well oppress his colleagues and interfere with their activities. Miliukov was, nonetheless, a man of many talents and great erudition, "unquestionably the most influential member of the Kadet party." It would be both useful and necessary to include him in the cabinet, as minister of foreign or internal affairs. Nicholas heard him out with seeming interest, and Shipov left feeling quite hopeful about Muromtsev's being commissioned to form a new ministry. Apparently the decision to dissolve the Duma instead of appointing a ministry including public men was settled only in early July, and largely by the behavior of the Duma itself.[141]

On June 20 the government had published an article calling upon the people to place their hopes for agrarian reform in the government, not the Duma. Outraged, the Duma decided on July 4 to turn to the people themselves with a defense of their agrarian project. Miliukov appreciated that this illegal step could serve as a pretext for dissolving the Duma and tried unsuccessfully, with Petrunkevich, to dissuade the Kadet Duma deputies from appealing to the people. Miliukov made one last effort to avert catastrophe with an appeal on July 6 in *Rech'* that the Duma refrain from answering the "unconstitutional act" of the ministers by acting unconstitutionally itself. "We are on the eve of civil war," he warned, for there could be no doubt about the consequences of a dissolution. This effort, too, failed. That same day the Kadets passed the appeal in the Duma, and two days later the tsar signed the ukaz dissolving it.[142]

In all his subsequent accounts of these negotiations Miliukov professed skepticism about the prospects of a ministry being formed and defended his own behavior. There probably was slight chance for a purely Kadet ministry, given the number of senior officials opposed to one. A coalition ministry containing bureaucrats and leaders from various parties was a more genuine possibility, and here Miliukov's behavior is open to criticism. His rejection of any such arrangement, partially prompted by awareness that the Duma would regard a coalition with suspicion, was also the product of arrogance and a doctrinaire attitude. He had no doubt of the superior qualifications of both his party and himself, and though he consistently denied that his intransigence was fueled by personal ambition, it is striking that virtually all accounts of the negotiations mention it.[143] Overestimating the degree of support behind Trepov and unwilling to compromise, Miliukov did nothing to enlist Stolypin's support for a ministry composed mainly of liberals. Vasilii Maklakov, who thought the Kadets could learn a good deal from experienced bureaucrats, blamed Miliukov's stand for "destroying the whole plan."[144]

The dissolution order published the morning of July 9, though expected at any time, caught the Kadet leadership and the Duma off guard. Stolypin, who had replaced Goremykin as head of the Council of Ministers, made sure that this would be so. On Friday, July 7, he asked Duma president Muromtsev to set aside Monday's session for his personal address, creating the impression that the Duma was at least safe for the weekend. He also took the precaution of posting troops to bar entrance to the Taurida Palace. When the announcement of the dissolution reached the offices of *Rech'* early Sunday morning, Miliukov bicycled around Petersburg rousing members of the central committee for an emergency meeting at the home of Petrunkevich.

The central committee had decided a month earlier to protest dissolution should such a step be taken; Petrunkevich and Vinaver proposed that the deputies refuse to leave the chamber and address some sort of manifesto to the population. Miliukov opposed this form of protest as unconstitutional. Dissolution was within the government's rights, and he favored compliance should it occur. The majority, however, strongly supported the suggestion that the party's deputies should refuse to vacate the Taurida Palace.[145] Stolypin's lockout spoiled this plan and a new form of protest had to be agreed to quickly.

The twenty or so Kadets gathered at Petrunkevich's home regarded the dissolution as a contravention of the Fundamental Laws, since no date had been named for elections to the new Duma. In response, they would call for a popular protest based on passive resistance: the refusal to pay taxes or furnish recruits to the government. Miliukov was asked to draft the text, which he then read to the group, asking if they appreciated that deputies taking such a step could be prosecuted. His position was in truth uncomfortable: not being a deputy, he could not sign the Duma appeal he had drafted and would not himself suffer the consequences. Petrunkevich declared that they knew the risk they were running and had resolved to proceed.[146] Approximately 120 Kadets, along with 80 Trudovik and Social Democratic deputies, then headed for Vyborg, Finland, where they could gather and deliberate beyond the reach of the Russian police.

Opposition to the manifesto among the Kadet group became more pronounced the following day. Many rightly considered the refusal to pay taxes or furnish recruits empty gestures, since direct taxes formed only a minute fraction of the state budget and the government would not be calling up conscripts for many months. As it became clear that many party members did not wish to support the manifesto, Miliukov urged that it be signed by all the deputies or dropped completely, since an appeal signed by only a portion of those present would lack significance.[147] The manifesto might very well have been shelved, but the mayor of Vyborg forced their hand by requesting that the gathering adjourn immediately. With misgivings, all eligible Kadets signed, believing that some public gesture on behalf of the Duma was necessary.[148] The text was spirited away for publication and dissemination, and the gathering at Vyborg dispersed.

As it turned out, the Vyborg Manifesto was indeed an empty gesture, though its signatories paid for their resolve with their political careers. The disorders anticipated by virtually everyone upon dissolution of the Duma did not materialize. The peasant population met the Duma's end passively or stoically, in some areas voicing anger at the dissolution, but only rarely attempting to act on the appeal made by their elected deputies. The few scattered outbursts and protests were easily quelled by the authorities. Although Miliukov cautioned against misconstruing the public calm as indifference toward the Duma, vainly searching for some sign of organized protest, it was clear that the Kadets had seriously misread the popular mood.[149]

The damage done to the Kadet party by the Vyborg Manifesto was enormous. Most tangibly, the government's decision to prosecute the signatories made them ineligible to run for future Dumas; over one hundred Kadets, including such prominent figures as Petrunkevich, Kokoshkin, Shakhovskoi, Vinaver, and Nabokov, lost the right to participate in the legislature. The party's sponsorship of an appeal to citizens to break the law also harmed its reputation profoundly, calling into doubt its responsibility, patriotism, and the credibility of its liberalism. A good deal of the opprobrium attached to its author. Petrunkevich recalled this several years later in a letter to Miliukov, in connection with a trial of several Kadets, expressing his distress that "all the accusations are in the main directed against you personally, you alone have to bear almost all the weight of the political struggle, all the blows, all the unscrupulousness of our opponents. The history of the Vyborg appeal, which was laid to your responsibility, is repeating itself."[150]

The Second Duma

In summer 1906 the Miliukovs took a dacha in Terioki, Finland, primarily to furnish a secure spot where the Kadets could meet and deliberate tactics. The most immediate—and difficult—question was the Vyborg Manifesto. To sound out the attitude in the country toward the manifesto, the leaders held meetings on August 2–4 with representatives of twenty-nine Kadet provincial committees. While representatives reported varying levels of support for or hostility toward the manifesto, almost all considered it unfulfillable. When the gathering then took up the question of concrete tactics, deep disagreements within the party were revealed. N. V. Teslenko expressed the views of the more militantly inclined with his proposal that the party endorse the Vyborg Manifesto, not "worry about legality," and energetically establish relations with left organizations. Iosif Gessen and Struve argued strongly that the party could neither implement the manifesto nor consider going underground.[151]

The deliberations at the fourth party congress, convened in Helsingfors on September 24–28, continued in the same vein. Miliukov gave the tactical report, his role being to persuade delegates to vote formal approval of the Vyborg Manifesto while at the same time agreeing not to act on it. Changed political conditions made it easier to engineer such a vote. The government had finally set dates for elections to a Second Duma, dispelling fears that it did not intend to convene one and thus undermining the arguments of those in favor of illegal actions. Miliukov maintained that the main task of the party must be preparation for the elections; it was not possible to campaign and conduct passive resistance simultaneously. Debate was heated, but a majority endorsed Miliukov's proposals. The congress also approved his proposal that the First Duma's answer to the speech from the throne serve as the basis of the party's electoral platform.[152]

That the Kadets had had to hold their congress in Helsingfors, having been denied permission to meet in the capitals, underlined the difficulty of their situation as an "unregistered" and therefore illegal party. The representatives to the August meetings had painted a uniformly depressing picture of the party's position in the provinces, speaking of official repression, demoralization, and the consequent "melting away" of membership.[153] Concerted efforts were now made to procure the party's legalization, in which Miliukov took active part; all ended in rejection. This meant that during the campaign and elections the Kadets were subject to all manner of restrictions and harassments. Their clubs were shut down, their campaign literature was confiscated, they were denied permission to hold public meetings, and, frequently, their candidates were disallowed on various pretexts. Miliukov, who received the most votes from the St. Petersburg party organization in the balloting for its candidates, was disqualified for having failed to establish proper residency in his district.[154]

He nonetheless played a decisive role in determining the campaign strategy, including proposed tactics in the Duma. By campaigning on the First Duma's answer to the throne, the party could remind electors of all that body had been prevented from doing for the people. Once in the Duma, Kadets would not avoid confrontation with the government, but must act less aggressively than in the First Duma: as he put it, their tactics would represent "not assault, but an orderly siege" [*ne shturm, a pravil' naia osada*]. The practicality of these proposals won general approval.[155]

Miliukov again took an active part in the campaign, speaking frequently at electoral meetings and defending the party's position on the pages of *Rech'*. He also wrote, in simple and straightforward language, the party's special brochure for the mass electorate, which explained that the Party of Popular Freedom (the Kadets) was the "true friend of the people." Only this party understood that the way to achieve in the Duma what the people wanted was not "threats and shouts" and not petitions, but use of all the Duma's lawful rights. The government understood this, and that was why it feared and persecuted the party.[156]

Despite generous government subsidies given right parties, and harassment of the unlegalized oppositional parties, the elections produced a Duma even more radical in composition than its predecessor. The left parties had this time decided against a boycott, resulting in election of approximately 180 revolutionary socialist and Trudovik deputies, as against 97 extreme rights, conservatives, and moderates. Socialist competition cut into the Kadet contingent, which fell from a high of 184 deputies at the end of the First Duma to 123 deputies in the Second. The Kadets were still the largest single party, their victory in both capitals proving their attractiveness to the urban electorate, but their position would be less dominant than it had been before. Moreover, the presence in the Duma of groups indifferent to its fate or actively seeking its destruction did not augur well for the restrained parliamentarism Miliukov recognized as crucial to the Duma's survival.[157]

The Second Duma opened February 20, 1907, and was dissolved June 3. The Kadets struggled to preserve it, avoiding provocative gestures such as another vote of no confidence in the government, and pushing for delay of particularly contentious bills in favor of reform projects less likely to divide the chamber, including bills on civil liberties and reform of local self-government. With the support of moderates they established committees that would review bills in a constructive fashion and reworked the Duma statute in an effort to ensure against unparliamentary actions and curtail endless, purely demonstrative debates. It was hoped that demonstrating the Duma's capacity for sober and creative legislative work would not only forward reform but make it that much harder for the government to justify a premature dissolution. There were, however, too many issues capable of causing serious conflict with the government, and too many deputies intent on bringing precisely those issues to the fore.

The most important questions for the fate of the Second Duma were agrarian reform and condemnation of revolutionary terror.[158] Miliukov did not have a great deal to do with the faction's handling of the former, but took an active part in determining its equivocal position on terror.

The attitude to be taken toward political terror had been passionately debated in liberal circles since 1903. Although no liberals engaged in or advocated the use of terror, many were reluctant to condemn it prior to October 1905, in part because they felt government oppression and brutality drove revolutionaries to resort to terror, and also because they realized that terror sometimes procured governmental concessions where peaceful means had failed. To condemn terror while enjoying the reforms it gained would be hypocritical, as Miliukov had noted in July 1905. After promulgation of the October Manifesto made peaceful, political work possible, removing any remaining justification for resort to terror, Octobrists and the moderates of the small Party of Peaceful Renewal were among those urging that terror must be condemned. Stolypin, from the start of the Second Duma, insisted that it denounce revolutionary terror.

The Kadets, for both tactical and moral reasons, were still unwilling to do so. They had not entirely shed their belief that cooperation with the left was essential to further reform; preservation of ties with the left required a circumspect stand on terror. Equally important, however, they considered the government chiefly responsible for continued, endemic violence in Russia. The government employed "terror" itself, in the form of punitive expeditions and Stolypin's notorious field courts-martial, still in operation at the start of the Second Duma. It also did not move decisively against pogromists or the death squads organized by the far right. Right-wing violence struck very close to home: the reactionary Union of the Russian People was responsible for the murder of two prominent Kadets, M. I. Gertsenshtein on July 18, 1906, and G. G. Iollos on March 14, 1907. A number of Kadet leaders received mailed death threats from the same organization, which also paid to have Miliukov beaten up on the street in broad daylight in April 1907.[159] In these circumstances, Miliukov and many Kadets argued, any condemnation of revolutionary terror would imply a justification of the government's behavior.[160]

During the Second Duma, the issue was further complicated by Kadet desire to avoid provocative behavior that might furnish the authorities with a pretext for dissolving the legislature, which was what deputies on the extreme right had in mind when they moved on March 8 that the Duma condemn revolutionary violence.[161] These considerations were discussed in the course of several meetings of the party central committee and Duma faction. On March 12, 1907, for example, Miliukov told his colleagues that *any* answer to the Right resolution on terror would be "very dangerous, [it would] only give grounds for attack. . . . The situation is thus, that the government wishes to obtain from the Kadets a condemnation of political murder, but then we will sever all connections with the extreme leftists; we should avoid discussion of murder in essence."[162]

Reluctant to take a clear-cut stand on terror, and fearful of the consequences should the Duma actually vote against a motion stating that it condemned terror, the party tried for some two months to prevent the issue being discussed at all. The Kadets managed to orchestrate a Duma refusal to vote on the motion denouncing revolutionary terror when it finally came up for debate in mid-May, but two days later the issue was raised again. Concern that the Duma would refuse to condemn political violence proved justified, as the Duma rejected no less than seven motions related to government illegality and to terror. These included the motions by the Octobrists, the Polish Kolo, and the Kadets, even though in all three the censure of left terror was so well concealed, Vasilii Maklakov later wrote, that one required a magnifying glass to detect it.[163]

In his memoirs, Miliukov came to the conclusion that Stolypin had a reason for insisting so strongly that the Duma condemn revolutionary terror: he needed such a gesture in order to ward off conservative pressures for another dissolution. Stolypin had in fact approached him personally on this question in January 1907, proposing that the Kadets persuade the Duma to condemn revolutionary murders, in exchange for the legalization of their party. When Miliukov explained this was impossible, Stolypin said he would be content with an article by Miliukov in *Rech'*, even an unsigned one, condemning political assassinations. Miliukov discussed this proposal with Petrunkevich, who insisted that any such deal would result in the ruin of Miliukov's own reputation and the "moral destruction of the party"; the matter was pursued no further.[164]

Despite the overall moderation of their behavior in the Second Duma, a storm of abuse engulfed the Kadets following its June 3 dissolution and the concomitant revision to the electoral law. The right and left press "dedicated their political articles to a relentless critique of Kadet tactics," I. V. Gessen wrote, "laying the whole responsibility on Miliukov." This was not altogether fair, Gessen believed, since Miliukov was absent from St. Petersburg during much of the Second Duma and not directing the faction's activity. Miliukov was in fact less involved in the affairs of the Kadet faction than was the case during the First Duma. His energies were at this time involved primarily in another, more personal affair.

Miliukov's relationship with the young Frenchwoman whom he had met in Chicago in late 1904 was renewed and took an unexpected turn.[165] He maintained in his memoirs that his involvement with Marie Petite did not exceed the bounds of the platonic until mid-1906, when she visited him in Russia, and that the affair was a very brief one. In fact, it embroiled him in a personal and family crisis that came close to destroying both his marriage and his career.

Anna Miliukova regularly wrote her friend Natalia Vernadskaia on the tortuous ups and downs of Miliukov's relationship with "the French girl." None of the letters are dated, but references to a tremendous quarrel on New Year's day, concerning Miliukov's refusal to terminate the affair; to the Duma's being in session; and a statement to the effect that "he has gone abroad and it has all started up again," suggest that the affair lasted no less than six months and perhaps continued for as long as a year.[166]

His feelings for the young woman were serious enough to cause him to leave home, despite his wish to minimize the "political scandal" it might cause. He returned to his family, saying he could not bear to be parted from the children, but left again a month later. Anna wrote, "Everything he says is completely contradictory. Now he says that he has liquidated the relationship . . . then he says that he will never leave her, that he feels himself connected to her. Then he says he doesn't know how he will end the whole affair but that it must be ended [words illegible] when he will go to her. Nothing is clear, definite. One has to wait, not knowing how it will all end."[167] Sometime in early 1907 Marie Petite returned to Paris but kept up a daily correspondence with Miliukov. They met again in Switzerland several months later when she accepted his invitation to join him in his travels in Europe over the Easter recess of the Second Duma. The affair apparently ended that summer. Miliukov returned to his family; he saw Marie Petite again in Paris, but by that time she was married. Later still, when he received word that she was gravely ill, he hurried to her side, only to find that she had already died. It was, he said in his memoirs, "one of the most painful experiences of my life."[168]

In 1905 Miliukov had returned to his homeland full of energy and confident he would have a role in the effort to win political liberty for Russia. What was astonishing was the number and variety of roles he filled: organizer, leader, tactician, mediator, and, not least, commentator. Drawing upon his friendships and connections from among the intelligentsia and zemstvo milieu, shuttling between Moscow and Petersburg, he helped to forge and preserve the unity of the widening opposition, then to establish the first constitutional party. Less than a year after his return he was one of the most prominent public figures in Russia, the leader of Russia's largest political party, editor of a widely read daily. For a brief time, it even appeared he might become part of the country's first popular cabinet.

His accomplishments were impressive, but there were mistakes and failures as well. The ambition that had helped propel him to the center of politics also helped to ruin negotiations for a liberal ministry. In lectures and almost daily pieces for *Rech'* he did as much as any individual in Russia to educate its citizens to the values of parliamentary versus violent struggle, to appreciation of the responsibilities as well as license of liberty, to respect for each other and for law. And yet he drafted the illegal Vyborg Manifesto and could not bring himself unequivocally to condemn political violence. As Ariadna Tyrkova perceptively observed, "In this moderate, restrained, rational Russian radical sat the maximalism that has played so many evil jokes with the Russian intelligentsia."[169]

The unhappy conclusion of the 1905 revolution also coincided, for Miliukov, with family crisis and the painful conclusion of his one, great love. Scars both personal and political would make themselves felt in the difficult years ahead.

CHAPTER SEVEN

The Search for Unity,
1907–1914

From the very start of the Second Duma the Kadets had feared for its existence. Nonetheless, its dissolution and the promulgation of a new electoral law sent shock waves through the party. The law of June 3 not only dealt a serious blow to Kadet prospects in future elections, but also, in the view of Miliukov and many other educated Russians, signaled the end of the revolution. How had a seemingly defeated and discredited government managed to regain the upper hand so quickly, and why had the revolution achieved so few of its goals?

Miliukov's first developed evaluation of the outcome of the revolution came in the form of an address to New York's Civic Forum, delivered before a huge audience at Carnegie Hall January 14, 1908. As the best-known spokesman in the United States of progressive Russian public opinion, he was invited by the Civic Forum to explain developments in Russia. Since Miliukov was by this time an elected deputy to the Third Duma, the trip had to be made over the Christmas recess. Travel to and from the United States by steamer required some three weeks, leaving just three days for his speech in New York and a whirlwind trip to Washington, where he met with members of Congress.[1]

In *Constitutional Government for Russia,* Miliukov set out to explain why a truly "national movement" for an end to autocracy, after its initial success in winning the October Manifesto, turned into virtual civil war and then gave way to political reaction.[2] He assigned the failure of the revolution to three agents, the revolutionaries, the court, and the nobility, all of whom had turned the "struggle for the constitution" into a violent class struggle, with all its "embitterment and mutual hatred."[3]

The revolutionaries, intoxicated by the victory of October 17, had fractured the national movement before it attained all its goals. Forgetting their Marxist doctrine and greatly overestimating their strength, they persuaded themselves that the advent of socialism was at hand, since the armed proletariat was strong enough to seize power itself. Despite the bloody failure of the Moscow uprising, "the revolutionary elements learned nothing." They furiously blamed the bourgeoisie for their defeat and worked to discredit the First Duma even before it was elected. Ill-conceived, unrealistic, and violent, the short-lived revolutionary phase "proved fatal for the success of the whole movement."[4]

Miliukov felt, however, that the deciding factor in the disappointing outcome of the revolution was the agrarian question, for it was this issue that swung the majority of the nobility to reaction. The autocracy had granted concessions, and honored them, only so long as it felt powerless to do otherwise. It found the support it had been lacking in the nobility, which now feared that the rising tide of rural unrest and violence would result in alienation of their land to the peasantry and the loss of their own privileged economic and social position. These two "decaying political powers" joined in defense of their interests. The tsar's government altered the franchise to the benefit of the nobility, subsidized formation of noble-dominated reactionary political parties, and changed its agrarian policy to conform with the landowners' wishes, all the while suppressing rural disorders with unbridled ferocity. The nobles, for their part, supported all the government's policies, giving it an "obedient" Duma and not disputing in principle the autocratic rights and privileges.

Neither party was capable of seeing that the political equilibrium thus achieved could only be temporary. The "external dramatic character" of the Russian revolution had been stifled, but the revolutionary movement itself had not. Not only had the causes of the revolution not been addressed, but class struggle had finally brought the masses to consciousness of the "real causes of their social misery"; there would certainly be renewed unrest in the villages. Although Miliukov suggested that a democratic solution would ultimately triumph, he regarded the near future with foreboding. "In short, wherever we turn or look, we only meet with new trouble to come, nowhere with any hope for conciliation and social peace."[5]

In coming years, Miliukov would refine his evaluation of the 1905 revolution, but he did not return to it at length until after the debacle of 1917. Then, reviewing the repetition of events of 1905–6—the rapid splintering of the society, the resurgence of class struggle, and the inability to follow a middle course—he grounded his analysis of the revolutionary process explicitly in Russian political culture. He had always underlined the significance of what he called a weakly developed "national tradition" in his country; by virtue of its frequent borrowings, Russia was curiously unconnected to its own past. In 1921, again on the occasion of addressing an American audience, Miliukov attached primary importance to a different sort of weakness, that of the ties holding Russia together.

> The fundamental difference which distinguishes Russia's social structure from that of other civilized countries, can be characterized as a certain weakness or lack of a strong cohesion or cementation of elements which form a social compound. You can observe that lack of consolidation in the Russian social aggregate in every aspect of civilized life: political, social, mental and national.[6]

That Russia's component parts were not strongly bonded by allegiance to the larger entity of the state could largely be traced to the workings of autocracy. The masses, "kept in a state of passive submission by a regime of force," remained, in a sense, "natural anarchists." The nobility, prevented from becoming a strong, internally cohesive social estate, was doomed to dependence on the crown against the peasantry. The intellectuals, forcibly isolated from the common people and denied practical experience in governing, developed an abstract cast of thought which "drove them to a sort of intellectual extremism." And finally, the national minorities, alienated and oppressed by the centralizing state, were pushed toward "separatist strivings." In each case, Miliukov implied, the political passivity imposed upon the various groups, and the barriers placed between them, ensured that "the aggregate was kept together by passive rather [than] by conscious desire to make one."[7] The strong arm of autocratic authority turned out to be the only glue holding Russia together; when that authority weakened or disappeared, the pieces came unstuck.

Although Miliukov did not fully elaborate this theme until after 1917, he could easily have done so earlier. For him, the period 1907–14 was a sustained lesson in the disunity of Russia, manifested in every conceivable way: between social classes and between ethnic groups, between the government and "society," between political parties in the Duma and outside it, and even within political parties, his own included. Much of his energy in these years was directed to preserving the unity of the Kadets, as well as to identifying the issues and tactics that might unite various Duma factions for the passage of reforms that could help knit the country together. And he became absorbed by the fight against a newly militant Russian nationalism, struggling not only to protect the rights of Russia's ethnic minorities, but to articulate a liberal and inclusive nationalism for the multinational state.

Tactics for the Third Duma

The Kadets were of two minds concerning how to campaign in the elections to the Third Duma, the principal topic of a party conference assembled in August 1907. One alternative was to attempt alliances with more moderate constitutionalists, definitively separating themselves from the left. Such a tactic was perhaps the best way of securing as many progressive deputies as possible for the Duma, since the new electoral law would work to the disadvantage of the Kadets and socialist parties. It was also ideologically congenial to those members of the party who had long felt that the Kadets needed to strengthen their commitment to a strictly legal, constitutional stance. For others, close cooperation with moderate groups would mean, in effect, to become Octobrists; the real enemies, they maintained, were not on the left. Miliukov worked to secure acceptance of a flexible electoral campaign free of formal alliances with any group, which would leave Kadets' options open in the Duma.[8] He shared most Kadets' skepticism regarding the staunchness of Octobrist constitutional convictions and concern that entering any sort of bloc with the Octobrists, or even with the small, more liberal Party of Peaceful Renewal, would be perceived as an endorsement of the Third of June coup: close association with them was not worth the risk of confusing or alienating the Kadet constituency. Close cooperation with the extreme left during elections was also not desirable in his view: he now harbored few illusions about the revolutionaries. He agreed with more militant Kadets that "kicking the left" was inappropriate in a period of ascendent reaction; by the same token, Constitutional Democrats could less than ever afford being bracketed with them.

Preserving a circumspect distance, however, in which Kadets would treat their erstwhile allies as "rivals" rather than "enemies," proved difficult given the lack of corresponding sensibilities on the part of much of the extreme left. Among Social Democrats, Plekhanov alone called for joint work among the opposition to avert a "Black Hundred" victory. Instead, the purely destructive Leninist line prevailed; unremitting Social Democratic attacks against the Kadets as bourgeoisie, class enemies, and double-dealers seemingly had the goal of harassing Kadets into adopting more radical positions while at the same time discrediting them utterly in the eyes of voters likely to support such positions.[9] Miliukov now countered such attacks bluntly, provoking a furor when he quoted a German fable to warn Kadets against saddling themselves with the left's misguided opinions: "An ass is an ass even though he temporarily finds himself on the back of a sage."[10]

The strident campaign was further characterized by far more massive government interference in the elections than before. Manipulation of the com-

ЕРТЬ.Л (24) ОКТЯБРЯ 1907 года № 7351.

Видъ волшебныхъ измѣненій милаго лица.
(Посвящ. П. Н. Милюкову).

1904 г. Друзья слѣва.

1905 г. Друзья слѣва.

1906 г. Сосѣди слѣва.

1907 г. Враги слѣва.

Cartoon from an Odessa newspaper (October 24, 1907) depicting evolution of Miliukov's attitude toward Russia's socialists, from "Friends on the left" in 1904 to "Enemies on the left" in 1907. Clipping from the Russian Pictorial Collection, Hoover Institution Archives, Stanford University.

plex provisions of the new electoral law in order to disqualify "suspect" electors, confiscation of ballots printed up by the party, and intimidation at polling places all helped to minimize election of Kadet candidates. The results were even worse than the party leadership had feared: only 56 of 449 deputies to the Third Duma were Kadets, as compared to 98 in the Second Duma and 154 in the First. This time, however, Miliukov's candidacy did not fall prey to governmental interference, perhaps in part because some officials believed that the Kadet leader was considerably more dangerous outside the Duma than in it, where "his chief shortcoming—tactlessness—frequently would put the party into an embarrassing position."[11] Miliukov won handily in St. Petersburg's second curia, with some 22,000 votes.

Disputes over tactics for the first session of the new Duma dominated the party's fifth congress, held in Helsingfors on October 24-27. Miliukov's tactical report was informed by two central propositions: that the revolutionary movement was over for the foreseeable future and that Russia still possessed, despite the June 3 violation of the Fundamental Laws, a fragile constitutional order. From this it followed that the Kadets, rather than acting in expectation of some "mythical" revolutionary upsurge, had to work within the present system. Eschewing the role of an irresponsible minority for that of a disciplined opposition, the party could pressure the Duma to exercise its rights in full, introduce reform bills which appeared to have some hope of acceptance, and support and amplify whatever progressive initiatives the Octobrists might introduce.[12]

The left minority criticized this defensive strategy and its implicit shift to the right. Instead, they advocated a strictly oppositional line in the Duma, stepping up the party's "nonparliamentary" activities in the countryside, and continued cooperation with the left rather than the Octobrists. Debate was more acrimonious, and affinity for the left position more widespread, than the 135-13 defeat of their resolution would suggest, for the left gave voice to a persistent fear that in adapting to a more restrictive political environment the Kadets would lose their identity and sense of mission.[13] With Miliukov assuring the congress that "we will not make friends with the Octobrists," delegates approved his resolutions on tactics. There was, in truth, no discernible alternative for a party committed to achieving change through parliamentary means, but holding less than 13 percent of the seats in the Duma. Support for Miliukov's tactical line, however, did not constitute an unreserved endorsement of his leadership: in the balloting for a new central committee he received 115 votes, coming in only sixteenth out of forty.[14]

Left Kadets need not have worried about overly cordial relations with the Octobrists, for the latter had no intention of "making friends" with their campaign rivals. While the Kadets gathered in Helsingfors, the Duma's new majority party was holding meetings in Petersburg with those to its right and pledging that no oppositional group would be represented on the Duma presidium.[15] Once the Duma opened, the Octobrists and their right allies made clearer still their intention to minimize the opposition's influence, seeing to it that they headed none of the Duma's twenty-four committees and were underrepresented on such important ones as judicial reform, budget, and education. Miliukov was seated on two innocuous committees, concerned with the Duma's statutes and its library, and on a special committee for drafting the Duma's address to the throne.[16]

Great importance was attached to this declaration, which in previous Dumas had been used to outline the chamber's political orientation and legislative intentions. Debate over the text produced by the special committee revolved primarily around whether to include loaded terms, such as "autocrat"—insisted upon by the moderate and extreme rights, and "constitution"—as demanded by the Kadets. In choosing to make an issue of these terms, both the Kadets and their opponents on the far right appreciated their potency as signifiers at a time of political transition, when the real nature of the country's "renovated order" was still disputed. The October Manifesto had created a new order, Miliukov argued, but so long as the Duma refused to utter the word "constitution," misunderstandings concerning Russia's political system would persist. "I suggest that if you now let slip that great honor which has fallen to your lot, finally to call by its true name that object towards which so many generations have striven, you will commit a crime before those who sent you."[17]

The Duma majority ignored this plea, as it did his exhortation to show greater sensitivity to the aspirations of Russia's national minorities by acknowledging them in its declaration. The Kadets had to be satisfied that the word "autocrat" was also omitted from the final text, and as a conciliatory gesture joined in passing the declaration, while the socialist parties and extreme right abstained.[18]

Stolypin then presented the government's program. Miliukov and a number of deputies unhappily discerned a shift away from the promises of the October Manifesto—a document not even mentioned by name in his speech—and toward restoration of order by whatever means necessary. Stolypin also struck a more nationalistic note as he dwelt on the need to restore the state's might and underlined the achievements of traditional, distinctively Russian autocratic authority, dismissing the feasibility of a parliamentary order with the words "one cannot affix some sort of alien flower to our Russian roots, our Russian stem."[19]

By emphasizing the restoration of order and nationalistic concerns, Stolypin more or less set the agenda for the first year of the Third Duma. The civil liberties promised in the October Manifesto, reform of the legal system and local self-government, and substantive social reforms would not be appreciably forwarded in the first year, which was instead preoccupied with demonstrations of antirevolutionary sentiment and questions of national defense. These concerns found concrete expression in the vote to fund construction of the strategically important Amur railroad, in extended debate over reform of the armed forces, and in favorable discussion of the bill to provide monetary aid to victims of terrorism.

But the antirevolutionary and nationalistic mood was also expressed by hostility toward the Kadets and the entire opposition, all of whom were routinely characterized as seditious and unpatriotic. Virtually all Kadet-sponsored interpellations, amendments, and bills were rejected or ignored. Miliukov, as leader of the Kadet party and head of its Duma faction, was a particular target of abuse, critiqued or derided in others' speeches and heckled and disrupted during his own.

The debates surrounding creation of the Duma's Committee on State Defense illustrate vividly the majority's attitude toward Miliukov and the Kadets. The Committee on State Defense was the brainchild of Guchkov. He hoped that by devoting itself to restoring the nation's military might—a pressing task following the losses in the war against Japan—the Duma would not only influence the direction of military reform but also deepen the court's appreciation of the positive role the legislature could play. By proposing that the opposition be excluded from the new committee, on the grounds that they could not be trusted with state secrets, he could highlight the patriotism of the parties of the center and right, as compared to parties of more suspect loyalties, while at the same time minimizing Kadet input on questions of national security.

In January 1908 a series of speakers from the moderate and extreme right, incensed by Miliukov's criticism of the Russian government in his Civic Forum address over the Christmas recess, used the debate over the proposal to close the committee's meetings to nonmembers to vilify the Kadets and their leader. Warning against the "poison that issues from the People's Freedom Party," they maintained that a party which had urged the population not to pay taxes or furnish recruits (an allusion to the Vyborg Manifesto) should be kept distant from the business of state defense. Russian affairs must be handled by real Russians, Pavel Krupenskii insisted, not the "new Christopher Columbus" and his Jew-loving confreres.[20] The reactionary V. M. Purishkevich advanced upon Miliukov from the speaker's tribune crying that he was a scoundrel and a blackguard and then declared himself pleased to "spit in the face of member of the Duma Miliukov." The Octobrists approved the motion to exclude Purishkevich for fifteen sessions for his conduct, but when Miliukov mounted the rostrum in the next session to defend his remarks and his party, they joined the right in promptly exiting the hall, forcing the chair to adjourn the session.[21] Although speakers from the Kadets and other opposition groups vigorously protested the imputations of disloyalty and the propriety of banning the minority from participation in the Defense Committee, the exclusionary proposals passed easily.[22]

The criticisms of Miliukov that were a staple of the first year's Duma sessions at times goaded him into injudicious responses. Twice during the spring his angry characterization of an opponent's allegations as "a lie" resulted in challenges to duels. The more serious challenge came from Guchkov, who had a reputation as a duelist; relations between these former university classmates were so thoroughly soured that Miliukov refused to offer a retraction. Seconds were appointed and formal protocols generated, to the great diversion of St. Petersburg society, before a compromise was at last found and the duel averted.[23]

For the most part, however, Miliukov endured the campaigns against him in the Duma and the press with remarkable composure. His restraint in responding to attacks against his patriotism, character, even his scholarship, and his courage in the face of physical threats and verbal assaults, won him respect. Bernard Pares, who found little to praise in Miliukov as a leader and tactician, nonetheless declared, "I have a profound admiration for him as a man, for his invariable coolness and courage, sticking bravely to his course, which disclaimed any violence, and indeed, for a wonderful personal gentleness under every kind of harassing from left and right."[24]

The faction as a whole displayed its discipline and clung doggedly to the cautious course mapped out by Miliukov and the central committee. The Kadets threw themselves into the work of committees and tried to avoid provocative gestures, refusing to support the Social Democrats' interpellation into the legality of the June 3 electoral law or to join them in voting against the entire budget of the Ministry of the Interior. A major gesture was their censure of political violence when debate began in February 1908 over the bill to provide compensation for victims of revolutionary terror. The Kadet faction had anticipated that the Rights would demand that the Duma condemn terror and resolved to abandon their earlier, equivocal position. The Duma majority rejected the Kadet resolution condemning all political violence in favor of one that deplored only revolutionary terror, but the gesture had been made, and noted.[25]

By the end of the first session, the Kadet faction was bruised but still intact and had, through hard work and sheer tenacity, improved its position. Miliukov and several other Kadets were elected to the important budget committee for the following session, the hostility of the Octobrists and moderate right had diminished appreciably, and Miliukov looked forward to accomplishing more in the second session, when substantive reforms would be on the agenda.[26]

Many members of the party, however, were less satisfied with these meager gains. In meetings arranged over the summer with provincial representatives and members of the Duma faction, at the party conference in October, and even at meetings of the central committee itself, in fall 1908, critics outnumbered those who felt the faction had done as much as possible under exceptionally difficult conditions. The faction did not seem sufficiently oppositional and outspoken, many felt; it was also disorganized and not pursuing any discernible program.[27]

In his tactical report for the October 1908 party conference Miliukov therefore tried to balance the widespread desire for a sharper, more confrontational posture in the Duma against his own belief that the Kadets were still too little inclined to compromise. In his opening remarks he acknowledged that the party must voice in the Duma the embittered mood of the country. He thought the faction could now act more independently, since it no longer had to fight for its legal place in the chamber or be concerned about the very existence of the Duma itself. Miliukov and a number of other faction deputies warned, however, that political alignments in the Duma had not changed fundamentally. Expectations had to correspond to those conditions, as did the faction's tactics: adopting a more independent line could not mean indulging in "thoughtless demonstrations."[28] Rodichev had best characterized the attitude of the majority of the leadership when he said bluntly, at the summer meeting with party representatives, "Our task now is not to spoil things for the future."[29]

The tactical changes outlined, and results predicted, were, in sum, very modest, but enough to mollify the conference delegates. The conference approved Miliukov's tactical report, expressing strong satisfaction with the "new note" he had sounded.[30] Miliukov and the central committee had again managed to preserve the unity of the party and, by agreeing to raise slightly the oppositional tone of the faction's pronouncements, secured approval for continuation of the restrained parliamentary conduct he wanted.[31]

As the above discussion demonstrates, Miliukov's ability in most cases to carry the day did not mean the party was his to command. Objections from both the right and left flanks of the party had to be addressed, concessions made or emphases shifted. His moderation and essential pragmatism in these years made it easier to win the majority's support, since dissenters were in the difficult position of having to formulate alternatives that seemed equally practical yet not ideologically divisive. But credit must also be given to the almost scholarly care with which Miliukov prepared and defended his proposals. He read voluminously, clipped and saved articles from a wide variety of periodicals, and took extensive notes during party meetings and sessions of the Duma, enabling him to back up his views with a formidable array of statistics and citations.³² His habit of preparing for every political meeting as though it were a seminar was well-suited to an organization sometimes referred to as the "party of professors."

Even so, Miliukov's views did not always prevail. One of his most substantial defeats concerned the party's negative vote on construction of the Amur railroad, an episode that also highlights the degree to which his concern for foreign policy set him apart from most of his Kadet colleagues in these years.

In March 1908 the Duma began discussion of a government request that it appropriate some 360 million rubles for construction of a railway along the left bank of the Amur river, a line characterized as necessary for the colonization and economic development of Eastern Siberia and protection of the Siberian frontier. The position the Kadets should take had been discussed extensively in central committee meetings. Most of the members opposed approving so vast a sum, arguing that the monies could be better spent on domestic needs closer to home. Miliukov was almost alone in favoring the appropriation. If it was demonstrated that the railroad was truly necessary for defense of the country, then it was impossible to vote against it. Preserving Russia's position in the East, he argued, "is a defensive, reasonable policy. To liquidate it owing to some sort of intelligentsia qualms is absolutely unthinkable."³³ The majority was unmoved by his arguments, deciding that the Kadet faction would vote against the appropriation and also rejecting his request that party members be permitted to present their own views on the issue in the Duma. He agreed to be bound by the decision, although he refused personally to vote against the appropriation, absenting himself from the Duma's April 1 roll call vote approving the construction funds.³⁴

Only a close observer of the vote would have guessed at Miliukov's support for the railroad, however, for he never made public his disapproval of the party's decision.³⁵ His reticence on the railroad vote was no doubt partially motivated by his disinclination ever to admit a defeat. But it was also in keeping with his more general efforts to prevent the party's internal disputes from becoming common knowledge. One consequence of this practice was that many outsiders imagined him to exercise more absolute sway over the party than was actually the case. It also meant that he found himself shouldering the blame, on occasion, for unpopular Kadet decisions he had himself opposed.

Substantive domestic reform was at last on the agenda in the Third Duma's second year, and the Kadet leadership had grounds for hoping that some of the bills to be considered might be passed in the form they desired. Their optimism did not extend to the most far-reaching project of the session, the bill to regularize the agrarian reforms Stolypin had enacted between the sitting of the First and Second Dumas by using article 87 of the Fundamental Laws. Stolypin had made unmistakably clear the importance he attached to his agrarian project, not only for improving the situation in the countryside, but for the rest of his reform program as well. The majority in the Duma had also indicated their support for a solution to the peasant question which had come to mean dissolution of the village commune and protection of the inviolability of private property. Kadets thus had no illusions about their ability to prevent passage of a bill they opposed. The question, rather, was how to oppose it, and what amendments, if any, they might successfully introduce.

Many of the Kadets' principal objections to the bill, touched on by Miliukov in a remarkable four-hour speech delivered over the course of two sessions, are well known.[36] One was its contravention of the new parliamentary order by violating the spirit of the Fundamental Laws. Article 87 was intended for enacting emergency decrees when the legislature was not in session, not as a means of bypassing the legislature in order to introduce a major reform. Another was the degree to which political considerations and class interests had shaped the contours of the Stolypin reforms. A third objection was the harshness of the bill: the dissolution of the commune would drive the poorest peasants off the land to fend for themselves however they could.

One of the most important critiques of the Stolypin legislation, however, was not specific to agrarian reform, but involved the question of how any social change could be effected by laws. All three of the principal Kadet speakers during the agrarian debates—Fedor Rodichev, Andrei Shingarev, and Miliukov—dwelt on the failure of the Stolypin legislation to correspond not only to the peasantry's main wish, which was to receive more land, but also to popular values. For this reason alone, they insisted, the reform could not ultimately be successful. In allowing for the forcible destruction of the commune and thus depriving peasants of their traditional communal rights, Rodichev argued, the bill violated the peasant sense of justice: "We need a law which will be just in the consciousness of all." Miliukov reminded the Duma of the reception of the law of November 9 in the village, where it was largely either not understood or not welcomed. More than half of the three hundred thousand peasants who had thus far separated from the commune had been able to do so only with the intervention of the local authorities, he claimed. Resort to coercion was not the way to return stability and peace to the countryside.

The Kadet defense of the commune struck some observers as scarcely consistent with liberalism, since dissolution of the commune would effect the final emancipation of the individual peasant and extend to him fuller equality before the law.³⁷ But in arguing that the agrarian reforms needed to take into greater account popular sensibilities, the Kadets were drawing on a reasoned approach to legislative reform as well as making a bid for peasant support for their party. As a proponent of reform through parliamentary means, Miliukov believed that law could be a mighty force for social change, a means of shaping new cultural values. But his belief in the social origin of values also made him realize, more than is usually appreciated, that law alone can not create new values, particularly when a law's provisions run entirely counter to a community's current values and is imposed from the "outside."

Miliukov most fully developed his argument on the limits of law as an agent of cultural change in his approach to nationality policy, but an early illustration of this view is provided by his approach to a less politically charged issue, that of combating alcoholism. In a speech to the Duma in March 1908, during discussion of proposals for tackling this problem, he drew on the history of legislative solutions to alcoholism attempted in other countries. In the United States, he said, draconian state laws against drinking, including outright prohibition, tended to result in widespread evasion of the law, not a decline in alcohol consumption. Much more effective was the "local option" approach, where a community determined its alcohol policy according to its own lights. The reason for the difference came down to respect for a given law: a prohibitive law is possible only when society is prepared to support the prohibition, "when society, by means of its own independent activity, creates in itself consciousness of those norms which are reflected in objective form in the posing of a law."³⁸

Miliukov and the Kadets were not contending that peasants should not share in the rights enjoyed by other citizens but that forcible dissolution of the commune by legislative fiat would not inculcate in the peasantry respect for private property. The Duma, however, ignored Kadet arguments and amendments, voting on November 15, 1908, to curtail debate on the bill, and passing it after its first reading in December; final passage, after the third reading, was on April 24, 1909. The party leadership tried to derive some consolation from the belief that their fight in the Duma had at least exposed the shortcomings of the law and absolved them, in popular perception, of responsibility for its implementation. Miliukov later claimed that through the Duma's peasant and clerical deputies, news of their efforts spread all over Russia, enhancing the opposition's reputation in the Third Duma.³⁹

The passage of the Stolypin agrarian bill marked a major turning point in the history of the "Third of June System," for the dominant coalition in the Third Duma had essentially been knit together by two issues, support for the government's efforts to restore order and Stolypin's agrarian reforms. By late fall 1908, with disorders quelled and the final passage of the agrarian law apparently assured, rifts in the coalition appeared and quickly widened.

The approximately fifty deputies of the extreme right opposed in part or in whole most of the remaining elements of Stolypin's reform program, including zemstvo and local court reform and laws securing civil liberties promised in the October Manifesto, seeing in them threats to the traditional order and the rights of the monarch and possible sources of renewed social instability. Rightist attacks against the Kadets and the opposition in the Duma, which had never abated, were broadened to include Octobrists and the Duma presidium. In the following year, an anti-Semitic campaign of incredible crudeness further poisoned the atmosphere of the Duma. In March 1910, when Miliukov took on the extremists by characterizing the Union of Russian People as a "union of murderers and pogromists," deputies on the far right added to their usual epithet, "Miliukov is a yid hireling," more intimidating catcalls: "We'll beat your snout!" "We'll knock out the last teeth!" Unable to control the extremists, Duma president N. A. Khomiakov resigned.[40]

Fault lines in the Duma majority appeared among the more convinced constitutionalists as well. The Octobrists had fully supported Stolypin's sequential approach to the task of "renewing" Russia, epitomized in his famous formula "first pacification, then reform." With the revolution vanquished and order restored, it was time to get on with the second part of that formula, but the government appeared to be dragging its feet. Many bills for realizing in law the civil liberties promised by the October Manifesto had yet to be introduced, and Duma efforts to compel a thorough reorganization of the armed forces had thus far had little effect. In winter 1908–9, the Octobrists began to step up their critique of government conduct, joining the Kadets and other opposition groups in support of interpellations concerning restrictions of the press in Moscow, unlawful conduct of the local administration in the Caucasus, and persecution of trade unions.[41]

These developments prompted more frequent cooperation between the Kadets, the Octobrists, and the Progressives (formerly the Party of Peaceful Renewal) over the next twelve months. In consequence, the period extending from February 1909 through January 1910 was the single most productive period for civil rights legislation. The greatest triumph was passage in May 1909 of three government bills on religion amended in a liberal spirit, concerning the rights of former clergy, of Old Believers, and of conversion from one faith to another; Miliukov helped in amending the latter two bills and delivered three speeches supporting them.[42] In November 1909 the Duma passed on second reading another liberally amended government bill, replacing the peasant *volost'* court with elected justices of the peace, with many Octobrists supporting Kadet efforts to eliminate, or at least lower, property requirements for justices. In January 1910 the Duma initiated and adopted a bill abolishing administrative exile in the empire.[43]

Unfortunately, all these victories were more apparent than real. Not one of the bills became law; some were rejected by the State council, others were not approved by the tsar, and others were held up indefinitely in committee through government inaction. There were other obstacles, as well, to continued cooperation between the "center" and moderate opposition that might have grown into something like a formal coalition. For one, there was serious dissension within the Octobrist faction, in part due to apprehensions that Guchkov's tactics were hurting the party in the eyes of its zemstvo constituency and the government. As a result of defections, the party of the center shrank from 148 deputies to 120 by fall 1909.

Second, intrigues against Stolypin were bearing fruit, as was demonstrated in what came to be called the "Naval Staffs Crisis." In April 1909, Nicholas decided not to approve a naval appropriations bill on which the Octobrists and Stolypin had expended considerable effort. That bill also contained the Duma's approval of naval staff personnel, a point which reactionary enemies of the premier and the lower house succeeded in representing to Nicholas as an effort to encroach on the royal prerogative. This humiliating defeat, coupled with problems passing other Stolypin reform projects, suggested the wisdom of shifting the emphasis in domestic policy toward goals less likely to provoke conservative opposition, and, concomitantly, cultivation of a conservative governmental majority for their support in the Duma.

That orientation was found in Russian nationalism, a theme Stolypin had already advanced in his programmatic address at the start of the Third Duma. Nationalism struck a responsive chord in many Duma deputies for a variety of reasons. Concern for the decline of national might, for preservation of both the moral and physical vigor of one's "race" or nation as embodied in "the people," had wide currency in Europe at the time.[44] Such concerns had special appeal for Russians, humiliated militarily by Japan and diplomatically by Austria's 1908 annexation of Bosnia-Herzegovina and only just emerging from revolutionary upheaval at home. Moreover, as Geoffrey Hosking has noted, in a period of political transition in Russia, when attempts were being made to establish centers of authority other than the autocracy, the idea of "the people" assumed a special importance; "nationhood was being sought as a new basis for political cohesion."[45]

A nationalistic domestic policy therefore seemingly had much to recommend it, both as a means of attracting support for Stolypin's ministry in the Duma and of disarming ultraconservative critics. The support was soon forthcoming. In October 1909 the moderate rights and National group in the Duma formally unified as the Russian National faction, numbering ninty-one deputies; a Nationalist Party was organized and made clear its devotion to the premier and to "the unity of the empire, the protection of Russians in all parts of the Empire, and Russia for the Russians."[46]

The Octobrists preserved their oppositional tone through fall 1909, but seeing the Duma's center of gravity shifting toward the Nationalist faction, and frustrated by their lack of progress with reform, eventually tried to renew their cooperative relationship with the Stolypin ministry. When Khomiakov resigned from the presidency of the Duma in March 1910, Guchkov put forward his own candidacy for the post. Miliukov felt this move was prompted at least as much by personal ambition as by a desire to improve the situation in the Duma, but the Kadets nonetheless hoped his presidency would draw Stolypin away from the Nationalists. Instead, Miliukov observed, the opposite occurred: "The government, and after it the center, evidently in the interests of self-preservation, embraced the whole program of militant nationalism."[47]

In Search of a Russian Nationalism

Nationalism, as an integrative force, was a rather problematic concept in a multinational empire. Promotion of an inclusive, all-Russian (*rossiiskaia*) national culture could easily give way to a more exclusive identification of Great Russian (*russkaia*) culture as the national one, characterized by arrogance toward and intolerance of the culture of the country's non-Russian populations, suspicions of their loyalties, and attempts to secure the predominance of Russians in all areas of the empire. This in fact became the tone of the "nationalist campaign" that began during the third year of the Third Duma, as expressed in the legislation on Finland, the proposal for creating zemstvos in six of the western provinces, and debate over expansion of elementary education. Flavored by the self-interested concerns of Great Russian landowning deputies from the empire's ethnically diverse borderlands, and heavily charged by the xenophobia and crude racism of the reactionary right, the nationalist legislation of the Third Duma was often aggressively, chauvinistically Great Russian.

The Kadets had not anticipated the "orgies" of chauvinism that characterized the first phase of the nationalist campaign, but they had been following the development of the nationalist mood with no little apprehension since late summer 1909. It was clear that the party had to work out a defined position on various nationalities questions, and do so with extreme caution. Kadet leaders rightly anticipated that even a restrained defense of the interests of national minorities would evoke counterattacks and imputations of lack of patriotism and indifference toward the integrity of the empire.[48]

External attack was not the only problem associated with the nationalities question, however, for the party leadership itself was divided on what its nationalities positions should be. The contentiousness of the issue did not stem solely from the obvious contradiction between what the party program demanded for nationalities—equality and cultural autonomy for all citizens without distinction on the basis of nationality—and what was politically expedient. A significant minority within the party leadership, for the most part on the party's right wing and influenced ideologically by Petr Struve, was profoundly interested in fostering a healthy Russian nationalism and concerned about the threat posed to a unified national culture and the empire's integrity by minority national movements. In the eyes of A. S. Izgoev, N. A. Gredeskul, Ariadna Tyrkova, D. D. Protopopov, and a number of others, the Kadet party was insufficiently nationalistic.[49]

At the same time, national minorities who supported the Kadet party, most especially Jews and Ukrainians, were increasingly irritated by the party's failure to advance their interests. The Kadets, Miliukov included, had done little more than counsel patience, pointing to the difficulties the party would experience in pushing minority issues in the Duma at the present time. But patience was wearing thin, as was confidence in the very nature of the liberal commitment to national minorities. In March and April 1909 Zionist Vladimir Zhabotinskii caused a furor with a series of articles castigating the Russian intelligentsia, and most especially the liberals, for ambivalence toward the Jews and a general disregard for the nationalities question. His charges received a seeming confirmation with the appearance in March 1909 of Struve's provocative article "The intelligentsia and the national visage." By stressing the contributions Jews had made to "Russian national culture" and welcoming Jewish assimilation, Struve seemed implicitly not to value non-Russian culture in and of itself. This article, too, caused consternation, since it issued from the pen of a prominent member of the Kadet central committee. At the November 1909 Kadet party conference, Ukrainian delegates criticized the party leadership for insensitivity toward Russia's national minorities, angrily warning that vagueness on the nationalities question was provoking mistrust among these groups that could translate into electoral losses.[50] Since the national minorities represented an important part of the Kadet constituency, such grievances could not be ignored.

Miliukov had long been interested in the question of the formation of national identity. Now, as the nationality question gained increasing political importance, he devoted more of his attention to it, not only in terms of specific policies on specific issues, but also theoretically. Although he did not systematically elaborate his views until 1925, in his book *Natsional'nyi vopros* (The national question), most of them may be found, at least in inchoate form, in the texts of his numerous Duma speeches on nationality questions, in various brief published pieces, and in the notes for two lectures on nationality and the state, which he apparently composed in 1912.[51]

In *Studies of Russian Culture* Miliukov had treated nationality as a sociological phenomenon—the product of social interaction—as distinct from a racial or ethnic one; he retained that basic perspective in all his subsequent writing on nationality. He also kept a firmly historical perspective, in his insistence that the national character or "national idea" was not something immutable, but rather subject to change over time. By the period of the Third Duma, however, Miliukov had significantly modified his thinking on nationality, as he inquired more deeply into the nature and genesis of national consciousness.

The importance of consciousness is reflected in the definitions of nation and nationality Miliukov offered in his 1912 lectures on nationalism, which differed from the definition used in the *Studies*. Whereas before he had stressed the importance of language for nationality, as "the singular and necessary means for uninterrupted psychological interaction," he now came to see language as a possible constituent element of nationality, but not a necessary one, the same being true of the other two most commonly identified indices of nationality, religion and ethnic origin. For proof of this contention, he suggested, one had only to look at the Ashkenazic and Sephardic Jews, speaking two languages but sharing a common nationality, or the Germans of Germany and Austria, claiming the same racial origin and speaking the same tongue, but not professing a common national identity.

Instead, the crucial determinant was a feeling of solidarity based upon two ties: belief in a shared history or tradition, and a sense of common values and goals in the present. Miliukov quoted with approval from Ernest Renan's celebrated 1882 lecture on the nation: "A nation is a great solidarity, achieved by consciousness of sacrifices which have been made in the past and which its members are prepared to make in the future." Both a nation and a nationality are, Miliukov added, consciously united by certain ideal goals or values; the only difference is that a nation has an "organ" for proclaiming and realizing its will, that is, a state, whereas a nationality might not.[52]

These definitions, by stressing the importance of consciousness, made nationality a voluntaristic and highly subjective thing—in fact, Miliukov followed Renan in asserting that it was possible to choose one's nationality.[53] They were also clearly politically useful to any effort to arrive at a workable concept of nation and nationality in a multinational state such as Russia. As E. J. Hobsbawm has pointed out, the concept of the nation as constituted by the deliberate political choice of its potential citizens, dating from the time of the American and French revolutions, bases its idea of patriotism on the state, not the nationality.[54] This is not to say that there are no objective criteria for determining what is or is not a nation or a nationality. Rather, such an approach recognizes the utility of a common language, ethnicity, religion, and territory for the social intercourse that over time can result in conscious solidarity, as compared to seeing these things as in themselves constituting nationality.[55]

One of the most sophisticated aspects of Miliukov's understanding of nationality was his appreciation of the degree to which the "national idea" was a construct. His investigation into the genesis of the Russian national idea had detailed the way the ideologues of the Muscovite state had drawn certain features from the Russian present and the Russian past to fashion a national identity that was then represented as something "eternal and immutable." A highly selective use of history, and even misreadings of it, along with a good dose of myth, characterizes any representation of a national character and its animating values. And the national idea, along with nationality itself, can alter over time. The means and the settings of social intercourse—language, religion, milieu—were not themselves static; the bonds and customs and values generated by and affecting that social intercourse could change as well. As Miliukov put it to the Duma in December 1909, "The nation is not race, the nation is not the totality of physical features which remain unchanging over centuries. The nation is adaptable, it changes, it expresses itself in the forms of current life, it prepares for the morrow."[56]

The very "plasticity" of nationality suggested the potentially great influence the modern state might exert upon it. The state could indeed harness the sense of national solidarity creatively, as in the case of German reunification. Equally, the state could exploit national feeling for more conservative or even destructive ends, an example being the multinational state which equates race with nationality and extols the primacy of the "ruling nationality." Miliukov proved something of a prophet with his 1912 observation that the national state can evoke the greatest passions and "commit the greatest crimes."[57] Still, nationality is not simply a creation and creature of the state. By the time consciousness of a distinct national identity has spread from the intelligentsia to the popular masses—and it is only then, at the end of the process, that one can speak of a genuine "national movement"—it has ceased to be a purely literary-cultural phenomenon, but has acquired a political dimension as well. At this point, Miliukov implies, the process is irreversible: once national consciousness becomes a "democratic" phenomenon, though it can be acted upon, it cannot be eradicated.[58]

This is why attempts at forcible assimilation of peoples becoming conscious of their nationality—in Ireland, in Austria-Hungary, and in the Russian empire—never succeed. Forced assimilation has an effect opposite to the one intended; coercion inevitably evokes a "conscious solidarity" antagonistic to the nationality doing the coercing.⁵⁹ As Miliukov warned the nationalists during the December 1909 debate on use of non-Russian languages in the lower courts, the slogan "Russia for the Russians" is "a slogan of disunity . . . it is a slogan that is not creative but destructive, and the destroyers are you (pointing to the right)."⁶⁰ Five months later, prior to the vote on the bill abrogating much of Finland's legislative autonomy, he spoke still more urgently about the dangers inherent in the Duma majority's militant Great Russian nationalism. Only an approach founded on accommodation of national differences could save the Russian state from "that national internecine strife and disintegration into which you are driving it. When that will be, we do not know. . . . But gentlemen, it *will happen*. And it is you and no one else who hastens this inevitable end."⁶¹

Miliukov nonetheless believed that the "Russian state entity" could be preserved by a just nationality policy that took into account the realities of the empire. He therefore rejected as unworkable any policy predicated on the belief that Russia was or could become a true national state (*Nationalstaat*) such as France and Germany were. On this point he decidedly parted company with Struve, who held that the existence of a dominant all-Russian culture throughout the empire meant that Russia was, for all its ethnic heterogeneity, a genuinely "national state."⁶² Miliukov's conviction that a number of non-Russian peoples had already become conscious of their own distinct identities meant it was too late to think in terms of a state where "nation and nationality coincide."

Similarly, he did not believe that a *Staatsnation* along the lines of Switzerland, one that was the sum of its nationalities, could be realized in Russia. Such a solution to Russia's nationality question was possible as recently as the 1860s when, he claimed, a Ukrainian or Jew could still feel himself to be a "Russian" as well. Then, most individuals would have been satisfied with a lifting of particularistic restrictions, on the principle of the equality of all before the law. Thanks to the policies of Russification, however, that time had passed; the demands now forwarded were not simply for individual rights but for rights of the national collective. The idea of a state nation could now be realized only in the form of a *Nationalitätenstaat*, a state of nationalities, a multinational state like Austria-Hungary. Genuine accommodation, rather than illusory hopes of assimilation, must shape a "healthy nationality policy."⁶³

The starting point, of course, was equality of all nationalities before the law—"the Alpha and Omega of all good government"—and full civil liberties, most especially freedom of expression.⁶⁴ Beyond this, there must be the right to use one's native tongue in schools, in court, and up to "that point where high culture begins"; that is, Russian would remain the language of state administration. Government officials in any given area should always know the local language. Administrative districts should be configured "along national boundaries" and it might also be desirable to organize voting in elections proportionally in order to "preserve the rights of minorities."[65] What he did not recommend was any form of federal system, something he had strongly opposed since 1905 as likely to threaten the cohesion of the state.[66]

Miliukov became the principal Kadet spokesman on questions of nationality. He spoke forcefully for use of non-Russian languages during debate over reform of the *volost'* court in December 1909, and over expansion of the system of elementary education, in fall 1910. He made nationality questions a prominent part of his critique of the government program in response to Kokovtsov's opening speech to the Fourth Duma, and introduced an interpellation on behalf of the Ukrainians, in January 1914, concerning the government's ban on commemoration of the anniversary of the poet Taras Shevchenko's birth. Miliukov was in fact the only head of a Russian political party to speak out publicly on behalf of Ukrainian culture.[67] Although he was not one of the Kadets' main fighters during the Beilis trial, that task being assumed by Vasilii Maklakov and Maksim Vinaver, he spoke out on other occasions against anti-Semitism; in March 1910, he was excluded from the Duma for one session for having called the presidium "base" for not suppressing the anti-Semitic outbursts of the extreme rights.[68] Outside the Duma, he wrote and lectured on the nationalities question; each year he composed the sections on nationalities contained in the annual party faction report and the *Rech' Yearbook*.

The concrete question that most involved him, however, was Finland, the issue which dominated the third year of the Duma. Miliukov gave no fewer than five major speeches on Finland between 1908 and 1912, and it is in them that he most fully articulated his understanding of both the integrative power and the limits of law.

Stolypin had first raised the question of "regularizing" Finland's position in spring 1908. In theory, Finland was joined to the empire only by a personal union: its grand duke was the Russian tsar. After the reforms of 1905–6, when the monarch ceased by himself to embody the state, Finland's anomalous status needed to be addressed. Stolypin, not unreasonably, wanted to bring Finland under the purview of the new state institutions, the Council of Ministers and the two legislative chambers. He was concerned, as well, to combat what he labeled Finnish "separatism." The most controversial issue concerned the role to be assigned to Finland's own legislature, the Diet. Miliukov believed that the Russian and Finnish legislatures should work together as equals on matters of "imperial concern," passing parallel legislation. The bill as amended by the Duma committee on Finland, however, gave the imperial legislative bodies an overriding right to deal with such matters. Furthermore, by defining "imperial concern" broadly to include such matters as taxes, associations, use of language, the press, and education, scarcely a shred remained of the autonomy guaranteed Finland in its 1809 constitution.[69]

Miliukov advanced every argument he could in his effort to persuade the Duma to recast the most offensive features of the bill. He appealed to the sense of noblesse oblige: "Remember that violence against defenseless nations committed in the name of physical might and the power of the state does not remain without consequences." He pointed out the harm passage of the bill would do to Russia's reputation, comparing the bill to the partitions of Poland and reminding the Duma that international legal opinion was on the side of Finland.[70] He offered a detailed historical account of the conditions under which Finland had been joined to Russia and the promise of Alexander I that the rights he had granted were "irrevocable."

In his eyes, the indifference toward such matters displayed in the Duma were indicative of Russian culture's weakly developed legal consciousness: it was grotesque that Octobrist V. K. von Anrep was applauded for declaring that "when dealing with a problem of such major national importance one should above all keep in mind the needs of the nation and the state, rather than elaborate legal rights."[71] This contempt for law was yet another instance of Russia's lack of connection with her past, the absence of ongoing "tradition." In Europe, where legal tradition did exist, a question comparable to that of Finland would not be decided without reference to the historical documents that formed part of the living law, "connecting the thread of time." In Russia, where "we don't want to remember even yesterday," where an "old state act" was just archival material, the archives contained "a whole cemetery of broken promises. Little Russia is there, so too is Georgia and the Baltic provinces, not to mention Poland. . . . For us to break promises seems in the nature of things."[72] Encroachment on Finnish rights could not be justified on the grounds that *salus rei publicae suprema lex esto* (the well-being of the state is the highest law). Even if one granted that the bill on Finland was vital to Russian state interests, the obligation to realize those interests by legal means was not thereby suspended.[73]

Finally, Miliukov insisted that the proposed legislation was not only unrealizable, but positively dangerous. It would turn friends into enemies and require force for its implementation, evoking resistance that would entail still more force. Even then, the goals of the bill would not be attained, because there were limits to the creative power of law. Returning to this subject later, during debate over further legislation directed against Finland, Miliukov urged the present government not to repeat the mistakes of the old regime in believing that "the impulses of the legislative will are, as it were, almighty." It was this illusion that prompted the government to assure the Duma that it could ignore the laws and customs of the Finns, "that this is a blank sheet on which you may write whatever you please." Wiser colonial administrators in other countries did not try to cross the boundaries of the attainable, understanding that the legislative will "operates within the rather tight confines of the actual conditions of life, the existing fabric of national, religious, social, and political relations. We would wish that the head of the government understand that these sociological givens constitute obstacles which are at times stronger than physical obstacles."[74]

Flexibility, respect for local sensibilities and for law, along with an appreciation of its limitations, were the best—the only—means of safeguarding Russian interests, for promoting national cohesion rather than disintegration.[75]

None of Miliukov's arguments, nor those of other speakers for the opposition, checked hectic passage of the bill exactly as it had emerged from committee: the Duma accomplished all three required readings in just four days, and by June 17 the bill had been signed into law. Nor did Miliukov's warnings about the destructiveness of an exclusively Great Russian nationalism staunch the flow of chauvinistic rhetoric epitomized in von Anrep's assertion that "we want the respect, we do not need the love of the nationalities."[76]

Instead, Miliukov's strong defense of the Finns elicited an ugly response. The Kadets were once again pilloried as proponents of revolution, unpatriotic, and enemies of the empire. The reactionary newspaper *Zemshchina* accused *Rech'* of having accepted a 250,000 ruble bribe from the Finns, and this damaging allegation was used in the Duma during debate over Finland.[77] Miliukov even received a death threat from the Union of Russian People on the eve of the final debates over the Finnish bill.[78] Petrunkevich was among those who had anticipated that advocacy for the Finns might seriously isolate the liberals, warning that "Finland could become for us what Poland was for Herzen."[79]

The Duma's behavior in spring 1910 disturbed Miliukov profoundly. In its treatment of Finland the Duma had gone beyond "all bounds of decency," he wrote several years later. "The servility of the State Duma, reaching its apogee from the time of the presidency of A. I. Guchkov, and the chauvinistic nationalism which damaged the Third Duma in the opinion of the whole civilized world, damaged it in the opinion of the country as well. The clearly powerless legislative chamber simply ceased to be taken account of."[80]

Because Miliukov habitually kept his innermost thoughts and feelings to himself and revealed little about his private life, his exact state of mind during this period can only be the subject of conjecture. It appears that his frustration, especially over the "national campaign," affected his mood and professional relations.

Domestic life was made easier by more comfortable finances; Miliukov's remuneration as a Duma deputy, his annual salary of 9,000 rubles from *Rech'*, and continuing book royalties meant that the years of hand-to-mouth existence were over. He and Anna bought property in the Crimea near the Petrunkeviches and a small dacha in Finland. The latter was particularly dear to him, especially after he had added a spacious study to accommodate his huge library. In all other respects, the Miliukovs continued to live extremely modestly. True *intelligenty*, they were not particularly interested in clothes, furnishings, or fine food. Most of their added income went into the coffers of the party, perennially short of funds, or to individuals in need of help: as soon as Miliukov received money "he passed it on to his friends," one acquaintance observed.[81]

The few surviving letters of Anna to her husband from this period, full of signs of affection, suggest that they had managed to repair their relations after the domestic upheavals of 1906–7. In one revealing letter of 1912, headed "Pavlunichka, my sweet, dear little master," Anna wrote: "Believe me, my dear, I love you with my whole heart, but a very great deal hinders expression and display and above all mine is not an easily expansive nature".[82] There was much to bind them besides the familiarity of more than twenty years' marriage, including many shared interests and deep love for their children. Miliukov, formidable though he could be, was comfortable with children in general and an affectionate father. He was in fact, one close friend maintained, almost two people. Severe and seemingly without "feeling" when at work, he drove himself tirelessly from early in the morning. Promptly at eight, however, "business" was put aside, and he was a different man, enjoying music and conversation, entering into others' concerns with interest. Although the Miliukovs did not themselves entertain often, being too busy and rather hopeless as hosts, they often visited and vacationed with close friends. Then, at leisure and among his intimates, Pavel Nikolaevich showed himself a warm friend and good companion.[83]

Little else gave cause for satisfaction. Frustrated in his hopes for reform, Miliukov also had to contend with criticism from virtually every quarter. The abusive campaigns of the Right heated up during the acrimonious debates on Finland, while the Social Democratic press continued to decry every instance of Kadet cooperation with moderate parties as evidence of a "bourgeois" sell-out. There was also criticism within the party. Besides the ongoing debate over whether the Kadets were sufficiently—or excessively—moderate, particular positions advocated by Miliukov came under fire. A number of Kadets felt that he focused the party's attention too narrowly on the Duma, to the neglect of the countryside, and disagreements erupted over his foreign policy positions.[84]

Disappointed hopes, constant criticism, and the burdens of leadership all took their toll. Miliukov the public man retreated further into the reserve that had always characterized his relations. That reserve had earlier been tempered not only by his "democratic" style—he had little use for formality or hierarchy in relationships—but also by a certain social gaucheness, making him appear rather shy than aloof, and an almost boyish energy and enthusiasm for any undertaking. The young professor who blushed furiously during his lectures had long since yielded to the assured public speaker, but the cold reserve, the absence of verve and of intuition which critics later recalled in memoirs, were apparently more recent developments. Iosif Gessen, for example, held that Miliukov's "lack of spirit" had not yet manifested itself in 1905, when his many talents combined with his "political fearlessness, inexhaustible patience, superhuman tirelessness . . . to make him the authoritative center of the liberation movement."[85]

By late 1909, although Miliukov's capacity for work remained, much of the animation was gone. Scattered indications of fatigue and stress appear in the sources: central committee meetings where he threw himself on critics or rebuffed suggestions sarcastically, and a serious falling out with long-time coeditor Gessen at *Rech'* in December 1911, due primarily to Miliukov's dictatorial handling of a disagreement over the paper's daily review of the press.[86] In summer 1911 his close colleague Maksim Vinaver wrote urging him to take a rest-cure at a German sanitorium, referring with concern to an earlier conversation concerning Miliukov's "shaky health."[87]

Miliukov's hardening reserve, tendency to bristle at criticism, and new abrasiveness can not have aided his efforts to preserve the unity of the central committee and broker compromises in the Duma. His deficiencies in this area, however, were partially remedied by Andrei Shingarev, a deputy from Voronezh. Shingarev had become the Kadets' most important spokesman during budget debates, but his role within the leadership also owed a great deal to personality. Warm-hearted and open, he was liked as well as respected. Sharing Miliukov's perspective on most issues, Shingarev worked to secure support for those positions and smooth out differences; he became "Miliukov's right hand." In the Duma, Ariadna Tyrkova recalled, people dealt much more willingly with him than with Miliukov, who "had no flexibility in intercourse with people, could not ameliorate a dispute with a little joke."[88] If Miliukov recognized this dimension of their professional relationship, he made no mention of it in his memoirs, simply noting, without elaboration, that Andrei Shingarev was "my closest friend."[89]

For Miliukov, the last fifteen months of the Third Duma were simply to be endured. The most that he hoped for was that the Duma would survive its five-year term without losing the few rights it had and without doing anything to further discredit itself. The political demise of Stolypin in spring

Andrei I. Shingarev. Vladimir Feofilovich Zeeler papers, Bakhmeteff Archive, Rare Book and Manuscript Library, Columbia University.

1911, as a consequence of the "Western Zemstvos Crisis," could not be greeted with rejoicing, since it demonstrated both the government's incomprehension of constitutionalism and the growing power of the reactionaries. Stolypin's assassination in September 1911, by a revolutionary who turned out to be an agent of the police as well, raised troubling questions about the "hypertrophy of the police," but did not mark any fundamental change in government policy; his successor, Minister of Finance V. N. Kokovtsov, lacked the authority to implement a new course.[90]

Meetings of the Kadet central committee became less frequent in this period, and the center of attention shifted away from bills in the Duma to activity outside it: lecture tours to the provinces, expanding the activities of the party press bureau, and organizing public gatherings, such as commemoration of the fiftieth anniversary of the emancipation of the peasantry. The party's organizational weakness outside the major cities was revealed by the leadership's stonewalling of requests that it try to convene a party congress. Although no congress had been held since fall 1907, most of the central committee strongly opposed attempting one. Given current repressive conditions, Miliukov reasoned, the representation at a congress would necessarily be small and "fortuitous," entailing the risk that its binding decisions concerning the party program might be correspondingly accidental in nature. For the time being, the leadership preferred to continue holding annual or semiannual party conferences, gatherings not empowered to alter the program or to reelect the central committee.[91] Whatever their differences, the members of the central committee believed themselves to be the proper caretakers of Kadet liberalism: they would not willingly relinquish control of the party to others.

Although Miliukov and most of the Kadet leadership had ceased to entertain hopes for the Third Duma, they were not, in 1912, wholly pessimistic. The main reason for this was the upcoming elections to the Fourth Duma, preparation for which was contributing in its own way to a general reanimation of the public already apparent from student protests and labor demonstrations in the wake of the Lena massacre of April 1912. The Kadets were not so naive that they expected an electoral victory for the opposition, but many hoped for the defeat of the Octobrists and election of a Duma more inclined to confront the government.[92]

That Miliukov still harbored hopes for improvement in the legislature was revealed by discussions in the party central committee concerning how to conduct the electoral campaign. Although he warned against promising voters too much, since he did not foresee a dramatically different Fourth Duma, he also opposed a militantly demonstrative campaign predicated on the assumption that the Duma's sole remaining value was as a tribune for making oppositional pronouncements. Instead, he urged that the party campaign *against* the record of the Third Duma, reminding voters constantly of all the lower chamber had failed to do, and *for* what he perceived, on the basis of recent travels in the provinces, to be the primary concerns of most citizens: an end to government illegality and arbitrariness, greater scope for local self-government, and a stop to the excesses against national minorities. In a relatively rare display of intransigence he declared that he would refuse to be the party's spokesman on the suffrage question if it decided, as Petrunkevich and several others urged, to make introduction of universal suffrage the central plank of its campaign platform.[93]

Although Miliukov's colleagues on the central committee did not evince any great enthusiasm for his proposed strategy, they agreed to its presentation to the next party conference, where it was duly endorsed. For his part, Miliukov no longer opposed campaigning together with Progressives and even, in some cases, Octobrists or candidates from the left, depending on local conditions.

Government interference in the campaigns, manifested this time not only in obstruction of "progressive" candidates but also in mobilization of the presumably conservative clerical vote, was more crude and widespread even than had been anticipated. For this reason, Kadets were more relieved than disappointed by the election results, for the right parties' contingent was not greatly enlarged from the last year of the Third Duma. The Kadets had increased slightly the size of their Duma faction, from 52 to 59; the party as a whole made a strong showing in both capitals, with Miliukov winning in St. Petersburg's second curia by an even larger margin than five years previously. The Progressives also fared relatively well, gaining 12 more deputies for a total of 48. The Octobrists were the principal losers: they fell from 120 to 98 deputies and their leader, Guchkov, was not reelected.[94]

Kadet Militancy and Discord: The Fourth Duma

The opening of the Fourth Duma nonetheless found Miliukov in a militant mood. The campaign and exposure to voters' opinions had apparently convinced him the party should adopt a more confrontational posture in the Duma, moving away from the politics of restraint he had advocated as recently as eight months earlier. His new militancy was signaled by his highly critical response to the programmatic declaration presented by Premier Kokovtsov in the opening sessions, which he characterized as lacking any coherent plan and riven by contradictions. Expressing dissatisfaction with every aspect of the government's conduct save S. D. Sazonov's foreign policy, Miliukov declared that three fundamental changes were required for a Duma that could really do something for Russia: change in the electoral law of June 3, reform of the State Council, and creation of a ministry responsible to the people's representatives.[95]

The unfastening of these three "padlocks" (*zamka*) became Miliukov's new slogan for the party, a theme he hammered at constantly in the pages of *Rech'*. Not surprisingly, a number of Kadets were displeased by this departure from the more modest demands forwarded in the Third Duma. Although the more combative stance corresponded to the mood of many provincial Kadets, it also exacerbated long-standing tensions with the right flank of the party.[96] Disagreements were soon out in the open, expressed in two challenges to Miliukov's leadership that threatened to split the party.

On December 8, 1912, Ariadna Tyrkova gave the central committee formal notice that several Kadets would be publishing a "nonparty" paper together with adherents of the Progressive party. A number of prominent Kadets had long been dissatisfied with the newspaper *Rech'*, which they considered too doctrinaire, too "European," and too reluctant to express viewpoints other than those of Miliukov and his supporters.[97] The new paper's organizers—among them Tyrkova, Protopopov, and Gredeskul, from the Kadets—were sympathetic to the program of national liberalism propounded by Petr Struve, but Tyrkova insisted that the paper would not be Struve's mouthpiece and, less frankly, that they were not attempting to effect changes in the party program; *Russkaia molva* (Russian talk) would simply provide a much-needed forum for discussion of topics and opinions that were being ignored. Since *Rech'* was not the official party organ, she argued, there ought not to be any objections to her undertaking.[98]

Tyrkova's announcement was a bombshell. Vladimir Vernadskii stated quite bluntly that dissatisfaction with *Rech'* was not confined to Tyrkova's coterie; he and Alexander Izgoev felt that a new paper should be welcomed as likely to promote the reanimation of the party. Most of those present, however, were less sanguine about the prospect of public airings of serious disagreements within the leadership. *Russkaia molva* might well produce a split in the party "even if that was not its founders' intention." Several demanded a vote on whether central committee members should be permitted to participate on a nonparty organ.[99]

Miliukov and Petrunkevich, recognizing that a negative vote would indeed precipitate a split, instantly opposed this proposal on the grounds that it was not the business of the central committee to pronounce judgment on a portion of its membership. At the same time, Miliukov declared that it was perfectly clear to him that "a fissure exists between certain sides and it will spread." He intended to resist this tendency: if *Russkaia molva* published a deeply divisive article, of the type of Struve's "The National Visage," it could not be allowed to go unchallenged. In the end, the majority rejected his suggestion that *Rech'* immediately take on the new paper, instead putting off the day of reckoning by waiting until *Russkaia molva* had demonstrated what line it would take.[100] When the anticipated critique of his orientation materialized in *Russkaia molva*, Miliukov promptly counterattacked.

Disapproval of Miliukov's line within the faction, apparent from the very start of the Fourth Duma, developed into an open conflict with M. V. Chelnokov in early spring of 1913. Chelnokov, a conservative Kadet from Moscow with a combative nature, had long chafed under the leadership of the man he privately referred to as "Miliuk Pasha."[101] Even before the opening sessions of the Fourth Duma he sharply criticized central committee "hegemony" over the party faction. Both Chelnokov and V. A. Maklakov were "opponents of democratic currents," N. N. Shchepkin wrote in some alarm to a friend in November, adding that Miliukov believed they were "preparing a break away from the party" in connection with a group from the Progressives.[102]

The controversy, which came to a head in early spring, involved Kadet participation on the Committee for Army and Navy Affairs, formerly the Committee on State Defense. Rather than excluding the entire opposition on principle, as the Third Duma had done, the right-Octobrist-dominated committee decided to make its own determinations about which deputies to seat. Accordingly, it voted against all the deputies named from the left parties and, of the Kadet nominees, rejected Miliukov but approved Chelnokov. Miliukov responded with a doctrinaire gesture, declaring on December 7, 1912, that members of the People's Freedom party would not work on the Defense Committee as long as representatives of all the other "democratic parties" were excluded. Chelnokov, who very much wanted to be on the committee, decided to contest this decision.

On February 17, Chelnokov informed the Moscow branch of the central committee that if he were not permitted to enter the Committee on Army and Navy Affairs he would accept the offer he had received from the Progressives to be elected to the committee by them. A Muscovite appeal to Miliukov on his behalf apparently produced no results, for on March 12 Chelnokov issued an ultimatum: he would leave the faction if it did not allow him to accept the Progressives' offer. Many members of the faction felt strongly that the party *should* be represented on the committee; a large majority endorsed Chelnokov's participation. Miliukov then issued his own ultimatum by resorting to a tactic he had never before employed—resigning as faction president. Only when Chelnokov had been prevailed upon not to take up the Progressives' invitation did Miliukov retract his resignation. Once this had been effected, Chelnokov wrote bitterly, "Mutual compliments followed, and calm descended."[103]

Those privy to this dispute had little doubt that a split in the party had been narrowly averted, for the conflict over participation on the Defense Committee was only a symptom of the deepening dissatisfaction of the right wing of the party with the orientation championed by Miliukov. In February Chelnokov told Dmitrii Shipov, a conservative Progressive, "In the faction many are against the hegemony of the left mood but can do nothing, fearing the authority of Miliukov and company. Obviously, the business is all the same moving toward a split in the party." In a long letter to Chelnokov of February 22, Shipov set out his views on the desirability of inducing Kadets of the type of "Struve, Maklakov, and so on" to leave the party, clearly assuming that they would join the Progressives. The root of the current discord was not disagreement over participation on the Committee on State

Defense, Shipov wrote, but rather the difference in "spiritual makeup" (*dukhovnyi uklad*) between Chelnokov and people like Miliukov.[104]

In employing the expression "spiritual makeup" in this context Shipov probably did not mean religiosity in the narrow sense, but the fact that Miliukov was a convinced atheist was not unimportant. Clearly, one affinity between a number of conservative Kadets and Progressives was their Christian faith; they could subscribe to the critique of the intelligentsia's lack of religious belief, and corresponding moral relativism, advanced by Struve and others in *Vekhi*. In the eyes of the right wing of the party, a fundamental shortcoming of Kadet liberalism, aside from the excessive radicalism of the Miliukov line, was its insufficient nationalism—and Russian nationalism, for many of these individuals, had a religious lining. Tyrkova, who characterized atheism as a "very dangerous disease," later asserted that Miliukov's speeches had no connection with Russian popular life, perhaps because he was "absolutely lacking in religious feeling."[105]

The challenges to his leadership, and the danger that the right wing of the party might go over to the Progressives, did not prompt Miliukov to rethink the stance he was urging upon the party. In early 1913, he was talking in central committee meetings of the almost "hopeless" situation in the Duma and recommending a further retreat from the tactics of restraint he had championed for the past five years. In a pessimistic outline of the tactical report he was preparing for the party's February 1913 conference, Miliukov described the Duma as being in a morass, unable to accomplish anything whatsoever, a condition due to the lack of a stable majority, the government's own lack of any well-defined course, and, above all, the general conviction that any positive measures actually passed would simply be squashed by the State Council. He urged that the Kadets shift their emphasis from "small deeds," in the form of continued legislative work, to "propaganda," by making demonstrative gestures in the Duma.[106]

The "sharper parliamentary tactics" advocated by Miliukov and his supporters on the central committee—most notably Shingarev, Rodichev, Shchepkin, and N. A. Nekrasov—had three elements: a concerted effort to force discussion of Kadet bills on civil liberties and universal suffrage, greater use of interpellations into government behavior, and more aggressive use of the Duma's budgetary rights. Kadet-sponsored bills on the inviolability of the individual, rights of association, freedom of the press, and freedom of conscience came up for preliminary consideration by the Duma in February 1913.[107] All four bills passed their first hurdle easily, being acknowledged by the Duma as worthy of consideration and sent to the appropriate committees; however, since no deadlines had been imposed they were, in effect, buried there.

If the civil liberties bills were largely demonstrative in nature, the controversial bill on universal suffrage was purely so. Aside from there being little ground for believing that a majority of the Duma desired immediate introduction of universal suffrage, the Fundamental Laws made an attempt to do so illegal: there was thus no question of the Duma even sending the bill to committee. By making this gesture the Kadets risked compromising their hard-won reputation for being level-headed, responsible legislators, a consideration which had caused Miliukov himself just one year earlier to oppose introducing a universal suffrage bill. Miliukov, however, by now shared the concern of Dmitrii Shakhovskoi, Nekrasov, and other more left-leaning Kadets about the disparity between the Duma's conduct and the increasingly oppositional mood of the country. He hoped that in addition to advertising the "democratic" nature of the Kadets, discussion of universal suffrage would put added pressure on the Octobrists to demonstrate their own democratic credentials.

Miliukov took care to characterize the bill before the Duma in as moderate a light as was possible, representing it as a starting point for an exchange of views on what changes to the existing suffrage law would be desirable. The question, after all, was of burning interest to the country and could not be ignored indefinitely without peril. Ending on a more provocative note, he asked if the Duma really wished to emulate the behavior of autocracy before October 1905, by its tardiness pushing the population to employ violent means of struggle and then deciding that it must employ violence itself to "pacify" the country.[108] The Kadet bill succeeded in evoking strong support from many peasant deputies for changes to the electoral law of June 3. The Duma, however, rejected not only the bill on universal suffrage but also the Kadet proposal that a committee be formed to consider more modest changes to the existing suffrage law.[109]

A more oppositional stance was elicited by the debates over the budget of the Ministry of Internal Affairs, traditionally the occasion when parties offered their assessment of the general state of the country. In spring 1913, the scathing evaluations of government policy by Progressives and Octobrists were almost indistinguishable from those offered by the Kadets, a common theme being the government's alienation of even the most moderate elements of society. Kadets had voted against portions of the budget of the Ministry of Internal Affairs for several years; now, declaring again that government policy was "anti-patriotic and anti-state," they moved that the Duma reject the ministry's budget in its entirety. Hopes that the Progressives would follow suit were not realized. The Duma finally passed, by a vote of 160 to 109, the Octobrist motion, which demanded the speediest possible implementation of reforms without calling for rejection of the budget.

Much the same pattern was followed for consideration of the budgets of the Ministries of Justice and Education, although here the Kadets moved only that the Duma reject the appropriations for the central organs of each ministry. Justifying the Kadet motion concerning the Ministry of Justice, Miliukov appealed to the Octobrists: "Words have lost their force . . . it is necessary to cross over from words to deeds." Once again, the Progressives and Octobrists declined to unite with the Kadets; the Duma passed motions expressing dissatisfaction with both ministries, but chose to withhold only token sums from each.[110]

Publicly, Miliukov characterized all these votes as victories of a sort, a sign that the faction's sharper tactical line was having an effect. It was true that the center was still forwarding demands for reform rather cautiously and irresolutely, he wrote in *Rech'*, but this vote showed that the Duma *was* a social force, and that "the government is completely isolated."[111] Whether he felt as satisfied in private is doubtful. The Octobrists had gone as far as he anticipated they would, but the Progressives had not. A "united opposition" in the Duma was still only a desideratum; Social Democratic deputies continued to attack the Kadets as upholders of class privilege and the tsarist regime, while the Trudoviks, now headed by the young lawyer Alexander Kerensky, provided only inconsistent support.

The government, moreover, showed no signs of responding positively to growing criticism. The public outcry over the 1912 Beilis murder case, unsavory both for its trumped-up evidence against the defendant and its charge that Jews engaged in the ritual murder of Christians, did not deter the Ministry of Justice from attempting to secure a conviction. Not a single substantive reform bill was introduced by the government during the first year of the Fourth Duma. Repeated appeals to the government to curtail rule by "extraordinary law" met no response, and repression in the provinces and the capitals continued unabated.

When Duma deputies returned to Petersburg in October 1913 after the summer recess, the atmosphere did not presage any improvement: rumors were rife that the government was considering reducing the Duma from a legislative to a consultative body.[112] Then in late January 1914 a conservative campaign against Kokovtsov resulted in his dismissal from the cabinet. The choice of the deeply conservative Ivan Goremykin, the bête noire of the First Duma, to succeed him as president of the Council of Ministers was an obvious sign of hostility toward the legislature.[113]

The government thus appeared to have settled upon a "new course" of more consistent reaction, a development that only added to the widespread unease that Russia was heading toward some new catastrophe. In these circumstances it was imperative that the Kadets try to mend their differences and arrive at some sort of agreement about what should be done, and with whom. Whether such an agreement was possible, however, was doubtful.

The Octobrists had recently given formal expression to their long-standing internal differences by breaking into three separate factions; some observers anticipated the imminent split of the Constitutional Democrats into "radical-democratic" and "national liberal" parties, perhaps at the party conference scheduled for late March. At any rate, in the weeks preceding the conference various groups and individuals made a concerted effort to build support for the orientation and tactics each deemed best.

The opening salvo from the more conservative wing of the party had already been fired in January, in an article by Struve in his journal *Russkaia mysl'*. Profoundly alarmed by the possible consequences of the government's increasing loss of authority, Struve warned against confrontational tactics that deepened the gulf between government and society while helping the left to incite a new, elemental mass movement. Such a movement would sweep aside moderate elements, and with them any hope for nonviolent solutions to Russia's problems. What was needed was a "regeneration of authority" (*ozdorovlenie vlasti*), to be accomplished by "the joint efforts of all progressive and at the same time *preservative* forces."[114]

Several weeks before the conference the Moscow liberal daily *Russkie vedomosti* (Russian gazette) began a spirited debate with Miliukov on his tactical line. While the editors did not echo Struve's advice about holding aloof from the left, they did question the wisdom of concentrating so exclusively on the systemic change embodied in undoing the "three padlocks." They believed this slogan should be supplemented by a concrete platform of "immediate practical tasks" if the opposition was to avoid driving away members of the public not yet committed to all their long-term goals.[115]

Miliukov fully shared Struve's fears about the perilous situation of the country and the disastrous repercussions to be expected from an "elemental" mass movement. He considered the approach promoted by conservative Kadets and the moderate *Russkie vedomosti*, however, mistaken on a number of counts. Whereas the conservative Kadets feared that too left a stance would initiate a repetition of the events of 1905–6, and therefore counseled that moderates remain studiously aloof from the left parties, Miliukov believed that the party had to respond to the leftward shift of the popular mood and make efforts to work with at least the Trudoviks. Second, he considered the prospect of winning over the Octobrists to some sort of firm alliance illusory. Finally, he felt such an alliance could accomplish almost nothing, so long as the State Council dismantled every Duma bill with impunity.

He made these differences explicit in his polemic with *Russkie vedomosti* and at two important central committee meetings in March shortly before the party conference. Chelnokov and Maklakov were, again, particularly outspoken; the latter's critique of the party faction in the Duma amounted to a rejection of virtually all of Miliukov's tactics.[116] Basically, Maklakov and Chelnokov were calling for tactics along the lines of Struve's envisioned union of progressive but "preservative" elements. They advocated working out a minimal program around which a moderate majority could unite wholeheartedly and an end to overtures to the Duma leftists, who, as Chelnokov put it, "don't come onto the rostrum without abusing us."

Miliukov countered in a spirit no less exasperated than that of his critics. The faction was not going to follow Maklakov because "otherwise it will cease to be the People's Freedom faction." The party's deputies were doing all they could to reach agreements with the Octobrists in every concrete instance, he insisted, but extended agreements with them were not possible. Miliukov also countered what he considered the Muscovites' dismissive attitude toward the leftists. What had to be taken into account was that "the democratic masses stand behind them, that we and the Trudoviks will have to share the peasants between us, and that therefore there might just be a basis for making advances to them." The opposition's task was not regeneration of authority but rather "isolation of the government." The majority of the St. Petersburg branch of the central committee agreed with Miliukov's definition of the party's immediate object; however, as Aleksandr Kornilov and others pointed out, the real difficulty lay in determining the *means* by which the government was to be isolated.[117]

Miliukov's understanding of the limits to "opposition" and the larger dilemma over means confronting Russian liberals were made explicit when the party conference convened March 23. In a departure from the customary practice, two proposals on tactics were presented: Miliukov gave the official report on behalf of the central committee, while N. V. Nekrasov offered proposals in his own name. Miliukov began with the assertion that the country demanded of the opposition more determined activity. He therefore called for increased efforts to unite the opposition in the Duma and in the country, with the goal of isolating the government; practical legislative work was suggested only conditionally as a means toward this end. Nekrasov, the most left-wing member of the central committee and long a staunch supporter of Miliukov's sharper tactical line, now argued that this did not go far enough. The party had to acknowledge that nothing could be done within constitutional limits and that it must therefore step beyond those limits. It should be willing to go as far as creating obstructions in the Duma and with the left organize demonstrations outside it. It needed, as well, to be more "democratic," exerting itself strenuously on behalf of workers, reworking its agrarian program, and demanding fulfillment of national minorities' aspirations for cultural autonomy.[118]

Nekrasov's presentation clearly spoke to all the pent-up frustrations of the delegates, for the conference responded with an ovation. Yet when debate began over his ten-point proposal, only two people supported it entirely. Instead, a series of speakers identified ideological and practical problems with the approach he proposed.

Miliukov argued that the reorientation of the party inherent in the Nekrasov proposal called into question the very meaning of constitutional democracy. "Constitutionalism is the quality with which we, as a party, came into the world," he argued; "if we foreswore it we would cease to exist as such, and the results of our many years of work would be lost." After a point by point critique of most of the proposed tactics as untimely or impractical, he concluded that the theses would "only introduce trouble and discord, and not the unity everyone is in need of." Fedor Kokoshkin took a similar view, maintaining that Nekrasov's proposals went "beyond the bounds of the party program." In the opinion of D. D. Protopopov, a more conservative Kadet, Nekrasov's line of argument was predicated on the unwarranted assumption that another revolution was inevitable.[119] So wholesale was the critique of Nekrasov's proposals that he withdrew them from formal consideration by the conference, which then passed Miliukov's tactical report virtually unamended.[120]

Nekrasov's speech had actually done Miliukov a great service. The emergence of a position left of Miliukov's had the effect of making his own proposals the middle route; if they did not thereby become positively attractive to conservative delegates, they at least became the lesser of two evils. By causing Miliukov to set out clearly his commitment to strictly legal and parliamentary methods of political struggle, uncertainty concerning how far he was prepared to take the party was dispelled. Nekrasov's proposal that the party step beyond the limits of constitutionalism also forced conference participants to clarify their own thinking on this vexed question. Despite the emotional appeal of the more heroic stance he outlined, the delegates were not prepared to embrace it. The fiasco of the 1906 Vyborg Manifesto had demonstrated the costs not only of misreading popular discontent, but also of confusing the difference between working with the Trudoviks and acting like the Trudoviks; Kadets did not wish to repeat those mistakes.

The March 1914 conference thus did not produce the split in the party many anticipated. Miliukov probably appreciated, however, that he had prevailed by default: the conference had united in rejecting Nekrasov's proposals, not out of enthusiasm for his own. The question now was whether his tactics could produce results.

"Isolation of the government" turned out to involve increasing opposition during debate over the budget. In a central committee discussion of tactics in February, Miliukov had referred to the possibility of voting against the entire state budget as too extreme a measure. Now, speaking for the Kadet faction in the session of April 26, he moved that the Duma take this step. He again pitched his appeal directly to the Octobrists, the "representatives of loyal and moderate circles," exhorting them to use their lawful budgetary rights to reject a governmental policy that was not only profoundly harmful to the state, but carried out in open alliance with the leaders of the Black Hundreds. This time, the Progressives backed the Kadets, also moving that the Duma refuse to give this government money. The Duma nonetheless voted by a large majority to proceed to examination of the budget.[121]

The more realistic hope that a majority of Octobrists would join the opposition in rejecting the budget of the Ministry of Internal Affairs was also disappointed. Denunciations from all sides of the Ministry's conduct were even fiercer than in the previous year, but the Octobrists announced that they could in principle deny only those appropriations whose loss would not harm local self-government. Although this was the most oppositional step yet taken by that group, one duly hailed in *Rech'*, it fell far short of what was needed to "isolate the government."[122] Moreover, the Octobrists undercut whatever urgency had been conveyed by the voting on the Interior budget by fully approving large military appropriations shortly thereafter. The center lacked sufficient independence and civic courage, Miliukov wrote bitterly several weeks later, "and the authorities understood this perfectly, never believing for a moment that mutual irritation could grow into a serious conflict."[123]

Had the Octobrists voted with the opposition the budget for the Interior would have failed, something no government could ignore. Whether such a step would have jolted the government into awareness that it must make substantive concessions, as Miliukov hoped, was another question. The demonstration might very well have persuaded Nicholas to dissolve the Duma and call for new elections, or return to his earlier idea of reducing it to a consultative body. Miliukov, with the majority of the Kadets and Progressives, had been prepared to take the risk; the Octobrists were not.

Instead, Miliukov experienced an altogether different sort of demonstration in the Duma. On May 13 the Right Octobrist N. P. Shubinskii unexpectedly raised the old insinuation that the Kadets had accepted a bribe from the Finns. The far right responded with applause and calls of "Bravo!" Miliukov angrily called Shubinskii a scoundrel. Shubinskii replied that he spit upon Miliukov. Purishkevich called Miliukov "a swine, a beast," and Kerensky, joining the fray, called Shubinskii a "bare-faced liar." Progressive A. I. Konovalov, presiding over the session in his capacity as Duma vice-president, asked that all four men be excluded for one session. The Duma duly voted to exclude Miliukov, Kerensky, and Purishkevich, but by a narrow margin failed to exclude the instigator of the incident, Shubinskii, which meant that a number of Octobrists refused to condemn their colleague's actions. Konovalov resigned from his position the same day, forcing a vote for a new Duma presidium.[124]

All of this must have seemed drearily familiar to Miliukov; the second year of the Fourth Duma was ending where the Third Duma had begun, with Octobrist-abetted insults to his party and himself. Some six years into the "Third of June" system, it appeared that little had really changed. The Duma had proved by turns unwilling or unable to pass needed reforms or halt administrative arbitrariness. In the case of legislation affecting national minorities it had not merely failed to oppose a divisive nationality policy, but outstripped the government in its Great Russian chauvinism. In truth, the institution Miliukov had counted upon to mend the rents in Russia's social fabric was rarely able to overcome its own factional divides. Not even increasingly widespread apprehensions that a crisis was in the making could induce the majority of Octobrists to join efforts to pressure the government through exercise of the Duma's legal rights.

If little forward movement was discernible in the Duma, neither had the Kadets advanced: Miliukov had succeeded in little more than holding his party together. In 1914, as labor unrest reached proportions reminiscent of the revolutionary period, the party was still replaying the debates of 1907 over whether to move closer to the Octobrists or the left. Denied legal status, its membership shrunk, and its finances in chronically bad shape, Russia's only avowedly liberal party was divided and demoralized on the eve of the country's greatest trial yet.[125]

CHAPTER EIGHT

The War Years

Of all Russian public figures, Miliukov was one of the best informed about foreign policy. He institutionalized discussion of foreign policy in the Duma—a subject formally outside the purview of the legislature—by raising it during the annual discussion of the budget of the foreign ministry.[1] He brought foreign policy issues before a wider public, editorializing regularly in *Rech'* on international diplomacy, publishing in *Rech'* his "letters from abroad," writing an annual review of Russia's conduct of foreign affairs for the *Rech'* yearbook, and lecturing widely.

Yet unlike his thinking on liberalism and nationalism, Miliukov's interest in foreign policy was not the natural outgrowth of his scholarship. With his sociological approach to history and disdain for the "history of events," foreign policy and diplomacy had scarcely figured in his scholarship. His famous conclusion of his magister's dissertation, that Peter had raised Russia to the rank of a European power at the cost of the "ruination of the country," seemingly reflected the conviction, common among the intelligentsia, that in Russia international power generally came at the direct expense of domestic well-being.[2]

The most obvious source of Miliukov's foreign policy preoccupations was his lifelong interest in the Balkans. As the Balkan question became a pressing interest to the European powers from 1908 on, his unrivaled knowledge of the region, its peoples, and its languages made him a confident commentator on developments in the area. That he nonetheless wrote almost nothing on foreign policy prior to that time and, when he began to concern himself with foreign policy, ranged over the whole spectrum of Russia's foreign policy signals the influence of other considerations in his growing interest in this topic. These considerations included the role of the Kadet party in the new order, the prestige and the future of the Russian state, and a commitment to pacifism.

Miliukov's very belief that the Constitutional Democrats should take a positive part in discussion of the state's foreign policy initially met with resistance from much of the party leadership. The party program contained no foreign policy provisions; in common with the Gladstonian liberalism of most of the British Liberal Party at that time, Kadets feared priorities that might place guns before butter. Moreover, the party's hostility toward the government and awareness that the Duma lacked any formal control over conduct of foreign policy made many Kadets feel their role should be confined to criticism.

These views were most fully aired in two gatherings of central committee members in early March 1909, in response to Miliukov's first effort to outline a positive foreign policy position for the party. A. M. Koliubakin, Nabokov, Shingarev, and others insisted that anything other than a critical position could only compromise the party. In any event, various speakers doubted that the Kadets would have the slightest affect on policy; Ariadna Tyrkova found particularly amusing Miliukov's conviction that "his editorials in *Rech'* influence Izvolskii and foreign affairs."[3]

Miliukov argued that advancing positive foreign policy positions would benefit the party by giving the lie to conservative charges that Kadets were deficient in patriotism. More significant, he believed Kadets *could* conceivably exercise a beneficial influence on the conduct of foreign policy, if only because European governments were beginning to take Russian public opinion into account. But to be heeded at all, it was essential that in the field of foreign policy they occupy truly "national" and "nonpartisan" positions, and offer constructive suggestions as well as criticism. Miliukov also took to task the traditional intelligentsia disdain for foreign policy; as a great state, Russia was "fated [*obrechena*] to conduct a great foreign policy."[4]

This 1909 exchange testified to the degree Miliukov's own thinking on national interests had altered. During the Russo-Japanese War he had insisted that support for the army translated into support for the government, a position that would only "muddle our political conduct and overshadow more urgent questions of domestic politics."[5] Now, he battled analogous attitudes held by most of his Kadet colleagues. The crucial difference, for Miliukov, seems to have been creation of the Duma. Because the citizenry's elected representatives enjoyed some share in state authority, they could and should become more state-minded. It was this supposition that underlay one of the most controversial of his "tactless" remarks, the declaration made in summer 1909, as member of a Duma delegation to London, that so long as a legislative assembly existed in Russia the opposition was "not an opposition *to* his Majesty, but the opposition *of* his Majesty." Although this remark caused such a commotion within Kadet ranks and leftist circles that he had more or less to disavow it, he did not disavow the statism that informed it.[6]

Struve, one of relatively few Kadets who approved Miliukov's pronouncement in London, was not among those who needed to be persuaded that care for Russia's might was a proper liberal concern.[7] Miliukov and Struve attached great significance to Russia's alliance with France and Great Britain, seeing in it both a safeguard against German threats to Russian security and interests and a potential reinforcement of parliamentarism at home. Both men, too, believed the emphasis in Russian foreign policy should shift from the Far East to where her real interests lay, the Balkans and Black Sea basin; however, their views on the sort of "great" foreign policy Russia should conduct, and the larger significance of that policy, differed markedly.

In his 1908 essay "Great Russia" Struve asserted that a state was not merely a system of relationships but a living thing, a personality, with its own laws of existence. The state's external power, far from being secondary to the question of its domestic well-being, was in fact its paramount concern. Strong and healthy states strive for power, with the weak falling prey to the strong. A good domestic policy was one that contributed to the state's external power, while a vigorous imperial policy stimulated national energies and cohesion, as demonstrated by Britain and Germany.[8] Miliukov, in contrast, rejected any conception of the state as an "organism" or personality, was highly suspicious of notions suggesting that the state observed laws peculiarly its own, and continued to believe that national energies were the source rather than product of a confident foreign policy. Finally, he was much more sensitive than Struve to the potentially dangerous consequences of an expansionist policy in the Balkans, at least until 1914.

Neo-Slavism was one orientation Miliukov initially shared with the right wing of the Kadets. In April 1908 a Society of Slavic Culture was opened in Moscow and a society of Slav Scholarship in St. Petersburg. Founders included Miliukov, Maklakov, Struve, and Pavel Dolgorukov from the Kadets, and such prominent Progressives and Octobrists as Shipov, Guchkov, and Duma president Khomiakov. The societies sponsored public talks and cultural evenings, including Miliukov's October 1908 lectures on Bosnia-Herzegovina. They also entered into the plans of neo-Slavist Karal Kramař, organizer of the Young Czech movement, to arrange international gatherings of Slavs; a Slavic Congress was held in Sofia in summer 1908 and in Prague in 1910. In these societies Miliukov stood out as the most "left" participant, and his enthusiasm for the larger neo-Slav movement soon faded. It was attracting, he felt, "the debris of old Slavophilism, usually people of conservative orientation." He distanced himself from neo-Slavism, refusing to attend either of the Slavic congresses abroad, although he did not sever his ties with the Slavic societies.⁹

As became clear in the aftermath of the Bosnia-Herzegovina crisis of 1908–9, the question of Russia's future policy in the Balkans did generate a nationally unifying idea, but not the sort Miliukov desired. In September 1908 the Austro-Hungarian government gave formal notice to Russia that it was annexing Bosnia-Herzegovina, over which it had exercised a protectorship since the Russo-Turkish War. Since the Serbs laid claim to much of the area, the Russian government did not welcome this move, but realized it was too weak to prevent it. Foreign Minister Aleksandr Izvolskii therefore tried to secure compensations for Serbia, Russia, and other states in exchange for recognizing the annexation; when Austria rejected his demands, Russia had no choice but to accede to its rival's unilateral act. The public was highly critical of the diplomatic mistakes that had resulted in Russia's humiliation—what Miliukov termed a "diplomatic Tsushima"—but appreciated the country could ill-afford war.¹⁰ In the years that followed, however, as nationalist passions in Russia mounted and military strength was rebuilt, public sentiment in favor of a more aggressive foreign policy grew as fear of the consequences of a possible war diminished. Resentment toward Austria, fear of a German *Drang nach Osten*, sympathy for the Balkan Slavs, and a desire to see Russia regain her prestige as a great power animated right Kadets, Progressives, and Octobrists alike in urging a more ambitious foreign policy in the Balkans. These views, variously called "national liberal" or "liberal Imperial," constituted the external policy component of the national liberalism that Struve, Maklakov, and other right Kadets wished to see the party develop domestically as well, in union with other moderate constitutionalists.¹¹

Miliukov had contacts with many of these individuals through the Society of Slavic Culture, but otherwise did not rush to embrace them. His reservations did not concern their imperialism per se, since he believed that Russia was a great power with interests to preserve. But the "realistic" imperialism they propounded appeared to him to border at times on the reckless. He questioned their uncritical enthusiasm for Slav interests, especially those of Serbia, and better appreciated the weaknesses of Russia's position concerning Constantinople and the straits than did many otherwise quite intelligent observers.¹² A third, and important point of difference between Miliukov and the foreign policy views of national liberals was his horror of war.

Miliukov had been involved in the pacifist movement since the period of the First Duma, when he was a member and vice-chairman of the Parliamentarian Union of Peace, lead by Christian Lange. He pinned his hopes for peace largely on broadening the scope of compulsory arbitration, a goal that seemed particularly crucial in the context of the continental armaments race spurred by British-German rivalry and renewed Balkan instability. In

1909 he joined the Society of Peace being organized by Prince Pavel Dolgorukov in Moscow and his former teacher, Maksim Kovalevskii, in Petersburg, and at their invitation prepared a seven-city lecture series on the pacifist movement.[13]

Miliukov's lectures, which he brought out in book form as *The Armed World and the Limitations of Armaments*, drew heavily on a recently published work by Norman Angell, *The Great Illusion*.[14] Instead of urging pacifism on moral grounds, Angell directed his appeal to reasoned self-interest, an approach which greatly impressed Miliukov. His own cast of thought inclined him to believe that the best hope for peace lay in "realistic argumentation" rather than invocation of moral imperatives, and he shared Angell's assumptions about the adaptiveness of human nature. Angell sought to demonstrate that the interdependence of modern, credit-based economies made it impossible to profit economically by war, whether through territorial annexation, imposition of indemnities, or the destruction of trade and commerce in the conquered territory. Second, he argued against what Miliukov termed the "psychological case" for war based on social darwinist presuppositions concerning the struggle for existence, the false analogy of the state as a personality, and a putatively unchanging, aggressive human nature, all leading to the conviction that armed conflict will never fade away. In fact, Angell held, the struggle for existence is not that of man against man, but humanity against nature, with victory going to the groups best able to specialize and cooperate. Neither is the level of aggression in human nature a constant, the disappearance from civilized societies of enslavement of the conquered and of wars of religion being two examples of the attenuation of resort to raw force in human affairs.

Finally, with Angell, Miliukov stressed that moderate pacifists were not arguing for immediate disarmament: so long as illusions concerning the profitability of war and unchangingly aggressive human nature persisted, peaceful states had to be prepared to defend themselves against their neighbors. For arms limitation agreements to be effective in the long run, they had to be accompanied by campaigns aimed at exposing these illusions. Only then would it be possible to end the arms race that virtually everyone agreed was not only economically burdensome but itself a powerful stimulus to resort to arms. This "realistic" form of pacifism was not yet widely embraced in Russia, Miliukov acknowledged, but he urged it upon his audiences as wholly in keeping with the values and goals of the Russian intelligentsia.[15]

In February 1912 Russia helped broker a secret alliance between Serbia and Bulgaria. The ostensible aim of the alliance was self-defense against possible Austrian aggression, but it clearly carried the risk of being turned to offensive purposes against the Ottoman Empire. In October of that year the offensive occurred, despite concerted efforts by Russia and the other European powers to avert it, as Bulgaria, Serbia, Montenegro, and Greece went to war against Turkey. To the surprise of virtually everyone, Turkey proved no match for the Balkan allies and in November turned to the Great Powers for help negotiating a peace. After protracted negotiations the Balkan allies and Great Powers acceded to Austria's demands that Serbia withdraw from the shores of the Adriatic and Montenegro give up the captured city of Skutari to the newly created Albanian state.

While the Russian government had in no way desired so dangerous a disruption of the status quo in the Balkans as was implicit in a Balkan war, Russian society had cheered on the Balkan allies' offensive against Turkey and celebrated their victories in the press and the streets of Petersburg. Public opinion was correspondingly outraged by the failure of Russian diplomacy to better defend Slav interests at the bargaining table, by threat of force if necessary.[16] Miliukov, who believed too strong a Russian defense of Serb claims could touch off a general war in Europe, now became one of the lone voices defending the restrained policies of Izvolskii's successor, S. D. Sazonov.

Sazonov was conducting Russian diplomacy as he should, Miliukov argued, in close concert with Russia's allies. Once war broke out, Russia and France secured for the Balkan states the opportunity to fight their opponents without outside intervention from other parties. Still, what the Balkan states and Europe wanted were not entirely identical; the interest of Europe was peace. In a Duma speech of December 1912, Miliukov spoke out against the provocative position taken by the majority of Duma speakers with their oft-repeated phrase "We don't want war, but we are not afraid." Miliukov warned the Duma, "You are not the masters of that war which 'you are not afraid of'; you don't know why it will be started, nor to what it will lead."[17]

In June 1913, on the eve of the Second Balkan War, Miliukov was more critical of Russian diplomacy, having learned of the secret Serb-Bulgarian treaty of February 1912: it seemed to him that Russia had been insufficiently aware that by making that alliance possible it had cleared the way for war with Turkey. But once that war began, he repeated, Russia and all the Great Powers had worked energetically and responsibly to keep the conflict from spreading, which he took as a heartening sign that appreciation of peace was gaining ground in Europe. He also defended the concessions Russia had countenanced for the sake of averting war, arguing that Serbia and the Balkan states had secured a great deal more than they perhaps appreciated, and largely thanks to Russia's support.

In surveying the tensions now threatening to compromise these successes,

Miliukov laid most of the blame on Serbia. The major bone of contention was the division of Macedonia between Serbia and Bulgaria as provided for in the February 1912 agreement. Miliukov regarded the agreement itself as indefensible; justice demanded an autonomous, intact Macedonian state. Since it was now too late for that, the interested parties needed to abide by their original agreement, and here Serbia was at fault: having occupied most of Macedonia during the war, it was unwilling to give up what it had taken. Miliukov's belief that Serbia was wholly unrealistic in its claims was reinforced by a visit he made to the Balkans in January 1913. From private discussions in Belgrade he had concluded that Serbian ambitions were growing over time—what was denied as a desiderata one week was insisted upon as a "vital interest" the next. The last means for avoiding fratricidal war were the upcoming discussions in Petersburg. Both Serbia and Bulgaria must come ready to make concessions, while Russia, in its role as mediator, must take care not to arouse European concerns by appearing to act unilaterally.[18]

The conflict Miliukov feared broke out days after this speech. The Bulgarian tsar, harboring grander territorial pretensions than did most of his cabinet, and fearful that Russian arbitration would back Serbian claims, took the desperate step of attacking Serbia and Greece. Bulgaria promptly found itself fighting not only all its former allies but Rumania and Turkey as well. The Second Balkan War, conducted with great savagery on all sides, ended some six weeks later with peace treaties stripping Bulgaria of all its gains from the previous war, largely to the advantage of Greece and Serbia.

Miliukov now embarked again for the Balkans, this time as a member of an international commission. In July 1913 the Education and Information Section of the Carnegie Endowment for International Peace decided to investigate the origins of the Balkan wars and the allegations concerning violations of the rules of war. Its goal was to foster "the replacement of violence by conciliation and justice in the regulation of international agreements." Baron d'Estournelles de Constant, chairman of the French branch of the Carnegie Institute, was the formal head of the project. The members of the investigatory commission, all of whom were known pacifists, included a French parliamentary deputy, Justin Godart; Samuel Dutton, of Columbia University; H. N. Brailsford, a British journalist; and Miliukov. Only the latter two, among those traveling to the Balkans, knew much of Balkan affairs or languages, and it was they who became objects of persecution.[19]

In Belgrade, Prime Minister Nicola Pasic refused to receive a commission including a "declared enemy" of Serbia—Miliukov. Unwilling to accept exclusion of one of its members, the commission immediately left for Salonika where it set about collecting documents and eyewitness reports and visited sites of alleged atrocities. After five days, on the request of the Greek authorities, the governor of Salonika asked the commission to leave; this time it was Brailsford who turned out to be the "enemy" of Greece. Godart and Miliukov then traveled to Athens, where within a few days Miliukov, too, was discovered to be "an enemy of Greece." At this point, it was decided that Miliukov would go on alone to Turkey, where he could count on the help of some of his acquaintances in gathering evidence and visiting sites, before joining Godart and Dutton in Sofia for ten days' investigative work. In September the commission members traveled to Paris to draw up their report.[20]

The result of their labors was a solid tome over five hundred pages long, comprised of the discussion of their findings, maps and photographs, and appendices. Four of the seven chapters of text were written by Miliukov—one providing the historical background on the wars, two chapters on nationalities and the war, and a chapter discussing violations of international law. Conscious of the novelty of their undertaking and the suspicions concerning their impartiality emanating from all the belligerents, the writers of the report were scrupulous in their attempts to weigh and verify testimony, place actions taken in context, and assign blame.[21]

There was no shortage of blame to go around. The most widely publicized atrocities had been those attributed to the Bulgarians, but as Miliukov wrote, "There is no clause in international law applicable to land war and to the treatment of the wounded, which was not violated, to a greater or lesser extent, by all the belligerents."[22] And while accounts of various atrocities frequently turned out to be exaggerated, evidence of excesses was abundant. Rape, pillage, torture and mutilations, forced religious conversions, expulsions of local populations from villages and towns, and wholesale massacres made up the sorry tale of both Balkan wars. The exceptionally widespread devastation reflected the fact that it was not the armies alone that were engaged in the conflict. "War is waged not only by the armies but by the nations themselves," Miliukov wrote.

> The local population is divided into as many fragmentary parts as it contains nationalities, and these fight together, each being desirous to substitute itself for the others . . . the object of these armed conflicts, overt or covert, clearly conceived or vaguely felt, but always and everywhere the same, was the complete extermination of an alien population.[23]

In some cases the savagery was apparently spontaneous, the action of ethnic and religious hatreds run rampant. In others, the extermination of a population by an advancing army appeared to have been systematic and premeditated. The Serbians and Greeks were the worst offenders, but in this, too, none of the combatants had clean hands.[24]

Miliukov's analysis for the report concerning the historical roots and immediate causes of the Balkan wars drew on his earlier work on nationality and national liberation movements. Briefly treating the conflicts among Balkan peoples for hegemony in the region, extending back to the tenth century, the debasing effects of some five centuries of Ottoman suzerainty, and the emergence of nationalist movements in the early nineteenth century, he called particular attention to the way mistaken attitudes toward nationality had compounded the Balkan tragedy. The most egregious sin was excessive nationalism; coupled to state interests it had given birth to ambitious but illegitimate "great national ideas," for a "Greater" Serbia, "Greater" Bulgaria or "Greater" Greece, conceptions which themselves involved transgressions against the claims and even the existence of other nationalities.[25] At the same time, the conflicts of the Balkans owed a good deal to an error of a different sort, that of underestimating or disregarding the strength of national consciousness. Attempts by Turkey and the various Slavic states to forcibly assimilate or "denationalize" other peoples, which only intensified their national feeling, was one illustration of this error. Another was furnished by the treaty-making of the European powers, drawing up territorial boundaries in the Balkans with a fine disregard for the national composition and sentiments of the regions involved. By provision of the 1878 Treaty of Berlin, the principality of Bulgaria had been dismembered and Macedonia left in the hands of the Turks. This grave error was, Miliukov insisted, "the origin and cause of all subsequent conflicts." The 1913 Treaty of Bucharest, concluding the Second Balkan War, only repeated this error; if not revised, the peace it established was unlikely to last.[26]

The members of the Carnegie commission ended their labors with no great optimism for the future. All parties had been guilty of gross inhumanity, the work of reconstruction would be enormous and costly, and there were no cure-alls to propose.[27] Despite the glowing praise of d'Estournelles de Constant for his critical contribution to the inquiry, Miliukov found himself wondering what they had accomplished: "On the one hand, a 'great step toward conciliation and justice'; on the other—hundreds of pages dotted with names of persons and places no one knew, with numbers, dates, half-literate accusations and confessions which no one would ever read. . . . It was as if one of us was not entirely serious."[28]

Even if he now harbored doubts about the efficacy of abstract pacifism, what he learned in the Balkans strengthened his support for a foreign policy of restraint. For one, the horrors of war were now more than ever clear, something he tried to impress upon Russian audiences through a series of public lectures on the Balkan wars.[29] For another, he believed the Balkan peoples had outgrown Russian tutelage; they had achieved their own liberation, and each now pursued its interests as it deemed necessary. Russia was therefore freed of the burden of constant care for the interests of Slavdom as a whole, and must guide itself by its own interests; "Russia must no longer fight because of the Slavs." He stuck to this unpopular line tenaciously over the next ten months, as the strident press campaign conducted between Germany and Russia in spring 1914 helped intensify international tensions produced by the changed Balkan status quo.

On the morning of June 16, 1914 (old style), Miliukov, then vacationing at his Finnish dacha, unfolded the newspaper, read the report of the murder in Sarajevo of the heir to the Austrian-Hungarian throne, and exclaimed, "This is war!" He was sure that the assassination would prove to be the work of "Serbian patriot-terrorists," and that it would furnish Austria the opportunity to deal with Serbia once and for all. Anxious to discover what line the government might take, he hurried to Petersburg. His conversations with Foreign Affairs official Prince Grigorii Trubetskoi led him to hope that Russia would not allow herself to be sucked into a possible war as protector of Serbia. The conflict, he believed, must be "localized," since the European alliance system made it highly likely that Russia's intervention in an Austro-Serbian conflict would pull in the other powers as well. Russia was not prepared for war, and her probable defeat would have incalculable consequences. Serbia must be made to understand that Russia would not fight for her.[30]

These views, which Miliukov argued forcefully from the pages of *Rech'* both before and after the Austrians finally delivered their ultimatum to Serbia on July 11/24, were decidedly out of step with the general mood. Aside from holding a more benign attitude toward Serbia than Miliukov did, much of the educated public believed that Russia's own national interests made a strong stand imperative. If Russia failed yet again to defend Serbia from German bullying she would lose all influence in the Balkans, invite further incursions against her interests by the Central Powers, and see herself lose the status of a great power. Russia's alliance with France and Britain should deter the Central Powers from aggression against Serbia; if it did not, Russia must be prepared to fight.[31] These views were prevalent among many Kadets, for the events of the previous two years had made inroads against party hostility toward a strong Balkan policy. Not all Russian liberals were ready to run the risk of war: Ivan Petrunkevich, in early July, wrote Miliukov expressing his unqualified approval of his position at a moment when everyone else had seemingly taken leave of their senses. "Let your voice now ring out alone," Petrunkevich encouraged him; if war came, Russia could not win. For the most part, however, the conciliatory stance Miliukov took in *Rech'* provoked more indignation than thought.[32]

Miliukov's prescience in arguing for "localization" of the Austro-Serbian conflict at almost any price is worth emphasizing, since it is his subsequent stand on continuation of the war until victory and Russia's right to the Dardanelles that is best remembered today. The stubborn self-assurance that caused him to ignore the public mood with such disastrous results in spring 1917 was the very quality that enabled him to brave the patriotic maelstrom in insisting upon peace in July 1914. Holding fast to that position in the face of criticism and abuse required no little courage.[33]

The War and National Unity

On July 15 Austria declared war on Serbia and began bombarding Belgrade. On July 17, in spite of German warnings and with great misgivings, Nicholas ordered a general mobilization; two days later, Germany declared war on Russia. That evening the authorities shut down *Rech'*, assuming it would continue its opposition to the war. Such fears were unfounded, for the confiscated paper—which was allowed to appear two days later—contained an unambiguously patriotic declaration from the Kadet central committee that Miliukov had helped draft: "No matter what our attitude toward the government's domestic policy, our first duty is to preserve the unity and integrity of our country, and to defend its position as a world power. . . . Let us postpone our domestic disputes; let us not give our adversary even the slightest excuse for relying on differences which divide us."[34]

Miliukov's dramatic about-face should not have surprised anyone who knew his views well. His pacifism had never been of the absolute or Tolstoyan variety, nor was it predicated on the belief that states did not have legitimate interests to defend. Russia was now involved in a war not of her making, and her citizens must join in a "sacred union" to do whatever they could to aid the national effort. When the government decided to convene a special one-day sitting of the Duma July 26 to vote war credits and demonstrate the nation's solidarity behind the war, Miliukov opposed the minority of Duma deputies, among them Kerensky and some left Kadets and Progressives, who wished to exploit the opportunity to press for fundamental reforms.[35] At the special Duma sitting, Miliukov declared for the Kadets that they were postponing parliamentary struggle during the fight to defend their native land, free Europe and Slavdom of German domination, and put an end to the armaments race. "We are united in this struggle; we set no conditions and demand nothing; on the scales of war we simply place our firm will for victory."[36]

As Miliukov's Duma declaration suggests, he thought it imperative to set out immediately what Russia was fighting for. Unification of Russian society around a common understanding of the origins of the war, its general goals for the Allies, and its significance for Russian interests was a task to which he devoted himself. With characteristic thoroughness he delved into French, German, and English literature on the war and its critics, closely followed legislative and public debate in the foreign press, and scrutinized diplomatic maneuvering. The results were a barrage of speeches and articles that could fill several volumes: writing on the origins and aims of the war became, for Miliukov, a sort of personal war industry.[37]

Serbian irresponsibility had triggered the conflict, he felt, but Germany was to blame for the war, and not just in the person of its capricious, ambitious Kaiser with his talk of Germans as the "salt of the earth" and the need for Germany to take its "place in the sun." Wilhelm was typical of a whole generation of Germans who had transformed Fichte's and Hegel's philosophical views on the state into a political doctrine of the supremacy of the state. By this thinking, the state was the source of all right and law and therefore not bound by any law, international or otherwise, in pursuit of its interests. For a generation schooled to believe in Germany's world civilizing mission, Germany's present might was not enough; they dreamed of economic and political domination of an area "from Berlin to Baghdad" and acquisition of a worthy colonial empire. German arms buildups had fueled the world armaments race, even as Germany's attempts at aggrandizement woke up its neighbors to their danger and resulted, with conclusion of the Anglo-Russian convention of 1907, in the very "encirclement" or isolation it so feared. Finally, with no firm ally left but Austria-Hungary, Germany was compelled to back that state's aggressive behavior in the Balkans or risk total isolation, and then to contemplate a preventive war before Russia had completed her own rearmament. The Austro-Serbian conflict could not be localized in 1914 because Germany did not desire it to be.[38]

Miliukov's explanation for the war, so similar in many respects to Fritz Fischer's later interpretation, represented a departure from his earlier reading of German intentions.[39] Up until the very declaration of war, the restraint exercised by Wilhelm in various international disputes and during the Balkan wars, as well as the anti-imperialism of Social Democrats in the Reichstag, had persuaded him that the views of extremists would not prevail in Germany. When Germany instead backed Austria's attack on Serbia, he conceived a near hatred for the German emperor for his deceptions and was angry with himself for letting his pacifism cloud his reason.[40] These feelings intensified his hostility toward Germany, which helps explain his energy in opposing antiwar sentiments—at home or abroad—or any talk of a negotiated peace. Only the complete defeat of the Central Powers, he held, would force the Germans to renounce their dreams of world power and enable the victors to dictate conditions that would avert future conflicts.[41]

The first great aim of the war, then, was the creation of an international league of states enjoying real powers to arbitrate disputes, regulate armaments, and sanction states violating international law. The second aim of the war was national liberation, which Miliukov initially interpreted in a rather more restrictive sense—as the grant of national autonomy to any nationality desiring it—than did many British and French commentators on war aims. His constraint here was natural, given the difficult question of Poland: to embrace the principle of complete national self-determination would mean to agree to Polish independence, something he was not reconciled to until later in the war. Miliukov thus initially envisioned a federal "United States of Austria" after the war rather than a multitude of fully independent Slav states, switching to the latter view after summer 1915.[42] Finally, Miliukov acknowledged the victorious states' rights to certain territorial desiderata. Once Turkey entered the war on the side of the Central Powers, he saw the chance for Russia to realize her centuries-old dream of controlling Constantinople and the Dardanelles. Prior to fall 1914 he had considered that goal unattainable as long as Turkey remained a factor in the European balance of power. By 1915, however, Russian possession of the straits—on the grounds of "vital state interests" and not Pan-Slavist pretensions—had become a veritable idée fixe, earning for him the nickname "Miliukov-Dardanel'skii."[43]

For a short while it appeared that the outbreak of war had indeed created the national solidarity Russia was so signally lacking. The strike movement, which had assumed enormous proportions by July 1914, melted away. Constitutionalists had declared a cessation of hostilities against the government and political differences between and within moderate groups were laid aside as individuals sought ways to aid in defense of their country. The government, too, appeared ready to promote national unity. Kadets were extremely pleased by the August 1 proclamation promising autonomy to Poland and by government willingness to sanction all-Russian public organizations, the Union of Zemstvos and the Union of Towns, for aid to the sick and wounded.[44]

Unfortunately, faith in government good will toward society was already being undermined by autumn 1914. A strict censorship regime hampered the press, while persecution of local public organizations, political "undesirables," and religious and national minorities continued unabated. The suspicion with which society's initiatives were still regarded was embodied in Minister of Internal Affairs Maklakov's refusal in November to authorize a congress of public organizations to discuss war needs, "since under the guise of delivering boots you will begin to make a revolution."[45] Miliukov was angered by the authorities' failure to honor the "sacred union," but opposed any strong public expressions of dissatisfaction. Airing grievances could impair the army's morale and play into the hands of reactionaries in the cabinet; he preferred behind-the-scenes efforts to foster cooperation and halt governmental abuses.

It was in this spirit that Miliukov and the other Duma faction leaders, the so-called "Council of Elders" (*senioren konvent*), entered into negotiations with the government to convene the Duma well before its next scheduled sitting in November 1915. Goremykin refused to receive the Council of Elders when they first raised the subject, but in mid-December was prepared to make a deal: in exchange for an abbreviated Duma session early in the New Year and the government's promise not to resort to article 87 of the Fundamental Laws to pass the 1915 budget, the Duma would pass the new war budget and demonstrate its unity with the government.

These conditions were agreed to, but at the closed meeting between the Duma Defense Committee and the Council of Ministers held the day before the opening of the three-day January sitting, Miliukov and Shingarev sharply voiced Kadet criticisms. Deploring Maklakov's attitude toward the press and national minorities and arbitrary administration in Russian-occupied Galicia and Bukovina, they held that the government's behavior was only strengthening centrifugal tendencies within Russian society. At least minimal concessions were needed to restore public confidence and unity. Goremykin made conciliatory noises and promised to introduce a bill for Polish autonomy.[46] The Duma session of January 27–29 went as agreed, but the government altered its policies not at all. Strict censorship and repressions continued; Russia's oldest public organization, the Free Economic Society, was shut down; no bill on Polish autonomy was introduced.[47]

Miliukov and the Kadet leadership were subsequently assailed for their passivity in January 1915, but these critiques were made with the benefit of hindsight. In December and January the leaders of the Duma factions did not as yet know that the provisions made for the front were almost as unsatisfactory as management of affairs in the rear. Nor would there have been significant support at that time within the Kadet party or the public at large for an unpatriotic exposure of governmental shortcomings that might harm the war effort. As Miliukov put it several months later, in January "the government received not the blows of a political opponent but the warnings of a temporary ally in the interests of the great national cause."[48] Although he never compared the events of late 1905 and the situation in winter 1914–15, the parallel was implicit in this remark. Kadets had been blamed in many quarters for pushing the regime to the right in the weeks after the October Manifesto by demanding more than the government could give as the price of their cooperation. Whatever the merits of this charge, it could not be repeated now: the party offered its support unconditionally and twice over.

Unfortunately, Miliukov acknowledged later, the truce society offered at the start of the war was taken as a capitulation.[49] He was nonetheless very slow in concluding that a change of tactics was necessary. In early spring the Progressives began a campaign for recall of the Duma before November for a regular sitting, but Miliukov, along with the majority of Kadets and the Octobrists, opposed this suggestion. By May, as reports of the successes of the Central Powers' offensive in western Galicia dispelled hopes for victory in the near future, general sentiment in favor of recalling the Duma for a long sitting began to mount, but still Miliukov resisted. He was finally converted to immediate reopening of the legislature when Duma president Mikhail Rodzianko returned from the front in mid-May with a shocking account of the losses in Galicia.[50]

The acrimonious debates characterizing the Kadet party conference held June 6–8 demonstrated the degree to which confidence in governmental good will and competence had evaporated. A number of left Kadets and provincial delegates roundly criticized the restrained tactics of the past six months and demanded that the party support the Progressives' proposal for "a ministry responsible to the Duma." Right Kadets like Maklakov, on the other hand, argued equally vehemently that opposition in wartime was inadmissible.[51]

Miliukov had to summon all his powers of persuasion and tact to win support for the central committee's more modest slogan of a "ministry enjoying the public confidence." Defending the party's earlier restraint, he agreed that the Duma now had an obligation to call for measures that would not only improve the situation at the front and the rear but also help bolster the sagging spirits of the population. But in setting Kadet tactics the overriding goal had to be kept in mind: party demands should be conceived realistically to aid national defense. A "responsible ministry" understood as one composed of public figures and answerable to the Duma was not a practical demand. He believed the population's confidence in the war effort could be restored if discredited members of the present cabinet were replaced with honest, capable bureaucrats responsive to public opinion. The central committee recommended calling for immediate convocation of the Duma and formation of a cabinet capable of guaranteeing "proper organization of the rear, maintenance of internal peace in the country, and the close cooperation of the government and society."[52] These resolutions passed, but divisions remained. Within days Petr Struve formalized his long-standing differences with the liberal party he had helped found by resigning from the central committee; shortly thereafter N. V. Nekrasov, the most prominent left Kadet, noisily did so as well.[53]

Just as the Kadets were finally resolved to go public with their critique, the regime began to act in a more conciliatory spirit; the continuing military setbacks of late spring and early summer made mobilization of the country for the war more critical than ever. The government created special commisions on munitions and other war needs which included both officials and representatives of the public. Four of the most hated ministers were dismissed. The moderate Prince N. B. Shcherbatov replaced Nikolai Maklakov as minister of internal affairs, and the popular and effective General Aleksei Polivanov succeeded V. A. Sukhomlinov as minister of war. And on June 13 an imperial rescript announced that in order to hear "the voice of the Russian people" the legislative bodies would be convened no later than August.

Miliukov was concerned that Goremykin retained his post, but otherwise greatly heartened by each concession. The "Council of Elders" agreed in a special meeting of June 13 that August was still too long to wait for the opening of the Duma; a delegation was selected to wait upon Goremykin to persuade him to advance the date, with Miliukov as its spokesman. He spoke "without inhibition" and at length. Goremykin made no promises, but shortly thereafter the opening of the Duma was moved up to July 19, the first anniversary of the beginning of the war.[54]

The Duma leaders' choice of Miliukov as their spokesman at this critical time signaled how profoundly his status and that of his party had changed: only a year before the majority had allowed the Octobrist Shubinskii to call him a traitor from the Duma tribune. Miliukov and the Kadets had proved their patriotism by their energetic support of the war effort and their political restraint. The partisan differences that had impeded creation of a moderate coalition in the Duma in time of peace did not now loom so large. On the second day of the Duma sitting, the Kadets and Octobrists threw their votes behind the Nationalists' formula for "a ministry enjoying national confidence," which won a 191–162 majority over the Progressives' motion that the Duma could only support a government that "announces its readiness to submit to its control and leadership." This vote provided a starting point for consolidation of a genuine coalition, and Miliukov now emerged as the natural leader of this effort.

It was, in a way, a return to the role he had filled so well in the headiest days of the liberation movement, when his abundant energies, organizational skills, and ability to broker compromises between disparate groups made him the main force for unity in the Union of Unions. As in 1905, his hope was that a united public opinion could persuade the supreme authority to honor its requests: he worked for a sharing of power from above rather than its seizure from below. In other respects, however, his role was more conservative than it had been in the past. He now sought political allies primarily to the right of the Kadets, among Progressives, Octobrists, and even a portion of the Nationalists, rather than to their left. And the reforms he sought, though still liberal in spirit, entailed working within the existing institutional arrangement rather than for its fundamental change. For the duration of the war he had laid aside his slogan of undoing the "three padlocks"—democratizing the electoral law of June 3, reforming the State Council, and making the ministries responsible to the legislature. These things would come as part of the postwar settlement, he assured Kadets.

Miliukov's organizing work for a moderate coalition took place under the imprint of personal tragedy. Until that time the war had claimed only one person dear to him, A. M. Koliubakin, a Kadet colleague and family friend who fell in battle in January 1915. Writing of this loss to his own son, Sergei, completing officers' training for the infantry, Miliukov told him, "We are mourning, but have reconciled ourselves to this sacrifice and have endeavored to make clear to wider circles its social significance. The death of Aleksandr Mikhailovich is a beautiful and sublime symbol of our attitude to this war." In the same letter he included news of his eldest son, Nikolai, already on active duty in the artillery, adding, "Kolia has instructed me to pass along that you are a 'blockhead' for not entering the artillery academy but that he kisses you all the same." On July 25 Miliukov received word that Sergei had been killed in action near Kholm. His grief was compounded by an acute feeling of guilt. Sergei had been given the option of accepting a relatively safe posting in the Far East; he asked his father's opinion, and Miliukov had replied that the real struggle was on the Austrian front. He never forgave himself for that advice, writing in his memoirs twenty-five years later "this was one of those wounds which do not heal. . . . It is bleeding even now."[55]

Political work, nonetheless, had to go on. Most important was the difficult job of devising a program capable of uniting a solid majority in the Duma. Faction leaders had begun discussing legislative activity in the Council of Elders prior to the Duma's opening, but only the Kadets had prepared a program.[56] On the first day of the Duma session Miliukov gave a speech outlining what his party saw as the most urgent concerns in addition to a ministry of confidence, including a bill on Polish autonomy and one extending equal rights to Jews, a political and religious amnesty, easing of the restrictive censorship, and restoration of labor unions.[57] This program would become the basic kernel of the Progressive bloc, the name assumed by the moderate coalition, but required emendation to prove acceptable to parties to the right of the Kadets. Miliukov, urging on his fellow faction leaders the necessity of uniting the Duma around a program quickly, was willing to compromise on many points. For example, though he insisted on inclusion of Polish autonomy and the Jewish question if the Kadets were to participate, he agreed to a watered-down formula for Jewish rights to keep the group of Nationalists headed by V. V. Shul'gin from refusing to join the bloc. Conciliatory tactics produced the hoped-for results; by mid-August the Duma bloc could count on a majority of 300 votes.[58]

A third organizational task concerned winning support in the State Council for the bloc program: a program backed by moderates of both legislative chambers would command far more attention. In August meetings were arranged between bloc representatives and interested members of the State Council; thanks to Miliukov's compulsive habit of note taking, a detailed record of the discussions exists.[59] Insuperable differences failed to materialize, since alarm at continuing military reversals imbued the participants with a sense of urgency: the German army entered Warsaw August 4, and Russia's "great retreat" from Poland began. It required only days to hammer out a preliminary agreement. Conservatives proved as willing to compromise as were moderates; as V. N. L'vov put it with some justice, "We are giving up a good deal—we are approaching liberalism." Wording of some points of the Duma program was altered—reference was made in the final draft, for example, to restoration of the "Little Russian" rather than "Ukrainian" press—but no point was removed altogether. The more serious disputes concerned not the program itself but what exactly was to be done with it when it was completed. It was finally decided on August 22 to sound out the cabinet and to refrain from publicizing the program in advance, on the grounds that the authorities would be more likely to adopt it if it they did not appear to be yielding to an ultimatum.[60]

The final program (which leaked into the press August 26) was moderate in that it avoided fundamental institutional change, but was nonetheless "approaching liberalism." The program opened with two basic demands. It called for "creation of a united government from people who enjoy the confidence of the country and have agreed with the legislative institutions on the implementation of a definite program at the earliest possible time." Second, it demanded "decisive changes in the methods of administration employed so far," including strict observance of legality. It then listed the eight most important measures for uniting the country for victory, among them an amnesty, an end to persecution on religious grounds, a bill on autonomy for Poland, restoration of labor unions and the labor press, equalization of peasants' rights with those of other classes, and "inauguration of a program aimed at the abolition of restrictions on the rights of Jews." The concluding section enumerated twelve less urgent measures, including a law on cooperative societies, and laws improving the pay and working hours of certain kinds of public and commercial employees.[61]

The Council of Ministers had been closely following the organization of the bloc in both legislative chambers and were divided over how to respond to this development. Goremykin, not surprisingly, thought the bloc an ill-concealed attempt to limit the power of the sovereign and declared he would fight it to the last. Most of the ministers, however, considered "five-sixths" of the bloc's program acceptable. After heated debate it was decided to meet with bloc members for "purposes of information" before making any recommendations to the tsar.[62] On August 27 four ministers met with nine representatives of the bloc. Miliukov, acting as chief spokesman for the bloc, explained that the demand for a new ministry of confidence was fundamental, the one on whose fulfillment depended all other points of the program. P. A. Kharitonov responded that agreement to this demand lay beyond the competence of the cabinet, but that he would communicate the bloc's wish that this view be made known to the sovereign. The ministers also queried the bloc's stress on strict observance of the law, with Minister of Internal Affairs Prince Shcherbatov observing, revealingly, that "the Russian people is in essence lawless." Miliukov countered with the assertion that the root evil of Russian life was administrative arbitrariness. As important as a reformist legislative program was, "the essence of the question of the restoration of domestic peace is found in the sphere of administration." All the bloc delegates strongly seconded his demand for an end to the present "dual power" of civil and military authorities, which was advancing the breakdown of internal order.[63]

For several days, hopes for the reconciliation of government and society on the program of the bloc remained high. Most of the ministers saw in it a reasonable basis for negotiation, although Goremykin advocated immediate prorogation of the legislature. The Council finally agreed to ask for prorogation, but also to petition the tsar for a change of ministry; Goremykin was to travel to *stavka* (military headquarters) the following day and report to the sovereign. Meanwhile, declarations of support for a ministry of confidence, many requesting that such a cabinet include individuals from outside the bureaucracy, were pouring in from public organizations and municipal councils all over the country. The Progressives had gone so far as to publish in their Moscow daily *Utro Rossii* (Dawn of Russia) the names of a possible "national" cabinet, headed by Duma president Mikhail Rodzianko and including representatives of various parties as well as three current ministers; among Kadets, Miliukov was listed for Foreign Affairs, Shingarev for Finance, and Vasilii Maklakov for Justice.[64] Bloc representatives meeting August 29 to discuss their next steps believed a new cabinet would indeed be formed.[65]

Despite the unprecedented alignment of opinion behind creation of a ministry of confidence, Nicholas rejected the proposal. Goremykin triumphantly returned to Petersburg with the instructions that the ministers were to remain at their posts and the legislature to be prorogued on September 3. Miliukov later concluded, probably correctly, that the sovereign's decision to ignore the reasoned appeal for a new government, supported even by his own ministers, probably owed a great deal to its unfortunate coincidence with another governmental crisis. In early August Nicholas had decided it was his duty in an hour of national peril to take over personal command of the armed forces from Grand Duke Nikolai Nikolaevich. This step, urged on him by the tsarina and Rasputin, was opposed by virtually all the cabinet save Goremykin, in part because they feared he would then be blamed for any further military misfortunes. Eight ministers sent a letter to the tsar August 21 begging him to reconsider his decision and, in light of their deep differences with Goremykin, expressing doubt about their ability to be of service to the country; Nicholas, deeply angered by their opposition, had refused to accept any resignations.[66] Now, a mere ten days later, the cabinet was again at loggerheads with Goremykin and requesting a change in government.

Looking back on the period of July and August 1915 several years later, Miliukov identified the tsar's refusal to effect a rapprochement between state and society at that time as a fatal turning point. Formation of the Progressive bloc was "the last attempt to find a peaceful way out of a situation which from day to day was becoming ever more threatening." Miliukov saw the bloc as a surrogate of the "sacred union" between the government and the country after the latter had been destroyed. A ministry of confidence implementing the bloc program, he was sure, could have improved internal administration of the country, allowed Russia to stay in the war until victory, and preserved the monarchy. Instead, the moment was lost; the internal situation steadily worsened; and when the regime finally agreed to the demand for a ministry of confidence, in February 1917, the revolution had already begun.[67]

Not all scholars have been as willing as Miliukov to believe that the bloc program and a new ministry would have been sufficient to sustain the population through so tremendous an ordeal as the war. All the same, most Western scholars have argued that the tsar's ultimate decision in late summer 1915 to ignore the moderate public's plea for a new cabinet, in conjunction with his decision to move to the *stavka* and assume command of the army, was a genuine turning point toward revolution. Taken together, these decisions deprived the government of needed public confidence and resulted in a power vacuum in the rear. That vacuum enabled the tsarina, counseled by Rasputin, to exercise a profoundly disruptive influence on the country's administration and thereby further discredit the dynasty.[68]

In September 1915, however, Miliukov did not know that this initial refusal to work with the bloc would prove to be permanent. While prorogation of the Duma until November without creation of a new government was a huge blow, he and most bloc members clung to the hope that the sovereign would soon reverse himself. "The political conjuncture which created the prorogation," Miliukov declared September 10, "is understood by all well-informed deputies as a transient moment, as the product of a fortuitous, temporary, brief victory of one of the contending sides."[69]

Almost immediately after prorogation of the Duma, government reaction again resumed. Nicholas began dismissing the ministers who had been most outspoken in opposing his decision to go to the front. The reopening of the Duma promised for November was postponed indefinitely. The whole situation was complicated by a stabilization at the front in late September. While improvement in the military situation meant the immediate national danger had passed, it also made it easier for the government to see substantive concessions to society as unnecessary. Throughout the fall, in meetings of the bloc and the Kadet central committee, it was Miliukov's thankless task to urge patience, restraint, and confidence that "we have a straight and open path before us to a brighter future." These counsels evoked no little anger and debate from Kadets and Progressives who desired to be doing something more concrete. Since no agreement was possible on various proposals forwarded, however, 1915 ebbed away with Russian moderates in a state of near suspended animation.[70]

Prospects improved in January when the seventy-seven-year-old Goremykin was finally let go, the presidency of the Council of Ministers going to an undistinguished bureaucrat, Boris Sturmer. Much as Miliukov and the bloc had desired the removal of this implacable opponent of the Duma, it was impossible to welcome his replacement by a man whose leading characteristics were, in the summary of one observer, a "third-rate intellect, mean spirit, low character, doubtful honesty, no experience, and no idea of State business."[71] He was, however, a crony of Rasputin and therefore had the backing of the tsarina, whose ill-judged meddling in governmental appointments would continue to increase.

The removal of Goremykin at least cleared the way for convocation of the Duma in February for a long sitting, restoring to political leaders a national forum and the long-postponed chance of enacting some of the bloc's program. In a move that surprised everyone, Nicholas decided to open the Duma session. After ten years' studied refusal to grace the legislature with the imperial presence, his visit was widely—and mistakenly—interpreted as a major gesture of conciliation.[72]

The opening session began with a lackluster speech by Sturmer and a reassertion of the program of the Progressive bloc by the Octobrist Sergei Shidlovskii, its titular head. On the second day Miliukov gave a long and somber speech outlining the evils the administration was visiting upon its own people. Nothing had been done about Poland, and Jewish pogroms were recurring. Mounting inflation was making the lot of working people intolerable. Transport and provisioning daily became more chaotic, while the government interfered with the sole effective efforts being made to establish order, those of the zemstvo and municipal unions. Everywhere and in everything the authorities appeared to be concerned more about their own prerogatives than about the war and the welfare of the country. The

Allies had mobilized their entire populations for the war effort, Miliukov noted, while in Russia "the government's jealous guardianship, motivated by fear of losing power, fetters all popular energies and hinders their development." He concluded on an uncharacteristically pessimistic note. "I know the way out, but I do not know how to get there. We have no means of solving this question through our own efforts, and are no longer willing to turn to the government. That is why, on the eve of what may be decisive events, I am more alarmed than ever before and leave this rostrum without an answer, and without the hope of receiving one from the present cabinet."[73]

The bloc had reiterated its demand for a new government, but since it could not make this change itself it had, of necessity, to focus on legislative work. The success of these efforts was exceedingly modest. It managed to pass through the Duma that spring only two major measures, a bill introducing a progressive income tax and one on cooperative societies, something Miliukov had identified in his speech as especially important legislation.[74] Three other bills Miliukov regarded as crucial to better organization of the country, those on creation of a *volost'* level zemstvo and revision of the zemstvo and municipal council statutes, mired down in committee thanks to the reservations of more conservative portions of the bloc. There was no progress at all on the still more controversial bloc points concerning amnesty, Polish autonomy, and national minorities, including the Jewish question.

Publicly, Miliukov defended the bloc's rather meager accomplishments as a genuinely important first step: the Duma had passed two important reform bills that would not have won majority approval in the pre-bloc era. Moreover, the bill on income tax had passed the State Council, and it appeared the bill on cooperatives would do so as well, which meant that for the first time in nearly five years both chambers were cooperating on reform. The very fact that the bloc was still intact when the Duma session ended June 20 had given the lie to all those who said it was a transient coalition.

Many Kadets looked upon the bloc with a more jaundiced eye. At the February party congress—the first national Kadet congress in eight years—more militant delegates had charged that Miliukov's temporizing tactics threatened to compromise the party itself, "not only in the broad democratic circles of the population, but also in the eyes of the liberal intelligentsia." The old complaint was resurrected—the Kadets were turning into "something close to Octobrists." Miliukov and the majority of the central committee managed to persuade the congress to vote for continued participation in the bloc, but a number of prominent Kadets still worried that endless postponement of the liberal agenda for the sake of preserving the bloc was ultimately a betrayal of liberal principles.[75] The situation was not improved by Miliukov's surprising decision to go abroad before the end of the spring session.

On April 16, 1916, Miliukov set off as part of a high-profile parliamentary delegation to Britain, France, and Italy. The trip had been initiated by the British with an eye to impressing upon the Russians the extent of their allies' war efforts and bolstering the parliamentarians' commitment to keeping Russia in the war; there were fears that influential court circles inclined toward a separate peace with Germany. Nine of the sixteen Duma deputies and members of the State Council in the delegation belonged to the Progressive bloc; Miliukov was the only leader of a faction to participate. The Kadet central committee had, with perfect justice, opposed his going, pointing out that as the head of the party faction and real leader of the bloc he was needed in the Duma. Miliukov brushed these objections aside, supported as always by Shingarev, whose participation was also objected to as untimely and who was similarly intent upon going.[76]

Their colleagues' concerns were well founded. Kadets critical of Miliukov's restrained policies exploited his absence to press for the demand for a responsible ministry and fuller use of the Duma's rights to battle the government. A left Kadet attempt to force a Duma vote on equal rights for Jews, a vote Miliukov had avoided as unwinnable, polarized the bloc and angered Kadet peasant deputies, some of whom quit the faction in protest.[77] Miliukov returned to St. Petersburg on June 17, just three days before the end of the Duma spring session, to find both his party and the bloc more divided than ever before.

Miliukov justified his participation in the delegation as an opportunity to enhance liberal influence at home by gaining for it European recognition. He also intended to advertise the "unanimity" of Russian public opinion regarding acquisition of the straits, while sounding out public opinion in the Allied countries on that issue and other aspects of the postwar settlement. He may also have had some idea of raising the question of attaching conditions to postwar loans to Russia during private conversations with members of Allied governments; liberal Russians had never entirely forgiven France for extending a massive loan to the tsarist government just prior to convocation of the First Duma, thereby freeing it from the necessity of coming to terms with the new legislature. At any rate, financial considerations figured prominently in Miliukov's argument that refraining from demanding implementation of the entire liberal program in wartime would not jeopardize its achievement after victory. In February 1916 he assured the delegates to the sixth Kadet congress that a reactionary government, not responsible to the Duma, would get no money after the war from either France or England. "The liquidation of the war will demand colossal sums which may be obtained only through foreign loans. And it is in this way, through the State Duma, that Russian liberalism will reach its goals and that our victory is assured."[78]

The delegation's trip was a great success, so far as its official organizers were concerned. The delegates everywhere received a warm welcome, toured munitions factories and were taken to the front, heard and gave patriotic speeches and toasts. Judging from his memoirs, Miliukov was deeply gratified by the attention paid him by English foreign minister Sir Edward Grey, receptions in the British House of Commons and French parliament, and presentation to King Victor Emmanuel of Italy and King George of Great Britain. (For the latter event he had to purchase a top hat, promptly passing it on to his old émigré friend Isaak Shklovskii as a souvenir; Miliukov never shed his dislike of formal attire.) He was able to report on his return that Allied public opinion understood and appreciated the Progressive bloc and was firm in its commitment to the alliance and war until victory, although the delegation's efforts to have published the secret agreement awarding Russia the straits were not successful.[79] These were rather nebulous achievements when weighed against the deterioration of relations in the bloc and the Kadet party during his absence. Nonetheless, rather than spending the Duma summer recess in political repair work, Miliukov chose to devote a good part of it to giving lectures at the Cambridge University summer school and in Norway.

The degree to which factionalism flourished and constructive activity broke down in the bloc and the Kadet party during Miliukov's travels highlights how important he had become to the practice of parliamentary politics in Russia. Conservative members of the bloc might fear that he was inveigling them into "liberalism," left and provincial Kadets might deplore his cautious conservatism, but no other figure had sufficient authority and skill to chart a generally acceptable course and reconcile recurring differences. At the same time, Miliukov's temporary abdication of his responsibilities in 1916, so reminiscent of his refusal to remain in Russia in fall 1904 at the time of the Banquet Campaign, demonstrates his shortcomings as a leader. Miliukov was not the first politician ever to seek relief from the intractable demands of domestic politics in a foreign visit or two. But political instinct should have told him that this was no time to abandon the home front. Political instinct, however, was something he frequently lacked.

The Storm Signal of Revolution

By fall 1916, Russia was again in a state of crisis. The crisis was not this time triggered by military reversals; the army was now adequately supplied and had even enjoyed some stunning successes against the Austrians over the summer. But the war's strain on the economy was increasingly making itself felt through spiraling inflation and scarcity of goods caused by deficiencies in the supply and transport system. High prices, shortages of basic commodities, and general war weariness made for a threatening public mood. Irritation was further exacerbated by the perception that the government was not only incompetent to address the problems but worse than indifferent to the plight of the urban population. Suspicions concerning the patriotism of the unpopular "German" empress and the circle around her were intensifying. Miliukov was shocked by his impressions of his native city on a visit there in early October: "If someone had told me twenty years ago that Moscow's mood would undergo such a metamorphosis I would have taken it as a foolish joke. The most inert and ignorant circles have begun to speak in the language of implacable revolutionaries." A massive strike of Petrograd workers on October 17–20, during which two regiments brought in to restore order mutinied and fired on the police, left no possible doubt about the gravity of the situation.[80]

Unfortunately, it was almost impossible to expect prompt and effective measures from the present government. Through 1916 the practice of dismissing the more "liberal" ministers and replacing them with conservatives or nonentities deemed more loyal to the royal couple had continued. That summer, in response to increasing administrative confusion in the country, Nicholas attempted to restore authority by creation of a "dictatorship of the rear." His choice for civil dictator was Boris Sturmer, a man eager to have the appointment and completely unequal to the task; what Miliukov termed the "paralysis of authority" continued.

On September 18 a vice-chairman of the Duma, the Octobrist Aleksandr Protopopov, was unexpectedly named minister of internal affairs. Many chose to interpret selection of a Duma member to this most powerful post as a gesture of reconciliation. Miliukov and a number of other bloc members had more misgivings. Protopopov was rumored to owe his elevation to intimacy with Rasputin, not in itself an encouraging sign. He had also shown appallingly poor judgment, as part of the Duma delegation to the Allies, by meeting in Stockholm with a German who wished to discuss the subject of a separate peace.[81] On October 19 Protopopov and leaders of the Duma factions met to sound one another out. As Miliukov's detailed notes of the extraordinary evening reveal, it began in acrimony and ended in bathos.

Protopopov, thoughtlessly appearing in the dress uniform of the gendarmes, requested that all discussion remain secret. Miliukov rejected this condition. Protopopov then declared he could not speak frankly and wondered why he was not being treated as a comrade. Miliukov hotly responded with an indictment of his behavior as minister thus far, concluding that "a man who persecutes the press and public organizations cannot be our comrade." Shingarev seconded him, pointing out that he was cooperating with

Sturmer, "a man with a definite reputation as a traitor." Protopopov tried to rebut their reproaches, repeating again and again that they were treating him badly and saying he thought he and Miliukov had become comrades on their trip abroad. In an effort to salvage the situation, Miliukov apologized for his heated remarks: "Perhaps this was truly a cry from the heart—a last cry." He tried carefully to explain the source of their concerns and confusion about Protopopov's intentions. In answer to Protopopov's declaration that he was a monarchist, Miliukov replied that they all were; the question concerned what *sort*—was he a proponent of unlimited or constitutional monarchy? Protopopov emotionally declared "Yes, I always was a monarchist, and now I have come know to the tsar personally and to love him. I don't know why, but he too has come to love me." Shingarev reminded him that besides love for the tsar there was love for the motherland, and that if the tsar was making mistakes the obligation of someone who loved him was to tell him so. I. N. Efremov and Rodzianko tried to explain the conviction of all those present that what was needed was not some "strong man" but a change of government. Finally I. I. Kapnist rose, went over to Protopopov and said firmly, "Aleksandr Dmitrievich, *resign* from your post." This too having produced no effect on Protopopov other than piteous indignation, the meeting broke up with the advice that he go home, lie down, "get some sleep."[82] The participants dispersed under the painful impression that Russia's minister of internal affairs was not only incompetent, but mentally unbalanced.

With a revolutionary situation developing in the capitals and the present ministers clearly incapable of handling the crisis, representatives of the Progressive bloc met repeatedly in the last weeks of October to try and agree upon a strategy for the Duma when it convened November 1. Virtually any course of action, including inaction, was fraught with risk. The Progressives and left Kadets argued that the Duma could afford to ignore the public mood no longer; it must attack the entire tsarist system if it did not wish to lose whatever influence it still enjoyed and with it the possibility of averting mass upheaval. The Nationalists argued the opposite, holding that any concerted stand against the government would only jeopardize the existence of the Duma and further inflame revolutionary passions. Miliukov, who believed that failure to vent popular indignation would drive the exasperated public into the arms of the extremists, proposed a middle course: concentrating the bloc's fire on the person of Sturmer in hopes of forcing his replacement with an individual able to inspire public confidence and work with the bloc. On October 24 he managed to secure the majority's tenuous adherence to this compromise tactic, embodied in his text for a bloc declaration of no confidence in Sturmer.[83]

It still remained to win over his own party. At the Kadet fall conference, held October 22–24, provincial delegates lashed out at Miliukov with unaccustomed ferocity. His travels abroad had made him poorly informed about the public mood, they charged; the patience of the people was exhausted. He saw the center of gravity in the parliamentary struggle with the government, when what was needed was organization of the masses and a rapprochement with the left. Miliukov responded with a plea that the Kadets not lose sight of their ultimate goal. There could be no question that a "terrible popular upheaval" would follow the end of the war; at that moment, when the government found itself with no source of support, it would finally reach out to the liberals:

> It will be our task not to destroy the government, which would only aid anarchy, but to instill in it a completely different content, that is, to build a genuine constitutional order. That is why, in our struggle with the government, despite everything, we must retain a sense of proportion. . . . To support anarchy in the name of the struggle with the government would be to risk all the political conquests we have made since 1905.

Summarizing the results of the conference, Prince Pavel Dolgorukov observed that after a prolonged and heated struggle "finally, as always, Miliukov succeeded in defeating his opponents and made them follow him." Nonetheless, the conference showed that "the party's left wing is growing constantly stronger and the attacks of this wing on the central committee of the party are acquiring an increasingly unrestrained character."[84]

It was this volatile combination of revolutionary passions, escalating apprehension, and the near breakdown of unity in the moderate camp that provided the impetus for the most notorious address in the history of the Duma, Miliukov's "Stupidity or Treason" speech of November 1, 1916. The day before the Duma's opening the Progressives shocked the moderates by pulling out of the bloc, on the grounds that far more was needed than denunciation of Sturmer's personal regime. At the opening session itself the ministers, notified by their informant within the bloc to expect unpleasantness, left the Duma chamber before any deputies took the floor.[85] Shidlovskii read the bloc's formal declaration, a toned-down version of Miliukov's draft text, which asserted the Allies' loss of confidence in Russia and the country's lack of confidence in Sturmer and demanded a new cabinet that could command national support. A hysterical speech by Kerensky followed, then Miliukov took the floor in an atmosphere electric with tension.

He began with a sketch of how public hopes for a reconciliation between state and society had been destroyed over the course of the war: "We have lost faith that the government can lead us to victory." Instead of creating a government of national unity as all her allies had done, Russia had witnessed the dismissal of every minister able to work with the legislature and the persecution of public organizations for support of the war effort. How was such a state of affairs to be explained? One answer was to be found in the rumors of treason in high places gaining currency everywhere; Miliukov then proceeded to discuss circumstances, actions, allegations that suggested these rumors were well founded.

He noted that Sturmer had freed Sukhomlinov, the former minister of war arrested and charged with treason. He noted the prevalence of pro-German propaganda in Russia recently decried by the British ambassador in Petrograd, which necessitated a judicial investigation. "At the time when we accused Sukhomlinov, as now, we did not possess the facts which were brought to light by the investigation. We had what we have today—the instinctive voice of the entire country and its subjective certainty." During his recent visit to the Allied countries, Miliukov went on, he had been told that the enemy had access to Russian state secrets. His most spectacular disclosures came from the foreign press. He cited the *Berliner Tagwacht* report concerning the scandal surrounding Sturmer's private secretary, Ivan Manasevich-Manuilov, who had been arrested on suspicion of treason but then released. Manasevich-Manuilov had been taking German bribes; his release was apparently to be explained by his passing on some of that money to Sturmer. He also quoted German newspapers expressing satisfaction with Sturmer's replacement of Sazonov as foreign minister and the appointment of Protopopov, and a Swiss paper's evaluation of those appointments as "der Sieg der Hofpartei, die sich um die junge Zarin gruppiert" [the victory of the court party grouped around the young tsarina], in this way managing to allude to the tsarina's influence on politics.

In the final, dramatic section of his speech, Miliukov enumerated the most harmful decisions of the Sturmer regime, pausing after each accusation to ask rhetorically "Is this stupidity or is it treason?" To each question the crowded Duma hall shouted in answer "Stupidity!" "Treason!" "Both!" Miliukov's own answer was that the root cause made no difference, since in either case "the consequences are the same."[86]

The degree to which Miliukov himself believed his implied charges and the strength of his evidence are impossible to establish. In his memoirs he observed that given a choice of stupidity or treason his listeners resolutely subscribed to the latter explanation "even in those aspects where I myself was not entirely sure," but did not identify which aspects he was uncertain of. His evidence, too, was a mixed bag. The most important came from Count Benckendorf, the Russian ambassador to Britain, concerning leaks of state secrets to the Germans since Sturmer's appointment as foreign minister and from Izvolskii, ambassador to France, who told him of Manasevich-Manuilov's involvement in the attempt to bribe *Novoe vremia* with German money. Some of it was apparently rumor and hearsay garnered from the Russian émigré colony in Lausanne; he never identified the nature of the evidence he said he had collected in Russia.[87] Miliukov believed his evidence warranted investigation into the claims that highly placed persons near or subordinate to Sturmer were forwarding Germany's interests; he seems to have suspected Sturmer's own complicity without having any very convincing evidence of guilt. That he nonetheless made a speech heavily implying treasonous activity on the part of a man whose behavior was, as it turned out, merely "stupid" testifies to how desperate he deemed the situation.[88]

Despite the authorities' prohibition against any reproduction of the speech in the press, its contents immediately became known. Tens of thousands of illicit mimeographed and typed copies were widely circulated, often with highly inflammatory additions to the original text. Much to his own surprise, Miliukov was transformed into a national celebrity. He received letters and telegrams of support from all over the empire. At a public meeting at the Petrograd Municipal Council several days after his speech his appearance produced a thunderous ovation. The Okhrana reported that "the hero of the hour is Miliukov; there is no doubt that his popularity in the Duma, bloc and his own faction has reached its zenith."[89]

There were, of course, people who saw his speech in quite a different light. In early December *Russkie vedomosti* reported rumors that the reactionary Union of Russian People, responsible in 1906 and 1907 for the murders of two prominent Kadets, was planning a similar end for Miliukov. Petrunkevich, deeply upset by this news, wrote Miliukov urging that he not underestimate his danger: "It is you and no one else who occupies an exclusive position in Russia. Standing above all and ahead of all you are everywhere visible." Stalwart young members of the party eagerly offered their services as bodyguards.[90]

The celebrity of the speech was further enhanced by attainment of its most immediate end, the dismissal of Sturmer. Sturmer had wished to prosecute Miliukov as a political criminal but received no support from his demoralized fellow ministers, who advised that he sue for slander. In the Duma the floodgates opened as speakers for almost every faction, even conservative ones, demanded Sturmer's removal. Shattered by the campaign against him, Sturmer advised the tsar that the Duma be prorogued; on November 8 Nicholas instead decided he must let his premier go. The jubilant Progressive bloc believed it had won its first victory. As Miliukov recounted months later, "It seemed this was, in effect, the first step toward ministerial responsibility in that an individual, having received a harsh judgment, was dismissed."[91]

Sturmer's successor was A. F. Trepov, a moderate bureaucrat who fully intended to try and work with the legislature. The left wing of the Duma was not similarly inclined to work with him, continuing to demand an entirely new cabinet and responsible ministry. Despite disappointment, Miliukov and the bloc decided to support Trepov. When the Mensheviks and Trudoviks mounted an obstructionist campaign during the premier's first visit to the Duma on November 19, bloc members pointedly voted to exclude them for eight sessions. The potential success of Trepov's good intentions and modest proposals for price-fixing in order to deal with the provisioning crisis were never tested. Trepov had incurred the tsarina's enmity by requesting Protopopov's dismissal; instead, on December 26, he was himself dismissed after less than two months in office.[92]

Even before that blow, however, the brief spurt of optimism evoked by Sturmer's dismissal had already spent itself. Sturmer was gone, but Protopopov remained, on November 5 provocatively banning scheduled congresses of the Union of Zemstvos and Union of Cities. The level of urban discontent over food and fuel shortages remained high. Increasingly, the conviction grew that only extra-parliamentary measures could stave off revolution. On December 16–17 the reactionary Duma deputy Purishkevich and two members of the Imperial family assassinated Rasputin. This deed was one of the chief topics of conversation at the Petrunkevich villa in the Crimea where the Miliukovs spent the Christmas holidays. Many of their hosts' guests warmly approved the "heroic action" of the conspirators. Miliukov considered it a disgraceful drama, "repulsive in its essence and its details." The Duma's fall session had opened with the "stupidity or treason" speech; Rasputin was killed the day after it closed. Looking back, Miliukov remarked that the Duma's session began and ended "with events which would have been impossible in the normal life of a state."[93]

C·H·A·P·T·E·R N·I·N·E

Miliukov Displaced

Scholars have often observed the degree to which the French Revolution weighed on the minds of Russians in the revolutionary period. The fate of the Girondists, the Thermidorian reaction, and the threat to the revolution from the right helped to color perceptions and inform decision-making. Yet there was not a single "French Revolution" from which to draw instruction. In 1915, Miliukov later wrote in his memoirs, he began to reread Taine's history of the French Revolution, and with an attitude very different from when he had compared it to that of Michelet in his student years; the Russian experience had already been sufficient to destroy, for him, the "mystique" of revolution.[1] In Miliukov's own history of the Russian Revolution, begun just months after the Bolsheviks seized power, the spirit of Taine is very much in evidence.

Taine's French Revolution is the product of a combination of circumstances: dearth, provoking unrest in the hungry mob; the lack of strong repression by the authorities, emboldening further disorders; and the diffusion of the doctrine of popular sovereignty, legitimizing the transformation of disorders into general rebellion. His Constituent Assembly is an unwieldy body cumbrously formed, lacking in both political experience and the power to address the shortages and grievances that precipitated the upheaval. Within this body the extremists enjoy the advantage, since "the prevailing theory is on the side of the revolutionists and they alone are determined thoroughly to apply it. This party, therefore, is the only one which is consistent and popular in the face of adversaries who are unpopular and inconsequent"; the moderates end up denying reason and common sense and abet the revolutionaries.[2] The extremists are utopians flourishing in a milieu of social decomposition. Armed by an exaggerated self-conceit and dogmatism convincing them of the absolute rightness of their ends and the permissibility of any means, they are not wanting in the necessary "resolution, audacity, rude energy" to seize the machinery of the centralized state.[3] For Taine there is nothing wonderful in the readiness of an aroused, ignorant, and brutalized people to follow the group whose doctrine of popular sovereignty promises them everything and flatters their self-esteem.

Miliukov's history of the Russian Revolution was the first written by a trained historian; the three volumes of part 1, concluding with the events of October 1917, he completed by summer 1918.[4] He fully appreciated that a "history" written so soon after the fact and without benefit of access to all relevant sources was a rather problematic undertaking. He thought these deficiencies were at least partially offset by his having been not only an eyewitness to, but a participant in, the events related. Moreover, his history was conceived as an analytical outline, "the bold strokes of a sketch," rather than a detailed recital of the facts. That analysis reflected very clearly his understanding of the revolution as a political one whose initial goal was successful prosecution of the war: his history largely concerns the actions—or inaction—of political groups and orientations striving to determine the nature of the state and its foreign policy. It is above all aimed at revealing the fatal mistakes of the moderate socialists vis-à-vis the ruthless extremism of the Bolsheviks, neither of whom showed any evidence of being informed by a sense of state consciousness (*gosudarstvennost'*).[5] By focusing on these political errors he suggests that the "deepening" of the political revolution into a social one, which for him meant the collapse of the war effort, growing economic chaos, and the disintegration of the Russian state itself, was not an irresistible process. Had moderate socialists shown more courage, more consistency, and greater care for the existence of the state, the tragedy engulfing Russia might have been averted.

February 27–March 3, 1917

The Duma went into recess on December 16, 1916, and did not meet again until February 14. During those two months between sittings members of the Duma could do little more than talk, trying to determine a plan of action to implement once the Duma opened, as well as responses to possible extraparliamentary developments. These concerned not so much an actual revolution as a coup, the forced abdication of Nicholas and his replacement by the heir, Aleksei. The bloodless overthrow of the monarch was in fact being planned, by Alexander Guchkov and several public figures and high-ranking officers, in hopes of saving the monarchy itself; rumors concerning such a step were widespread. Miliukov and other members of the bureau of the Progressive bloc, meeting with zemstvo and municipal leaders, decided the Duma could take no part in any plot, but that in the event of the tsar's overthrow Aleksei must be acknowledged as sovereign, with the Grand Duke Michael Alexandrovich appointed as regent.[6]

Miliukov continually urged patience upon workers and his own colleagues as severe food shortages fueled the strike movement in Petrograd and the Duma's convocation approached. He opposed mounting strong protests against the January 27 arrest of all the workers' delegates to the Central War Industries Committee, and on February 9 appealed to workers not to participate in a mass demonstration planned for the day of the Duma's opening; it was, he warned, a police provocation. The Okhrana, closely following all developments, gave it as their opinion that Miliukov feared responsibility for a possible false step: "The theme constantly recurring in all his conversation is the danger of making a wrong decision 'for which it will be necessary to answer before history and the whole civilized world.'" Once the Duma convened, Miliukov again appealed for calm, insisting that "the word and the vote are for the time being our only weapons."[7]

The events in Petrograd that turned into the Russian revolution began on Thursday February 23, as street disorders over lack of bread combined with a procession in honor of International Women's Day and a large strike to protest food shortages. Over the next two days the crowds grew larger and more aggressive, strikes shut down more and more enterprises, and economic demands were supplemented by overtly political ones. On the evening of February 25 Nicholas telegraphed from the *stavka* that the disorders were to be stopped immediately, with force if necessary. The following day troops fired on the crowds and managed to disperse them although one unit, ominously, mutinied. Whether Miliukov shared the belief of many observers that the immediate danger was over by that evening is impossible to determine, but he remembered vividly that on the morning of Monday February 27, as he and Anna walked up Potemkin Street to the Duma, they heard the smack of stray bullets in the nearly empty streets. The general revolt of the city's garrisons had begun; by evening the city would be in the hands of the insurgents.[8]

The Miliukovs were already aware that the Duma had been prorogued. Duma president Mikhail Rodzianko had telephoned this alarming news to faction heads the previous evening; the scheduled session would open in the morning, the decree of prorogation would be read out, and the Duma would then have to decide what to do. Rather than simply dispersing after the announcement, however, many agitated deputies moved from the session hall to an adjoining room and began to deliberate as a "private" gathering. News of the spreading soldiers' revolt was already filtering in.[9]

The meeting was heated and confused. It was variously proposed that they ignore the decree and reconvene the regular Duma session, that they go and appease the soldiers, that those gathered take power themselves and form a government. Miliukov found none of these proposals acceptable, but freely admitted he had no concrete suggestions. Participants finally agreed that the Duma would not defy the prorogation but instead empower the Council of Elders to appoint a committee to act on the Duma's behalf. After protracted talks Miliukov and eleven other individuals were selected to the "Temporary Committee of Duma Members for the Restoration of Order in the Capital and Establishment of Relations with Individuals and Institutions," a name in itself redolent of indecision.[10] Meanwhile, thousands of protesters, soldiers, officers, and other citizens streamed to the Taurida Palace bringing information, pledging support, seeking protection, and above all expecting that the Duma would take charge. Many looked to Miliukov, the undisputed head of the Progressive bloc, for a decisive answer. His dilemma in those hours was captured by the radical journalist Nikolai Sukhanov, author of the most detailed eyewitness account of the revolution. "Up and down the Ekaterininskii Hall, all alone, walked P. N. Miliukov, the central figure of bourgeois Russia. . . . His whole appearance suggested that he did not know what to do. Various people went up to him, spoke to him, reported to him. He gave them answers, unwillingly and vaguely. His interlocutors left him, and again he walked alone."[11]

That evening, the decision was made: the Temporary Committee would establish a government. A number of circumstances contributed to this step. By late evening the insurgents were in control of many governmental buildings and the Winter Palace, and several ministers had been arrested. According to Sukhanov, the first formal pledge of support from the army was critical; that evening Miliukov received a phone call from the Preobrazhenskii regiment, placing itself at the disposal of the Duma's Temporary Committee and requesting orders.[12] Also important was the decision that day of members of socialist parties to set up in the Taurida Palace a soviet of workers' deputies on the model of the revolutionary Petersburg Soviet of 1905; the Temporary Committee faced the possibility that the Soviet might immediately claim power. In the early morning hours the Committee issued a statement about its decision to organize a new government and an appeal to the population to avoid disorder, looting, and bloodshed. It also appointed Duma members to oversee provisioning, transport, and military organization of the capital.[13]

On February 28 regiment after regiment presented itself at the Taurida Palace, pledging loyalty to the Duma. They expected a reception and celebratory speeches, for which Rodzianko, Kerensky, and Miliukov were frequently pressed into service. In his speech to the Lifeguard Grenadiers Miliukov developed the themes of organization and undivided authority, topics already of grave concern to him, given the anarchy of the moment and the threat posed by the Petrograd Soviet. He told the troops that "we must first of all be organized, united, and subordinated to one authority. This authority is the Temporary Committee of the State Duma. It is necessary to submit to it and to no other authority, for dual authority is dangerous and threatens to split and divide our forces." He also urged the soldiers to retain their discipline: "Only together with your officers will you be strong. . . . If the whole army were to become a disorganized mob, a small group of organized enemy [forces] would be sufficient to break us up." He pursued the same theme before troops elsewhere that day; in each case the men responded enthusiastically and with cheers, pledging themselves to the Duma.[14] For a brief time this reserved and erudite man, who in Viktor Chernov's estimation "never spoke the language of the people, the worker, the peasant, the soldier," bridged the psychological distance between himself and the crowd. "I was astounded," recalled his colleague Prince Pavel Dolgorukov, "by the confidence and aplomb with which he greeted the men, walking through the ranks, and chatting with the officers and men."[15]

Once hopes of averting a revolution he had not wanted were gone, Miliukov's earlier indecision vanished. Critical decisions concerning the form and composition of the government, the source of its authority, and its relationship to the new Soviet were yet to be made, and he did his utmost to see them resolved in the manner he deemed best for the war effort and the country. In those chaotic days he drove himself relentlessly, conferring, negotiating, exhorting, drafting statements, only occasionally snatching a moment of rest. When Maurice Paleologue next saw him, a week later, he found him "aged by ten years."[16]

Miliukov played a key role in determining the composition of the government, although few of the ministers were surprises: these were largely individuals who had figured in lists of putative coalition cabinets worked up by various groups since the first days of the Progressive bloc. His most significant intervention concerned the choice of premier. The Octobrist Mikhail Rodzianko assumed that as president of the Duma and of its Temporary Committee he would head the government. Miliukov regarded Rodzianko as an energetic and well-meaning person of conservative opinions, little authority, and even less judgment; he had no intention of seeing him as head of the cabinet.[17] He instead promoted the candidacy of Prince Georgii L'vov, a man he scarcely knew personally but who seemed in many respects an ideal candidate. L'vov enjoyed tremendous authority in society as president of the Union of Zemstvos. He was also known to stand consciously outside politics; in this respect he answered perfectly Miliukov's conviction that the new government should be perceived as truly "national," standing above and outside purely party or class interests. Unfortunately, L'vov also proved to be disinclined to assert any authority at all, entertaining a sort of Slavophile faith in popular wisdom and hostility toward bureaucracy per se. Miliukov had perhaps imagined he would be better able to influence L'vov than he would Rodzianko, but it was Kerensky who came to dominate the malleable premier. Miliukov later admitted to friends that in promoting L'vov he had made a great mistake.[18]

Other ministers included Octobrist leader Guchkov for Army and Navy, a logical choice considering his old role in the Duma Defense committee; Centrist Vladimir L'vov as Procurator of the Holy Synod; and Miliukov's close friend Andrei Shingarev for Agriculture. Miliukov would take Foreign Affairs.

Rather less predictable ministerial choices were Alexander Kerensky, Nikolai V. Nekrasov, and M. I. Tereshchenko. Some people anticipated that one of the Kadets' preeminent jurists, Vasilii Maklakov or Vladimir Nabokov, would take the Justice portfolio, but most Committee members deemed participation of the political left in the cabinet important for its popular acceptance. Kerensky, vice-chair of the new Petrograd Soviet, was a moderate socialist and eager to enter the government (unlike the only other socialist approached, the Menshevik N. S. Chkheidze, who flatly declined appointment as minister of labor). Nekrasov was somewhat surprising as minister of transport, not so much by virtue of his qualifications—an engineer by profession, he was a highly capable man and knowledgeable about railroads—as for personal reasons. As leader of the left wing of the Kadet party, he had long been a bitter critic of Miliukov's; his acrimonious resignation from the Kadet central committee in 1915 had also generated a good deal of ill-will among the party leadership. Why Miliukov did not object to the candidacy of an individual so unlikely to support him in the cabinet is something of a mystery, but he may have believed that Nekrasov's leftist reputation would be helpful.[19] Finally, there was M. I. Tereshchenko, a wealthy young financier from Kiev whose appointment as finance minister provoked general surprise. Miliukov discovered only later that Kerensky, Nekrasov, and Tereshchenko had the common bond of membership in the same Masonic lodge. They quickly came to form a "triumvirate" within the cabinet, directed against Miliukov.[20]

Before composition of the new government could be formalized and announced, its source of legitimacy and general program had to be determined. These questions, as it turned out, involved defining its relationship not only to the Duma but also to the Petrograd Soviet, which by February 28 had called upon the population of the capital to rally to the Soviet and proclaimed its task as "the organization of the popular forces."[21] Miliukov and most of the members of the Temporary Committee would have much preferred to be commissioned by the tsar to form a new government. Instead, they were forced to act outside the law. In these circumstances support of the new government by the popular Petrograd Soviet appeared crucial. The Soviet might well have chosen to create a government itself, but the socialists forming its Executive Committee had already decided that in a "bourgeois" revolution it would leave formation of a provisional government to bourgeois groups, while reserving for itself the right to "state the demands which in the name of the entire democracy it was presenting to the Government created by the revolution." On the evening of March 1 the Duma Temporary Committee began negotiating with representatives of the Executive Committee of the Soviet about the program and mandate of what would be the Provisional Government. The most active participants from the Soviet side were Nikolai Sukhanov, N. D. Sokolov, and Iu. M. Steklov. Miliukov was virtually sole negotiator for the Temporary Committee. According to Sukhanov, "He spoke for the entire Duma committee; everyone considered this a matter of course. It was clear that Miliukov here was not only a leader, but the *boss*."[22]

The deputies for the Soviet had prepared a nine-point program the new government must adopt as the condition for the Soviet's support. The first three demands were desiderata Kadets had long worked for: a political amnesty; grant of the civil liberties promised in the October Manifesto but only partially realized; and removal of disabilities and privileges stemming from nationality, religion, or social origin. Miliukov had no trouble with the fourth demand that preparation begin immediately for the convocation of a constituent assembly elected on "four-tailed" suffrage; from the outset, the new government understood its role as that of a temporary caretaker. Less welcome but still acceptable were dissolution of the police and their replacement with a militia, and the promise that military units which had participated in the revolution would keep their weapons and not be sent to the front. The point dealing with the military he substantially amended. He insisted that its extension of full civil rights to soldiers be limited to their off-duty hours, and on inserting a clause which retained strict military discipline in the structure and carrying out of military service; after much wrangling the Soviet deputies also agreed to strike out the proviso that officers were to be elected.[23]

The one point Miliukov categorically refused to accept was a pledge by the new government not to take any steps to predetermine the future form of government. The socialists desired a republic, whereas Miliukov wanted a limited constitutional monarchy. Sukhanov, who had expected Miliukov to put up a fight for monarchy, was nonetheless surprised that "he should make this the most contentious point of all our terms." Miliukov tried to convince the deputies of the Soviet that retention of the dynasty, as represented by Aleksei and the regency of Michael, would pose no threat to democracy, since "one was a sick child, the other a thoroughly stupid man." Since agreement on this point proved impossible, it was temporarily shelved; the discussants moved on to other points in the Soviet program and finally to the question of what the Temporary Committee, in its turn, expected of the Soviet. Again, Sukhanov was somewhat surprised by the nature of Miliukov's demands. As he recalled it, Miliukov was less concerned with extracting a pledge of support for the government than with securing Soviet insistence that citizens refrain from violence and disorder and that soldiers heed their officers and have confidence in them. The agreements were finalized the following evening; Miliukov, Steklov and Sukhanov wrote out the final drafts together.[24]

The program and declarations approved on March 2 and published the following morning were a very imperfect compromise. The Soviet Executive Committee had secured the government's approval of most of its points in exchange for a declaration exhorting citizens to eschew violence and anarchy, calling upon soldiers to follow their officers in order to defend the revolution, and extending to the new government a most grudging and conditional support: the Soviet declaration to the people held that "to the extent that" the government worked to honor its promises and obligations "the democracy should lend it support."[25]

The unsatisfactory nature of both the eight-point program and the Soviet declaration naturally raises the question of why Miliukov and his colleagues ever agreed to them. By promising an amnesty that extended even to terrorists, the government made possible the return to the capital of revolutionaries openly dedicated to its overthrow. The abolition of the police and its replacement by local militias with elected officers had the effect of depriving the regime of the means of ensuring order, while the promise that the mutinous Petrograd troops could stay in the capital saddled it with an undisciplined soldiery that soon swelled the ranks of extremist parties.

Obviously, part of the explanation lies in the exigencies of the moment. Both documents were drawn up by exhausted men amid conditions of incredible chaos; the full implications of various points and phrases would be apparent only later.[26] The promise to the Petrograd troops, Miliukov noted, was dictated by the expectation that they would shortly be called upon to defend the capital from advancing loyalists. Moreover, the acceptability of the initial list of Soviet demands owed a good deal to what it did *not* contain, namely, stipulations concerning the conduct of the war, agrarian reform, and the right of national self-determination. Miliukov could only be grateful for such omissions and perhaps feared that protracted negotiations would result in a broadening of demands. In any event, speed seemed to him imperative. He believed that the longer the vacuum in power was allowed to exist, the greater anarchy would grow.

A last but cardinal issue had yet to be resolved, the status of the tsar and the dynasty. Retaining Nicholas himself was, of course, out of the question; Miliukov and most others committed to preserving the monarchy believed that the most acceptable arrangement was his abdication in favor of the heir, under the regency of the Grand Prince Michael.[27] Early on March 2, it was decided someone would have to go to Nicholas, now at Pskov since his train from the *stavka* had not been allowed to continue to the capital, and secure the abdication along these lines. Guchkov and V. V. Shul'gin set off that afternoon by special train. In the meantime, Miliukov tried to prepare the public to accept this arrangement. In an interview that day with a correspondent for Reuters he asserted that the government was firmly decided upon Michael's regency.[28] That afternoon in the Duma's Ekaterininskii Hall he announced to the assembled crowd the composition of the new government and certain provisions of its still unfinalized program. The hall displayed only moderate enthusiasm for most of the ministers, the exceptions being Kerensky and Miliukov himself: these names evoked stormy applause. When someone called out, "Who elected you?" Miliukov responded, "Nobody elected us, since if we had sat down to wait for an election by the people . . . our enemy would have had time to organize and defeat you and us. We were elected by the Russian revolution." This adroit answer produced prolonged applause. The most difficult moment came when he announced the regency.

> You ask about the dynasty. I know beforehand that my answer will not satisfy all of you. But I will tell it to you. The old despot who brought Russia to the brink of ruin will either voluntarily renounce the throne, or else be deposed. (Applause.) The power will be transferred to the regent, the Grand Duke Michael Alexandrovich. (Prolonged bursts of indignation, exclamation: "Long live the republic!" "Down with the dynasty!") (Weak applause, drowned by new bursts of indignation.) The heir will be Aleksei. (Cries: "This is the old dynasty!") Yes ladies and gentlemen, this is the old dynasty, which perhaps you do not like and which perhaps I do not like either. But [the question of] who it is that we love is beside the point right now. We cannot leave unanswered and undecided the question concerning the form of government . . . if we start arguing about this now instead of reaching an immediate decision, then Russia will find itself in a state of civil war which will only revive the ruined regime.

Miliukov went on to explain that the government would be convening a constituent assembly, at which time the freely elected representatives of the people could decide this question as they saw fit. Pressed for more details about the program, he decided it was time to end his remarks, making excuse that his voice—which was indeed hoarse from all the speeches of the last few days—was giving out. The good mood of the gathering was restored: Miliukov received tremendous applause and was lifted and carried out of the hall.[29] Still, general displeasure over his announcement about the monarchy mounted throughout the afternoon. That evening a sizable crowd of officers made their way to the Taurida Palace and insisted that they dare not return to their men if Miliukov did not retract his remarks about the regency and succession of Aleksei. Unwilling to repudiate this position, he agreed to release a statement to the press declaring that his remarks on the monarchy were an expression of his own personal opinion.[30]

In the early morning hours of March 3 members of the Provisional Government received disturbing news from Guchkov and Shul'gin. Upon reaching Pskov, they discovered that Nicholas had already made up his mind to abdicate; his generals had persuaded him that to do otherwise would cause civil strife that would endanger the war effort. But he had also decided, on further reflection, to change the act of abdication in favor of his son to one in favor of his brother Grand Duke Michael, since he did not wish to lay this burden on a sickly child from whom he would then be separated. Nonplussed by this unexpected development, the two Duma deputies concurred, departing for Petrograd as soon as the necessary papers were drawn up and signed.[31] Miliukov was subsequently very bitter about the act of abdication, which in bypassing the child Aleksei helped seal the fate of the monarchy; he saw in it not a sacrifice made for the benefit of the war effort but another instance of the tsar's customary selfishness: "Nicholas II did not wish to risk the fate of his son, preferring to risk his brother and Russia to an unknown future."[32]

Upon receipt of the report cabled by Guchkov and Shul'gin, members of the new government, Rodzianko, and several others hurriedly gathered to determine a course of action. All but Miliukov were of the opinion that the revolutionary mood of the moment would not tolerate accession to the throne of an adult Romanov. The Grand Duke Michael was informed of the situation and a meeting arranged for later in the morning. At Miliukov's insistence, it was agreed that he and Kerensky would present the arguments for and against acceptance of the throne; Michael could then decide for himself. Kerensky spoke briefly, Miliukov at length and with passion: everything, he believed, was at stake. The transition to the new order required a strong governmental authority, he argued, but the government could be strong only if buttressed by a symbol of authority to which the masses were accustomed. That symbol was the monarchy. "The Provisional Government by itself, without the support of this symbol, will simply not survive until the opening of the Constituent Assembly."[33]

Guchkov and Shul'gin joined the meeting shortly before noon. Miliukov expected they would back him up but found them very reluctant to do so—Guchkov, who had almost been set upon at the railroad station when he announced that Michael would be tsar, had also concluded that the dynasty was finished. Infuriated by what he took as the general cowardice or incomprehension of all those present, Miliukov refused to yield. As Shul'gin recalled it, "This man, usually so polite and self-controlled, would not allow anyone to speak; he interrupted those who were objecting to him, interrupted Rodzianko, Kerensky, everyone. . . . White as a sheet, his face bluish-grey from lack of sleep, completely hoarse from making speeches in barracks and at street meetings, he croaked away raspingly."[34] Unable to deny the popular antagonism toward monarchy in the capital, Miliukov went so far as to advocate bringing in troops from Moscow to back up Michael. He wrote later, "I was sure that this solution was comparatively safe. But even if it were dangerous, and even if the situation in Petrograd really was that bad, then we still had to take the risk: this was the only solution." But no one else wished even to discuss a step that might precipitate civil war, and the debate at last came to an end.[35] Michael, who had sat silent throughout, required little time for consideration before announcing that he could accept the supreme authority only in the event that it was offered him by the Constituent Assembly. Vladimir Nabokov and other jurists quickly drafted the text of his renunciation of the throne, which indicated that full power was vested in the Provisional Government until the Assembly could be convened.[36] In his history of the revolution Miliukov wrote of this decision, "The representatives of the Duma, 'The Duma of June 3,' in essence decided the fate of the monarchy. They created a situation which was defective at its very source, a situation from which all subsequent errors of the revolution flowed."[37]

Many of the individuals who witnessed Miliukov's efforts to preserve the monarchy at least until convocation of the Constituent Assembly would later conclude that he had been right to stress its importance for the new government. Had the government been backed by the symbolic authority of a tsar, a personal embodiment of the unity of Russia, the revolution might have developed very differently. Yet virtually all believed, as they had in March 1917, that the monarchy could not have been saved at that time. Popular hostility toward it was too acute, while the organized forces for its defense did not exist.[38] That Miliukov recognized clearly, before almost anyone else, the consequences of the end of the monarchy was a testament to his prescience; that he failed to appreciate the practical impossibility of retaining the monarchy testified to the limitations of his understanding.

Prior to the meeting with Michael, Miliukov had made his participation in the new government contingent upon the grand duke's acceptance of the crown. These hopes dashed, Miliukov and Guchkov both announced their resignations at the conclusion of the morning's work. Prince L'vov immediately asked Nabokov to use his influence with Miliukov to induce him to stay in the government. Nabokov needed no urging, since he believed that with Miliukov's resignation the Provisional Government would be losing "the only person who could direct foreign policy and who was known to Europe. Essentially, his exit would have been a veritable catastrophe." The joint efforts of Nabokov and other members of the Kadet central committee to persuade him of his responsibility to remain in the cabinet succeeded; that evening Miliukov attended the session of ministers, where he found Guchkov as well.[39] Nearly eleven years after his unsuccessful efforts to negotiate a strictly Kadet cabinet he reluctantly agreed to enter a government whose members had just helped defeat him on an issue he considered of paramount importance.

Minister Miliukov

Despite his old predictions that a second Russian revolution would be elemental and destructive and that a revolution in the midst of war would spell disaster, despite even the huge blow to stability represented by the elimination of the monarchy, Miliukov harbored higher hopes for the new order than did some of his colleagues.[40] His optimism was in part a matter of temperament, but in the first weeks of the Provisional Government it was not difficult to persuade oneself that things were off to a good start. Resistance by supporters of the tsarist regime never materialized; the near absence of bloodshed accompanying the change of order produced an initial sense of euphoria.[41]

As pledges of loyalty and support poured in from around the country, the government immediately set about realizing the easiest of its tasks, the repeal of odious laws and the proclamation of promised rights. An amnesty was declared, and capital punishment abolished; the main censorship administration was done away with; restrictions on rights due to religion and national origin were enumerated and declared null and void. A manifesto on Finland repealed the laws violating the Finnish constitution, including the discriminatory legislation Miliukov had fought so hard in the Third Duma, and guaranteed its cultural autonomy. The question of Polish independence

Vladimir N. Nabokov, passport photo. Courtesy the Nabokov Archives, Montreux.

was more complicated, since most of Russian Poland was under enemy occupation, but on March 16, on Miliukov's insistence, the government published an appeal to Poles promising creation of an independent Polish state "comprising all lands in which the Polish people constitute the majority of the population," to be united with Russia in a "free military alliance."[42]

In the early weeks of the revolution prospects also appeared promising for the Constitutional Democrats, the only non-socialist party still intact. Kadets all over the country played a prominent role in establishing "Committees of Public Safety" to assume the tasks of local government, party organizations were created or reanimated in tens of dozens of locales, and new liberal dailies set out to attract provincial readership. An almost celebratory spirit pervaded the seventh Kadet congress, convened in Petrograd March 25, which also demonstrated its united support for Miliukov. Prince Evgenii Trubetskoi, recently returned to the party he had quit in 1906 as too radical, introduced Miliukov to the congress as "our dear unifier" and "valiant leader" (*doblestnyi vozhd'*). Mikhail Mandel'shtam, long a critic of the party's excessive moderation, now proclaimed that Miliukov's wartime leadership—from unification of the Duma to the speech against Sturmer—embodied a true understanding of "state and national interests."[43]

Miliukov in fact took little part in party affairs at this time, given the demands of his official position. His first concern as foreign minister was to secure international recognition of the new government. On March 4 he cabled Russia's diplomatic representatives abroad, assuring them the new government would strictly observe all existing treaty obligations and devote itself to the achievement of victory in the war. A more official declaration followed two days later, and within the week the United States and the Allied powers had formally recognized the Provisional Government as Russia's legitimate authority.[44]

The repatriation of political émigrés was another delicate issue requiring Miliukov's attention. The Provisional Government's grant of amnesty gave thousands of Russian citizens living in foreign exile the right to return home; among them were people implacably opposed to the war, whose repatriation Miliukov scarcely desired. He therefore covertly tried to pursue a policy of selective admissions. On March 10 he instructed Russian embassies and consulates to provide all possible assistance to émigrés desiring to return to Russia, but the following day sent a secret telegram saying passports were not to be issued to individuals identified in Allied or Russian proscription lists as spying for Germany or opposing the war. When Trotsky was detained by the British, en route from the United States to Russia, Miliukov asked that they keep him and his comrades until "further information about them had been obtained." Delaying tactics could not work indefinitely; the Soviet received complaints and demanded that the foreign minister "adopt urgent measures assuring the return of all political emigrants, without exceptions, to Russia." Miliukov had little choice other than to request that Trotsky be allowed to resume his trip and that no distinctions be drawn "between political emigrants who are pacifists and non-pacifists."[45]

The Provisional Government felt similarly constrained to allow the return of Lenin and other "defeatists" via Germany by train. Miliukov apparently underestimated the threat posed by Lenin, believing that Lenin's very "importation" by Germany would wholly discredit him in the eyes of the public. He also considered Lenin's views on the war too extreme to enjoy real influence, an impression reinforced by the cool reception afforded Lenin's initial pronouncements upon his return. Paleologue noted Miliukov's elation April 5 after the Bolshevik leader's debut at the Petrograd Soviet: Lenin argued the pacifist cause so heatedly, Miliukov said, "and with such effrontery and lack of tact, that he was compelled to stop and leave the room amidst a storm of booing. He will never survive it."[46]

Miliukov made minimal changes in the running of the foreign policy establishment. He dispensed with much of the formality and ritual characteristic of the office, including liveried doorkeepers and sumptuous receptions. It was prudent to do so, since tsarist pomp in hungry Petrograd would have offended popular sensibilities, but the unadorned and workaday environment established in the Ministry also suited him personally, with his notorious dislike of formal dress and elaborate protocol. When work kept him late at the ministry, as it often did, he spent the night in a small room for servants; Anna on occasion brought him lunch wrapped in newspapers.[47]

More important, he made few changes in personnel beyond replacing several highly conservative ambassadors and bringing into the ministry a number of private persons—most notably the liberals Boris Nol'de as deputy minister and Petr Struve to direct a newly created Economic Department. Miliukov did not distrust all servants of the old regime as some of his fellow ministers did, but rather appreciated both the value of bureaucratic expertise and the virtue of continuity in administration.[48]

All these details and demands consumed a tremendous amount of energy, but were, ultimately, secondary to the question of the war. Almost immediately upon taking office, Miliukov found his interpretation of Russia's war aims challenged by the Petrograd Soviet. In trying to meet that challenge he discovered that the Provisional Government not only did not enjoy the autonomy it formally claimed, but also that it was not always willing to utilize even such power as it had. He also discovered, to his chagrin, that his influence in a cabinet whose composition had been largely of his own making was limited.

The Soviet's views on war aims were first expressed in its famous March 14 "Appeal to the Peoples of the World" in which the "Russian democracy" proclaimed that the time had come to launch a determined struggle against the acquisitive ambitions of the governments of all countries and for the people to take into their own hands the right to decide questions of war and peace. The Appeal urged the populations of the Central Powers to overthrow the autocratic yoke in their own countries and join the Russian people in putting an end to the butchery.[49]

In order to counter such views, Miliukov seized upon the deliberations in the U.S. Senate over entering the war to publicly outline his position on war aims. In a press conference on March 23, he welcomed the imminent entry of the "mighty republic" on the side of the Allies as something that would not only hasten victory but provide a tremendous *moral* boost to the war effort. Endorsing Woodrow Wilson's characterization of the primary goals of the war as the prevention of future wars and the liberation of subject peoples, he stressed that these were and always had been the Allies' own goals. In particular, Russia desired the removal of Turkey from Europe, the restructuring of Austria-Hungary, and the creation of an independent Czechoslovakia. Talk about Allied support of "annexations" therefore rested on misunderstandings, including even the question of Constantinople. Constantinople, he claimed, was not truly a Turkish city but rather a dominion in which the Turks remained "an alien element," while for Russia control of the city and the straits constituted protection of "the doors to our home."[50]

Miliukov seems truly not to have appreciated how provocative these announcements would appear to much of the left. Kerensky was furious; according to Nabokov, when Kerensky arrived at the next cabinet meeting with the offending issue of *Rech'*, "he burst into unnatural laughter, tapped his fingers on the newspaper, and repeated, 'No, no, this trick will not work.'" He angrily accused Miliukov of pursuing his own foreign policy rather than that of the Provisional Government.[51] The Soviet, too, took strong exception to Miliukov's views. It demanded from the government an immediate public statement on Russian war aims in line with the formula "peace without annexations and indemnities" and assurances that steps for concluding a general peace would be taken immediately.

In cabinet discussions over the following days held with the "Contact Committee"—the body established to provide a regular link between the Soviet Executive Committee and the Provisional Government—Miliukov found himself arguing not only with the Soviet representatives, but with Kerensky, Tereshchenko, Nekrasov, and Vladimir L'vov as well. Again defending the territorial agreements with the Allies as being consonant with Russia's liberationist war aims, he also argued—with rather more foundation—that their hopes about the response to the Soviet Appeal were misplaced. The majority of socialists in Germany were first and foremost nationalists; they were not going to desert their government in war. He also thought it fruitless to ask the Allies to begin peace negotiations on the basis of "no annexations or indemnities," while unilaterally repudiating the territorial claims in the treaties would only raise doubts in the West about Russia's commitment to stay in the war.[52]

His arguments made little impression on the Soviet representatives, most of whom firmly believed that the Russian Revolution would provide a powerful international impetus for a just peace. Within the cabinet, Nekrasov, Tereshchenko, and Prince L'vov pressed for accommodation. Miliukov therefore reluctantly drafted a Declaration on War Aims, issued by the government on March 27, that made substantial concessions to the Soviet. It declared that Russia did not desire domination over other nations, seizure of their national possessions, or forcible occupation of foreign territories. Rather ambiguously, however, it also declared that the Russian people would not permit their country "to emerge from this great struggle humiliated and sapped in its vital forces."[53] He also managed to ensure that the

Declaration be issued as a statement to the citizens of Russia rather than to the Allies, hoping in this way to minimize its diplomatic implications. These compromises did not resolve the fundamental differences over the war or diffuse the personal antagonisms dividing the cabinet. When the issue of war aims was again taken up, it touched off a governmental crisis.

On April 13 newspapers carried an announcement that the Provisional Government was preparing a note on its revised war aims to be submitted to the Allied powers. In fact, no such note had been discussed; Kerensky had made a misleading statement to the press in order to force the issue. When Miliukov discovered that Kerensky was responsible for the announcement, he demanded a retraction. At a stormy session of the cabinet it was agreed that the announcement must be disavowed, but the ministers also saw justice in Kerensky's contention that it was time to present the Allies with a formal statement concerning war aims. The announcement of a note, followed by a retraction, had already made such a step unavoidable: the Soviet declared April 17 that it would not approve the government's bond issue until a statement was sent.[54]

Miliukov drafted a note to accompany the Declaration of War Aims, which was to be transmitted to the Allies. The entire cabinet discussed, amended, and finally approved the text of the note. Before dispatching it, Miliukov emphasized that this approval meant the government was united behind the document and accepted responsibility for its contents. All agreed; as Kerensky later put it, the wording of the note "should have satisfied the most violent critic of Miliukov's 'imperialism.' "[55]

Instead, publication of the note in the Petrograd press on April 20 touched off massive street disorders, the beginning of the "April crisis." Angry demonstrations, demanding the resignation of "Miliukov-Dardanel'skii" (an allusion to Miliukov's position on the straits), began in the afternoon. They were soon met by counter-demonstrations organized in his support. General Lavr Kornilov, commander of the Petrograd military district, wished to suppress the disorders, but Premier L'vov refused to resort to the "violence" of the former regime. Late in the day the cabinet and representatives of the Soviet met in an unsuccessful effort to work out a compromise. In a meeting of the Soviet, there were numerous calls for the resignations of Miliukov and Guchkov; a handful of Bolshevik deputies demanded that the Soviet itself assume power.[56]

On April 21 the demonstrations grew larger and more threatening. Some of the demonstrators, including soldiers from the Petrograd garrison, were armed; three people were killed in clashes between different groups. To help diffuse the crisis, Nekrasov and Tsereteli composed a supplementary statement to Miliukov's note, clarifying its references to fulfillment of treaty obligations as being meant in the spirit of the March 27 Declaration; the government and Soviet approved this text. The Soviet Executive Committee also succeeded in ending the disorders without resort to force. Countermanding Kornilov's instructions to bring out artillery and troops, it banned all demonstrations for forty-eight hours and denounced anyone resorting to arms as a traitor to the revolution.

The events of April 20 and 21 revealed the weakness of the Provisional Government, the authority of the Petrograd Soviet, and widespread hostility toward Miliukov's foreign policy line; however, the conclusions to be drawn from all this varied. The effect of the April crisis on Kerensky, Nekrasov, and Tereshchenko was to harden their determination to oust Miliukov as minister of foreign affairs and bring members of the Soviet into the cabinet to enhance the government's popularity and authority. Prince L'vov and ministers less opposed to Miliukov also thought creation of a coalition cabinet the only way to resolve the contradictions of dual power; on April 26 the government issued a statement to the population expressing its intention to bring new "actively creative forces" into the cabinet.[57]

Miliukov's response to the April crisis was decidedly different. He had demonstrated from the start his customary courage: on April 20, when angry soldiers and workers surged around his government car and forced it to stop, he rose calmly, folded his arms, and began giving a speech. This cool display of nerve impressed the crowd, and the car was soon allowed to proceed. In official deliberations later that day he alone, among cabinet members, urged calling out the troops to suppress the disorders.[58] The government's reluctance to do so was in his opinion an irresponsible failure to exercise the power it had, while the Soviet's countermand of Kornilov's orders was an arrogation of power to which it had no legal right.

He also had a very different take on the demonstrations themselves: if his views on war aims were unpopular with part of the capital's population, the strong demonstrations on his behalf showed there were many who supported them. Believing that he was pursuing policies that upheld Russia's honor and interest, he had no trouble in determining which part of the population should be heeded. Given these perspectives, Miliukov thought coalition a disastrous idea. Socialists in the cabinet would make it even more subject to Soviet control, while socialist ministers would feel obliged to espouse class politics that would intensify civil strife and jeopardize the war effort. The result would be a cabinet more internally divided and paralyzed than was the present one. What was needed was not coalition but a firm demand that the Soviet cease interfering in government and undermining its credibility.[59]

The Soviet Executive Committee was divided over the question of entering the government and did not agree to begin negotiations until the end of the month. The eight conditions it set included official support for peace

Miliukov, minister of Foreign Affairs, 1917. Courtesy Russian Pictorial Collection, Hoover Institution Archives, Stanford University.

"without annexation or indemnity" and democratization of the army. Rather than demanding Miliukov's exclusion altogether, it was proposed that he relinquish Foreign Affairs and take over the Ministry of Education from A. A. Manuilov.[60] Miliukov had actually considered such a move several weeks before, having become aware that the Allies had reservations about his ability to deal with the Soviet. Now, the circumstances were different. Opposed to coalition in principle and unwilling to remain in a cabinet that would be committed to Soviet views on the conduct of foreign policy, he angrily resigned during a cabinet meeting May 2.[61]

Miliukov hoped that all the Kadet ministers would resign as well, thus forcing a reconsideration of the idea of coalition. But while much of the Kadet leadership shared his concerns about the effectiveness of a coalition cabinet, most also believed some sort of compromise with the Soviet was necessary. It could be hoped that the presence of members of the Soviet in the cabinet would make it more supportive of the government, and that liberal ministers would still be able to influence decision making. After extended debate the Kadet central committee voted 18 to 10 in favor of participating in a coalition cabinet; Nekrasov had already declared he would remain in the cabinet regardless of the party's decision. However, efforts to persuade Miliukov to retract his resignation were unsuccessful and the new cabinet was formed without him. His ministerial career had lasted exactly eight weeks.[62]

The Need for Firm Authority

The euphoric period of the Russian Revolution ended with the armed demonstrations of the April crisis and formation of the first coalition cabinet. That body was destined to last no longer than its predecessor; by a peculiar rhythm, as Miliukov noted in his history of the revolution, each cabinet of the Provisional Government lasted but two months, while the interregnum between the cabinet that was collapsing and the one that was replacing it became longer and more traumatic.[63] This "constant and progressive disintegration of power" took place within a context of deteriorating economic conditions, mounting urban and rural violence, and social and political polarization.

Polarization was reflected in the two fundamentally different responses that developed to the problem of restoring state authority. The first, reduced to its essentials, held that authority could be strong only if it enjoyed broad popularity. Satisfaction of the demands and grievances of different parts of the population could not therefore be wholly delayed until the Constituent Assembly was elected and convened. The peasant desire for land, worker demands for an eight-hour day and greater control over production, the claims to greater political autonomy forwarded by Ukrainians and other national minorities, and the general desire for a speedy end to the war all had to be addressed if the government were to enjoy—and merit—confidence. While there was no consensus within the Soviet itself or among socialists in general about how these steps were to be undertaken, or how far the revolutionary regime could preempt the decisions of the Constituent Assembly, all agreed upon the need for speedy implementation of some social reforms.[64]

An entirely different view insisted that any far-reaching measures of political or social reconstruction had to be delayed. For such measures to be legitimate and be accepted by the entire population they had to have the sanction of the people's will as expressed in an elected constituent assembly; organization of fair elections would take time. Furthermore, such far-reaching measures, however sanctioned, would inevitably cause dissension, instability, and a fall in agricultural and industrial productivity, all of which could be fatal to the war effort. Concern for the state as it fought a difficult war required patience, subordination to the authority of the Provisional Government, and the postponement of major social and political changes. The fact that proponents of such views came largely from officers and the propertied classes added a class dimension to the political and ideological orientations underlying the two perspectives on bolstering government authority.

Before April 1917 Miliukov would almost certainly have devoted his energies to mediating between these two basic perspectives. Reconciling differences, finding compromise formulas, preserving or seeking grounds for unity had been his most customary role not only within the Kadet party but within Russian politics: in the Union of Liberation and the Union of Unions, during the first two Dumas, and in organizing the Progressive bloc. And the role of conciliator was not merely purely personal: it stemmed from his conception of the nature and function of liberalism in Russia.

After his resignation from the government, however, he virtually abandoned this role both for himself and his party as he became convinced that compromise was no longer possible. The "middle ground" that many Kadets and moderate socialists continued to seek did not exist, he believed, primarily because socialists could not bring themselves to break decisively with the elements who did not care about the preservation of the state, most especially the Bolsheviks. He had thought Lenin's views too extreme to win popular support; instead, Bolshevik popularity grew and government authority diminished.

Personal bitterness no doubt contributed to this bleak appraisal. The humiliation of his ouster from his ministry, and of being supplanted in influence by Kerensky, a man he despised, was compounded by the sense that almost no one had behaved as they should. Guchkov had abruptly resigned April 29 instead of helping him resist Soviet pressure, Nekrasov had intrigued to displace him from foreign affairs, while the Kadets' decision to remain in the cabinet represented a reversal of their stand at the March party congress, when Mandel'shtam declared that participation of the Party of Popular Freedom in a government that did not include Miliukov was simply "unthinkable."[65]

In addition, the lessons perhaps suggested to Miliukov by Taine's *French Revolution* are again apposite: against the backdrop of unbridled popular passions Taine chronicles the failure of nerve of those in authority and the hunger for power of the Jacobins. The king could have been saved at the Tuileries, wrote Taine, if he had been willing to fight, and the Jacobins routed as Lafayette urged. But with the governing as with the governed, "all notion of the State was lost." Constitutionalists' volition "evaporated"; horrified at shedding blood, they forgot that their duty to maintain society and civilization at times required use of force. The Jacobins, in contrast, were unburdened by any scruples concerning bloodshed. They also understood that in a centralized state such as France, he who seizes the lever at the center can control the whole machine.⁶⁶

After the "July Days," when an uprising encouraged by the Bolsheviks almost toppled the government, Miliukov's attitude toward conciliation and demand for firm authority became even more pronounced, shifting him decidedly to the right and dividing him from many of his Kadet colleagues. One of the best illustrations of this was the Moscow State Conference convened August 12 by Kerensky, now head of the Provisional Government.

The Moscow conference, attended by representatives of parties, public organizations, and local and state governing bodies, was conceived as a forum for discussing new programs and especially for developing national unity. Tsereteli, Chkheidze, and other Soviet spokesmen made a strong show of support for the new coalition government, echoing Kerensky's call for restoration of the army's fighting capacity, the need to place the interests of the country as a whole above those of specific classes or groups, and even his insistence that to protect the revolution the government must be prepared to fight its enemies on the left as well as the right.⁶⁷

Miliukov's response to these avowals was revealing. Speaking to the conference on August 14, he said he saw scant evidence that the government had shed the "ideological and organizational dependence" that had kept it from taking the steps needed for the salvation of the country. Events had forced moderate socialists to acknowledge that there were criminals and traitors among the Bolsheviks, he observed, but they had yet to admit that the basic idea of Bolshevism—the transformation of foreign war into civil war in the interests of revolution—was itself "criminal." The government talked about the principle of the state, order, and firm authority but what measures did it propose taking to guarantee order and protect the inviolability of the individual and of property? Nor could there be much confidence that it would implement the measures the military command had pointed out were necessary for the "moral regeneration" of the army (these included curtailment of the activities of soldiers' committees and restoration of the death penalty). Miliukov ended his speech with a pledge of support for the new coalition cabinet that was also a warning: "The future will depend on the use to which the government puts the support which we give it voluntarily and without quarrels." There was little in either the tone or the content of this speech to distinguish it from the pronouncements of Maklakov, Struve, and Guchkov.⁶⁸

In early September, Miliukov's hopes for a strengthening of governmental authority plummeted in the aftermath of what is usually referred to as the "Kornilov rebellion" or the "Kornilov Affair."⁶⁹ On the evening of August 26, Kerensky told his stunned cabinet that General Lavr Kornilov, commander-in-chief of Russia's armed forces, was marching on the capital with the intention of overthrowing the government. Kerensky secured cabinet consent to its "suspension" and a grant of extraordinary powers, which he used to notify Kornilov by telegram in the early hours of August 27 that he had relieved him of his command. Kornilov furiously denied that he was acting against the government and refused to resign. Efforts by Miliukov and others that day to mediate between Kerensky and Kornilov did not succeed in averting a public rupture: an announcement that Kornilov was attempting the armed overthrow of the government was transmitted to the press late that evening. Kornilov issued a declaration of his own, maintaining that Kerensky's statement was a lie and that a great "provocation" was taking place. He also instructed officers to disregard government orders to halt the advance. Whatever his original intentions, he was now in open revolt against the Provisional Government.[70]

On August 28 Miliukov and the Kadets redoubled efforts to find some sort of face-saving compromise that would allow for creation of a strong government without an actual overthrow of Kerensky, a step they feared would inaugurate outright civil war. The plan they devised appeared promising: if Kerensky authorized an individual whom Kornilov trusted, such as General M. V. Alekseev, to form a new government of which Kerensky would be a part, Kornilov could yield with honor intact and armed conflict would be avoided. Miliukov secured Alekseev's support for this plan, which also had the backing of the majority of the cabinet.[71] Kerensky, however was reluctant to surrender his powers and by the following day saw no need to do so, as it became clear that early reports had overestimated Kornilov's strength and that the Soviet and parties to the left would support the government. Most of Kornilov's troops, on learning that they were opposing the Provisional Government, refused to continue. The revolt dissolved in confusion; on September 1 Kornilov surrendered and was placed under arrest.

The repercussions of the "Kornilov Affair" were enormous.[72] The officer corps believed either that Kerensky had manipulated Kornilov into appearing to revolt in order to discredit him, or had weakly reneged on a prior agreement with the general in the face of Soviet pressure, as Kornilov himself maintained; in either case, they despised Kerensky and would not in future defend his government. Radical socialists, soldiers, and workers believed a counterrevolutionary conspiracy had been narrowly thwarted; their hostility toward the officers and privileged classes correspondingly intensified, undermining what was left of morale at the front. This hostility definitely encompassed the chief party of the "bourgeoisie," the Kadets; they, and Miliukov especially, were widely suspected of being part of the conspiracy.[73]

Miliukov denied then and always that he or his party participated in any plot to overthrow the government, noting Kadet efforts to mediate during the crisis and maintaining that on several occasions he personally warned Kornilov against attempting a military revolt.[74] There is little reason to doubt these denials, either on the basis of the circumstantial and contradictory evidence that exists on the Kornilov Affair or on his own past record: he was not, by nature or conviction, a plotter.[75] At the same time, Miliukov believed replacement of the weak second coalition with a strong government was urgently required; if means could have been found for persuading Kerensky to consent to formation of a provisional civil-military dictatorship including Kerensky and Kornilov, he would have been delighted. Miliukov's open admiration for Kornilov in the weeks before the crisis and his refusal to condemn him unequivocally once it began was enough to taint him in the public eye. Kerensky demanded on August 30 that the head of the Kadet party temporarily leave the country, or at least go to some spot far from Petrograd, fearing that his presence in either capital would excite public opinion against inclusion of Kadets in the new coalition cabinet he was trying to organize. Miliukov chose to travel to the Crimea.[76]

Virtually the only group to benefit from the Kornilov Affair was the Bolsheviks. Their energetic contribution to organizing the defense of Petrograd when it appeared menaced by "counterrevolution" helped restore the popularity they lost after the July revelations about their German contacts; on September 25 the Bolsheviks won a majority in the Workers' Section of the Petrograd Soviet. When Miliukov rejoined his colleagues in the capital in early October, he found an atmosphere charged by alarm over the German advance toward the city, the virtual nonexistence of government authority, and the growing strength of the Bolsheviks. A majority on the Kadet central committee now felt that cooperation with the moderate socialists was the only way to shore up the government until convocation of the Constituent Assembly, whose elections had finally been set for November 12. Kadets had already joined, in Miliukov's absence, a third coalition cabinet with a more frankly socialist program than any of its predecessors. They were presently involved with organizing the party's electoral campaign and with work in the Council of the Republic, or pre-parliament, a large conference convened October 7 by Kerensky in a last-ditch effort to marshal support for the government.[77]

Miliukov looked on these activities with dismay. He continued to believe that supporting the socialists' program and introducing social reforms would achieve, at best, a phantom unity. Instead, he urged that the party actively campaign for its own program and try to attract to itself other groups genuinely committed to order, law, and the interests of the whole nation.[78] Miliukov attended all the remaining sessions of the pre-parliament but spoke only once, on the subject of foreign policy. There, he came out in support of

Foreign Minister Tereshchenko's conduct of foreign policy and against the abstract utopianism of the Leninist line, acidly observing that it had more affinity with Slavophilism than internationalism in its conviction that "a 'new word' will issue from Russia that will regenerate the decaying West"; it was not for Russia to teach the leading democracies of the world how to conclude a just peace.[79] This position was the opposite of conciliatory.

In the middle weeks of October, as delegates to the pre-parliament debated, inhabitants of the capital followed daily bulletins about the German advance and rumors of an imminent Bolshevik-led uprising. Miliukov and other members of the Kadet central committee met each day at 6 P.M. with Kadet ministers in the cabinet for discussions, but a feeling of hopelessness gripped many; the atmosphere was very reminiscent of the weeks prior to the February revolution. Then, on the afternoon of October 24, Kerensky appeared before the pre-parliament to announce that a Bolshevik attempt to overthrow the Provisional Government was already under way. His appeal to the gathering for its support during the crisis evoked stormy applause, but the resolution it passed deplored the insurrection without expressing any support for the government. After this astonishing vote of no confidence, the session broke up in confusion. The behavior of the Council of the Republic appeared to confirm Miliukov's worst predictions about socialist statesmanship.[80]

After October

On October 25–26 the Bolsheviks overthrew the Provisional Government in Petrograd. An editorial in *Rech'* of October 26, almost certainly by Miliukov, read in part:

> Thus the die is cast. A country which is exhausted and tormented by three years of war, which has experienced the convulsions of revolution, which is reduced to misery, which has reached the last degree of economic and industrial disintegration, a country deprived of a firm and solid government, a country which has become the arena of anarchic and pogrom movements—this unfortunate, perishing country will have to undergo a new stage on her road to Golgotha. We have already entered upon a new era of vivisectional experimentation over her.[81]

Kadet attempts in the first confused days to halt or fight the Bolshevik takeover came to nothing, although virtually no one among them imagined that the Bolsheviks would long retain the power they had usurped. Kerensky had managed to elude arrest and travel to Gatchina, where he intended to marshal forces loyal to the Provisional Government for a march on the capital; the Kadet central committee, on October 29, urged all institutions and organizations to unite against the Bolshevik seizure of power, while discussing ways and means of doing so. Miliukov, for his part, left almost immediately for Moscow, where the attempt to proclaim soviet rule was meeting much stiffer resistance than in Petrograd.

It is impossible to determine precisely what Miliukov did during the next few weeks. By November 2, after several days of fierce fighting, the Bolsheviks and their supporters had carried the day in Moscow and repulsed the pro-government advance on Petrograd under General Krasnov. Kadets were not agreed about what steps should be taken next. A number of prominent party members, among them Nikolai Astrov and N. V. Teslenko in Moscow and V. D. Nabokov in Petrograd, inclined toward passive resistance until the scheduled convocation of the Constituent Assembly on November 28, to which the new government had committed itself and which would, presumably, repudiate it. But with ministers of the Provisional Government under arrest, the editorial offices of *Rech'* smashed, and the Kadets' Moscow offices closed by the Bolsheviks, others shared Miliukov's belief that more forceful opposition to the new regime was required. In mid-November General Alekseev traveled incognito to cossack territory on the Don to begin organizing such a force. Miliukov, who had been in contact with Alekseev, would naturally have desired to play a part in this effort. He also had reason to fear for his freedom should he remain in Bolshevik-controlled territory: on November 17, in Petrograd, armed sailors had turned up at Miliukov's and Shingarev's apartments to arrest them (the Kadet party as a whole was outlawed ten days later). Thus, despite his election as one of seventeen Kadet deputies to the Constituent Assembly, in the latter part of November Miliukov headed not for the capital but south, for the Don. Shingarev, who had also been elected to the Assembly, decided instead to go to Petrograd, where he was arrested the day of its opening meeting.[82]

The situation on the Don proved to be a good deal less favorable for establishment of an anti-Bolshevik movement than any of its would-be organizers had appreciated. True, Ataman General Kaledin, head of the Don cossacks, was fiercely anti-Bolshevik and welcomed Alekseev and other Russian officers, but his control over his own men and territories was nominal. War-weariness on the part of younger cossack troops, social hostilities between land-rich cossacks, on the one hand, and poor tenant peasant farmers, urban workers, and miners, on the other, and intensifying regional particularism all meant that much of the local population was less than willing to combat Bolsheviks at home, let alone join a national campaign to liberate and reunify all Russia. In fact, no one as yet had any clear idea of what "Soviet power" meant, nor what its opponents intended to put in its stead.

Furnishing an answer to the latter question was part of the task Miliukov envisioned for himself and the handful of other liberals who had journeyed south to help organize an anti-Bolshevik movement. To be truly "national" that movement could not be purely military and negative, in the sense of defeating the usurpers by force; it must have a civil dimension and positive goals as well. General Alekseev shared this view, and in mid-December, after his small force had won its first victory by expelling the Bolsheviks from Rostov, authorized creation of a "Political Council" by Miliukov, Petr Struve, G. Trubetskoi, and others. Miliukov quickly drafted a Declaration of Purpose, an appeal that could serve both to define the basic goal of the "Volunteer" movement, as the south Russian force was now called, and attract new recruits to the cause.[83]

The Declaration did not differ greatly from the themes of his speeches and articles over the course of the year, dwelling as it did on the unity of the Russian state and the necessity of putting aside differences in order to fight for free and democratic government, law, and national honor. Just as Russians from every walk of life had rallied during the Time of Troubles to repel the invader from their homeland, so now all the people of Russia must unite to save their country.[84] The goals identified in the Declaration of Purpose were those Miliukov held most dear, but he may also have reasoned that invoking such abstractions as freedom and love of country, while avoiding the more contentious issues of regional autonomy and social reforms, was the best means of building a broad movement in a deeply divisive time. Two years later, surveying in emigration the collapsing fortunes of the anti-Bolshevik movement, he would come to the conclusion that this position had been a mistake: reluctance to address the issues of most immediate importance to the bulk of the population had contributed to perception of the movement as an alien rather than genuinely popular concern. In late 1917 and throughout the following year, however, he continued to believe that so long as the state was in peril resolution of other questions must be left to the future.[85]

Even as the Volunteer Army struggled to "win the right to existence" in the Don, as General Anton Denikin put it, Miliukov and the civilians of the Political Council were forced to defend their place among the Volunteers. General Kornilov, who arrived in the Don in early December, got along badly with Alekseev and did not share his appreciation for the civilians' administrative and organizational skills, his experiences of the previous months having left him with small stomach for politicians. Kornilov wanted the movement entirely under military control, threatening at one point to quit the Don and set up his own army in Siberia. Anxious to avoid a split in the movement and to keep the popular Kornilov with the Volunteers, Miliukov and the other civilians managed after intense discussions to effect a compromise. Kornilov would take over military command of the Volunteers; Alekseev, with the Political Council, would manage civil affairs; and Ataman Kaledin would head the cossacks. The Political Council, which included senior officers, Miliukov, and a number of other liberal civilians, was primarily responsible for organizing desperately needed economic support and for relations with foreign and local governments and with Russian society.[86]

This arrangement was not destined to last very long. The addition of Kerensky's former aide Boris Savinkov and three other socialists to the Political Council in January, a step Kaledin and Alekseev felt important to give it a more representative cast, infuriated Kornilov and his supporters; after more stormy meetings the Council was downgraded to purely consultative status. Kornilov also displayed his disregard for the "politicians" by drafting, without their knowledge, a new political program for the Volunteers. Although the program was basically liberal in spirit, pledging full and equal civil rights for all citizens and promising to pass authority to a constituent assembly, Miliukov was troubled by the military chief's trespass on an area of civilian competence. Kornilov was behaving like an "adventurer," he wrote Alekseev; his action threatened to destroy public support for the Volunteer Army.[87]

The January advance through the Don of the numerically superior Bolshevik forces finally put an end to this uneasy situation. After fighting during which both sides behaved with unprecedented brutality, the city of Taganrog passed to Bolshevik control; they now prepared to close in on Rostov, headquarters of the Volunteer Army. Ataman Kaledin, unable to rally his cossacks, committed suicide January 29. The death of the Volunteers' staunchest local ally made their already precarious position in the Don untenable; on February 9 Alekseev and Kornilov began evacuating their army, numbering only about five thousand men and lacking sufficient food and arms, to the Kuban. Both generals strongly discouraged the civilian members of the Political Council from accompanying the army on what came to be known as the "Ice March," a heroic, six-hundred mile ordeal of almost constant fighting and terrible privation during which Kornilov himself was killed. Struve and Trubetskoi determined to make their way back to Moscow; Miliukov, however, decided to remain in Rostov, which Bolshevik forces occupied February 10.[88]

The following two months were extraordinarily difficult ones. The Bolsheviks lost no time in arresting and executing the newly selected cossack leaders; Miliukov and the Rostov Kadets had to remain in hiding. Cut off from friends and constructive activity, he worked on his history of the revolution. He also had ample time to reflect on the many setbacks to the anti-Bolshevik cause for which he had entertained such high hopes. Quite aside from the disappointments of his experience in the Don, there was tragic news from the north. On January 5 in Petrograd Bolshevik sailors wantonly murdered Andrei Shingarev and Fedor Kokoshkin, convalescing under detention in the Mariinskii Hospital. The senseless death of his two dearest friends grieved him profoundly.[89] A blow of another sort was the Soviet central government's conclusion of a separate peace with the Central Powers on March 3, 1918 (new style), at Brest-Litovsk.

Miliukov's attitude toward the Germans, however, was about to change in dramatic fashion. In the months after Brest-Litovsk the Germans continued their push through Ukraine and into the Don, driving the Bolsheviks from Rostov in late April. Miliukov and remaining local Kadets could now emerge from hiding, and were struck not simply by the Germans' restoration of order in the city, but by what they learned of German cooperation with the autonomous, anti-Bolshevik governments established in Kiev by Hetman Pavlo Skoropadskii and in Novocherkassk by the new Don ataman, P. N. Krasnov. Krasnov's cossacks received arms from the Germans, something the Volunteers were very much in need of. The Volunteers were also dangerously short of funds; Alekseev had written Miliukov on May 10 that if he did not receive money soon he would be forced to dissolve the army.[90] Miliukov now began to think it possible that the Volunteers, too, could cooperate with the Germans, receiving material assistance and backup military support to enable them to drive the Bolsheviks out of Moscow.

He did not come to this startling reorientation lightly. He blamed the Germans entirely for starting the war and had lost a beloved son in that conflict. He was also alive to the fact that he had done as much as anyone in Russia to propagandize the dangers inherent in German hegemonic pretensions and the consequent necessity of continuing the fight against them until total victory. A great deal had changed, however. Russia was now out of the war, the Germans occupied large portions of formerly Russian territory, and the Allies were not in a position to offer substantive help. There could be no question of the Volunteers attempting to fight on their own both Germans and Bolsheviks simultaneously, and of the two, the latter were for Miliukov unquestionably the greater evil. The Bolsheviks threatened not only liberal values but the very existence of the Russian nation-state. He therefore wrote Alekseev confidentially in mid-May about his new approach, expressing his intention to go to Kiev to sound out German representatives and his hope that the general would undertake to bring the army around to these views.[91]

With the backing of the Kadets in Rostov and strong misgivings on the part of Alekseev, who thought trying to "reorient" the Volunteers almost hopeless, Miliukov arrived in Kiev May 28/June 10. He first spent ten days in meetings with various liberals and conservatives from the capitals, local Kadets, and members of Skoropadskii's government. Many believed the Germans were more interested in reaching some sort of arrangement with the Bolsheviks than with helping their opponents reunify Russia, but those to whom he communicated his plans believed they were worth pursuing. Miliukov apparently suspected that the Kadet central committee in Moscow would oppose his actions, for on May 31 he sent it a letter backdated to May 25 and addressed from Rostov so as not to "prematurely reveal" his trip.[92]

On June 8/21 Miliukov met with the chief of German military intelligence in the Ukraine, Major Hasse. The tone of the conversation was friendly, but Miliukov presented a remarkably stiff set of conditions for a man whom the German might reasonably consider a supplicant. His fundamental goal, he told Hasse, was the reunification of Russia, and not along federal lines; border areas would exercise regional autonomy but there must be a single, unitary territory and citizenship with sole sovereignty vested in the central government. His party was prepared to acknowledge that Ukraine constituted an exceptional case, with claims to political autonomy, but it would not be an independent state merely joined to Russia. The reunification of Russia also presupposed review of the treaty of Brest-Litovsk: with the exception of Poland, whose independence was for Kadets "a matter of honor," they insisted upon restoration of Russia's former frontiers. When Hasse observed that it would be difficult for his country to renounce what had been won at great sacrifice, Miliukov coolly countered that it should be quite easy. A number of Germany's political parties opposed its annexations in the east, and in the case of certain Baltic territories the treaty had simply been an enormous mistake—Germany would be confronted by an aroused nationalism that would embroil it in "a whole century of quarrels and complications."[93]

The men also discussed the issues of Russia's future government and alliances. The Germans had made it clear that they would deal only with "monarchist parties"; not surprisingly, Miliukov himself favored restoring monarchy, provided it was a "popular monarchy" (*narodnoe monarkhestvo*) with a parliamentary government, not an autocratic one. In response to Hasse's pertinent questions whether the people would accept any sort of monarchy and the conservative officers a constitutional one, Miliukov thought problems from either quarter would be minimal. He admitted that overcoming anti-German sentiment would be harder, but he thought most officers would understand the necessity of taking into account "objective facts." What was crucial for acceptance of a new regime was that Russia's liberation from the Bolsheviks be accomplished by *Russians*: the Volunteer Army would need supplies, materiel, and protection of their western flank as they approached the capital, but they would fight for Moscow themselves. Concerning formal relations with Germany, he had stated prior to the meeting that he was unalterably opposed to any sort of alliance; the most he could agree to was "benevolent neutrality" and trade agreements. Nor could he offer the guarantees Hasse desired for the future because that would depend entirely on German behavior toward Russia—"Above all, we are Russians and we serve Russia." They then parted, Hasse reiterating that their discussion had been purely personal and nonbinding, but that he would relay Miliukov's views to higher authorities; should they prove acceptable, direct negotiations could begin.[94]

Miliukov's audacious plan rested on a large number of assumptions, some of whose tenability was questionable. So far as the attitude of the great bulk of the population was concerned, he believed they were tired of fighting and of disorder, and basically desired the reunification of a great Russian state: if that reunification was not achieved by the enemy, a democratic form of government was established, and due provision made for the rights of the national minorities, most of the population would not oppose it. Implicit in this view were two further suppositions: that the people's role in the final outcome would be largely passive, and that social issues, including the question of land ownership, were not the critical determinants of popular opinion. The subsequent history of the civil war proved that at least the last of these assumptions, concerning the secondary importance of social policies as compared to political ones, was mistaken.

Second, Miliukov believed that German aid to the Bolsheviks in the past did not mean they were wedded to continued cooperation with Lenin's government; the Germans were bound to realize that the long-term danger posed them by a Bolshevik regime preaching international revolution outweighed the short-term benefits to be derived from exploiting a weak and dismembered Russia. There were indeed many high-ranking German officers and senior officials worried about the menace of Bolshevism, but Berlin also confronted new strategic concerns. The seizure in June by Czech soldiers of key points of the Trans-Siberian railway, which inaugurated a new phase of the Russian civil war, also raised the possibility of Allied reactivization of the eastern front. In these circumstances, continued German dominance in Ukraine and the existence of a Bolshevik regime hostile to the Allies appeared far more advantageous than a reunified Russia promising only neutrality.[95] Hasse told Miliukov at their next meeting that Germany was not interested in discussing revision of the Brest-Litovsk treaty; by mid-July Miliukov's hopes that the Germans would help in the reunification of Russia had vanished.[96]

Finally, Miliukov was wrong about his own party's willingness to acknowledge what he termed "accomplished facts." Even as he was deciding to approach the Germans, a Kadet party conference convened in Moscow in mid-May voted for continued commitment to the Allies. Following the conference, the Kadets organized a "National Center" for creation of an anti-

German coalition in support of the Volunteers and preparation of an uprising in the capitals. When rumors reached Moscow that it was not only Kievan Kadets but the leader of the party who was in favor of a German "orientation," Miliukov's astonished colleagues at first refused to believe them. Maksim Vinaver was dispatched south in early June to explain the party's position to Kadets in Kiev. He met with Miliukov shortly after his first, friendly conversation with Hasse, to learn that he was indeed in contact with the Germans and had no intention of altering his course.[97]

Vinaver's report on his findings, along with Miliukov's written statement explaining his "German policy" and critiquing the party's tactics, caused an uproar. The central committee meetings of July 10 and July 26 (new style), devoted almost entirely to the question of Miliukov and the German orientation, were among the stormiest in the party's history.[98] Most—but not all—of the Kadets in Moscow rejected Miliukov's new approach. It was clear that if they could not resolve the differences over this question, the last remaining nonsocialist party in Russia would split irrevocably.

The disagreement was primarily over means rather than ends, as Nikolai Astrov pointed out. Most of the party leadership shared Miliukov's goals of a resurrected state and central government authority, and reunification along former frontiers. Some also supported constitutional monarchy. But many, Astrov included, did not share Miliukov's belief that Germany would help achieve those goals, his lack of confidence in Allied support, or even his newfound conviction that Russia was incapable of reentering the war on *anyone's* side. Many also believed cooperating with the Germans would destroy relations the party was building with other anti-Bolshevik groups on the Volga and in Siberia. The objections of some Kadets, most especially Pavel Dolgorukov and Fedor Rodichev, had less to do with practicality than principles. The party was morally and ideologically committed to the Allies: utilitarian motives could not justify "tossing aside moral values."

Those who supported Miliukov at least in part pointed out that he had demanded not a reorientation of the party, but only the freedom to sound out the Germans. Since the Germans were in control of a good part of Russian territory and no one could be sure that they would reject his conditions for cooperation, it was a logical demand. They also shared his reservations about the Allies: help from that quarter had thus far been disappointing and it was doubtful that they genuinely desired resurrection of a strong and united Russia. For these reasons, and for the sake of preserving party unity, Pavel Novgorodtsev, A. G. Khrushchev, and several others opposed the resolution introduced by Astrov forbidding contacts with the Germans by individual members of the party. Reminding those assembled of how important Miliukov was for the party and the country, Novgorodtsev pleaded for a spirit of forbearance: "Russia is now truly, physically perishing and we can therefore understand Pavel Nikolaevich's passionate desire to save her." Astrov's resolution nonetheless passed unanimously, with five abstentions.[99]

This resolution, amounting to a public condemnation of their leader, revealed just how angry many of his colleagues were. Clearly what rankled was the manner in which he had proceeded, as well as the German orientation itself. He had for some seven months failed to inform the party of his views or activities, Dolgorukov noted bitterly, had decided on a course of action without first consulting his comrades, and had ignored their inquiries and directives.[100] This was not in fact the first occasion when Miliukov had acted more like a private individual than the leader of his party, but the stakes now were particularly high. His unsanctioned overtures to the Germans threatened to split the Kadets, and for this many of his colleagues could not forgive him. In light of the tensions generated in the leadership by his orientation, Miliukov resigned as head of the party.[101]

Miliukov never regained his former authority as the leader of Russian liberalism, although his open breach with the party proved only temporary. The possibility of rapprochement came very soon; with the collapse of Miliukov's negotiations with the Germans in July, and Germany's own declining military fortunes, the German "orientation" ceased to exist. In October 1918, as a deputy from Kiev to the Kadet conference in Ekaterinodar, Miliukov not only admitted that he had been wrong, but generously declared, "I am glad that I was mistaken!" Since the ability to acknowledge mistakes had never been Miliukov's most salient characteristic, the gathering responded warmly to this apology.[102]

Some colleagues still had reservations about him, however, and he found himself in the minority at the conference on several important tactical issues. Few shared his conviction that only a monarchy could reestablish authority in Russia, while he argued against the general inclination to endorse a temporary military dictatorship under General Denikin, now the head of the Volunteer forces. His own experience caused him to doubt that the generals would allow civilians much influence in the movement, and the Volunteers were indisputably conservative. By identifying themselves too closely with the army, the Kadets ran the risk of being saddled with responsibility for reactionary policies they had not formulated. Support for a dictatorship passed by a vote of 43 to 14, which meant that Miliukov's return to party work coincided with Kadet commitment to a policy he opposed. And despite his genuine satisfaction in being restored to his old colleagues, his position was not a comfortable one: noting in his diary a small slight by Vinaver, he wrote revealingly "I cannot demand from these people particular delicacy in respect to my person."[103]

Miliukov therefore eagerly accepted an invitation in early November to take part in a conference of anti-Bolshevik public figures in Jassy, the temporary capital of Rumania. The object of the conference, organized by a rather obscure figure attached to the French consulate in Kiev, was to coordinate the anti-Bolshevik movements of southern Russia in order to facilitate dealings with the Allied powers.[104] Miliukov went as a delegate for both the National Center and the Council for the National Unification of Russia, a body he had helped organize among supporters of monarchy immediately after the Ekaterinodar party conference.[105]

The conference was yet another exercise in frustration. Despite the obvious need to present a united front to the Allies in requesting their aid, the twenty-one Russian delegates could not reconcile their differences. Miliukov, swallowing his reservations about a military dictatorship, championed Denikin, but a minority of delegates on the right insisted on monarchy, whereas a minority on the left held out for a civilian directory. The conference thus did nothing to forward any agreements, and the Allied representatives did not even bother to transmit its final communiqué, written by Miliukov, to their respective governments.[106] Miliukov went briefly to Odessa in late November when the conference moved its meetings there, then departed on December 3 for Paris as part of its subsidiary delegation sent to talk directly with the Allied heads of state. The only result of his trip to the French capital was a personal humiliation: Clemenceau had him expelled from the city, on the grounds of having had dealings with the Germans.[107]

Rather than return home Miliukov directed his steps to London, a city where he had many influential contacts and hoped to have better luck in pleading the case for aid to the anti-Bolshevik forces around Denikin.[108] He became involved there with the "Russian Liberation Committee" organized by Ariadna Tyrkova and her husband Harold Williams, giving lectures and publishing articles to propagandize the anti-Bolshevik cause and justify British aid and intervention in Russia—work his colleagues still in Russia considered extremely valuable.[109]

The decision to settle in London completed the two-year process of Miliukov's displacement. In February 1917 he had been at the revolution's very center, politically and personally, negotiating, mediating, addressing audiences ranging from soldiers and socialist intellectuals to a grand prince and Duma deputies. Within months he found himself out of government and, increasingly convinced that no ideological middle ground existed, shifting to the right. In December 1917 he moved from the capitals to the periphery, to South Russia; in 1918 he moved further still, to independent Ukraine and toward his German orientation, in the process becoming ever more estranged from the majority of his party. By early 1919 he was living abroad, no longer the leader of Russian liberalism and directing his appeals primarily to foreigners.

In the summer and early fall of 1919, when a decisive military confrontation with the Bolsheviks appeared near, Tyrkova, Struve, and a number of other prominent liberals returned to Russia; Kadet leaders in Ekaterinodar talked about organizing Miliukov's return, as well. Miliukov, however, chose not to go. Keenly following the campaigns of Denikin's Volunteers and the other White armies from afar, continuing his publicity work, he did not doubt their eventual victory or suspect that he would never see his homeland again.

Conclusion

Miliukov's achievements as a historian, including his role in articulating and disseminating the sociological approach known as the Moscow school of historiography, deserve a book of their own. He was one of the pioneers of modern, archive-based historical scholarship in Russia, a contribution embodied in his huge study of the economic reforms of Peter the Great. He wrote what is perhaps still the best study of the development of Russian historical thought, an essay that is also an exploration of one of his most persistent themes, Russia's creative reworking and transformation of borrowed ideas. His three-volume *Studies of Russian Culture*, the most widely read overview of Russian history since that by Karamzin, profoundly influenced the way a generation of Russians looked at their past. Certain theses of that work, especially his formulation of the idea that in Russia the state proceeded and created society, continue to figure in the work of Western scholars of Russia today.[1]

My focus, however, has been primarily on the relationship between Miliukov's historical thought and his political views. It might be assumed that an individual who turned his efforts to shaping his country's future after some two decades of studying its past would bring some of his historical perspectives to his political views. And in fact, Miliukov's historical thought is central to understanding his political thought: his constitutionalism and liberalism, and also his understanding of nationality and national identity. Miliukov's entire worldview was historical and historicist; consciousness of past origins and of processes of change informed his values and his goals at every turn.

Miliukov was both a self-proclaimed positivist and a radical empiricist. Encyclopedic in his interests and eclectic in his methodology, he championed a monistic perspective on the historical process and at the same time dwelled on the multiplicity of causes. Explaining the historical process as the interaction of the factors of universal "law," material milieu, and human volition, he attempted to consider everything: the universal and the particular, the dynamic and the static, the "determined" and the adventitious. Central to Miliukov's sociological perspective was his belief in the increasing complexity and interdependence of all social phenomena, a belief informed as much by French positivism as by his early reading of Marxism, and one of cardinal importance to his views on constitutionalism.

As Miliukov's historical horizons broadened, his views on the role of the individual in making history altered subtly. From the beginning of his scholarly career, the process of change was his main focus, but he initially played down the role of conscious human activity as an agent of change, as opposed to larger, unconscious and impersonal forces, and was reserved about doctrines of progress. After 1892, however, as his interests began to shift toward exploration of ideas and mentalities, Miliukov afforded greater weight to the influence of human volition. He at the same time became more confident about the inexorable march of human progress, which he defined not so much as mastery of the physical environment as the spread of "consciousness," that is, of a rational and enlightened perspective that enabled human beings to appraise the possibilities and limitations of their powers realistically. Progress could never be achieved by the enlightenment of the few; it was only when "consciousness" had genuinely reached the many that human society could bridge the historical abyss between articulation of ideals and their actual realization.

Consciousness presupposed more rational and secular modes of thinking, but also included two other elements: a more historicist understanding of social phenomena and a heightened social awareness. As human beings came to appreciate the purely historical origins of values, customs, conventions, and theories, they became free to discard or remake those which no longer corresponded to the reality of their own day. And concomitant with the gradual democratization of the political process, which Miliukov took to be paradigmatic of Western political development, came greater appreciation of the connection between a polity's political and economic health, on the one hand, and its social health, on the other.

Miliukov's interpretation of the historical process, and the pattern of political development, informed his conviction that Russia could and would experience a constitutional regime. His belief in universal historical "laws" and the interconnectedness of all social phenomena led him to an understanding of constitutionalism as a form of governmental order that was not predicated on the political traditions of a given culture, but rather on the complexity of its social and economic development. He had, moreover, specifically Russian evidence for believing that his country was ready to adopt constitutionalism. This was not because of any putative Russian tradition of self-governance, such as the *veche* or *zemskii sobor*; the "usable past" Miliukov discovered was not so much the existence of a tradition or institution, but the absence of either. Miliukov argued that Russia was, and always had been, a singularly protean nation. It adopted, reworked, and discarded institutions and ideas at a dizzying rate, thereby repeatedly severing its connections with its past.

The result, in Miliukov's view, was the absence of any organic tradition and the creation of a "national type" whose chief characteristic was its "plasticity." Russians were preeminently borrowers, and the absence of traditions to act as obstacles to change, coupled with the culturally generated adaptiveness of the national type, meant that Russia was unusually well suited for a rapid transformation of its political order.

The eurocentrism of Miliukov's reading of the probable future course of Russian development has been the tenet of his political thought most vulnerable to criticism. He has been charged with entertaining a typically Westernizer notion of Russia as a tabula rasa, one resting on a normative dismissal of Russia's own, traditional institutions and an overly rationalistic faith in the possibility of transplanting the institutional products of a given country's culture in alien soil. There is a good deal of truth in these accusations; Miliukov deeply admired Western democratic political orders and was unflaggingly confident that Russia eventually would enjoy such an order, too. At the same time, it is worth stressing that Miliukov coupled his cosmopolitan perspective on constitutionalism with a perceptive reading of Russian history that stressed the dynamic character of Russia's entire cultural experience. He did not believe that he was positing the sudden "modernization" of a stagnant society or urging the substitution of borrowed for indigenous practices, for he had demonstrated that Russia was, and had been, in an almost constant state of change, and that its putatively traditional institutions and "national ideology" were in fact themselves borrowed.

A belief in the blessings of a constitutional order does not necessarily make one a liberal, and Miliukov, Russia's "quintessential liberal," came to liberalism only gradually, and after exploring and rejecting more radical orientations. Indeed, if we choose to define liberalism as encompassing more than the combination of the desire for human freedom, belief in the rule of law, and a preference for evolutionary as compared to revolutionary change, if being a liberal requires a belief in the primacy of the individual and absolute values, then Miliukov never was a liberal.

Just as Miliukov's historical approach was avowedly sociological, his liberalism was sociological rather than philosophical in its foundations. He considered classical liberalism ill-equipped to deal with the phenomenon of the modern democratic, interventionist state and rejected both neo-idealism and theories of natural law as tenable bases for twentieth-century liberalism. The views he had worked out by 1903 bear a striking resemblance to the "new liberalism" being developed at the turn of the century by certain English and French thinkers, among them Hobson, Hobhouse, and Fouille. These theorists turned to sociology for a "science of society" that would provide a new understanding of community and guidelines for social progress, while accommodating the liberal belief in the freedom of the individual.

"Sociological liberalism" tended to argue that liberties are not a product of the nature of the individual but are generated by society and are, therefore, not absolute but liable, with society, to change. At the same time it sought to show that a large measure of individual freedom is a functional good for society as a whole, and one of the constituent elements of social progress.

Working within the same sociological tradition, but applying it to study of the origins and evolution of Russian liberalism, Miliukov developed a liberal theory similar to, but not derived from, that of his European contemporaries. Insisting on liberalism's "intellectual" rather than class origins in Russia, on its humanitarian ethos, and on its relatively early shift from an individualistic to a more communitarian perspective, he sought to demonstrate two things: that Russian liberalism was a "progressive" doctrine that would improve the lot of the many and not just the few and that it was part of the genuine Russian intelligentsia tradition, not merely a borrowed and unsuitable political creed. Its superiority to socialism, he argued, lay in its more modest but realistic goals: Russian liberalism worked "not for the better future, but for the better present."

Miliukov's treatment of the evolution of Russian liberalism broadened liberalism's potential appeal, as did his identification of support for constitutionalism with genuine liberalism. He expended considerable effort on showing that a constitution was not only desirable but practicable for Russia. One of his most persuasive arguments was drawn from his familiarity with Bulgaria, whose constitutional experience supported his contention that exposure to constitutional life could effectively school the most politically unlettered population.

The importance Miliukov attached to demonstrating that a goal was not simply an ideal reveals his whole political orientation. Despite his faith in human rationality, which could cause him seriously to underestimate the power of nonrational motivations and customs and occasionally to be doctrinaire, his was a pragmatic approach to politics. He truly believed that politics was the art of the possible, and that the hallmarks of effective politics were the ability to distinguish between the desirable and the feasible and the ability to act to achieve the feasible, which included knowing how, and when, to compromise. His 1921 evaluation of Lenin's power as consisting in his "realism and ability to act" was not the fruit of a belated recognition of the impracticality of the Russian intelligentsia; from as early as 1903 he had been urging both practicality and action on the liberation movement.[2]

His initial contribution to programmatic and organizational considerations was the program he wrote for the zemtsy, published in the first issue of *Osvobozhdenie*. Moderate and even cautious in its proposals, this program anticipated almost perfectly the demands the zemstvos would eventually advance at their November 1904 congress. Miliukov's insistence that political rights had to be won, and legislative processes determined, before social issues could be resolved was to be characteristic of his approach to reform for many years to come.

Miliukov's practical orientation provided the foundation for one of his most important contributions to Russian politics from 1905 until the February revolution, his role in seeking to unify all or parts of "progressive" Russia. When he returned to Russia in April 1905, having finally chosen politics over scholarship, he did so with a conscious mission to promote the organizational cooperation of liberals and leftists. Characteristically, he approached this task by making a twofold appeal to history. He sought first to legitimize collaboration between socialists and liberals by demonstrating how some of their values and aspirations had converged. Then he warned that failure to collaborate would enable autocracy to counter any progressive challenge by exploiting divisions in public opinion—just as it had many times in the past. Miliukov argued that no government faced with the sorts of crises confronting Russia in 1905–6—military, economic, and revolutionary—could ignore the concerted pressure of the opinion of its entire educated elite indefinitely. He was confident that the majority of socialists appreciated, or could be brought to appreciate, the desirability of working with constitutionalists to achieve political and social reforms without encouraging mass violence. He devoted his publicistic talents to promoting these views, played an extremely important role in organizing and holding together the Union of Unions, and tried, less successfully, to curb the radicalism of the first two Dumas.

After the experience of the Second Duma and the acrimonious electoral campaign to the Third, Miliukov concluded socialists were incapable of learning from their mistakes; he did not recover his faith in the possibility of forging a durable alliance between liberals and socialists until emigration. When he again exercised his talents for coalition building in Russia, in the midst of the military debacles of summer 1915, as founder and leader of the Progressive bloc, he looked to the right for support. He devised a political program that would secure certain liberal goals but could be acceptable to both more conservative politicians and the government itself, negotiated its acceptance by various public groups, and worked assiduously to keep it from falling apart. Had Nicholas listened to the majority opinion of his ministers and worked with the bloc, the erosion of confidence in the authorities that finally brought down the regime might very well have been averted.

Miliukov played a comparable role within the Constitutional Democratic Party. Trying to keep it from straying too far to left or right, he also sought to keep it together. In emigration Vasilii Maklakov would charge that the effort to preserve Kadet unity had been mistaken, causing "vacillation, an avoidance of clear positions, which made the party seem insincere."[3] Reconciling internal differences did come at a political cost, most particularly in the case of the party's attitude toward political terror. The Kadets, however, managed to avoid the fate of their moderate political opponents and allies. By the outbreak of the February revolution the Nationalists, Octobrists, and Progressives had divided or ceased to exist, leaving the Kadets as the only constitutionalist party in a position to influence events.

Miliukov's place in Russian politics also came at great personal cost. As the leader of a "centrist" party in a frequently polarized political climate, he was subject to incredible vituperation from both the right and the left. Opponents questioned and excoriated his character, values, leadership, and patriotism in the Duma and partisan press. Once he was physically attacked, and several times threatened with death. He was also frequently criticized within his own party as insufficiently or excessively moderate, too preoccupied with the narrow world of the Duma, or too pacifistic or imperialistic in his foreign policy views. The constant barrage of criticism, the burden of leadership, and the demands of his publicistic work combined to make him increasingly intolerant of dissenting viewpoints, reserved to the point of coldness, and disinclined to yield on a position. He also became less adept at gauging and responding to shifts in public opinion, a talent that had contributed to his authority and effectiveness in the early part of his political career.

It might also be argued that Miliukov's work on the nationality question was part of his larger effort to contribute to political unity. His interest in nationality was lifelong, growing out of his historical investigations into the origins of the Muscovite "national idea" and his research into Slavic self-identity in the Balkans. After 1908, as Great Russian nationalism increasingly figured in Stolypin's policies and the policies of the Third Duma as well, Miliukov tried to oppose this with a "constitutional nationalism" of his own. Sociological in its approach, it treated nationality not as a question of race or ethnicity, but of self-identity: nationality was constructed over time and subject to change. National identity was therefore adaptable, but once national consciousness within a given group became a mass phenomenon, it could not be suppressed or eradicated. This meant that attempts at forcible assimilation of Russia's national minorities would not contribute to the unity of the state, but rather the reverse: the only possible "Russian nationalism" had to be based on respect, equality, and broad cultural autonomy. Although Miliukov's efforts to demonstrate the disintegrative effects of chauvinistic nationalism had little practical influence on the nationality policies of the period, his thoughtful approach to nationality policy is one of his most impressive liberal achievements.

The fundamental change in Miliukov's political place in Russia came in 1917. Concern for the war effort and fear of revolution had helped make him more conservative after July 1914, but in the early weeks of the revolution he was still a negotiator, capable of compromise, as his role in establishing the Provisional Government showed. After the April crisis, however, in the context of the increasing polarization of political views, the disintegration of the military front, and the unraveling of the economy and state authority, he refused compromise. The man who had done more than any other in 1905 and again in 1915 to reconcile and unite competing parties and views now set himself against coalitions and "conciliation."

Convinced that only strong government could save the state, he believed a middle road no longer existed: the choice was "Lenin or Kornilov." While the behavior of most Russian socialists gave little reason to believe they could finally bring themselves to contain the most destructive forces on the left, Miliukov's refusal even to try cooperation ensured that he himself had no creative role to play in 1917. After the Bolshevik seizure of power, he continued to reject cooperation with socialists and to believe that resurrection of a united Russian state required postponement of divisive social reforms. His effort to secure German help in 1918 to liberate and reunify Russia threatened finally to split the Kadets; although he made his peace with his colleagues and continued to work for the anti-Bolshevik cause, he ceased to be a leader of liberalism in Russia.

Epilogue

> Life took from him so many personal attachments and smashed so many intellectual undertakings, and towards the end it plunged sharply off into other channels so that he long remained alone. . . . Such a rich life, and such a solitary death!
> —P. N. Miliukov, "In Memory of A. I. Herzen" (1900)

Like Alexander Herzen, the Russian thinker whom he most deeply admired, Paul Miliukov ended his days in France after decades of exile. Like Herzen, he came to know the endless recriminations and feuds of exile life, the frustration of outliving a once great intellectual influence, the repeated dashing of almost every hope for Russia. And he experienced, as Herzen did, the death or estrangement of almost all the individuals with whom he had shared those hopes. Yet he would certainly have said of himself, as he asserted of Herzen, that neither successive disappointments nor his own changing perspectives reduced him to thoroughgoing skepticism, to the surrender of ideals; there was always "something positive in which he believed."[1]

In early 1921 the Miliukovs settled in Paris, a residence they imagined would be only temporary. They had lost virtually all their possessions, but Miliukov's international reputation and command of foreign languages enabled him to earn a livelihood through scholarly writing, lecturing, and journalism; he began immediately to collect a new library. Nothing, however, could fill the void left by their daughter. Their son, Nikolai, had joined them in emigration sometime before, but Natasha—"Taka"—had not. Early in 1919 she had married a widower with five children; a year later, having twice fled from cities about to fall to the Bolsheviks, Natasha was a widow. She nonetheless hesitated to leave Russia, in part because she saw no viable future as an ill-educated and dependent young woman in a foreign land. Enrolling in a polytechnical institute in Petrograd, she wrote her parents the next summer that though she worried about their disapproval and about acting in a "Bolshevik manner" she did believe in a future for those willing to work and to learn, while the very demands of study and daily existence caused her "to live with all the energies of my soul, to be cheerful and full of the joy of living." She died a year later of dysentery, at the age of twenty-four.[2]

Even as Natasha was trying to build a life in Soviet Russia, her father was debating with fellow émigrés how they could most effectively hasten the end of Soviet power. Among liberals and conservatives there was little disagreement concerning the provisional nature of the Bolsheviks' tenure: they were a strictly destructive element, incapable of managing a state or of productive economic activity, which meant that for all their recourse to terror and repression they could not remain in power indefinitely. Miliukov also shared the conviction of the majority of the émigrés that dictatorship was an integral feature of Bolshevik rule rather than the temporary product of extreme situations or a given leader's influence, and that the regime therefore could not evolve into a genuinely democratic system.[3] The major question dividing liberals in the early years of the emigration was not so much who was to replace the Bolsheviks, although strong differences existed, as to *how* Russia was to be liberated from their rule.

The complex answer Miliukov worked out in 1920–21 divided him from the majority of the emigration. It stemmed necessarily from his answer to another question: Why had the Bolsheviks won the civil war? He invoked again some of the historical factors that had contributed to the failure of the 1905 revolution, including the general population's lack of state consciousness and Russia's weak social cohesion. To these products of centuries of autocratic rule he added more immediate and fortuitous factors, among them the mistakes of the other socialist parties, the combination of German aid to the Bolsheviks and allied stinginess toward the anti-Bolshevik forces, Bolshevik demagogy and ruthlessness, and strategic military errors committed by the Whites.

As important as were all these factors, however, Miliukov believed the Whites' own political and programmatic mistakes had been critical to Bolshevik victory. The Whites had seriously misread popular wishes and failed to respond to them, so that when the war's outcome hung in the balance the population either actively sided with the Bolsheviks or at best refused to fight them. And the masses did so, he now concluded, not out of simple credulity—although he still stressed the Bolsheviks' bad faith—but in conscious defense of their own interests as they understood them. The peasants wanted land, the minorities wanted real self-government, and virtually everyone resented the remnants of class inequality and rule from above which haunted the White cause. The Whites' support for these perspectives had been too uncertain and had come too late, allowing the Bolsheviks to appear the only truly "democratic" choice.

In effect, the people had chosen, and any hopes that the Bolsheviks could be displaced had to rest on the people making a new choice. The emigration therefore needed a "new tactic," Miliukov declared. It must foreswear unequivocally all thought of organizing armed intervention in Russia from abroad, instead doing what it could to encourage the growth of a popular, anti-Bolshevik democratic movement within Russia. It must develop a program in line with what the revolution had effected and the people wanted. Some form of national representative assembly would eventually decide political, social, and economic questions, but in the meantime liberals must make clear their total commitment to four major points: republican government, peasant ownership of the land, a genuinely federative structure for the multinational Russian state, and an end to old government arbitrariness and rule from above. Finally, in seeking allies, the Kadets could work only with those who accepted these points, which essentially meant moderate socialists.[4]

Miliukov's "new tactic," which he persuaded the Paris Kadets to endorse in December 1920, represented a rather startling switch from his position of 1917–18, when he had stood for monarchy, an undivided Russian empire, and postponement of major social changes until the decisions of the constituent assembly were made. Yet in one sense, at least, his new tactic was not so much a reversal as a return to positions he had held before the Great War. Sweeping social reform regained an important place in his thought alongside the political liberties he had more consistently supported, while some of his confidence in the independent activity of the common people was restored. In his 1905 book *Russia and Its Crisis*, Miliukov had quoted Turgenev: "The mission of the educated class in Russia is to transmit civilization to the people, in order that they may themselves hereafter decide what they shall accept or repudiate." In 1921, in the preface to his revised history of the Russian revolution, Miliukov stressed that not all the popular choices of the revolution were bad ones, so that hope for the future was not lost: "If, from the darkness of that non-existence in which we lie buried under the rubble of a ruined world, we can manage to fix our gaze on that bright point of light in the distance, the thought of it will help lighten the most stubborn pessimism and, perhaps, inspire all those who are drowning in despair with the desire to go on living in order to work for their native people in new ways, ways chosen by the people itself."[5]

Miliukov's new tactic finally split the Kadet party. Although some considered it an essentially sound diagnosis of past mistakes and a more realistic starting point for future action, others disputed the political realism of attempting joint work with the left politicians who had shown so little judgment in 1917–18. Still others believed that a counsel against armed intervention in Russia was equivalent to resigning themselves and Russia to indefinite Bolshevik misrule. Finally, many were profoundly offended by Miliukov's indictment of the White movement, a seemingly insensitive dismissal of the sacrifices of those who had fought in the White armies. By a vote of 9–7 on June 2, 1921, despite Miliukov's counsel against taking any decisive steps, the Kadet central committee officially rejected the new tactic. On July 28, after a large meeting of émigré Kadets in Paris also voted against adopting it, Miliukov left the central committee to form a separate sub-group calling itself the Democratic Group of the Party of People's Freedom.[6]

A minority of Kadets entered the new group, Maksim Vinaver being the only prominent "founding father" to join him. Efforts by Vladimir Nabokov and several other party leaders to effect a reconciliation were unsuccessful, in part because of the abuse heaped on Miliukov by critics within the party, in part because of his own hardheadedness. The split between "right" and "left" wings of the Constitutional Democratic Party, for so many years threatened, was made formal in 1924 when Miliukov and his followers established an independent group, the Republican Democratic Alliance (Respublikansko-Demokraticheskoe Ob"edinenie, or RDO), which attracted some moderate socialists and several hundred left Kadets. Miliukov worked mightily on behalf of his new organization in the years that followed, founding clubs in various cities, writing pamphlets, giving speeches, but its membership dwindled year by year as hopes for an end to Bolshevik rule receded. In truth no émigré group, whatever its proposed tactics concerning Russia, was in a position to affect either the western governments' policies toward the Soviet Union or the climate of opinion in the homeland.[7]

Miliukov's move leftward did not endear him to the great majority of the emigration, including a number of former colleagues. Fedor Rodichev, for example, who reproached him for having only "glass" instead of a soul, severed their relations. Petr Struve, who insisted that no "positive achievements" had issued from the revolution, saw in Miliukov's overtures to the left an example of the intelligentsia's chronic failure to learn from its mistakes.[8] Reactionary émigrés, for whom Miliukov's contributions to undermining monarchy loomed much larger than did his efforts in March 1917 to save it, frankly detested him. Their attacks were most frequently verbal or printed—the scurrilous little articles common from the Third Duma days were regular fare in right-wing publications—but on several occasions took more violent form. The most tragic of these occurred on March 28, 1922, in Berlin, where Miliukov had come at Nabokov's invitation to deliver a public lecture to the large Russian émigré community of that city. At the conclusion of the talk two right-wing members of the audience leaped to their feet and opened fire on Miliukov. Although the gunmen failed to hit their intended target, they wounded four others and killed Nabokov, who had thrown himself on one of the attackers.[9]

Nabokov's murder shocked and grieved Miliukov, but in other respects the organizational and personal ruptures caused by his political positions appeared to leave him unmoved. He had not wished to split his party, but he would not alter his views to avert that result or soften the tone of his pronouncements to assuage his comrades' sensibilities: he had abandoned once and for all the role of mediator and conciliator. As one close colleague of these years saw it, Miliukov did not himself break with anyone; "He was rooted, like a sturdy, low-growing oak. People parted from him, people came to him, but no one could dislodge the root on which he stood." The very equanimity with which he accepted ruptures in relationships, the lack of personal rancor in his polemics, suggested to some that he truly was without feeling. He did not choose to defend himself against such charges or to exhibit the pleasure he felt when a breach was healed. Nor did many people know that he anonymously provided financial assistance from his modest means to a number of his more impoverished former colleagues, their political hostility notwithstanding.[10]

Politics, though a consuming interest, was not Miliukov's sole or even primary occupation in emigration. His literary output was remarkable, and by no means confined to the editorials he wrote three to four times a week for his paper *Poslednie novosti*—frequently dedicated to events in the Soviet Union and how the emigration should respond to them—and pamphlets for the RDO. He also wrote encyclopedia entries, historical sketches, and a number of full-length articles, including extended responses to Vasilii Maklakov's indictment of Kadet liberalism, as well as eight books on historical and topical subjects.[11] In 1938, when he assumed editorship of the monthly journal *Russkie zapiski*, he began publishing installments of his memoirs of the liberation movement and First Duma, under the name "Fateful Years" (*Rokovye gody*).

As always, writing and scholarship occupied only part of his energies. The material needs of Russians, especially in the early 1920s, were pronounced, and both Miliukovs worked to raise money for the relief of famine in the Soviet Union and refugee aid. They also subscribed completely to the shared émigré belief that "Russia Abroad" must keep alive the culture that was being destroyed or discarded in the Soviet Union. To this end, both worked to advance the educational opportunities of Russian emigrants. With his old teacher Paul Vinogradov and others, Miliukov helped collect funds to support academics and lectured on Russian history at various institutions; Anna focused particularly on women's higher education, eventually becoming president of the Russian branch of the International Organization of

Miliukov aboard the SS *America*, October 1921, his fourth visit to the United States. UPI/Corbis–Bettmann.

University Women. They participated actively in the annual "Day of Russian Culture" celebrated throughout the diaspora on the anniversary of Pushkin's birth, and from 1922 to 1928 Miliukov helped lead the effort to sustain a viable émigré press and publishing industry as president of the Union of Russian Writers and Journalists in Paris.[12]

However, Miliukov's most important contribution to émigré life and the history of "Russia Abroad" was his editorship of the Paris daily *Poslednie novosti*, the most long-lived and widely read of all Russian émigré publications. The paper was established in April 1920; a year later Miliukov succeeded M. L. Gol'dshtein as editor, a position he retained until 1940 when the paper ceased publication. Subsidies from Thomas Masaryk's Czech government helped out in the early years, but thanks to the high quality of contributors and shrewd management *Poslednie novosti* soon became self-supporting. Miliukov attached particular importance to the editorials and articles dedicated to his "democratic" line—perhaps the pieces least attended to by the readership—as well as to detailed and responsible reporting of events in the Soviet Union. The paper also provided coverage of French and international news, affairs of the émigré community, and lighter fare, including serialized detective novels in translation. Poetry, short stories, essays, and literary criticism by luminaries of prerevolutionary Russia and younger, émigré authors—Marina Tsvetaeva, Vladimir Sirin-Nabokov, I. A. Bunin, V. F. Khodasevich, Nina Berberova, to name a few—appeared regularly. Autobiographical pieces and memoirs by prominent prerevolutionary figures were also staples. By the late 1920s *Poslednie novosti* had achieved a daily press run of approximately 23,000 and was read all over the Russian diaspora and by at least a few figures in the Kremlin. Soviet censorship prevented the vast majority of Russians from ever seeing the paper, which meant it could not duplicate the role of *Osvobozhdenie* in stimulating a liberation movement, as Miliukov perhaps initially hoped to do.[13] But in a real sense *Poslednie novosti* served not only as the unofficial "paper of record" of the first wave of the Russian emigration but also constituted a sort of archive of early twentieth-century Russian culture and history.

The paper's generous treatment of its contributors was also a tangible support of cultural effort. *Poslednie novosti* offered a profit-sharing plan and health insurance to regular staffers and a minimum payment for free-lance pieces far higher than "market" conditions required. As one émigré author later recalled, the honorarium for a single short story could keep a struggling writer afloat for a month: "Willy-nilly one misses, if not his editorials, then Miliukov's ability to conduct a commercial enterprise honorably and profitably."[14]

For virtually all émigrés the second decade of exile was even more difficult than the first. Stalin's "revolution from above" deepened their isolation from their homeland, while the world depression made life more pinched and penurious. For Miliukov, advancing old age brought not only worsening health but the deaths of more and more of the people who linked him to the old life in Russia, including, in 1935, that of Anna Miliukova.[15] Finally, like all Russian émigrés, he was deeply affected by Europe's political destabilization and the spread of dictatorial regimes.

Early in the 1930s, Miliukov began to fear the spread of fascism. He spoke out consistently against any kind of dictatorship, against the racism underlying national socialism, and warned of the dangers of appeasement.[16] His grief at the death of Masaryk and Czechoslovakia's protracted demise was extreme. In Masaryk's success he had seen the living embodiment of what he had tried to achieve in Russia; friends agreed that he was altered by the Czech tragedy, somehow spiritually battered. Nonetheless he refused to doubt that the great democracies would eventually fight fascism; optimism, for Miliukov, was a chronic condition. And though he numbered the Soviet Union among the regimes that had misappropriated and abused the word "democracy," he could not for a moment share the view of those émigrés who were prepared to look upon fascist dictatorships benevolently, or at least to deem them less evil than the communist variety. Nor could he sympathize with the view that a war against Russia would be partially welcome in that it would surely finish off the Soviet regime.[17]

He moved to Vichy in late 1939; after the Nazi occupation in June 1940—in the course of which his papers, books, and possessions, all still in Paris, were seized—he went on to Montpelier, then eventually to the village of Aix-les-Bains in Savoy. He had had invitations to come to the United States and accept an academic position, but turned them down: he wished to be near the action, to be able to follow the course of fighting. His own health was by then precarious, and with his sources of income gone he lived, like many other émigrés, in near destitution. One long-time colleague visiting him found him shockingly thin and frail, but still driving himself relentlessly. He wrote constantly, slept little, and ate but one meal a day, with total indifference to what he consumed. His prized possession was an ancient radio on which he listened to concerts and broadcasts about the war. With the German invasion of the Soviet Union Miliukov suspended all criticism of the Soviet regime—as he had done twenty-seven years earlier for the tsarist regime—and hoped unequivocally for a Russian victory. In the shabby hotel room that was his home in the last years of his life he hung a huge map of the Eastern front, plotting with colored pins the movements of armies. The war was almost his only topic of conversation, and he spoke unembarrassedly of "our front, our army, our troops."[18] The heroic resistance to the invaders mounted by the peoples of Russia impressed him profoundly.

Paul Miliukov died March 31, 1943, two months after the Soviet victory at Stalingrad.[19]

Notes

Preface

1. P. N. Miliukov, *Vospominaniia* (New York, 1955; reprint, Moscow, 1991), p. 121.
2. P. N. Miliukov, *Istoriia vtoroi russkoi revoliutsii*, 3 vols. (Sofia, 1921–24). Miliukov details the history of this work, originally completed in 1918 and then revised abroad, in an introduction dated December 27, 1920. The English translation, by Richard and Tatiana Stites and Gary M. Hamburg, is *The History of the Russian Revolution*, 3 vols. (Gulf Breeze, Fla., 1978–1987).
3. P. B. Struve, review of *Ocherki po istorii russkoi kul'tury*, vol. 1, *Novoe slovo* 1 (October 1897): 89–94.
4. Miliukov's opposition to entering the Great War is noted in D. C. B. Lieven, *Russia and the Origins of the First World War* (New York, 1983), pp. 122–24.
5. Two such assessments by outsiders are Dmitrii Shipov, *Vospominaniia i dumy o perezhitom* (Moscow, 1918), pp. 456–57, and V. I. Gurko, *Features and Figures of the Past: Government and Opinion in the Reign of Nicholas II* (Stanford, Calif., 1939), pp. 428–31. An example of a Kadet who found Miliukov's leadership oppressive is S. P. Mansyrev, "Moi vospominaniia o Gosudarstvennoi Dume (1912–1917 g.)," in *Istorik i sovremennik* (Berlin), 2 (1922): 5–45. Vasilii Maklakov, in contrast, maintained that Miliukov's perpetual groping for a middle line made it impossible for him to lead (*Vlast' i obshchestvennost' na zakate staroi Rossii* [*vospominaniia*] 3 vols. in 1 [Paris, 1936], pp. 488–89).
6. V. A. Obolenskii, *Moia zhizn', moi sovremenniki* (Paris, 1988), p. 443.
7. The two Miliukov personal archives—*lichnye fondy*—in Moscow are referred to in the bibliography. They contain nearly 6,000 files for the years 1859–1938, ranging in size from a single sheet of paper to many hundreds of pages and including such materials as drafts of articles and speeches, his notes of meetings, newspaper cuttings, and professional and party correspondence. The Miliukov collection in the Bakhmeteff ar-

chive of Columbia University is also large, although most of its materials relate to the period after 1918.

8. There are a number of similarities of style and behavior between Miliukov and Wilson, including the fondness of each for female company and the way each man combined bold goals with a desire to temper and restrain reformist followers.

9. Miliukov, *Vosp.*, p. 175.

10. I. V. Gessen, *V dvukh vekakh: Zhiznennyi otchet* (Berlin, 1937), p. 224.

11. The biography by Thomas Riha, *A Russian European: Paul Miliukov in Russian Politics* (Notre Dame, Ind., 1969), was the first full-length study of any twentieth-century Russian liberal and is particularly valuable for its use of Miliukov's post-1929 writings. A new biography covering the years to 1905, the first volume of a projected three-volume study, is Natalia G. Dumova's *Liberal v Rossii: Tragediia nesovmestimosti. Istoricheskii portret P. N. Miliukova* (Moscow, 1993).

12. There is still no comprehensive history of liberalism in Russia. George Fischer's *Russian Liberalism* (Cambridge, Mass., 1958), does not go beyond 1905; Victor Leontovitsch, *Geschichte des Liberalismus in Russland* (Frankfurt, 1957), concentrates on what he calls "conservative liberalism," largely ignoring the Kadets. A fine work by Andrzej Walicki, *Legal Philosophies of Russian Liberalism* (Oxford, 1987), addresses a little-studied aspect of Russian liberal thought. V. V. Shelokhaev has recently published the first full-length study of Russian liberalism by a Russian scholar, *Russkii liberalizm* (Moscow, 1995), and Shmuel Galai is currently working on a history of the Constitutional-Democratic Party. The shortcomings of Kadet liberalism are trenchantly explored by Richard Pipes in his two-volume biography *Struve* (Cambridge, Mass., 1970 and 1980). Several stimulating essays on Russian liberalism and the Kadets are contained in Charles Timberlake, ed., *Essays on Russian Liberalism* (Columbia, Mo., 1972). Also of note are Michael Karpovich, "Two Types of Russian Liberalism: Maklakov and Miliukov," in *Continuity and Change in Russian and Soviet Thought*, ed. Ernest J. Simmons (Cambridge, Mass., 1955): 129–43; Marc Raeff, "Some Reflections on Russian Liberalism," *Russian Review* 18 (July 1959); Donald Treadgold, "The Constitutional Democrats and the Russian Liberal Tradition," *Slavic Review* 10 (1951): 85–94; and Judith Zimmerman's article on the views of a minority within the Kadet party, "Russian Liberal Theory, 1900–1917," *Canadian-American Slavic Studies* 1 (Spring 1980): 1–20. Monographs and articles examining the policies, organization, and composition of the Constitutional-Democratic Party for discrete periods of time—by Terence Emmons, V. V. Shelokhaev, N. G. Dumova, William Rosenberg, Iu. A. Avrekh, Shmuel Galai, Raymond Pearson, and Judith Zimmerman—are listed in the bibliography.

13. The only extended study of Miliukov's historical thought is the recent work by M. G. Vandalkovskaia, *P. N. Miliukov, A. A. Kizevetter: Istoriia i politika* (Moscow, 1992). Geoffrey Hosking notes Miliukov's efforts to articulate a "constitutional nationalism" in his book *The Russian Constitutional Experiment: Government and Duma, 1907–1914* (Cambridge, 1973), pp. 107–18; an overview of his thought on nationalities is by C. Jay Smith, "Miliukov and the Russian National Question," in *Russian Thought and Politics*, ed. Hugh McClean (Essay Index Reprint Series), (Cambridge, Mass., 1971), pp. 395–420.

14. "History may have its whims, but it also has its laws; and if the law of Russian history is progress, as we have tried to demonstrate, political reform may not be avoided. To deny it is to despair of the future of Russia" (Paul Miliukov, *Russia and Its Crisis* [Chicago, 1905], p. 564).

15. Miliukov had a long life in exile—he died in France in 1943, at the age of eighty-four—but his original scholarship and political significance belong to the period spent

in Russia. I discuss in the epilogue his changing appraisal of the revolution, his views of the Soviet state and possible evolution of its society, and his fortunes in the Paris emigration. By treating these topics in the epilogue I mean to suggest not that they are without interest, but rather that Miliukov's life in emigration, from 1919, is part of a different story, the cultural history of "Russia Abroad."

Chapter One: Youth and Student Years

1. Unfortunately, the sole source on Miliukov's childhood and youth is his memoirs; there are no accounts in any way relating to Miliukov before his second year at Moscow University. Miliukov did not want to commit himself to the task of writing his memoirs until he had "nothing useful left to do"; he began them in Montpelier, France, in 1939 when he was eighty-one years old, already in failing health, and without access to those personal papers and books which could have helped correct the vagaries of memory. He was able to bring the account only through January 1918 before his death in 1943. The manuscript was edited by Michael Karpovich and Boris Elkin and published in two volumes as *Vospominaniia* (New York, 1955). Citations come from the one-volume reprint edition, *Vospominaniia* (Moscow, 1991) (hereafter cited as "*Vosp.*"). The complete manuscript of the text is in the Bakhmeteff Archives of Columbia University. The manuscript contains approximately eight pages of text relating to his personal life, as well as thirty-three rough draft pages unrevised before his death, which the editors omitted. I cite the manuscript copy of the memoirs as "Miliukov, *Vosp.* MS."

The extent to which Miliukov omitted, edited, or confused the events of his early life, or attributed to this period views or sentiments arrived at later, is largely a matter for conjecture. After the year 1886 external evidence that can corroborate or modify an account in the memoirs is increasingly available; unfortunately, this evidence suggests that the memoirs are occasionally, though by no means consistently, inaccurate.

2. Miliukov later looked into this claim, which his grandfather had so ardently pursued, and was unable to ascertain whether his branch of the Miliukov family could rightly claim noble descent (*Vosp.*, p. 33). But on being elected to the Third Duma, Miliukov did give his *soslovie* (social class) as "noble" (*dvorianin*) (RGIA, f. 1278, op. 9, ed. khr. 513, l. 1, "Chlena gosudarstvennoi dumy Miliukova," October 30, 1907).
3. Miliukov, *Vosp.*, p. 34.
4. Ibid., pp. 35–37. Alexander was fatally shot following some drinking bout in the regiment, and his death seems to have made little impression on the family.
5. Ibid., pp. 28–29, 37.
6. Ibid., pp. 30, 34–35, 43, 47–48.
7. Ibid., pp. 37–39, 44–45.
8. Ibid., p. 37.
9. Ibid., pp. 33–34, 37, 42–43.
10. Ibid., pp. 40–41, 45–47.
11. Ibid., pp. 51–52. For an appraisal of the nature of Tolstoian classicism and its underlying assumptions see Patrick L. Alston, *Education and State in Tsarist Russia* (Stanford, Calif., 1969), pp. 87–101. See also Allen Sinel, *The Classroom and the Chancellery: State Educational Reform in Russia under Count Dmitry Tolstoi* (Cambridge, Mass., 1973).
12. Miliukov acquired the love poetry of Sappho; the verse of Anacreon; Aristotle's *Metaphysics*; the tragedies of Sophocles and Euripedes; and Virgil, Terence, and Horace; later, he added Catullus, Cicero, and his favorite, Tacitus (Miliukov, *Vosp.*, pp. 52–55).

Miliukov slowly and lovingly assembled an enormous personal library; financial constraints eventually forced him to sell the portion of it that he was able to take from Russia to the University of California, Berkeley, in the late 1920s; see Wojciech Zalewski and D. Jelik, "The Miliukov Collection: Early Collecting of Russica in California Academic Libraries," *Libri* 34, no 3 (1984): 186–97. The sizable part of his library that remained in Russia became part of what is today the "Russkii fond" of the Saltykov-Shchedrin Library in St. Petersburg.

13. Miliukov, *Vosp.*, pp. 54–55; I. V. Gessen, "P. N. Miliukov kak zhurnalist," in *P. N. Miliukov: Sbornik materialov po chestvovaniiu ego semidesiatiletiia, 1859–1929*, ed. S. A. Smirnov et al. (Paris, 1929), p. 196.

14. Alan Wildman, "The Russian Intelligentsia of the 1890s," *American Slavonic and East European Review* 19 (April 1960): 157, 161, discusses the student circle as part of the larger Russian intelligentsia tradition of the circle, "the nurturing bed of Russian intelligentsia ideas and values."

15. Miliukov, *Vosp.*, pp. 56–58. P. D. Dolgorukov, a long-time political associate of Miliukov in the Kadet party, alludes briefly to his older brother Nikolai's Slavophile leanings and friendship with Miliukov in his book *Velikaia razrukha* (Madrid, 1964), p. 304.

16. Miliukov, *Vosp.*, pp. 53, 55.

17. Miliukov, "Russia," *The Athenaeum* (London), July 2, 1892, p. 25.

18. Miliukov, *Vosp.*, p. 55; some twenty-two years later, in a lengthy review article surveying the origins and development of sociology, Miliukov credits Spencer and Auguste Comte with giving sociology its methodology and agenda, although he felt neither could actually be considered a founder of the science of society. See P. N. Miliukov, "Novaia kniga po sotsiologii," *Mir Bozhii*, December 1899, pp. 196–215.

19. Miliukov, *Vosp.*, pp. 61–62. For a detailed treatment in English of Russia's involvement in Balkan politics and conflicts in this period, see B. H. Sumner, *Russia and the Balkans, 1870–1880* (Oxford, 1937).

20. Among those who have noted Miliukov's gifts as an organizer are Bernard Pares, *The Tale of a Wandering Student* (Syracuse, N.Y., 1948), p. 125, and A. A. Kizevetter, *Na rubezhe dvukh stoletii (vospominaniia 1881–1914)* (Prague, 1929), p. 293.

21. Miliukov, *Vosp.*, pp. 62–66.

22. Ibid., p. 67. On his courage see, for example, O. Gruzenburg, "Staromu drugu," in Smirnov et al., eds., *P. N. Miliukov*, pp. 185–86, and Gessen, *V dvukh vekakh*, pp. 284–85.

23. James McClelland, "Diversification in Russian-Soviet Education," in *The Transformation of Higher Learning, 1860–1930*, ed. Konrad H. Jarausch (Chicago, 1983), p. 183. On Russian universities in this period, and how the two university statutes affected them, see also P. A. Zaionchkovskii, *Rossiiskoe samoderzhavie v kontse XIX stoletiia* (Moscow, 1970), pp. 309–34; Alston, *Education and State*, pp. 44–57; and Samuel D. Kassow, *Students, Professors, and the State in Tsarist Russia* (Berkeley, Calif., 1989), p. 30, n. 38.

24. Moscow University had 1060 students in 1858; by the late 1870s this number was almost 1600, and by 1885 it exceeded 3000. See P. N. Miliukov, "Universitety v Rossii," in F. A. Brokgauz and I. A. Efron, *Entsiklopedicheskii slovar'*, vol. 34 (St. Petersburg, 1902), p. 799 (hereafter cited as "Brokgauz and Efron" by volume and page).

25. Miliukov, lecture notes, "Tat'ianin den' i Moskovskii universitet," in GARF, f. 579, op. 1, d. 3404, l. 30, and his article "Moskva i Tat'iana," *Poslednie novosti* (Paris), January 24, 1928, p. 2; "tat'ianin den'" was the traditional day of festivities honoring the university's foundation. Miliukov wrote up his university reminiscences for a volume

commemorating Moscow University's 175th anniversary. See P. N. Miliukov, "Moi universitetskie gody," in *Moskovskii universitet, 1755–1930: Iubileinyi sbornik*, ed. V. B. El'iashevich et al. (Paris, 1930), pp. 262–74 (hereafter cited as *Moskovskii universitet*).

26. According to V. R. Leikina-Svirskaia, *Intelligentsiia v Rossii vo vtoroi polovine XIX veka* (Moscow, 1971), p. 58, in 1880, 146 students were enrolled in the history and philology *fakul' tet* at Moscow University.

27. Miliukov, *Vosp.*, pp. 69–70, and "Moi universitetskie gody," pp. 264, 266. Natalia Dumova, *Liberal v. Rossii*, pp. 27–30, noting the much more positive accounts of Ger'e's teaching offered by other former students, suggests that Miliukov's recollections were colored by his professor's subsequent public criticisms of the conduct of the Kadets in the First Duma.

28. Miliukov, "V. O. Kliuchevskii," in *V. O. Kliuchevskii: Kharakteristiki i vospominaniia* (Moscow, 1912), p. 189. The Russian word for science, *nauka*, could be used in the broad sense of the German *Wissenschaft*, to include such intellectual disciplines as history, philosophy, and theology.

29. On the scientism of the nihilists and the prevailing enthusiasm for science, see Alexander Vucinich, *Social Thought in Tsarist Russia: The Quest for a General Science of Society, 1861–1917* (Chicago, 1976), pp. 3–8.

30. Miliukov, *Vosp.*, p. 69, and "Moi universitetskie gody," p. 263. Troitskii influenced several generations of Moscow University students by introducing them to English empiricism and preaching the primacy of inductive over deductive reasoning; see V. V. Zernovsky, *A History of Russian Philosophy* (New York, 1953), 2:714, and "M. M. Troitskii," in Brokgauz and Efron, 33a:879–81.

31. M. M. Kovalevskii describes this circle of young professors in "Otryvki iz vospominanii," in *Moskovskii universitet*, pp. 275–93; biographical data on these individuals has been drawn from the relevant volumes of Brokgauz and Efron, and from *Entsiklopedicheskii Slovar' tovarishchestva Bratiia A. i I. Granat i Ko.*, 7th ed., 58 vols (Moscow, 1910–1948).

32. Kovalevskii, "Otryvki," p. 278. Miliukov's sociological orientation is discussed in Chapter 3.

33. Miliukov, "Moi universitetskie gody," pp. 262–63, and *Vosp.*, pp. 68, 73.

34. Miliukov to Kovalevskii, February 20, 1892, in the Bakhmeteff Archive of Russian and East European History and Culture at Columbia University (hereafter, BAR), M. M. Kovalevskii papers, box 1, and Miliukov, *Vosp.*, pp. 73–74.

35. Miliukov, *Vosp.*, p. 76, and Vasilii Maklakov, "Otryvki iz vospominanii," in *Moskovskii universitet*, pp. 309–11.

36. Maklakov, "Otryvki," p. 310.

37. Miliukov, *Vosp.*, pp. 76, 92–94.

38. A short biographical sketch on Kliuchevskii was written by M. K. Liubavskii, the successor to his chair at Moscow University, for the collection issued in Kliuchevskii's honor shortly after his death. See Liubavskii, "Vasilii Osipovich Kliuchevskii," in *V. O. Kliuchevskii*, pp. 5–25. Other biographical works include M. V. Nechkina, *Vasilii Osipovich Kliuchevskii* (Moscow, 1974) and Robert F. Byrnes, *V. O. Kliuchevskii, Historian of Russia* (Bloomington, Ind., 1995).

39. Miliukov, "V. O. Kliuchevskii," pp. 194–96; *Vosp.*, p. 77; and "Moi universitetskie gody," p. 268.

40. Kliuchevskii did teach a course in methodology in 1884–85, but it was not repeated. Mimeographed copies of student notes on the course exist, and it is discussed at length in Nechkina, *Vasilii Osipovich Kliuchevskii*, pp. 254–67. Kliuchevskii's elliptical and derivative discussion of the subject matter, purpose, and value of history, occupying

less than thirty pages in the first volume of the *Kurs russkoi istorii*, scarcely does justice to his methods and views. On the school around Kliuchevskii, see Terence Emmons, "Kliuchevskii's Pupils," *California Slavic Studies* 14 (1992): 68–98. My exploration of Miliukov's role in the formation and dissemination of the Moscow school of historiography was inspired by this elegant and thoughtful essay.

41. Miliukov, "V. O. Kliuchevskii," p. 189. In the theoretical introduction to the printed *Kurs*, Kliuchevskii argues that history itself is the source of study for the general cultural development of mankind, and that the history of a given nation provides a sort of case study for investigation of processes that reveal the mechanics of all historical life. See V. O. Kliuchevskii, *Sochineniia* (Moscow, 1959), 1:26.

42. Miliukov, "V. O. Kliuchevskii," pp. 190, 192. Two brief English-language treatments of Kliuchevskii's historical approach are Emmons, "Kliuchevskii's Pupils," and Alfred Rieber's introduction to the English translation of V. O. Kliuchevskii's *Kurs russkoi istorii* (Moscow, 1937): *A Course in Russian History: The Seventeenth Century*, trans. Natalie Duddington (Chicago, 1973), pp. xiii–xl. See also P. A. Kireeva, *V. O. Kliuchevskii kak istorik russkoi istoricheskoi nauki* (Moscow, 1966), which attempts a reconstruction of Kliuchevskii's course on historiography.

43. Miliukov felt Kliuchevskii's clerical, "non-intelligentsia" background, which distinguished him from the majority of his gymnasium-educated colleagues, was part of the key to understanding his social aloofness, as well as his interpretation of Russian history. In "V. O. Kliuchevskii," pp. 203–7, Miliukov suggests that Kliuchevskii was more truly at home in the cultural world (*byt'*) of Muscovy, and something of a stranger to the world of his own day. See also Miliukov, "V. O. Kliuchevskii, kak lichnost'," *Poslednie novosti*, January 24, 1932, pp. 2–3.

44. In Russian, *sam dokhodi!* See Iu. V. Got'e, "V. O. Kliuchevskii kak rukovoditel' nachinauiushchikh uchenykh," in *V. O. Kliuchevskii*, p. 180.

45. Miliukov, *Vosp.*, pp. 77–78, and "V. O. Kliuchevskii," pp. 195–96. Miliukov's characterization of Kliuchevskii as a teacher is corroborated by, for example, A. A. Kizevetter, "V. O. Kliuchevskii kak prepodavatel'," in *V. O. Kliuchevskii*, pp. 164–76, and Got'e's essay in the same collection.

46. It is also important that Kliuchevskii, though he offered a course in historiography, rarely explicitly critiqued alternate approaches to the study of the past; as V. I. Syromatnikov, "V. O. Kliuchevskii i B. N. Chicherin," in *V. O. Kliuchevskii*, pp. 61–62, puts it, "He had business only with history, not with historians."

47. Miliukov, "Moi universitetskie gody," p. 266, and *Vosp.*, pp. 78, 94.

48. Miliukov, *Vosp.*, p. 71.

49. A time-honored means for supplementing slender student budgets was to make a précis of a lecture course, which was then hectographed and sold; Miliukov created such a précis for Troitskii's course on the history of Greek philosophy. See Miliukov, "Moi universitetskie gody," p. 263, and *Vosp.*, pp. 69 and 75. During this academic year the Miliukov brothers lived apart from their mother in a rooming house on Maroseika (Miliukov, *Vosp.* MS, pp. 102–3).

50. Miliukov, *Vosp.*, p. 79. The financial difficulties Miliukov experienced as a student were not uncommon; for a discussion of the material privations of university students and their self-help organizations, see Kassow, *Students*, pp. 57–72, 77–85.

51. In *Vosp.*, p. 58, Miliukov mistakenly recounts this episode as having occurred in 1876 when he was still in gymnasium. For a vivid picture of student life in Moscow in the 1880s and the chronically bad relations of the university neighborhood with the Okhotnyi Riad area, see Kizevetter, *Na rubezhe*, p. 10.

52. Miliukov, *Vosp.*, pp. 58–59; Dostoevskii had in fact suspended publication of the highly successful *Diary* by this time.
53. See Fedor Dostoevskii, *Pis' ma* (Moscow, 1959), 4:355–57, for Miliukov's letter of April 8, 1878.
54. Miliukov, *Vosp.*, p. 59. The letter to Dostoevskii and his response are discussed in detail in Dumova, *Liberal v Rossii*, pp. 37–46.
55. See Dostoevskii, *Pis' ma*, 4:16–17, for his answer of April 18, 1878.
56. Miliukov, *Vosp.*, p. 59.
57. Alston, *Education and State*, pp. 112–13, and Zaionchkovskii, *Rossiiskoe samoderzhavie*, pp. 309–16.
58. Miliukov, *Vosp.*, pp. 79–80, and "Moi universitetskie gody," pp. 268–69. See also G. V. Vernadskii, *Pavel Nikolaevich Miliukov* (Petrograd, 1917), p. 4. This pamphlet by Vernadskii, clearly meant to popularize Miliukov's image, is nonetheless valuable in being the first biographical work on Miliukov; it corroborates a number of the episodes Miliukov recounts much later in his memoirs.
59. Miliukov, *Vosp.*, p. 81. The "active fighters" were the members of the People's Will, a conspiratorial revolutionary organization of the late 1870s which employed terror. On March 1, 1881, after several failed attempts, the revolutionaries assassinated the tsar.
60. Miliukov, *Vosp.*, pp. 79–80, and "Moi universitetskie gody," pp. 272–73. Shakhovskoi's account is contained in his fragmentary "Avtobiografiia," in *Russkie vedomosti, 1869–1913* (Moscow, 1913), pp. 196–200.
61. Miliukov, "Moi universitetskie gody," p. 272.
62. Shakhovskoi, "Avtobiografiia," pp. 196–97.
63. Miliukov, "Moi universitetskie gody," p. 274.
64. Miliukov, *Vosp.*, pp. 82–83, and *Vosp.* MS, p. 103; see also Dumova, *Liberal v Rossii*, pp. 69–70.
65. Miliukov, *Vosp.*, pp. 85–91.
66. Miliukov, "Moi universitetskie gody," p. 274.
67. The subject of "generational" differences appears with some frequency in Miliukov's writing, and was something he was obviously conscious of. See "Moi universitetskie gody," p. 274; "Russian Literature," *The Athenaeum* (London), July 4, 1891, pp. 29–30; *Vosp.*, pp. 176–77, 191; and "Rokovye gody," *Russkie zapiski* (Paris), August–September 1938, p. 109, and October 1938, pp. 132–34. On the question of generational identity, see Terence Emmons, *The Formation of Political Parties and the First National Elections in Russia* (Cambridge, Mass., 1983), pp. 62–72, who points out that most of the Kadet leaders were "men of the eighties."
68. The student movement did not die out completely during this decade, but there would be no major disorders at Moscow University until 1887; for the student movement and university life in these years, see Zaionchkovskii, *Rossiiskoe samoderzhavie*, pp. 309–34, and G. I. Shchetinina, *Universitety v Rossii i ustav 1884 g.* (Moscow, 1976)
69. Miliukov, *Vosp.*, pp. 92–93 and 440. Miliukov described Vinogradov as one of his dearest friends at the university. The relationship cooled during the years of the liberation movement, apparently because Vinogradov felt Miliukov's political views were too radical.
70. The thesis was for the degree of *kandidat*, a special honors degree which entailed writing a thesis based on original research, equivalent to an undergraduate senior honors thesis or the *diplomnaia rabota* written by Russian students in their fifth year at the university. See G. G. Krichevskii, "Uchenye stepeni v universitetakh dorevoliutsionnoi Rossii," *Istoriia SSSR*, no. 4 (1985): 141–52. Miliukov probably incorporated some

of the arguments of this thesis into his article "Knigi pistsovye i perepisnye," in Brokgauz and Efron, 40:457–59.

71. The report noted that "in investigatory methods the author reveals remarkable ability in dealing with material as difficult and unyielding as the Moscow cadastral books, [as well as] in clearly analyzing and grouping the data presented by them. The author supports all his positions with a great deal of statistical data and tables" (RGIA, Archive of the Ministry of Education, f. 733, op. 149, d. 680, god 1883, l. 23).

72. Miliukov, *Vosp.*, pp. 93–94. Miliukov mistakenly gives 1882 as the year of his completion of the undergraduate degree; the Ministry of Education formally approved his candidacy December 31, 1883 (RGIA, f. 733, op. 149, d. 680, god 1883, l. 141a).

73. Henry W. Longfellow, "A Psalm of Life," in *The Complete Poetical Works of Henry Wadsworth Longfellow*, Cambridge Edition (Boston, 1922), pp. 2–3; Miliukov, *Vosp*, p. 95.

74. Miliukov, *Vosp.*, p. 95.

75. Miliukov, *Vosp.*, pp. 96–97, 121; a description of his departure for Riazan' is contained in GARF, f. 102, 3 d-vo, d. 251, cited in N. V. Shirokova, *Partiia "Narodnogo prava"* (Saratov, 1972), p. 166.

76. The English term "master" is somewhat misleading, since the Russian degree of *magistr* was essentially the equivalent of the U.S. degree of doctor of philosophy. Preparation for the *magistr* examinations generally took three years, with an additional three years being devoted to the writing of the dissertation, which had to be published before it could be publicly defended. The degree of *magistr* was abolished after the revolution and replaced by the more modest degree of *kandidat*. The doctoral degree, after 1884, required publication and defense of a book-length dissertation, but did not entail further course work or exams, which remains the case in Russia today. See Krichevskii, "Uchenye stepeni," pp. 142–52.

77. Miliukov, *Vosp.*, pp. 97–98.

78. Lecturers were not paid a salary, but an honorarium based on the number of students enrolled in their courses: since few students had time to take electives, lecturers rarely managed to make even the 300 rubles a year that constituted the average student stipend (Miliukov, "Universitety v Rossii," in Brokgauz and Efron, 34:788–800). There was a considerable literature generated on the subject of the meager remuneration of lecturers and other university positions below the rank of full professor; see Kassow, *Students*, pp. 32–33, 36.

79. Miliukov, "Rasprostranenie universitetskogo obrazovaniia v Anglii, Amerike i Rossii," *Russkoe bogatstvo*, March 1896, p. 117.

80. Miliukov's originality in establishing the heuristic rubric of the juridical school—also referred to as the state school—was noted by Gary M. Hamburg in his paper "The Problem of the State School in Russian Historiography," presented at the December 1988 convention of the American Historical Association. Hamburg contends that no such "school" ever existed, on the grounds that the approaches of scholars usually considered as constituting this school have more differences than similarities.

81. Miliukov, "Iuridicheskaia shkola v russkoi istoriografii (Solev'ev, Kavelin, Chicherin, Sergeevich)," was first published in *Russkaia mysl'*, June, 1886, pp. 80–92, and reprinted in Miliukov, *Iz istorii russkoi intelligentsii* (St. Petersburg, 1902).

82. Miliukov, "Iuridicheskaia shkola," pp. 91–92.

83. The memoirs are rather confusing on the subject of these lectures. Miliukov claims that the candidate was required to give two, but that friends advised him to combine his two topics in some fashion; his second topic, on the origins of the *razriadnaia kniga*, was later published but apparently never delivered as a talk: (Miliukov, *Vosp.*, pp. 98–99,

and P. N. Miliukov, "Drevneishaia razriadnaia kniga offitsial'noi redaktsii [po 1565 g.],"
in *Chteniia v Imperatorskom Obshchestve istorii i drevnostei rossiiskikh pri Moskovskom universitete* [Moscow, 1902]).
84. Iu. V. Got'e, "Universitet (Iz zapisok akademika Iu. V. Got'e)," *Vestnik Moskovskogo Universiteta, seriia 8: Istoriia*, no. 4 (July–August 1982): 13–27.
85. Miliukov outlined his pedagogic approach in "Rasprostranenie universitetskogo obrazovaniia," p. 114.
86. Kizevetter, *Na rubezhe*, p. 87.
87. A. A. Kizevetter, quoted in P. N. Miliukov, "Dva russkikh istorika," *Sovremennye zapiski* (Paris) 51 (1933): 323.
88. Women were not admitted to regular Russian universities, but in the 1870s "higher courses" for women were organized in four cities, St. Petersburg, Moscow, Kiev, and Kazan; on the obstacles to higher education for women in this period see Richard Stites, *The Women's Liberation Movement in Russia: Feminism, Nihilism, and Bolshevism, 1860–1930* (Princeton, 1978), pp. 168–73.
89. Miliukov, *Vosp.*, pp. 99–100; Anna Zhikareva, "Anna S. Miliukova: Zhiznennyi put'," *Poslednie novosti*, April 5, 1935, p. 2. The short article by Zhikareva, continued in the April 8 issue of *Poslednie novosti*, is a rare source of information on Miliukov's domestic life other than the memoirs.
90. Miliukov, *Vosp.*, pp. 100–101; Zhikareva, "Anna S. Miliukova," emphasizes Anna's trepidations about sacrificing her independence by marrying.
91. Andrei Belyi, in *Na rubezhe dvukh stoletii* (Moscow, 1930), pp. 102–62, devotes an entire chapter of his memoirs to characterizations of his popular father's university colleagues, dismissing their "liberalism" for its "insincerity of pose and indistinctness of ideology."
92. Miliukov, *Vosp.*, pp. 102–3, and Zhikareva, "Anna S. Miliukova."
93. Fischer, *Russian Liberalism*, pp. 18–19. For a study of early Russian liberalism through the period of the Great Reforms, see Gary M. Hamburg, *Boris Chicherin and Early Russian Liberalism, 1828–1866* (Stanford, Calif., 1992); a brief characterization of professorial liberalism at the turn of the century is in Kassow, *Students*, pp. 6–8.
94. Miliukov, *Vosp.*, p. 102.
95. Ibid., pp. 112–13; Zhikareva, "Anna S. Miliukova."
96. Miliukov, *Vosp.*, pp. 111–12, and GARF, f. 579, op. 1, d. 4b, l. 1, copy of court order of July 25, 1886. The brothers were taken to court over some of their mother's long-standing debts, but settled all accounts after selling the family dachas at Pushkino.
97. See for example Gessen, *V dvukh vekakh*, p. 200, and the following articles contained in Smirnov et al., eds., *P. N. Miliukov*: V. Obolenskii, "Miliukov kak politik," p. 103; V. Miakotin, "P. N. Miliukov, kak istorik," pp. 39–40; and Gruzenburg, "Staromu drugu," pp. 180–82.
98. Kizevetter describes the pleasant gatherings at Vinogradov's, with Miliukov excitedly expounding his archival discoveries, in *Na rubezhe*, pp. 71–72.
99. Miliukov provides two significantly different accounts of how he arrived at his topic, both of which must be read with a degree of caution. At his dissertation defense, aware of the controversy that his findings had already provoked, he insisted on the absence of any a priori assumptions, dwelling instead on how the materials had shaped the topic and his conclusions: the transcript of the defense speech was published in *Russkaia mysl'*, July 1892, pp. 57–66. In his memoirs, with no need to defend himself before a scholarly audience, and influenced by his later studies of the cultural side of the Petrine reforms, Miliukov claimed that in selecting the topic he was interested in determining the extent to which violence had been a necessary part of reforms that were not only

crucial to the existence of the state but also historically logical (*Vosp.*, pp. 105–6). The dissertation defense appears to be the more accurate version.

100. Miliukov, "Deux historiens russes: S. F. Platonov et A. A. Kizevetter," *Le Monde Slave*, March 1933, p. 454. "Dva russkikh istorika" is a longer version of this article.

101. Miliukov, *Vosp.*, pp. 108–9; Platonov was married to the sister of one of Miliukov's close childhood friends, N. N. Shamonin. Platonov arranged to have Miliukov's dissertation published serially in the journal of the Ministry of Education, and also arranged for him to review Lappo-Danilevskii's *Organizatsiia priamogo oblozheniia v Moskovskom gosudarstve* (St. Petersburg, 1892) for the prestigious imprint of the Academy of Sciences.

102. In his unpublished memoir of the years 1889–92, E. B. Shmurlo discussed the stimulating community of younger historians at St. Petersburg University, including Platonov, Lappo-Danilevskii, Druzhinin, N. D. Chechulin, I. A. Shliapkin, and several others; cited in L. I. Demina, "'Zapiski' E. F. Shmurlo ob istorikakh peterburgskogo universiteta (1889–1892)," *Arkheograficheskii ezhegodnik za 1984 god* (Moscow, 1986), p. 254.

103. Miliukov, "Dva russkikh istorika," p. 319, and *Vosp.*, p. 109. This subject is taken up in more detail in Chapter 3.

104. Miliukov, *Vosp.*, pp. 109–10, and "Pamiati V. A. Miakotina," *Poslednie novosti*, October 8, 1937, p. 2. On Semevskii, see Michael Petrovich, "V. I. Semevskii, Russian Social Historian," in *Essays in Russian and Soviet History*, ed. J. Curtiss (Leyden, 1963), p. 70.

105. Miliukov, *Vosp.*, p. 78, and "V. O. Kliuchevskii, kak lichnost'"; Kizevetter, *Na rubezhe*, pp. 60–62. See also Nechkina, *Vasilii Osipovich Kliuchevskii*, pp. 371–74.

106. Emmons, "Kliuchevskii's Pupils," p. 70, and Nechkina, *Vasilii Osipovich Kliuchevskii*, p. 375. The dissertations were by Miliukov (1892), M. K. Liubavskii (1894), N. A. Rozhkov (1900), M. M. Bogoslovskii (1902), A. A. Kizevetter (1903), and Iu. B. Got'e (1906); Liubavskii also defended a doctoral dissertation under Kliuchevskii, in 1901.

107. Kliuchevskii, following M. P. Pogodin, theorized a mass movement of Russian tribes from south to north following the Kiev period. Miliukov, consulting the evidence provided by historical linguistics and archaeological remains, argued that no such mass movement had occurred. See Miliukov, *Vosp.*, p. 104, and his article based on this course, "Kolonizatsiia Rossii," in Brokgauz and Efron, 45a:740–46.

108. Miliukov, *Vosp.*, p. 104.

109. Ibid., pp. 106–7.

110. Miliukov to Kliuchevskii, March 10, 1891, in GARF, f. 579, op. 1, d. 6390, l. 1.

111. Kliuchevskii to Miliukov, April 22, 1892, in GARF, f. 579, op. 1, d. 6390, l. 5.

112. Kliuchevskii to Miliukov, May 5, 1892, in GARF, f. 579, op. 1, d. 6390, l. 3; Kliuchevskii's usual salutation was "Respected Pavel Nikolaevich."

113. This option was provided for in the 1884 university statute, but required a unanimous vote of the faculty—obviously, Kliuchevskii had voted in Karelin's favor. See Krichevskii, "Uchenye stepeni," p. 148.

114. Miliukov, *Vosp.*, p. 107.

115. The substance of the dissertation defense was written up by V. Storozhev in his article "Istoricheskaia khronika," *Istoricheskoe obozrenie* (St. Petersburg) 5 (1892): 198–215. The text of Miliukov's speech is in *Russkaia mysl'*, July 1892, pp. 57–66.

116. Maklakov, "Otryvki iz vospominanii," pp. 302–4; Kizevetter, *Na rubezhe*, p. 278; the complete text of Kliuchevskii's examination is in Kliuchevskii, *Sochineniia*, 8: 177–83.

117. Miliukov, *Vosp.*, pp. 107–8; Kliuchevskii's refusal to recommend award of a doc-

toral degree on the basis of Miliukov's dissertation is discussed briefly in Nechkina, *Vasilii Osipovich Kliuchevskii*, pp. 375–76.

118. I am indebted to Edward L. Keenan for first suggesting this parallel, after reading a draft of the manuscript.

Chapter Two: Political Awakening

1. Miliukov, *Vosp.*, p. 110. Kliuchevskii wrote his former student in October 1892 to inform him that on the basis of his high evaluation of Miliukov's monograph on the reforms of Peter the Great, he had been awarded the first Solev'ev prize in history; see GARF, f. 579, op. 1, d. 4614, l. 4.
2. Holders of the *magistr* were frequently named extraordinary professors, which entitled them to a higher rate of pay (Krichevskii, "Uchenye stepeni," p. 148).
3. Kliuchevskii was booed and hissed in the classroom after describing the late emperor as the "tsar of peace"; the episode produced a small scandal at the university. Miliukov rather thought that Kliuchevskii, too, suspected him of writing the anonymous squib (Miliukov, *Vosp.*, p. 122, and Kizevetter, *Na rubezhe*, pp. 244–46).
4. Miliukov, *Vosp.*, pp. 112–13.
5. Miliukov, "K. K. Arsen'ev," *Poslednie novosti*, May 4, 1929, pp. 2–3.
6. Among the journal's contributors were Leo Tolstoy, N. K. Mikhailovskii, V. P. Vorontsov, V. G. Korolenko, and Maksim Gorkii (Viktor Chernov, *Zapiski sotsialista revoliutsionera* [Berlin, 1922], p. 147; Miliukov, *Vosp.*, p. 113; and *Russkaia periodicheskaia pechat', 1702–1898* [Moscow, 1959], p. 616).
7. Ivan I. Petrunkevich, who would play a significant part in promoting Miliukov's leadership of the Kadets, began attending Gol'tsevs' "at homes" after his arrival in Moscow in August 1890. He mentions meeting Miliukov there (I. I. Petrunkevich, *Iz zapisok obshchestvennogo deiatelia* [Berlin, 1934], p. 267).
8. Miliukov, *Vosp.*, p. 118. He subsequently gave the same course at Moscow University in 1894–95 when Kliuchevskii was on leave. The lectures were published in hectographed form as P. N. Miliukov, *Lektsii po "Vvedeniiu v kurs Russkoi istorii"* (Moscow, 1894–95, hectograph) (hereafter cited as *Lektsii*).
9. Miliukov, *Vosp.*, p. 119. A more complete treatment of Miliukov's reading of Russian history is presented in Chapter 3.
10. Miliukov, *Lektsii*, pt. 2, p. 4.
11. Miliukov, *Vosp.*, p. 118. That the curriculum be expanded to include history courses covering the nineteenth century would be one of the demands made by student strikers at St. Petersburg University in 1905 (Kassow, *Students*, p. 257).
12. Miliukov, *Lektsii*, pt. 2, p. 4. Part 1 of volume 3 of the *Ocherki po istorii russkoi kul'tury* (St. Petersburg, 1903), which examines the origins and evolution of the Russian "national idea," was not part of the original lecture course; Miliukov worked these ideas out well after the period under review. (See Chapter 4.)
13. Miliukov, *Lektsii*, pt. 1, p. 209.
14. Ibid., pt. 3, p. 7.
15. Ibid., pt. 1, pp. 203–10.
16. Miliukov, *Vosp.*, pp. 115–16. Miliukov wrote the articles in Russian, and they were translated into slightly stilted English by Brayley Hodgetts, who had written on Russian history.
17. Miliukov, "Russia," *The Athenaeum*, July 5, 1890, p. 25, and July 4, 1891, p. 29.

18. Although it would be preferable to avoid using this untranslated Russian word, English equivalents—zemstvo men (and women), zemstvo activists, individuals working in the zemstvos—are cumbersome. I will therefore follow what appears to be current, standard practice: employment of the unitalicized Russian word.

19. Miliukov makes no mention of such meetings in his memoirs; his participation in them is mentioned in the diary of K. K. Arsen'ev, cited in N. M. Pirumova, *Zemskoe liberal'noe dvizhenie* (Moscow, 1977), p. 187.

20. Miliukov, "Russia," July 5, 1890, p. 25.

21. Miliukov, "Russia," *The Athenaeum*, July 7, 1894, p. 23.

22. Miliukov, "Russia," *The Athenaeum*, July 6, 1889, p. 27. Several years later, Miliukov was invited to Tolstoy's to discuss with him "the general meaning of history." Tolstoy proved an attentive listener, but the cryptic remarks with which he rejected "science" convinced Miliukov that "I would never understand Tolstoy" (*Vosp.*, pp. 114–15).

23. Miliukov, "Russia," July 4, 1891, p. 30.

24. Miliukov, "Russia," July 6, 1889, p. 27.

25. Ibid; Miliukov, "Russia," July 5, 1890, p. 26, and July 2, 1892, p. 25.

26. Miliukov, "Russia," July 6, 1889, p. 27.

27. Miliukov, "Russia," July 5, 1890, p. 26.

28. Miliukov, "Russia," July 2, 1892, p. 25.

29. On the famine's influence in politicizing Russian society see, for example, Arthur P. Mendel, *Dilemmas of Progress in Tsarist Russia* (Cambridge, Mass., 1961), pp. 119–27.

30. Miliukov was elected to membership in the Committee on Literacy of the Moscow Society for Agriculture on February 9, 1893. Within a year, he had been named to the Committee's revision committee and as a delegate to the section on popular instruction of the Russian Congress of Agriculturalists and All-Russian Exhibition of Agriculture scheduled for December 20, 1895; see GARF, f. 579, op. 1, d. 2503 and d. 2504.

31. Miliukov, *Vosp.*, p. 114. The text of the lecture is contained in P. N. Miliukov, "Razlozhenie slavianofil'stva," in *Iz istorii russkoi intelligentsii*, 2d ed. (St. Petersburg, 1903), pp. 266–306; it was originally printed in *Voprosy filosofii i psikhologii* 3 (1893): pp. 46–96.

32. Miliukov was commissioned to write the article on Slavophilism for Brokgauz and Efron. See Miliukov, "Slavianofil'stva," in Brokgauz and Efron, 30:307–14.

33. Miliukov, "Razlozhenie slavianofil'stva," p. 303.

34. Ibid., p. 269.

35. Ibid., pp. 290, 303. Danilevskii, as Miliukov put it, had two, irreconcilable personas: that of the calm, dispassionate man of science, and that of the angry patriot. He looked to science for the foundation of his theory but ended up with the metaphysical conception of the world-historical type.

36. Danilevskii denied the theory of evolution, both for biology and for sociology; Leont'ev, fearing the decay of Russian nationalism, advocated "freezing" it (Miliukov, "Razlozhenie slavianofil'stva," pp. 276, 279, 283).

37. For Miliukov, Solov'ev's identification of religion with progress was the last, logical conclusion from the humanitarian world-historical tendencies of the original Slavophilism (ibid., pp. 299, 302). Solov'ev published a rejoinder to Miliukov's lecture which affirmed Miliukov's exposition of his theory, but rejected the characterization of it as in any way "Slavophile." See V. M. Solov'ev, "Zamechaniia na lektsiiu P. N. Miliukova," in *Sobranie sochinenii V. A. Solev'eva* (St. Petersburg, n.d.), pp. 458–62.

38. Miliukov, "Razlozhenie slavianofil'stva," p. 304.

39. Ibid., pp. 267, 306. Fischer, *Russian Liberalism*, p. 70, interprets this reference to "democratic liberalism of the newest type" as evidence of Miliukov's commitment to liberalism at this time.
40. Leont'ev was openly and cynically amoral, arguing, Miliukov said, that "*all means are good*" for achievement of his end, since "'politics are not ethics.'" Although Danilevskii envisioned Russia's further development into a cultural-historical type, Miliukov considered his practical aims to be essentially the same as Leont'ev's (Miliukov, "Razlozhenie slavianofil'stva," pp. 285, 288–90).
41. Ibid., pp. 302, 305.
42. Miliukov's conception of the historicity, and therefore relativity, of values, still tentative in form in 1893, would be more explicitly developed by 1900, when he asserted in volume 2 of *Ocherki po istorii russkoi kul'tury* (Studies of Russian Culture) that spiritual culture is "the product of *human society*"; see Miliukov, *Ocherki po istorii russkoi kul'tury*, 2d ed. (St. Petersburg, 1899), 2:2 (emphasis added). In 1920 he stated, a propos of morality in Soviet Russia, "New generations evolve new forms of moral and intellectual culture" (Miliukov, *Russia Today and Tomorrow* [New York, 1921], pp. 386–87).
43. My discussion of Dewey is indebted to James Kloppenburg's remarkable book *Uncertain Victory: Social Democracy and Progressivism in European and American Thought, 1870-1920* (Oxford, 1986). Kloppenburg's subject is two generations of thinkers looking for a "via media" in philosophy. Kloppenburg argues: "Discarding accepted distinctions between idealism and empiricism in epistemology, between intuitionism and utilitarianism in ethics, and between revolutionary socialism and laissez-faire liberalism in politics, they converged toward a *via media* in philosophy and toward the political theories of social democracy and progressivism" (p. 3).
44. As the lectures for the Pedagogical Institute demonstrated, Miliukov was, by 1893, a convinced democrat. As early as 1888 Dewey made explicit his belief in the connection between morality and democracy in his book *The Ethics of Democracy*. In Kloppenburg's estimation, "It is impossible to exaggerate the importance of the democratic ideal in Dewey's thought" (*Uncertain Victory*, p. 140).
45. John Dewey, *Reconstruction in Philosophy* (New York, 1920), pp. 197–98.
46. This attitude is implicit in his diatribes against the influence of Tolstoy and explicit in his 1909 response to the symposium *Vekhi*. There, he maintained that the *Vekhi* participants' call for a process of "internal self-perfection" before perfection of institutions was not only ethically mistaken, but politically indefensible. "'People, and not institutions'—such, before the triumph of free institutions, is the ideological slogan of all reactions" (Miliukov, "Intelligentsiia i istoricheskaia traditsiia," in *Intelligentsiia v Rossii*, ed. K. Arsen'ev et al. [St. Petersburg, 1910], p. 105).
47. John Dewey, *Ethics*, pp. 281–84, cited in Kloppenburg, *Uncertain Victory*, p. 121. Robert E. MacMaster, "In the Russian Manner: Thought as Incipient Action," *Harvard Slavic Studies* 4 (1964): 263–80, suggests it was a characteristic of the intelligentsia to turn Western political notions into directives for action.
48. A detailed examination of Miliukov's reluctance to condemn political terror is presented in my forthcoming article "Politics, Morality, and Violence: Kadet Liberals and the Question of Terror, 1902–1911," *Russian History* 22 (Winter 1995): 455–80.
49. Pipes, *Struve*, 1:61.
50. Miliukov, "Russia," *The Athenaeum*, July 6, 1895, p. 24.
51. Ibid. The artel' was a group or association of peasants organized for labor.
52. Miliukov, "Russia," *The Athenaeum*, July 4, 1896, p. 25, and July 6, 1895, p. 25.

53. Publication of volume 1 of the *Ocherki po istorii russkoi kul'tury* convinced many readers that Miliukov was a Marxist, at least in economics (Miliukov, *Vosp.*, p. 138). Georgii Plekhanov, for instance, in a letter to P. B. Akselrod of March 2, 1894, referred to Miliukov and Lappo-Danilevskii as "ours" (cited in Shirokova, *Partiia "Narodnogo prava,"* p. 94).

54. Miliukov first became familiar with economic materialism as an undergraduate, primarily through the work of Achille Loria, reading volume 1 of *Kapital* somewhat later in Bakunin's translation (Miliukov, *Vosp.*, p. 76).

55. Miliukov, "Russia," July 6, 1895, p. 25. Plekhanov's work was published under the pseudonym Beltov.

56. Miliukov, "Russia," July 7, 1894, p. 24.

57. Ibid. The determinism of the young Marxists is similarly noted in Leopold Haimson, *The Russian Marxists and the Origins of Bolshevism* (New York, 1966), p. 53.

58. Miliukov, "Russia" July 6, 1895, p. 25, and July 7, 1894, p. 24. On Struve's *Kriticheskie zametki k voprosu ob ekonomicheskom razvitii Rossii* (St. Petersburg, 1894) and its reception, see Pipes, *Struve*, 1:101–17.

59. "In this dispute over principles the study of the actual facts of Russian contemporary life was comparatively relegated to a place of secondary importance, just as the development of a program from the teachings of the marxists was practically ignored" (Miliukov, "Russia," July 4, 1896, p. 26).

60. Miliukov, "Russia," July 7, 1894, p. 24. Mikhailovskii's views at this time are discussed in James H. Billington, *Mikhailovsky and Russian Populism* (Oxford, 1958), pp. 164–70.

61. Miliukov, "Russia," *The Athenaeum*, July 1, 1893, p. 27, and July 6, 1895, p. 25.

62. Ibid.

63. Miliukov, "Russia," July 7, 1894, p. 24.

64. Miliukov, *Vosp.*, pp. 103, 110. Scholars have tended to take Miliukov at his word. See Fischer, *Russian Liberalism*, p. 71, and Riha, *A Russian European*, p. 38, who argues that Miliukov's reputation in the 1890s was "more radical than his actual beliefs."

65. The United Council was founded at the end of the 1880s and set about uniting Moscow student organizations under its aegis, then broadened its sights to attract students all over Russia. Unlike more moderate organizations, it advocated illegal tactics and the redirection of student protest from purely university and student concerns to national, political ones. On the Council, see Norman Naimark, *Terrorists and Social Democrats* (Cambridge, Mass., 1983), pp. 225–30.

66. Chernov, *Zapiski*, p. 126.

67. Ibid., p. 175.

68. Miliukov, *Lektsii*, pt. 1, pp. 167–69. For an exposition of Chicherin's views on the origins of the commune, see Hamburg, *Boris Chicherin*, pp. 87–88, 159–60.

69. Chernov, *Zapiski*, p. 166.

70. Ibid., pp. 170–71.

71. Ibid., pp. 172–73.

72. Ibid., pp. 173–74.

73. Much later, when it was clear that the differences between Miliukov and the agrarian socialists involved far more than tactics, Chernov still believed that their overtures to Miliukov had not rested on a simple misunderstanding of his views: "I do not think that at that time P. N. Miliukov had fully succeeded in coming to know himself. He was, probably, in the power of an illusion which brought him close to us" (*Zapiski*, p. 175).

74. As V. V. Zenzinov later recalled, "In P. N. Miliukov's high reputation in our eyes there figured as well, to no small degree, the circumstance that he was accounted a seditious privat-dotsent" ("Iz pokoleniia v pokolenie," in Smirnov et al., eds., *P. N. Miliukov*, p. 160).
75. V. I. El'iashevich, "Iz vospominanii starogo moskovskogo studenta, 1892–1896 gg." in *Pamiati russkogo studentchestva: Sbornik vospominanii* (Paris, 1934), p. 109. S. I. Mitskevich, *Na grani dvukh epokh: Ot narodnichestva k marksizmu* (Moscow, 1937), p. 123, echoes El'iashevich's characterization of the use of student parties in the years 1892–94 to disguise gatherings for political debate.
76. El'iashevich, "Iz vospominanii," pp. 109–10. Disputes at these gatherings were sometimes acrimonious; at one party, Miliukov became embroiled with an ardent student Marxist who attacked his depiction of Russian history because it exaggerated the role of the state, minimized class struggle, and denied that Russia's development had been and would be identical to that of the West (Mitskevich, *Na grani dvukh epokh*, p. 124).
77. RGIA, f. 878, op. 1, d. 40, l. 55. Kizevetter also refers to this paper as being the main reason for Miliukov's exile to Riazan' (*Na rubezhe*, p. 246).
78. Miliukov, *Vosp.*, p. 120.
79. Miliukov's involvement in *Narodnoe pravo* is somewhat problematic, since the sole source testifying to this is the memoir written by the old Bolshevik S. I. Mitskevich, who was not himself a party member. Miliukov makes no mention of having been a member of the party, but many of his activities of this period are omitted from his memoirs. He never denied Mitskevich's assertion that he joined *Narodnoe pravo*, but may not have known that such a claim had been made.
80. The only full-length study of the party is Shirokova, *Partiia*; the party is also discussed in some detail in Norman Naimark, *Terrorists*, pp. 235–38, and Galai, *The Liberation Movement in Russia, 1900–1905*, (Cambridge, 1973), pp. 58–65.
81. Shirokova, *Partiia*, pp. 62–72. The text of the program is contained in V. O. Aptekman, "Partiia Narodnogo Prava," *Byloe*, no. 7 (1907): 177–204.
82. Shirokova, *Partiia*, p. 66.
83. The term "close to the party" is Shirokova's. In her list of persons associated with the party she does not always distinguish between those who were actually members and those who were not, nor does she explain how she identified actual members; see Shirokova, *Partiia*, p. 105 and appendix.
84. Mitskevich, *Na grani dvukh epokh*, p. 123.
85. When Miliukov was subjected to administrative exile in February 1895 he was not charged with having been a member of the illegal *Narodnoe pravo*; however, Shirokova cites police records indicating that in fall of that year A. I. Bogdanovich, a member of *Narodnoe pravo*, planned to visit Miliukov in Riazan' to discuss setting up a new party press; he apparently never made it to Riazan', an informer having tipped off police about his intentions. Shirokova *Partiia*, pp. 129–31, 147.
86. Among those who have noted the similarities are Galai, *Liberation Movement*, p. 64; Haimson, *Russian Marxists*, p. 50; and Naimark, *Terrorists*, p. 238.
87. Aptekman, "Partiia Narodnogo prava," p. 180. A list of members is contained in Shirokova, *Partiia*, pp. 182–95.
88. In his memoirs, Miliukov says that in the 1880s "moderate liberalism" was the only tenable position open to him (*Vosp.*, p. 103). Since the memoirs' next explicit characterization of his political views asserts his "liberalism" in 1905, the reader is forced to infer that Miliukov was a liberal throughout this period.

89. Ibid., p. 116.
90. I. I. Stepanskii offers an interesting treatment of educational and self-improvement movements in the 1890s in "Liberal'naia intelligentsia v obshchestvennom dvizhenii Rossii na rubezhe XIX-XX vv.," *Istoricheskie zapiski*, no. 109 (1983): 64-94.
91. On *Posrednik* (Intermediary) and the St. Petersburg Literacy Committee, see Jeffrey Brooks, *When Russia Learned to Read: Literacy and Popular Literature, 1861-1917* (Princeton, 1985), pp. 337-42.
92. A similar organization was established at the end of 1894 in St. Petersburg as a "special department for assisting self-education" under the St. Petersburg Pedagogic Museum. It did not attempt such active guidance of its readers as the Moscow Commission did, and was not as large an undertaking. See Miliukov, "Rasprostranenie universitetskogo obrazovaniia," pp. 111-12.
93. Zhikareva, "Anna S. Miliukova," p. 2; Miliukov, *Vosp.*, pp. 116-17.
94. This trip to France, spent on the Riviera in the company of the French slavicists Jules Legras and Paul Boyer and their families, was made possible by the money awarded with the Solev'ev prize in history (Miliukov, *Vosp.*, pp. 110-11, 117). Miliukov's appraisal of the English extension movement is contained in P. N. Miliukov, "Letnii universitet v Anglii," *Mir Bozhii*, May 1894, pp. 194-206, and "Rasprostranenie universitetskogo obrazovaniia," especially pp. 79-101.
95. Kizevetter, *Na rubezhe*, pp. 286-88; Miliukov, *Vosp.*, p. 117. Kizevetter was very active in university extension, and his memoirs are the most important firsthand account of the movement. Curiously, Miliukov gives the extension movement only cursory treatment in his own memoirs, although this was his chief activity in 1893 and 1894, and a project very dear to his heart.
96. Kizevetter, *Na rubezhe*, pp. 289-90.
97. Ibid., pp. 290-91; Miliukov, "Rasprostranenie universitetskogo obrazovaniia," pp. 103-4.
98. "Kommissiia po organizatsii domashnego chteniia v Moskve," in *Mir Bozhii*, May 1894, p. 232.
99. Information on subscribers exists only for the year 1895; the overwhelming majority were aged 18-30 and lived outside the two capitals. Women constituted only 27 percent of subscribers, which surprised the organizers, given the high attendance by Russian women at popular lectures and the large numbers of women participating in university extension programs abroad (Miliukov, "Rasprostranenie universitetskogo obrazovaniia," pp. 105-8).
100. Kizevetter, *Na rubezhe*, pp. 290-91.
101. Miliukov, "Rasprostranenie universitetskogo obrazovaniia," p. 104; "Otchet Kommissiia po organizatsii domashnego chteniia," pp. 234-35.
102. Kizevetter, *Na rubezhe*, p. 291. The manuscript of Mint's *Logic*, which was part of a popular English textbook series, had been translated into Russian, but Miliukov found the translation so faulty that he retranslated it; Anna also translated books for the library (Miliukov, *Vosp.*, p. 117; Zhikareva, "Anna Sergeevna Miliukova," p. 2).
103. Miliukov, "University Extension," in Brokgauz and Efron, 34:806-8. In 1899, 16 percent of those working through the programs submitted written work for evaluation, which was almost identical to the ratios for the Cambridge program.
104. Kizevetter, *Na rubezhe*, p. 298.
105. Miliukov, "Rasprostranenie universitetskogo obrazovaniia," pp. 79, 107.
106. Speech to a meeting of the society "Gramotnost'" in early 1895, in GARF, f. 579, op. 1, d. 3372, 1. 2.

107. Miliukov, "Rasprostranenie universitetskogo obrazovaniia," pp. 115–16, 118, and *Vosp.*, p. 117.
108. Kizevetter, *Na rubezhe*, p. 300.
109. Copies of Miliukov's prospectus are contained in GARF, f. 579, op. 1, d. 3398, ll. 1–2.
110. Both the vice-governor and the bishop subsequently experienced difficulties for having attended (and, in the case of Chaikovskii, enthusiastically applauded) such incendiary talks; Chaikovskii's applause apparently cost him a promotion. I. Demidov, a gymnasium student in Nizhnii Novgorod at the time of the lectures, described the audience and the impression the lectures made on him and his fellow students in "P. N. Miliukov, kak uchitel'," in Smirnov et al., eds., *P. N. Miliukov*, pp. 153–59; also see Kizevetter, *Na rubezhe*, p. 300.
111. Miliukov later admitted that in these lectures he strongly implied that "revolution and constitution go together," although he maintained that such an idea was not truly characteristic of his thought (Miliukov, "Rokovye gody," October 1938, p. 131). Notes on both lecture series, taken down by a gendarme and sent to the police in St. Petersburg, are contained in RGIA, f. 733, op. 194, d. 1597.
112. GARF, f. 102, 3 d-vo, 1895, d. 251, t. I, cited in Shirokova, *Partiia*, p. 164.
113. Durnovo to I. V. Delianov, minister of education, memorandum, February 22, 1895, in RGIA, f. 733, op. 194, d. 1597, l. 44.
114. According to Kizevetter, the commission began winding down its activities after 1905, but Orlova continued to correspond with Miliukov on commission business after this date, and between 1907 and 1909 the commission brought out a journal, *Kriticheskoe obozrenie* (The critical review—not to be confused with the journal of the same name edited by Kovalevskii and Miller). Its stated goal was to "raise the activity of evaluating contemporary literature to the level of a genuine science" (*Kriticheskoe obozrenie*, no. 1 [1907], and BAR, P. N. Miliukov Personal Archive, Catalogued Correspondence: E. I. Orlova). ("P. N. Miliukov Personal Archive" is hereafter abbreviated "Miliukov.")
115. Kizevetter, *Na rubezhe*, pp. 292, 296.
116. Delianov, minister of education, to Count Kapnist, supervisor of the Moscow Educational District, February 6, 1895, in RGIA, Arkhiv Ministerstva Imp. Dvora, op. 468/2417, razriad 1, d. 10, karton 8788.
117. Miliukov, *Vosp.*, p. 121.
118. Miliukov to M. M. Kovalevskii, March 3, 1895, in BAR, M. M. Kovalevskii papers, box 2.
119. GARF, f. 579, op. 1, d. 3402.
120. Durnovo to I. D. Delianov, January 25, 1895, in RGIA, f. 733, op. 194, d. 1597, ll. 5–6.
121. Delianov to Durnovo, rough draft of confidential letter, March 3, 1895, in RGIA, f. 733, op. 194, d. 1597, l. 48.
122. Delianov to Kapnist, March 3, 1895, in RGIA, f. 733, op. 194, d. 1597, l. 51.
123. Durnovo to Delianov, February 22, 1895, and circular from Durnovo to Governors, January 25, 1895, in RGIA, f. 733, op. 194, d. 1597, ll. 34, 44.
124. Lieutenant General Petrov, director of police, to Delianov, March 13, 1895, in RGIA, f. 733, op. 194, d. 1597, l. 72.
125. Miliukov to Kovalevskii, March 3, 1895, in BAR, M. M. Kovalevskii papers, box 1.
126. Miliukov, *Vosp.*, p. 121.
127. Miliukov to M. M. Kovalevskii, March 3, 1895, in BAR, M. M. Kovalevskii papers, box 1.

128. That Miliukov was able to serve his administrative exile in a city that would prove so congenial was largely due to the efforts of his wife; Anna went to the capital and "roused liberal Petersburg." She enlisted an influential ally in the person of Baroness Ikskul', who arranged a meeting with Delianov. As a result of this meeting, Miliukov was allowed to choose his own place of exile, settling on Riazan' as the provincial city closest to Moscow (Miliukov, *Vosp.*, p. 121; Zhikareva, "Anna Sergeevna Miliukova," p. 2).
129. Miliukov, *Vosp.*, pp. 121, 123.
130. Ibid., pp. 168–69; Zhikareva, "Anna Sergeevna Miliukova," p. 2.
131. Letter to Miliukov from the Riazan' Archive Commission, May 21, 1900, in BAR, Miliukov, Catalogued correspondence, box 3.
132. Letter to Anna Miliukova from a Riazan' friend (signature indecipherable) June 5, 1900, in BAR, Miliukov, Catalogued correspondence, box 3.
133. The most important testimony to this effect is that of Kizevetter, *Na rubezhe*, p. 87, and Got'e, "Universitet," pp. 13–27.
134. The most critical assessment by a colleague comes from Ariadna Tyrkova-Vil'iams, *Na putiakh k svobode* (New York, 1952), pp. 304–5, who described Miliukov as coldly logical, personally reserved, and ambitious; see also Obolenskii, *Moia zhizn', moi sovremenniki*, pp. 442–43, who asserted that "the open coldness of Miliukov paralyzed any personal feelings of sympathy or love toward him. And indeed, he had no need of them." I. V. Gurko, who despised the Kadets in general, describes Miliukov's personal qualities as "boundless ambition, vanity, self-assurance, doctrinairism, and political amorality" (*Features and Figures*, p. 429).
135. Miliukov, *Vosp.*, p. 121.
136. Miliukov, "Russia," July 6, 1895, p. 25.
137. Miliukov, "Russia," July 4, 1896, p. 25.
138. Miliukov had met Dragomanov in Paris in 1893 while summering in France and been deeply impressed by him; it is likely that Dragomanov recommended him as his successor (*Vosp.*, p. 111).
139. Ibid., pp. 124–25. Miliukov then went to Paris for further preparation for his courses before joining the family in Switzerland for the remainder of the summer.

Chapter Three: Miliukov's Historical Thought

1. Miliukov, *Lektsii*, pp. 2, 4.
2. Miliukov, *Vosp.*, p. 88.
3. Miliukov, "Istoriosofiia g. Kareeva," *Russkaia mysl'*, November 1887, pp. 92–93, and Miliukov, *Ocherki po istorii russkoi kul'tury*, 2d ed. (St. Petersburg, 1896), 1:7. (All subsequent references to volume 1 of this work come from this edition, unless otherwise noted.) For a discussion of the Comtean positivism of the later nineteenth century, as opposed to other strains of positivism, see Philip Abrams, *The Origins of British Sociology, 1834–1914* (Chicago, 1968).
4. Miliukov, *Ocherki*, 1:7–8.
5. Ibid., p. 7.
6. Ibid., p. 9. In a review written while still in graduate school Miliukov called the deductive approach "very tempting," adding, "We can't despair at the possibility of doing this, but it is a very difficult business" ("Istoriosofiia," p. 91).
7. Miliukov, *Ocherki*, 2d ed., 2:2–3.

8. In subsequent editions of the *Studies of Russian Culture*, Miliukov expended considerable thought in explaining the exact nature of his views on economic materialism, having been charged, variously, with "trivializing" it and with being an "unwitting" economic materialist (*Ocherki*, 1:14; preface to the third edition of vol. 1, reprinted in 6th ed. [St. Petersburg, 1909], p. 308; and 2d ed., 2:3).

9. Miliukov, *Ocherki*, 1:13–14. Vucinich remarks this same pluralist view in Kovalevskii, who also opposed Gabrial Tarde's psychological interpretation of social change and Lilienfeld's organismic models of social structure as theories of key causes in social dynamics. See Vucinich, *Social Thought in Tsarist Russia*, p. 164. Miliukov shared Kovalevskii's estimation of the theories of these two thinkers; in general, it is clear that his sociological views were greatly influenced by Kovalevskii. See Miliukov, "Novaia kniga po sotsiologii," pp. 208–9.

10. Miliukov, *Ocherki*, 5th ed., 2:5. (All subsequent references to volume 2 are to this edition, unless otherwise noted.) Miliukov later wrote of Kliuchevskii that he was excessively schematic. See Miliukov, "Dva russkikh istorika," p. 320.

11. Miliukov, *Ocherki*, 1:15; the adjective "sociological" was not used in the theoretical introduction to the 1894 lecture course, but was already present in the second edition of the *Ocherki*. Miliukov's ingredients for the working of the historical process—sociological laws, milieu, and individual human actions—resemble to a certain extent Kliuchevskii's characterization of social life as the product of the dynamic relationship of the human individual, the human community, and the physical environment. The key difference was their differing views on the idea of universal laws. See Kliuchevskii, *Sochineniia*, 1:21.

12. Miliukov, *Ocherki*, 2:5.

13. I examine Miliukov's lengthy exposition of the process of the formation of a "national idea" in greater detail later in this chapter.

14. Miliukov, "Russia," July 4, 1896, p. 26.

15. Miliukov, "Novaia kniga po sotsiologii," p. 213; *Ocherki*, 1:17.

16. P. B. Struve, review of *Ocherki po istorii russkoi kul'tury*, *Novoe Slovo*, no. 1 (October 1897): 89–94. Struve praised Miliukov as the best among a very fine new generation of historians, but his evaluation of Miliukov's *Ocherki* was more severe than that of any other contemporary. He found Miliukov weak on epistemology, said he trivialized economic materialism, and also considered volume 2 of the work to be more narrative than analytical. In this review—and the polemic on Russian household industry that followed—very probably lay the seeds of the later rivalry between Struve and Miliukov. See also Struve, "Istoricheskoe i sistematicheskoe mesto russkoi kustarnoi promyshlennosti (Otvet P. N. Miliukovu)," pt. 1, *Mir Bozhii*, no. 2 (February 1898): 188–200.

17. Miliukov, *Ocherki*, 1:7; see also his denial of "the miracle of the freedom of will" in "Iuridicheskaia shkola," p. 88.

18. Vucinich, *Social Thought in Tsarist Russia*, p. 233, identifies this attitude as being typical of Russian social theorists of the period.

19. Miliukov, *Ocherki*, 1:7, "Istoriosofiia," pp. 93–94.

20. The text of Miliukov's speech at his defense is contained in the section "Istoricheskaia khronika," in *Istoricheskoe obozrenie*, no. 5 (1892): 203.

21. Miliukov, "V. O. Kliuchevskii," p. 189.

22. Miliukov, *Ocherki*, 1:2.

23. Ibid. U.S. scholars called the general reorientation in history writing, from the last decades of the nineteenth century, the "new history." For a contemporary's appraisal, see Harry Elmer Barnes, *The New History and Social Studies* (New York, 1925), espe-

cially pp. 13–17, 29–36. According to Barnes the new history was synthetic and primarily interested in establishing not how things once were but how they came about. It eschewed concentration on political, narrative history, enlarging the scope of historical inquiry and drawing upon the methodologies of the social sciences. Among orientations within the new history Barnes particularly distinguished the "collective psychological," an approach well-established in France and represented in the work of Tarde, Lucien Levy-Bruhl, Alfred Fouillée, Charles Seignobos, and Emile Durkheim; Miliukov was familiar with the work of all these individuals.

24. Miliukov, *Ocherki*, 1:19.

25. Ibid., pp. 4–5. Miliukov's attempt to distinguish strictly between pure and applied science was directed in part against the consciously "subjective" approach of the sociology of Mikhailovskii and P. A. Lavrov, which held that in the social sciences, as opposed to the natural sciences, the introduction of value judgments is not only unavoidable but desirable—unavoidable, because the social sciences deal with the phenomenon of human will and intentionality, and desirable because the aim of sociology is not merely to establish the truth but to aid in the improvement of society. For discussions of subjective sociology, see Vucinich, *Social Thought in Tsarist Russia*, pp. 23–26, and Billington, *Mikhailovsky*, pp. 25–41. Miliukov's strictures against the scholar's introducing practical considerations into an investigation also help explain his admiration for the "dynamic sociology" of Lester Ward, who elaborately demarcated the proper tasks of pure and applied sociology. Miliukov particularly recommended Ward's *Dynamic Sociology* (New York, 1903) (Miliukov, *Ocherki*, 6th ed., 1:20; on Ward, see also his article "Novaia kniga po sotsiologii," p. 206).

26. Miliukov most clearly reveals this assumption in the introductory remarks to his book *Glavnye techeniia russkoi istoricheskoi mysli*, 2d ed. (Moscow, 1898), p. 2; see also Miliukov, *Ocherki*, 2d ed., 2:2–7, and vol. 3, pt. 1, pp. 15–17.

27. Miliukov, *Ocherki*, 1:222.

28. Miliukov, *Lektsii*, pt. 1, p. 14, and *Ocherki*, 1:7.

29. Miliukov, "Istoriosofiia," p. 95.

30. Miliukov, *Lektsii*, pt. 1, pp. 14–15.

31. Miliukov, *Russia and Its Crisis*, p. 564. Miliukov's faith in progress is demonstrated by his 1917 eulogy for Maksim Kovalevskii. He noted that in 1910 Kovalevskii had slightly reworked the Comtean understanding of sociology, changing the definition of sociology from "the science of order and progress of human societies" to "the science of development and organization of human societies," which reflected his awareness that "the internal arrangement of human society is not always 'order,'" and that "'progress' is not always progress in the sense of positive movement forward." In the same breath, Miliukov insisted that Kovalevskii not only believed but *knew* that "no force could arrest the positive course of history." See Miliukov, "M. M. Kovalevskii kak sotsiolog i kak grazhdanin," in *M. M. Kovalevskii: Uchenyi, gosudarstvennyi i obshchestvennyi deiatel' i grazhdanin*, ed. K. Arsen'ev et al. (Petrograd, 1917), pp. 138, 143.

32. H. Stuart Hughes, *Consciousness and Society: The Reorientation of European Thought, 1890–1930* (New York, 1977), p. 16; Hughes calls this reorientation, as a whole, the "revolt against positivism." For an analysis of German debate on the question of historical knowledge, see Maurice Mandelbaum, *The Problem of Historical Knowledge* (New York, 1938).

33. On the Annales school, see Georg G. Iggers, *New Directions in European Historiography*, rev. ed. (Middletown, Conn., 1984), pp. 43–79. Iggers suggests that Durkheim's theory of knowledge, with its shift of emphasis from the individual to the

collectivity and its belief in "social facts" often capable of direct observation by the historian or social scientist, was part of the intellectual tradition of the Annales school. He also divides the Annales school into two periods; the first of these, lasting until approximately 1945, was more interested in mentalities and less quantitative in its approach than has been true of the postwar period. Miliukov and the Moscow school came closer to the earlier period, dominated by Marc Bloch and Lucien Febvre.

34. Ibid., p. 44.

35. Michael Karpovich, "Klyuchevskii and Recent Trends in Russian Historiography," pt. 1, *Slavonic Review* 21 (March 1943): 38.

36. This contextual approach to the study of ideas was first discussed in his unsigned review of *Vlast' Moskovskikh gosudarei: Ocherki iz istorii politicheskikh idei drevnei Rusi v kontse XVI veka*, by M. D'iakonov, *Russkaia mysl'*, October 1889, pp. 425–27, where Miliukov complained that the autocracy examined by D'iakonov wasn't a "phenomenon of political life, but one of political literature, not a fact but an idea." It was also apparent in his main charge against the juridical school, which he accuses of lacking "real" content for its formal schemas. See Miliukov, "Iuridicheskaia shkola," p. 91.

37. Miliukov, *Vosp.*, pp. 73–75.

38. Michael Karpovich, "P. N. Miliukov kak istorik," *Novyi zhurnal* (New York), no. 6 (1943): 368.

39. Miliukov reviewed history books for *Russkaia mysl'* from 1886 to 1894, also writing a regular column surveying current issues of history periodicals. These unsigned reviews are identified in the bibliography of Miliukov's work compiled by B. A. Evreinov in *P. N. Miliukov: Sbornik materialov*, pp. 313–51.

40. S. A. Solov'ev, *Sobrannye sochineniia* (St. Petersburg, 1882), p. 1060, Kliuchevskii, *Kurs russkoi istorii*, 4:265–66.

41. P. N. Miliukov, *Gosudarstvennoe khoziaistvo Rossii v pervoi chetverti XVIII stoletiia* [sic] *i reforma Petra Velikogo*, 2d ed. (St. Petersburg, 1905), "Preface" to the first edition, pp. xi–xii, and p. 544.

42. Miliukov, *Vosp.*, p. 105.

43. Miliukov, *Gosudarstvennoe khoziaistvo*, p. 546. The controversy on this point had as much to do with data used as with the conclusion drawn. Miliukov, by comparing population estimates drawn from tax lists of 1688 and 1710, estimated a 20 percent drop in the population for this period. Critics pointed out that the 1710 figures had been suspect even in Peter's own day, and that the population estimates from the 1721 tax lists present a far less bleak picture of the costs in mortality of the Petrine reforms. See M. Bezobrazov, *Russkoe obozrenie*, April 1892, cited in an unsigned review, "Novyi trud o petrovskoi reforme," *Vestnik Evropy*, no. 8 (1892): 813–33.

44. Unsigned review, "Novyi trud o petrovskoi reforme," p. 830.

45. Miliukov, *Gosudarstvennoe khoziaistvo*, p. 542. It is interesting that the scholars who took greatest umbrage at this diminution of Peter's role—Presniakov, Pavlov-Sil'vanskii, Platonov, Bestuzhev-Riumin—were all products of the "Petersburg school" of Russian history writing. On Pavlov-Sil'vanskii's early critique of Miliukov's treatment of Peter, see Thaddeus C. Radzilowski, *Feudalism, Revolution, and the Meaning of Russian History: An Intellectual Biography of Nikolai Pavlovich Pavlov-Silvanskii* (Boulder, Colo., 1994), pp. 42–46. Platonov felt that even Miliukov's more generous representation of Peter in the *Ocherki* still unduly minimized his creative role. See S. F. Platonov, *Lektsii po russkoi istorii* (St. Petersburg, 1915).

46. Nicholas Riasanovsky, *The Image of Peter the Great in Russian History and Thought* (Oxford, 1985), p. 184.

47. Pavlov-Sil'vanskii, several years after publication of Miliukov's dissertation, discovered in the Petersburg archives a collection of draft reform projects extensively marked up in Peter's own hand, which proved that Peter had in fact taken a very active role in creating the reforms. See N. V. Pavlov-Sil'vanskii, "Proekty reform v zapiskakh sovremennikov Petra Velikogo," *Zapiski istoriko-filologicheskogo fakul'teta Imperatorskogo S. Petersburgskogo universiteta*, no. 42 (St. Petersburg, 1897), especially pp. 50–52, 55–56, 76–77. Miliukov acknowledged Pavlov-Sil'vanskii's findings in his article on Peter and the reforms "Petr veliki," in Brokgauz and Efron, 23a:487–95. See also Miliukov, *Ocherki*, 2d ed. vol. 3, pt. 1, pp. 134–86, and *Ocherki*, Jubilee ed. (Paris, 1930), 3:157–217; and P. N. Miliukov et al., *Histoire de Russie* (Paris, 1932), 1:267–427.
48. In 1929 V. A. Miakotin recalled the stir created by publication of Miliukov's dissertation, saying that it was received by the historical community with "respectful amazement." See Miakotin, "P. N. Miliukov kak istorik," p. 40.
49. For Kliuchevskii's and E. V. Iakushkin's critiques of Miliukov's dissertation, see Chap. 1. Also, Miliukov, "Istoriosofiia," p. 91.
50. M. N. Pokrovskii, no great admirer of Miliukov, considered both of Miliukov's monographs on state finances indispensable. See Pokrovskii, *Ocherki istorii russkoi kul'tury*, 5th ed. (Petrograd, 1923), p. 162. A more recent assessment of Miliukov's dissertation is contained in E. V. Anisimov, *Podatnaia reforma Petra pervogo* (Moscow, 1982).
51. M. M. Bogoslovskii, *Oblastnaia reforma Petra velikogo v provintsii* (St. Petersburg, 1902); A. A. Kizevetter, *Posadskaia obshchina v Rossii XVIII stoletiia* (Moscow, 1903).
52. Miliukov, *Spornye voprosy finansovoi istorii moskovskogo gosudarstva* (Moscow, 1892), a book-length essay responding to A. S. Lappo-Danilevskii's *Organizatsiia priamogo oblozheniia v Moskovskom gosudarstve* (St. Petersburg, 1892). Miliukov differed with Lappo-Danilevskii by concluding that the *prikaz* administration had become not only more specialized but also more centralized, and in maintaining that this aided, not hindered, the conduct of the wars of the late seventeenth and early eighteenth centuries, as well as the Petrine reforms.
53. Miliukov, *Spornye voprosy*, pp. 2, 4.
54. Ibid., pp. 5–6. Miliukov's hostility to the heuristic employment of "types" perhaps accounts for his lack of interest in the work of Max Weber. Miliukov's only reference to Weber is to his article on the phenomenon of "pseudo-constitutionalism" and the liberation movement, "Russlands Übergang zum Scheinkonstitutionalismus," *Archiv für Socialwissenschaft und Politik*. See Miliukov, *Ocherki*, 6th ed., 1:219.
55. Miliukov, *Ocherki*, 1:22.
56. The book was based on Miliukov's 1886–87 course on historiography at Moscow University, which took his interpretation to his own day. According to P. A. Kireeva, it was only in the late 1870s and early 1880s that Russian higher educational institutions began to offer courses in historiography; the first such courses were offered by K. N. Bestuzhev-Riumin, M. O. Koialovich, Kliuchevskii (1887–88), and Miliukov (Kireeva, *V. O. Kliuchevskii*, pp. 6–7).
57. Miliukov, *Glavnye techeniia*, pp. 1–2.
58. Ibid., p. 1.
59. Ibid., p. 22.
60. Ibid., p. 31.
61. Ibid., pp. 37, 39.
62. Ibid., pp. 42–43.
63. Ibid., p. 69.

64. Ibid., p. 147. For a contemporary appraisal, see the unsigned review in *Russkaia mysl'*, April 1897, p. 165. Miliukov claimed that this debunking of the legend of Karamzin caused him some trouble from the historical establishment in St. Petersburg, particularly Bestuzhev-Riumin (*Vosp.*, p. 105).
65. According to Picheta, Solov'ev had noted Karamzin's dependence on Shcherbatov, but Miliukov "brilliantly and thoroughly developed" this insight. See V. I. Picheta, *Vvedenie v russkuiu istoriiu: Istochniki i istoriografiia* (Moscow, 1922), p. 107.
66. Miliukov, *Glavnye techeniia*, p. 192.
67. Ibid., p. 259, 292.
68. Martin Malia, *Alexander Herzen and the Birth of Russian Socialism* (Cambridge, Mass., 1961), p. 80, notes the importance Russians attached to the historical aspects of Schelling's philosophy, adding that this was the aspect least emphasized by Schelling himself.
69. Miliukov, *Glavnye techeniia*, pp. 311-22, 338. Miliukov devoted twelve pages to an exposition of Schellingism, including the question of how to reconcile the idea of the "lawfulness" of the historical process with the idea of personal freedom and moral worth.
70. Ibid., p. 392. His characterization of Kireevskii's reaction to Schelling is similar to that by Abbott Gleason, although Gleason more carefully underlines that Kireevskii was not a "Slavophile" at this time. See Abbott Gleason, *European and Muscovite* (Cambridge, Mass., 1972), pp. 114-15.
71. One of these historiographical pieces was his 1899 encyclopedia article on Russian history writing, which suggested that Kliuchevskii's main shortcoming was the absence of the "vital nerve" an integral, social worldview gives to scholarly work. Miliukov, "Istochniki russkoi istorii i russkaia istoriografiia," in Brokgauz and Efron, 28:444-45. Nechkina believes this remark helped prolong the estrangement between Kliuchevskii and Miliukov. See Nechkina, *Vasilii Osipovich Kliuchevskii*, p. 410.
72. P. N. Miliukov, "Liubov' u idealistov tridtsatykh godov," in *Iz istorii russkoi intelligentsii*, 2d ed., p. 105.
73. Ibid.
74. Malia, *Alexander Herzen*, p. 450 n. 73, is somewhat dismissive of this essay, holding that Miliukov took Herzen's rationalizations of his sentiments too literally.
75. Miliukov, "Liubov' u idealistov," p. 143.
76. Ibid., pp. 160, 163-64. Miliukov here takes a very thoughtful look at Natasha's sufferings and how the upbringing of young women of her class in the 1830s made for such difficulties: denied sufficient education to be prepared to keep up in thought with young men, they were also excluded from the debates "where young men decided the 'true nature' of woman and woman's love."
77. Ibid., p. 116.
78. It is Miliukov's emphasis on "life" consciously seeking to mirror art that makes this study, in my view, similar to the semiotic approach. According to that view, "Ideal representations, borrowed from books or spontaneously created in the process of literary life, were transformed into real behavior and actual life histories. Their reality became, in turn, inseparable from their artistic representations in letters, diaries, roles adopted by members of artistic groups, and, finally, literary images. Art and reality, the model and its projection in real life, are in continual interaction" (Boris Gasparov, "Introduction," in *The Semiotics of Russian Cultural History*, ed. Alexander D. Nakhimovsky and Alice Stone Nakhimovsky [Ithaca, N.Y., 1985], p. 19).
79. The only review I could find of this piece refers to it as "long and extremely cu-

rious." See the unsigned review of *Iz istorii russkoi intelligentsii*, in *Istoricheskii vestnik* 91 (March 1903): 1167.

80. In his memoirs, Miliukov maintained that while writing the lecture course that formed the foundation of *Ocherki*, he was greatly influenced in his conceptualization by two general histories of Russia written by foreigners for a non-Russian audience. Mackenzie Wallace, in his book *Russia*, and Anatole Leroy-Beaulieu, in his book *L'empire des tsars*, both asked "What is it most important to know about Russia in order to understand it?" Miliukov set himself the same practical, pedagogic task in writing his own survey of Russian cultural history for a nonspecialized—but Russian—audience. His rendering of Russian history for a foreign audience is his book *Russia and Its Crisis*.

81. Unsigned review of Miliukov's *Ocherki po istorii russkoi kul'tury*, vol. 1, in *Russkaia mysl'*, November 1896, p. 516.

82. The course was subsequently offered at Moscow University and an authorized hectograph made of it (see Chap. 2, note 8). The first version of the *Ocherki* began appearing in serial form in *Mir Bozhii* in 1895.

83. The three-volume English language edition, *Outlines of Russian Culture*, conveys an entirely inaccurate impression of the work as a whole, since it is actually an abridgement of the three parts of volume 2 alone, the part of *Ocherki* most concerned with "culture" strictly conceived, that is, high culture.

84. Miliukov, *Ocherki*, 1:17. This statement represents a retreat from his bolder assertion, in *Lektsii*, pt. 1, p. 17, that "the ancient, Kievan period of our history is separated from more recent times not only chronologically, but actually." Usually considered the first fully articulated scholarly objection to the connection of Kievan and Russian history is Mychaylo Hrushevsky's 1902 article, "The Traditional Scheme of 'Russian' History and the Problem of a Rational Organization of the History of Eastern Slavs," in *From Kievan Rus' to Modern Ukraine: Formation of the Ukrainian Nation* (Cambridge, 1984), pp. 355–64.

85. *Ocherki* has little in the way of footnotes, so there is no way of determining exactly how Miliukov arrived at his population estimates for the pre-imperial period. Still, his guess that Russia's population was stable or declining from the end of the sixteenth century to the death of Peter does fit the general European demographic trend for this period posited by scholars today; see E. A. Wrigley, *Population and History* (New York, 1969), pp. 77–79.

86. Miliukov, *Ocherki*, 1:114. This contention was not original to Miliukov, having been elaborated by Chicherin in the 1850s in his master's thesis, *Oblastnye uchrezhdeniia Rossii v XVII-m veke*; see Hamburg, *Boris Chicherin*, pp. 84–87.

87. Miliukov, *Ocherki*, 1:114–15, 164–67, 177–80. Michael Hittle notes that Miliukov ignored the circumstance that many European cities had their origins as the administrative centers of medieval rulers or as centers of Roman power. He also suggests that many Russian cities had "more in the way of economic enterprise than Miliukov was prepared to acknowledge." See J. Michael Hittle, *The Service City: State and Townsmen in Russia, 1600–1800* (Cambridge, Mass., 1979), p. 7.

88. Edward Keenan, for example, has noted the ways in which Muscovite political culture was "admirably suited to Muscovy's needs." See Edward L. Keenan, "Muscovite Political Folkways," *Russian Review* 45 (April 1986): 119.

89. Miliukov, *Ocherki*, 5th ed., 2:1.

90. Ibid., p. 398 (emphasis in the original).

91. Ibid., pp. 9, 399.

92. Ibid., p. 393.

93. Ibid., p. 391. Miliukov's treatment of the official church betrays his own dismissive attitude toward that institution. In general, this volume of the *Ocherki* is the weakest and the most dated, being highly marked by Miliukov's preference for the realistic genres in art and literature of the nineteenth century.
94. Ibid., pp. 392–93.
95. Ibid., p. 7.
96. Ibid., pp. 24, 26, 33–176, 179.
97. Ibid., pp. 10, 149, 161, 244. It is important to note that Miliukov carefully distinguished between Russian Orthodoxy in particular and Eastern Orthodoxy in general, observing that the latter's level of spiritual attainment was much higher. The Church was *also* a victim of ancient Russia's low level of cultural development.
98. The general exception was architecture, since "architecture is the most material aspect of art and must answer to conditions of climate, available materials, popular customs" (Miliukov, *Ocherki*, 2:211).
99. See, for example, Richard Pipes, *Karamzin's Memoir on Ancient and Modern Russia* (New York, 1974), p. 8; Anatole Mazour, *Modern Russian Historiography* (Princeton, N.J., 1958), p. 134; and Riha, *A Russian European*, p. 55. I am inclined to agree with Michael Karpovich, who felt that Miliukov's book on historiography is equally brilliant and enduring. See Karpovich, "P. N. Miliukov kak istorik," p. 368.
100. Miliukov, *Ocherki*, 2d ed., vol. 3, pt. 1, p. 3.
101. Ibid., 2:7, and 2d ed., vol. 3, pt. 2, p. 16.
102. Ibid., 2d ed., vol. 3, pt. 1, pp. 7, 10. Miliukov also stresses the religious coloration of national distinctions as they first come to be recognized.
103. Ibid., pp. 9–10.
104. Ibid., pp. 11–12. For Miliukov, the press is of great importance here, since it furnishes the means for a high degree of interaction between members of a given society: "For the creation of the public opinion of modern times the press is just as necessary a means as language for the national consciousness of all times."
105. Ibid., p. 24.
106. Ibid., 3d ed., vol. 3, pt. 1, pp. 25–26, 35–46. The discussion of the Third Rome theory was one of the features of *Ocherki* considered most novel and compelling by contemporaries; a more recent support of Miliukov's argument concerning the south Slav and Bulgarian origins of the theory is presented in Dmitri Stremooukhoff, "Moscow, the Third Rome: Sources of the Doctrine," in *The Structure of Russian History*, ed. Michael Cherniavsky (New York, 1970), p. 117.
107. Hrushevsky allowed for more Kievan cultural and institutional influence on Muscovy than Miliukov did, but their formulations of the origins and nature of the view connecting Kievan history to "Russian" history are strikingly similar. Consider these three points in Hrushevsky's argument: (1) "This is an old scheme which had its beginnings in the historiographical scheme of the Moscow scribes, and at its basis lies the genealogical idea"; (2) "The genealogical approach may have satisfied the Moscow scribes, but modern science looks for *genetic* connections and thus has no right to unite the 'Kievan period' with the 'Volodimir period' (emphasis added); (3) "The Volodimir-Moscow state was neither the successor nor the inheritor of the Kiev state; it grew out of its own roots" (Hrushevsky, "The Traditional Scheme of 'Russian' History," pp. 356–57).
108. Miliukov, *Ocherki*, 3d ed., vol. 3, pt. 1, pp. 78, 92.
109. It was also from the Time of Troubles that the European influence on Russian life and thought grew ever larger (ibid., pp. 75–76).

110. Ibid., pt. 2, pp. 135–43.
111. Ibid., 2d ed., vol. 3, pt. 2—this is the subject of the entire second book of volume 3. The exposition in the *Ocherki* stopped at the end of Catherine's reign, perhaps out of censorship considerations. But in the lecture course upon which the *Ocherki* was based, Miliukov traced the development of social consciousness up to his own day, concluding with a survey of the penetration of this thought from the capitals to the provinces. He saw this as a harbinger of progress, since the provinces were coming to form a "reservoir of social feeling" that would increasingly supply an organic quality to development: "The time will come when the development of Russian culture will cease depending on accidental causes" (Miliukov, *Lektsii*, pt. 3, p. 162). Miliukov also carried his analysis to his own day in *Russia and Its Crisis*; see Chapter 5.
112. V. A. Miakotin, "Kurs russkoi istorii P. N. Miliukova," *Russkoe bogatstvo*, November 1896, p. 17, and M. Pomialovskii, review of volume 1 of *Ocherki*, in *Istoricheskii vestnik* 87 (February 1902): 689.
113. N. V. Pavlov-Sil'vanskii, *Feodalizm v drevnei Rusi* (St. Petersburg, 1907), p. 24. Pavlov-Sil'vanskii's dispute with Miliukov on the subject of feudalism was part of his larger critique of Miliukov's "break" with the historiographic tradition of Solov'ev, Chicherin, and others who saw greater similarity between European and Russian development than Miliukov allowed for. For a thoughtful discussion of this issue, see Vandalkovskaia, *P. N. Miliukov, A. A. Kizevetter*, pp. 185–210.
114. "P.B.," "Neskol'ko zamechanii ob 'Ocherkakh po istorii russkoi kul'tury' g. Miliukova," *Russkoe bogatstvo*, August 1898, pp. 1–21, pp. 10–11. (It is worth mentioning that this was not P. B. Struve).
115. Miliukov was not at first persuaded by Pavlov-Sil'vanskii's thesis, maintaining that the existence in Russia of certain feudal characteristics did not mean Russia had had a feudal order; see P. Miliukov, "Feodalizm v Rossii," in Brokgauz and Efron, 70:548–50. He incorporated Pavlov-Sil'vanskii's findings on feudalism in the fifth edition of volume 1 of the *Ocherki* (St. Petersburg, 1904), which was the most substantive revision of any part of the work before the revolution. In emigration, volume 1 would again be the most revised; Miliukov planned its transformation into two new volumes, only the first of which he managed to publish before his death: *Ocherki po istorii russkoi kul'tury*, vol. 1, pt. 1 (Paris, 1937); part 2 was edited by N. E. Andreev and finally published in 1964 by the Hague.
116. Miliukov, *Ocherki*, 2d ed., vol. 3, pt. 1, p. 21.
117. Ibid., p. 26.
118. Ibid., p. 18.
119. In a very revealing phrase, Miliukov describes the foreign suburb in Moscow in the seventeenth century as "a small oasis of Europe amid a cultural desert" (ibid., 3d ed., vol. 3, pt. 1, p. 101).
120. Miliukov tended, especially in volume 3 of *Ocherki*, to describe views of past times in anachronistic terms, as when he talks about "Muscovite constitutionalists of the sixteenth century" in pt. 1, p. 62. Scholars of Miliukov's generation were less cautious, in general, in the use of such terms, but I think this is primarily a reflection of considered choice of words for a popular audience.
121. Ibid., Jubilee ed., vol. 3, pts. 1 and 2. I take up the evolution of Miliukov's thinking on nationalism as a potentially progressive phenomenon in Chapter 7.
122. Compare, for instance, J. R. Green, *A Short History of the English People*, 4 vols. (New York, 1895); Karl Lamprecht, *Deutsche Geschichte*, 12 vols. (Berlin, 1891–1909); and Alfred Rambaud, *Histoire de la civilisation francaise*, 2 vols. (Paris, 1885–87).

123. Only James Billington's *The Icon and the Axe* (New York, 1966), can compare with the extent of the treatment of the history of the Church and religiosity as they contributed to, or adversely affected, Russian thought and creativity.
124. Kliuchevskii and Solov'ev recognized the defense considerations underlying the autocratic form of government, but neither linked this to the poverty and low population level of the Great Russian territory as the cause for the development of autocracy.
125. An interesting treatment of modernization theory, cultural imperialism, and "impact-response" models of change in Western historiography on China is contained in Paul A. Cohen, *Discovering History in China* (New York, 1984); there are a number of suggestive parallels for the Western student of Russian history.
126. Miliukov, "Liubov' u idealistov," p. 144.
127. Miliukov, *Ocherki*, 3d ed., vol. 3, pt. 1, pp. 138–40.
128. See Chapter 5.
129. Miliukov, *Ocherki*, 2d ed., vol. 3, pt. 1, pp. 11–12.
130. Ibid., 2:245, 264; see also Miliukov, *Russia and Its Crisis*, pp. 28–29.
131. Miliukov, *Ocherki*, 5th ed., 2:304–28.
132. Ibid., 3d ed., vol. 3, pt. 1, pp. 91–92.
133. Karpovich, "Klyuchevskii and Recent Trends in Russian Historiography," pp. 36, 38.
134. Kliuchevskii, *Kurs russkoi istorii*, 4:8.

Chapter Four: Scholarship and Opposition

1. The expression used by Miliukov, *gody skitanii*, is equivalent to the German *Wanderjahre*.
2. Miliukov, *Vosp.*, pp. 125–26.
3. Ibid. Details on Karavelov are drawn from Richard J. Crampton, *Bulgaria, 1878–1918; A History* (Boulder, Colo., 1983), pp. 30, 50–53, 77–79, 146, 164, and Cyril Black, *The Establishment of Constitutional Government in Bulgaria* (Princeton, N.J., 1943), pp. 85–87, 121, 261. On Malinov, who was to be a leader of the pro-Russian faction in the National Assembly in 1917, see Robert Johnson, *Tradition versus Revolution: Russia and the Balkans in 1917* (Boulder, Colo., 1977), pp. 19, 48–55.
4. Miliukov's book on the Bulgarian constitution is replete with stories of political deals, compromises, and miscalculations, many of which clearly came from inside sources. It first appeared in three installments in the journal *Russkoe bogatstvo* and was also published in a volume of collected articles and as a separate volume, in Bulgarian translation; I have used the serialized text. P. N. Miliukov, "Bolgarskaia konstitutsiia," *Russkoe bogatstvo*, August 1904, pp. 193–216; September 1904, 26–69; October 1904, 28–59.
5. Miliukov to Aleksandra V. Gol'shtein, n.d., in BAR, Miliukov, Catalogued correspondence.
6. Miliukov, *Vosp.*, pp. 126–27; Crampton, *Bulgaria*, pp. 166–73, 229–33.
7. Miliukov, *Vosp.*, p. 127. He intended to ask for permission to travel to St. Petersburg to see if he could settle the affair, a request that was apparently denied (Miliukov to Gol'shtein, BAR, Miliukov, Catalogued correspondence).
8. On the Macedonian question, see Crampton, *Bulgaria*, pp. 233, 235, 237, 251.
9. P. Miliukov, "Pis'mo iz Makedonii," *Russkie vedomosti*, no. 159 (1898): 3. The letters appeared in nos. 159, 168, 181, 183, 277 (1898), and nos. 4, 7, 15, 21, 28, 36, 44, 60, 85 (1899).

10. Miliukov, "Pis'mo iz Makedonii," no. 277 (1898), relates that for these people, Russia's call for disarmament, which resulted in the Hague conference, was inexplicable and upsetting: they did not see its humanitarian motives, understanding only that Russia could not fulfill its "Macedonian mission" under world peace.
11. Miliukov, *Vosp.*, pp. 127–32.
12. Apparently Miliukov could have returned home at least four months before he did, but put off his return in order to excavate in Macedonia, then evaluate his findings (Anna Miliukova to N. Vernadskaia, n.d., in ARAN f. 518, op. 7, d. 332, l. 22). Shortly after his return to Russia he left again in summer 1899 to participate in digs in Macedonia and what is now Albania (Miliukov, *Vosp.*, pp. 132–35).
13. Miliukov, *Vosp.*, p. 127.
14. Ibid. The Bulgarians demonstrated their appreciation of his partisanship in 1929, when the Bulgarian government funded the jubilee edition of the *Ocherki*, issued in honor of Miliukov's seventieth birthday. His foreign policy views are examined in detail in Chapter 8.
15. See Chapters 3 and 7.
16. Miliukov, "Bolgarskaia konstitutsiia," pt. 2, p. 26, and pt. 3, p. 56. Among the features of the Bulgarian constitution endorsed by Miliukov were its unicameral legislature, provisions for the legislature's supervision of the behavior of the executive branch, and its right to initiate legislation ("Bolgarskaia konstitutsiia," pt. 1, pp. 208–14, and pt. 3, pp. 50–52). He felt its main shortcomings concerned insufficient limitations on monarchical prerogatives, insufficient means for reversing legislative violations of the constitution, and the party "spoils system" in distributing government offices (pt. 1, pp. 200, 207; pt. 2, pp. 33–64; and pt. 3, pp. 38–39, 48, 55–56).
17. Ibid, pt. 2, p. 28.
18. Ibid., pt. 3, p. 30.
19. Miliukov, *Vosp.*, p. 135. While still in Sofia, Miliukov had requested permission to live in St. Petersburg, which was denied (Anna Miliukova to N. Vernadskaia, n.d., in ARAN, f. 518, op. 7, no. 332, l. 22).
20. Klaus Frolich, *The Emergence of Russian Constitutionalism, 1900–1904: The Relationship between Social Mobility and Political Group Formation in Pre-revolutionary Russia*, trans. Suzanne M. Read (The Hague, 1981), pp. 48–49; on the student strike movement of 1899, see Kassow, *Students*, pp. 90–119.
21. Miliukov, *Vosp.*, p. 135.
22. Ekaterina Kuskova, a former Social Democrat who was one of the founders and leaders of the Union of Liberation, described the radicalization of Russian society at the beginning of the twentieth century in an article titled "Heel to the left." See Kuskova, "Kren nalevo," *Sovremennye zapiski* 44 (1930): 366–95.
23. That Miliukov experienced no difficulty in legally publishing works in Russia of a nonpolitical nature, despite being barred from teaching and under observation by the police, illustrates the inconsistencies of tsarist censorship. The financial arrangements with *Mir Bozhii* are discussed in Anna Miliukov to N. Vernadskaia, n.d., in ARAN, f. 518, op. 7, no. 332, l. 35.
24. Iuzhakov's letter of January 22, 1901, to Miliukov opened with the inauspicious declaration, "To your categorical question, do you have an absolute veto concerning articles, I just as categorically answer, *no, you do not.*" A day later Iuzhakov wrote defensively, "I very much regret the insistence with which you stand on your point of view. I have been a member of various editorial boards for twenty-five years now and think that this gives sufficient foundation for editorial conduct" (BAR, Miliukov, Arranged corre-

spondence, box 3). Miliukov refers to his reputation for tactlessness in "Rokovye gody," September 1938, p. 112.

25. Miliukov, *Vosp.*, pp. 136–37.

26. A brief account of the publishing history of *Mir Bozhii* is contained in "Marksistskaia periodicheskaia pechat', 1896–1906 gg.," *Krasnyi arkhiv* 18, (1926): 177–84. In 1904 the journal was renamed *Sovremennyi mir* and eventually came to be regarded, unambiguously, as a Social Democratic organ.

27. N. Severnyi to Miliukov, January 19, 1900, in BAR, Miliukov, Arranged correspondence, box 3.

28. Miliukov, *Vosp*, p. 137. On the strong-willed Davydova, see Tyrkova-Vil'iams, *Na putiakh*, p. 37.

29. A contributor to both journals favorably contrasted the atmosphere at *Mir Bozhii* with the more sober and weighty conclaves of the journal *Russkoe bogatstvo*, where literature and all other departments took a back seat to political questions (L. Vrangel', "'Russkoe bogatstvo' i 'Mir Bozhii,'" *Novyi zhurnal* [New York], no. 69 [1962]: 163, 168.

30. Vrangel', "'Russkoe bogatstvo,'" pp. 165–66. On Mikhailovskii's declining years—the time when Miliukov knew him—see Billington, *Mikhailovsky*, pp. 172–82.

31. Miliukov, *Vosp.*, pp. 138, 182, and "Pamiati V. A. Miakotina," p. 2. A description of the arguments that frequently broke out between the two men at gatherings in the Mikhailovskii home is in Vrangel', "'Russkoe bogatstvo,'" p. 164. The Miliukovs and Miakotins nonetheless remained close friends throughout their lives.

32. Miliukov later described, with some sarcasm, the exclusivity of the radical intelligentsia (*Vosp.*, pp. 227–28). I. V. Gessen felt Miliukov's tolerance and disinclination toward "cliquishness" greatly contributed to his speedy rise as leader of the liberals in 1905. See Gessen, *V dvukh vekakh*, p. 203.

33. The nature of Miliukov's involvement in the Free Economic Society in 1899–1902 is unclear; in his memoirs he does not mention belonging to it at this time. That he must have been fairly active is suggested by a letter written to him by Count Petr Geiden, the society's president, inquiring whether Miliukov would be willing to be elected secretary of the society: "It is important that we choose a candidate not only as desirable as you, but one desirous of accepting election" (Count Geiden to Miliukov, August 11, 1901, in BAR, Miliukov, Arranged correspondence, box 3).

34. Miliukov, *Vosp.*, pp. 135, 182, and "Rokovye gody," *Russkie zapiski* (Paris), November 1938, p. 138. In his memoirs Miliukov mistakenly identifies this organization as the creation of the Literary Fund, an older organization that also benefited writers but never assumed the frankly political character of the Writers' Union. See V. R. Leikina-Svirskaia, *Russkaia intelligentsiia v 1900–1917 godakh* (Moscow, 1981), pp. 135–37.

35. Galai, *Liberation Movement*, pp. 99–101. The most detailed account of the history and activities of the Writers' Union is found in Jonathan Sanders, "The Union of Unions" (Ph.D. diss., Columbia University, 1986), pp. 52–66.

36. *Severnyi kur'er*, March 17, 1900, p. 2, cited in Sanders, "Union of Unions," p. 53, and Miliukov, *Vosp.*, p. 138.

37. Quoted in Alexander Kaun, *Maxim Gorky and His Russia* (New York, 1931), p. 281.

38. The other members of the bureau were V. Ia. Bogucharskii, V. I. Charnoluskii, N. A. Rubakin, and A. A. Nikonov. Information on the bureau and projected organization comes from a letter of Bogucharskii to Belokonskii cited in Sanders, "Union of Unions," p. 66.

39. The gist of his presentation is reported in *Severnyi kur'er*, November 13, 1900,

cited in Sanders, "Union of Unions," p. 57. The congress itself is treated briefly in Leikina-Sverskaia, *Russkaia intelligentsiia*, p. 137.
40. Miliukov, *Vosp.*, p. 138, and "Rokovye gody," *Russkie zapiski* (Paris), June 1938, p. 116.
41. GARF, f. 102 00, 1900 g., d. 108, cited in Shatsillo, *Russkii liberalizm*, p. 53.
42. BAR, Miliukov, Arranged correspondence, box 3.
43. Paris Okhrana Archive, Hoover Library, Stanford, Calif., File 17: "P. N. Miliukov," Report of July 1902, describing Miliukov's activities in 1900.
44. Miliukov, *Vosp.*, p. 138, and "P. L. Lavrov (Nekrolog)," pt. 2, *Mir Bozhii*, March 1900, pp. 32–34.
45. Miliukov, *Vosp.*, pp. 138–39, and "Rokovye gody," *Russkie zapiski* (Paris), April 1938, p. 113.
46. A certain vagueness in Miliukov's description in his memoirs of his arrest creates the impression that the talk was given shortly after Lavrov's death on February 6, 1900, and that he was therefore arrested in February of 1900, not 1901; however, in a letter to Natalia Vernadskaia Anna Miliukova refers to his having been arrested suddenly (Miliukov, *Vosp.*, p. 140, and "Rokovye gody," April 1938, pp. 112–14; Anna Miliukova to N. Vernadskaia, February 8, 1901, in ARAN, f. 518, op. 7, d. 332, l. 11; the note to Anna is cited in Dumova, *Liberal v Rossii*, p. 199).
47. Miliukov, *Vosp.*, p. 140.
48. Ibid., pp. 139–40. In his memoirs, Miliukov says he was in prison for six months; in a different account he makes it three ("Rokovye gody," April 1938, p. 111). The latter version appears to be the correct one.
49. Miliukov, *Vosp.*, pp. 139–40, and Miliukova to N. Vernadskaia, February 24, 1901, in ARAN, f. 518, op. 7, no. 332, l. 8.
50. A discussion of the circumstances leading up to the demonstration is contained in Shatsillo, *Russkii liberalizm*, p. 129.
51. The demonstration and its aftermath is described in Kaun, *Maxim Gorky and His Russia*, pp. 321–23, and Kassow, *Students*, pp. 127–32. The demonstration is also described at length by one participant who was arrested, Tyrkova-Vil'iams, in *Na putiakh*, pp. 64–74.
52. Frolich, *Russian Constitutionalism*, p. 50. Among contemporaries who identified the Kazan' Square incident as the turning point in their attitude toward the autocracy were Tyrkova-V'iliams, *Na putiakh*, p. 90, and Gessen, *V dvukh vekakh*, pp. 159–60.
53. Galai, *Liberation Movement*, p. 115; Miliukov, *Vosp.*, pp. 140–41.
54. According to N. M. Pirumova, the "Petrunkevich group" had tried to set up precisely such a newspaper abroad in 1895–96 and again in 1897; following these failures, the group shelved the idea of a newspaper until 1901 (*Zemskoe liberal' noe dvizhenie*, pp. 214–16, 221–23).
55. In George Fischer's opinion, 1901 should be regarded as the beginning of the "new liberalism" in Russia: prior to that time, Russian liberalism was not a movement but "a state of mind, a hazy cluster of political ideals and programs" (*Russian Liberalism*, pp. 119, 129). Nathan Smith, tracing the origins of the Kadet party, takes the founding of *Osvobozhdenie* as the beginning of constitutional democracy. See Nathan Smith, "The Constitutional-Democratic Movement in Russia, 1902–1906" (Ph.D. diss., University of Illinois, 1958), p. 31.
56. The sketchiness of the sources allows for some disagreement concerning when certain steps were taken and agreements reached in the founding of *Osvobozhdenie*. The only full-scale account by a participant is the history of the Union of Liberation by Dmitrii Shakhovskoi, "Soiuz osvobozhdeniia," pt. 2, *Zarnitsy*, no. 2 (1909): 81–171.

The most important scholarly treatments are contained in Frolich, *Russian Constitutionalism*, pp. 93–100; Pipes, *Struve*, 1:310–16; Galai, *Liberation Movement*, pp. 116–19, 131; and Shatsillo, *Russkii liberalizm*, pp. 64–76. Useful information is also to be found in E. D. Chermenskii, *Burzhuaziia i tsarizm v pervoi russkoi revolutsii*, 2d ed. (Moscow, 1970), pp. 27–31.

57. Vernadskii was a professor of mineralogy at Moscow University and close personal friend of Petrunkevich. Miliukov and Vernadskii do not appear to have been especially close at this time, but their wives were intimate friends, which frequently brought the two men together. See ARAN, f. 518, op. 7, no. 332, "Letters of Anna S. Miliukova to N. Vernadskaia, 1897–1917."

58. Petrunkevich, *Iz zapisok*, pp. 336–37.

59. Ibid., p. 337.

60. Miliukov, *Vosp.*, p. 141, and "Rokovye gody," June 1938, pp. 116–17. In the memoir account of this incident Miliukov incorrectly states that the Union of Liberation had already been founded in Switzerland by this time—the organizational meeting in Switzerland took place two years later, in summer 1903.

61. On Struve's intellectual development during this period see Pipes, *Struve*, 1:252–63, 274–79, and, especially, chapter 12.

62. Shakhovskoi, "Soiuz osvobozhdeniia," pp. 86–87. It is unclear when the crucial question of the editor was settled. According to Shmuel Galai, the basic agreement was reached as early as April 1901, when Struve met with Petrunkevich in Tver'. ("A Note on the Establishment of the Liberation Movement," *Russian Review* 37 [July 1978]: 312). Accepting this date would call into question Miliukov's account of the initial approach made to him, since he was in prison until mid-April. Frolich believes the agreement was reached in early fall, as does Shatsillo; see Frolich, *Russian Constitutionalism*, pp. 93–94, and Shatsillo, *Russkii liberalizm*, p. 75, and "Novoe o 'Soiuz osvobozhdeniiia,'" p. 137. Richard Pipes argues that Struve was acting independently until March 1902, when a firm commitment was finally worked out with the Petrunkevich group (*Struve*, 1:311–18).

63. The organizational work done by Bogucharskii, Shakhovskoi, and others is described in Galai, *Liberation Movement*, pp. 118–19; Frolich, *Russian Constitutionalism*, pp. 95–96; and Shakovskoi, "Soiuz osvobozhdeniia," p. 87.

64. The Finnish circle was later transformed into the St. Petersburg branch of the Union of Liberation and was largely responsible for organization of the so-called "Culinary Committee," which served as a surrogate for the banned Union of Writers (Galai, *Liberation Movement*, pp. 166–67; Gessen, *V dvukh vekakh*, pp. 167–68).

65. Miliukov does not mention the Finnish circle in his memoirs and says his cooperation with *Osvobozhdenie* began when he was asked to help draft its programmatic article, in early spring 1902 (*Vosp.*, p. 164). This does not preclude his having taken some part in the circle, however, since he omits many activities and affiliations from this period in his memoir accounts.

66. Miliukov, *Vosp.*, pp. 164–65. Kizevetter, *Na rubezhe*, pp. 336–37, describes a meeting in Moscow at the home of V. I. Vernadskii, where Miliukov's article and the program and distribution of the new journal were discussed. Participants included the Petrunkevich brothers, Vernadskii, Shakhovskoi, Novgorodtsev, Bogucharskii, and Kizevetter; Miliukov's article and the journal's program were approved by all present.

67. A third article, "An Open Letter from a Group of Zemstvo Activists," also appeared in the first issue. More conservative than the other two major articles, it called for reform while condemning equally governmental anarchy and anarchy from below.

See "Otkrytoe pis'mo ot gruppy zemskikh deiatelei," *Osvobozhdenie*, June 18/July 1, 1902, pp. 13–14.

68. P. B. Struve, "Ot redaktora," *Osvobozhdenie*, June 18/July 1, 1902, pp. 1–2, 3.

69. Ibid., p. 2.

70. Ibid., pp. 5, 6.

71. [Miliukov], "Ot russkikh konstitutsionalistov," *Osvobozhdenie*, June 18/July 1, 1902, p. 9.

72. Ibid., pp. 7–8.

73. Ibid., p. 8.

74. Ibid., pp. 9–10. "Supreme control" presumably refers to the principle of a ministry responsible to the people's representatives.

75. Ibid., pp. 11–12.

76. Ibid., p. 12.

77. Struve, "Ot redaktora," p. 2; P. Struve and S. Frank, "Ocherki filosofii kul'tury," pt. 1, *Poliarnaia zvezda*, December 22, 1905, p. 110, cited in Judith Zimmerman, "Between Revolution and Reaction: The Constitutional Democratic Party, October 1905 to June 1907" (Ph.D. diss., Columbia University, 1967), p. 82.

78. By liberalism I mean specifically the three currents contained within the liberal Constitutional Democratic Party itself. Characterizations of the Kadet left wing, associated with Moscow lawyer M. L. Mandel'shtam and later with Nikolai Nekrasov, and the more theoretical right wing, whose chief spokesman was Struve, are to be found in Zimmerman, "Between Revolution and Reaction," pp. 66–82. Employing the term liberalism more broadly, Donald Treadgold, *Lenin and His Rivals* (Cambridge, Mass., 1958), pp. 117–18, identifies three groups of liberals, which had coalesced by 1898: the moderate "Slavophiles" of the Shipov type; moderate "empiricists" such as Vasilii Maklakov; and "those who, following Miliukov, were radical on rationalist and westernizing grounds."

79. See, for instance, Miliukov, *Russia and Its Crisis*, pp. 523, 560–61, and the article "Protivorechiia bolshevistskoi agitatsii protiv dumy," in *God bor'by: Publitsisticheskaia khronika, 1905–1906* (St. Petersburg, 1907).

80. Miliukov, "'Partii' ili 's"ezdy'?" *Syn otechestva*, April 21, 1905, p. 2; the text is reprinted in Miliukov, *God bor'by*, pp. 38–41.

81. For the publication history of *Osvobozhdenie*, including estimated circulation figures and the means by which it was distributed, see Shatsillo, *Russkii liberalizm*, pp. 94–102. Tyrkova-Vil'iams was caught, arrested, and convicted the first time she tried to smuggle copies of the paper into the country; liberationist friends organized her escape abroad (Tyrkova-Vil'iams, *Na putiakh*, pp. 131–69).

82. Cited in Shatsillo, *Russkii liberalizm*, p. 84.

83. Twelve articles and letters signed with the initials "ss," Miliukov's pseudonym in *Osvobozhdenie*, appeared in the journal. Of these, only the articles are listed in the published bibliography of Miliukov's work; Miliukov's important letters of February 16, 1903, and March 7, 1904, are omitted, as is the unsigned article "Ot russkikh konstitutsionalistov" ("Bibliografiia pechatnykh trudov Pavla Nikolaevicha Miliukova [1886–1930]," compiled by B. A. Evreinov, in Smirnov et al., eds., *P. N. Miliukov*, pp. 313–58).

84. Miliukov, *Vosp.*, p. 166.

85. The two pieces for *Osvobozhdenie* are "Ot russkikh konstitutionalistov" and "Chto takoe konstitutsiia Loris-Melikova?" November 18, 1902. The Serbian article, "Srednevekovoi ugolok v sovremennoi Evrope (iz poezdki v Staruiu Serbiiu)," *Zhurnal dlia vsekh*, no. 3 (pp. 329–46), no. 4 (pp. 467–80), and no. 5 (pp. 579–88.) The historical works included part 1 of volume 3 of the *Ocherki*, *Natsionalizm i obshchestvennoe mne-*

nie (St. Petersburg, 1901); the revised, third edition of volume 2 of the *Ocherki, Tserkov' i shkola*, and the first six installments of the second part of the third volume of the *Ocherki*, serialized in *Mir Bozhii* in 1901–2. Other historical works include the collection *Iz istorii russkoi intelligentsii*; encyclopedia articles on Russian universities, Russian feudalism, and the physiocrats in Russia, all for the Brokgauz and Efron encyclopedia; and the edition of the *razriadnaia kniga* he supervised for the Moscow University Imperial Society of History and Russian Antiquities: *Drevneishaia Razriadnaia Kniga ofitsial'noi redaktsii (po 1565 g.)* (Moscow, 1901). Full publication details are contained in the bibliography.

86. Batiushkov to Miliukov, May 1, 1900, in BAR, Miliukov, Catalogued correspondence, box 3. Also present at the meeting were several other historians, including Lappo-Danilevskii and Ol'denburg. In the memoirs, Miliukov mistakenly dates the meeting to summer 1901 (*Vosp.*, pp. 141–42).

87. Miliukov to Charles Crane, April 25, 1902, in BAR, Miliukov, Catalogued correspondence, box 3, and Miliukov, *Vosp.*, p. 142.

88. According to Riha, *A Russian European*, p. 59, n. 85, Miliukov knew, in addition to his native Russian, Sanskrit, Latin, Greek, Lithuanian, French, German, English, Bulgarian, Serbo-Croatian, Turkish, Finnish, Czech, Polish, Ukrainian, Norwegian, Armenian, and modern Greek. Italian should also be added to the list.

89. Miliukov, *Vosp.*, pp. 142–43, 164. Miliukov's whereabouts following the February meeting in Tver' are difficult to determine. He states in his memoirs that he was already out of the country when founders and supporters of *Osvobozhdenie* gathered in Moscow (in April 1902) for the final editing of his program article. If the memoirs are reliable on his being abroad at the time of the Moscow gathering, his "summer trip" to England lasted no less than six months—from at least April to the end of September, when he returned to Russia.

90. Ibid., pp. 142, 164.

91. In an undated letter to Natalia Vernadskaia, Anna Miliukova describes her husband's return home, which produced an endless stream of visits from friends and colleagues, and preparations for his prison term, which was to commence October 1, 1902 (ARAN f. 518, op. 7, no. 332, l. 39).

92. Miliukov, *Vosp.*, p. 143, and Zhikareva, "Anna Sergeevna Miliukova," p. 2.

93. Miliukov, *Vosp.*, pp. 143–45.

94. The text of the letter is published in *V. O. Kliuchevskii: Pis'ma, Dnevniki, Aforizmy i mysli ob istorii* (Moscow, 1968), p. 197. This collection was compiled by P. A. Kireeva and A. A. Zimin, under the editorship of Kliuchevskii's biographer, M. V. Nechkina; archival citations for individual documents are not included. See also Nechkina, *Vasilii Osipovich Kliuchevskii*, p. 410.

95. Kliuchevskii to Miliukov, early 1903, in *V. O. Kliuchevskii: Pis'ma, Dnevniki, Aforizmy*, pp. 197–98.

96. Miliukov, "V. O. Kliuchevskii," pp. 212–16. On their secret discussions concerning the Bulygin Duma, see Chapter 6.

97. Miliukov, *Russia and Its Crisis*, pp. 516–17.

Chapter Five: Russian Liberalism

1. Shakhovskoi to Struve, early November 1902, in TsPA [RTsKhID], f. 279, k. 13, l. 28, cited in Shatsillo, *Russkii liberalizm*, pp. 78–80. On the May zemstvo congress, see Galai, *Liberation Movement*, pp. 145–51; Sergei Witte was then minister of finance.

2. Struve first advanced the call for convocation of a zemskii sobor' in an editorial in *Osvobozhdenie*, November 2, 1902, pp. 149–50; he developed his ideas fully in the editorial of December 2, pp. 185–89.
3. Miliukov, "K ocherednym voprosam," pt. 1, *Osvobozhdenie*, February 16/March 1, 1903, pp. 289–91; P. B. Struve, "K ocherednym voprosam," ibid., pp. 291–92. In the opinion of Klaus Frolich, this exchange was the turning point of the organizational development of Russian constitutionalism. See Frolich, *Russian Constitutionalism*, p. 318, n. 267.
4. Miliukov, "K ocherednym voprosam," p. 289.
5. Ibid., pp. 289–90.
6. Ibid., pp. 290–91.
7. Struve, "K ocherednym voprosam," pp. 291–92.
8. In "K ocherednym voprosam," Miliukov called their future organization "liberal" and therefore for the first time numbered himself—if somewhat indirectly—among the liberals. Russian liberals actually tended to refrain from characterizing themselves as "liberal," since this word had acquired a rather negative connotation, but I believe Miliukov would have identified himself as a liberal earlier if he had considered himself to be such. On the history of the use of the word "liberal" in Russia, see Charles Timberlake, "Introduction: The Concept of Liberalism in Russia," in *Essays on Russian Liberalism*, pp. 1–17.
9. For a rebuttal of the old argument holding that changing social composition pushed liberalism to the left, see Gregory Freeze, "A National Liberation Movement and the Shift in Russian Liberalism, 1901–1903," *Slavic Review* 28 (March 1969): 81–91.
10. Gessen, *V dvukh vekakh*, pp. 199–200, 279. A Jew who converted to Christianity, Gessen wrote that he found philo-Semitism as offensive as anti-Semitism; Miliukov was a rarity among the intelligentsia in being simply free of prejudice.
11. A discussion of the manifesto is contained in Frolich, *Russian Constitutionalism*, pp. 23–24.
12. "ss" [Miliukov], "Derzhavnyi maskarad," *Osvobozhdenie*, March 19/April 1, 1903, pp. 321–23.
13. For a treatment emphasizing the role of the economic crisis in the mobilization of social groups for political organization, see Frolich, *Russian Constitutionalism*, pp. 46–48. The effect of the pogrom on consolidating the ranks of the radical intelligentsia in St. Petersburg is discussed in Galai, *Liberation Movement*, pp. 167–68.
14. Among participants of the Schaffhausen conference who wrote descriptions of the meetings were Shakhovskoi, "Soiuz osvobozhdeniia," pp. 105–7, and Petrunkevich, *Iz zapisok*, pp. 337–39. For scholarly accounts of the conference see Galai, *Liberation Movement*, pp. 177–81, 185–87; Pipes, *Struve*, 1:333–35; Frolich, *Russian Constitutionalism*, pp. 212–19; and Shatsillo, *Russkii liberalizm*, pp. 157–77.
15. According to Shakhovskoi, the spirit of the decisions made at the Schaffhausen conference was embodied in an article on the agrarian question "K agrarnomu voprosu," *Osvobozhdenie*, October 19/November 1, 1903, pp. 153–58 ("Soiuz osvobozhdeniia," p. 106). The article presents as an axiom of the liberation movement the conviction that "political liberalism and socioeconomic democratism, the demand for political freedom and the demand for democratic social reform, cannot be separated from one another in the general program" (p. 153).
16. On the protracted and delicate business of organizing the Union of Liberation, and for the only primary source on its founding congress, see Shakhovskoi, "Soiuz osvobozhdeniia," pp. 105–7, 110–17.

17. The original Russian text of the program is contained in Terence Emmons, "The Statutes of the Union of Liberation," *Russian Review* 33 (January 1974): 82–83; it differs in several places from the text published in *Listok Osvobozhdeniia*, November 19/December 2, 1904.
18. Shakhovskoi, "Soiuz osvobozhdeniia," p. 113; Shatsillo, "Novoe o 'Soiuze osvobozhdeniia,' " *Istoriia SSSR*, no. 4 (1975): 143.
19. Miliukov, *Vosp.*, p. 146. Subsequent visits were paid in 1904–5, 1908, 1921–22, and 1928.
20. Miliukov, *Vosp.*, p. 150.
21. P. N. Miliukov, *Russia Today and Tomorrow* (New York, 1922), p. 8.
22. Miliukov grew very fond of the entire Crane family. He paid warm tribute to his American patron in an obituary, "Charles R. Crane," *Poslednie novosti*, February 18, 1939, p. 2, as well as in the memoirs, *Vosp.*, pp. 147–48.
23. John Franklin Jameson to Miliukov, May 30, 1905, in BAR, Miliukov, Arranged correspondence, box 3.
24. Miliukov, *Vosp.*, pp. 148–49. In the opinion of a correspondent to *Osvobozhdenie* writing from Chicago, in Miliukov's "superb history . . . Americans could not fail to hear the muffled roar of the historic wave of the liberation movement" ("tt," "Lektsii P. N. Miliukova," *Osvobozhdenie*, August 2/15, 1903, p. 70).
25. In the book's preface, written in February 1905, Miliukov says that the first four chapters were set in print in late 1903. The long chapters on liberalism and socialism were entirely recast on a much larger scale. The seventh chapter, "The Crisis and the Urgency of Reform," was an addition based on his lectures at the Lowell Institute in fall 1904 (*Russia and Its Crisis* pp. v–vi).
26. Ibid., pp. 21, 158–61.
27. Ibid., p. 29.
28. Ibid, p. 340.
29. Ibid., pp. 226, 249; emphasis in the original.
30. Ibid., pp. 341, 366–76.
31. Ibid., pp. 281–82.
32. Ibid., pp. 321–22, 398–99, 424–28, 560–61. Miliukov's exposition of the socialists' move toward a more practical and accommodating stance between 1881 and 1891 rested almost entirely on materials written and published abroad by socialists in foreign exile. It therefore expresses the views of individuals who were, in many cases, out of touch with the activities and inclinations of socialists in Russia. For a treatment of this period drawing on internal sources, see Naimark, *Terrorists*.
33. Miliukov, *Lektsii*, pt. 3, p. 160.
34. Miliukov, *Vosp.*, p. 152; in his memoirs, he incorrectly dates his Boston lectures to fall 1903.
35. Miliukov to Charles Crane, August 15, 1903, in BAR, Miliukov, Catalogued correspondence, box 3 and *Vosp.*, p. 150.
36. Miliukov summarized his observations of the doomed rebellion in "S makedonskoi granitsy," *Russkie vedomosti*, October 1, 1903.
37. Anna Miliukova to Natalia Vernadskaia, n.d., in ARAN, f. 518, op. 7, d. 332, l. 93. Anna did not publish these memoirs, and no copy of the manuscript appears to have survived.
38. Miliukov, *Vosp.*, pp. 152–54. Miliukov's closest friend among the exile community was I. V. Shklovskii, a long-time correspondent for *Russkie vedomosti*, whose London home was a gathering place for Russians of diverse political views. See Miliukov, "Privet

staromu drugu," *Poslednie novosti*, April 2, 1932, p. 2, and "Pamiati I. V. Shklovskogo-Dioneo," *Poslednie novosti*, March 10, 1935, p. 3.

39. Miliukov wrote two accounts of this meeting, both long after the fact. The first is in *Russia Today and Tomorrow*, p. 48; the year of the meeting is incorrectly given as 1901. He wrote a slightly more detailed account for Boris Nikolaevskii, at the latter's request, in 1928: "Moia vstrecha s Leninym," in Hoover Institution Archives, Nikolaevsky collection, box 794, file 13. Here, the meeting is dated—again incorrectly—to winter 1901–2.

40. Miliukov's friends among journalists included the radicals George Perris and A. G. Gardiner and the renowned liberal journalist H. W. Massingham. Among his friends in the scholarly community were two men who shared his interest in the Balkans, Henry N. Brailsford and Robert Seton-Watson. Miliukov also became friendly with Ramsay MacDonald, then just beginning his political career. See Miliukov, *Vosp.*, pp. 154–55.

41. Pares, *Wandering Student*, p. 125.

42. My main sources for discussion of the "new liberalism" are Michael Freeden, *The New Liberalism: An Ideology of Social Reform* (Oxford, 1978), and Stefan Collini, *Liberalism and Sociology: L. T. Hobhouse and Political Argument in England, 1880–1914* (Cambridge, 1979). Also of interest is H. V. Emy, *Liberals, Radicals, and Social Politics, 1892–1914* (Cambridge, 1973).

43. Freeden, *New Liberalism*, p. 6.

44. Collini, *Liberalism and Sociology*, p. 1. William Logue, *From Philosophy to Sociology* (Dekalb, Ill., 1983), argues that French liberal theorists were independently working through an almost identical shift from philosophy to sociology during this period.

45. Logue, *From Philosophy to Sociology*, p. 215; Freeden, *New Liberalism*, p. 110; Collini, *Liberalism and Sociology*, pp. 124–25, 186.

46. Miliukov, *Russia and Its Crisis*, pp. 223–26, 335–37.

47. Miliukov, *Glavnye techeniia*, p. 39.

48. P. N. Miliukov, "Sub"ektivnoe i sotsiologicheskoe obosnovanie svobody pechati," in *V zashchitu slova: Sbornik statei*, 2d ed. (St. Petersburg, 1905), p. 24.

49. Miliukov first made this point in "Iuridicheskaia shkola," p. 87; see also his favorable appraisal of Plekhanov's *On the Monist View in History*, in his survey "Russia," July 7, 1894, p. 24.

50. Miliukov, *Russia and Its Crisis*, p. 224.

51. Ibid., pp. 223, 335–37, 340. Michael Freeden, *New Liberalism*, p. 42, cites the 1906 observation of L. G. Chiozza Money, a liberal M.P., that "the period 1865–1900 . . . may be termed the period of Unconscious Socialism. With the twentieth century begins a period of Conscious Socialism."

52. Miliukov, *Russia and Its Crisis*, p. 339.

53. Miliukov, *Ocherki*, vol. 1, 2d ed., p. 17.

54. Miliukov, *Russia and Its Crisis*, pp. 339, 527. Miliukov's critique of the future-mindedness of revolutionary socialists is very close to his critique of Solov'ev's brand of Christian-idealist future-mindedness. See Miliukov, "Razlozhenie slavianofil'stva," p. 305.

55. In his opening speech to the founding congress of the Constitutional Democratic Party, October 12, 1905, Miliukov declared, "Our party stands closest to those groups among the Western intellectuals who are known under the name of 'social reformers.' . . . our program is undoubtedly the most Left of all those put forward by Western European groups analogous to us" (Miliukov, in *Konstitutsionno-demokraticheskaia partiia: S'ezd 12–18 oktiabria 1905 g.* [St. Petersburg, 1905], p. 7).

56. "ss" [Miliukov], "Izolgalis'!" *Osvobozhdenie*, January 19/February 1, 1904, p. 265.
57. P. B. Struve, "Voina," *Osvobozhdenie*, February 5/18, 1904.
58. P. B. Struve, "Pis'mo k studentam," *Listok Osvobozhdeniia*, February 11/24, 1904, pp. 2–3.
59. "ss" [Miliukov], "Voina i russkaia oppozitsiia," pt. 1, *Osvobozhdenie*, March 7/20, 1904, pp. 329–30.
60. Ibid., p. 330.
61. P. B. Struve, "Voina i russkaia oppozitsiia," *Osvobozhdenie*, April 2/15, 1904, p. 331.
62. "ss" [Miliukov], "Voina i russkaia oppozitsiia," pt. 2, *Osvobozhdenie*, April 2/15, 1904, pp. 378–79.
63. "So far as 'worldview,' is concerned," Miliukov wrote, "I fear that neither I nor the 'many with me' can stand, one hundred years later, on the point of view of the Fichtean 'Speeches to the German People'" (ibid.).
64. Ibid., p. 378.
65. Ibid.
66. On the war and public response to defeats, see J. N. Westwood, *Russia against Japan: A History of the Russo-Japanese War* (London, 1986), and Shmuel Galai, "The Impact of War on the Russian Liberals in 1904–5," *Government and Opposition*, no. 1 (1965): 91–92.
67. "Liberal," "Zadachi konstitutsionnoi partii v dannyi moment," *Osvobozhdenie*, June 25/July 8, 1904, p. 383.
68. "ss" [Miliukov], "Ocherednye zadachi russkikh konstitutsionalistov," *Osvobozhdenie*, July 19/August 1, 1904, pp. 36–39.
69. Shakhovskoi, "Soiuz osvobozhdeniia," p. 127.
70. "ss" [Miliukov], "Novyi kurs," *Osvobozhdenie*, October 2/15, 1904.
71. Ibid.
72. Galai, *Liberation Movement*, p. 211; Shakhovskoi, "Soiuz osvobozhdeniia," pp. 128–29.
73. The report documenting the efforts of Colonel Motojiro Akashi to further the Russian revolutionary movement is published in Motojiro Akashi, *Rakka ryusui: Colonel Akashi's Report on His Secret Cooperation with the Russian Revolutionary Parties during the Russo-Japanese War* (Helsinki, 1988). The volume also contains summaries of conversations Akashi had with Zilliacus, which suggest that the Union of Liberation and Socialist Revolutionary Party did *not* know that the Paris Conference was being funded by the Japanese. On this question see also Pipes, *Struve*, 1:363–64, and Galai, *Liberation Movement*, pp. 215–16.
74. Petrunkevich was also in Paris and met regularly with the Union of Liberation delegates, but did not take formal part in the conference. Miliukov used the alias "Aleksandrov." See Miliukov, *Vosp.*, p. 168.
75. The most comprehensive scholarly accounts of the Paris Conference are by K. F. Shatsillo, "Iz istorii osvoboditel'nogo dvizheniia v Rossii v nachale XX veka," *Istoriia SSSR*, no. 4 (1982): 51–70, and Shatsillo, *Russkii liberalizm*, pp. 237–58; see also Galai, *Liberation Movement*, pp. 214–19; Pipes, *Struve*, 1:363–66; and Sanders, "Union of Unions," pp. 144–53. Miliukov's accounts are in *Vosp.*, pp. 168–70, and "Rokovye gody," June 1938, pp. 122–27.
76. Miliukov, *Vosp.*, pp. 168–69; Miliukov rejected Struve's proposal that Poland's constitutional charter—granted in 1815 by Alexander I and abrogated by Nicholas I—be restored. For an overview of Miliukov's position on the Polish question, see C. Jay Smith, "Miliukov and the Russian National Question," *Russian Thought and Politics*,

ed. Hugh McLean (Cambridge, Mass., 1957): 395–420. The text of the resolution is contained in *Listok Osvobozhdeniia*, November 19/December 2, 1904.

77. In his account of the Paris Conference, Chernov claimed that Miliukov objected to the demand for universal suffrage on more than tactical grounds, declaring that he personally preferred a limited franchise based on educational qualifications. Miliukov's justification of this position rested on his fear that peasants would elect "land captains and *popy* [village priests]" who would swamp the intelligentsia representatives in the parliament. See Viktor Chernov, *Pered burei* (New York, 1953), p. 45. Shatsillo makes no mention of any such remarks.

78. Shatsillo, "Iz istorii," p. 60.

79. K. F. Shatsillo discovered, in the archive of the journal *Osvobozhdenie*, jottings from the conference in Miliukov's handwriting, which make possible a partial reconstruction of his positions. See Shatsillo, *Russkii liberalizm*, p. 238, and "Iz istorii," p. 57.

80. Shatsillo, "Iz istoriia," p. 62.

81. An English translation of the text of the Declaration is contained in Miliukov, *Russia and Its Crisis*, pp. 524–25.

82. Shatsillo, "Iz istorii," p. 61.

83. Ibid., pp. 65, 68, and Galai, *Liberation Movement*, p. 217.

84. TsPA [RTsKhID], f. 279, k. 9, l. 20, cited in Shatsillo, "Iz istorii," p. 66.

85. Miliukov, *Russia and Its Crisis*, p. 384.

86. The other vice-chairman was R. Dmowski of the Polish National League; Zilliacus was elected chairman and Struve and Bogucharskii were secretaries. All the members of this "bureau" were on the editorial committee that drafted the conference Declaration (Shatsillo, "Iz istorii," p. 57).

87. Stolypin's disclosure on the Paris Conference is in *Gosudarstvennaia duma: Stenograficheskie otchety*, III, 2, sess. 50 (February 11, 1909), col. 1426–48 (hereafter cited as GDSO). Miliukov's defense of his participation, and the Right's interpellation, came in the following session (cols. 1557–76). Later still, in émigré polemics over liberal mistakes, Vasilli Maklakov would charge that at the Paris Conference Russian liberalism made a disastrous choice, entering into "a formal union with revolution" (*Vlast' i obshchestvennost' na zakate staroi Rossii* [Paris, 1936], 2:327). Miliukov vehemently rejected Maklakov's characterization of the Paris Conference as a "union" of liberals with revolution, along with his entire argument concerning the maximalism of the liberals' posture. In the memoirs, he emphasized that all the groups meeting in Paris preserved their complete independence and suggested that he made it his business to see to it that this independence was formally acknowledged by the participants in the congress resolutions. See Miliukov, *Vosp.*, p. 169.

88. Miliukov, "Rokovye gody," June 1938, p. 128.

89. Shakhovskoi, "Soiuz osvobozhdeniia," pp. 130–32. Sanders, "Union of Unions," p. 159, says that Bogucharskii, Dolgorukov, and Miliukov were all present at this important meeting, but it is unlikely that Miliukov had arrived in Russia by this time. Miliukov was apparently the member of the Union of Liberation delegation to the Paris Conference charged with bringing the conference declaration and protocol to Russia, but those documents became available to the second congress of the Union only on the final day of its sessions.

90. The main published sources for the second congress of the Union of Liberation are Shakhovskoi, "Soiuz osvobozhdeniia," pp. 130–36, and I. P. Belokonskii, *Zemskoe dvizhenie* (Moscow, 1914), pp. 210–11. Significant archival sources are drawn on in the account by Shatsillo, *Russkii liberalizm*, pp. 264–70.

91. Shakhovskoi, "Soiuz osvobozhdeniia," p. 135.
92. Shakhovskoi, *Russkii liberalizm*, pp. 135–37. All three documents were published in *Listok Osvobozhdeniia*, November 19/December 2, 1904.
93. Members elected to the council by the second congress of the Union of Liberation are listed in Shatsillo, "Novoe o 'Soiuze osvobozhdeniia,'" p. 143.
94. Kuskova, "Kren nalevo," p. 389.
95. Shakhovskoi, "Soiuz osvobozhdeniia," p. 140.
96. Miliukov, "Zadacha zemskogo s"ezda," *Pravo*, no. 48 (1904): 4. The article is reprinted in Miliukov, *God bor' by*.
97. An English translation of the resolutions of the zemstvo congress is contained in Miliukov, "Present Tendencies of Russian Liberalism," *Atlantic Monthly*, March 1905, pp. 410–12. For a detailed account of the proceedings of the zemstvo congress, see Galai, *Liberation Movement*, pp. 227–31.
98. Ariadna Tyrkova-Vil'iams, who was living with the Struves in Paris at the time, recalled this discussion in a diary entry of January 8, 1905. See GARF, f. 629, op. 1, d. 16, l. 15.
99. Miliukov, *Russia and Its Crisis*, p. 530; the dates referred to in the quotation are Gregorian.
100. For an evaluation of the campaign, see Terence Emmons, "Russia's Banquet Campaign," *California Slavic Studies* 10 (1977): 45–86. "Four-tailed" suffrage refers to voting that is universal, secret, equal, and direct.
101. Miliukov, *Russia and Its Crisis*, p. 531.
102. Ibid., p. 131.
103. Miliukov, "Present Tendencies," p. 413; the article is dated January 26, 1905.
104. Gessen says friends and colleagues asked him to try to persuade Miliukov to remain; Miliukov answered, "Don't worry, Iosif Vladimirovich! I'll return in time, but it's essential to go to America" (Gessen, *V dvukh vekakh*, p. 200).
105. Miliukov, *Vosp.*, p. 171.
106. Ibid., p. 150. In the memoirs, Miliukov erroneously dates his Lowell Institute Lectures to fall 1903 instead of fall 1904.
107. Jane E. Good, "America and the Russian Revolutionary Movement, 1888–1905," *Russian Review* 41 (July 1982): 282.
108. Miliukov, *Vosp.*, p. 173.
109. Ibid., pp. 174–75.

Chapter Six: The Revolution of 1905

1. Miliukov, *Vosp.*, p. 189.
2. "Obrashchenie Struve k III s"ezdu 'Soiuza osvobozhdeniia,'" in RTsKhID, f. 279, op. 1, d. 47, l. 1. Struve declared that he personally considered the idea of an armed uprising utopian, but that he might be completely mistaken, since conditions of struggle were changing every month.
3. The preparatory work on the program, the program itself, and the proceedings of the third congress are described in Shakhovskoi, "Soiuz osvobozhdeniia," pp. 150–58; Miliukov emphasizes differences at the congress in his account in "Rokovye gody," *Russkie zapiski*, December 1938, pp. 120–21.
4. Miliukov, "Rokovye gody," August–September 1938, pp. 117–21, and *Vosp.*, pp. 186–87.

5. Miliukov outlined his views on the relative merits of a bicameral and unicameral legislature in "Demokratizm i vtoraia palata," *Russkoe bogatstvo*, July 1905, pp. 193–210.
6. Miliukov, *Vosp.*, p. 186.
7. Miliukov's talk before fashionable society at the Morozov mansion prompted Margarita Morozova, a young and attractive widow, to invite him frequently to her home for tête-à-têtes. She was, he said, "interested in the speaker personally," but they soon discovered that they differed on nearly all aesthetic and philosophical questions, and the meetings came to an end. Miliukov does not mention in his memoirs that he was in fact deeply attracted to her; in November 1905 he sent her a declaration of love, which she found unwelcome, judging by the rough draft, preserved in the archives, of her reply. While they never did discuss politics, the ostensible cause for the invitations, Morozova gave Miliukov several thousand rubles toward formation of a new political party (Miliukov, *Vosp.*, pp. 189–92, and "Rokovye gody," October 1938, pp. 130–34, and the Morozova papers, in OR RGB, f. 171, kart. 2, ed. khr. 1, esp. ll. 6–8, and kart. 3, ed. khr. 14, ll. 1–2).
8. Miliukov, *Vosp.*, pp. 182–83.
9. The remaining eleven All-Russian unions established between January and early May 1905 were the Agronomists and Statisticians; Pharmaceutical Assistants; Clerks and Bookkeepers; Equal Rights for Jews; Writers and Journalists; Lawyers; Government, Municipal, and Zemstvo Employees; Teachers; Veterinary Surgeons; Zemstvo Activists; and Railway Workers and Employees, the largest of the unions (Galai, *Liberation Movement*, pp. 246–48). The only complete history of the professional union movement is Sanders's "Union of Unions."
10. The congress is described in *Pravo*, May 1, 1905, and in the *Manchester Guardian*, April 29, 1905, pp. 9–10.
11. "A Journalistic Congress," *Manchester Guardian*, April 24, 1905, p. 10. Sanders has identified the author as Harold Williams, a knowledgeable observer of Russia who later married Kadet central committee member Ariadna Tyrkova ("Union of Unions," p. 519).
12. Miliukov's two articles on the purposes and organization of professional unions are "'Partii' ili 'soiuzy'?" and "'Politicheskie' ili 'professional'nye' soiuzy?" in *Syn otechestva*, April 21 and May 5, 1905, reprinted in Miliukov, *God bor' by*, pp. 34–41 and 41–47. They represent part of a polemic on the nature of the unions conducted by Miliukov, Grigorii Landau (a leader of the Jewish Democratic Group), and the young Marxist historian Nikolai Rozhkov.
13. Miliukov, "'Partii' ili 'soiuzy'?" pp. 35–36.
14. Ibid., pp. 40–41, and "'Politicheskie' ili 'professional'nye' soiuzy?" pp. 45–46.
15. Miliukov, "'Politicheski' ili 'professional'nye' soiuzy?" pp. 44–45.
16. "Materialy k pervomu delegatskomu s″ezdu Soiuz soiuzov," in GARF, f. 518, op. 1, d. 1; Dmitrii Sverchkov, "Soiuz soiuzov," *Krasnaia letopis'*, no. 3 (1925): 149. The accounts in Miliukov's memoirs of his participation in the union movement suffer from many omissions; he does not, for instance, mention that he was chairman of the first congress of the Union of Unions. See Miliukov, *Vosp.*, p. 195, and "Rokovye gody," November 1938, p. 140.
17. Sverchkov, "Soiuz soiuzov," pp. 150–51.
18. The incident was reported in *Osvobozhdenie*, June 8/June 21, 1905, pp. 363–64; Miliukov's accounts are in "Rokovye gody," November 1938, pp. 142–43, and *Vosp.*, p. 196.

19. Miliukov, "Rokovye gody," November 1938, p. 143. Miliukov displayed unusual animosity toward Charnoluskii, Fal'bork, and Lutugin in his memoirs, referring to Lutugin as a hypocrite and "vulgarian" and Fal'bork as "that intolerable chatterbox and liar" (*Vosp.*, p. 227).
20. On Trepov's appointment, see Abraham Ascher, *The Revolution of 1905*, 2 vols. (Stanford, Calif., 1988, 1992), 1:104–5.
21. The text of the appeal is reprinted in Sverchkov, "Soiuz soiuzov," p. 153.
22. Miliukov, *Vosp.*, p. 198.
23. GARF, f. 518, op. 1, d. 2, l. 1.
24. On the Coalition Congress see Chermenskii, *Burzhuaziia i tsarizm*, pp. 66–70, and Roberta T. Manning, *The Crisis of the Old Order in Russia: Gentry and Government* (Princeton, N.J., 1982), pp. 106–8.
25. Miliukov was in fact part of a small group before whom Sergei Trubetskoi and the rest of the deputation rehearsed their presentation of the petition to the tsar (Miliukov, *Vosp.*, p. 197, and "Rokovye gody," November 1938, pp. 143–44). His article commemorating the first anniversary of the deputation is "Deputatsiia koalitsionnogo s"ezda 6 iunia 1905 g.," *Rech'*, June 6, 1906, reprinted in *God bor'by*, pp. 8–12.
26. Miliukov, "Soiuznoe dvizhenie i 'soiuz soiuzov'" (n.d.), reprinted in *God bor'by*, pp. 50–51.
27. Sverchkov, "Soiuz soiuzov," p. 154; Miliukov, *Vosp.*, pp. 195–96.
28. Miliukov to Struve, in RTsKhID, f. 279, op. 1, d. 84, l. 23. The letter is undated, but since it refers to the zemstvo deputation that is to meet with the tsar on the following day, it must have been written June 5, 1905.
29. Ibid.
30. Miliukov, "Ballotirovat' i ballotirovat'sia li?" reprinted in *God bor'by*, pp. 32–33.
31. Miliukov to Struve, [September 1904?], in RTsKhID, f. 279, op. 1, d. 84, l. 11.
32. The decisions of the London congress and the split between Bolshevik and Menshevik factions of the Social Democratic Party were discussed by "N-ch" in "Raskol v russkoi sotsial demokratii," *Osvobozhdenie*, June 8/June 21, 1905, pp. 356–57.
33. A. Kornilov to P. Struve, July 14, 1905, in RTsKhID, f. 279, op. 1, d. 66, ll. 253–54.
34. Apparently Miliukov toured the northern cities in May, between the first and second congresses of the Union of Unions, and lectured in the south in mid-June (*Vosp.*, p. 192, and undated letter to Struve, in RTsKhID, f. 279, op. 1, d. 84, l. 22).
35. Miliukov told an audience in Kursk that in the ten years since Nicholas had been petitioned by zemtsy to grant a representative assembly, he had progressed merely from "senseless" replies to "hypocritical ones" (cited in P. D. Dolgorukov to Struve, July 17/30, 1905, in RTsKhID, f. 279, op. 1, d. 78, ll. 162–63).
36. Miliukov's account of his lecture tour includes his personal guidelines for "public speaking before the masses" (*Vosp.*, pp. 192–93). On Miliukov as a speaker, see Tyrkova-Vil'iams, *Na putiakh*, pp. 411, 415; she characterizes him as an orator who appealed to his listeners' reason rather than emotions, one "able to expound the most complex questions . . . so clearly that they became intelligible to the most unsophisticated minds."
37. Prince Peter Dolgorukov, writing to Struve about the importance of arranging talks on social questions in both the capitals and the provinces, said that "Miliukov's lectures have been of tremendous use" (P. D. Dolgorukov to P. B. Struve, Karlsbad, July 30/August 12, 1905, in RTsKhID, f. 279, op. 1, d. 78, l. 174). Other liberationists lecturing in the provinces included Iakushkin, Kizevetter, and Novgorodtsev; Shakhovskoi

characterized the whole undertaking as a great success ("Soiuz osvobozhdeniia," p. 157).
38. Miliukov, "Rokovye gody," October 1938, pp. 135–38, and *Vosp.*, pp. 192–94.
39. On the events in Odessa see Ascher, *Revolution of 1905*, 1:170–74.
40. "ss" [Miliukov], "Rossiia organizuetsia," *Osvobozhdenie*, July 13, 1905, pp. 396–98.
41. Sverchkov, "Soiuz soiuzov," pp. 156–57, and Miliukov, *Vosp.*, p. 199. The Unions of Professors, Writers, and Secondary School Teachers supported Miliukov's resolution for participation in the elections; the four abstaining unions—Peasants, Equality for Jews, Veterinarians, and Elementary School Teachers—wished the decision to be postponed until the next congress.
42. Chermenskii, *Burzhuaziia i tsarizm*, p. 103.
43. Miliukov, *Vosp.*, pp. 201–2; Petrunkevich mentions Miliukov as part of this committee, but mistakenly attributes its formation to the September congress of representatives of zemstvos and city councils (*Iz zapisok*, p. 393).
44. Miliukov, *Vosp.*, pp. 201–2, and "Rokovye gody," December 1938, pp. 124–25.
45. Miliukov, *Vosp.*, pp. 202–3. Kliuchevskii's participation in the Peterhof conference and meetings with Miliukov are discussed in Nechkina, *Vasilii Osipovich Kliuchevskii*, pp. 460–67.
46. For an analysis of the statutes of the "Bulygin Duma" see Emmons, *Political Parties*, pp. 10–13.
47. Miliukov, "Politicheskoe znachenie zakona 6-go avgusta," *Syn otechestva*, August 7, 1905, reprinted in *God bor' by*, p. 70, and *"Iskonnaia nachala" i "trebovanie zhizni" v russkom gosudarstvennom stroe*. (Rostov on Don, 1905), pp. 17–21, 23.
48. Miliukov, "Gosudarstvennyi akt," reprinted in *God bor' by*, pp. 64–66.
49. Miliukov, "Politicheskoe znachenie," p. 72.
50. L. Trotsky, *Sochineniia*, 2:196–205, cited in I. Deutscher, *The Prophet Armed: Trotsky, 1879–1921* (London, 1954), p. 121.
51. Miliukov, *Vosp.*, pp. 204–5.
52. Sanders, "Union of Unions," pp. 954–55.
53. Miliukov, *Vosp.*, p. 221.
54. An account of the fourth congress and the text of its resolutions are contained in Shakhovskoi, "Soiuz osvobozhdeniia," pp. 164–69.
55. Miliukov, "Rokovye gody," *Russkie zapiski*, January 1939, p. 122, and *Vosp.*, p. 207.
56. Protocols of the organizing committee, in GARF, f. 523, op. 1, d. 34, ll. 6, 12, 20. Miliukov's brother Aleksei, a member of the Union of Engineers and Technicians, attended two sessions on behalf of the Moscow bureau of the Union of Unions.
57. Ibid., l. 22.
58. Ibid., ll. 2, 5, 9, 10.
59. Ibid., ll. 6, 12, and *Otchet tsentral'nogo komiteta Konstitutsionno-demokraticheskoi partii (Partii Narodnoi svobody) za dva goda (s 18 oktiabria 1905 g. po oktiabr' 1907 g.)* (St. Petersburg, 1907), p. 17. The fullest treatment of these organizational steps is in Shmuel Galai, "The Kadet Quest for the Masses," in *New Perspectives on Modern Russian History*, ed. Robert B. McKean (London, 1991), pp. 89–91, and V. V. Shelokhaev, *Kadety—glavnaia partiia liberal'noi burzhuazii v bor'be s revoliutsiei 1905–1907 gg.* (Moscow, 1983), pp. 55–57.
60. Miliukov, *Vosp.*, p. 208, and "Rokovye gody," January 1939, p. 122.
61. "Vstupitel'naia rech' P. N. Miliukova," in *Konstitutsionno-demokraticheskaia par-*

tiia: S'ezd 12–18 oktiabria 1905 g. (Moscow, 1905) (hereafter cited as *S'ezd 12–18 oktiabria*). The text of the speech is also reproduced in Miliukov, *God bor' by*, pp. 97–101.
62. *S'ezd 12–18 oktiabria*, p. 3.
63. The version in *God bor' by*, p. 100, which renders this line "protivnikom biurokraticheskoi tsentralizatsii i ministerstva," is a misprint.
64. *S'ezd 12–18 oktiabria*, p. 5.
65. Ibid., p. 7.
66. Gessen, *V dvukh vekakh*, p. 205.
67. The text of the statement is in *Pravo*, no. 52 (1905): 57–58.
68. Miliukov, *Vosp.*, p. 209.
69. Maklakov, *Vlast' i obshchestvennost'*, 2:431. Miliukov later wrote that he did not recall uttering the famous phrase "Nothing has changed; the war continues," but might well have done so. By his own account, he told an excited crowd at the hall of the Moscow Artistic-Literary Circle that the manifesto was a popular victory that still required defense: "If only to hang on to what we have already won, we must not forsake the battle stations" (*Vosp.*, pp. 209–10).
70. Miliukov, *Vosp.*, pp. 209–11. His detailed analysis of the manifesto, and the report by Sergei Witte published together with the manifesto, is reproduced in *God bor' by*, pp. 72–78.
71. *S'ezd 12–18 oktiabria*, pp. 23–26.
72. Miliukov, "K. D. kak posredniki mezhdu terrorom snizu i terrorom sverkhu," *Rech*, April 8, 1906, reprinted in *God bor' by*, p. 261.
73. The second congress of zemstvo and municipal congress representatives convened September 13–15 in Moscow; for Guchkov's debate with Miliukov, see *Russkie vedomosti*, September 17, 1905, and Miliukov, "Rokovye gody," January 1939, pp. 119–21. Miliukov's reversal of his position on Polish autonomy, which he opposed mentioning at the Paris Conference, was the result of an agreement worked out by liberationists and Poles at a congress of April 8–9, 1905. There, he was willing to support Polish autonomy so long as its limitations were clearly spelled out. The protocols of the conference, organized by Aleksandr Lednitskii and Dmitrii Shakhovskoi, are contained in RTsKhID, f. 279, op. 1, d. 39.
74. On foundation of the Octobrists, see Emmons, *Political Parties*, pp. 104–25.
75. In his tactical report to the second party congress, Miliukov told delegates that at the party's founding he had opposed efforts to increase its membership by trying to attract those to their right, and welcomed organization of the Octobrists "in the interests of the purity of our own party." Reports on the proceedings are contained in Raymond Pearson, ed., *Vtoroi vserossiiskii s'ezd Konstitutsionno-demokraticheskoi partii 5–11 yanvarya 1906 g.* (New York, 1986), p. 15 (hereafter cited as "*Vtoroi s'ezd*").
76. *Otchet tsentral' nogo komiteta*, p. 3; Miliukov, *Vosp.*, p. 227.
77. Gessen, *V dvukh vekakh*, p. 212; Miliukov, *Vosp.*, p. 228.
78. An example of criticism from an old friend is the article by V. Miakotin, "O gosudarstvennoi dume," *Russkoe bogatstvo*, August 1905, p. 98. For the charge that the Kadets broke up the liberation movement before it realized its goals, see Ekaterina Kuskova, "Otvet na vopros: kto my?" *Bez zaglaviia*, 1906, pp. 86–87.
79. On Kadet efforts to court the nonaligned socialists, and differentiation within these groups, see Emmons, *Political Parties*, pp. 78–88.
80. A second important consideration was Witte's insistence on appointing as minister of internal affairs P. N. Durnovo, a known reactionary with an unsavory personal reputa-

tion (A. I. Guchkov, "Iz vospominanii A. I. Guchkova," *Poslednie novosti*, August 9, 1936, p. 2; D. Shipov, *Vospominaniia i dumy o perezhitom* [Moscow, 1918], pp. 334–49).
81. Miliukov actually wrote four accounts of this meeting; though they differ on details, the substance is the same. See Miliukov, "Politika Gr. Vitte. (Pis'mo v 'Correspondance Russe')," in *God bor' by*, pp. 180–86; *Tri popytki: K istorii russkogo lzhe-konstitutsionalizma* (Paris, 1921), pp. 23–25; "Rokovye gody," *Russkie zapiski*, February 1939, pp. 128–31; and *Vosp.*, pp. 219–21.
82. Miliukov, *Vosp.*, pp. 219–220, and "Rokovye gody," February 1939, pp. 129–30.
83. Miliukov, *Vosp.*, p. 220, and "Rokovye gody," February 1939, p. 131.
84. *Pravo*, November 20, 1905, p. 3703.
85. Miliukov, *Vosp.*, p. 222.
86. *Pravo*, November 20, 1905, p. 3705.
87. Ibid., pp. 3662–63; Miliukov, *Vosp.*, pp. 223–24.
88. Sessions of the Kadet central committee of November 13 and 23, 1905, in GARF, f. 523, op. 1, d. 27, ll. 19–20, 34.
89. Miliukov to Margarita Morozova, (undated, but shortly before December 1, 1905), in OR RGB, f. 171, kart. 2, ed. khr. 1, ll. 6–8.
90. Details of the newspaper's publishing history are in Gessen, *V dvukh vekakh*, pp. 218–21, and Miliukov, "Rokovye gody," *Russkie zapiski*, April 1939, pp. 130–37.
91. Miliukov, untitled article, *Narodnaia svoboda*, December 1, 1905, reprinted in *God bor' by*, p. 164.
92. Ibid., p. 165.
93. Ibid., p. 169.
94. Miliukov, untitled article, *Svobodnyi narod*, December 8, 1905, reprinted in *God bor' by*, p. 171.
95. Miliukov, *Svobodnyi narod*, December 14, 1905, reprinted in *God bor' by*, p. 175.
96. Ascher, *Revolution of 1905*, 1:322.
97. Miliukov, *Vosp.*, p. 234.
98. The proceedings of the first few days of the congress were reported in detail in supplements to *Pravo*, January 29, 1906, pp. 1–22, and February 19, 1906, pp. 25–26; two other important sources on the congress are its semiofficial daily *Biulleten'* and its formal resolutions (*postanovleniia*); these are reproduced and accompanied by a detailed discussion of the second congress by Raymond Pearson in *Vtoroi s'ezd*; Miliukov's report is also reprinted in *God bor' by*, pp. 102–10.
99. *Vtoroi s'ezd*, p. 41.
100. Richard Pipes remarks that "the delegates proceeded to manifest the schizophrenic nature of Russian liberalism by passing a series of mutually exclusive resolutions" (*Struve*, 2:30; see also Emmons, *Political Parties*, pp. 58–59).
101. *Vtoroi s'ezd*, pp. 223–28.
102. Ibid., pp. 196–209. Akchurin, the representative of the Tatar group of Kazan, pointed out that from the Muslim perspective the Kadet commitment to the principle of equality for women contradicted a different Kadet principle, that of freedom of religious belief and practice. The congress adopted a special resolution stating that the party acknowledged Muslim rights.
103. Ibid., pp. 175, 179. The change concerned the remuneration to be given landowners whose land was expropriated for sale to the peasantry: the land was to be valued at a "just" rather than market price.
104. Tyrkova-Vil'iams, *Na putiakh*, pp. 252–53; Kizevetter, *Na rubezhe*, pp. 412–18; Maklakov, *Vlast' i obshchestvennost'*, p. 511.

105. Iosif Gessen discusses in detail his years on *Rech'* in *V dvukh vekakh*, especially pp. 217–24, 260–70, 275–83; Miliukov's brief characterization of the paper is in *Vosp.*, pp. 238–39; see also Thomas Riha, "Riech': A Portrait of a Russian Newspaper," *Slavic Review* 22 (1963): 663–82.
106. Numbers for the composition of the First Duma differ from source to source and also changed over the course of its existence, as deputies continued to arrive from outlying parts of the empire and also changed their party affiliations in the Duma. Emmons estimates that by the end of the First Duma the Kadets had approximately 170–80 deputies, out of 478 total (*Political Parties*, pp. 355–56).
107. Ibid., p. 366.
108. For example, in his response to the socialist journal *Bez zaglaviia*, Miliukov pointed out that the Kadets did not recognize any group as having a monopoly on the right to "express the opinions of the country" and realized full well that they had been elected on the basis of a restricted franchise. See Miliukov, "Upreki 'sleva,'" *Rech'*, April 5, 1906, reprinted in *God bor'by*, pp. 251–52.
109. *Protokoly III obshcheimperskogo delegatskogo s'ezda partii narodnoi svobody (konstitutsionno-demokraticheskoi)* (St. Petersburg, 1906), p. 42 (hereafter cited as *Protokoly III s'ezda*).
110. Miliukov, *God bor'by*, pp. 216, 225, 234, 247.
111. The leadership was also torn on the question of tactics, approving Miliukov's tactical report on the eve of the congress only after "fierce debate" and once he had agreed to a number of amendments (central committee meeting of April 19, 1906, in GARF, f. 523, op. 1, d. 27, l. 43).
112. *Protokoly III s'ezda*, pp. 9, 11, 13.
113. Ibid., pp. 16, 18–20.
114. Ibid., pp. 25–55.
115. Ibid., pp. 55–56.
116. Since the October Manifesto had promised that no law would be enacted without the Duma's approval, both promulgating the Fundamental Laws and prohibiting their amendment by the legislature violated that promise; see Ascher, *Revolution of 1905*, 2:63–71.
117. *Protokoly III s'ezda*, pp. 161–62.
118. The literature on the First Duma, both partisan and scholarly, is voluminous. Two important works by Kadets are V. A. Maklakov, *Pervaia gosudarstvennaia duma* (Paris, 1939), and M. M. Vinaver, *Konflikty v pervoi dume* (St. Petersburg, 1907). Important scholarly treatments include those in Ascher, *Revolution of 1905*, vol. 2; Chermenskii, *Burzhuaziia i tsarizm*; S. M. Sidelnikov, *Obrazovanie i deiatel'nost' pervoi gosudarstvennoi dumy* (Moscow, 1962); Startsev, *Russkaia burzhuaziia*. See also the assessment offered by Richard Pipes in *Struve*, 2:39–43.
119. Bernard Pares, *My Russian Memoirs* (London, 1931), pp. 106, 121–22.
120. Tables reflecting the shifting makeup of groups or party factions in the First Duma are presented in Emmons, *Political Parties*, pp. 355–56.
121. Miliukov, *Vosp.*, p. 244.
122. The circumstances of the text's composition are discussed in Vinaver, *Konflikty*, pp. 16–17, 33–43.
123. V. N. Kokovtsov, *Out of My Past: The Memoirs of Count Kokovtsov*, trans. Laura Matveev (Stanford, Calif., 1935), pp. 135–36. The text of the Duma's answer to the throne is in *Pravo*, May 8, 1906, pp. 1766–68.
124. Vinaver, *Konflikty*, pp. 55–58.

125. Miliukov, *Vosp.*, p. 245, and "Rokovye gody," *Russkie zapiski*, June 1939, p. 116. Rash steps averted by Miliukov, and other Kadets, included a resolution against Goremykin for refusing to receive a Duma delegation and the proposal to dispense with sending the bill on abolishing the death penalty through committee, or even on to the upper house (Vinaver, *Konflikty*, pp. 66–67, 78–80, 89–91).

126. Miliukov, "Duma v narodnoi soznanii," *Rech'*, June 8, 1906, reprinted in *God bor' by*, pp. 373–75.

127. Miliukov, "Pervyi mesiats dumskoi raboty," *Rech'*, May 30, 1906, reprinted in *God bor' by*, pp. 358–59.

128. Miliukov, "Glavnoe delo dumy i krainiia partiia," *Rech'*, May 10, 1906, and "Revoliutsionery sprava," *Rech'*, May 17, 1906, reprinted in *God bor' by*, pp. 350, 433–34; see also "Gubernatorskaia agitatsiia protiv dumy," *Rech'*, May 30, 1906, pp. 434–36.

129. Miliukov, "Presledovanie sotsialisticheskoi pechati," *Rech'*, June 15, 1906, reprinted in *God bor' by*, pp. 377–78.

130. Miliukov, "Protivorechiia 'bolshevistskoi' agitatsii protiv dumy," *Rech'*, May 11, 1906; "Chto razumeiut s. d. fraktsii pod podderzhkoi' dumy?" *Rech'*, May 12, 1906; and "Spory o mestnykh komitetakh v dume i v levoi pechati," *Rech'*, May 27, 1906, all reprinted in *God bor' by*, pp. 446, 449–50, and 463.

131. Miliukov, "Protivorechiia 'bolshevistskoi' agitatsii protiv dumy," reprinted in *God bor' by*, pp. 447–48; see also his reference to the "sectarian ideology of the Russian revolutionary intelligentsia" in "Cherez dumu ili mimo dumy?" *Rech'*, May 28, 1906, and to the efforts of Social Democrats to preserve the purity of their "true-believer" (*pravovernye*) followers, in "Dva puti organizatsii obshchestvennykh sil," *Rech'*, July 5, 1906. These articles are reprinted in *God bor' by*, pp. 466, 476.

132. Miliukov, "Glavnoe delo dumy i krainiia partiia," reprinted in *God bor' by*, p. 350.

133. Miliukov, "Novoe ministerstvo," *Rech'*, April 20, 1906, reprinted in *God bor' by*, p. 310.

134. Miliukov, "Obsuzhdenie otvetnogo adresa," *Rech'*, May 3, 1906, and "Nakanune krizisa," *Rech'*, July 9, 1906, reprinted in *God bor' by*, pp. 406, 382.

135. That day, Miliukov published an article spelling out his reasons for insisting on a Kadet cabinet. See "Nevozmozhnost' koalitsionnogo ministerstva," *Rech'*, June 16, 1906, reprinted in *God bor' by*, pp. 490–92.

136. Miliukov, "Moe svidanie s gen. Trepovym," *Rech'*, February 17, 1909, p. 2, and *Vosp.*, pp. 251–52; in the latter version, Miliukov quotes Trepov as using the term "regicides" rather than "bombists."

137. Kokovtsov, *Out of My Past*, pp. 146–47.

138. *The Memoirs of Alexander Iswolsky* (London, n.d.), pp. 186–87; I have altered the transliterations of Russian names and terms to conform to current usage.

139. Izvolskii later maintained that Stolypin had sincerely desired the participation of public men, but Shipov, who met with Stolypin several times, shared Miliukov's skepticism about his real intentions (Izwolsky, *Memoirs*, p. 212; Miliukov, *Vosp.*, pp. 255–56; Shipov, *Vospominaniia*, p. 459).

140. Shipov, *Vospominaniia*, pp. 448–50.

141. Ibid., pp. 456–57; Miliukov, *Vosp.*, pp. 260–61.

142. Miliukov, "Priblizhenie razviazki," *Rech'*, July 6, 1906, reprinted in *God bor' by*, p. 381; Vinaver, *Konflikty*, pp. 170–76.

143. For Miliukov's dismissive appraisal of the ministerial caliber of the Trudoviks see his article "Est' li pochva v dume dlia K. D. ministerstva?" *Rech'*, June 18, 1906, reprinted in *God bor' by*, p. 493.

144. Maklakov, *Pervaia gosudarstvennaia duma*, p. 202.
145. Central committee meeting of June 4, 1906, in GARF, f. 523, op. 1, d. 27, l. 124, and M. M. Vinaver, *Istoriia vyborgskogo vozzvaniia* (*Vospominaniia*) (Petrograd, 1917), p. 7. Vinaver's history of the Vyborg appeal was written in 1910, then read and corrected by Petrunkevich, Miliukov, Kokoshkin, and Shakhovskoi, to be preserved as the "sole authorized account of the events of July 9–10, 1906."
146. Miliukov, *Tri popytki*, p. 63, and *Vosp.*, p. 266; Vinaver, *Istoriia vyborgskogo vozzvaniia*, p. 10.
147. Vinaver, *Istoriia vyborgskogo vozzvaniia*, pp. 22–23, 30, 33; Miliukov, *Vosp.*, pp. 266–68.
148. Miliukov later justified the Vyborg Manifesto as intended to provide an outlet for the general indignation, so as to "avert armed clashes on the streets of the capital" (Miliukov, *Tri popytki*, pp. 62–63). A translation of the text of the manifesto is contained in Ascher, *Revolution of 1905*, 2:205–6.
149. Miliukov, "Pod pervym vpechatleniem," *Rech'*, July 10, 1906, and "Tishina pered burei i lozungi momenta," *Rech'*, July 16, 1906, both reprinted in *God bor'by*, pp. 525, 532.
150. Petrunkevich to Miliukov, April 22, 1914, in GARF, f. 579, op. 1, d. 5372, l. 17, and Dolgorukov, *Velikaia razrukha*, p. 321. For a study of the Vyborg episode suggesting that it intensified Kadet distrust of the masses, debasing the policies of the party, see Raymond Pearson, "The Vyborg Complex," *Irish Slavonic Studies* (1980), p. 81.
151. "Protokoly soveshchanie 2 avgusta 1906 g. ts-go k-ta K. D. partii s predstaviteliami gubernskikh komitetov," in GARF, f. 523, op. 1, d. 27, ll. 192–96.
152. No protocols of the fourth congress exist, but Miliukov presented his views on the response to the manifesto and the points of his report at central committee meetings of September 19 and September 22, 1906, in GARF, f. 523, op. 1, d. 28, ll. 10–11, 15; the resolutions of the congress are contained in the weekly *Vestnik partii narodnoi svobody*, September 30, 1906, pp. 1585–91.
153. "Protokoly soveshchanie 2 avgusta 1906 g. ts-go k-ta K. D. partii s predstaviteliami gubernskikh komitetov," in GARF, f. 523, op. 1, d. 27, ll. 148–79.
154. Persecution of the party in St. Petersburg is described in D. D. Protopopov, *Ocherk deiatel'nosti S-Peterburgskoi gruppy partii Narodnoi svobody, 1 oktiabria 1906–1 noiabria 1907* (St. Petersburg, 1908), pp. 4–12. The list of party candidates for St. Petersburg is printed in *Rech'*, November 12, 1906, p. 3.
155. Meetings of the central committee of October 20 and 29, in GARF, f. 523, op. 1, d. 28, ll. 45, 72–87, and Miliukov, *Vosp.*, pp. 275–76.
156. Some 240,000 copies were printed of his popular brochure: *Pered vyborami v novuiu dumu; Otchet tsentral'nogo komiteta K. D. partii za dva goda s 18 oktiabria 1905 g. po oktiabr' 1907 g.* (St. Petersburg, 1907), pp. 44–46; for a detailed account of the elections, see S. A. Smirnov, *Kak proshly vybory vo 2-iu gosudarstvennuiu dumu* (St. Petersburg, 1907), including the foreword by Miliukov, "Obshchii obzor izbiratel'noi kampanii."
157. Figures for the composition of the Second Duma are those reproduced in Miliukov, *Vosp.*, p. 277; see also Emmons, *Political Parties*, pp. 365–71, who estimates lefts at 175 and the Kadets at 108.
158. In summer and fall 1906 the Stolypin government promulgated a series of agrarian reforms, the most important of which was the law of November 9, 1906, allowing peasants to separate from the village commune and claim their share of communal allotment land as their private property. For an extremely clear and even-handed discussion of this complex set of laws see Ascher, *Revolution of 1905*, 2:264–91.

159. Miliukov, *Vosp.*, pp. 282–83; Gessen, *V dvukh vekakh*, p. 238; and Kizevetter, *Na rubezhe*, pp. 456–57.

160. See A. A. Kizevetter, *Napadki na partii Narodnoi svobody i vozrazheniia na nikh* (Moscow, 1906), pp. 53–54, and Miliukov, "Smertnye kazni i politicheskoe ubiistvo," *Rech'*, May 19, 1906, and "Pochemu nevozmozhna 'podderzhka' pravitel'stva," *Rech'*, May 30, 1907.

161. Miliukov devoted a *Rech'* article of May 16, 1907, to the extreme right's efforts to have the Duma dissolved; it is reproduced in P. N. Miliukov, *Vtoraia duma* (St. Petersburg, 1908), p. 221. On the proposals of the far right in the Second Duma see Alfred Levin, *The Second Duma: A Study of the Social Democratic Party and the Russian Constitutional Experiment*, 2d ed. (Hamden, Conn., 1966), pp. 270–78, and Maklakov, *Vtoraia gosudarstvennaia duma*, (Paris, 1948), pp. 204–30.

162. "Protokoly parlamentskoi fraktsii 17 fev.–14 dek. 1907 g.," in GARF, f. 523, op. 1, d. 1, 47, and 63. A third tactical consideration, for Miliukov in particular, was preservation of the unity of the party itself; there was nothing like consensus among Kadets on the attitude to be taken toward terror. See Tyrkova-Vil'iams, *Na putiakh*, pp. 282–83, 300, 340; Gessen, *V dvukh vekakh*, pp. 226, 242; and Kizevetter, *Na rubezhe*, pp. 460–70.

163. GDSO, II, 1, sess. 38 (May 15, 1907), cols. 608–9, and sess. 40 (May 17, 1907), cols. 758–68, and Maklakov, *Vtoraia duma*, p. 220; see also Ascher, *Revolution of 1905*, 2:322–26.

164. Miliukov, *Vosp.*, pp. 281–82. Lenin's response to the rumors concerning Miliukov's 1907 meeting with Stolypin demonstrates that liberals did have a basis for fearing that repudiation of terror would discredit them in the eyes of the left. Miliukov declared in print that no deal had been struck, but Lenin portrayed the interview otherwise: "And Miliukov chats at an audience with Stolypin: 'As you see, Your Excellency, I disrupted the revolution, and tore the moderates from it . . .' Stolypin: 'Hm, yes, I'll look into the legalization of your party. You know, Pavel Nikolaevich, you should split up the working rabble, and I'll hit them with a club. . . . It's a bargain, Pavel Nikolaevich'" (cited in Riha, *A Russian European*, p. 149).

165. In his memoirs, Miliukov hints at a number of romantic involvements he could have disclosed to his readers had he cared to; his liaison with Marie Petite is the only one he ever publicly acknowledged (*Vosp.*, pp. 173–74). The editors of his memoirs deleted from the manuscript passages concerning his youthful involvement with two other women, one during his third year as an undergraduate; see *Vosp.* MS., pp. 46, 102–3, and BAR, Miliukov, box 8. Letters to Miliukov in the Bakhmeteff Archive suggest he briefly became involved with a married Russian woman sometime during the course of his Bulgarian exile. The letters were accidentally placed in a file marked "P. G. Vinogradov"; they were signed with a single, illegible initial, so that I was not able to establish the identity of the woman, who had returned with her husband to the Kiev area by 1899, at the time the letters were written. It has also been rumored that Miliukov had an affair, sometime between 1906–1910, with Ariadna Tyrkova-Williams, the only woman on the Kadet party central committee. Tyrkova-Williams referred in her diary to some sort of rumors apparently circulating in 1909 of a nature to cause Anna Miliukova to behave coldly toward her, but wrote that she did not know what the rumors were and did not intend to find out; nothing else in the diary, which she kept only sporadically, suggests that her relations with Miliukov were ever intimate. See GARF, f. 629, op. 1, d. 16, "Diary of A. Tyrkova-Vil'iams," particularly the entry for November 20, 1909, l. 43. In her own memoirs, which display a great deal of animosity

toward Miliukov, she refers to a "weakness for the ladies" he shared with Vasilii Maklakov (*Na putiakh*, pp. 240, 351).
166. Anna Miliukova to Natalia Vernadskaia, ARAN, f. 518, op. 7, d. 332, ll. 52, 53, 73–75, 85–86, 88, 99.
167. Anna Miliukova to Natalia Vernadskaia, n.d., ARAN, f. 518, op. 7, d. 332, ll. 51–52.
168. Miliukov, *Vosp.*, pp. 284, 174.
169. Tyrkova-Vil'iams, *Na putiakh*, p. 413.

Chapter Seven: The Search for Unity

1. Miliukov, *Vosp.*, pp. 296–99.
2. Paul Milyoukov [*sic*], *Constitutional Government for Russia* (New York, 1908), pp. 8–9.
3. Ibid., p. 27.
4. Ibid., pp. 8, 11, 15.
5. Ibid., pp. 27–28.
6. Miliukov, *Russia Today and Tomorrow*, p. 8.
7. Ibid., pp. 8–17.
8. GARF, f. 523, op. 1, d. 28, ll. 26–27.
9. On the Social Democratic electoral campaign and disagreements over tactics among revolutionary groups, see Alfred Levin, *The Third Duma, Election and Profile* (Hamden, Conn., 1973), pp. 67–71.
10. *Rech'*, September 21, 1907, p. 2, and Miliukov, *Vosp.*, p. 290.
11. This was the opinion of Sergei Kryzhanovskii, drafter of the new electoral law. See S. Kryzhanovskii, *Vospominaniia* (Berlin, n.d.), p. 97.
12. See Miliukov's tactical report, and his comments during ensuing debate in P. Miliukov, "Doklad ts. kom. V s"ezdu partii Narodnoi Svobody," *Vestnik partii Narodnoi svobody*, no. 43 (1907): cols. 1835–36, and no. 49 (1907): col. 2140.
13. Ibid., col. 2154.
14. GARF, f. 523, op. 1, d. 255, l. 11.
15. Ben-Cion Pinchuk, *The Octobrists in the Third Duma, 1907–1912* (Seattle, Wash., 1974), p. 42.
16. *Otchet fraktsii narodnoi svobody* (St. Petersburg, 1908), pp. 7, 34, 43.
17. GDSO, III, 1, sess. 5 (November 13, 1907), col. 147.
18. Ibid., col. 248.
19. Ibid., sess. 7 (November 16, 1907), cols. 311–12, 349–54.
20. Ibid., sess. 23 (January 25, 1908), col. 1492, and sess. 24 (January 29, 1908), col. 1525. A pamphlet distributed at this time by members of the Union of Russian People (N. Krivskii, *Vtoroe pravitel'stvo* [*Poezdka Miliukova v Ameriku i ee znachenie*] [n.p., 1908]) alleged that Miliukov had traveled to New York to obtain a loan from Jewish bankers to finance the revolution in Russia, promising them eastern Siberia once the Kadets took power (pp. 1, 4).
21. GDSO, III, 1, sess. 22 (January 22, 1908), cols. 1417–19 and 1422, and sess. 23 (January 25, 1908), cols. 1507–8; Miliukov published the text of his undelivered speech in a pamphlet with that name, P. Miliukov, *Neproiznesennaia rech'* (St. Petersburg, 1908).
22. GDSO, III, 1, sess. 23 (January 25), 1908, cols. 1513–17, 1522, 1539.

23. For the altercation between Count Vladimir Bobrinskii and Miliukov, see GDSO, III, 1, sess. 42 (March 27, 1908), cols. 1100–1101, 1107, and sess. 43 (March 28, 1908), cols. 1205–18; for that between Guchkov and Miliukov, see sess. 58 (May 2, 1908), cols. 2662–66. The protocols generated for the duel with Guchkov are contained in Miliukov's archive in GARF, f. 579, op. 1, d. 500, ll. 8–9, and d. 501, ll. 1–2; Miliukov's account of both challenges is in *Vosp.*, p. 295.

24. Pares, *Wandering Student*, pp. 126–27.

25. Failing to condemn terror, several speakers warned in a faction meeting of November 21, 1907, would be to risk destruction of both the Duma and the party (GARF, f. 523, op. 1, d. 1, l. 148). The text of the Kadet motion is in GDSO, III, 1, sess. 27 (February 8, 1908), col. 1873.

26. *Tret' ia gosudarstvennaia duma: Fraktsiia Narodnoi svobody v period 15 okt. 1908 g.–2 noia. 1909 g. Otchet fraktsiia* (St. Petersburg, 1909), p. 18. In an interview given to reporters shortly before the opening of the second session, moderate right leader P. N. Krupenskii declared that attitudes toward the Kadets had changed, since they had "worked a great deal and honorably" in the previous session. See *Rech'*, October 1, 1908, p. 4.

27. Records of the conference of the Kadet Duma faction with representatives of provincial groups, June 1 and 2, 1908, and the party conference of October 20–21, 1908, are to be found in GARF, f. 523, op. 1, d. 6, ll. 84–87, 91–93, and d. 7, l. 76, and protocol of the central committee meeting of October 11, 1908, in GARF, f. 523, op. 1, d. 29, ll. 167–70.

28. Kadet party conference of October 21–22, 1908, in GARF, f. 523, op. 1, d. 7, l. 74.

29. Meeting of the Kadet faction with provincial representatives of the party, June 2, 1908, in GARF, f. 523, op. 1, d. 6, l. 94

30. Kadet party conference of October 21–22, 1908, in GARF, f. 523, op. 1, d. 7, ll. 74–76.

31. Miliukov's tactical line continued to satisfy most provincial delegates for some time; Pavel Dolgorukov, reporting to the Moscow branch of the Kadet central committee on the party conference of November 14–15, 1909, said that criticism of the faction's tactics by provincial representatives had nearly disappeared. See GARF, f. 523, op. 1, d. 245, ll. 12–13.

32. The huge collection of Miliukov's papers held in GARF, containing more than 5,000 folders, includes dozens of files of clippings, copies of reports to committees, and notes he made during meetings; on his habit of note-taking, see also Tyrkova-Vil'iams, *Na putiakh*, p. 414.

33. Central committee meetings of February 23 and March 9, 1908, in GARF, f. 523, op. 1, d. 29, ll. 87–90, 102–10.

34. GDSO, III, 1, sess. 46 (April 1, 1908), cols. 1586–90.

35. He later wrote, for example, that the opposition did not care to purchase its "right to criticize" problems in military organization by voting for the Amur railroad (P. N. Miliukov, "Politicheskie partii v Gosudarstvennoi dume za piat' let," in *Ezhegodnik gazety Rech', 1911 g.* [St. Petersburg, 1911], p. 81).

36. The text of Miliukov's two speeches is in GDSO, III, 2, sess. 8 (October 31, 1908), cols. 617–53, and sess. 9 (November 2, 1908), cols. 772–94.

37. See Walicki, *Legal Philosophies*, p. 400.

38. GDSO, III, 1, sess. 30 (February 19, 1908), cols. 2110–23.

39. Miliukov, *Vosp.*, p. 318.

40. GDSO, III, 3, sess. 87 (March 31, 1910), col. 2520.
41. Pinchuk, *Octobrists*, pp. 84–86.
42. GDSO, III, 2, sess. 112 (May 13, 1909), sess. 113 (May 15, 1909), and sess. 117 (May 23, 1909).
43. L. Nemanov, "Itogi deiatel'nosti tretei gosudarstvennoi dumy," in *Ezhegodnik gazety Rech'*, *1912 g.* (St. Petersburg, 1912), pp. 103, 105, 109; P. N. Miliukov, "Obshchee politicheskoe polozhenie," in *Tret'ia Gosudarstvennaia duma: Fraktsiia Narodnoi svobody v period 10 okt. 1909 g.–5 iiunia 1910 g. Otchet fraktsii* (St. Petersburg, 1910), p. 19; Pinchuk, *Octobrists*, pp. 96–97.
44. See, for example, Robert J. Scally, *The Origins of the Lloyd George Coalition: The Politics of Social-Imperialism, 1900–1918* (Princeton, N.J., 1975), pp. 173–75.
45. Hosking, *Russian Constitutional Experiment*, p. 106.
46. Robert Edelman, *Gentry Politics on the Eve of the Russian Revolution: The Nationalist Party, 1907–1917* (New Brunswick, N.J., 1980), pp. 94–95.
47. Miliukov, "Politicheskie partii v Gosudarstvennoi dume za piat' let," pp. 85–86.
48. Central committee meetings of October 21 and November 7, 1909, in GARF, f. 523, op. 1, d. 30, ll. 26–32, 35–41.
49. Diary of Tyrkova-Vil'iams, entry for January 17, 1910, in GARF, f. 629, op. 1, d. 16, l. 43.
50. V. S. Diakin, *Samoderzhavie, burzhuaziia, i dvorianstvo 1907–11 gg.* (Leningrad, 1978), pp. 170–71. For an excellent treatment of the relationship between Ukrainian nationalists and the Kadet party in this period, see Olga Andriewsky, "The Politics of National Identity: The Ukrainian Question in Russia, 1904–1912" (Ph.D. diss., Harvard University, 1991), especially pp. 325–420.
51. GARF, f. 579, op. 1, d. 3514. This folder contains thirty-seven sheets of notes, undated, outlining two lectures, "Natsionalizm i natsional'nyi vopros" and "Natsional'nost' i gosudarstvo." The notes in the folder are not in order, and the remarks frequently elliptical, but so far as I have been able to reconstruct the texts of the lectures, they appear to embody most of the points Miliukov developed in *Natsional'nyi vopros: Proiskhozhdenie natsional'nosti i natsional'nye voprosy v Rossii* (Prague, 1925). That the lectures were written in 1912 can be concluded from a governmental memo of September 22, 1912, refusing Miliukov permission to give a lecture titled "Natsional'nost' i gosudarstvo" in the city of Grodno; see GARF, f. 579, op. 1, d. 1343, l. 5.
52. Miliukov, "Natsionalizm i natsional'nyi vopros," in GARF, f. 579, op. 1, d. 3514, l. 26; Ernest Renan, *Qu'est ce que c'est une nation?* (Paris, 1882).
53. Writing in 1925, Miliukov compared Durkheim's 1915 definitions of the nation and nationality with definitions dating from the first half of the nineteenth century, observing that "now we speak of nationality as the basis of statehood, as a sort of moral essence possessing the national will; nationality becomes active . . . voluntaristic" (*Natsional'nyi vopros*, p. 79).
54. E. J. Hobsbawm, *Nations and Nationalism since 1780: Programme, Myth, Reality*, 2d ed. (Cambridge, 1992), pp. 87–88.
55. Miliukov, "Natsionalizm i natsional'nyi vopros," 1. 37.
56. GDSO, III, 3, sess. 26 (December 4, 1909), col. 2986.
57. Miliukov, "Natsional'nost' i gosudarstvo," l. 20.
58. Ibid., ll. 32–33; see also *Natsional'nyi vopros*, pp. 64–65, 80–83, 92–99.
59. Miliukov, "Natsional'nost' i gosudarstvo," ll. 30–31.
60. GDSO, III, 3, sess. 26 (December 4, 1909), col. 2990.
61. Ibid., sess. 117 (May 22, 1910), col. 2089 (emphasis in the original).

62. For Struve's thinking on Russian nationhood, see Pipes, *Struve*, 2:210–13.
63. Miliukov, "Natsional'nost' i gosudarstvo," ll. 22a, 31–33.
64. Ibid., l. 34; the quotation comes from his Duma speech supporting his amendment to qualify Yiddish and Ukrainian as languages of instruction in elementary schools. See GDSO, III, 4, sess. 18 (November 12, 1910), cols. 1238–58.
65. Miliukov, "Natsional'nost' i gosudarstvo," l. 34.
66. Miliukov preferred "decentralization" to federalism; *Vosp.*, p. 206.
67. Andriewsky, "Politics of National Identity," p. 365, n. 97.
68. The Kadets twice introduced formal protests against use of anti-Semitic expressions in the Duma, on February 18, 1909, and May 1914; see Miliukov's remarks in GDSO, IV, 2, sess. 89 (May 20, 1914), cols. 1163–64.
69. The problems associated with defining Finland's position are discussed in Hosking, *Russian Constitutional Experiment*, pp. 107–15.
70. GDSO, III, 3, sess. 74 (March 17, 1910), cols. 940, 970, and sess. 117 (May 22, 1910), col. 2088.
71. Ibid., sess. 116 (May 21, 1910), col. 2002.
72. Ibid., sess. 117 (May 22, 1910), cols. 2072–73.
73. Ibid., col. 2075.
74. The text of Miliukov's speech, delivered in the Duma October 29, 1911, during debate on a bill to equalize the rights of Russians in Finland with those of the Finns, is reproduced as "Ravenstvo grazhdan i narushenie prav," in *Tret' ia gosudarstvennaia duma: Sessiia 5-aia. Fraktsiia Narodnoi svobody period 15 oktiabria 1911 g.–9 iiunia 1912 g.* (St. Petersburg, 1912), pp. 10–20.
75. GDSO, III, 3, sess. 117 (May 22, 1910), cols. 2077–78, 2082, 2089.
76. On Octobrist attitudes toward Finland, see Pinchuk, *Octobrists*, pp. 118–22, who points out that not all Octobrists supported the excesses of the Finnish bill: twenty-three joined the opposition in protesting the bill by walking out of the Duma prior to the final vote.
77. GDSO, III, 3, sess. 74 (March 17, 1910), col. 958. *Rech'* promptly filed suit for libel, but had to wait some four years for resolution of the case. Although the Kadets were able to prove that they had not accepted a bribe, they did not convince the court that the editors of *Zemshchina* had knowingly made a false accusation and therefore lost their suit; see *Rech'*, April 19, 1914.
78. Diary of Tyrkova-Vil'iams, entry of May 20, 1910, in GARF, f. 629, op. 1, d. 16, l. 47. Anna Miliukova took this threat seriously, as did Tyrkova, who wrote "if it weren't for Iollos and Gertsenshtein [two prominent Kadets murdered by the U.R.P.] this would only be disgusting, but it is impossible not to be afraid." See also Gessen, *V dvukh vekakh*, p. 285.
79. Diary of Tyrkova-Vil'iams, entry of November 10, 1909, in GARF, f. 629, op. 1, d. 16, l. 40.
80. Miliukov, "Politicheskie partii v Gosudarstvennoi dume za piat' let," p. 86.
81. Cited in R. G. Vinaver, "Vozhdi kadetskoi partii," *Novyi zhurnal* (New York), no. 10 (1945): 259.
82. Miliukov, *Vosp.*, pp. 313–15; Anna Sergeevna Miliukova to P. N. Miliukov, August 13, 1912 in GARF, f. 579, op. 1, d. 5070, l.7 and ll. 3–12, 36, 41, 43 (dating from 1909–14); Gessen, *V dvukh vekakh*, pp. 201, 276.
83. Vinaver, "Vozhdi kadetskoi partii," pp. 260–62.
84. See, especially, the central committee meeting of November 7, 1909, in GARF, f. 523, op. 1, d. 30, ll. 35–48.

85. Gessen, *V dvukh vekakh*, pp. 201–2.
86. The falling-out with Gessen is discussed in a letter of Petrunkevich to Miliukov of December 19, 1911. See GARF, f. 579, op. 1, d. 5372, ll. 2–3; see also Tyrkova-Vil'iams, *Na putiakh*, p. 406.
87. Vinaver to Miliukov, July 25, 1911, in GARF, f. 579, op. 1, d. 3948, l. 1.
88. Tyrkova-Vil'iams, *Na putiakh*, p. 376. A similar representation of Shingarev and his role is in Obolenskii, *Moia zhizn', moi sovremenniki*, pp. 446–47.
89. Miliukov, *Vosp.*, p. 478.
90. Miliukov's most sustained evaluation of Stolypin's tenure is in *Rech'*, September 6, 1911; this was virtually the only time that he acknowledged that Stolypin was not solely responsible for many of the policies carried out during his tenure. His most detailed evaluation of the final year of the Third Duma is "Obshchee politicheskoe polozhenie i gruppirovka partii," in *Tret'ia gosudarstvennaia duma: sessiia 5-aia*, pp. 3–15.
91. Plenary meeting of the central committee, October 22, 1911, in GARF, f. 523, op. 1, d. 30, ll. 113–117. The Kadets managed to hold eleven party conferences between June 1908 and March 1914 (V. V. Shelokhaev, *Ideologiia i politicheskaia organizatsiia rossiiskoi liberal'noi burzhuazii 1907–1914 gg.* (Moscow, 1991), p. 15.
92. Miliukov, "Obshchee politicheskoe polozhenie i gruppirovka partii," pp. 3–15.
93. Central committee meetings of October 11 and November 13, 1911, in GARF, op. 1, d. 30, ll. 119–27.
94. The statistics, based on a total of 442 deputies identified, come from P. Miliukov, "The Representative System in Russia," in *Russian Realities and Problems*, ed. J. Duff (Cambridge, 1917), p. 32. For a description of the electoral campaign and evaluation of its results see A. Izgoev, "Ot tretei dumy k chetvertoi," in *Ezhegodnik gazety Rech' na 1913 god* (St. Petersburg, 1914), pp. 193–95.
95. GDSO, IV, 1, sess. 11 (December 13, 1912), col. 603.
96. The most detailed personal account of the Kadet faction in the first two years of the Fourth Duma is S. P. Mansyrev, "Moi vospominaniia o Gosudarstvennoi Dume (1912–1917g.)," in *Istorik i sovremennik* (Berlin) 2 (1922): 5–45; Mansyrev credits Miliukov with holding the faction together at a time when most Duma factions were splitting, but also blames him for tactics he condemned as shortsighted and needlessly unproductive.
97. Diary of Tyrkova-Vil'iams, entry of January 17, 1910, in GARF, f. 629, op. 1, d. 16 l. 43.
98. Central committee meeting of December 8, 1912, in GARF, f. 523, op. 1, d. 31, ll. 7, 10–11.
99. Ibid., ll. 7, 12, 14–15.
100. Ibid., ll. 16–17.
101. Tyrkova-Vil'iams, *Na putiakh*, p. 350.
102. N. N. Shchepkin to N. M. Shchepkin, November 15, 1912, cited in Avrekh, *Tsarizm i chetvertaia duma*, pp. 208–9.
103. Mansyrev, "Moi vospominaniia o Gosudarstvennoi dume," p. 41, and Avrekh, *Tsarizm i chetvertaia duma*, pp. 210–12.
104. Avrekh, *Tsarizm i chetvertaia duma*, p. 212 and GARF, f. 579, op. 1, d. 914, l. 1.
105. Tyrkova-Vil'iams, *Na putiakh*, pp. 57, 412.
106. Central committee meetings of January 27 and February 1, 1913, in GARF, f. 523, op. 1, d. 31, ll. 18, 23, 35, 38.
107. The text of Miliukov's speeches are in GDSO, IV, 1, sess. 22 (February 13, 1913), cols. 1595–1610, and sess. 24 (February 27, 1913), cols. 1799–1815.

108. GDSO, IV, 1, sess. 24 (February 27, 1913), cols. 1805, 1808, 1815. Miliukov took up the subject again on March 8 (sess. 27), cols. 2168–86.
109. The vote on the suffrage bill was 196 to 31 (GDSO, IV, 1, sess. 27 [March 8, 1913], col. 2064).
110. GDSO, IV, 1, sess. 56 (May 28, 1913), cols. 253–54, and sess. 57 (May 29, 1913), cols. 317–18.
111. Unsigned editorial in *Rech'*, May 24, 1913, p. 1.
112. In October 1913 Minister of Internal Affairs Nikolai Maklakov and the tsar discussed the possibility of dissolving the Duma if it did not improve its conduct, or even changing the Fundamental Laws to eliminate the need for Duma approval of laws. The letters between Maklakov and the tsar are in *Padenie tsarskogo rezhima* (Petrograd, 1917), 5:194–96; for former Minister of Justice I. Shcheglovitov's testimony concerning the cabinet's opposition to making the Duma a purely consultative body, see ibid., 2:435–37.
113. *Rech'*, March 18, 1914, p. 2.
114. P. B. Struve, "*Ozdorovlenie vlasti*" part 2, *Russkaia mysl'*, January 1914, p. 152 (emphasis added).
115. *Russkie vedomosti*, March 15, 1914.
116. GARF, f. 523, op. 1, d. 245, ll. 179–181.
117. Ibid., d. 31, ll. 114, 117–18.
118. Ibid., d. 16, ll. 8–9.
119. Ibid., ll. 15–26.
120. For the text of the proposals passed by the conference, see *Rech'*, March 26, 1914, p. 4.
121. The text of Miliukov's speech is in GDSO, IV, 2, sess. 67 (April 26, 1914), cols. 1179–97.
122. Unsigned editorial in *Rech'*, May 4, 1914, p. 2, and "Za nedeliu," *Rech'*, May 5, 1914, p. 3.
123. *Rech'*, June 15, 1914, p. 2.
124. GDSO, IV, 2, sess. 83 (May 13, 1914), cols. 605–9.
125. There were 346 Kadet organizations in the empire in 1905–7, 100 in 1908–9, and only 80 in 1913–14 (Shelokhaev, *Ideologiia i politicheskaia organizatsiia rossiiskoi liberal'noi burzhuazii*, p. 10).

Chapter Eight: The War Years

1. On the efforts of Foreign Minister Aleksandr Izvolskii to enlist the support of the Duma in foreign policy questions, see David MacLaren McDonald, *United Government and Foreign Policy in Russia, 1900–1914* (Cambridge, Mass., 1992), pp. 120–25.
2. Prior to the Third Duma, Miliukov's only scholarly pieces on Russian diplomacy were two review essays, "Novyi istorik dvenadtsatogo goda," *Russkaia mysl'*, February 1887, pp. 145–55, and "Vostochnaia politika Imperatora Nikolaia," *Russkaia mysl'*, June 1877, pp. 15–33.
3. Meeting of March 9, 1909, in GARF, f. 523, op. 1, d. 30, ll. 2–11, and diary of Ariadna Tyrkova-Vil'iams, entry for March 5, 1909, in GARF, f. 629, op. 1, d. 16, l. 37.
4. Central committee meeting of March 1, 1909, in GARF, f. 523, op. 1, d. 30, ll. 2–11, and P. Miliukov, "Otnosheniia inostrannoi pechati," *Rech'*, April 9, 1908, where

Miliukov quoted a London *Times* editorial to the effect that Duma debates of foreign affairs "give Russian policy more weight in Europe."
5. "ss" [Miliukov], "Voina i russkaia oppozitsiia," pt. 2, *Osvobozhdenie*, April 2/15, 1904, p. 379.
6. Miliukov explained his remarks in articles in *Rech'* of July 30 and September 10, 1909; for the hostile reaction of more radical Kadets, see also Mikhail Mandelshtam, *1905 god v politicheskikh protsesakh* (Moscow, 1931), p. 162. In view of the uproar caused by Miliukov's remarks, the central committee asked him to prepare a special report on the London trip for presentation to the fall party conference; see GARF, f. 523, op. 1, d. 30, ll. 21–22.
7. In a central committee meeting of November 7, 1909, Struve declared that the point of view Miliukov expressed in London was "completely correct both pedagogically and methodologically." See GARF, f. 523, op. 1, d. 30., ll. 44–46.
8. P. B. Struve, "Velikaia Rossiia: Iz razmyshlenii o probleme russkogo mogushestva," *Russkaia mysl'*, January 1909, pp. 143–57. For an analysis of Struve's confusion of cause and effect in seeing national cohesion as the product of an expansionist policy, see Pipes, *Struve*, 2:90–92.
9. On the Slavic Societies and the neo-Slav movement see Miliukov, *Vosp.*, pp. 309–10, and articles in *Rech'* of October 28, 1908, p. 2.
10. Miliukov's most detailed evaluation of the mistakes made by Izvol'skii in handling the annexation was his article "Diplomaticheskaia Tsushima," reproduced in P. N. Miliukov, *Balkanskii krizis i politika A. P. Izvol'skogo* (St. Petersburg, 1910), pp. 132–57. This volume also contains the texts of his related foreign policy lectures and editorials in *Rech'*.
11. See Lieven, *Russia and the Origins of the First World War*, pp. 122–29; Dietrich Geyer, *Russian Imperialism: The Interaction of Domestic and Foreign Policy, 1860–1914* (New Haven, 1982), pp. 294–96, 298–300; and Pipes, *Struve*, 2:180–86.
12. Miliukov, *Balkanskii krizis*, p. 155.
13. Miliukov, *Vosp.*, pp. 310–11; besides the capitals, he lectured in Ekaterinoslav, Taganrog, Astrakhan, Vilnius, and Riga (P. N. Miliukov, *Vooruzhennyi mir i ogranichenie vooruzhenii* [St. Petersburg, 1911], p. 3).
14. Sir Norman Angell, *The Great Illusion: A Study of the Relation of Military Power in Nations to Their Economic and Social Advantage* (London, 1910); the main arguments are summarized in part 1, chapter 3; part 2, chapter 2; and part 3, chapter 2. Miliukov summarizes Angell's arguments in *Vooruzhennyi mir*, pp. 142–62.
15. Miliukov, *Vooruzhennyi mir*, pp. 3–12, 139–41. His discussion of contemporary pacifism also draws heavily on the work of Alfred Fried, especially *Die Grundlagen des revolutionären Pacifismus* (Tübingen, 1908).
16. McDonald, *United Government*, pp. 182–83, 189.
17. GDSO, IV, 1, sess. 11 (December 13, 1912), cols. 610–11.
18. Ibid., cols. 1027, 1038–44; in his memoirs, Miliukov makes no mention of his January visit to Belgrade, but discusses in some detail a trip to Sofia and through Serbian-occupied Macedonia during the April 1913 Duma recess, when he met with the Bulgarian tsar Ferdinand and the Serbian heir to the throne, Alexander (*Vosp.*, pp. 356–58).
19. Miliukov, *Vosp.*, p. 359, and d'Estournelles de Constant, "Introduction," *Report of the International Commission to Inquire into the Causes and Conduct of the Balkan Wars* (Washington, D.C., 1914), pp. 3–12 (hereafter cited as *Report of the Commission*). The

commission also included one Austrian and two Germans, but none of these participated in the investigation itself.

20. Miliukov, *Vosp.*, pp. 360–64. Miliukov kept a journal on this trip that details a number of interviews not included in the memoir account, including a conversation with N. V. Gartvig, head of the Russian mission in Belgrade. Gartvig, who was very pro-Serb, talked about an Austrian-Bulgarian agreement with the aim of destroying Serbia; Miliukov insisted that there had been no such agreement. Milukov also mentions twice offering to resign from the commission, a step Dutton ruled out; see GARF, f. 579, op. 1, d. 3542, ll. 6–7, 13.

21. The authors of the various chapters were not identified. George F. Kennan, using the Carnegie Endowment's archives, identifies the authors in his introduction to the reprint edition of the Carnegie report, "The Balkan Crises: 1913 and 1993," in *The Other Balkan Wars* (Washington, D.C., 1993), p. 8. Brailsford wrote the chapter on the wars and the noncombatant population, Dutton wrote that on the economic devastation caused by the wars, and Godart wrote the chapter on the wars' social and moral consequences.

22. *Report of the Commission*, p. 208.

23. Ibid., p. 148.

24. Ibid., pp. 149–51, 154–55, 163–71, 186–87, 206.

25. Ibid., pp. 38–39, 206.

26. Ibid., pp. 31–32, 40, 69, 206–7.

27. Beyond urging on everyone tolerance and mutual respect, Miliukov and the other authors could forward only two concrete suggestions: that in any future war international commissions of inquiry should accompany belligerent armies, to monitor compliance with the conventions of war, and that any loans extended by governments to the Balkan states include provisions limiting or excluding expenditure on armaments (ibid., pp. 234, 264).

28. D'Estournelles de Constant to Miliukov, March 2, 1914, in GARF, f. 579, op. 1, d. 1457, ll. 19–20, and Miliukov, *Vosp.*, p. 364.

29. Miliukov's personal archive contains prospectuses dating from 1913–14 for two series of seven public lectures, "Uzhasy voiny i novoe ravnovesie na Balkanakh," and "Voina i mir na Balkanakh"; see GARF, f. 579, op. 1, dd. 1769 and 1789.

30. Miliukov, *Vosp.*, pp. 384–86, and unsigned *Rech'* editorials of July 1, 6, 8, 12, and 14–19, 1914; his weekly resume "Za nedeliu," for June 30, p. 2, and July 14, p. 2, and his signed article warning against irresponsible French incitement to war, "Frantsuzskii natsionalizm i vooruzheniia," *Rech'* July 15, 1914, pp. 2–3.

31. In cabinet meetings held during the July crisis these sentiments came to prevail over the other consideration that had informed the conduct of foreign affairs since 1905, that war carried too high a risk of provoking revolution; see Lieven, *Russia and the Origins of the First World War*, pp. 140–46, and McDonald, *United Government*, pp. 204–7.

32. Petrunkevich to Miliukov, July 6/19, 1914, in GARF, f. 579, op. 1, d. 5372, l. 22.

33. After Austria issued its ultimatum to Serbia, *Novoe Vremia* printed an article alleging that Miliukov had recently met with officials in Vienna, allowing readers to infer that his lack of support for Serbia was the product of some sort of deal with her enemies (Gessen, *V dvukh vekakh*, p. 325).

34. Miliukov, *Vosp.*, pp. 390, 394, and *Rech'*, July 22, 1914, p. 1.

35. Miliukov titled this section of his memoirs the "Sacred Union" (*sviashchennoe edi-*

nenie); see Miliukov, *Vosp.*, pp. 394–95. On the attitude of the Duma leftists, see Alexander Kerensky, *Russia and History's Turning Point* (New York, 1965), pp. 129–30.

36. GDSO, IV, extraord. sess. (July 26, 1914); the English text of Miliukov's speech is in *Documents of Russian History, 1914–1917*, ed. Frank Golder (New York, 1927), pp. 35–36.

37. In addition to his four articles on the war for the *Rech'* yearbook of 1915, individual *Rech'* articles, and public and Duma speeches, Miliukov published "Neitralizatsiia Dardanell i Bosfora," in *Voprosy mirovoi voiny*, ed. M. I. Tugan-Baranovskii (Petrograd, 1915), pp. 532–48; "Territorial'nye priobreteniia Rossii," in *Chego zhdet Rossiia ot voiny: Sbornik statei*, ed. N. N. Mikhailov (Petrograd, 1915), pp. 49–63; "Vstuplenie neitral'nykh gosudarstv," "Tseli voiny," and "Voina i mezhdunarodnoe pravo," in *Ezhegodnik gazetoi Rech' na 1916 g.* (Petrograd, 1916), pp. 1–196; "Konstantinopol' i prolivy," *Vestnik Evropy*, January 1917, pp. 354–82; February 1917, pp. 227–59; and April-May-June 1917, pp. 525–48; and *Pochemu i zachem my voiuem?* (Petrograd, 1917).

38. Miliukov's fullest explication of German thinking and the origins of the war were his two essays "Proizkhozhdenie voiny" and "Diplomaticheskaia istoriia voiny," in *Ezhegodnik gazetoi Rech' na 1915 g.* (Petrograd, 1915), especially pp. 1–21, 33–34, 54–55, 70–71, 85–89.

39. Miliukov did not raise the question of German industrialists' support for annexationist demands, as Fritz Fischer does, but the accounts are very similar in stressing that it was not just the military in Germany that supported an extravagant "world power" policy pursued with conspicuous disregard for the rights of other nations; cf. Fritz Fischer, *Germany's Aims in the First World War* (New York, 1967).

40. See Miliukov's testimony in *Padenie tsarskogo rezhima*, 6:367, and *Vosp.*, pp. 364–65, 389–90.

41. See, for example, P. Miliukov, "Tseli voiny," in *Ezhegodnik gazetoi Rech' na 1916 g.* (Petrograd, 1916), pp. 29–30.

42. P. Miliukov, "Soedinennye shtaty Avstrii," *Rech'*, September 4, 1914, p. 2.

43. Miliukov's fullest defense of Russian acquisition of the straits is the 1917 series "Konstantinopol' i prolivy," in *Vestnik Evropy*. His prewar position on the straits is presented in his evaluation of Sazonov's foreign policy in 1912. See GDSO, IV, 2, sess. 104 (April 13, 1912), cols. 2218–42.

44. On Miliukov's role in the founding of the Union of Towns, and the important role played by Kadets in this organization, see the excellent study by Natalia G. Dumova, *Kadetskaia partiia v period pervoi mirovoi voiny i Fevral'skoi revoliutsii* (Moscow, 1988), pp. 34–40, 47. Many Kadets believed that members' war work in the Union of Towns could also help reanimate local Kadet organizations; Dumova suggests this in fact occurred.

45. Miliukov, *Vosp.*, pp. 401–2; Okhrana report of November 4, 1914, cited in Raymond Pearson, *The Russian Moderates and the Crisis of Tsarism, 1914–1917* (London, 1977), p. 24.

46. Three accounts of the closed Defense Committee meeting with the ministers, differing slightly on details, exist: that given by Miliukov in his report to the June 1915 Kadet party conference, published in *Krasnyi Arkhiv* (Moscow, 1933), 59:113–14; the testimony given by Miliukov and Shingarev to the 1917 investigatory commission, in *Padenie tsarskogo rezhima*, 6:309–11 and 7:21–22, 27; and the account given in Miliukov, *Vosp.*, p. 397.

47. Miliukov's declaration of Kadet support for the government is in GDSO, IV, 3, sess. 1 (January 27, 1915), cols. 49–52.
48. Miliukov's report to the Kadet party conference, in *Krasnyi Arkhiv*, 59:116.
49. P. Miliukov, *Taktika fraktsii Narodnoi svobody vo vremia voiny* (Petrograd, 1916), p. 9.
50. Miliukov, *Vosp.*, p. 402. An Okhrana report of June 4, 1915, suggests that Miliukov in fact agreed in late May to support a Duma recall only under pressure from other Kadets; see Pearson, *Russian Moderates*, p. 35. For an account of the loss of Galicia in the course of a six-week campaign, see Norman Stone, *The Eastern Front, 1914–1917* (New York, 1975), pp. 136–43.
51. "Kadety v dni Galitsiiskogo razgroma 1915 g.," in *Krasnyi Arkhiv*, 59:131–32.
52. Miliukov's report to the conference and concluding speech of June 8, in *Krasnyi Arkhiv*, 59:118–20, 141, 143–44.
53. Nekrasov charged the central committee with being unrepresentative, intolerant of dissenting opinions, and out of touch with the population; his resignation generated a good deal of ill-will among party leaders; see central committe meeting of June 18, 1915, in GARF, f. 523, op. 1, d. 32, ll. 178–80.
54. Miliukov's testimony in *Padenie tsarskogo rezhima*, 6:312–14; *Rech'* July 4, 1915, p. 1; and *Vosp.*, p. 403. The narrative is somewhat confused in his memoir account; Miliukov recalls telling Goremykin at their July meeting that Maklakov and Sukhomlinov must be dismissed, but they had already been replaced by that time.
55. Miliukov to Sergei P. Miliukov, January 31, 1915, in GARF, f. 579, op. 1, d. 6462, ll. 7–8; *Vosp.*, pp. 398–99 and *Rech'*, July 25, 1915.
56. At a central committee meeting of June 10, even before the rescript promising an earlier convocation of the Duma, Miliukov had urged the necessity of preparing legislation and thinking about what would happen in the Duma session. The Kadets needed to have more talks with the Octobrists and initiate talks with the Progressives, though he cautioned against relying on the latter; see GARF, f. 523, op. 1, d. 32, ll. 176–77.
57. GDSO, IV, 3, sess. 4 (July 19, 1915), cols. 92–109.
58. The Kadets came to see August 6 as the founding date of the Progressive bloc, for it was on that date that the two Octobrist and Center fractions agreed to demand that the Duma's session be a long one, and to begin negotiating on a program. The far left deputies refused to join the bloc, as did part of the Nationalists; the extreme right deputies were not invited to participate (*Chetvertaia Gosudarstvennaia Duma: Fraktsiia narodnoi svobody. "Voennye sessii" 26 iiulia 1914–3 sentiabria 1915 g.* [Petrograd, 1916], pp. 29–30). See also Miliukov, *Vosp.*, pp. 405–6, 409, and V. V. Shul'gin, *The Years*, trans. Tonya Davis (New York, 1991), p. 315.
59. In his account of the formation of the bloc, V. I. Gurko describes the Nationalist P. N. Krupenskii as its initiator. Gurko's version of events differs from Miliukov's in other important respects: according to his recollection, in August members of the Duma and State Council met and agreed to form a bloc, with Gurko, Miliukov, Shul'gin, and Baron Meller-Zakomelskii commissioned to draft a program (V. I. Gurko, *Features and Figures of the Past: Government and Opinion in the Reign of Nicholas II*, trans. Laura Matveev (Stanford, Calif. 1939), pp. 571–74). Miliukov, in contrast, says the Duma had worked out its own program in advance of meetings with the State Council and assigns no organizing role to Krupenskii (*Vosp.*, pp. 321–22, 326–27). Miliukov's notes of these meetings, from August 1915 until early 1917, were published in *Krasnyi Arkhiv*, vols. 50/51, and 52 (Moscow, 1932–33), pp. 122–60, 144–96. The originals of the notes are contained in GARF, f. 579, op. 1, d. 1276 and d. 1278.

60. *Krasnyi Arkhiv*, 50/51:122–44.
61. A draft program of the bloc in Miliukov's handwriting is preserved in his personal archive. It contains several points not included in the final program, on review of the police statutes and on freedom to convert from one faith to another. See "Minimum uslovii, neobkhodimykh dlia vosstanovleniia doveriia strany k vlasti," in GARF, f. 579, op. 1, d. 3425, ll. 1–3.
62. Miliukov testified in 1917 that the initial impetus for attempting to build a coalition had perhaps come from A. V. Krivoshein, minister of agriculture, who cherished hopes of being named premier and considered it necessary to have the support of a majority in both chambers. See *Padenie tsarskogo rezhima*, 6:312, and *Vosp.*, pp. 411–12, and Gurko, *Features and Figures of the Past*, pp. 575–76. The most detailed record of discussion in the Council of Ministers is I. Iakontov, "Tiazhelye dni: Sekretniia zasedaniia soveta ministrov 16 iiulia-2 sentiabria 1915 g.," in *Arkhiv Russkoi Revoliutsii* (Berlin, 1926), 18:106, 111, 119–25.
63. The notes on this meeting are reproduced in *Krasnyi Arkhiv*, 50/51:145–50.
64. *Utro Rossii*, August 13, 1915. The list included Polivanov, Krivoshein, and Ignat'ev, who were to retain their ministerial posts; Guchkov as minister of internal affairs; the Progressives Konovalov and Efremov as minister of trade and state comptroller; and the Kadet N. I. Nekrasov for Communications.
65. *Krasnyi Arkhiv*, 50/51:150–54.
66. P. N. Miliukov, *Rossiia na perelome* (Paris, 1927), 1:14; Avrekh argues that the two events were not merely coincidental but connected. See I. Ia. Avrekh, *Tsarizm nakanune sverzheniia* (Moscow, 1989), pp. 93–105.
67. P. Miliukov, *Bolshevism: An International Danger* (London, 1920), p. 68.
68. See, for example, Richard Pipes, *The Russian Revolution* (New York, 1990), pp. 224–28, and Thomas Riha, "Miliukov and the Progressive Bloc in 1915," *Journal of Modern History* 32 (1960): 16–24. Pearson identifies the bloc's failure in September 1915 as fatal for the fortunes of Russian moderates, but does not suggest that a bloc victory would have made much difference to the war effort or public opinion in the long run (*Russian Moderates*, pp. 60–64, 176–79).
69. From an interview in *Russkie vedomosti*, September 10, 1915, cited in V. S. Diakin, *Russkaia burzhuaziia i tsarizm v gody pervoi mirovoi voiny (1914–1917)* (Leningrad, 1967), p. 123.
70. *Rech'* editorial of October 19, 1915; protocol of the plenary central committee meeting of October 5, 1915, in GARF, f. 523, op. 3, d. 10, ll. 11–12; records of the nine bloc meetings held from October 25 through November 26, *Krasnyi Arkhiv*, 52:144–84.
71. The appraisal of Sturmer was recorded by French ambassador Maurice Paleologue, *An Ambassador's Memoirs*, trans. F. A. Holt (New York, 1925), 2:166.
72. On hopeful interpretations of the tsar's decision to open the Duma, see the unsigned editorial in *Rech'*, February 10, 1916, and that in the influential *Novoe Vremia*, February 10, 1916, p. 1. Paleologue reports Sazonov as exclaiming "That's what I call sane policy! Good liberalism!" (*Ambassador's Memoirs*, 2:188–89).
73. The text of Miliukov's speech is in GDSO, IV, 4, sess. 18 (February 10, 1916), cols. 1304–23.
74. Ibid., cols. 1314–15. In addition to approving 172 minor items, the Duma bloc also passed a bill curtailing censorship of "political" information; for an extended treatment of bloc legislative efforts see Michael Hamm, "The Progressive Bloc" (Ph.D. diss., University of Indiana, 1976), pp. 92–189.

75. GARF, f. 523, op. 3, d. 5, ll. 18–21, 41–42. The sixth party congress, whose protocols were never published, is discussed in detail by A. Ia. Avrekh, *Raspad tret'- eiiunskoi sistemy* (Moscow, 1985), pp. 221–32, and Pearson, "Sixth Kadet Congress," pp. 210–29. The elderly Petrunkevich retired as central committee president at the sixth party congress, which then chose Miliukov as formal head of the party.

76. Central committee meeting of March 30, 1916, in GARF, f. 523, op. 3, d. 9, ll. 47–58.

77. The peasants were angry because the Kadet effort on behalf of the Jews took the form of an amendment to the bill equalizing peasants' rights with those of other estates, which might have jeopardized the peasant bill. A treatment of the controversy over Jewish rights and the concurrent challenges to Miliukov's leadership within the Kadet party is in Pearson, *Russian Moderates*, pp. 93–97; on bloc handling of the Jewish question, see also Hamm, "The Progressive Bloc," pp. 156–81.

78. Miliukov, *Vosp.*, pp. 418–19, and Okhrana report of February 29, 1916, published in *Burzhuaziia nakanune Fevral'skoi revoliutsii*, ed. B. B. Graves (Moscow, 1927), p. 80.

79. Miliukov's impressions from his trip are to be found in *Vosp.*, pp. 418–33, and in a published portion of the diary he kept on the trip, *Krasnyi Arkhiv*, 54/55:14–43; his report to the Duma's Army and Navy Committee on his return was published in *Krasnyi Arkhiv*, 58:3–23.

80. Paleologue, *Ambassador's Memoirs*, 3:65, 74, 83; Miliukov's remarks are in Graves, *Burzhuaziia nakanune*, pp. 142–43.

81. Miliukov, *Vosp.*, p. 433.

82. Miliukov's detailed handwritten notes of the meeting are contained in GARF, f. 579, op. 1, d. 524, ll. 1–9. They were later published by the Progressive bloc; the text is contained in A. Shliapnikov, *Semnadtsati god* (Moscow, 1923), pp. 99–107. Protopopov's remarks included a hint about legalizing the Kadet party, which Miliukov and Shingarev ignored entirely.

83. The record of the meetings of the bloc of October 22 and 24 are contained in *Krasnyi Arkhiv*, 56:99–106. Miliukov's personal archive contains three drafts of the bloc declaration; the third and longest version bears a note in his handwriting, "discussed in the meeting of 24 October"; see GARF, f. 579, op. 1, dd. 402 and 404.

84. The very slim published report on the conference is in *Rech'*, October 27, 1916, pp. 1–2. A more revealing report, by the Okhrana, is in Graves, *Burzhuaziia nakanune*, pp. 145–48. See also Riha's discussion in *A Russian European*, pp. 261–62.

85. Paleologue, *Ambassador's Memoirs*, 3:91. The government's informant was Krupenskii.

86. The official stenographic report of the speech was heavily censored; the full text was later legally published under various titles, two of which are *Rech' P. N. Miliukova 1 noiabria 1916 g.* (Petrograd, 1917) and A. S. Rezanov, *Shturmovoi signal P. N. Miliukova* (Paris, 1924), pp. 43–61. The text of the speech is contained in GARF, f. 579, op. 1, d. 462.

87. Miliukov, *Vosp.*, pp. 441, 445.

88. For a study of the allegations in Miliukov's speech demonstrating most of them to be wrong, see S. I. Mel'gunov, *Legenda o seperatnom mire* (Paris, 1957), pp. 279–318.

89. *Rech'*, November 11, 1916; Okhrana report of November 8, 1916, cited in Pearson, *Russian Moderates*, p. 116.

90. Petrunkevich to Miliukov, December 3, 1916, GARF, f. 579, op. 1, d. 5372, l. 52.

91. Miliukov's testimony in *Padenie tsarskogo rezhima*, 6:347–48; on Sturmer's report to the tsar see Diakin, *Russkaia burzhuaziia*, pp. 242–43.

92. Bloc meetings of November 9 and 14, 1916, *Krasnyi Arkhiv*, 56:117–20 and 126–31; Miliukov, *Vosp.*, pp. 446–47; GDSO, IV, 5, sess. 6 (November 19, 1916), cols. 240–51.
93. Miliukov, *Vosp.*, p. 447.

Chapter Nine: Miliukov Displaced

1. On the influence of the French revolution see John Keep's "1917: The Tyranny of Paris over Petrograd," *Soviet Studies* 20 (July 1968): 22–45. See also Pipes, *The Russian Revolution*, p. 447; Jane Burbank, *Intelligentsia and Revolution: Russian Views of Bolshevism, 1917–1922* (New York, 1986), pp. 20–21, 59–61; and Miliukov, *Vosp.*, p. 404.
2. Hippolyte Adolphe Taine, *The French Revolution*, 3 vols., trans. John Durand (New York, 1878–85), 1:1–21, 125.
3. Ibid., 2:6, 13, 48–52.
4. Publication of the history was interrupted by Petliura's seizure of Kiev in December 1918. Miliukov partially revised the three volumes of part 1 in exile; they finally appeared in Sofia between 1921–1924 as *Istoriia vtoroi russkoi revoliutsii*. An intended part 2, on the civil war, was never written, but the second volume of his *Rossia na perelome* is a history of the civil war.
5. Miliukov, *Istoriia vtoroi russkoi revoliutsii*, 1:117, 122.
6. On rumors concerning a coup and the planned response by the Progressive bloc see Miliukov, *Istoriia vtoroi russkoi revoliutsii*, 1:21–23, and *Vosp.*, pp. 449–50; Miliukov reaffirmed his lack of knowledge of the actual plot in a letter to Petrunkevich, October 2, 1919, in RZIA, f. 5856, op. 1, d. 184, ll. 5–6. On the plot itself, see A. I. Guchkov, "Vospominaniia," *Poslednie novosti*, September 13, 1936, p. 3, and the account he gave to Nikolai Bazily in 1932, printed in *Aleksandr Ivanovich Guchkov rasskazyvaet*, ed. V. I. Startsev (Moscow, 1993), pp. 17–23; see also Diakin, *Russkaia burzhuaziia*, pp. 298–303.
7. Miliukov, *Vosp.*, pp. 449–50, and *Istoriia vtoroi Russkoi revoliutsii*, 1:23–26; Okhrana report of February 4, 1917, cited in Pearson, *Russian Moderates*, p. 136; GDSO, IV, 5, sess. 20 (February 15, 1917), col. 1340.
8. Miliukov, *Vosp.*, p. 454.
9. Mikhail Rodzianko, "Gosudarstvennaia duma i Fevral'skaia 1917 goda revoliutsiia," in *Fevral'skaia revoliutsiia: Revoliutsiia i grazhdanskaia voina v opisaniakh belogvardeitsev*, ed. S. A. Alekseev, 2d ed. (Moscow, 1926), pp. 38–39.
10. A translation of the notes of the unofficial meeting of the Duma made by an unnamed participant and list of members of the Temporary Committee are published in the collection assembled by Robert Paul Browder and Alexander F. Kerensky, *The Russian Provisional Government 1917, Documents* (Stanford, Calif., 1961), 1:45–47 (hereafter cited as *PG Documents*). The committee included representatives of all factions save the extreme right. Also see Miliukov, *Istoriia vtoroi russkoi revoliutsii*, 1:27–29.
11. N. Sukhanov, *Zapiski o revoliutsii* (repr. ed., 6 vols. in 3; Moscow, 1991), 1:83.
12. In his memoirs, Miliukov dates the pledge of the Preobrazhenskii regiment to the Duma February 28, whereas Sukhanov has it as February 27 (Miliukov, *Vosp.*, p. 457; Sukhanov, *Zapiski*, 1:96–97).
13. Alexander Kerensky, *Russia and History's Turning Point* (New York, 1965), p. 201; the texts of the two declarations by the Temporary Committee, issued at 2:00 A.M.

February 28, are in *PG Documents*, 1:50. The list of commissars appeared in *Rech'*, March 5, 1917, p. 2.

14. The text of Miliukov's speech to the Grenadiers is in *PG Documents*, 1:51–52; see also Miliukov, *Vosp.*, p. 457, and Kerensky, *Russia and History's Turning Point*, pp. 201–2.

15. Victor Chernov, *The Great Russian Revolution*, trans. Philip E. Mosely (New Haven, Conn., 1936), p. 172; Dolgorukov, *Velikaia razrukha*, pp. 12–13.

16. Paleologue, *Ambassador's Memoirs*, 3:244.

17. According to V. V. Shul'gin, Miliukov simply drew up the whole list of ministers himself (*Dni* [Belgrade, 1925], pp. 222–24). Virtually all accounts agree that Miliukov was instrumental in L'vov's selection as premier and minister of the interior; see Chernov, *The Great Russian Revolution*, pp. 177–78, and Rodzianko, "Gosudarstvennaia duma," pp. 56–57. The most detailed analysis of Miliukov's displacement of Rodzianko is that by Tsuyoshi Hasegawa, *The February Revolution: Petrograd 1917* (Seattle, Wash., 1981), pp. 442–58.

18. In his memoirs Miliukov characterized L'vov as a poor choice but also insisted that Rodzianko was "equally impossible"; he told Nabokov that he often agonized whether it would not have been better to select Rodzianko (Miliukov, *Vosp.*, pp. 457–60; V. D. Nabokov, *The Provisional Government*, in *V. D. Nabokov and the Russian Provisional Government, 1917*, ed. Virgil D. Medlin and Steven L. Parsons [New Haven, Conn. 1976], p. 85).

19. The Kadet central committee's anger over Nekrasov's resignation is evident in a letter from Petrunkevich to Miliukov of July 14, 1915, in GARF, f. 579, op. 1, d. 5372, ll. 29–30.

20. The most complete characterizations of various ministers come from Vladimir Nabokov, who served as Head of the Chancellery in the first Provisional Government (Nabokov, *Provisional Government*, pp. 93–94, 100–101). See also Miliukov, *Istoriia vtoroi russkoi revoliutsii*, 1:43–44, and *Vosp.*, pp. 464–65, where he refers to Tereshchenko as "a novice known to no one," attributing the choice of Tereshchenko to Guchkov's influence. Guchkov, however, thought Miliukov must have been primarily responsible for selecting Tereshchenko as well as Nekrasov and Kerensky (*Aleksandr Ivanovich Guchkov rasskazyvaet*, pp. 13–14).

21. Miliukov, *Istoriia vtoroi russkoi revoliutsii*, 1:43; the text of the Soviet's proclamation "To the People of Petrograd and Russia," is in *PG Documents*, 1:78.

22. Sukhanov, *Zapiski*, 1:53, 116.

23. Ibid., pp. 141–57; Miliukov, *Istoriia vtoroi Russkoi revoliutsii*, 1:45–47, and *Vosp.*, pp. 462–63; Miliukov's account is corroborated by that of Shul'gin, *Dni*, pp. 227–31.

24. Sukhanov, *Zapiski*, 1:152–59, 174–75, and Miliukov, *Istoriia vtoroi russkoi revoliutsii*, 1:46.

25. "From the Executive Committee of the Soviet of Workers' and Peasants' Deputies," in *PG Documents*, 1:136–37.

26. Sukhanov, describing drafting of the final version of the government program, provides the most vivid illustration of this factor: "The revision was laborious, with many hesitations and corrections. I remember that we took a long time groping for the phrasing of [the] last pledge. 'Reforms and measures'—could you say that? We shrugged our shoulders and said it" (*Zapiski*, 1:175–76).

27. The dynastic question was apparently decided on March 1; Paleologue's diary entry for that date refers to a "secret conference" of leaders of liberal parties held that evening, which resolved on the abdication of Nicholas, but also on retention of the monarchy (*Ambassador's Memoirs*, 3:233).

28. Miliukov, *Istoriia vtoroi russkoi revoliutsii*, 1:45–46; his remarks to Reuters were reported in *Russkie vedomosti*, March 3, 1917.
29. The text of Miliukov's speech, reported in *Izvestiia revoliutsionnoi nedeli*, March 2, 1917, is reproduced in *PG Documents*, 1:129–33.
30. Miliukov's statement was printed in *Izvestiia revoliutsionnoi nedeli*, March 3, 1917; see *PG Documents*, 1:133; see also his *Vosp.*, p. 466.
31. Shul'gin, *Dni*, pp. 267–71, and Guchov, "Iz vospominanii," *Poslednie novosti*, September 15, 1936, p. 2.
32. Miliukov, *Istoriia vtoroi russkoi revoliutsii*, 1:49.
33. Kerensky, *Russia and History's Turning Point*, pp. 214–16; Miliukov, *Istoriia vtoroi russkoi revoliutsii*, 1:50, and *Vosp.*, pp. 468–69.
34. Shul'gin, *Dni*, pp. 271–76.
35. Miliukov, *Vosp.*, pp. 468–69.
36. Kerensky, *Russia and History's Turning Point*, p. 216; Shul'gin, *Dni*, pp. 303–7. A discussion of the legal niceties of the act of renunciation is given by Nabokov, who was called in to help draft it (Nabokov, *Provisional Government*, pp. 48–55). The text of the act is contained in *PG Documents*, 1:116.
37. Miliukov, *Istoriia vtoroi russkoi revoliutsii*, 1:54.
38. Nabokov, *Provisional Government*, p. 51; Rodzianko, "Gosudarstvennaia duma," p. 32. Not surprisingly, Vasilii Maklakov did not share this later pessimism, arguing that "the forces of the state" could have retained Michael on the throne and reconciled the population to parliamentary monarchy: V. Maklakov, "Introducion," in *La Chute du régime tsariste* (Paris, 1927), p. 10. Allan Wildman's research into the attitudes of soldiers at this time suggests that Miliukov was mistaken in believing units from Moscow could and would support the dynasty (Allan K. Wildman, *The End of the Russian Imperial Army: The Old Army and the Soldiers' Revolt (March–April 1917)* [Princeton, N.J., 1980], pp. 203–10).
39. Nabokov, *Provisional Government*, pp. 48, 55–56.
40. A number of moderates felt they had a responsibility to hide their misgivings in the early phase of the revolution; Iosif Gessen, for example, extolled the revolution and its brilliant future in *Rech'* "without believing a word I wrote" (Gessen, *V dvukh vekakh*, pp. 362–63). Guchkov was singular in openly airing his pessimism from the start. Miliukov, *Vosp.*, p. 477, and Nabokov, *Provisional Government*, pp. 85–86.
41. The most detailed treatment of the first weeks of the Provisional Government is that by V. I. Startsev, *Vnutrenniaia politika vremennogo pravitel'stva pervogo sostava* (Moscow, 1980), pp. 111–61.
42. The initial acts of legislation are enumerated in Miliukov, *Istoriia vtoroi russkoi revoliutsii*, 1:61–65; the text of the first proclamation of the Provisional Government, made March 6, 1917, is contained in *PG Documents*, 1:157–58; for the texts of the Proclamation to the Poles and the Manifesto on Finland see *PG Documents*, 1:321–23 and 334–35.
43. According to the party journal, *Vestnik Partii Narodnoi svobody*, May 25, 1917, p. 17, more than 180 local party committees were active by the end of April. On the Kadet role in the organization of Committees of Public Safety, coalition bodies they frequently dominated, see A. Ia. Grunt, *Moskva, 1917: Revoliutsiia i kontrrevoliutsiia* (Moscow, 1976), pp. 49–58, and E. N. Burdzhalov, *Vtoraia Russkaia revoliutsiia: Moskva. Front. Periferiia* (Moscow, 1971), pp. 163, 189, 198, 207–11. The speeches by Mandel'shtam, Trubetskoi, and Miliukov are contained in *Rech'*, March 28, 1917, pp. 3–5, which reported extensively on the three-day congress. The effective display of

solidarity was bolstered by the decision to postpone consideration of divisive issues such as agrarian reform to the next party congress.

44. Miliukov, *Vosp.*, pp. 486–89; Paleologue, *Ambassador's Memoirs*, 3:254–55, 268–69. The United States was the first to extend formal recognition, on March 9; Miliukov received the formal declarations from the ambassadors of Britain, France, and Italy at the Mariinskii Palace on March 11 (after having led them through the palace in search of a suitable room, groping for light switches en route, as Paleologue recalled).

45. Miliukov is completely silent on this subject in his memoirs, which suggests he was not satisfied with his own handling of the repatriation problem. The texts of his official cables instructing Russian embassies to assist all émigrés with their return are in A. Popov, ed., "Diplomatiia vremennogo pravitel'stva v bor'be s revoliutsei," *Krasnyi arkhiv* 20 (1927): 3–38; on his secret cable, see Dumova, *Kadetskaia partiia*, 107–10. The Soviet's protest about hold-ups in the return of political émigrés is in *PG Documents*, 2:1088–89.

46. Nabokov, *Provisional Government*, p. 119, and Paleologue, *Ambassador's Memoirs*, 3:304.

47. Paleologue, *Ambassador's Memoirs*, 3:268–69, 271; Dolgorukov, *Velikaia razrukha*, p. 16; and Miliukov, *Vosp.*, pp. 480–81.

48. Miliukov, *Vosp.*, p. 480; Pipes, *Struve*, 2:233.

49. The text of the appeal is printed in *PG Documents*, 2:1057–58.

50. *Rech'*, March 23, 1917, p. 2.

51. Nabokov, *Provisional Government*, pp. 114–15. For a treatment of the differing foreign policy views of Kerensky and Miliukov, and a thoughtful handling of their relations, see Richard Abraham, *Alexander Kerensky: The First Love of the Revolution* (New York, 1987), pp. 163–65, 171–88.

52. For accounts of these meetings, see Miliukov, *Istoriia vtoroi russkoi revoliutsii*, 1:85; I. Tsereteli, *Vospominaniia o fevral'skoi revoliutsii* (Paris, 1963), 1:66–67; and Nabokov, *Provisional Government*, p. 115. Miliukov's position clearly owed something to Allied pressure. Paleologue told him that the Soviet demands on peace negotiations amounted to the defection of Russia; if realized, they would be an "eternal disgrace" to the Russian people (*Ambassador's Memoirs*, 3:295). The return of Irakli Tsereteli and other antiwar socialists from exile had a huge impact on Soviet views on peace; see Rex A. Wade, *The Russian Search for Peace: February–October 1917* (Stanford, Calif., 1969). pp. 13–50.

53. The text of the Declaration is in *PG Documents*, 2:1045–46.

54. Nabokov maintained that the communiqué was a deliberate falsehood; Kerensky claimed that the press had garbled his statement that the government "was about to consider the question of dispatching a note to the Allies" on Russia's new war aims (Nabokov, *Provisional Government*, pp. 121–22; Kerensky, *Russia and History's Turning Point*, pp. 245–46). The texts of the announcement in the press and the retraction are in *PG Documents*, 2:1096–97.

55. Nabokov, *Provisional Government*, pp. 122–23; Alexander Kerensky, *The Catastrophe* (New York, 1927), p. 135.

56. The cabinet's rejection of Kornilov's proposal was described by Admiral Kolchak, who was present at the meeting; see *PG Documents*, 3:1240–41, and Kerensky, *Russia and History's Turning Point*, p. 247. An account of the Soviet attitude is in Tsereteli, *Vospominaniia fevral'skoi revoliutsii*, 1:86–96.

57. Kerensky, *Russia and History's Turning Point*, pp. 246–47; the text of the government's declaration is in *PG Documents*, 3:1249–51.

58. Obolenskii, *Moia zhizn', moi sovremenniki*, pp. 526–27, and A. I. Guchkov, "Iz vospominaniia," *Poslednie novosti*, September 23, 1936, p. 2.
59. Miliukov's assessment of support for his foreign policy views is contained in the speech he gave to a private conference of former Duma deputies (*Rech'*, May 5, 1917, p. 3). Some of his objections to coalition were also made in his opening speech to the Kadet eighth party congress and his rejoinder to Nekrasov's critique of that speech (*Rech'*, May 10, 1917, pp. 3–4, and May 11, 1917, p. 3).
60. The Socialist Revolutionary Viktor Chernov, who led the campaign against Miliukov, claims that he proposed moving Miliukov to Education (Chernov, *The Great Russian Revolution*, pp. 201, 205–6).
61. Nabokov mentions that Miliukov earlier considered handing over Foreign Affairs to Tereshchenko (who in fact replaced him there) and becoming minister of education (*Provisional Government*, p. 121). George Buchanan, the British ambassador, believed Miliukov had no influence in the Soviet and should be replaced (*My Mission to Russia*, 2:109). Paleologue, in contrast, considered Miliukov the only minister capable of keeping Russia in the war, but in early April his influence was superseded by the arrival in Russia of the French socialist Albert Thomas, an admirer of Kerensky who helped work for Miliukov's ouster (*An Ambassador's Memoirs*, 3:312–15, 329).
62. Miliukov, *Vosp.*, pp. 500–501, and *Istoriia vtoroi russkoi revoliutsii*, 1:108–11; and Nabokov, *Provisional Government*, pp. 123–25. For a discussion of Kadet debate over participation in a coalition see Rosenberg, *Liberals*, pp. 114–16.
63. Miliukov, *Istoriia vtoroi russkoi revoliutsii*, 1:57.
64. A rich body of literature exploring popular attitudes and demands in 1917, and the response to them of various socialist parties, has developed over the last two decades. Among the most influential works have been David Mandel's treatment of working-class views in Petrograd, *The Petrograd Workers and the Fall of the Old Regime. From the February Revolution to the July Days, 1917* (New York, 1983) and *The Petrograd Workers and the Soviet Seizure of Power: From the July Days 1917 to July 1918* (New York, 1984); Diane Koenker's exploration of working-class views in Moscow, *Moscow Workers and the 1917 Revolution* (Princeton, N.J., 1981); and Wildman's work on the views of soldiers, *The End of the Russian Imperial Army*.
65. On May 4, 1917, Miliukov half-humorously told a gathering of former Duma deputies, "I can say with a clean conscience that I did not leave, I was *ousted* [Ne Ia ushel, a menia ushli]" (P. N. Miliukov, "Pochemu Ia ushel iz Vremennogo Pravitel'stva?" in his *Rossiia v. plenu tsimmervalda* [Petrograd, 1917], p. 1 [emphasis added]). For his perspective on the part played by Nekrasov and the French representative Albert Thomas in Kerensky's ascendancy and his own defeat, see Miliukov, *Vosp.*, pp. 490–92, 498–500; on his anger at Guchkov's abrupt resignation, which strengthened the case for bringing in new ministers to form a coalition, see p. 503. Mandelshtam's declaration at the seventh congress is reported in *Rech'*, March 28, 1917, p. 5.
66. Taine, *French Revolution*, 2:157–58, 179–80.
67. The stenographic account of the conference is contained in *Gosudarstvennoe soveshchanie* (Moscow, 1930). Miliukov's detailed treatment of the conference is in his *Istoriia vtoroi russkoi revoliutsii*, 2:115–25. See also Rosenberg, *Liberals*, pp. 214–18.
68. For the text of Miliukov's August 14 speech and Tsereteli's rejoinder see *Gosudarstvennoe soveshchanie*, pp. 128–38.
69. Secondary works dealing extensively with Kadet involvement in the Kornilov affair include Miliukov's own, *Istoriia vtoroi russkoi revoliutsii*, 2:152–291; Rosenberg, *Liberals*, pp. 196–233; George Katkov, *The Kornilov Affair* (London, 1980); N. Ia.

Ivanov, *Kornilovshchina i ee razgrom* (Leningrad, 1965); and N. G. Dumova, "Maloizvestnye materialy po istorii kornilovshchiny," *Voprosy istorii*, no. 11 (1968): 69–93, and her *Kadetskaia partiia*, pp. 170–98. For an overview of the voluminous literature on the Kornilov affair see Jørgen Munck, *The Kornilov Revolt*, trans. Torben Schmidt (Århus, Denmark, 1987).

70. The texts of Kerensky's and Kornilov's declarations are contained in Kerensky's work on the Kornilov affair, *Delo Kornilova* (Ekaterinoslav, 1918); the English translation is *The Prelude to Bolshevism: The Kornilov Rebellion* (London, 1919), pp. 215–17. Richard Pipes argues that there was no Kornilov conspiracy and that the insurrection existed only from the moment that Kornilov refused to comply with Kerensky's order (*The Russian Revolution*, pp. 439–67).

71. Miliukov, *Istoriia vtoroi russkoi revoliutsii*, 2:251–52; in corroboration of his account of this plan, Miliukov reproduces in his text the account of F. F. Kokoshkin—one of the Kadets who helped devise it—originally printed in *Russkie vedomosti*, September 1, 1917. Kerensky says he turned down Miliukov's and Alekseev's offers to mediate, made on August 28, but makes no mention of the proposal that he surrender his powers to Alekseev (*Prelude to Bolshevism*, pp. 218–22, and *Russia and History's Turning Point*, pp. 353, 385).

72. The failed rebellion and the related end of the "second coalition" government marked the end of one stage of the revolution and inaugurated a new one, which Miliukov termed "the agony of authority" (*Istoriia vtoroi russkoi revoliutsii*, 2:290–91).

73. On how Kerensky, the Kadets, and the whole principle of continued coalition with the "bourgeoisie" were discredited by the Kornilov affair, see Alexander Rabinowitch, *The Bolsheviks Come to Power: The Revolution of 1917 in Petrograd* (New York, 1978), pp. 152–62, 165–67. On popular mistrust of Miliukov and the Kadets see also Gessen, *V dvukh vekakh*, p. 373.

74. Miliukov, *Istoriia vtoroi russkoi revoliutsii*, 2:174, 183.

75. Other than Kornilov's talks with Miliukov and several other Kadets in July and August, the main evidence adduced by Soviet historians in arguing the complicity of Miliukov and the Kadets in a plot is as follows: Kadet central committee meetings of August 11 and 20, where Miliukov and several other party leaders spoke about the desirability of creating a dictatorship; the fact that the Kadet ministers resigned when Kerensky demanded that the cabinet vote him extraordinary powers to deal with the insurrection; a suppressed *Rech'* editorial for September 1 which called on the population to support the new government created with Kornilov; and a letter to Miliukov from General Alekseev, in mid-September, asking him to organize financial support for the arrested officers' families and hinting at disclosures that might otherwise be made about the connection of various individuals with the activities of Kornilov; the most recent summary is in Dumova, *Kadetskaia partiia*, pp. 188–208. None of these circumstances prove complicity; the protocols of the August 20 central committee meeting, in fact, show that Miliukov and most of those present would have welcomed peaceful establishment of a dictatorship but thought that a military action would probably precipitate civil war. See GARF, f. 523, op. 2, d. 20, ll. 8–19.

76. Kerensky, *Russia and History's Turning Point*, pp. 406–12. No information exists on Miliukov's activities during his enforced stay in the Crimea, which he does not mention in his memoirs; it might be supposed that he spent at least some time there with the Petrunkeviches.

77. Miliukov returned to Petrograd only on October 10; on his return, and Kadet

activities during his absence, see Nabokov, *Provisional Government*, pp. 149–54. The program of the third coalition government is printed in *PG Documents*, 3:1714–17.

78. According to Miliukov, at the Kadet tenth party congress, held October 14–15, the majority of the delegates supported his views against the more conciliatory approach of the central committee (*Istoriia vtoroi russkoi revoliutsii*, 3:145–46). Accounts of the congress and its resolutions are in *Russkaia vedomosti*, October 15 and 17, 1917.

79. Miliukov presents a detailed account of the pre-parliament in *Istoriia vtoroi russkoi revoliutsii*, 3:120–78, 203–12; on his speech of October 16, see especially pp. 162–65. The full stenographic account of his speech is in GARF, f. 579, op. 1, d. 2270; excerpts from the speech are in *Rech'*, October 17, 1917.

80. Nabokov, *Provisional Government*, pp. 155–57; Miliukov, *Istoriia vtoroi russkoi revoliutsii*, 3:203–11; *Rech'*, October 25, 1917, p. 2. Passage of the resolution of the Menshevik Internationalists and Socialist Revolutionaries apparently owed something to confusion during the voting; a resolution expressing full support for the government, put forward by the cooperative movement delegates and supported by the Kadets, never came to a vote.

81. *Rech'*, October 26, 1917, p. 1; the English translation is in *PG Documents*, 3:1798.

82. For a general discussion of Kadet activity and attitudes in the first weeks after the coup see Rosenberg, *Liberals in the Russian Revolution*, pp. 263–77.

83. A. S. Lukomskii, "Vospominaniia," in *Beloe dvizhenie: General Kornilov* (Moscow, 1993), pp. 229.

84. The text of the Declaration was published December 27, 1917, in the Kadet paper in Rostov, *Donskaia rech'*.

85. For Miliukov, the process of rethinking liberal strategies in the civil war began late in 1919 as it became clear that the White Armies would not be liberating Russia. In a report to a conference of Kadets in Paris in late April–early May 1920, he listed disregard of local interests and failure to acknowledge passage of land to the peasants as two of the cardinal mistakes of the past two years; see the protocols of the Paris Kadet Committee and Group, May 6 and 7, 1920 in BAR, S. V. Panina Archive, subject files, box 13.

86. A. I. Denikin, *Ocherki Russkoi smuty* (Paris, 1922), 2:187–90, and Lukomskii, "Vospominaniia," pp. 227–28. According to Lukomskii, in addition to Kaledin, Kornilov, and Alekseev, the council included three other generals—Denikin, Romanovskii, and himself—and Struve, Miliukov, Fedorov, Prince Grigorii Trubetskoi, and Boris Savinkov; Denikin, because of Savinkov, refused to participate. In Denikin's account, Savinkov and three other socialists were added later.

87. Denikin, *Ocherki russkoi smuty*, 2:193–94, and Miliukov to Alekseev, n.d., BAR, Miliukov, catalogued correspondence, box 1.

88. Denikin, *Ocherki russkoi smuty*, 2:219–24, 233, and Lukomskii, "Vospominaniia," pp. 235–40.

89. Miliukov, *Vosp.*, p. 186, and "A. I. Shingarev," in *Pamiati pogibshchikh*, ed. N. I. Astrov et al. (Paris, 1929), pp. 26–44. Both men had been arrested November 27, the day the Constituent Assembly was to first convene, in consequence of an edict outlawing the Kadet party. The killings had not been authorized and the perpetrators were later tried, but the deaths of Shingarev and Kokoshkin greatly intensified Kadet hatred of the Bolsheviks; see Rosenberg, *Liberals in the Russian Revolution*, pp. 282–86.

90. Alekseev to Miliukov, May 23, 1918, cited in Peter Kenez, *Civil War in South Russia, 1918* (Berkeley, Calif., 1971), p. 158.

91. Miliukov to Alekseev, May 3/16, 1918, and Miliukov to Alekseev, n.d., in BAR, Miliukov, Catalogued correspondence, box 1.

92. Miliukov, "Dnevnik," pp. 1–9. This information, and most of the account of Miliukov's talks with German representatives, is drawn from his lengthy unpublished diary covering his civil war activities through 1920. One copy of the typed manuscript, cited as "Dnevnik," is in the Miliukov collection of the Bakhmeteff Archive, box 10. A second copy, with slightly different pagination, is in fond 5856, dela 13–15, of the *Russkii zagranichnyi istoricheskii arkhiv* (RZIA) in Moscow—that is, the so-called Prague Archive, which is now part of the complex of the State Archive of the Russian Federation (GARF). Short excerpts from the manuscript, one dealing with Miliukov's negotiations with the Germans, have been published as "Dnevnik P. N. Miliukova," *Novyi Zhurnal* (New York) 66 (1961): 173–203, and 67 (1962): 180–218; whenever possible, citations will refer to the published portions.

93. Miliukov, "Dnevnik," *Novyi Zhurnal* 66 (1961): 177–78, 180–81.

94. Ibid., 173–74, 178–82, 184.

95. After Brest-Litovsk, some 40,000 Czech soldiers who had been fighting the Central Powers with Russia secured Soviet permission to leave the country by heading east on the Trans-Siberian railway. For a brief discussion of the causes of their revolt and the help they gave anti-Bolshevik forces on the Volga and in Siberia, see Evan Mawdsley, *The Russian Civil War* (Boston, 1987), pp. 46–49, 99–100. On German thinking on Russia at this time, see Oleh S. Fedyshyn, *Germany's Drive to the East and the Ukrainian Revolution, 1917–1918.* (New Brunswick, N.J., 1971), esp. pp. 158–83, 242–43; he argues that despite German anti-Bolshevik sentiment, especially among the military, and desire to establish closer relations with Russian monarchists in Ukraine, differences on a reunited Russia essentially precluded cooperation.

96. Miliukov, "Dnevnik," *Novyi Zhurnal* 66 (1961): 190–93.

97. GARF, f. 523, op. 2, d. 23, central committee meeting of June 28/July 10, 1918, l. 26, and Miliukov, "Dnevnik," pp. 27–28, 31–38.

98. Miliukov's account of his conversation with Vinaver, and the text of his critique of Vinaver's tactical report, are in his "Dnevnik" (RZIA copy), pp. 27–28, 32–38. The protocols of the central committee meetings of June 28/July 10 and July 13/26 and the text of Vinaver's report are in GARF, f. 523, op. 2, d. 23, ll. 25–55.

99. GARF, f. 523, op. 2, d. 23, ll. 39–43.

100. Ibid., l. 32.

101. Dolgorukov, *Velikaia razrukha*, p. 119.

102. Miliukov, "Dnevnik," *Novyi Zhurnal* 67 (1962): 185.

103. Ibid, 184–88.

104. On the conference see Robert H. McNeal, "The Conference of Jassy: An Early Fiasco of the Anti-Bolshevik Movement," in *Essays in Russian and Soviet History in Honor of Gerold Tanquary Robinson*, ed. J. S. Curtiss (New York, 1963), pp. 221–36.

105. Other prominent members of the Council for National Unification of Russia included former Progressive leader P. P. Riabushinskii, former minister of agriculture A. V. Krivoshein, and E. N. Trubetskoi (Miliukov, "Dnevnik," pp. 239–40, and his *Rossiia na perelome*, 2:80–81).

106. McNeal, "The Conference of Jassy," p. 232.

107. Miliukov, "Dnevnik," pp. 364–65, 414. The delegation first stopped in Constantinople to meet with the commander of French forces there, arriving in Paris on December 26; after Miliukov's expulsion, its various members went their separate ways.

108. Miliukov to Petrunkevich, February 16, 1919, in RZIA, f. 5856, op. 1, d. 184, l. 1.

109. Miliukov to M. M. Fedorov, August 8, 1919, and National Center to Miliukov, July 22, 1919, cited in N. G. Dumova, *Kadetskaia kontrrevoliutsiia i ee razgrom (Oktiabr' 1917–1920 gg.)* (Moscow, 1982), pp. 236–37.

Conclusion

1. Good examples are the work of Richard Pipes, *Russia under the Old Regime* (New York, 1974), and Robert Tucker's work on processes of state-building in Soviet Russia, including his "Stalinism as Revolution from Above" in Robert C. Tucker, ed., *Stalinism: Essays in Historical Interpretation* (New York, 1977), pp. 77–108.
2. Miliukov, *Istoriia vtoroi russkoi revoliutsii*, 3:184.
3. Maklakov, *Vlast' i obshchestvennost'*, pp. 484–87.

Epilogue

1. P. N. Miliukov, "Pamiati A. I. Gertsena," in *Iz istorii russkoi intelligentsii*, pp. 169–75.
2. Natasha managed to send her parents five letters between September 9, 1919, and June 21, 1921. They are contained in RZIA f. 5856, op. 1, ed. khr. 217, ll. 1–21. With their accounts of new-found love and efforts to make a personal life, care for sick friends, and find work and shelter during the upheavals of civil war and reconstruction, they are deeply moving documents. On Natasha's death see R. Vinaver, "Vozhdi kadetskoi partii," p. 262.
3. Miliukov's first extended analysis of Bolshevism was *Bolshevism: An International Danger* (London, 1920). Intended to promote foreign support for the anti-Bolshevik forces in Russia, it stressed Bolshevism's international orientation. For a brief treatment of the development of his views on Bolshevism's Russian roots see G. M. Hamburg, "Miliukov and the Coming of the October Revolution," in Paul N. Miliukov, *The Russian Revolution*, vol. 3, trans. G. M. Hamburg (Gulf Breeze, Fla., 1987), pp. vii–xxvii.
4. The "Notes on a New Tactic" Miliukov presented to the group of Paris Kadets was later published as "Chto delat' posle krymskoi katastrofy," *Poslednie novosti*, July 7, 1921; an abbreviated version of the article is reprinted in P. N. Miliukov, *Emigratsiia na pereput' e* (Paris, 1926), pp. 132–36.
5. Miliukov, *Russia and Its Crisis*, p. 280, and *Istoriia vtoroi russkoi revoliutsii*, vol. 3, pp. 9–10.
6. Miliukov's account of how the split came about is in "M. M. Vinaver kak politik," P. N. Miliukov et al., *M. M. Vinaver i russkaia obshchestvennost nachala XX veka* (Paris, 1937), pp. 36–50; see also the articles by Petr Ryss, "Krizis liberalizma" and "V poiskakh sotsial'noi bazy," *Poslednie novosti*, June 7 and 12, 1921. A thoughtful handling of the Kadets' parting of the ways is Rosenberg, *Liberals in the Russian Revolution*, pp. 445–63.
7. Among Miliukov's most important published pieces on the views and activities of his political group are the report he gave to the founding meeting of the Prague Russian Democratic Club, "Rossiia i demokraticheskaia emigratsiia" *Poslednie novosti*, July 6 and 7, 1923; *Tri platformy Respublikansko-Demokraticheskikh Ob"edinenii (1922–24)* (Paris, 1925); *Emigratsiia na pereput' e* (Paris, 1926). The fortunes of the RDO are touched on in Jens Petter Nielsen, *Miliukov i Stalin: O politicheskoi evoliutsii P. N. Miliukova v emigratsii (1918–1943)* (Oslo, 1983), but no study of the group has ever been made.

8. On Rodichev see the recollections of N. K. Vakar, "Miliukov v izgnanii," *Novyi zhurnal* (New York), no. 6 (1943): 369–70; on the unpopularity of Miliukov's position with most Kadets and the more conservative majority of the emigration see Dmitrii Meisner, *Mirazhi i deistvitel'nost'* (Moscow, 1966), pp. 138, 166–73; although Meisner's memoirs must be used with a degree of caution, they provide a generally sympathetic portrait of the emigration. On Struve's attitude toward Miliukov, see Pipes, *Struve*, 2:342. An in-depth comparison of the early views of Struve and Miliukov on the revolution is Burbank, *Intelligentsia and Revolution*, pp. 113–69.

9. On Nabokov's murder and Miliukov's tributes to his old friend see *Poslednie novosti*, March 30 and 31, April 1 and 6, 1922; March 28, 1923; and March 28, 1925. Critics made much of Miliukov's "cowardly" failure to attend Nabokov's funeral on the grounds of having received further death threats from extremist émigrés in Berlin; see Andrew Field, *VN. Vladimir Nabokov. His Life in Art* (New York, 1986), pp. 74–75. That the family did not consider Miliukov's conduct remiss is suggested by the absence of rancor toward him on the part of Vladimir V. Nabokov, the dead man's devoted son and a man notoriously unrestrained in expression of personal dislikes; see for example his autobiographical work *Speak, Memory: An Autobiography Revisited* (New York, 1966).

10. Vakar, "Miliukov v izgnanii," pp. 370–71; Meisner, *Mirazhi i deistvitel'nost'*, pp. 197–98, suggests that Miliukov simply ceased to care about "conventions" or what the public thought of him.

11. Maklakov charged that the excessive radicalism of Russian liberals in the years 1904–06 made impossible the collaborative work with society genuinely desired by the government and thus brought on the revolution; Miliukov's rebuttals, which constitute his most detailed appraisal of Kadet liberalism, are "Sud nad kadetskim 'liberalizmom,' " in *Sovremennye zapiski* (1930), 41: 347–71, and "Liberalizm, radikalizm, i revoliutsiia," *Sovremennye zapiski* (1935), 57:285–315. In addition to his three-volume history of the 1917 revolution and first work on Bolshevism, Miliukov's books in the first decade of emigration include *Tri popytki* (Paris, 1921); the book based on his 1921 lectures in the United States, *Russia Today and Tomorrow* (New York, 1922); *Natsional'nyi vopros. Proiskhozhdenie natsional'nosti i natsional'nye voprosy v Rossii* (Prague, 1925); *Emigratsiia na pereput'e* (Paris, 1926); and a two-volume study of Bolshevism and the civil war, *Rossiia na perelome* (Paris, 1927), which first appeared as *Russlands Zusammenbruch* (Berlin, 1926). His books in the second decade of emigration include the three-volume *Histoire de Russie* (Paris, 1932) which he edited with Charles Seignobos; *La politique extérieure des soviets* (Paris, 1934), a study of Russian foreign policy from Nicholas II to Stalin; and *Zhivoi Pushkin* (Paris, 1937).

12. On the cultural mission of the emigration, including differing views concerning the nature of the culture that was to be preserved, see Marc Raeff, *Russia Abroad: A Cultural History of the Russian Emigration, 1919–1939* (Oxford, 1990), especially pp. 47–117. On Anna's activities in the emigration see Zhikareva, "Anna S. Miliukova: Zhiznennyi put'," *Poslednie novosti*, April 8, 1935. Tellingly, a significant portion of Miliukov's correspondence as president of the Union of Writers and Journalists dealt with the pressing financial needs of émigré writers; "Pis'ma P. N. Miliukova," RZIA f. 5856, op. 1, d. 242b.

13. Miliukov's statement of purpose to readers on assuming the editorship, promising that the paper would be "non-party" and devoted to democratic ideals, is "Nashi zadachi," *Poslednie novosti*, March 1, 1921; see also his "Politicheskaia deiatel'nost' 'Poslednoi novosti,' " in P. N. Miliukov et al., *Iubileinii sbornik gazety "Poslednie no-*

vosti," *1920–1930*. On the paper and its place in the émigré daily press see Raeff, *Russia Abroad*, pp. 82–84, and Robert H. Johnson, *"New Mecca, New Babylon": Paris and the Russian Exiles, 1920–1945* (Montreal, 1988), pp. 35, 39–43.

14. A vivid description of *Poslednie novosti* and detached but sympathetic view of Miliukov is V. S. Yanovsky, *Elysian Fields: A Book of Memory*, trans. Isabella and V. S. Yanovsky (DeKalb, Ill., 1987), especially pp. 219–30.

15. Friends agreed that Miliukov took Anna's death very hard, which caused many to consider all the more "tactless" his marriage months later to an émigré considerably his junior; see Meisner, *Mirazhi i deistvitel' nost'*, pp. 197–98.

16. Examples are his editorials on Nazi racism and the perversion of German democracy and culture, *Poslednie novosti*, April 1, 1933, July 1, 1934, and January 30, 1937, and his preface to R. M. Blank, *Adolf Hitler: Ses aspirations, sa politique, sa propagande et les "Protocoles des sages de Sion"* (Paris, 1938).

17. Vakar, *"Miliukov v izgnanii,"* pp. 374–77; Meisner, *Mirazhi i deistvitel' nost'*, pp. 164, 231. On émigré attitudes toward fascism and the potentially desirable consequences of an attack on the Soviet Union by an anti-communist regime see Johnson, *New Mecca, New Babylon*, pp. 117–23, 166 and Pipes, *Struve*, 2, pp. 413–20, 435–37.

18. Don Aminado, *Poezd na tret' em puti* (New York, 1954), pp. 319–20, and Vakar, "Miliukov v izgnanii," p. 378.

19. The evident willingness of the Soviet people to continue fighting under the most appalling conditions strongly colored Miliukov's short piece entitled "Pravda bol'-shevizma" ("The Truth of Bolshevism") which circulated in hectographed form before being published in *Russkii patriot* (Paris), November 11, 1944. Written in the last weeks of his life, it was a response to the article "Pravda anti-bol'shevizma" by Mark Vishniak, then residing in New York, who criticized émigrés for allowing their Russian patriotism to cloud their recognition of the real nature of Stalin and the Soviet system. Miliukov insisted that at a time of national peril there could be no middle ground between Hitler and Stalin, that one had to choose unconditionally. Moreover, he did not defend the Stalin regime as merely the lesser of two evils, arguing that the war effort compelled the conclusion that he and other émigrés had been wrong about Bolshevism; it *had* been able to evolve, to establish a government capable of defending the country and evoking the ardent support of its citizens. This piece naturally provoked consternation among those who respected Miliukov's twenty-year opposition to both Bolshevik ends and means, but allowance should be made for the exceptional circumstances of its composition. Vishniak's treatment of the Miliukov piece, his response, and the uproar they engendered is in his *Gody emigratsii, 1919–1969* (Stanford, Calif., 1970), pp. 165–66, 192–96. Johnson, *New Mecca, New Babylon*, pp. 170–78, provides an interesting discussion of the huge impact of the Soviet war effort on the thinking of many émigrés.

Selected Bibliography

The following is not a complete list of all the materials, published and unpublished, consulted for this study. I have included here major archival collections and titles of works frequently cited in the text; full references for other sources are to be found in the endnotes. I have followed much the same rule in deciding which works by Miliukov to include in the bibliography. Many short articles, editorials, reviews, speeches, and manuscript pieces not listed here are cited in the notes. The bibliography of Miliukov's published works and his major speeches, (1886–1930), compiled by B. Evreinov, is in *P. N. Miliukov: Sbornik materialov po chestvovaniiu ego semidesiatiletiia, 1859–1929*, ed. S. Smirnov (Paris, 1929): 313–58, but even this list is not complete.

Archival Sources

Gosudarstvennyi Arkhiv Russkoi Federatsii (GARF), Moscow:
 Fond 518 Soiuz soiuzov
  523 Konstitutsionno-Demokraticheskaia Partiia
  579 P. N. Miliukov
  629 A. V. Tyrkova
Otdel Rukopisei, Rossiiskaia Gosudarstvennaia Biblioteka (OR RGB), Moscow:
 Fond 171 Morozov
  218 Peshekhonov
Russkii Zagranichnyi Istoricheskii Arkhiv (RZIA), Moscow:
 Fond 5856 P. N. Miliukov (1892–1939)

Rossiiskii Tsentr khraneniia i izucheniia dokumentov noveishei istorii (RTsKhID), Moscow:
  Fond 279 Redaktorstvo zhurnala *Osvobozhdenie*
Arkhiv Rossiiskoi Akademii Nauk (ARAN), Moscow:
  Fond 518 Akademik V. V. Vernadskii
Rossiiskii Gosudarstvennyi Istoricheskii Arkhiv (RGIA), St. Petersburg:
  Fond 733 Delo departamenta narodnogo provsveshcheniia
       1276 Sovet Ministrov
       1278 Gosudarstvennaia Duma
Hoover Institution Archives on War, Revolution, and Peace, Stanford, California:
  Miliukov MS (a history of Russian foreign policy, 1900-1940)
  E. I. Murav'eva Papers
  Russia. Departament politsii. Zagranichnaia agentura, Paris. (Okhrana Archive)
  Konstitutsionno-demokraticheskaia Partiia

Bakhmeteff Archive of Russian and East European History and Culture (BAR), Columbia University, New York:
  P. N. Miliukov Personal Archive
  M. M. Kovalevskii Collection
  S. V. Panina Archive

Miliukov's Published Works

"A. I. Shingarev." In *Pamiati pogibshikh*, edited by N. I. Astrov et al. Paris, 1929.
Balkanskii krizis i politika A. P. Izvol'skogo. St. Petersburg, 1910.
"Bolgarskaia konstitutsiia," Parts 1-3. *Russkoe bogatstvo*, August 1904, pp. 193-216; September 1904, pp. 26-69; October 1904, pp. 28-59.
Bolshevism: An International Danger. London, 1920.
["ss," pseud.] "Chto takoe konstitutsiia Loris-Melikogo?" *Osvobozhdenie*, November 18/December 1, 1902, p. 173.
Constitutional Government for Russia. New York, 1908.
"Demokratizm i vtoraia palata." *Russkoe bogatstvo*, July 1905, 193-210.
["ss," pseud.] "Derzhavnyi maskarad." *Osvobozhdenie*, March 19/April 1, 1903, pp. 321-23.
"Dnevnik P. N. Miliukova." *Krasnyi arkhiv* 44-45 (1932): 3-48. (Miliukov's journal of the 1916 visit of the Duma delegation to the Allies.)
"Dnevnik P. N. Miliukova." *Novyi Zhurnal* (New York), 66 (1961): 173-203; 67 (1962): 180-218. (Excerpts from the diary Miliukov kept from 1918 to 1920, from the manuscript contained in the Miliukov collection in the Bakhmetev Archive.)
"Dva russkikh istorika." *Sovremennye zapiski* (Paris) 51 (1933): 311-35.
"Doklad tsentral'nomu komitetu v s"ezdu partii Narodnoi Svobody." *Vestnik partii narodnoi svobody*, 1907, pp. 1833-40.
Emigratsiia na pereput'i. Paris, 1926.
["ss," pseud.] "Fiasko 'Novogo Kursa.'" *Osvobozhdenie*, November 10/23, 1904, pp. 162-63.
Glavnye techeniia russkoi istoricheskoi mysli. 2d ed. Moscow, 1898.
God bor'by: Publitsisticheskaia khronika, 1905-1906. St. Petersburg, 1907.
Gosudarstvennoe khoziaistvo Rossii v pervoi chetverti XVIII veka i reforma Petra Velikogo. St. Petersburg, 1892.
["ss," pseud.] "Idti ili ne idti v gosudarstvennuiu dumu." *Osvobozhdenie*, August 6/19, 1905, pp. 417-18.

Selected Bibliography 363

"The Influence of English Political Thought in Russia." *Slavonic and East European Review* 5 (1926): 258–70.
"Intelligentsiia i istoricheskaia traditsiia." In *Intelligentsiia v Rossii*, edited by K. Arsen'ev et al., pp. 89–191. St. Petersburg, 1910.
"Istochniki russkoi istorii i russkaia istoriografiia." In F. A. Brokgauz and I. A. Efron, *Entsiklopedicheskii slovar'*, vol. 28, pp. 430–36. St. Petersburg, 1899.
Istoriia vtoroi russkoi revoliutsii. 3 vols. Sofia, 1921–24.
"Istoriosofiia g. Kareeva." *Russkaia mysl'*, November, 1887, pp. 90–102.
"Iuridicheskaia shkola v russkoi istoriografii (Solov'ev, Kavelin, Chicherin, Sergeevich)." *Russkaia mysl'*, June 1886, pp. 80–92.
Iz istorii russkoi intelligentsii. 2d ed. St. Petersburg, 1903.
["ss," pseud.] "Izolgalis'!" *Osvobozhdenie*, January 19/February 1, 1904.
["ss," pseud.] "K ocherednym voprosam." *Osvobozhdenie*, February 16/March 1, 1903, pp. 289–91.
"K redaktoru 'Russkikh vedomostei.'" *Russkie vedomosti*, September 17, 1905.
"K voprosu o sostavlenii razriadnykh knig." *Zhurnal Ministerstva Narodnogo Prosveshcheniia*, May 1889, pp. 165–95.
"Kolonizatsiia Rossii." In F. A. Brokgauz and I. A. Efron, *Entsiklopedicheskii slovar'* vol. 15, pp. 740–46. St. Petersburg, 1895.
"Konstantinopol' i prolivy." Parts 1–3. *Vestnik Evropy*, January 1917, pp. 354–81; February, pp. 227–59; and April-May-June, pp. 525–47.
Lektsii po "Vvedeniiu v kurs russkoi istorii." Moscow, 1894–95.
"Letnii universitet v Anglii: Iz poezdki v Kembridzh." *Mir Bozhii*, May 1894, pp. 194–206.
"Liberalizm, radikalizm, i revoliutsiia." *Sovremennye zapiski* (Paris) 57 (1935): 285–315.
"M. M. Kovalevskii, kak sotsiolog i kak grazhdanin." In *M. M. Kovalevskii: Uchenyi, gosudarstvennyi i obshchestvennyi deiatel' i grazhdanin*, edited by K. Arsen'ev et al., pp. 136–43. Petrograd, 1917.
"M. M. Vinaver, kak politik." In *M. M. Vinaver i russkaia obshchestvennost' nachula XX v.*, pp. 19–52. Paris, 1937.
"Natsionalizm protiv natsionalizma." In *Po vekham: Sbornik statei ob intelligentsii i "natsional' nom litse,"* pp. 37–42. Moscow, 1909.
Natsional' nyi vopros (Proiskhozhdenie natsional' nosti i natsional' nye voprosy v Rossii). Prague, 1925.
Neproiznesennaia rech'. St. Petersburg, 1908.
"Novaia kniga po sotsiologii." *Mir Bozhii*, December 1899, pp. 196–215.
["ss," pseud.] "Novyi kurs." *Osvobozhdenie*, October 2/15, 1904, p. 113.
["ss," pseud.] "Ocherednye zadachi russkikh konstitutsionalistov." *Osvobozhdenie*, July 19/August 1, 1904, p. 38.
Ocherki po istorii russkoi kul' tury. 3 vols. St. Petersburg, 1896–1918 (7 editions). Jubilee ed. Paris, 1930–37.
[unsigned] "Ot russkikh konstitutsionalistov." *Osvobozhdenie*, June 18/July 1, 1902, 7–12.
"'Ottalkivanie' ili 'pritiazhenie.'" In *Po vekham: Sbornik statei ob intelligentsii i "natsional' nom litse,"* pp. 76–81. Moscow, 1909.
"Petr Velikii i ego reforma." *Na chuzhoi storone* (Paris), 10 (1925): 5–28.
Piat' etnograficheskikh kart Makedonii, s tektsom P. N. Miliukova. St. Petersburg, 1900.
"Pierre le Grand et sa Reforme." *Le Monde Slave*, February 1925, pp. 157–85.
"Pis'ma iz Makedonii." *Russkie vedomosti*, nos. 159, 168, 181, 183, 277 (1898) and 4, 7, 15, 21, 28, 36, 44, 60, 85 (1899).

Political Memoirs, 1905–1917. Edited by Arthur P. Mendel, Translated by Carl Goldberg. Ann Arbor, Mich., 1967.
"Present Tendencies of Russian Liberalism." *Atlantic Monthly*, March 1905, pp. 404–14.
"Rokovye gody." Parts 1–16. *Russkie zapiski* (Paris), April 1938, pp. 109–18; May, pp. 109–19; June, pp. 115–31; July, pp. 126–36; August–September, pp. 108–24; October, pp. 128–38; November, pp. 135–49; December, pp. 116–25; January 1939, pp. 117–28; February, pp. 120–34; March, pp. 101–12; April, pp. 127–39; May, pp. 106–20; June, 111–21; July, pp. 104–20; August–September, pp. 96–111.
Rossiia na perelome. 2 vols. Paris, 1927.
["ss," pseud.] "Rossiia organizuetsia." *Osvobozhdenie*, July 13/26, 1905, pp. 396–98.
Rossiia v plenu u Tsimmerval'da. Petrograd, 1917.
"Russia." *The Athenaeum* (London), July 6, 1889, pp. 27–29; July 5, 1890, pp. 25–27; July 4, 1891, pp. 29–32; July 2, 1892, pp. 25–27; July 1, 1893, pp.27–30; July 7, 1894, pp. 22–25; July 6, 1895, pp. 24–25; July 4, 1896, pp. 26–27.
Russia and England. London, 1920.
Russia and Its Crisis. Chicago, 1905.
Russia Today and Tomorrow. New York, 1922.
"Slavianofil'stvo." In F. A. Brokgauz and I. A. Efron, *Entsiklopedicheskii slovar'*, vol. 30, pp. 307–14. St. Petersburg, 1900.
Spornye voprosy finansovoi istorii moskovskogo gosudarstva. Moscow, 1893.
"Sub"ektivnoe i sotsiologicheskoe obosnovanie svobody pechati." In *V zashchitu slova: Sbornik statei*, pp. 10–26. 2d ed. St. Petersburg, 1905.
"Sud' nad kadetskim 'liberalizmom.'" *Sovremennye zapiski* (Paris) 41 (1930): 347–71.
Taktika fraktsii narodnoi svobody vo vremia voiny. Petrograd, 1916.
"Territorial'nye priobreteniia Rossii." In *Chego zhdet Rossiia ot voiny: Sbornik statei*, edited by N. N. Mikhailov, pp. 49–62. Petrograd, 1915.
Tri platformy respublikansko-demokraticheskikh ob"edinenii. Paris, 1925.
Tri popytki: K istorii russkogo lzhe-konstitutsionalizma. Paris, 1921.
"Tseli voiny." *Ezhegodnik gazetoi Rech' na 1916 g*. Petrograd, 1916.
["ss," pseud.] "Voina i russkaia oppozitsiia." *Osvobozhdenie*, March 7/20, 1904, pp. 329–30; April 2/15, 1904, pp. 378–79.
Vooruzhennyi mir i ogranichenie vooruzhenii. St. Petersburg, 1911.
Vospominaniia (1859–1917). 2 vols. New York, 1955. Reprint (2 vols. in 1). Moscow, 1991.
Vtoraia duma. St. Petersburg, 1908.
"Vvedenie." In *Nuzhdy derevni po rabotam komitetov o nuzhdakh sel'sko-khoziaistvennoi promyshlennosti*, edited by K. Arsen'ev et al., vol. 1, pp. 1–40. St. Petersburg, 1904.
"Zadacha zemskogo s"ezda." *Pravo*, no. 48 (1904): 4.

Other Published Sources

Akashi, Motojiro. *Rakka ryusui: Colonel Akashi's Report on His Secret Cooperation with the Russian Revolutionary Parties during the Russo-Japanese War*. Edited by Olavi K. Falt and Antti Kujala. Translated by Inaba Chiharu. Helsinki, 1988.
Aminado, Don. *Poezd na tret'em pute*. New York, 1954.
Alston, Patrick L. *Education and State in Tsarist Russia*. Stanford, Calif., 1969.
Andriewsky, Olga. "The Politics of National Identity: The Ukrainian Question in Russia, 1904–1912." Ph.D. diss., Harvard University, 1991.
Ascher, Abraham. *The Revolution of 1905*. Vol. 1, *Russia in Disarray*. Vol. 2, *Authority Restored*. Stanford, Calif., 1988, 1992.
Avrekh, A. Ia. *Raspad tret'eiiunskoi sistemy*. Moscow, 1985.

———. *Stolypin i tret'ia duma*. Moscow, 1968.
———. *Tsarizm i chetvertaia duma, 1912–1914 gg*. Moscow, 1981.
Barnes, Harry Elmer. *The New History and Social Studies*. New York, 1925.
Beloe dvizhenie: General Kornilov. Moscow, 1993.
Black, Cyril E. *The Establishment of Constitutional Government in Bulgaria*. Princeton, N.J., 1943.
Browder, Robert Paul, and Alexander Kerensky. *The Russian Provisional Government, 1917*. 3 vols. Stanford, Calif., 1961.
Burbank, Jane. *Intelligentsia and Revolution. Russian Views of Bolshevism, 1917–1922*. Oxford, 1986.
Charques, Richard. *The Twilight of Imperial Russia*. London, 1958.
Chermenskii, E. D. *Burzhuaziia i tsarizm v pervoi russkoi revoliutsii*. 2d ed., revised with additions. Moscow, 1970.
Chernov, Viktor. *Pered burei*. New York, 1953.
———. *Zapiski sotsialista-revoliutsionnera*. Book 1. Berlin, 1922.
Churchill, Rogers B. "Paul Nikol. Milyukov." In *Some Historians of Modern Europe*, edited by Bernadotte E. Schmidt, pp. 324–48. Chicago, 1942.
Collini, Stefan. *Liberalism and Sociology: L. T. Hobhouse and Political Argument in England, 1880–1914*. Cambridge, 1979.
Crampton, Richard J. *Bulgaria, 1878–1918*: A History. Boulder, Colo., 1983.
Denikin, A. I. *Ocherki russkoi smuty*. 5 vols. Paris, 1922.
Dolgorukov, Pavel Dm. *Velikaia razrukha*. Madrid, 1964.
Dostoevskii, F. M. *Pis'ma*. Vol. 4 (1878–81). Moscow, 1959.
Druzhinin, N. "Recollections and Thoughts of a Historian." *The Soviet Review* (New York) 4, no. 1 (1963): 22–46.
Dumova, N. G. *Kadetskaia kontrrevoliutsiia i ee razgrom (Oktiabr' 1917–1920 gg.)*. Moscow, 1982.
———. *Kadetskaia partiia v period pervoi mirovi voiny i Fevral'skoi revoliutsii*. Moscow, 1988.
———. *Liberal v Rossii: Tragediia nesovmestimosti. Istoricheskii portret P. N. Miliukova*. Moscow, 1993.
———. "Maloizvestnye materialy po istorii kornilovshchiny." *Voprosy istorii*, no. 11 (1968): 69–93.
Dumova, N. G., and V. G. Trukhanovskii. *Cherchill' i Miliukov protiv sovetskoi Rossii*. Moscow, 1989.
Edelman, Robert. *Gentry Politics on the Eve of the Russian Revolution: The Nationalist Party, 1907–1917*. New Brunswick, N.J., 1980.
El'iashevich, V. B. "Iz vospominanii starogo moskovskogo studenta, 1892–1896 gg." In *Pamiati russkogo studentchestva: Sbornik vospominanii*, pp. 106–14. Paris, 1934.
El'iashevich, V. B., A. A. Kizevetter, and M. M. Novikov, eds. *Moskovskii Universitet, 1755–1930. Iubileinyi sbornik*. Paris, 1930.
Elkin, B. I. "Paul Miliukov." *Slavonic and East European Review* 23, no. 62 (1945): 137–41.
Emmons, Terence. *The Formation of Political Parties and the First National Elections in Russia*. Cambridge, Mass., 1983.
———. "Kliuchevskii's Pupils." *California Slavic Studies* 14 (1992): 68–98.
———. "Russia's Banquet Campaign." *California Slavic Studies* 10 (1977): 45–86.
Erofeev, N. D. "Liberal'nye narodniki zhurnala 'Russkoe bogatstvo' v 1905 g." *Vestnik Moskovskogo Universiteta, seriia 9: Istoriia*, no. 3 (May–June 1973): 32–46.
Ezhegodnik gazetoi Rech'. St. Petersburg, 1912–16.

Fischer, George. *Russian Liberalism*. Cambridge, Mass., 1958.
Freeden, Michael. *The New Liberalism: An Ideology of Social Reform*. Oxford, 1978.
Freeze, Gregory. "A National Liberation Movement and the Shift in Russian Liberalism, 1901–1903." *Slavic Review* 28 (March 1969): 81–91.
Frolich, Klaus. *The Emergence of Russian Constitutionalism, 1900–1904: The Relationship between Social Mobility and Political Group Formation in Pre-Revolutionary Russia*. Trans. Suzanne M. Read. The Hague, 1981.
Galai, Shmuel. "The Impact of the War on the Russian Liberals in 1904–5." *Government and Opposition* 1 (1965): 85–109.
——. "The Kadet Quest for the Masses." In *New Perspectives on Modern Russian History*, edited by Robert McKean, pp. 80–93. London, 1991.
——. *The Liberation Movement in Russia, 1900–1905*. Cambridge, 1973.
——. "A Note on the Establishment of the Liberation Movement." *Russian Review* 37 (July 1978): 308–12.
——. "The Role of the Union of Unions in the Revolution of 1905." *Jahrbücher für Geschichte Osteuropas* 24, no. 4 (1976): 512–25.
——. "The Tragic Dilemma of Russian Liberalism as Reflected in Ivan Il'ich Petrunkevich's Letters to His Son." *Jahrbücher für Geschichte Osteuropas* 29 (1981): 1–29.
Gessen, I. V. *V dvukh vekakh: Zhiznennyi otchet'*. Berlin, 1937.
Goldenweiser, Alexis. "Paul Miliukov—Historian and Statesman." *Russian Review* 16 (January 1957): 3–14.
Good, Jane E. "America and the Russian Revolutionary Movement, 1888–1905." *Russian Review* 41 (July 1982): 273–87.
Gosudarstvennaia duma: Stenograficheskie otchety. St. Petersburg, 1906–17.
Got'e, Iu. V. "Universitet" (Iz zapisok akademika Iu.V. Got'e). *Vestnik Moskovskogo Universiteta, seriia* 8: Istoriia, no. 4 (July–August 1982): 13–27.
Graves, B. B., ed. *Burzhuaziia nakanune Fevral'skoi revoliutsii*. Moscow, 1927.
Gurko, V. I. *Features and Figures of the Past: Government and Opinion in the Reign of Nicholas II*. Translated by Laura Matveev. Edited by J. E. Wallace Sterling, Xenia Joukoff Eudin, and H. H. Fisher. Stanford, Calif., 1939.
Haimson, Leopold H. *The Russian Marxists and the Origins of Bolshevism*. Cambridge, Mass., 1955.
Hamburg, G. M. *Boris Chicherin and Early Russian Liberalism, 1828–1866*. Stanford, Calif., 1992.
——. "Miliukov and the Coming of the October Revolution." In Paul N. Miliukov, *The Russian Revolution*, vol. 3., edited and translated by G. M. Hamburg, vii–xxvii. Gulf Breeze, Fla., 1987.
Hamm, Michael. "The Progressive Bloc." Ph.D. diss., University of Indiana, 1976.
Hasegawa, Tsuyoshi. *The February Revolution: Petrograd, 1917*. Seattle, Wash., 1981.
Hobsbawm, E. J. *Nations and Nationalism since 1780: Programme, Myth, Reality*. 2d ed. Cambridge, 1992.
Hosking, Geoffrey A. *The Russian Constitutional Experiment: Government and Duma, 1907–1914*. Cambridge, 1973.
Iggers, Georg. *New Directions in European Historiography*. Revised edition. Middletown, Conn., 1984.
Izwolsky, Alexander. *The Memoirs of Alexander Izwolsky*. London, n.d.
Johnston, Robert H. *"New Mecca, New Babylon": Paris and the Russian Exiles, 1920–1945*. Montreal, 1988.
Karpovich, Michael. "Klyuchevski and Recent Trends in Russian Historiography," pt. 1, *Slavonic Review* 21, (March 1943): 31–39.

———. "P. N. Miliukov kak istorik." *Novyi zhurnal* (New York), no. 6 (1943): 362–68.
———. "Two Types of Russian Liberalism: Maklakov and Miliukov." In *Continuity and Change in Russian and Soviet Thought*, edited by Ernest J. Simmons, pp. 129–43. Cambridge, Mass., 1955.
Kassow, Samuel D. *Students, Professors, and the State in Tsarist Russia*. Berkeley, Calif., 1989.
Katkov, George. *The Kornilov Affair*. London, 1980.
Kaun, Alexander. *Maxim Gorky and His Russia*. New York, 1931.
Kenez, Peter. *Civil War in South Russia, 1918*. Berkeley, Calif., 1971.
Kerensky, Alexander. *The Prelude to Bolshevism*. London, 1919.
———. *Russia and History's Turning Point*. New York, 1965.
Kireeva, P. A. *V. O. Kliuchevskii kak istorik russkoi istoricheskoi nauki*. Moscow, 1966.
Kizevetter, A. A. *Napadki na partii Narodnoi svobody i vozrazheniia na nikh*. Moscow, 1906.
———. *Na rubezhe dvukh stoletii (vospominaniia 1881–1914)*. Prague, 1929.
———. *P. N. Miliukov*. Moscow, 1917.
Kliuchevskii, V. O. *Pis'ma. Dnevniki. Aforizmy i mysli ob istorii*. Moscow, 1968.
———. *Sochineniia*. 8 vols. Moscow, 1959.
———. *V. O. Kliuchevskii: Kharakteristiki i vospominaniia*. Moscow, 1912.
Kloppenburg, James. *Uncertain Victory: Social Democracy and Progressivism in European and American Thought, 1870–1920*. Oxford, 1986.
"Kommissiia po organizatsii domashniago chteniia v moskve." *Mir Bozhii*, May 1894, pp. 231–36.
Konstitutsionno-demokraticheskaia partiia: S'ezd 12–18 oktiabria 1905 g. Moscow, 1905.
Konstitutsionno-demokraticheskaia partiia: III gosudarstvennaia duma: Otchet fraktsii narodnoi svobody. 5 vols. St. Petersburg, 1908–1912.
Kornilov, A. "P. N. Miliukov." In *Novyi Entsiklopedicheskii Slovar' Brokgauz-Efrona*, vol. 26, pp. 543–46. St. Petersburg, n.d.
Leikina-Svirskaia, V. R. *Intelligentsiia v Rossii vo vtoroi polovine XIX veka*. Moscow, 1971.
———. *Russkaia intelligentsiia v 1900–1917 godakh*. Moscow, 1981.
Levin, Alfred. *The Second Duma: A Study of the Social Democratic Party and the Russian Constitutional Experiment*. New Haven, Conn., 1940.
Lieven, D. C. B. *Russia and the Origins of the First World War*. New York, 1983.
Logue, William. *From Philosophy to Sociology*. Dekalb, Ill., 1983.
Lunacharskii, A. *Tri kadety*. n.p., [1907?]
Maklakov, V. A. *Pervaia gosudarstvennaia duma*. Paris, 1939.
———. *Vlast' i obshchestvennost' na zakate staroi Rossii (vospominaniia)*. 3 vols. Paris, 1936.
———. *Vtoraia gosudarstvennaia duma (vospominaniia sovremennika)*. Paris, 1948.
Manning, Roberta T. *The Crisis of the Old Order in Russia: Gentry and Government*. Princeton, N.J., 1982.
Mazour, Anatole. *Modern Russian Historiography*. Princeton, N.J., 1958.
McClelland, James C. *Autocrats and Academics: Education, Culture, and Society in Tsarist Russia*. Chicago, 1979.
McDonald, David M. *United Government and Foreign Policy in Russia, 1900–1914*. Camnbridge, Mass., 1992.
McNeal, Robert H. "The Conference of Jassy: An Early Fiasco of the Anti-Bolshevik Movement." In *Essays in Russian and Soviet History in Honor of Geroid Tanquary Robinson*, edited by J S. Curtiss, pp. 221–36. New York, 1963.

Meisner, Dmitrii. *Mirazhi i deistvitel' nost': Zapiski emigranta.* Moscow, 1966.
Mendel, Arthur. *Dilemmas of Progress in Tsarist Russia: Legal Populism and Legal Marxism.* Cambridge, Mass., 1961.
Miakotin, V. A. "Kurs russkoi istorii P. N. Miliukova." *Russkoe bogatstvo,* November 1896, 1–20.
Mitskevich, S. I. *Na grani dvukh epokh: Ot narodnichestva k marksizmu.* Moscow, 1937.
Nabokov, V. D. *V. D. Nabokov and the Russian Provisional Government, 1917.* Edited by Virgil Medlin and Steven L. Parsons. New Haven, Conn. 1976.
Naimark, Norman M. *Terrorists and Social Democrats.* Cambridge, Mass., 1983.
Nechkina, M. V. *Vasilii Osipovich Kliuchevskii.* Moscow, 1974.
Nielsen, Jens Petter. *Miliukov i Stalin: O politicheskoi evoliutsii P. N. Miliukova v emigratsii (1918–1943).* Oslo, 1983.
Obolenskii, V. A. *Moia zhizn', moi sovremenniki.* Paris, 1988. (Written in 1937).
Otchet tsentral'nogo komiteta Konstitutsionno-demokraticheskoi partii za dva goda (s 18 oktiabria 1905 g. po oktiabr 1907 g. St. Petersburg, 1907.
Padenie tsarskogo rezhima. 7 vols. Leningrad, 1924–27.
Paleologue, Maurice. *An Ambassador's Memoirs.* Trans. F. A. Holt. 3 vols. New York, 1925.
Pares, Bernard. *The Fall of the Russian Monarchy.* New York, 1939.
———. *My Russian Memoirs.* London, 1931.
———. *A Wandering Student: The Story of a Purpose.* Syracuse, N.Y., 1948.
P.B. "Neskol'ko zamechanii ob 'Ocherkakh po istorii russkoi kul'tury' g. Miliukova." *Russkoe bogatstvo,* August 1898, 1–21.
Pearson, Raymond. "Miliukov and the Sixth Kadet Congress." *Slavonic and East European Review* 52 (April 1975): 210–29.
———. *The Russian Moderates and the Crisis of Tsarism, 1914–1917.* London, 1977.
———. *Vtoroi vserossiiskii s'ezd Konstitutsionno-demokraticheskoi partii 5–11 yanvarya 1906 g.* New York, 1986.
———. "The Vyborg Complex." *Irish Slavonic Studies,* 1980, pp. 73–91.
Petrunkevich, Iv. *Iz zapisok obshchestvennogo deiatelia: Vospominaniia.* In *Arkhiv russkoi revoliutsii* 21. Berlin, 1934.
Picheta, V. I. *Vvedenie v russkuiu istoriiu: Istochniki i istoriografiia.* Moscow, 1922.
Pinchuk, Ben-Cion. *The Octobrists in the Third Duma, 1907–1912.* Seattle, Wash., 1974.
Pipes, Richard. *The Russian Revolution.* New York, 1990.
———. *Struve.* Vol. 1, *Liberal on the Left, 1870–1905.* Vol. 2, *Liberal on the Right, 1905–1944.* Cambridge, Mass., 1970 and 1980.
Pirumova, N. M. *Zemskoe liberal'noe dvizhenie:* Sotsial'nye korni i evoliutsiia do nachala XX veka. Moscow, 1977.
Pomialovskii, M. Review of volume 1 of *Ocherki russkoi kul'tury. Istoricheskii vestnik* 87 (February 1902): 688–91.
Protokoly III obshcheimperskogo delegatskogo s"ezda partii narodnoi svobody (konstitutsionno-demokraticheskoi). St. Petersburg, 1906.
Protopopov, D. D., ed. *Ocherk deiatel'nosti S-Peterburgskoi gruppy partii Narodnoi svobody, 1 oktiabria 1906–1 noiabria 1907.* St. Petersburg, 1908.
Rabinowitch, Alexander. *The Bolsheviks Come to Power: The Revolution of 1917 in Petrograd.* New York, 1978.

Radzilowski, Thaddeus C. *Feudalism, Revolution, and the Meaning of Russian History: An Intellectual Biography of Nikolai Pavlovich Pavlov-Silvanskii.* Boulder, Colo., 1994.
Raeff, Marc. *Russia Abroad: A Cultural History of the Russian Emigration, 1919–1939.* New York, 1990.
———. "Some Reflections on Russian Liberalism." *Russian Review* 18 (July 1959): 218–30.
Report of the International Commission to Inquire into the Causes and Conduct of the Balkan Wars. Washington, D.C., 1914.
Rezanov, A. S. *Shturmovoi signal P. N. Miliukova.* Paris, 1924.
Riasanovsky, Nicholas. *The Image of Peter the Great in Russian History and Thought.* Oxford, 1985.
Rieber, Alfred. "Introduction." In V. O. Kliuchevsky, *A Course in Russian History: The Seventeenth Century,* xiii–xxi. Chicago, 1973.
Riha, Thomas. "Miliukov and the Progressive Bloc in 1915." *Journal of Modern History* 32 (1960): 16–24.
———. "*Riech'*: A Portrait of a Russian Newspaper." *Slavic Review* 22 (1963): 663–82.
———. *A Russian European: Paul Miliukov in Russian Politics.* Notre Dame, Ind., 1969.
Rodichev, F. I. "The Liberal Movement in Russia, 1855–1917." *Slavonic and East European Review* 2 (1923): 1–13, 249–262.
Rosenberg, William. *Liberals in the Russian Revolution, 1917–1921.* Princeton, N.J., 1974.
Rubinstein, N. L. *Russkaia Istoriografiia.* Moscow, 1941.
Sanders, Jonathan, "The Union of Unions." Ph.D. diss., Columbia University, 1986.
Schapiro, Leonard. *Russian Studies.* New York, 1987.
Schmidt, Bernadotte E., ed. *Some Historians of Modern Europe.* Chicago, 1942.
Shakhovskoi, D. I. *Avtobiografiia.* Moscow, [1917?].
———. "Soiuz osvobozhdeniia," *Zarnitsy,* no. 2 (1909): 81–171.
Shatsillo, K. F. "Iz istorii osvoboditel'nogo dvizheniia v Rossii v nachale XX veka (O konferentsii liberal'nykh i revoliutsionnykh partii v Parizhe v sentiabre–oktiabre 1904 goda)." *Istoriia SSSR,* no. 4 (1982): 51–70.
———. "Novoe o 'Soiuze osvobozhdeniia.'" *Istoriia SSSR,* no. 4 (1975): 132–45.
———. *Russkii liberalizm nakanune revoliutsii, 1905–1907 gg.* Moscow, 1985.
Shelokhaev, V. V. *Ideologiia i politicheskaia organizatsiia rossiiskoi liberal'noi burzhuazii, 1907–1914 gg.* Moscow, 1991.
———. *Kadety—glavnaia partiia liberal'noi burzhuazii v bor'be s revoliutsiei, 1905–07 gg.* Moscow, 1983.
Shipov, D. *Vospominaniia i dumy o perezhitom.* Moscow, 1918.
Shirokova, V. V. *Partiia "Narodnogo prava."* Saratov, 1972.
Shul'gin, V. V. *Dni.* Belgrade, 1925.
Skif, N. [pseud.] "G. Miliukov i slavianofil'stvo." *Russkii vestnik,* no. 1 (1903): 269–317.
Smirnov, S. A., et al., eds. *P. N. Miliukov: Sbornik materialov po chestvovaniiu ego semidesiatiletiia, 1859–1929.* Paris, 1929.
Smith, C. Jay. "Miliukov and the Russian National Question." In *Russian Thought and Politics,* ed. Hugh McClean, pp. 395–420. Cambridge, Mass., 1957.
Smith, Nathan. "The Constitutional-Democratic Movement in Russia, 1902–1906." Ph.D. diss., University of Illinois, 1958.
Stone, Norman. *The Eastern Front, 1914–1917.* New York, 1975.
Stepanskii, A. D. "Liberal'naia intelligentsiia v obshchestvennom dvizhenii Rossii na rubezhe XIX–XX v.v." *Istoricheskie zapiski* no. 109 (1983): 64–94.

———. "Obshchestvennye organizatsii Rossii na rubezhe XIX–XX vv." Ph.D. diss., Moscow State University, 1982.
Stockdale, Melissa K. "Politics, Morality, and Violence: Kadet Liberals and the Question of Terror, 1902–1911." *Russian History* 22 (Winter 1995): 455–80.
Storozhev, V. N. "Istoricheskaia khronika." *Istoricheskoe obozrenie*, no. 5 (1892): 198–215.
Struve, P. B. Review of *Ocherki po istorii russkoi kul' tury*. *Novoe Slovo*, no. 1 (October 1897): 89–94.
Sukhanov, Nikolai. *Zapiski o revoliutsii*. 6 vols. 1922. Reprint edition (6 vols. in 3). Moscow, 1991.
Timberlake, Charles E., ed. *Essays on Russian Liberalism*. Columbia, Mo., 1972.
Treadgold, Donald W. *Lenin and His Rivals*. New York, 1955.
Tuck, R. "Paul Miliukov and Negotiations for a Duma Ministry." *American Slavic and East European Review* 10 (1951): 117–29.
Tyrkova-Vil'iams, A. "The Cadet Party." *Russian Review* 12 (July 1953): 173–86.
———. *Na putiakh k svobode*. New York, 1952.
———. "Russian Liberalism," *Russian Review* 10 (January 1951): 3–14.
Vakar, N. P. "P. N. Miliukov v izgnanii." *Novyi zhurnal* (New York), no. 6 (1943): 369–78.
Vandalkovskaia, M. G. *P. N. Miliukov, A. A. Kizevetter: Istoriia i politika*. Moscow, 1992.
Vernadskii, G. V. *Pavel Nikolaevich Miliukov*. Petrograd, 1917.
Vinaver, M. M. *Istoriia vyborgskogo vozzvaniia (Vospominaniia)*. Petrograd, 1917.
———. *Konflikty v pervoi dume*. St. Petersburg, 1907.
Vinaver, R. G. "Vozhdi kadetskoi partii." *Novyi zhurnal* (New York), no. 10 (1945): 250–62.
Vishniak, Mark. *Gody emigratsii, 1919–1969*. Stanford, Calif., 1970.
Von Laue, T. H. "The Chances for Liberal Constitutionalism in Russia." *Slavic Review* 24 (1965): 34–46.
Vrangel', L. "'Russkoe bogatstvo' i 'Mir Bozhii.'" *Novyi zhurnal* (New York), no. 69 (1962): 161–69.
Vucinich, Alexander. *Social Thought in Tsarist Russia: The Quest for a General Science of Society, 1861–1917*. Chicago, 1976.
Wade, Rex. *The Russian Search for Peace: February–October 1917*. Stanford, Calif., 1969.
Walicki, Andrzej. *Legal Philosophies of Russian Liberalism*. Oxford, 1987.
Wildman, Allan K. *The End of the Russian Imperial Army: The Old Army and the Soldier's Revolt (March–April 1917)*. Princeton, N.J., 1980.
———. "The Russian Intelligentsia of the 1890s." *American Slavonic and East European Review* 19 (April 1960): 156–79
Witte, S. *Vospominaniia*. 3 vols. Moscow, 1960.
Yanovsky, Vassily. *Elysian Fields. A Book of Memory*. Trans. Isabella Yanovsky and Vassily Yanovsky. De Kalb, Ill., 1987.
Zaionchkovskii, P. A. *Rossiiskoe samoderzhavie v kontse XIX stoletiia*. Moscow, 1970.
Zhikareva, A. "Anna S. Miliukova. Zhiznennyi put'." *Poslednie novosti*, April 5 and April 8, April 1935.
Zimmerman, Judith, "Between Revolution and Reaction. The Constitutional Democratic Party, October 1905 to June 1907." Ph.D. diss., Columbia University, 1967.
———. "Russian Liberal Theory, 1900–1917." *Canadian–American Slavic Studies* 1 (Spring 1980): 1–20.

Index

Agrarian question, 171, 177, 181–82; Miliukov's views on, 142–43
Alekseev, General M. V., 260, 263–64, 265, 266
Amur railroad, 177, 180, 338n.35
Angell, Norman, 212
Annales school, 60, 308n.33
Annenskii, N. F., 87, 93
Anti-Semitism, 106, 107, 177, 202
April Crisis (April 20–21, 1917), 254–55
Archduke Franz Ferdinand, assassination of, 217
Armed World and Limitation of Armaments, 212
Astrov, Nikolai I., 263, 269–70
Athenaeum, 31, 32, 33, 36, 51
Autocracy, 97, 107, 119, 176; Miliukov's views on, 30, 73, 75, 171–72, 281
Azef, Evno, 120

Balkan Wars (1912–13), 212–13; Miliukov on, 213–16
Banquet campaign (1904), 125
Beilis trial, 202
Belinskii, V. G., 4, 67–68
Belyi, Andrei, 20
Black Hundreds, 157, 158, 206
Bloody Sunday (January 9, 1905), 129
Bogdanovich, A. Iu., 86–87
Bogucharskii, V. Ia., 92–93, 120, 123, 147

Bolsheviks, 158, 173; Kadet response to their power seizure, 262–63; Miliukov on, 134, 137–39, 158, 259; in Petrograd Soviet, 261. *See also* Social Democrats
Bolshevism, Miliukov's views on, 259, 266, 281, 357n.3, 359n.19
Bosnia-Herzegovina crisis (1908), 210–11
Brailsford, H. N., 214–15
Buckle, Thomas Henry, 54
Bulgaria, 51, 82, 212–14, 215; constitutionalism of, as example for Russia, 84, 119, 124, 316n.16; liberalism of, 84–85; Miliukov's partiality for, 83
Bulygin Duma, 135–37, 139–41

Carnegie Commission on Balkan Wars (1913), 214–16
Chaadaev, P., 66, 71
Charnolusskii, V. I., 88, 135
Chelnokov, M. V., 198–200, 203
Chernov, Viktor M., 39–41, 121, 302n.73
Chicherin, Boris N., 18, 39
Chuprov, A. I., 8, 17, 20, 44
Civic forum address by Miliukov (January 1908), 177
Civil war, and anti-Bolshevik movement (1917–20), 263–66, 269, 271–72; Miliukov's analysis of outcome, 281–82, 358n.11
Class struggle, 99, 118, 171

Coalition cabinet, formation of, (April–May 1917), 255–56
Commission for Organization of Home Reading. *See* University Extension
Comte, Auguste, 5, 9, 25–26, 53–54, 59, 292n.18
Conference of Jassy (1918), 270–71
Constituent Assembly, 133, 135, 136, 146, 148, 149, 244, 257, 263
Constitution, 89–90, 104, 124, 148–49, 176
Constitutional Democratic Party (Kadets, Party of People's Freedom): founding of, 139–40, 142–43; organization and legal status, 164, 207, 250–51, 263, 342n.125, 351n.43; central committee, 145, 152, 154, 162, 175, 195–96, 204, 209, 222, 256–57, 269–70, 348n.75; left wing of, 175, 201, 218, 222, 234; right wing of, 186, 197–200, 203–4, 211, 222; agrarian program, 142, 152, 181–82; nationality policy and national minorities, 185–86, 224, 332n.102; on civil liberties, 146, 183–84, 200, 224, 244; on foreign policy, 180, 209–11, 217; on a ministry responsible to Duma, 222; on monarchy, 149, 248, 270; on political amnesty, 149, 159, 224; on political violence, 149, 166–67, 178; and legal tactics, 154, 163, 164, 204–5; liberalism of, 144, 181–82, 203; relations with Octobrists, 147, 173, 175–77, 201–2, 206–7, 229; and Progressives, 197, 198–200, 222–23; attitudes toward the Left, 147–48, 150, 166, 173, 204–5, 234; attitudes toward the government, 146, 148–49, 209–10; in First Duma, 153, 155–56, 161; in Second Duma, 164–67; in Third Duma, 175–79, 180, 182, 183–84; in Fourth Duma, 197, 199–202, 205–7; and World War I, 218, 223, 224, 268–69; in Russian revolution (1917), 250–51, 256–57, 260–61; and civil war, 262–65, 268–69, 269–70; split in emigration, 282–283; criticism of party, 147–48, 156, 163, 167, 173, 177, 186, 192, 206–7, 260; historiography on, 290n.12
—Congresses: founding congress, 143–46; second congress (January 1906), 151–52; third congress (April 1906), 153–55; fourth congress (September 1906), 164; fifth congress (October 1907), 175; sixth congress (February 1916), 229; seventh congress (March 1917), 250–51; tenth congress (October 1917), 355n.78
—Conferences: October 1908, 179; November 1909, 186, 343n.6; March 1914, 204–5; June 1915, 222; May 1918, 268; October 1916, 233–34; in Ekaterinodar (October 1918), 270. *See also* Kornilov Affair; Miliukov, Pavel Nikolaevich; Vyborg Manifesto
Constitutional Government for Russia, 170
Constitutionalists, 94–97, 104, 118, 119, 142–43
Controversial Questions in the History of Muscovite State Finances (Spornye voprosy finansovoi istorii moskovskogo gosudarstva), 63–64, 310n.52
Council for National Unification of Russia (1918), 271
Council of Elders, Duma, 221, 241
Council of Ministers, and Progressive bloc, 225–27
Council of the Republic (1917), 261–62, 355n.80
Crane, Charles, 100, 127

Danilevskii, Nikolai, 34–35, 300n.35
Dardanelles, Miliukov's views on, 220, 254
Day of Russian culture, 286
Declaration of Purpose, Volunteers (1917), 264
"Decline of Slavophilism" (*Razlozhenie slavianofil'stva*), 33–35
Delianov, I. D. (minister of education), 47
Democracy, 20, 105, 244; Miliukov's views on, 30–31, 77–78, 114–15, 268
Denikin, General Anton I., 264, 270
Dewey, John, 35–36
Dolgorukov, Prince Nikolai D., 4–5
Dolgorukov, Prince Pavel D., 143, 210, 212, 269
Dolgorukov, Prince Petr D., 120–21, 123
Dostoevsky, Fedor, 4, 5; Miliukov's letter to, 12–13
Dragomanov, M. P., 51, 306n.138
Duma, First (1906): appeal to people, 161; composition of, 333n.106; dissolution of, 161–62; electoral campaign, 152–53; Miliukov's role in, 155–57, 160
Duma, Second (1907): elections and composition of, 164–65; and issue of terror, 165–67
Duma, Third (1907–12): address to throne, 176; anti-revolutionary mood of, 176–77; coalition efforts by, 183–84; Committee on state defense, 177–78; elections and composition, 173, 175; and extreme right, 177, 183; Miliukov's

Duma, Third (*cont.*)
  views on, 185, 192, 194; nationalist campaign of, 184–85, 190–92
Duma, Fourth: and budget debates, 201–2, 205–6; committee on Army and Navy, 199–200, 221; elections and composition of, 196–97; and foreign policy, 213, 218; government reaction to, 202; prorogued (January 1917), 240. *See also* Progressive bloc
Duma, Temporary Committee of (February 1917), 241, 244–45
Duma delegation to allies, 1916, 230–31, 232
Durnovo, P. N. (minister of interior), 47, 48
Dutton, Samuel, 214

Economic materialism, 37, 54–55
Event-oriented history, 29, 53, 58, 208

Fal'bork, G. A., 88, 135
Famine, trans-Volga (1891), 33, 36, 41
"Fateful Years" (*Rokovye gody*), 284
Feudalism, Russian, 74, 314n.115
Finland, 91, 93, 129, 163, 193; status within empire, 190–92, 249
Fischer, Fritz, 219, 345n.39
Fischer, George, 20
Freeden, Michael, 112
Free Economic Society, 43, 87, 131, 221, 317n.33
French Revolution, 158, 238–39, 258–59
Friends of liberation, 93, 319n.64
From the History of the Russian Intelligentsia (*Iz istorii russkoi intelligentsii*), 67–68
"From the Russian constitutionalists," ("Ot russkikh konstitutsionalistov"), 94–97
Fundamental laws, 154–55, 175; article 87, 221

Galicia (1915), 221, 222
Geiden, P. A., 147, 160
Generational identity, 7–8, 15–16, 26, 32
Ger'e, V. I., 7, 24, 293n.27
German romanticism, 66
Gessen, Iosif V., 106, 145, 147, 153, 164, 194
Godart, Justin, 214–15
Gol'tsev, V. A., 29, 42, 49
Goremykin, I. L. (premier, 1905–6, 1914–16), 155–56, 159, 202, 221; dismissal of, 228; and Progressive bloc, 225–26
Gorkii, Maksim, 88

Government, "new course" (1914), 202
Great Illusion, The, 212
Great reforms, 105, 110
Gredeskul, N. A., 186, 198
Guchkov, Aleksandr I., 16, 148, 149, 184, 197, 210, 259; and abdication of tsar, 246–48; challenges Miliukov to duel, 1908, 178; founds Octobrists, 147; Miliukov on, 185, 192; organizes Duma defense committee, 177–78; plans palace coup, 239–40; president of Third Duma (1910–11), 185; in Provisional Government, 243, 249, 258

Harper, William, 99, 111
Hasse, Major, and negotiations with Miliukov (1918), 267–68, 269
Herzen, A. I., 192, 280; Miliukov on, 47, 67–68, 76, 280
Higher education, women's, 297n.88
History of the Russian Revolution (*Istoriia vtoroi russkoi revoliutsii*), xi, 239, 289n.2; publication of, 349n.4
Hobhouse, L. T., 112
Hobsbawm, E. J., 187
Hobson, J. A., 112
Hrushevsky, Mykhalo, 313n.107

Ianzhul, I. I., 20, 43
Ice March (1918), 265
Intelligentsia, Russian, 13, 71, 87, 105, 143, 156, 180, 200, 208; Miliukov as member of, 106, 169, 193, 283; Miliukov's views on, 74, 75, 172, 188, 282
Iuzhakov, S. N., 86
Izgoev, A. L., 186, 198
Izvol'skii, A. P. (foreign minister, 1906–10), 160, 211, 235

Jewish question, 186, 228–29, 348n.77
Juridical school, 18, 296n.80

Kaledin, Ataman, 263, 265
Karamzin, N. M., 65–66
Kavelin, K. D., 61
Kazan Square demonstration (1901), 91
Kerensky, Alexander F., 202, 206, 218, 234, 242; enters Provisional Government, 243; as head of government, 259, 261–62; and Kornilov Affair, 260–61; Miliukov on, 258; and against monarchy, 247; war aims of, 253–55
Khomiakov, N. A., 183, 210
Kizevetter, A. A., 19, 23, 25, 45, 47
Kliuchevskii, V. O.: and Bulygin Duma, 140; historical approach of, 7, 10, 60,

Kliuchevskii, V. O. (cont.)
80, 293n.40, 307n.11; on Miliukov's work, 25, 63; personal relations with Miliukov, 16, 19, 21, 23–26, 28, 101–2; as teacher, 10–11, 23
Kloppenburg, James, 301n.43
Kokoshkin, Fedor F., 130–31, 148, 152, 163, 205; in First Duma, 155–56; murder of, 265–66, 355n.89
Kokovtsev, V. N. (minister of finance, 1904–14; premier, 1911–14), 160, 195, 202
Koliubakin, A. M., 209, 224
Konovalov, A. I., 206–7
Kornilov, Aleksandr I., 94, 138, 204
Kornilov, General Lavr G., 254, 264–65
Kornilov Affair (1917), 259–60; Kadet role in, 261, 354n.75
Kovalevskii, Maksim M., 8, 9, 49, 130, 212; influence on Miliukov, 25, 307n.9
Kramář, Karel, 210
Kriticheskoe obozrenie, 8
Krupenskii, P. N., 177, 346n.59
Kuskova, E. D., 93, 124, 147

L'vov, Prince G. E., 149, 225, 242–43, 253, 255, 350n.18
L'vov, V. N., 225, 243
Lappo-Danilevskii, A. S., 63–64
Lavrov, Petr L., 89, 308n.25
Law of June 3, 1907, 170
Lenin, V. I., 173, 251; Miliukov meets with (1903), 112; on Miliukov's "deal" with Stolypin, 336n.164; views on, 251, 277
Leontev, Konstantin, 34
"Liberal," use of term, 97, 322.n8
Liberalism, Russian, 20, 35, 91–92, 225, 297n.91, 318n.55; currents within, 97–98, 320n.78; and European new liberalism, 112–13, 115; and liberal nationalism, 198, 200, 211; Miliukov's characterization of, 114–15; as not "bourgeois," 109–10, 144; shifts leftward (1903), 104–5; and socialism, 109–10; and social reformism, 322n.15, 144. *See also* Constitutional Democratic Party; Miliukov, Pavel Nikolaevich; Struve, Petr B.; Union of Liberation
Liberals, Russian, 36, 37, 39, 42, 101, 103, 143, 146, 229; and anti-Bolshevik movement, 264; and constitutionalism, 105; and national minorities, 122, 186, 192; and revolutionaries, 138–39, 151; and war, 217
Lowell Institute lectures (1904), 126

Macedonia, 111, 214; Macedonian question, 82–83
Main Currents in Russian Historical Thought (*Glavnye techeniia russkoi istoricheskoi mysli*), 64–66
Maklakov, Nikolai (minister of internal affairs, 1912–15), 220, 221, 223
Maklakov, Vasilii A., 9, 25, 41, 145, 167, 210; critiques of Kadet liberalism, 115, 326n.87, 358n.11; critiques Miliukov line in Fourth Duma, 198, 203; on saving monarchy (1917), 351n.32; supports national-liberal foreign policy, 211; wartime views of, 222
Mandel'shtam, M. L., 251, 258, 320n.78, 343n.6
Marxist-Populist debate, 36–39; Miliukov on Marxism in Russia, 110
Masaryk, Thomas, 100, 286–87
Miakotin, Venedikt, 23, 32, 74, 87, 93, 131, 133, 317n.31
Mikhailovskii, N. K., 9, 38, 42, 308n.25
Miliukov, Aleksei Nikolaevich, 21, 132
Miliukov, Nikolai Pavlovich, 21, 224, 280
Miliukov, Pavel Nikolaevich (1859–1943)
—biography: family, 1, 12, 21, 50, 86, 193–94; early education, 2–4; at Moscow University (1877–95), 7–18, 39–40, 47–50; dissertation on Peter I, 21–22, 24–25; generational identity, 16, 26; arrests and imprisonments, 14, 89–90, 100–102, 141; death threats and attacks against, 166, 192, 236, 283–84, 340n.47; romantic attractions, 15, 167–69, 328n.7, 336n.165; marriage to Anna S. Smirnova (1886), 19–20; finances, 12, 18, 29, 50, 86, 193, 280, 284; in Riazan exile (1895–97), 49–51; settles in Finland (1901), 91, (1905), 129; in south Russia (1917–18), 263; in Kiev (1918), 266; in London (1919), 271; in Paris, 280; last years and writings in emigration, 287, 355n.11
—travels abroad: Balkans (1897–98), 82, 83, (1903) 111, (1913) 213–16, 343n.18, 344n.20; Conference of Jassy (1918), 270–71; England (1902), 100, (1903–4) 111–12, (1909, with Duma delegation) 209–10, (1916) 231; France (summer 1893), 43, (1904) 120, (1918) 271; Italy, 15; Norway (1916), 231; with parliamentary delegation to Allies (1916), 230–31; Turkey (1898–99), 83, (1913) 215; United States (1903), 108, 111, (1904–5),

Miliukov, Pavel Nikolaevich
—travels abroad (cont.)
126–27, (1908) 170, (1921–22) 285;
Vienna (1897), 57
—personal characteristics: ambition, 162,
168, 306n.134; courage, 6, 218, 255;
doctrinairism, 148, 162, 199; eclecticism, 79–80; gentleness, 178; independence, 26–27, 126, 218, 230, 269–70;
lack of political instinct, 231;
as leader, 47, 125–26, 175, 179–80,
289n.5; optimism, 49, 249, 287; organizational skills, 5, 44, 223; overbearing,
147, 161; pragmatism, 148–49, 165,
179; radicalism, 42, 52, 128, 135–37,
169; reserve, 50–51, 193–94, 284,
306n.134; tactlessness, 86, 175, 209–
10; tolerance, 77, 80, 87, 106, 317n.32
—intellectual characteristics: religious sensibilities, 2, 5, 161, 200; ethical views, 3,
26, 32–33, 35–36, 115, 301n.42; as rationalist, 76–77; as positivist, 25–26,
53–54; as Westernizer,
30–31, 77–78, 314n.119; command
of foreign languages, 100, 321n.88;
as speaker, 138, 194, 241, 329n.36;
patriotism, 48, 117, 218, 268, 270, 287;
pacifism, 211–12, 216, 218; love of music, 2, 21, 50; and archeology, 50, 83;
diary, 356n.92; personal archives, 289–
90n.7; library, 291–92n.12
—as editor: Granat encyclopedia, 86; *Mir
Bozhii*, 86–87; *Narodnuiu svoboda*, 150;
Poslednie novosti, 286; *Rech'*, 153, 198;
Russkaia mysl', 29; *Russkaia zapiski*, 284
—as educator: teaching, 11, 17–19, 48;
in America, 108–11, 126–27; in Bulgaria, 82; in emigration, 284; popularity
as teacher, 40–41, 303n.74; on role of
education, 45–46; on democratization
of education, 45–46; launches university
extension, 43–46; on political education,
xv, 84, 156–58, 276
—historical thought: archival scholarship, 273; on causality, 54–55; on deductive method, 54–55, 306n.6; on economic materialism, 37–38, 54; and
epistemology, 60; and eurocentrism, 60,
79, 275; and historicism, 77, 79, 273;
on history as science, 53, 57–58; and
cultural history, 69, 75; and philosophical history, 57, 79; and scientific history,
8, 59, 66, 76–77; on history of events,
53, 58, 60, 79; on history of ideas, 60,
64, 66, 67–68; on historical laws, 53,
54; on historical process, 55, 77–78;
on progress, 59–60, 274, 290n.14,
308n.31; on historical types, 63–64,
310n.54; on theory in history, 64–67;
sociological views, 8, 54, 57–58, 80;
uses of history, 58–59, 80; on Juridical
school of historiography, 18, 74; and
Moscow school of historiography, 11,
18–19, 22–23, 26, 80; on Petersburg
school of historiography, 22; on Karamzin, 65–66, 311n.64; on idealism,
66–68; on Kievan history, 69, 84,
312n.84; "Third Rome" theory, 73,
313n.106; on role of state in Russian
history, 30, 69–70, 75, 77, 273; on
Russia's protean nature, 30, 76, 109; influence of his historical views on his political thought, 77–79, 273–77. *See also*
Muscovite Russia; Orthodox church;
Peter the Great
—political views: on democracy, 30–31,
77–78, 114–15; on liberty, 97, 114,
158; on freedom of press, 157–58; on
human rights, 113–14; on natural law,
113–14; on power and limits of law,
182, 191–92; on political violence, 40,
89, 140, 166–67; on the state, 36–37,
114, 188, 209–10, 258, 259, 264; on
constitutionalism, 114, 138, 274–75; on
constitutional order, 95–96, 176; on
unicameral legislature, 131; on Marxism,
37–38, 110; on Populism, 38–39; on
Russian socialism, 110–11; on Slavophilism, 33–35; on social reform, 36–37,
95–96, 115, 264, 268; his shift right
(1917), 259, 279
—and liberalism: on development of liberalism, 113–15; on history of Russian liberalism, 109–10; on qualities of new
Russian liberalism, 98, 114–15; on
closeness of liberalism and socialism in
Russia, 109–11; on liberalism and class
interests, 144; his early liberalism, 20,
26, 303n.88; first identification as liberal
(1903), 105, 322n.8; nature of his liberalism, 42, 52, 115, 275–76
—on nationality and nationalism: on national feeling, 117; on nationalism and
national identity, 186–90; on nationality
question, 186–90, 278–79; "Nationality and the State" (1912), 187–89,
339n.51; on nationality as sociological
phenomenon, 71–72, 187; as Kadet
spokesman on nationality question, 190;

Miliukov, Pavel Nikolaevich
—on nationality and nationalism (*cont.*)
on slavophile nationalism, 33–35; on national identity in Balkans, 84; on national minorities, 176; on early panslavism, 5; on slavic societies, 210; on Muscovite national idea, 71–73; on "plasticity" of Russian nationality, 78, 109, 275; on Finland, 190–92, 249; on Poland, 120–21, 147, 221, 224, 249–50, 267, 331n.73; on Ukraine, 190, 267
—political activities: in Narodnoe Pravo party (1894), 41–42; among St. Petersburg intelligentsia (1899–1901), 88–89; at Paris conference (1904), 120–22; in union movement (1905), 133–37; composes Appeal to People, 135–36; composes Vyborg Appeal, 162–63; in peace movement, 211–12; organizes Progressive bloc (1915), 223–26, 347n.62; "Stupidity or Treason" speech, 234–36; organizes Provisional Government, 241–46; as minister of foreign affairs (March 2–May 2, 1917), 251–56, 352n.52; in civil war, 263–70; at Conference of Jassy, 270–71; and Russian Liberation Committee, London (1919), 271; in emigration, 281–84; his role as unifier in Russian politics, 128–29, 137, 250–51, 258, 278, 284, 341n.96
—and Constitutional Democrats: on party's founding, 143–44; on leftism of Kadets, 144; on constitutionalism of Kadets, 205; in central committee, 175, 195–96, 348n.75; role in First Duma, 151–52, 154–56; and negotiations for public cabinet, 159–62; tactics in Second Duma, 164–67; as Kadet faction head in Third and Fourth Dumas (1907–12), 175, 177, 178–79, 196, (1912–14) 197–206, 341n.96; his wartime caution, 223–24, 231, 234; in 1917, 250–51, 255, 256, 258, 260–63; resigns as party head (1918), 270; his "new tactic" (1920–21), 282–83; Kadet criticisms of him, 179, 193, 197–99, 203–4, 233–34, 269–70, 283
—foreign policy views: on Russo-Turkish war, 5–6; on Russo-Japanese war, 115–18; on Far East, 180, 210; Balkan influence on his views, 83, 216–17; and Balkan policy of restraint, 211, 213–14, 217–18; on arms limitations, 211–12; on Kadet party's foreign policy views,

180, 209–11, 217; on war aims in World War I, 218–20, 345n.37; on Constantinople and Dardanelles, 220, 230–31, 252–53; on Germany's war blame, 219; on Allies, 230–31, 269; critique of Petrograd Soviet position, 253, 262; his "German orientation," 266–68; on Russia's war effort in World War II, 287
Miliukov, Sergei Pavlovich, 50, 224
Miliukova, Anna Sergeevna, 19, 111, 252, 284–85, 287, 297n.90, 306n.128; relations with husband, 168, 193; in women's movement, 144–45
Miliukova, Natasha Pavlovna, 86, 280–81, 357n.2
Mill, J. S., 17, 59
Miller, Vsevelod F., 8, 9
Ministry of public figures: negotiations (1906), 159–62; in 1915, 226, 347n.64
Mir Bozhii, 50, 85, 86
Monarchy, and Miliukov: efforts to preserve it (1917), 246–49; views on it (1918, 1920–21), 267, 270, 282
Morozova, Margarita, 328n.7
Moscow Conference (August 1917), 259
Moscow general strike (1905), 143–44
Moscow literacy committee, 33
Moscow school of historiography, 22, 26, 60, 80
Moscow University, 6–7, 8–9, 12–13, 14–16, 20, 39–41, 293n.26
Moscow uprising (1905), 150–51, 171
Moscow Young Professors, 8–9, 17, 20–21
Muromtsev, Sergei A., 130, 160–61
Muscovite Russia, 65–66, 73–75, 312n.88

Nabokov, Vladimir D., 145, 160, 163, 248, 249, 263; murder of (1922), 283–84, 358n.9; as treasurer of *Rech'*, 153
Narodnaia svoboda, 150
Narodnaia volia, 10, 41, 295n.59
Narodnoe Pravo party (1894), 41–42, 303n.85
National Center (1918–19), 268–69, 271
Nationalist campaign, Third Duma, 185
Nationalists: in Third Duma, 184–85; in Fourth Duma, 233; in Progressive bloc, 223–24
Nationality, Russian, 34, 185, 188, 189, 207
Nationality Question (*Natsional'nyi vopros*), 186, 339n.51

Nekrasov, Nikolai V., 200; and proposed tactics (1914), 204–5; leaves Kadet central committee, 222, 346n.53; in Provisional Government, 243, 253, 254, 255, 257
Neo-slavism, 210
"New Course," Sviatopolk-Mirskii, 119
New history, 62, 80, 307–8n.23
New liberalism, 112–13
Nicholas II (1894–1917), 46, 47, 82, 101, 149, 228, 236, 342n.112; abdication, 246, 247; Miliukov's views on, 138, 246, 247, 329n.35; and Progressive bloc, 226–27
Nizhnii Novgorod, lectures in (1895), 46–47
Novgorodtsev, Pavel I., 130, 269–70

October Manifesto, 145–46, 176, 183
Octobrist party (Union of 17 October), 167, 183, 184; founding, 147; in first year of Third Duma, 175–76; Duma committee on state defense, 177–78, 199; and national campaign, 185, 190–92; in Fourth Duma, 197, 201–2, 206–7; and Progressive bloc, 223, 228; faction splits, 203; Miliukov's views on, 147, 173, 175, 185, 204, 206, 331n.75
"Opposition of his Majesty," 209–10
Orlova, Elizaveta, 43–44
Orthodox church, Russian, Miliukov's thought on, 5, 70–71, 313n.97
Osvobozhdenie: founding, 91–94, 318–19nn.56,62; program of, 94–98; circulation and distribution, 98, 100, 320n.81; Miliukov's contributions to, 94, 98–99, 106, 126, 320n.83; and 104–5, 107, 115–18, 286. See also Struve, Petr B.
Outlines of Russian Culture, 312n.83

Palace revolution (planned 1916–17), 239–40
Paleologue, Maurice (French ambassador), 242, 251, 353n.61
Pares, Bernard, 112, 155, 178
Paris conference (1904), 120–23, 326n.87
Paris Kadets, 283
Party of Peaceful Renewal (Progressive Party), 183
Pavlov-Sil'vanskii, N. P., 22, 74
Peasant commune, 38, 39–40; Miliukov's views on, 37, 181–82
People, Russian (*narod*), Miliukov on, 78, 172, 268, 282

People's Freedom party. See Constitutional Democratic Party
People's Will. See *Narodnaia volia*
Peshekhonov, A. V., 88, 131
Petersburg school of historiography, 22, 309n.45
Peter the Great, Miliukov on, 21, 61–63, 71, 73–74, 297n.99, 310n.47
Petite, Marie, 127, 167–68
Petition to tsar (1905), 136, 329n.25
Petrunkevich, Ivan I., 29, 123, 160, 163, 198, 217, 236; and First Duma, 155; and Kadets, 143, 348n.8; meets Miliukov, 299n.7; *Osvobozhdenie*, 92–94; and Petrunkevich group, 131, 318n.54; and *Rech'*, 153; and Union of Liberation, 131; and Vyborg Manifesto, 162–63
Pipes, Richard, 332n.100
Platonov, S. F., 22, 298n.101
Plehve, V. K., 101, 118, 119
Plekhanov, G. B., 37, 111, 173, 302n.53
Polarization, 1917, 257–58
Polish question, 120–122, 220, 229, 249–50, 331n.73
Political Council, and Volunteers (1917–18), 265, 355n.86
Populism, 7, 35, 38–39
Populists, 36, 110
Positivism, 25–26, 53
Poslednie novosti, 286
Potemkin mutiny (1905), 139
Pravo, 106, 124
Pre-parliament. See Council of the Republic
Professional Unions, 131–34, 328n.9
Progressive bloc: organized, 223–25, 346n.59; and legislative efforts, 229–30; debates strategy (1916), 233; program, 225; Miliukov on, 227, 229
Progressive Party (Party of Peaceful Renewal), 183, 199–200, 201–2; and Duma budget debates (1914), 206; during war, 222, 226
Prokopovich, S. N., 93, 147
Protopopov, A. D. (minister of interior, 1916), 232–33, 237
Protopopov, D. D., 198, 205
Provisional Government: organized, 242–44; program, 244–45; laws and acts, 249–50; foreign policy, 253–54, 262; April crisis, 254–57; Miliukov resigns from, 353n.65; Kornilov Affair, 259–60; third coalition, 261; overthrown, 262; masons in, 243; Miliukov on, 257

Public opinion, Miliukov's writing on, 72, 74, 117–18, 125, 313n.104
Purishkevich, V. M., 177, 206, 237

Rasputin, Grigorii, 232, 237
Rech', 153, 165, 169, 263; accused of bribe-taking, 192, 340n.77; antiwar line (1912–14), 217; closed (1914), 218, (1917), 263; Kadet critiques of, 198
Renan, Ernest, 187
Republican Democratic Alliance (RDO), 283, 357n.7
Revolutionaries, 138, 150–51, 171
Revolution of 1905, Miliukov on, 150–51, 154, 170–72
Right, extreme, 165, 166, 177, 183
Rodichev, Fedor I., 179, 181, 200, 269, 283
Rodzianko, Mikhail V. (Duma president, 1911–17), 222, 226, 240
Rousseau, Jean-Jacques, 7
Russia Abroad, 284–85, 291n.15
Russia and Its Crisis, 109, 282
Russian Liberation Committee, 271
Russian Revolution (1917), Miliukov's views on, 238–39, 257–58, 262
Russkaia molva, 198
Russkaia mysl', 20–21, 28, 29; under Struve, 203
Russkie vedomosti, 50, 83, 203
Russkie zapiski, 284
Russkoe bogatstvo, 39, 85, 317n.29; circle, 87–88, 147–48
Russo-Japanese war (1904–5), 118, 135, 142; Miliukov's views on, 115–17, 121, 135–36

Savinkov, Boris V., 89, 265
Sazonov, S. D. (foreign minister, 1911–16), 213, 214
Schellingism, Miliukov on, 66, 311n.69
Science (*nauka*), enthusiasm for, 8–10, 293n.28
Science of society. *See* Sociology
Semiotics, 68
Serbia, 211, 218; Serbian-Bulgarian alliance, 212–14; Miliukov's views on, 214, 215, 217, 219
Shakhovskoi, Prince Dmitrii I., 14, 29, 92–93, 118–19, 124, 129–30, 131, 143, 163
Shchepkin, Nikolai N., 199, 200
Shcherbatov, Prince N. B. (minister of interior, 1915), 223, 226
Shidlovskii, S. I. (head of Progressive bloc), 228, 234

Shingarev, Andrei I., 181, 194, 221, 243, 263; murder of, 265–66, 355n.89
Shipov, Dmitrii, 147, 148, 160, 199–200, 210
Shklovskii, I., 231, 323n.38
Shubinskii, N. P., 206, 223
Shul'gin, V. V., 224, 247
Skoropadskii government, Ukraine, 266–67
Slavic Congresses, 210
Slavophilism, 33, 38
Social cohesion, Russia's lack of, 108, 172
Social Democrats, 122, 134, 138; polemics against Kadets, 147, 153, 173; in Fourth Duma, 202; German, 219
Socialist Revolutionaries, 87, 121, 139
Society of Slavic Culture, 210
Sociology, 8, 34–35, 57–58; and approach to history, 9–10, 22, 55, 58–59, 79; and nationality, 73, 187–88, 192; and new liberalism, 112–15; subjective, 56, 57, 308n.25
Solov'ev, S. M., 7, 61–62
Solov'ev, V. M., 20, 33, 34–35, 300n.37
Soviet, Petersburg (1905), 149, 150; Petrograd (1917), 241–42, 243–45, 249; contact committee, 253; war aims, 252–54; during April crisis, 254–55; at Moscow Conference, 259
Spencer, Herbert, 5, 292n.18
State council (upper house of legislature), 156, 197, 200, 203
State Economy of Russia in the First Quarter of the Eighteenth Century and the Reforms of Peter the Great, 61–63
Stepniak-Kravchinsky, S. M., 111
Stolypin, P. A. (minister of internal affairs and premier, 1906–11), 122–23, 162; agrarian reforms, 180–82, 335n.158; meets with Miliukov (1906), 160, (1907) 167; nationality policies, 184–85, 190–91; naval staffs crisis, 184; on terror, 167; at Third Duma, 176; assassination of, 194–95; Miliukov on, 341n.90
Storozhenko, N. I., 8, 20, 31, 44
Struve, Petr B., 36, 38, 124–25, 137, 164, 265, 272; critique of *Studies*, 56, 307n.16; and central committee, 222; on creating a liberal party, 103–5, 129; in emigration, 283; on foreign policy, 210, 211; and liberalism, 94–98; and nationalism, 117, 186, 189; and national liberalism, 198; and *Osvobozhdenie*, 92–93, 99; at Paris conference, 120–21; on regeneration of authority (1914), 203; on Russo-Japanese war, 116–18

Student circles, 4, 292n.14
Studies of Russian Culture (*Ocherki po istorii russkoi kul'tury*), 50, 68–76, 100–101, 187, 273
"Stupidity or Treason" speech (November 1, 1916), 234–36
Sturmer, Boris V. (premier, 1916), 228; as civil dictator, 232; Miliukov's campaign against him, 233–36; dismissed, 236
Sukhanov, N. N., 241, 350n.26
Sukhomlinov, V. A., 223, 235
Sviatopolk Mirsky, Prince P. D., 124

Taine, Hippolyte, 7, 238–39, 258–59
Tereshchenko, M. I. 243, 253
Third of June system, 182, 207
Tolstoy, Leo, 32, 300n.22
Tradition, Russia's lack of, 74–75, 78, 109, 191, 275
Trepov, A. F. (minister of interior, fall 1916), 236–37
Trepov, D. F., 135; and ministry negotiations (1906), 159–60
Troitskii, M. M., 7–8, 16, 293n.30
Trotsky, Leon, 141, 251
Trubetskoi, Prince Evgenii N., 250–51
Trubetskoi, Prince G. N., 217, 265
Trudoviks, in First Duma, 155–56, 162–63; and 198, 202, 203, 204, 205
"Truth of Bolshevism" (*Pravda bol'shevizma*), 359n.19
Tseretelli, Irakli G., 254, 255
Tsushima, Battle of (1905), 135
Tyrkova-Vil'iams, Ariadna, 169, 186, 194, 200, 272, 320n.81; challenges *Rech'*, 197–98; and relations with Miliukov, 336–37n.165; and Russian Liberation Committee, 271

Union of Liberation: Schaffhausen conference (July 1903), 107; founding congress (January 1904), 107–8; second congress (October 1904), 123; third congress (March 1905), 129; fourth congress (August 1905), 142; program, 107, 129; on Russo-Japanese war, 115–16; relations with Left, 120, 123, 138; Petersburg branch of, 131, 137, 147; and zemtsy, 103, 105, 120, 131
Union of Russian People, 166, 236
Union of 17 October. *See* Octobrist party
Union of Towns, 220, 237
Union of Unions: first congress, 134; second congress (May 1905), 135–37; third congress (July 1905), 105, 139; Appeal to the People, 135–36, 140; Miliukov as chair, 99, 139; Constitutional Democratic Party, 142, 144; Miliukov in, 99, 108, 120–22, 125–26.
Union of Zemstvos, 220, 237
United Council, Moscow University, 39–41, 302n.65
Universal suffrage, 105, 107, 121, 156, 196, 200–201; Miliukov's views on, 96, 105, 122, 144–45, 152, 326n.77
University autonomy (1905), 142
University Extension, 43–47, 304n.99, 305n.114
University of Chicago lectures, 100, 109–11, 126–27

Vernadskii, V., 92, 198, 319n.57
Vestnik Evropy, 29
Vestnik partii narodnoi svobody, 153
Vinaver, Maksim, 133, 163, 194; in First Duma, 155–56, 162; in Kadet central committee, 152, 269, 270; in RDO (1921), 283
Vinogradov, Paul, 9, 19, 41, 44–45, 284, 295n.69
Vishniak, Mark, *Pravda anti-bol'shevizma*, 359n.19
von Anrep, V. K., 191–92
Vyborg Manifesto, 162–64, 177, 205; Miliukov on, 335n.148

Ward, Lester, and dynamic sociology, 308n.25
Williams, Harold, 271, 328n.11
Witte, Sergei (premier, 1905–6), 103, 146, 155; and public cabinet, 148–49
Women's suffrage, 144–45, 152
World War I, and Russia, 223, 225, 228, 231, 233, 235, 260, 261, 266; Miliukov against, 216–18; on war aims, 219–20, 252–53; on "truce" with government, and sacred union, 218–19, 220–22, 227; his predictions on postwar Russia, 230, 234; his fear of revolution, 232, 233, 240. *See also* "Stupidity or Treason" speech
Writers Union (1899–1901), 87–88, (1905), 131, 133

Zemstvo congresses (November 1904), 124–25, (May 1905), 136; and municipal congresses (September 1905), 147, (November 1905), 148–49
Zemstvo constitutionalists, 139–40, 143, 144
Zemstvos, and Miliukov, 31–32, 95–97, 124
Zhabotinskii, Vladimir, 186
Zilliacus, Koni, 120–21

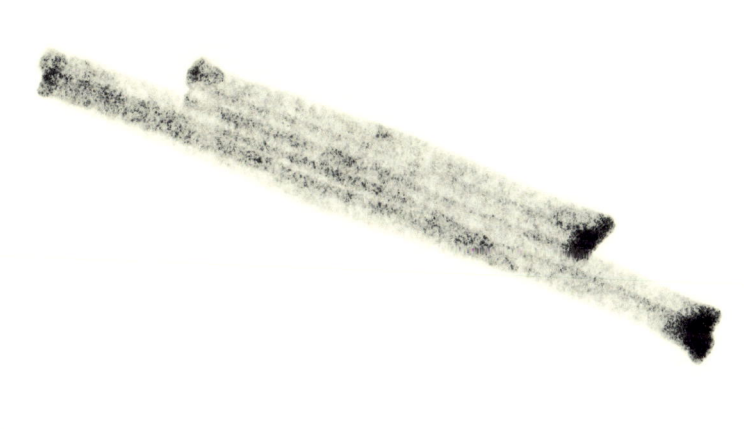

WITHDRAWN